SECOND EDITION

ENCYCLOPEDIA OF

American Farm

Implements & Antiques

©2004 **by** C.H. Wendel

Published by

kp krause publications
An F+W Publications Company

700 East State Street • Iola, WI 54990-0001
715-445-2214 • 888-457-2873
www.krause.com

Our toll-free number to place an order or obtain
a free catalog is (800) 258-0929.

Library of Congress Catalog Number: 2004092436

ISBN: 0-87349-568-3

Designed by Stacy Bloch

Edited by Tom Collins

Printed in United States of America

Table of Contents

Introduction

Since the 1997 introduction of this book, we have acquired additional materials that made this Second Edition possible. The many new illustrations include a sizable showing of wagons and carriages. The biggest change for the Second Edition is an extensive database. Under each section is a listing of all the trade names we could find.

For instance, under Corn Shellers, there are nearly 300 different trade names, along with their manufacturers. This makes it relatively easy to identify the Favorite as being built by Marseilles Mfg. Company, and so on. Included in the listings is the year we first found reference to this entry. In many instances a particular machine or implement might have been built for some years before and/or after this listing. Thus, the year shown is done so in a relative sense, rather than an exclusive one.

In the same way, a 1905 patent number on a machine doesn't necessarily mean that it was built in 1905. All it tells us that it was not built before 1905.

Building the database for the Second Edition was a formidable task that took months of work. After some health problems, I was forced to limit my daily schedule. This gave me a lot of idle time, so working on the database filled in many hours that would have been wasted by watching endless news programs and soap operas. I was able to acquire some very early implement directories that provided lots of new information. These have been carefully gleaned for anything that would expand our knowledge of farm implement manufacturers and their products.

Despite all the information and data in this book, there is still much more to be found. We have spent most of a lifetime collecting literature on early farm equipment. Even so, our collection is woefully inadequate, especially for certain implements.

Some companies survived for only a short time, probably fading away before their first catalog was issued. Other companies were notably stingy with their catalogs. For many, magazine advertisements were the primary

means of getting their sales message to the farmer. Some companies worked through a drummer, or a traveling salesman, and others displayed their goods at county fairs and similar events.

Local hardware stores, blacksmith shops, and implement dealers often made the decision for a community by stocking those makes which had a personal appeal.

Current prices for collectible farm machinery are virtually impossible to determine. Prices vary considerably from one auction to another, even in the same geographic area. Perhaps one auction was well advertised and was held on a beautiful day. Another might have been on a cold, foggy day when all but the hardy souls stayed home.

Let it be said that collectible farm machinery prices are on the rise. Today, the decrepit remains of an old sulky plow might bring up to $100, even though a nice example of the same plow likely sold for under $20, just a few years ago.

It never ceases to amaze this writer that we had so many talented workers in our past. For instance, the wheelwright usually learned the trade after a long apprenticeship. Today, not very many of us would be capable of making a set of wheels, even with a shop full of expensive woodworking machines. The early wheelwright of the 1880s used chisels, mallets, drawknives, spoke shaves, and other hand tools.

We might look at the intricate castings in some early machines. Patternmakers and iron founders conspired to produce parts that are completely foreign to our world of welded fabrication. Little wonder that many of us have become interested in vintage farm machinery. Perhaps a few of us, like myself, have become completely enamored with the quiet beauty and serenity of these pages from the past.

Hopefully, we will eventually be able to produce yet another edition of this book. In that regard, we encourage anyone having old farm machinery literature, history, and photographs to write: C. H. Wendel, c/o Krause Publications, 700 E. State Street, Iola, WI 54990-0001.

We hope you will enjoy this book for many years to come.

C. H. Wendel
Jan. 6, 2003

Trademarks

This section contains dozens of trademarks gleaned from the pages of the *Patent Office Gazette*. They are arranged alphabetically by companies. While many of these companies will be found within this book, others are not referred to, simply because their trademark applications are the only information within our files. The trademark listings can prove valuable in several ways. First, they provide a facsimile of the mark that might have been used on a specific machine. Looking at Avery Co., for instance, you can get a conception of its "Yellow Fellow" trademark. Another interesting feature is that most trademarks include the date when it was first used. For instance, under Grand Detour Plow Co., it's "Grand Detour" trademark was used since 1837. That phrase nails down the first use of the mark, obviously and makes it plain that the Grand Detour plow had its first public life at that time.

Trademark listings also manifest a number of interesting companies for which we have no other record. One example is the "Monitor" trademark of Minneapolis Plow Works, filed in 1898 and "used since August 1875." Our research thus far has never found a clue regarding this company. Also of interest, there are many trademarks that appear in farm equipment literature that we have never located, despite a perusal of the *Patent Office Gazette* from 1872 onward. Having a trademark doesn't necessarily mean that the trademark is registered and this must have happened to some extent. On the other hand, International Harvester Co., in particular, seems to have registered every mark it had, with dozens appearing in the following section, plus many others for tractors and other equipment.

Farm machinery trademarks did not become popular with manufacturers until the 1880s and following years. Much of the impetus came from farm equipment trade magazines. Editorials encouraged the use of a trademark for the sake of product identity. The idea took root and many different marks emerged in the following years; some are quite interesting. In this section, the mark is shown underneath is the company name, followed by the year the mark was first used and the year it was filed with the U.S. Patent Office.

HODGES

Acme Harvester Co., 1870/1893, Peking, Ill.

AMSCO

American Seeding Machine Co., 1918/1920, Springfield, Ohio.

SUPERIOR

American Seeding Machine Co., 1868/1923, Springfield, Ohio.

ADRIANCE

Adriance, Platt & Co., 1878/1912, Poughkeepsie, N.Y.

HOOSIER

American Seeding Machine Co., 1867/1911, Richmond, Ind.

Hi-Yield

American Steel Products Co., 1916/1817, Macomb, Ill.

ASPINWALL

Aspinwall-Watson Co., 1884/1925, Houlton, Maine.

B.F. Avery & Sons, 1869/1920, Louisville, Kty.

Harvest-All

Avery Farm Machinery Co., 1937/1937, Peoria, Ill.

MONITOR

Baker Manufacturing Co., 1874/1892, Evansville, Wisc.

BALDWIN

Baldwin Harvester Co., 1927/1927, Independence, Mo.

MATCHLESS

Aultman & Taylor Machinery Co., 1893/1911, Mansfield, Ohio.

YELLOW FELLOW

Avery Co., 1900/1922, Peoria, Ill.

THE BAIN

The Bain Wagon Co., 1852/1923, Kenosha, Wisc.

Monitor

Baker Manufacturing Co., 1874/1948, Evansville, Wisc.

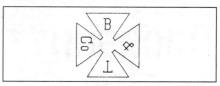

Belcher & Taylor Agricultural Co., 1894/1894, Chicopee Falls, Mass.

THE CHAMPION

Cecil Billups, 1876/1913, Norfolk, Va.

6

IMP Sr&Jr

Bucher & Gibbs Plow Co., 1873/1896, Canton, Ohio.

Burch Plow Works Co., 1897/1919, Crestline, Ohio.

AGITATOR

J.I. Case Threshing Machine Co., 1880/1990, Racine, Wisc.

BIRDSELL

Birdsell Manufacturing Co., 1855/1932, South Bend, Ind.

IMPERIAL

Bucher & Gibbs Plow Co., 1873/1896, Canton, Ohio.

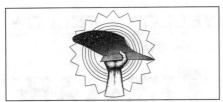

J.I. Case Plow Works, 1902/1910, Racine, Wisc.

Chattanooga Implement & Manufacturing Co., 1906/1908, Chattanooga, Tenn.

COCKSHUTT

Cockshutt Plow Co., Limited, 1877/1949, Brantford, Ontario, Canada.

Cutaway Harrow Co., 1912/1925, Higganum, Conn.

TEXAS RANGER

Deere & Co., 1875/1895, Moline, Ill.

JOHN DEERE

Deere & Co., 1847/1897, Moline, Ill.

DeLaval Separator Co., 1916/1920, New York, N.Y.

TREKKER

Crossman & Sielcken, 1910/1916, New York, N.Y.

KC

Deere & Co., 1918/1918, Moline, Ill.

HOOF

Deere & Co., 1914/1914, Moline, Ill.

D.H.Co.

Deering Harvester Co., 1897/1900, Chicago, Ill.

COMBINE MILKER

DeLaval Separator Co., 1947/1956, Poughkeepsie, N.Y.

ANNU-OILED

Dempster Mill Manufacturing Co., 1925/1925, Beatrice, Neb.

Dunham Co., 1881/1912, Berea, Ohio

COLTI-PACKER

Dunham Co., 1914/1914, Berea, Ohio.

Eagle Manufacturing Co., 1944/1945, Appleton, Wisc.

DUNHAM COLTI-PACKER

Dunham Co., 1917/1918, Berea, Ohio.

DUNHAM

Dunham Co., 1881/1912, Berea, Ohio.

KELLY DUPLEX

Duplex Mill & Manufacturing Co., 1885/1911, Springfield, Ohio.

Elgin Windmill Co., 1938/1939, Elgin, Ill.

Elgin

Elgin Windmill Co., 1890/1939, Elgin, Ill.

TWO-IN-ONE

Emerson-Brantingham Co., 1926/1926, Rockford, Ill.

"EMPIRE"

Empire Plow Co., 1890/1925, Cleveland, Ohio

Farm Tools, Inc., 1937/1938, Mansfield, Ohio

SUCCESS

J.A. Engel & Co., 1907/1907, East Peoria, Ill.

Empire Cream Separator Co., 1905/1918, Bloomfield, N.J.

ENTERPRISE

Enterprise Manufacturing Co., 1867/1924, Philadelphia, Pa.

A.T. Ferrell & Co., 1879/1951, Saginaw, Mich.

STAR

A.T. Ferrell & Co., 1879/1951, Kendallville, Ind.

G & D Manufacturing Co., 1904/1948, Streator, Ill.

PULVER-PLOW

Garden City Feeder Co., 1922-1923, Racine, Wisc.

Gleanor Manufacturing Co., 1923/1926, Independence, Mo.

SKIMMASTER

Galloway Co., Inc., 1937/1938, Waterloo, Iowa.

GARDEN CITY

Garden City Feeder Co., 1922/1923, Pella, Iowa

Gesting Wagon Co., 1878/1915, St. Louis, Mo.

Gleanor Combine Harvestor Corp., 1923/1928, Independence, Mo.

Globe Milker Inc., 1945/1945, Des Moines, Iowa.

Grain King

Grain King Manufacturing Co., 1918/1926, Minnesota Transfer, Minn.

Ideal

B.F. Gump Co., 1912/1919, Chicago, Ill.

TORNADO

Williamson R. Harrison, 1885/1911, Massillon, Ohio.

Gordon Bean and Pea Harvester Co., 1918/1920, Elizabeth City, N.C.

Grand Detour Plow Co., 1837/1916, Dixon, Ill.

E.J. RUBOTTOM PLOW

P.B. Hackley, 1904/1922, Berkeley, Calif.

CHAMPION.

Hench & Dromgold Co., 1881/1916, York, Pa.

O. V. B.

Hibbard, Spencer, Bartlett & Co., 1884/1896, Chicago, Ill.

LIFETIME

Holt Manufacturing Co., 1922/1923, Stockton, Calif.

DIAMOND

International Harvester Co., 1897/1920, Chicago, Ill.

KENTUCKY

International Harvester Co., 1893/1920, Chicago, Ill.

PLANO

International Harvester Co., 1893/1915, Chicago, Ill.

HOCKING VALLEY

Hocking Valley Manufacturing Co., 1869/1925, Lancaster, Ohio.

MONITOR

Huntley Manufacturing Co., 1886/1913, Silver Creek, N.Y.

HOOSIER

International Harvester Co., 1867/1920, Chicago, Ill.

ONCE OVER AND ITS ALL OVER

International Harvester Co., 1925/1925, Chicago, Ill.

McCORMICK

International Harvester Co., 1880/1915, Chicago, Ill.

INTERNATIONAL

International Harvester Co., 1903/1915, Chicago, Ill.

CHAMPION

International Harvester Co., 1860/1913, Chicago, Ill.

McCORMICK-DEERING

International Harvester Co., 1922/1926, Chicago, Ill.

TITAN

International Harvester Co., 1910/1913, Chicago, Ill.

DEERING

International Harvester Co., 1879/1915, Chicago, Ill.

LITTLE GENIUS

International Harvestor Co., 1915/1915, Canton, Ohio.

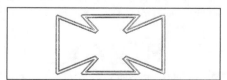

International Harvester Co., 1895/1926, Chicago, Ill.

LITTLE CHIEF

International Harvester Co., 1920/1920,
Chicago, Ill.

International Harvester Co., 1900/1913,
Chicago, Ill.

International Harvester Co., 1911/1913,
Chicago, Ill.

International Harvester Co., 1887/1913,
Chicago, Ill.

International Harvester Co., 1913/1913,
Chicago, Ill.

TOM THUMB

International Harvester Co., 1908/1913,
Chicago, Ill.

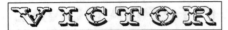

International Harvester Co., 1912/1913,
Chicago, Ill.

DAISY

International Harvester Co., 1812/1913,
Chicago, Ill.

NEW SOUTHERN

International Harvester Co., 1908/1913,
Chicago, Ill.

RIVAL

International Harvester Co., 1892/1913,
Chicago, Ill.

RIVAL

International Harvester Co., 1908/1913,
Chicago, Ill.

International Harvester Co., 1881/1913,
Chicago, Ill.

MILWAUKEE

International Harvester Co., 1887/1913,
Chicago, Ill.

STEEL KING

International Harvester Co., 1908/1913,
Chicago, Ill.

HANDY ANDY.

International Harvester Co., 1870/1914,
Chicago, Ill.

VOLUNTEER

International Harvester Co., 1883/1920,
Chicago, Ill.

JOHNSTON

International Harvester Co., 1871/1894,
Batavia, N.Y.

WEBER

International Harvester Co., 1845/1914,
Chicago, Ill.

KEYSTONE

International Harvester Co., 1912/1914,
Chicago, Ill.

I.H.C.

International Harvester Co., 1904/1913,
Chicago, Ill.

SPEED KING

International Harvester Co., 1923/1928,
Columbus, Ohio

LIGHTNING

International Harvester Co., 1895/1900,
Kansas City, Mo.

Joliet Manufacturing Co., 1923/1923, Joliet, Ill.

IDEAL

John F. Langdon, 1906/1913, Kansas City, Kan.

STROUD

Little Red Wagon Manufacturing Co.,
1899/1924, Omaha, Neb.

Massey Harris Harvester Co. Inc., Batavia, N.Y.

MONARCH

La Crosse Plow Co., 1898/1900, La Crosse, Wisc.

LA CROSSE

La Crosse Plow Co., 1898/1900, La Crosse, Wisc.

Little Red Wagon Manufacturing Co.,
1899/1924, Omaha, Neb.

LILLISTON

Lilliston Implement Co., 1911/1948, Albany, Ga.

Meadows Manufacturing Co., 1903/1911,
Pontiac, Ill.

Linstroth Wagon Co., 1905/1905, St. Louis, Mo.

Minneapolis-Moline Power Implement Co.,
1934/1947, Minneapolis, Minn.

MONITOR

Minneapolis Plow Works, 1875/1898,
Minneapolis, Minn.

MONITOR

Moline Implement Co., 1874/1927, Moline, Ill.

McDONALD

Moline Plow Co., 1911/1922, Moline, Ill.

Minneapolis-Moline Power Implement Co., 1931/1932, Hopkins, Minn.

CLIPPER

Massey-Harris Co., Inc., 1938/1938, Racine, Wisc.

HUSKOR

Minneapolis-Moline Power Implement Co., 1934/1950, Hopkins, Minn.

Minneapolis Steel & Machinery Co., 1919/1919, Minneapolis, Minn.

Moline Implement Co., 1925/1925, Moline, Ill.

CRESCENT

Moline Plow Co., 1896/1900, Moline, Ill.

HERCULES

Moline Plow Co., 1913/1922, Moline, Ill.

Moline Plow Co., 1905/1905, Moline, Ill.

NH

New Holland Machine Co., 1940/1956, Lancaster Co., Pa.

New Idea Spreader Co., 1899/1930, Bellevue, Ohio

Moline Plow Co. 1897/1899, Moline, Ill.

Moline Plow Co., 1870/1893, Moline, Ill.

SATTLEY

Montgomery Ward & Co., Inc., 1891/1929, Chicago, Ill.

O.K. UNLOADER

F.E. Myers & Bros. Co., 1902/1922, Ashland, Ohio.

Automaton

New Holland Machine Co., 1947/1947, New Holland, Pa.

NEW IDEA

New Idea Spreader Co., 1899/1930, Coldwater, Ohio.

Ohio Cultivator Co., 1905/1905, Bellevue, Ohio.

OSBORNE

D.M. Osborne & Co., 1894/1894, Auburn, N.Y.

PAPEC

Papec Machine Co., 1901/1916, Shortsville, N.Y.

PEERLESS

Peerless Husker Co., Inc., 1906/1923, Buffalo, N.Y.

Surge

Pine Tree Milking Machine Co., 1925/1925, Chicago, Ill.

Hydramatic

Oliver Corp., 1947/1947, Chicago, Ill.

Oliver Chilled Plow Works, 1905/1905, South Bend, Ind.

D.M. Osborne & Co., 1893/1894, Auburn, N.Y.

OSBORNE

D.M. Osborne & Co., 1890/1895, Auburn, N.Y.

PERFECTO

Parlin & Orendorff Co., 1915/1915, Canton, Ill.

Pine Tree Milking Machine Co., 1918/1918, Chicago, Ill.

Roderick Lean

Pittsburgh Forgings Co., 1894/1955, Coraopolis, Pa.

LIGHT RUNNING PLANO

Plano Manufacturing Co., 1885/1894, Chicago, Ill.

RED JACKET

Red Jacket Manufacturing Co., 1881/1891, Davenport, Iowa.

EVOLUTION

Roderick Lean Manufacturing Co., 1911/1912, Mansfield, Ohio.

RONNING

Ronning Motor Co., 1912/1923, Minneapolis, Minn.

ROSS

E.W. Ross Co., 1850/1924, Springfield, Ohio.

St. Joseph Manufacturing Co., 1894/1896, Mishawaka, Ind.

LIGHT RUNNING JONES

Plano Manufacturing Co., 1894/1894, Chicago, Ill.

Plano Manufacturing Co., 1898/1898, Chicago, Ill.

RED JACKET

Red Jacket Manufacturing Co., 1881/1912, Davenport, Iowa.

Rome Plow Co., 1932/1956, Cedartown, Ga.

CORNBINE

Rosenthal Manufacturing Co., 1941/1944, West Allis, Wisc.

ECONOMY KING

Sears, Roebuck & Co., 1913/1914, Chicago, Ill.

HEXAGON

Sears, Roebuck & Co., 1922/1923, Chicago, Ill.

James B. Sedberry, 1920/1921, Texarkana, Ark.

Silver Manufacturing Co., 1890/1918, Salem, Ohio.

South Bend Iron Works, 1892/1892, South Bend, Ind.

Superior Drill Co., 1868/1892, Springfield, Ohio.

BLACK HAWK

D.M. Sechler Implement & Carriage Co., 1907/1912, Moline, Ill.

BLACK HAWK

D.M. Sechler Implement & Carriage Co., 1897/1899, Moline, Ill.

MOTO·MILKER

Sharples Milker Co., 1919/1921, Toronto, Canada

Sharples Separator Co., 1916/1919, West Chester, Pa.

WOLVERINE.

Marvin Smith Co., 1895/1899, Chicago, Ill.

HORN

Daniel E. Speicher, 1903/1920, Urbana, Ind.

SAMSON

Stover Manufacturing Co., 1899/1903, Freeport, Ill.

IDEAL

Stover Manufacturing Co., 1898/1898, Freeport, Ill.

Farmhand

Superior Separator Co., 1948/1948, Hopkins, Minn.

Union Corn Planter Co., 1871/1896, Peoria, Ill.

"V&K"

Vaile-Kimes Co., 1915/1915, Dayton, Ohio.

CHAMPION.

Warder, Bushnell & Glessner Co., 1860/1901, Chicago, Ill.

NEW CENTURY

Walter A. Wood Mowing and Reaping Machine Co., 1900/1901, Hoosick Falls, N.Y.

Wyatt Manufacturing Co., 1945/1946, Salina, Kan.

Weber Wagon Co., 1895/1896, Chicago, Ill.

ACE

U.S. Wind Engine & Pump Co., 1925/1925, Batavia, Ill.

DIABOLO

United Engine Co., 1912/1916, Lansing, Mich.

EMPIRE

United States Butter Extractor Co., 1895/1895, Newark, N.J.

Vega Separator Co., 1919/1920, Fostoria, Ohio.

Alfalfa Grinders

Prior to 1900, farmers were becoming increasingly aware of new terms, such as "feed efficiency." Simply, this meant getting all possible gain from a given amount of livestock feed. Manufacturers claimed that by grinding alfalfa, the feeding value could be doubled. As a result, a few companies offered special alfalfa grinders, also known as "alfalfa comminuters." Regardless of the name, the primary goal was to provide farmers with a means of gaining better feed efficiency from alfalfa and other crops. Eventually, it was possible to achieve the same results from a hammer mill that could also be used for other feed grinding, so the sales of alfalfa grinders were rather limited. On the vintage farm equipment scene, the value of these machines cannot be accurately determined.

In 1906, the Silver Manufacturing Co., Salem, Ohio, was offering a rather large portable alfalfa grinder. It likely was an ancestor of the "hay choppers," which eventually would assume a niche in the farm equipment market. This one could blow the ground alfalfa into a bin or into a barn. The problem was that large quantities of this material were prone to spontaneous combustion; chopped hay was the cause of many barn fires.

Appleton Manufacturing Co., Batavia, Ill., sold its Alfalfa Reducer in 1917 and for a few years before and after that time. The machine shown here was of the stationary variety, requiring that the hay be fed into the cutters via a hand feeder. Cut hay dropped from the hopper, although a sacking elevator could be attached. Hammer-mills and other multi-use machines limited the market for this specialized design.

Although Stover Manufacturing & Engine Co., Freeport, Ill., is probably best known for its gasoline engines, this company also built many other farm machines, especially in the 1900-1930 period. The Stover Comminuter appeared about 1915 and remained on the market for several years, with this style being made in 1918. Two sizes were available, with the No. 55 shown here being capable of processing three to five tons of alfalfa hay per day of 10 hours and requiring six to 12 horsepower for efficient operation. The larger No. 56 Comminuter was intended for commercial operators.

Trade Names			
Appleton	Appleton Mfg. Co.	Batavia, IL	1917
Monarch	Silver Mfg. Co.	Salem, OH	1906
Scientific	Foos Mfg. Co.	Springfield, OH	1905
Stover	Stover Mfg. Co.	Freeport, IL	1915

Alfalfa Planting & Harvesting Implements

Many implements were built specifically for the alfalfa crop. These included alfalfa harrows, alfalfa loaders, alfalfa rakes and many other items. To avoid needless repetition, these specialized items are categorized under their generic headings, such as hay loaders, rakes, harrows and the like.

Trade Names			
Dain's Power Lift	Dain Mfg. Co.	Ottumwa, IA	1905
Iowa	Hay Tool Mfg. Co.	Council Bluffs, IA	1905
Rancher	E. Children's Mfg. Co.	Council Bluffs, IA	1905

Did You Know?

Early corn planters, especially those prior to the automatic check-row designs, command $500 or perhaps much more.

B

Balers

Up to the 1940s, balers were generally called "hay presses." Apparently, the change in terminology came about together with the advent of the automatic pick-up balers. These were completely mobile machines intended for direct baling in the field. By comparison, hay presses were generally a portable unit that could be moved from farm to farm, with the hay or straw being brought to the hay press vis-à-vis the baler. Since the majority of the machines included in this book are portable hay presses and to avoid redundancy, balers are also included in this section.

Barn Equipment

A great many items could rightfully be placed within this category, although this book separates various categories, such as Dairy Equipment, Haying Equipment and the like. Until about 1900, the average barn was about the same as it had been for hundreds of years, containing ample room for hay storage, stalls for livestock, harness, milk stools and little else. With the coming of farm mechanization came the introduction of great labor-saving devices such as litter carriers, carts and other devices intended to lessen work for the farmer.

Butler Mfg., Co., Kansas City, was one of many companies offering an extensive line of galvanized tanks and other equipment. A 1907 advertisement demonstrates stock fountains, galvanized hog troughs and its Improved K.C. Water Elevator. The latter has acquired collectible status, with good examples fetching more than $100 by antique dealers.

Lightning rod equipment had become quite popular by 1900, particularly in those areas in which thunderstorms were frequent and oftentimes severe. Curiously, many early manufacturers advertised their wares in the farm equipment journals of the day. One of these was the Des Moines, Iowa, firm of Dodd & Struthers. Its 1905 advertisement illustrates a static generator that it furnished to all of its retailers. It was intended to demonstrate the proclivities of lightning and also how it could be tamed with the use of lightning rods.

Firms like J.E. Porter Co., Ottawa, Ill., specialized in barn and farmstead equipment. This 1907 offering for the Porter Litter Carrier was one example. The carrier was mounted on an iron track and featured a raising and lowering device to make work easier for the farmer.

Litter carriers became quite popular with the advent of large barns, particularly the dairy barn. The majority of Midwestern farms of 1900 had at least a small herd of milk cows. R. Herschel Manufacturing Co., Peoria, Ill., offered its Standard Carrier in 1909. It used a solid wire cable from which the carrier was suspended.

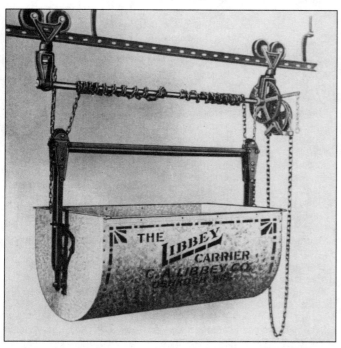

C.A. Libbey Co., Oshkosh, Wis., offered its version of the ideal litter carrier in the 1920s. It featured a simple chain-operated device for raising and lowering the carrier. Track systems were available for almost any situation and included accessories, such as right angle curves, switches and other configurations to permit travel to all portions of a barn.

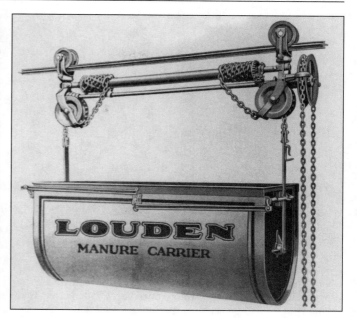

Louden Machinery Co., Fairfield, Iowa, offered a huge line of barn and dairy equipment, including cattle stalls, stanchions, hay carriers and several different styles of litter carriers. The model shown here from a catalog of the 1920s was typical of the line. Most carriers were designed with a track system extending outdoors for dumping the loaded unit, either onto a dung heap or into a waiting manure spreader. Either way, the savings in labor was well worth the investment.

Bean Harvesters

By the 1890s, several companies were offering bean harvesters as a means of mechanizing what was otherwise a back-breaking job. The plants were cut just under the soil and the vines were gently windrowed. Usually, the cut beans were then cocked by forking them into small stacks for drying. After a suitable time, they were threshed. In most instances, the early offerings were intended for use with edible beans, since soybeans had not yet become an important crop. Very few bean harvesters are still in existence, so those still left should rank some value in the farm antiques market, but we have found no indication of their value.

Gale Manufacturing Co., Albion, Mich., offered its Albion Bean Harvester in 1894. It was designed to straddle two rows, cutting them and leaving them in windrows to be loaded onto a wagon. As previously noted, some farmers preferred cocking the beans first for better drying, while others hauled them directly to a waiting bean thresher.

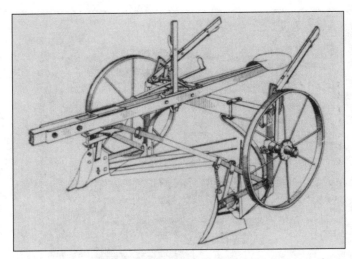

Caledonia Bean Harvester Works, Caledonia, N.Y., announced its New Caledonian Bean Harvester to the 1889 implement trade, noting that it was the result of "Twenty-three Year's Experience." That would put the beginnings of this machine back to 1866. Edible bean production was centered primarily in the Eastern states, gaining little prominence in the Western and Midwestern areas.

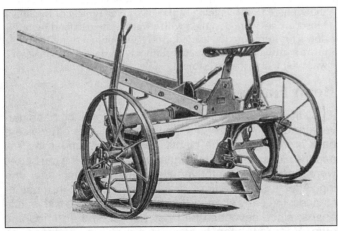

Miller's Bean Harvester, as advertised in 1898, was the product of F.W. Miller Manufacturing Co., LeRoy, N.Y. Advertising of the day noted it to be the "oldest and best and beyond competition." The company also made numerous other implements, including plows, cultivators and land rollers.

Wiard Plow Co., Batavia, N.Y., offered its Universal Bean Harvester as late as 1916. It could be purchased with an all-steel frame or a wooden frame, as desired, and could also be supplied with cast-iron or steel wheels, again at the whim of the purchaser. Eventually, the combine took over the job of harvesting edible beans, as well as soybeans, and the bean harvester became obsolete.

Trade Names

Adsit	Curtis Mfg. Co.	Albion, NY	1892
Akron	Akron Cultivator Co.	Akron, OH	1922
Albion	Gale Mfg. Co.	Albion, MI	1892
Bailor	Bailor Cultivator Co.	Atchison, KS	1924
Baldwin's American	Donaldson Bros.	Mt. Clemens, MI	1909
Bidwell	C. H. Bidwell Thresher Co.	Batavia, NY	1892
Boston	Sterling Mfg. Co.	Sterling, IL	1922
Caledonia	J. L. Owens Co.	Minneapolis, MN	1909
Champion	Champion Drill Co.	Avon, NY	1892
Chautauqua	Chautauqua Planter Co.	Jamestown, NY	1905
Common Sense	Lyndsey P. Thomas	Lowell, MI	1892
Detroit	American Harrow Co.	Detroit, MI	1905
Donaldson	Donaldson Bros.	Mt. Clemens, MI	1922
Eagle	Eagle Mfg. Co.	Davenport, IA	1892
Excelsior	D. D. Bromley	Waterport, NY	1892
Famous Ohio	Ohio Cultivator Co.	Bellevue, OH	1909
Fox	Lehr Agricultural Co.	Fremont, OH	1892
Gale	Gale Mfg. Co.	Albion, MI	1915
Giant	A. P. Dickey Mfg. Co.	Racine, WI	1892
Giant	Donaldson Bros.	Mt. Clemens, MI	1909
Holly	Patterson Mfg. Co.	Holly, MI	1915
Johnson's	A. Johnson	Waterport, NY	1892
Killefer	Killefer Mfg. Co.	Los Angeles, CA	1924
Kraus	Akron Cultivator Co.	Akron, OH	1909
Kraus	Charles Amos & Co.	Detroit, MI	1905
Lehr	Lehr Agricultural Co.	Fremont, OH	1905
Little Giant	Howland Mfg. Co.	Pontiac, MI	1905
Little Giant	Patterson & Brown Bros. Mfg. Co.	Holly, MI	1909
Little Giant	Wells Cultivator Co.	Milford, MI	1892
Luckey Improved	Luckey & Co.	Paris, TN	1892
McWhorter	McWhorter Mfg. Co.	Riverton, NJ	1905
Miller	F. W. Miller	Caledonia, NY	1892
Miller	Le Roy Plow Co.	Le Roy, NY	1905
New American	American Harrow Co.	Detroit, MI	1892
New Caledonian	Caledonia Bean Harvester Works	Caledonia, NY	1905
Ohio	Ohio Cultivator Co.	Bellevue, OH	1905
Owens	J. L. Owens Co.	Minneapolis, MN	1905
Parker	Parker Plow Co.	Richmond, MI	1915
Peerless	Donaldson Bros.	Mt. Clemens, MI	1922
Reed	Reed Mfg. Co.	Kalamazoo, MI	1905
Rowell	J. S. Rowell Mfg. Co.	Braver Dam, WI	1905
Savage's Improved	H. M. Smith & Co.	Richmond, VA	1892
Segment	Moore Plow & Implement Co.	Greenville, MI	1905
Sterling	Sterling Mfg. Co.	Sterling, IL	1909
Toledo	Toledo Plow Co.	Toledo, OH	1915
Turner	Geo. O. P. Turner	Churchville, NY	1892
Westinghouse	Westinghouse Company	Schenectady, NY	1892
Wiard's Universal	Wiard Plow Co.	Batavia, NY	1905
Wilder	York's Foundry & Machine Co.	Honeoye, NY	1913

Bee Hives & Supplies

Although bee-keeping is ordinarily considered to be a very specialized industry, farmers often kept a few hives of bees to help pollinate their crops, as well as providing an inexpensive source of delicious honey. Rather than depend on the chances of finding a "honey tree," commercially made bee hives were a method of harvesting a valuable product. In addition to hives, a few companies manufactured the other necessities, such as supers, smokers, honey extractors and other supplies.

Kretchmer Manufacturing Co., Council Bluffs, Iowa, was established in 1864. This firm pioneered many different farm-related items, including its Iowa seed-corn sorters. However, a 1910 advertisement indicates that the company was ready to supply virtually any need for bee culture.

Trade Names

Aspinwall	Aspinwall Mfg. Co.	Jacksom, MI	1909
Back Lot	Standard Churn Co.	Wapakoneta, OH	1945
Beeware	G. B. Lewis Co.	Watertown, WI	1945
Coolsmoke	G. B. Lewis Co.	Watertown, WI	1945
Dadant's	Dadant & Sons	Hamilton, IL	1905
Edson	Wyman L. Edson	Union Center, NY	1892
Everybody's	D. Stutzman	Ligonier, IN	1892
Falcon	W. T. Falconer Mfg. Co.	Jamestown, NY	1905
Kretchmer	Kretchmer Mfg. Co.	Council Bluffs, IA	1909
Leahy	Leahy Mfg. Co.	Higginsville, MO	1909
McCune	Wm. McCune & Co.	Sterling, IL	1892
New American	A. G. Hill	Kendallville, IN	1905
Root	A. I. Root Co.	Medina, OH	1945
Simplicity	W. T. Falconer Mfg. Co.	Jamestown, NY	1892

Bob Sleds & Sleighs

By definition, a bob sled or bob sleigh consists of two sets of runners, one behind the other. These are connected with a reach, built in such a way that the two sections can oscillate independently of each other. Sleighs, on the other hand, are simply a pair of runners mounted to a solid frame. Generally, sleighs were used for transporting people and bob sleds were used for transporting goods of every sort.

Sleighs are highly valued today, especially those built along fancy lines, with upholstered seats and other niceties. It is not uncommon for a nicely restored sleigh to bring more than $1,000, but, as with many antique items, the value depends somewhat on the region. Items commonly used in an area are more plentiful, thus keeping the price somewhat lower. Bob sleds or bob sleighs in good condition commonly bring $500 or more. Establishing a general price figure is difficult, since these are seldom seen on the antique market.

From my collection comes an 1877 circular for James Goold & Co., Albany, N.Y. Established in 1813, this company illustrated its 1816 model on the front of its brochure. The 1816 model looks little different than those built some 60 years later! A sleigh of this vintage would certainly be a valuable piece today, since only a handful of sleighs of its age still exists.

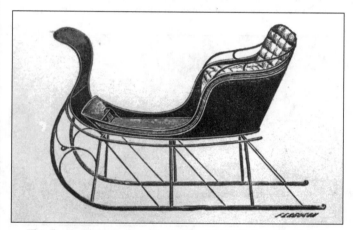

This Portland Cutter from the 1877 catalog of James Goold & Co., illustrates the state-of-the-art in sleighs. Sleighs were generally of the same basic design, with subtle cosmetic changes that could dramatically alter the appearance of the finished product. Relatively few Midwestern farmers of the 1870s were wealthy enough to own a cutter such as this. Most of those who could afford one didn't buy one. It was either a buggy, if the roads were permissible, or a bob sled, if they weren't.

Recognizing the reluctance of many farmers to invest in a cutter or sleigh, various firms offered a conversion kit. By removing the wheels from the buggy and replacing them with runners, the conversion was made from summer to winter. Pioneer Manufacturing Co., Columbus, Ohio, offered this conversion kit, "adjustable to fit any buggy, carriage, light delivery or express wagon…not too heavy for a light buggy or too light for a moderately heavy vehicle." In 1888, this kit sold for $5, plus freight.

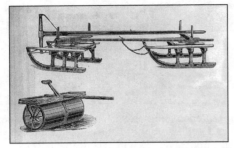

Castree-Mallery Co., Flint, Mich., offered various implements for 1887, including the bob sleigh pictured here. Usually, these were designed so that the front runners could turn beneath the reach, enabling the sled to make short turns. The length could be varied by moving the back set of runners ahead or back on the reach pole.

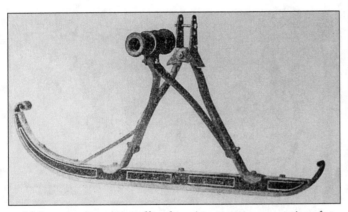

Numerous companies offered carriage-runner conversions for buggies and light wagons. Lansing Wagon Works, Lansing, Mich., was one such firm, offering three different styles for 1910. The same company also made Lansing wagons and Clark buggies. Despite the low cost, compared to a factory-built sleigh, conversion kits never gained great popularity.

Pioneer Implement Company, Council Bluffs, Iowa

Loosely defined, a cutter is a one-horse sleigh. Pioneer, like numerous other wagon makers, offered various cutter styles. Their 1903 dealer catalog notes, "You can sell cutters the first day it snows."

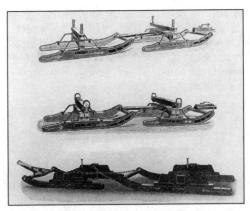

Bob sleds or bob sleighs were built by many different wagon makers. Some of these were then jobbed to other companies, such as Frost & Wood at Smiths Falls, Ontario, Canada. The latter offered several styles in its 1910 catalog, each designed for a specific purpose. The Ontario Sloop was the most common style, followed by the heavy teaming and logging sled. For extra heavy work, especially for logging, the Midland style was available. It used a wide track design to provide better stability.

Moline Plow Co., Moline, Ill., bought out the T.G. Mandt Co., Stoughton, Wis., in 1906. Mandt vehicles dated back to 1865—and at least into the early 1920s, this wholly owned subsidiary was known as the Mandt Wagon Branch of Moline Plow Co. Its offerings of 1920 included several styles of the Mandt oscillator sleds as shown. In addition, there were at least two styles of anti-tip sleds using a wider track pattern.

Evans Manufacturing Co., Hammond, N.Y., was producing several styles of bob sleighs at the turn of the century. Included was this flexible lumbering version. Instead of the usual bolster mountings for a standard wagon box, the lumbering style was furnished with heavy rings at each end of the bolsters for securing logs and other items.

Over time, certain standards developed in all phases of the farm implement industry. For instance, this Evans bob sleigh of 1905 was built with the track in New York Standard-style or 35 inches from center to center of the runners. However, the standard style was sometimes a disadvantage. If the runners broke through the snow pack on one side, the sled would upset. Then, there was nothing to do but tip the sled back to its proper orientation, reload the cargo and make another attempt. Wide-track sleds had the advantage of providing greater stability.

Boilers

By the 1880s, leading agriculturists were promoting the concept of cooking livestock feed to make it more palatable and more nutritious. The idea had been around for centuries but gained new impetus at this time. Numerous companies emerged with their own ideas of the ideal boiler, cooker or steam generator. Eventually, farmers decided that the advantages were heavily outweighed by the investment in time and labor.

The Austin Steam Generator of 1889 was designed as a multi-purpose unit. It could be used for cooking feed, slaughtering hogs, heating water for laundry and bath use and various other purposes. This company built many different products in its long history, eventually concentrating on the manufacture of road building machinery. The manufacturer, F.C. Austin Co., was located in Chicago.

Crippen's Agricultural Boiler was patented in 1899; this 1903 advertisement shows it in use for scalding hogs as part of the slaughtering and butchering process. Its advertising notes that "the above boiler is a revolution of the old sled for butchering, as one person can butcher and hang a hog weighing 400 pounds." This combination outfit could also be used for smoking meat, drying fruit and, with its attached pump, and also served as a hand-operated orchard sprayer. It was built by H.M. Crippen, Athens, Ohio.

Davis Gasoline Engine Works Co., Waterloo, Iowa, offered this Northwestern Improved Return Draft Steam Feed Cooker in 1906. By that time, W.F. Davis, the company's founder, left for other endeavors; the company was then in control of the Cascaden interests at Waterloo. Like other feed cookers of its time, this one consisted of a small boiler that was intended to be portable, although it probably took Dad, the boys and the hired man working in unison to move it any distance.

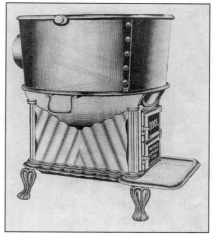

The Hartman Co., Chicago, offered this Majestic Feed Cooker as late as 1919. This one was on the order of a large cast-iron cauldron set inside of a metal jacket; the latter being attached to a rather ordinary box heater. The whole outfit was very simple and buyers were instructed to specify whether they would be burning wood or coal, so that the proper grates would be included. In 1919, this complete outfit sold for $20, plus freight.

Bone Cutters

The grinding of bones is of early origin. The ground material was often returned to the soil as fertilizer; commercially, it was then reduced to bone-black. Farmers and farm wives of the late 1800s were aware that ground bones were an excellent supplement to the diet of their laying hens, since the extra calcium meant better eggs with harder shells. Thus, these machines enjoyed brief popularity until oyster shells and similar products became available on a commercial basis. Bone cutters are seldom found, and, despite many queries and research, we were unable to find a current market value. However, it can be presumed that, due to their scarcity, bone cutters can now fetch $100 and perhaps much more, depending on the machine, its complexity, age and overall condition.

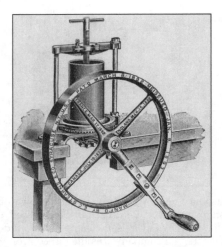

The Webster & Hannum bone cutter was a tabletop variety, with the processed material dropping from the table above into a waiting basket. This one had patents dating back to 1892 and was made by E.C. Stearns & Co., Syracuse, N.Y. The adjustable handle is an interesting feature. It could be removed entirely if any sort of belt power was available.

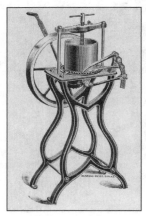

Webster & Hannum bone cutters, like most other makes, were available in several sizes. The larger units featured an automatic feed mechanism, and this was a great advantage. The crank handle was adjustable and could be removed entirely for use with a belted power. Unfortunately, the average farm of 1895, the year that this mill was advertised, had no power except a strong arm.

In an 1897 advertisement, P.A. Webster, Cazevonia, N.Y., noted that his Premier Green Bone Cutter was "a great revolution in bone cutters…" It had been personally tested and recommended by individuals, as well as by some popular magazines of the day. According to its maker, "not only a woman but a child can cut bones with ease…"

Curiously, Detroit Engine Works, Detroit, added bone cutters to its line about 1910, continuing with them for a few years. This one could be operated by hand or could be powered by an engine. For the latter, three bolts were removed and the crank wheel could be slid off the belt pulley. The company noted that it wasn't necessary to sharpen the knives every week and, further, that there was no need "for your neighbor to have a better [cutter] than you."

The majority of the bone cutters were for green bones, but Enterprise Manufacturing Co., Philadelphia, also offered a series of Dry Bone Mills, with this one being of 1910 vintage. In addition to dry bones, this mill could reduce corn, roots, bark and other materials as desired. Even though it is small in physical size, this hand-operated model weighed some 60 pounds

Trade Names			
Adam	Adam's Steel & Wire Works	Joliet, IL	1905
Adam	Wm. E. Pratt Mfg. Co.	Chicago, IL	1915
Crown	Ralph W. Fry	Easton, PA	1931
Crown	Wilson Bros.	Easton, PA	1905
Daisy	Ralph W. Fry	Easton, PA	1931
Daisy	Wilson Bros.	Easton, PA	1905
Detroit	Detroit Engine Works	Detroit, MI	1910
Enterprise	Enterprise Mfg. Co.	Philadelphia, PA	1910
Harrison	Leonard D. Harrison	New Haven, CT	1892
Humphrey	Humphrey & Sons	Joliet, IL	1905
Mann	F. W. Mann Co.	Milford, MA	1905

Trade Names (cont..)			
Newell	Newell Universal Mill Co.	New York, NY	1892
Nonpareil	L. J. Miller	Cincinnati, OH	1892
Philips	C. C. Philips	Philadelphia, PA	1892
Pratt	Wm. E. Pratt Mfg. Co.	Chicago, IL	1924
Premier	P. A. Webster	Cazenovia, NY	1897
Standard	Standard Green Bone Cutter Co.	Milford, MA	1913
Stearns	E. C. Stearns & Co.	Syracuse, NY	1905
Stover	Stover Mfg. Co.	Freeport, IL	1913
Tornado	W. R. Harrison & Co.	Massillon, OH	1913
Victor	Foster & Williams Mfg. Co.	Racine, WI	1913
Webster & Hannum	E. C. Stearns & Co.	Syracuse, NY	1892

Broom Corn Equipment

Before factory-made brooms were widely available, some farmers raised broom corn, cut it, dried it and did all those special things to make it suitable for durable brooms. All of the equipment was very specialized, so it is not often found today. Since it is virtually worthless for anything but its very specialized purpose, the value of this equipment is not usually as high as might be thought. For instance, a broom vise, used to compress and form the head of the broom might bring anywhere from $75 and up; a broom cutter to trim the bottom end of the broom might bring $50 or more, and the actual broom-making machine might not bring more than $200.

Since the broom-making business was and is very specialized, some of the machines used in this process give little clue as to their actual purpose. This 1884 illustration shows a broom corn scraper, apparently used in the early stages of the preparation process to clean the fibers of leaves and other undesirable debris. More than likely, this device was limited mainly to larger broom-making operations than ordinarily found in a farm broom-making shop.

Trade Names			
Acme	G. D. Colton & Co.	Galesburg, IL	1905
Galesburg	G. D. Colton & Co.	Galesburg, IL	1905
Genesee	Genesee Mfg. Co.	Mt. Morris, NY	1905
Stapples Universal	Little Giant Hay Press Co.	Dallas, TX	1905
Whitman's Hercules	Whitman Agricultural Co.	St. Louis, MO	1892

Bunchers

Originally, the buncher was intended to bunch or windrow seed clover and seed alfalfa for its trip to the threshing machine. Eventually, the buncher was used for other purposes, including the flax harvest and the pea harvest. It could also be used in down grain that was flattened by a wind or due to adverse soil and weather conditions. Use of these devices was rather limited, so they are now found only on rare occasions.

It took me considerable time to get a satisfactory image of this illustration, since the original left much to be desired. However, even this rather poor-quality image shows a heavy crop windrowed on the left, but a light crop on the right has been bunched. This device was made by the Side Delivery Buncher Co., Toledo, Ohio; the illustration is from a 1903 advertisement.

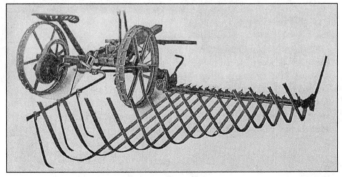

A 1905 advertisement of the Side Delivery Buncher Co., shows its Clover Buncher and Hay Windrower as attached to a mower. This unit could be attached to virtually any mowing machine. The cut material gathered on the buncher until full; the operator then raised the vertical fingers to the left, allowing the "bunch" to slide off behind the mower.

Did You Know?

Cast-iron lids from seed boxes are a rarity; on average, they sell from $20 to $30.

Port Huron Engine &Thresher Co., Port Huron, Mich., was a well-known manufacturer of traction engines, threshers and other farm machinery. Its 1907 announcement of a buncher was somewhat afield of its usual endeavors; it is not believed that Port Huron continued with bunchers for any length of time. This one was especially designed for harvesting peas, but could also be used with other crops.

While most bunchers were of a side-delivery design, the American buncher (shown in this 1903 advertisement) used a rear delivery system. The company offered two varieties—the American and the Improved Prairie Buncher. These units were designed particularly for the harvest of seed clover or seed alfalfa and were used primarily in areas amenable to these seed crops. American Buncher Manufacturing Co., was located in Indianapolis.

Did You Know?

Today, vintage flour mills often sell at a considerable figure; a nicely restored small mill might bring up to $1,000. However, a mill with a poor framework or a broken stone will bring but a fraction of that figure.

C

Cane Mills

Cane mills are used to squeeze the juice from sorghum cane or sugar cane. The extracted juice is then reduced to a syrup in a suitable evaporator pan. Many communities had at least one such cane mill to provide a source of corn syrup and sorghum for the kitchen. Eventually, most of this work was taken over by commercial refiners. But even today, a few cane mills remain for the annual production of these products. As with many kinds of farm equipment, cane mills and related items have almost no value to someone uninterested in them, but have substantial value to those who wish to perpetuate and preserve the art.

Blymyer Iron Works Co., Cincinnati, Ohio

Prior to the 1880s, cane mills were rarely found on farms. Commercial establishments were found in nearby towns. Aside from animal power, there was no way to operate the crushing rolls, unlike commercial establishments with steam engines. Companies like Blymyer probably were established around a foundry business, making the heavy cane mill a natural addition.

N.O. Nelson & Co., St. Louis, Mo.

By the 1880s, several companies were offering cane mills, sometimes calling them sorghum mills. This one was made by N.O.

Nelson & Co., St. Louis. It was a powered mill and could be driven either by attaching a belt pulley to the countershaft or by driving it from the tumbling rod on a horsepower.

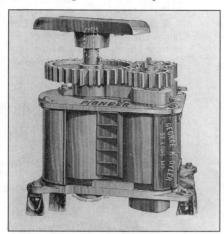

George K. Oyler Co., St. Louis, Mo.

An 1887 advertisement shows the Pioneer Cane Mill as built by George K. Oyler Co., St. Louis. This one was attached to four sturdy posts set in the ground. The large casting at the very top carried one or two sweep arms. One or more horses was hooked to the sweeps and walking "round-and-round," they turned the massive iron rolls.

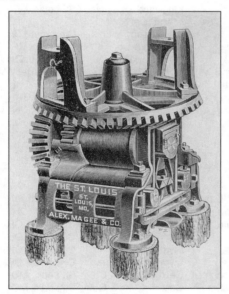

Alex. Magee and Co., St. Louis, Mo.

In an 1887 issue of *Farm Machinery*, an extensive article detailed the various makes and models of cane mills built in St. Louis. Included was The St. Louis, made by Alex. Magee & Co. Rather than use vertical rolls, this one featured horizontal crushing rolls. Sweep arms were attached to the large gear atop the mill, and the horsepower used to operate the mill was genuine animate horsepower.

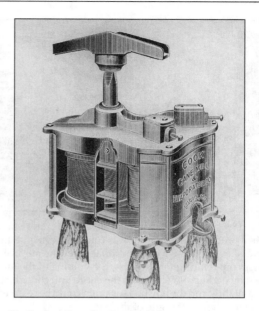

George K. Oyler Co., St. Louis, Mo.

A 1907 advertisement details the vertical cane mill from Cook Cane Mill & Evaporator Co., St. Louis. During the 1880s, the Cook mill and the Cook evaporator appear to have been built and sold by Geo. K. Oyler Co., St. Louis, with Cook eventually coming to dominate the market. Thousands of these mills were built, but only a few remain. The sorghum cane was first stripped of its leaves and heads and the stalks were fed through the rolls. The offal came out the other side, while the sweet juices were caught in a vessel below.

A 1922 catalog of Cook Cane Mill & Evaporator Co., illustrates numerous sizes and styles of cane mills, with this Superior model being one of the largest. Squeezing all the juice from the cane required considerable power, but by the 1920s this could be derived from various sources. Eventually, the popularity of the home-made product declined and commercially produced syrups came to a dominant position.

Did You Know?

The value of early ear-corn cutters can be more than $100 for one in good condition.

Did You Know?

Old cream cans, sometimes known as shipping cans, can often bring $20 to $40 or much more for an unusual or unique design.

By the 1880s, Cook's Rocking Portable Evaporator was an established product. The operator was constantly busy stoking the fire and skimming the foam and offal from the surface of the boiling syrup. During this process, the volume of the juice was reduced by perhaps 90%. Finally, the entire unit could be rocked or tilted slightly and the finished sorghum could be released from a convenient tap on the side of the pan.

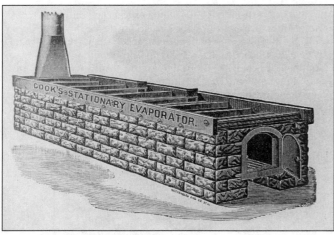

For permanent locations, Cooks' Stationary Evaporator could be set up, using either the best quality of galvanized steel or even better, a cold-rolled copper pan. Gates were used to regulate the flow of juice, and, as the juice boiled down in its section, it was transferred to the next and so on, until finally being released into waiting barrels and finally into jars. The first cold autumn day was an ideal time to sample the new batch of sorghum over a platter of buckwheat pancakes!

Trade Names

Aurora	Blymyer Iron Works	Cincinnati, OH	1905
Bounty	C. S. Bell Co.	Hillsboro, OH	1909
Bounty	James L. Haven Co.	Cincinnati, OH	1892
Champion	C. S. Bell Co.	Hillsboro, OH	1909
Chattanooga	Chattanooga Plow Co.	Chattanooga, TN	1905
Climax	C. S. Bell Co.	Hillsboro, OH	1909
Colon	Blymyer Iron Works	Cininnati, OH	1905
Columbus	Southern Plow Co.	Columbus, GA	1905
Cook's Star	Cook Cane Mill & Evaporator Co.	St. Louis, MO	1905
Cresson	George V. Cresson Co.	Philadelphia, PA	1905
Cyclone	Pearl River Foundry & Agric. Works	Jackson, MS	1892

Trade Names (cont...)

Domestic	C. S. Bell Co.	Hillsboro, OH	1909
Eclipse	C. S. Bell Co.	Hillsboro, OH	1909
Economist	C. S. Bell Co.	Hillsboro, Oh	1909
Economist	James L. Haven Co.	Cincinnati, OH	1892
Eureka	Blymyer Iron Works	Cincinnati, OH	1905
Export	Chattanooga Plow Co.	Chattanooga, TN	1909
Falls City	Brennan & Co.	Louisville, KY	1892
Farmer's Choice	C. S. Bell Co.	Hillsboro, OH	1909
Farrell	Farrell Foundry & Mach. Co.	Ansonia, CT	1905
Forest King	J. A. Field Mfg. Co.	St. Louis, MO	1892
Garland	Blymyer Iron Works	Cincinnati, OH	1905
Gem	American Seeding Machine Co.	Richmond, IN	1913
Gem	Brennan & Co.	Louisville, KY	1892
Globe	C. S. Bell Co.	Hillsboro, OH	1909
Gold Medal	C. S. Bell Co.	Hillsboro, OH	1909
Golden's	Golden's Foundry & Machine Co.	Columbus, GA	1905
Graham	Graham Foundry & Machine Co.	Graham, VA	1892
Great Western	Blymyer Iron Works	Cincinnati, OH	1905
H. V.	Hocking Valley Mfg. Co.	Lancaster, OH	1913
Horizontal	Kingsland & Douglas Mfg. Co.	St. Louis, MO	1892
Invincible	Kingsland & Douglas Mfg. Co.	St. Louis, MO	1892
Jewell	Blymyer Iron Works	Cincinnati, OH	1905
Kentucky	Brennan & Co.	Louisville, KY	1892
La Adela	Blymer Iron Works	Cincinnati, OH	1913
Little Giant	McMaull Machine & Foundry Co.	Ronceverte, WV	1892
Lombard	Lombard Iron Works	Augusta, GA	1905
Lone Star	C. S. Bell Co.	Hillsboro, OH	1909
Lone Star	James L. Haven Co.	Cincinnati, OH	1892
Missouri	Kingsland & Douglas Mfg. Co.	St. Louis, MO	1892
Monarch	C. S. Bell Co.	Hillsboro, OH	1909
National	Newell Universal Mill Co.	New York, NY	1892
New Live Oak	Blymyer Iron Works	Cincinnati, OH	1905
New South	C. S. Bell Co.	Hillsboro, OH	1909
New South	James L. Haven Co.	Cincinnati, OH	1892
Niles	Blymyer Iron Works	Cincinnati, OH	1905
Ohio	Blymyer Iron Works	Cincinnati, OH	1905
Opal	Blymyer Iron Works	Cincinnati, OH	1905
Oyler Economist	Geo. K. Oyler & Co.	St. Louis, MO	1892
Oyler Pearl	Geo. K. Oyler & Co.	St. Louis, MO	1892
Oyler Pioneer	Geo. K. Oyler & Co.	St. Louis, MO	1892
Oyler's Plantation	Geo. K. Oyler & Co.	St. Louis, MO	1892
Paragon	C. S. Bell Co.	Hillsboro, OH	1909
Parker	Ripley Foundry & Machine Co.	Ripley, OH	1913
Peerless	Cook Cane Mill & Evaporator Co.	St. Louis, MO	1905
Pioneer	C. S. Bell Co.	Hillsboro, OH	1909
Pioneer	James L. Haven Co.	Cincinnati, OH	1892
Planter's Choice	Cook Cane Mill & Evaporator Co.	St. Louis, MO	1905
Planter's Choice	Geo. K. Oyler & Co.	St. Louis, MO	1892
Prairie Queen	J. A. Field Mfg. Co.	St. Louis, MO	1892
Rockford	Rockford Well Drill Co.	Rockford, IL	1905

Trade Names (cont...)

Schofield	J. S. Schofield's Sons Co.	Macon, GA	1905
Seward	Seward Co.	Bloomington, IN	1892
Southern Queen	Cook Cane Mill & Evaporator Co.	St. Louis, MO	1905
St. Louis	Alex Magee & Co.	St. Louis, MO	1887
Star	C. S. Bell Co.	Hillsboro, OH	1909
Star	J. A. Field Mfg. Co.	St. Louis, MO	1892
Star	N. O. Nelson & Co.	St. Louis, MO	1880
Stonewall	S. R. White's Sons	Norfolk, VA	1913
Tiger	J.S. Schofield's Sons & Co.	Macon, GA	1892
Topaz	Blymyer Iron Works	Cincinnati, OH	1905
Victor	Blymyer Iron Works	Cincinnati, OH	1905
Western	C. S. Bell Co.	Hillsboro, OH	1909
Western	Geo. K. Oyler & Co.	St. Louis, MO	1892
Wilder	J. K. Wilder & Son	Monroe, MI	1892
Winship	Winship Machine Co.	Atlanta, GA	1892

Cement Mixers

While not truly a farm implement, small cement mixers became very popular in the early 1900s. No longer did farmers have to rely on plank or stone floors; they could now mix concrete by themselves for enduring walls, floors or for other purposes. With the development of the cement mixer, it was but a short time until there were a few in almost every community. When it came time for a major concrete job, everyone pitched in to help. Although drum mixers are still made at the present time, the older machines, especially those with their own gasoline engine, can oftentimes bring several hundred dollars. However, in these cases, the buyer usually places much more value on the engine than on the mixer itself.

Cherokee Manufacturing Co., Cherokee, Iowa

An unusual cement mixer design was the 20th century, offered in 1912 by Cherokee Manufacturing Co., Cherokee, Iowa. This one dry-mixed the materials for the first six feet of travel, at which point water was added for the final part of the mix. When it emerged at the rear of the machine, the concrete dropped into waiting wheelbarrows. According to advertising of the time, the company used its own engine, an example of which is shown in this illustration.

Cement Tile Machinery Co., Waterloo, Iowa

Cement Tile Machinery Co., Waterloo, Iowa, helped popularize the cement mixer with this 1913 version. The drum was loaded with sand, gravel, cement and water in certain proportions; after a short mixing time, it was ready to be discharged into a waiting wheelbarrow. The engine appears to have come from Waterloo Gasoline Engine Co., in Waterloo.

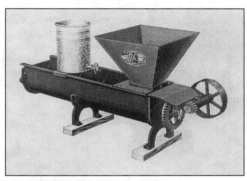

Hartman Co., Chicago, Ill.

Continuous mixers enjoyed a certain popularity (as shown by this Majestic from Hartman Co., Chicago. This $40 outfit was illustrated in its 1919 catalog. Mixing concrete was a very labor intensive job, requiring one man to scoop sand, another man or two with gravel, another with cement and water, someone to run the machine, several more to push loaded wheelbarrows to the site and still more men to level and smooth the new concrete.

Standard Scale & Supply Co., Pittsburgh, Pa.

Standard Scale & Supply Co., had a factory at Pittsburgh but also maintained offices in New York, Chicago and Philadelphia. Its Standard Low Charging Mixer of 1912 used a drum design, vaguely familiar with today's "ready-mix" trucks. From the position shown, the drum turned clockwise. After being loaded, the mixer operated for a suitable time, after which a discharge door on the opposite end of the drum was opened. Depending on the circumstances, the entire load could be discharged at once or parceled out to waiting wheelbarrows.

Jaeger Machine Co., Columbus, Ohio

Jaeger Machine Co., Columbus, Ohio, became widely known for its famous Jaeger Line of mixers and other construction equipment. This offering of 1920 included a gasoline engine mounted in the house at the rear of the machine and usually consisting of an engine of 2 to 3 horsepower. Many thousands of these batch mixers were sold by Jaeger and many other companies, with a substantial number being owned by a group of farmers within a neighborhood.

Associated Manufacturers, Waterloo, Iowa

Beginning about 1912 and continuing for several years, Associated Manufacturers in Waterloo, Iowa, offered its Amanco concrete mixer. Advertising of the time noted that it would "meet the needs of the farmer and small contractor." This one sold for $115, complete with a 2-1/4 horsepower Associated engine. The mixer was of the continuous design. On today's market, a complete unit, like this one, could bring somewhat more than just the value of the engine; the latter would by itself likely fetch more than $300 in reasonably good condition.

Trade Names

20th Century	Cherokee Mfg. Co.	Cherokee, IA	1912
Acme	Acme Road Machinery Co.	Frankfort, NY	1915
Acme	Colgan Machy. & Supply Co.	Columbus, OH	1913
Amanco	Associated Manufacturers	Waterloo, IA	1915

Trade Names (cont...)

Anchor	Cement Tile Machinery Co.	Waterloo, IA	1913
Associated	Associated Manufacturers	Waterloo, IA	1920
Austin	F. C. Austin Co.	Chicago, IL	1922
Automix	Gilson Bros. Co.	Fredonia, WI	1931
Baby Grand	Hall-Holmes Mfg. Co.	Jackson, MI	1913
Big-an-Little	Jaeger Machine Co.	Columbus, OH	1915
Bloom	J. S. Bloom Mfg. Co.	Independence, IA	1922
Bolte	Bolte Mfg. Co.	Kearney, NE	1913
Boss	American Cement Machine Co.	Keokuk, IA	1922
Bragstad	Bragstad Concrete Machinery Co.	Canton, SD	1913
Broncho	Lansing Co.	Lansing, MI	1922
Buch	Buch Mfg. Co.	Elizabethtown, PA	1939
Buffalo	Buffalo Concrete Mixer Co.	Buffalo, NY	1913
Bull Dog	Raber & Lang Mfg. Co.	Kendallville, IN	1924
Bull Dog	R & L Concrete Machy. Co.	Kendallville, IN	1931
Champion	Champion Mfg. Co.	Cedar Rapids, IA	1915
Cherokee	Cherokee Foundry & Mfg. Co.	Cherokee, IA	1922
Clinton	Valley Mfg. Co.	Clinton, IA	1922
Clover Leaf	Clover Leaf Machinery Co.	South Bend, IN	1909
Clover Leaf	Cherokee Foundry & Mfg. Co.	Cherokee, IA	1922
Coltrin	Howe Scale Co.	Chicago, IL	1922
Contractor's Helper	Cement Tile Machinery Co.	Waterloo, IA	1915
Crescent	Raber & Lang Mfg. Co.	Kendallville, IN	1913
Cropp	Cropp Concrete Macy. Co.	Chicago, IL	1913
Culvert Molds	Russell Grader Mfg. Co.	Minneapolis, MN	1913
Dandie	Koehring Machine Co.	Milwaukee, WI	1922
Dunn	W. E. Dunn Mfg. Co.	Chicago, IL	1913
Elmco	E. F. Elmberg Co.	Parkersburg, IA	1922
Eureka	Eureka Machine Co.	Lansing, MI	1922
Ever Ready	Iowa Spreader & Engine Co.	Waterloo, IA	1922
Farmer's Friend	C. D. Edwards Mfg. Co.	Albert Lea, MN	1924
Gauntt	F. G. Gauntt Mfg. Co.	Fort Wayne, IN	1913
Gilson	Gilson Bros. Co.	Fredonia, WI	1931
Grand	Hall-Holmes Mfg. Co.	Jackson, MI	1913
H & Z	Hertzler & Zook Co.	Belleville, PA	1931
Handy	Bolte Mfg. Co.	Kearney, NE	1922
Hartwick	Hall-Holmes Mfg. Co.	Jackson, MI	1913
Helm	Helm Brick Machine Co.	Traverse City, MI	1913
Helper	Stewart Mfg. Co.	Waterloo, IA	1924
Ideal	Ideal Concrete Machinery Co.	South Bend, IN	1913
Ingeco	Worthington Pump & Machy. Co.	Cudahy, WI	1922
Iowa	Iowa Foundry & Mfg. Co.	Fort Dodge, IA	1915
Jaeger	Jaeger Machine Co.	Columbus, OH	1920
John Deere	Deere & Co.	Moline, IL	1931
Jumbo	Nelson Bros.	Saginaw, MI	1931
Keller	Keller Concrete Machinery Co.	Kearney, NE	1913
Koehring	Koehring Machine Co.	Milwaukee, WI	1913

Trade Names (cont...)

Lay	Van Dolsen Mfg. Co.	Shelbyville, IN	1924
Little Giant	Ballou Mfg. Co.	Belding, MI	1915
Little Mixer	Jaeger Machine Co.	Columbus, OH	1924
Little Wonder	Waterloo Cement Machy. Corp.	Waterloo, IA	1915
Low Down	Elite Mfg. Co.	Ashland, OH	1913
Majestic	Hartman Co.	Chicago, IL	1919
Milwaukee	Milwaukee Concrete Mixer Co.	Milwaukee, WI	1922
Monarch	Monarch Mfg. Co.	Grand Rapids, MI	1913
Money Maker	Cement Tile Machinery Co.	Waterloo, IA	1915
Mountville	Mountville Mfg. Co.	Mountville, PA	1931
Multiplex	Multiplex Concrete Machy. Co.	Elmore, OH	1913
Multnomah	R. M. Wade & Co.	Portland, OR	1931
National	National Mixer Co.	Rochester, NY	1913
New Holland	New Holland Machine Co.	New Holland, PA	1945
New State	Demorest Mfg. Co.	Enid, OK	1913
Nims	Barron & Cole Co.	New York, NY	1913
Northfield	Cement Tile Machinery Co.	Waterloo, IA	1915
Northfield	Northfield Iron Co.	Northfield, MN	1922
Northwestern	Northwestern Steel & Iron Works	Eau Claire, WI	1913
Onli	Philip Bernard Co.	Sioux City, IA	1931
Overturff	C. W. Overturff	Dumont, IA	1922
Peerless	Peerless Brick Machine Co.	Minneapolis, MN	1913
Perfection	Cement Tile Machinery Co.	Waterloo, IA	1913
Polygon	Waterloo Cement Machy. Corp.	Waterloo, IA	1913
Pony	Gehl Bros. Mfg. Co.	West Bend, WI	1922
Pony	Pony Mixer Co.	West Bend, WI	1945
Remmel	Remmel Mfg. Co.	Kewaskum, WI	1924
Republic	Republic Iron Works	Tecumseh, MI	1922
Rex	Chain Belt Co.	Milwaukee, WI	1922
Rippley	Rippley Hardware Co.	Grafton, IL	1913
S & S	Cement Tile Machinery Co.	Waterloo, IA	1913
S. S. S.	Standard Scale & Supply Co.	Pittsburgh, PA	1915
Sandow	Sandy McManus Inc.	Waterloo, IA	1915
Sandusky	Plowman Tractor Co.	Waterloo, IA	1922
Schramm	Chris D. Schramm & Son	Philadelphia, PA	1922
Scientific	Bauer Bros. Co.	Springfield, OH	1913
Sheldon	Sheldon Mfg. Co.	Nehawka, NE	1924
Sheldon's	Sheldon Engine & Sales Co.	Waterloo, IA	1922
Simplicity	Cement Tile Machinery Co.	Waterloo, IA	1913
Simplicity Jr.	Turner Mfg. Co.	Port Washington, WI	1915
Smith	Contractors Supply & Equipment Co.	Chicago, IL	1909
Somers	Somers Bros. Mfg. Co.	Urbana, IL	1913
Standard	Standard Scale & Supply Co.	Pittsburgh, PA	1912
Standard	Standard Scale & Supply Co.	Pittsburgh, PA	1915
Standard Jr.	Baker Mfg. Co.	Springfield, IL	1915
Steel King	American Cement Machine Co	Keokuk, IA	1922
Sterling	Sterling Pattern Works	Sterling, IL	1913

Trade Names (cont...)

Stewart	Miller Products Co.	Waterloo, IA	1931
Stewart	Stewart Mfg. Co.	Waterloo, IA	1922
Swift	Swift Mfg. Co.	Waterloo, IA	1931
Systematic	Republic Iron Works	Tecumseh, MI	1922
Triumph	Sears, Roebuck & Co.	Chicago, IL	1931
United	United Engine Co.	Lansing, MI	1915
Van Duzen	Van Duzen-Roys Co.	Columbus, OH	1915
Vandolco	Porter Mirror & Glass Co.	Shelbyville, IN	1931
Vim	Vim Tractor Co.	Slinger, WI	1924
Wade	R. M. Wade & Co.	Portland, OR	1939
Waterloo Boy	Deere & Co.	Moline, IL	1922
West Bend	Babson Mfg. Corp.	Chicago, IL	1931
Whitney	St. Johns Foundry Co.	St. Johns, MI	1922
Whitworth	Monarch Self-Feeder Co.	Cedar Falls, IA	1913
Winner	Cement Tile Machinery Co.	Waterloo, IA	1915
Winner	Miller Products Co.	Waterloo, IA	1931
Winner	Stewart Mfg. Co.	Waterloo, IA	1922
Wonder	Waterloo Cement Machy. Corp.	Waterloo, IA	1915
X-L ALL	X-L-All Mfg. Co.	Chicago, IL	1913

Churns

Butter churns have a long history and, in some form or other, go back to the beginning of butter. However, the 1880s saw new developments, necessitated by the rapid settlement of the Midwest and Western states. The transportation system at the time was poorly developed, so the transport of sweet milk or cream was nearly impossible. To best use this cash commodity, the cream was separated from the milk, with the cream being converted into butter.

Like many aspects of American life, this too came to an end. Of interest, though, many farmers churned their own butter, at least occasionally, during World War II, due to the scarcity of many commodities. The author churned many a batch with an old Dazey churn. Sometimes, it was easy, taking but 15 or 20 minutes. Other times, it was a lot of cranking, taking 45 minutes or more to get that ripened cream to turn into butter. Today's prices vary widely. An ancient box or barrel churn can oftentimes fetch $500 or more, while the smaller and more common paddle churns often sell for $50 or more.

Did You Know?

A simple 7-inch foot-operated lathe from W.F. & John Barnes Co., sold for $40 in 1903; today, its value as a collectible could be $400.

H.G. Batcheller & Son, Rock Falls, Ill.

This barrel churn of 1887 was built in many variations by numerous companies. Most consisted of a wooden barrel with a removable lid. Once it was loaded with ripened sour cream, it was slowly turned until the conversion to butter came; this could take nearly an hour. Of course, after the job was done came the task of thoroughly cleaning up the churn so as to leave it sweet and clean for the next batch. This one was made by H.G. Batcheller & Son, Rock Falls, Ill.

C. Mears & Son, Bloomsburg, Pa.

Numerous companies of the 1880s and onward made churns as well as a "dog power" to do the work. In this 1892 advertisement, C. Mears & Son, Bloomsburg, Pa., offered a combination of its "Washer," "Propeller Churn" and "Dog Power." Its claim was that a 40-pound dog could operate either machine with no problem at all.

Anyone having additional materials and resources relating to American farm implements is invited to contact C.H. Wendel, in care of Krause Publications, 700 E. State St., Iola, WI 54990-0001.

Goshen Churn and Ladder Co., Goshen, Ind.

Many small churns were available for household use. These included the inimitable Dazey churn with its glass jar, as well as many others with a metal or wood container. Of the latter, the Oval Churn of Goshen Churn & Ladder Co., Goshen, Ind., typifies the lot. This one of 1903 was intended for making fresh butter for the household, as compared to making larger quantities for private or commercial sale.

M. Rumely Co., LaPorte, Ind.

Among its many other interests in 1913, the M. Rumely Co., LaPorte, Ind., offered its Rumely Home Creamery as part of its line. Ostensibly, the company was much more famous for its Ideal threshers and OilPull tractors than for its churns; consequently, it wasn't in the churn business for very long. The advertising accompanying the Rumely Home Creamery pointedly noted that it could "add creamery profits to the farmer's profits" to woo potential purchasers.

Trade Names			
Acme	H. H. Palmer Co.	Rockford, IL	1905
American	American Woodenware Mfg. Co.	Toledo, OH	1905
Ames	Ames Plow Co.	South Framingham, MA	1915
Anti-Bent Wood	Standard Churn Co.	Wapakoneta, OH	1915
Ash Dash	Buckeye Churn Co.	Sidney, OH	1915
Ash Dash	M. Brown & Co.	Wapakoneta, OH	1913
B & W	D. H. Burrell & Co.	Little Falls, NY	1905
Batcheller Faultless	H. F. Batcheller & Son	Rock Falls, IL	1892
Belle	John McDermaid	Rockford, IL	1905
Belle	John McDermaid	Rockford, IL	1931

Trade Names (cont...)

Bent Wood	M. Brown & Co.	Wapakoneta, OH	1905
Blanchard	Porter Blanchard Sons Co.	Nashua, NH	1892
Bluffton	Bluffton Mfg. Co.	Bluffton, IN	1892
Boss	H. H. Palmer Co.	Rockford, IL	1905
Boss	H. McDermaid	Rockford, IL	1892
Boss	Wyman L. Edson	Union Center, NY	1892
Boyd	John Boyd	Chicago, IL	1892
Brammer	H. F. Brammer Mfg. Co.	Davenport, IA	1892
Brown	M. Brown & Co.	Wapakoneta, OH	1913
Buckeye	Buckeye Churn Co.	Sidney, OH	1905
By-Lo	Standard Churn Co.	Wapakoneta, OH	1924
Challenge	Mason Mfg. Co.	Canton, OH	1913
Champion	Champion Churn Works	Toledo, OH	1892
Champion	E. R. Gwinner & Co.	Cincinnati, OH	1905
Charm	American Woodenware Mfg. Co.	Toledo, OH	1905
Cherry	J. G. Cherry	Cedar Rapids, IA	1892
CP	Creamery Package Mfg. Co.	Chicago, IL	1905
Crystal	Crystal Creamery Co.	Lansing, MI	1892
Curtis	Cornish, Curtis & Greene	Fort Atkinson, WI	1892
Dairy Box	Creamery Package Mfg. Co.	Chicago, IL	1905
Dairy Queen	Hunt, Helm & Ferris	Harvard, IL	1913
Dash	M. Brown & Co.	Wapakoneta, OH	1915
Davis	Ames Plow Co.	Boston, MA	1892
Davis Swing	Vermont Farm Machine Co.	Bellows Falls, VT	1905
Dazey	Dazey Churn Co.	St. Louis, MO	1913
Disbrow	Davis-Watkins Mfg. Co.	Chicago, IL	1922
Elward's	Winchester & Partridge Mfg. Co.	Whitewater, WI	1892
Eureka	Aquatic Cream Separator Co.	Rochester, NY	1905
Fairy	H. H. Palmer Co.	Rockford, IL	1905
Fargo	Fargo Creamery Supply House	Lake Mills, WI	1905
Fargo's Dairy Box	Fargo Creamery Supply House	Lake Mills, WI	1905
Favorite	Blakeman & Dobson Mfg. Co.	Rockford, IL	1892
Favorite	Dobson Mfg. Co.	Rockford, IL	1905
Favorite	H. P. Deuscher Co.	Hamilton, OH	1892
Fenner Revolving	R. W. Fenner	South Stockton, NY	1905
Fenner's	R. W. Fenner	South Stockton, NY	1892
Fyler's	Sidney Holmes	Grafton, VT	1892
Gem	Mason Mfg. Co.	Canton, OH	1915
Goshen Oval	Goshen Churn & Ladder Co.	Goshen, IN	1905
Grand Detour	Grand Detour Plow Co.	Dixon, IL	1905
Haney & Campbell	Haney & Campbell	Bellevue, IA	1892
Hero	American Woodenware Mfg. Co.	Toledo, OH	1905
I. X. L.	American Woodenware Mfg. Co.	Toledo, OH	1915
Ideal	H. H. Palmer Co.	Rockford, IL	1905
Iowa	J. G. Henderson & Co.	Keokuk, IA	1892
Lever	One Minute Mfg. Co.	Newton, IA	1909
Little Wonder	Blue Valley Mfg. Co.	Manhattan, KS	1909
New Owatonna	Owatonna Fanning Mill Co.	Owatonna, MN	1913

Trade Names (cont...)

O. K.	John S. Carter	Syracuse, NY	1892
O. K.	Standard Churn Co.	Wapakoneta, OH	1915
One Minute	One Minute Churn Co.	New York, NY	1905
Oval	I. X. L. Pump Co.	Goshen, IN	1892
Prima	Buckeye Churn Co.	Sidney, OH	1922
Pritchard	Mosely & Pritchard Mfg. Co.	Clinton, IA	1892
Rectangular	A. H. Reid Creamery & Dairy Supply	Philadelphia, PA	1913
Rectangular	Creamery Package Mfg. Co.	Chicago, IL	1905
Reid	A. H. Reid Creamery & Dairy Supply	Philadelphia, PA	1905
Richmond Cedar	Richmond Cedar Works	Richmond, VA	1915
Roe	D. H. Roe & Co.	Chicago, IL	1892
Sanitary	Superior Churn & Mfg. Co.	Northville, MI	1924
Shoyou	Schulte Bros.	Oregon, MO	1913
Sidney	Buckeye Churn Co.	Sidney, OH	1892
Simplex	D. H. Burrell & Co.	Little Falls, NY	1913
Smathers	Smathers Mfg. Co.	Brevard, NC	1945
Spain	Dairymen's Supply Co.	Philadelphia, PA	1913
Star	H. McDermaid	Rockford, IL	1892
Star	Wyman L. Edson	Union Center, NY	1892
Sterling	Novelty Iron Works	Sterling, IL	1922
Stoddard	Creamery Package Mfg. Co.	Rutland, VT	1913
Stoddard	Mosely & Stoddard Mfg. Co.	Rutland, VT	1892
Stoddard	Stoddard Mfg. Co.	Rutland, VT	1905
Sturges & Burn	Sturges & Burn Mfg. Co.	Chicago, IL	1905
Surprise	Vermont Farm Machine Co.	Bellows Falls, VT	1922
Union	American Woodenware Mfg. Co.	Toledo, OH	1905
Union	American Woodenware Mfg. Co.	Toledo, OH	1915
Union	Baldwin Woodenware Co.	LaFayette, IN	1892
Union	Baldwin Woodenware Co.	Lafayette, IN	1892
Union	Union Mfg. Co.	Toledo, OH	1892
Vermont	Vermont Farm Machine Co.	Bellows Falls, VT	1913
VFM	Vermont Farm Machine Co.	Bellows Falls, VT	1905
Victor	Duplex Wind Mill Co.	Brooklyn, WI	1892
Whitney's Improved	Schulte Bros.	Oregon, MO	1913
Willis	Henry M. Willis	East Williston, NY	1892
Wilson	H. McK. Wilson & Co.	St. Louis, MO	1892
Wilson's	Flint Cabinet Creamery Co.	Flint, MI	1892

Cider Mills

The cider mill, as illustrated here, had taken its general form by the 1860s. Two major components were needed, the grinder, which reduced the apples to a pulpy mass, and the press, which squeezed out the juice. Fresh apple cider has long been a delicacy, with a fair portion being made into apple wine, hard cider and other products. Only a few styles and sizes are shown here; today's values vary widely. A small single drum unit might sell for $50 to $100, while a fancy double-drum unit might bring twice that figure. Again, the value is largely dependent on the condition of the machine, as well as its popularity in a given area.

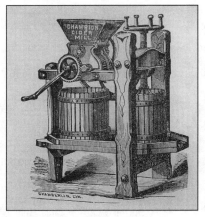

P. P. Mast & Co., Springfield, Ohio

An 1887 advertisement shows the Champion Cider Mill from P.P. Mast & Co., Springfield, Ohio. This one was made in three different sizes and was of the double-drum design. While one person fed apples into the hopper, another turned the crank, reducing them to pulp and filling the slatted open drum below. While this was taking place, another person was busy squeezing the juice from the pulp, using a heavy lever on the top of the feed screw. A barrel or vat below the floor of the mill caught the delicious apple juice. Exactly a year later, the identical engraving is shown in an advertisement from the Superior Drill Co., also at Springfield.

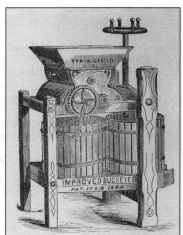

P. P. Mast & Co., Springfield, Ohio

The Improved Buckeye Cider Mill from P.P. Mast & Co., was patented already in 1864. It was a big machine, and, with enough manpower, it could reduce many bushels of apples to cider in a short time. This Springfield, Ohio, company pioneered a great many farm implements, in addition to the cider mill shown here.

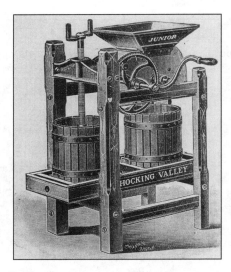

Hocking Valley Manufacturing Co., Lancaster, Ohio

A pioneer farm implement builder, the Hocking Valley Manufacturing Co., was located in Lancaster, Ohio. Its implements and machines were built to the highest standards rather than building to a price. This 1904 example shows its Junior cider mill; it featured a cast-iron case for the grinder, along with other important features. Virtually all these machines were built to last a lifetime; in fact, a substantial number have survived for several lifetimes.

A. B. Farquhar Co., York, Pa.

The American Cider Mill of A.B. Farquhar Co., featured a substantial flywheel to assist the grinding of the apples. Of course, this added still more weight to the machine, but added weight was not a deterring factor in most early farm-machine design. Note the heavy wooden bar on the floor. It was furnished with the machine. After turning the screw down by hand as far as possible, the lever raised the pressure still more, until almost all the juice was extracted, leaving a rather solid cake of pumice at the bottom. This was hauled away for livestock feed. Meanwhile, a full drum was moved under the screw while the empty one went back beneath the grinder.

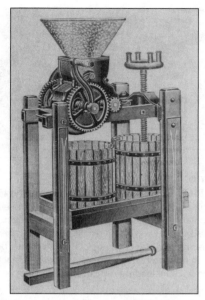

By the 1920s, the cider mill had undergone noticeable changes. Many of them were of much lighter design, and, while still substantial, the lighter design also lowered the price. This Majestic double-tub cider mill of 1920 came from the Hartman Co., in Chicago. It sold for the princely sum of $19.85, plus freight.

Hartman Co., Chicago, Ill.

For household use, Hartman Co., of Chicago, offered this single-tub design in 1920. It was priced at only $13.75, but the lower price meant a sacrifice in convenience. With this unit, the tub was filled from the grinder and then squeezed by the screw. As an additional inducement, Hartman offered easy credit terms with a full year to pay.

Trade Names

Name	Company	Location	Year
American	A. B. Farquhar Co.	York, PA	1905
American	Advance Mfg. Co.	Hamilton, OH	1892
Americus	Whitman Agricultural Co.	St. Louis, MO	1892
B & B	Boomer & Boschert Press Co.	Syracuse, NY	1892

Trade Names (cont...)

Name	Company	Location	Year
Banner	Greenville Implement Co.	Greenville, MI	1905
Bantam	Hocking Valley Mfg. Co.	Lancaster, OH	1913
Bay State	Ames Plow Co.	South Framingham, MA	1915
Buckeye	American Seeding Machine Co.	Springfield, OH	1913
Buckeye	P. P. Mast Co.	Springfield, OH	1892
Buckeye Jr.	Keystone Farm Machine Co.	York, PA	1905
Buckeye Medium	Keystone Farm Machine Co.	York, PA	1905
Buckeye Sr.	Keystone Farm Machine Co.	York, PA	1905
Butterworth	New Jersey Agricultural Works	Trenton, NJ	1892
Can"t Clog	Eagle Machine Co.	Lancaster, OH	1922
Champion	American Seeding Machine Co.	Springfield, OH	1913
Daniel's	Daniels Machine Co.	Woodstock, VT	1913
Diamond	New Winona Mfg. Co.	Winona, MN	1915
Eagle Jr.	Eagle Machine Co.	Lancaster, OH	1905
Eagle Medium	Eagle Machine Co.	Lancaster, OH	1905
Eagle Sr.	Eagle Machine Co.	Lancaster, OH	1905
Empire State	G. J. Emeny Co.	Fulton, NY	1905
Excelsior	Brennan & Co.	Louisville, KY	1892
Excelsior	S. R. White's Sons	Norfolk, VA	1913
Excelsior	S. R. White's Sons	Norfolk, VA	1915
Excelsior	Wytheville Foundry & Machine Co.	Wytheville, VA	1892
Farmers Favorite	Cutaway Harrow Co.	Higganum, CT	1892
Farmer's Favorite	Cutaway Harrow Co.	Higganum, OH	1909
Favorite	Greenville Implement Co.	Greenville, MI	1905
Favorite	S. R. White's Sons	Norfolk, VA	1913
Freeman	S. Freeman & Sons Mfg. Co.	Racine, WI	1915
Graham	Graham Foundry & Machine Co.	Graham, VA	1892
H & Z	Hertzler & Zook	Belleville, PA	1931
Haven's	James L. Haven Co.	Cincinnati, OH	1892
Hench & Dromgold	Hench & Dromgold Co.	York, PA	1905
Hocking Valley	Hocking Valley Mfg. Co.	Lancaster, OH	1892
Home	Hydraulic Press Mfg. Co.	Mt. Gilead, OH	1905
Hutchinson	H. N. Hubbard	New York, NY	1892
Hutchinson	Whitman Agricultural Co.	St. Louis, MO	1905
Hutchinson's	S. R. White & Bro.	Norfolk, VA	1892
Hutchison	S. R. White's Sons	Norfolk, VA	1913
Hydraulic	Boomer & Boschert Press Co.	Syracuse, NY	1913
Iamit	Keystone Farm Machine Co.	York, PA	1909
Improved Buckeye	Superior Drill Co.	Springfield, OH	1892
Improved Champion	Superior Drill Co.	Springfield, OH	1892
Improved Favorite	Tiffin Agricultural Works	Tiffin, OH	1892
IXL	James L. Haven Co.	Cincinnati, OH	1892
Jersey	New Jersey Agricultural Works	Trenton, NJ	1915
Junior	Brennan & Co.	Louisville, KY	1892
Kentucky	Brennan & Co.	Louisville, KY	1892

Trade Names (cont...)			
Keystone	Keystone Farm Machine Co.	York, PA	1905
Keystone Hutchinson	Keystone Farm Machine Co.	York, PA	1905
Look & Lincoln	Look & Lincoln	Marion, VA	1892
Monitor	Whitman Agricultural Works	Auburn, ME	1892
Morjuice	Crown Mfg. Co.	Phelps, NY	1931
Mount Gilead	Hydraulic Press Mfg. Co.	Mount Gilead, OH	1913
National	Ames Plow Co.	Boston, MA	1905
New Monitor	Whitman Agricultural Co.	St. Louis, MO	1892
Oasis	Silver Mfg. Co.	Salem, OH	1924
Orchard Queen	Puffer-Hubbard Mfg. Co.	Minneapolis, MN	1915
Over	Ewald Over	Indianapolis, IN	1892
Senior	Brennan & Co.	Louisville, KY	1892
St. Clair	Sucker State Drill Co.	Belleville, IL	1892
Standard	Red Cross Mfg. Co.	Bluffton, IN	1913
Telegraph	F. F. Drinkhouse	Phillipsburg, NJ	1905
Tracy	A. J. Tracy Co.	New York, NY	1892
Triumph	Geo. S. Comstock	Mechanicsburg, PA	1892
United	United Engine Co.	Lansing, MI	1924
Valley Chief	S. R. White's Sons	Norfolk, VA	1931
White's Excelsior	S. R. White & Bro.	Norfolk, VA	1892
White's Favorite	S. R. White & Bro.	Norfolk, VA	1905
Whitman	Whitman Agricultural Co.	St. Louis, MO	1913

Clover Hullers

Clover was recognized as an important crop in England as early as 1650. With the earliest settlements in America, clover became an important forage crop, its greatest problem being that of securing the seed. Eventually, farmers learned to cut the first crop for hay. Then, if the seed failed to develop on the second crop, all was not lost for the season. Secondly, by cutting the second crop, the seed heads ripened more uniformly, resulting in a much better chance at getting a yield. For many years, a yield of two bushels of seed per acre was worthwhile, while four or five bushels was an excellent return. Getting as high as eight bushels of seed per acre was a virtual bonanza.

A study of early U.S. Patent Office records shows a small amount of activity up to the 1850s. However, the most significant development was that of John Comley Birdsell, who was granted his first clover-huller patent in 1855. He commenced building hullers on his farm at that time, continuing at West Henrietta, N.Y., until 1863, when he moved to South Bend, Ind. Testifying to his designs, the Birdsell hullers saw little change from 1881 until the end of the company in 1931. At that time, it was bought out by Allis-Chalmers Manufacturing Co.; the latter was developing an All-Crop combine that could successfully harvest clover seed right in the field. That put an end to the need for clover hullers.

Several other manufacturers built clover hullers in competition with the Birdsell. While some may have matched it in quality, it is unlikely that any exceeded it. Others attempted to market combination machines—that is, a grain thresher and clover huller in a single unit. These met with mediocre success.

John C. Birdsell, West Henrietta, N.Y.

This New Birdsell clover huller of 1895 marked the 40th anniversary of the first Birdsell huller in 1855. John C. Birdsell gained his first huller patent that year, beginning the manufacture of clover hullers on his farm near West Henrietta, N.Y. This continued until 1863 when he moved the entire operation to South Bend, Ind. A major factor in this move might well have been the fact that, at the time, Indiana was the leading producer of seed clover.

John C. Birdsell, West Henrietta, N.Y.

The Birdsell Clover Huller of the 1920s was built in several sizes and could be equipped in several different ways. The machine shown here with its feed board swung back over the top for transportation was a hand-fed machine, requiring people to fork the clover toward the threshing cylinder. However, it was equipped with a wind stacker to carry away the leaves and stems. Birdsell huller owners never ceased to praise their machines. One owner from Elgin, Ill., reported to the company that he had a machine built in 1860, and it had been in used every season for 55 years, with not more than $5 in expense during that time.

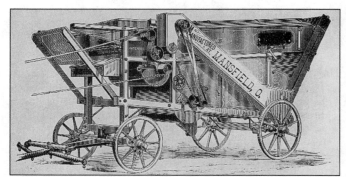

Aultman & Taylor Machinery Co., Mansfield, Ohio

Aultman & Taylor Machinery Co., Mansfield, Ohio, illustrated its clover huller in an 1893 catalog. Its salient feature was the method of driving both cylinders with a single belt. The upper cylinder was designed to remove the heads from the stems, with the hulling or rubbing out of the seeds being achieved in the lower cylinder. For many hullers, a capacity of five or six bushels per hour was the maximum; even the largest machines only had a capacity of perhaps 15 bushels per hour.

Newark Machine Co., Newark, Ohio

Newark Machine Co., Newark, Ohio, offered its Victor Double Huller in this 1895 advertisement. The clover was fed by hand into the threshing cylinder, with the straw passing out over vibrating racks to the rear. Hulling was achieved in a drum beneath the threshing cylinder. Since much of the seed escaped with its husk the first time through, a large tailings or return elevator carried it back for a second pass. After this, the seed went through a small re-cleaner seen here on the side of the machine.

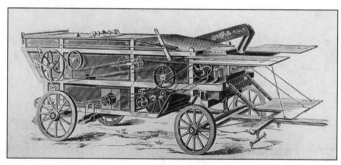

Orrville Machine Co., Orrville, Ohio

As otherwise noted, a few companies attempted to market a combination grain thresher/clover huller on a single frame. One of these was the New Combined Champion from Orrville Machine Co., Orrville, Ohio. This 1895 model had already been on the market for 20 years, but little further information has been found on this machine after the early 1900s. The market was limited first to those who would likely be harvesting clover seed; most of these farmers preferred a thresher for threshing and a clover huller for hulling.

M. Rumely Co., LaPorte, Ind.

A few of the large threshing-machine builders opted into the clover-huller market. One of these was the M. Rumely Co., LaPorte, Ind.; after 1914, this was known as the Advance-Rumely Thresher Co. This 1904 model was built largely along the lines of the Rumely grain threshers and it is likely that a great many parts were interchangeable. The re-cleaner is obvious above the left rear wheel. Re-cleaning was necessary to help remove weed seed and other foreign material left behind by the huller.

Reeves & Co., Columbus, Ind.

Reeves & Co., Columbus, Ind., was another large thresher manufacturer that entered the clover-huller business, at least for a brief time. Reeves was bought out by Emerson-Brantingham Co., Rockford, Ill., in 1912. Thus, the company's career in the huller business was rather brief, if, in fact, it continued up to the time of the E-B takeover. With the advent of the Allis-Chalmers All-Crop combine in the 1930s, clover hullers quickly fell into obsolescence, since farmers were able to harvest the seed crop directly in the field. One man with an All-Crop combine instantly replaced the large crew needed with the time-honored clover huller.

Trade Names			
Ashland	Ashland Clover Huller Co.	Ashland, OH	1892
Avery	Avery Co.	Peoria, IL	1913
Birdsell	Allis-Chalmers Mfg. Co.	Milwaukee, WI	1939
Birdsell	Birdsell Mfg. Co.	South Bend, IN	1892
Campbell	Schoharie Co. Agricultural Works	Central Bridge, NY	1892
Case	J. I. Case Threshing Machine Co.	Racine, WI	1922
Champion	Orrville Machine Co.	Orrville, OH	1892
Gaar-Scott	Gaar, Scott & Co.	Richmond, IN	1892
Hagerstown	Hagerstown Steam Engine & Mach.	Hagerstown, MD	1892
Hawkeye	Groton Bridge & Mfg. Co.	Groton, NY	1892
Matchless	Aultman & Taylor Machinery Co.	Mansfield, OH	1892
Minneapolis	Minneapolis Threshing Mach. Co.	Hopkins, MN	1922
Monitor Jr.	Birdsell Mfg. Co.	South Bend, IN	1909
New Racine	Belle City Mfg. Co.	Racine, WI	1924
Peerless	Geiser Mfg. Co.	Waynesboro, PA	1905
Reeves	Reeves & Company	Columbus, IN	1905
Robinson	Robinson & Co.	Richmond, IN	1913
Rumely	M. Rumely Co.	LaPorte, IN	1905
Scientific	Illinois Thresher Co.	Sycamore, IL	1924
Simplicity	Illinois Thresher Co.	Sycamore, IL	1924
Victor	Newark Machine Co.	Newark, OH	1905
Victor	Blair Mfg. Co.	Newark, OH	1915
Victor	Newark Machine Co.	Newark, OH	1905
Westinghouse	Westinghouse Company	Schenectady, NY	1892

Combines

The word "combine" is actually an abridgment of the earlier term, "combined harvester-thresher." The idea of combining the two operations of harvesting the standing grain and taking the grain to the bin, while leaving the straw in the field, had been extant for many years prior to the 1900 Holt.

This machine gained but slight interest, but the company persisted and finally was completely successful by 1915. International Harvester was another major player at the time and was hard at work developing a combine of its own. Other companies took notice of the new developments and, by the early 1920s, there was a number of companies with combines in the field.

It is not the purpose of this book to delineate the entire development of the combine industry. That has been done in various other books, especially the author's book *150 Years of International Harvester* (Crestline/Motorbooks, 1981). This title provides an in-depth look at Harvester's long struggle to market a completely successful machine. This came rather slowly, despite the fact that Harvester poured more money into new product research than almost any other American farm-implement maker.

To completely overlook the combine in this book would likewise, be a grave error, so the author had chosen a middle-ground to present a few examples of early combine design, doing so in a limited space, lest other significant machines and implements be left out completely.

Until the development of the Allis-Chalmers All-Crop combine in the early 1930s, virtually all combines used the time-honored spike-tooth cylinder featured in the threshing machine. The early machines were big, heavy and rather complicated. It could well be said that these early combines were essentially a small threshing machine mounted so that a cutterhead could feed the cut grain into the cylinder. The All-Crop combine constituted the first major change in combine design and heralded a new era for the combine.

Another significant design emerged from the work of Curtis C. Baldwin of Kansas. Already in 1913, he developed his vacuum thresher, followed later by more-or-less conventional designs. The Baldwin combines gained a considerable reputation, finally being acquired by Allis-Chalmers.

Not to be forgotten was the significant work of Massey-Harris Co., developing the first successful self-propelled combine in the late 1930s. From this first design sprang today's ultra-modern machines.

Holt Manufacturing Co., Stockton, Cal.

Caterpillar combines were a direct descendant of the Holt combine, development of which began as early as 1900. This 1930 model epitomized combine development of the time, even including Timken roller bearings to reduce friction and consequent

power losses. Holt Manufacturing Co., was an early pioneer in the combine business, but opted to concentrate on its tractor and construction machinery business, selling the combine line to John Deere in 1935.

Curtis C. Baldwin Co., Joplin, Mo.

The Savage combined tractor-harvester-thresher was a 1920 design of Curtis C. Baldwin. At the time, Joplin, Mo., was hoping to acquire a new factory to be built for this unique machine. For reasons unknown, this design did not meet with great success, although later Baldwin designs were very popular, especially in the wheat belt.

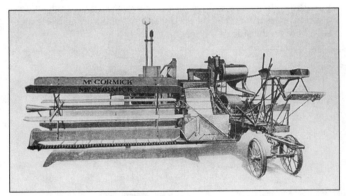

International Harvester Co., Chicago, Ill.

The McCormick Harvester-Thresher of 1920 was capable of harvesting from 15 to 20 acres per day. It was ordinarily furnished with a four-cylinder engine, but could also be furnished with a ground-drive, omitting the engine. In this case, anywhere from eight to 12 horses were required to pull and operate the machine.

Avery Farm Machinery Co., Peoria, Ill.

Avery Farm Machinery Co., at Peoria, Ill., developed a combine in the 1920s, continuing to market it in small numbers into the 1930s. Like virtually all combines of the time, it cut the grain and delivered it sideways to the threshing cylinder. Avery offered several sizes and styles, with headers ranging up to 16 feet in width.

Minneapolis-Moline Co., Minneapolis, Minn.

Minneapolis-Moline Co., resulted from a 1929 merger; prior to that time, one of the partners, Minneapolis Threshing Machine Co., had been busy developing a combine. As with most others of 1930, the cut grain was delivered by a conveyor into the cylinder. To leave the field and travel down a road, the header was detached and remounted on its own wheels for separate transportation from the threshing unit.

Massey-Harris Harvester Co., Batavia, N.Y.

Massey-Harris Harvester Co., was headquartered in Toronto, Ontario, Canada, but had a factory at Batavia, N.Y. Massey developed its own combine during the 1920s, marketing this big No. 9 Combined Reaper-Thresher in 1927. It was made in 12-foot and 15-foot sizes. Its smaller machine, the No. 6, used a 10-foot cut.

Massey-Harris Harvester Co., Batavia, N.Y.

Massey-Harris tested its No. 20 self-propelled combine in late 1937. Limited production of this machine ensued in the 1938-40 period. Originally tested in Argentina, the No. 20 was especially designed for and marketed on the West Coast. Even though production was limited and the machine had its shortcomings, it marked the beginning of the new era of self-propelled combines.

Massey-Harris Harvester Co., Batavia, N.Y.

Massey-Harris No. 21 self-propelled combines first emerged in 1940. Even though the demands of World War II were great, the company was able to build a limited number of these machines during the war, since they were able to bring in the crop, even with the limited manpower then available. Thus came the famous Massey-Harris Harvest Brigade. These combines were to be sold only to custom operators who would harvest at least 2,000 acres of grain per season and under the supervision of Massey-Harris.

Deere & Co., Moline, Ill.

Deere & Co., Moline, Ill., was another of the major companies to enter the combine business during the 1920s. Its No. 1 combine of 1928 is shown here, being pulled by a John Deere Model D tractor. The combine is equipped with its own independent engine, as evidenced by the high intake pipe and the high exhaust well above the dust zone of the combine. At this point in time, two men were required—one to drive the tractor and the other at the controls of the combine.

Advance-Rumely Thresher Co., LaPorte, Ind.

Advance-Rumely Thresher Co., LaPorte, Ind., came forth with its combine in the mid-1920s. It followed the same general design as others of the period, with a side-mounted header, independent engine and heavy construction. The Rumely was offered in numerous sizes and styles, even including a special hillside model. Rumely was absorbed by Allis-Chalmers in 1931.

Nichols & Shepard Co., Battle Creek, Mich.

Of all the old-line thresher manufacturers, Nichols & Shepard at Battle Creek, Mich., was one of the most conservative in its designs. However, while many of the thresher builders refused to get into the combine business, N&S came out with its own design in the 1920s, offering several sizes and styles. This rugged machine typifies the N&S design and apparently was sold to some extent, particularly in the wheat belt. Nichols & Shepard merged with others to form the Oliver Farm Equipment Co., 1931.

Allis-Chalmers Mfg, Co., Milwaukee, Wis.

Allis-Chalmers ventured forth with its All-Crop Harvester in 1931. Early production saw the need for further changes; by 1932 the All-Crop had come into its own realm as the combine to imitate. Soon, the side-mounted header came to an end. In its place came the direct-cut machine, such as the All-Crop. Another innovation was the standard use of a PTO shaft on this light-weight machine, obviating the necessity of an auxiliary engine. Only the earliest of the All-Crop combines were equipped with the steel wheels shown here; the remainder used rubber tires. One exception may have been the production of a few All-Crop combines on steel during World War II, due to the scarcity of rubber.

Did You Know?

Old sickle grinders sometimes have a substantial antique value, occasionally selling for $50 or more.

J. I. Case Co., Racine, Wis.

In 1940, J.I. Case Co., offered this Model F combine as part of its overall line. Case had pioneered in the threshing machine business and had been building combines since the 1920s. However, Case, like most others, was soon to adopt the in-line method of combining grain, just as had been pioneered by the Allis-Chalmers All-Crop. The Case Model F combine shown here cut a 54-inch swath.

Wood Bros. Thresher Co., Des Moines, Iowa

Wood Bros., Thresher Co., Des Moines, Iowa, was a well-known threshing machine manufacturer. During the 1930s, the Wood brothers developed several new and innovative machines, including this all-steel combine with a 5-foot cut and using a threshing cylinder the full width of the machine. However, Wood Bros. was a small company compared to Case, International Harvester and others. Thus, it faced tremendous competition and World War II, severely limited farm-equipment production. Eventually, Wood Bros. was taken over by the Farm Equipment Division of Ford Motor Co.

Trade Names			
Advance-Rumely	Advance-Rumely Thresher Co.	LaPorte, IN	1929
All-Crop	Allis-Chalmers Mfg. Co.	Milwaukee, WI	1939
Allis-Chalmers	Allis-Chalmers Mfg. Co.	Milwaukee, WI	1936
Avery	Avery Power Machinery Co.	Peoria, IL	1929
Baby	Holt Mfg. Co.	Stockton, CA	1915
Baldwin	Baldwin Mfg. Co.	Nickerson, KS	1922
Best	Best Mfg. Co.	San Leandro, CA	1909
Blewett	Northwest Harvester Co.	Spokane, WA	1915

Trade Names (cont...)

Case	J. I. Case Threshing Machine Co.	Racine, WI	1924
Caterpillar	Deere & Co.	Moline, IL	1936
Caterpillar	Holt Mfg. Co.	Stockton, CA	1915
Centrifugal	National Farm Machy. Co.	Wichita, KS	1936
Clipper	Massey-Harris Co.	Racine, WI	1939
Corn Belt	Allis-Chalmers Mfg. Co.	Milwaukee, WI	1939
Deering	International Harvester Co.	Chicago, IL	1919
Gleaner	Gleaner Combine Harvester Corp.	Independence, MO	1929
Gleaner Baldwin	Gleaner Combine Harvester Corp.	Independence, MO	1929
Grain Master	Oliver Farm Equipment Co.	Chicago, IL	1936
Hainke Harvester	Combine Harvester Corp.	Kensington, KS	1939
Harrington	Harrington Mfg. Co.	Harrington, WA	1929
Harris	Harris Mfg. Co.	Stockton, CA	1924
Harris	Idaho Harvester Co.	Moscow, ID	1924
Harvest-All	Avery Power Machinery Co.	Peoria, IL	1939
Holley Side Hill	Holt Mfg. Co.	Stockton, CA	1915
Holt	Holt Mfg. Co.	Stockton, CA	1909
Houser & Haines	Houser & Haines Mfg. Co.	Stockton, CA	1909
Huber	Huber Mfg. Co.	Marion, OH	1939
John Deere	Deere & Co.	Moline, IL	1929
Massey-Harris	Massey-Harris Harvester Co.	Batavia, NY	1924
McCormick	International Harvester Co.	Chicago, IL	1919
McCormick-Deering	International Harvester Co.	Chicago, IL	1929
Minneapolis-Moline	Minneapolis-Moline Co.	Minneapolis, MN	1936
M-M Harvestor	Minneapolis-Moline Co.	Minneapolis, MN	1936
Northwest	Northwest Harvester Co.	Spokane, WA	1913
Oliver	Oliver Farm Equipment Co.	Chicago, IL	1936
Port Huron	Port Huron Thresher Co.	Port Huron, MI	1931
Red River Special	Nichols & Shepard Co.	Battle Creek, MI	1929
Rotary	Rotary Farm Equipment Co.	Wichita, KS	1936
Spokane	Spokane Harvester Co.	Spokane, WA	1909
Standard	Holt Mfg. Co.	Stockton, CA	1915
Wood Bros.	Wood Bros. Thresher Co.	Des Moines, IA	1929

Corn Binders

Although limited activity probably took place sooner, there were no commercially practical corn binders prior to 1890. At that time, D.M. Osborne Co., Auburn, N.Y., came out with a practical machine. About the same time, McCormick Harvesting Machine Co., Chicago, introduced a unique push-type corn harvester, but it was not a success. Despite this, McCormick later went on to claim that it had built the first "corn harvester." Technically, at least, that may have been true; in practical terms, though, it was Osborne who led the field.

Agriculturists of the 1880s were promulgating the concept of converting standing corn into silage, regarding the latter as very palatable and nutritious for livestock. The idea caught on; during the 1890s, there was a flurry of activity to build corn binders for harvesting the standing corn. Likewise, there was a boom in the ensilage cutter business (of course, the business of erecting silos was doing quite well, too).

There's little to be said about corn binders—their purpose is obvious and for those who have worked around them, lugging those heavy bundles of green corn was hard work. However, there was little other choice until the field cutter began impacting the market in the 1940s. Today, a good corn binder is not easy to find. They were completely useless for any other purpose, so the great majority were scrapped. A corn binder in reasonably good condition will bring in excess of $200 today. A nicely kept one in original condition might bring substantially more.

International Harvester Co., Chicago, Ill.

An early advertisement of International Harvester Co., illustrates McCormick's "Self-Binding Corn Harvester." The term was later shortened simply as "corn binder." McCormick claimed it was the first on the market, although it appears that Osborne at Auburn, N.Y., was the first with a commercially successful machine. International Harvester continued to offer this machine at least up to 1953.

Deering Harvester Co., Chicago, Ill.

Deering Harvester Co., Chicago, was a strong competitor to the McCormick interests. In 1899, Deering came out with this "horizontal corn binder." It was uniquely different, in that it cut the standing corn, laid it down for binding and discharged the finished bundles. Despite its unique design, the Deering was eminently successful and remained in the Harvester line for many years. The artist's rendition gives the reader an idea of how it was done. It's more than a little unlikely that the farmer would have been dressed in suit coat, vest and tie, nor would one have been accustomed to seeing fancy, fine-boned driving horses pulling the binder.

Milwaukee Harvester Co., Milwaukee, Wis.

The Milwaukee corn binder of 1902 was a vertical design and came from Milwaukee Harvester Co., Milwaukee. In 1902, this company became a part of International Harvester. The Milwaukee corn binder also remained in the IHC line for some years, partially because the company maintained separate product lines under a single corporate umbrella into the early 1920s.

Aultman-Miller & Co., Akron, Ohio

Aultman-Miller & Co., Akron, Ohio, was well known for its Buckeye line of mowers, reapers and other implements. In the late 1890s it came out with its own corn binder, illustrating it in its 1901 catalog. My copy is written in German. This was not uncommon, since many immigrants were not conversant in the English language. To give the best possible impression of its machine, Aultman-Miller noted that "it is grounded on the right principles," to loosely translate the German version.

Frost & Wood Ltd., Smith's Falls, Ont.

Frost & Wood at Smith's Falls, Ontario, Canada, offered a rather complete line of harvesting equipment, including this 1910 ver-

sion of its corn and sunflower binder. Certain areas of the northern United States and southern Canada were well suited for raising sunflowers, thus this company's reference to the crop.

D. M. Osborne & Co., Auburn, N.Y.

D.M. Osborne & Co., Auburn, N.Y., was the first to successfully market a corn binder, doing so in 1890. Its machine was on exhibit at the Chicago World's Fair of 1893. No wonder this 1900 version was called the Osborne Columbia Corn Harvester. Note the interesting design of the cast-iron drive wheel.

Johnson Harvester Co., Peoria, Ill.

Johnston Harvester Co., Batavia, N.Y., illustrated this version of its corn binder in 1908. By that time, many farmers, especially dairy farmers, were convinced of the value from ensilage, so there was a ready market for silos, silo fillers, corn binders and related equipment.

Acme Harvester Co., Peoria, Ill.

Acme Harvester Co., Peoria, Ill., was a relatively small competitor in a land of giant manufacturers. Nevertheless, Acme offered this corn binder in 1914. It featured an all-steel design and this would be the trend of the future. Acme only remained in business for a few years.

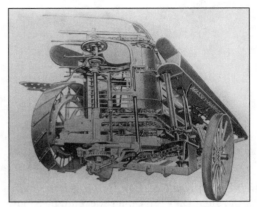

Massey-Harris Harvester Co., Ltd., Toronto, Ont.

Massey-Harris was based in Toronto, Ontario, Canada, and its equipment was widely sold in Canada. However, the company also made many excursions into the United States, the most famous being its 1928 purchase of the J.I. Case Plow Works at Racine, Wis. Prior to that time, Massey-Harris had acquired a few smaller concerns, so the company's status was well established when this No. 3A corn binder was offered to the market in 1919.

Emerson-Brantingham Co., Rockford, Ill.

International Harvester divested itself of the Osborne factories in 1918, having acquired this operation some years before. In turn, Emerson-Brantingham bought up the Osborne line, offering it virtually intact for a few years. Included was the E-B Osborne corn binder of 1919 shown here. However, Emerson-Brantingham fell into financial hard times and only survived until 1928.

John Deere Harvester Works, Moline, Ill.

John Deere slowly and deliberately built its product line over the years. Until about 1912, numerous products were jobbed

from other manufacturers and sold by the various John Deere branch houses. Eventually, the company acquired enough companies and developed enough of its own products to become a full-line company with everything being sold under the John Deere name. Such was the case with this John Deere corn binder of 1927.

J. I. Case Co., Racine, Wis.

When J.I. Case Co., bought out Emerson-Brantingham in 1928, it also acquired the Osborne line that E-B had bought only a few years before. For several years after the acquisition, Case continued to market many Osborne machines under the Case-Osborne trademark. Included was this attractive corn binder that featured all-steel construction. This machine continued on the market until after World War II.

Trade Names			
Acme	Acme Harvesting Machine Co.	Peoria, IL	1915
Adriance	Adriance, Platt & Co.	Poughkeepsie, NY	1905
Champion	International Harvester Co.	Chicago, IL	1905
Deering	International Harvester Co.	Chicago, IL	1905
E-B	Emerson-Brantingham Co.	Rockford, IL	1919
Empire	Seberling, Miller & Co.	Doylestown, OH	1913
Independent	Independent Harvester Co.	Plano, IL	1919
John Deere	John Deere Harvester Works	Moline, IL	1919
Johnston	Johnston Harvester Co.	Batavia, NY	1905
Kellogg	Kellogg Harvester Co.	Chicago, IL	1905
Massey-Harris	Massey-Harris Harvester Co.	Batavia, NY	1919
McCormick	International Harvester Co.	Chicago, IL	1905
Milwaukee	International Harvester Co.	Chicago, IL	1905
Minnesota	Minnesota State Prison	Stillwater, MN	1929
Moline	Moline Plow Co.	Moline, IL	1919
New Century	Walter A. Wood	Hoosick Falls, NY	1905
New Ideal	International Harvester Co.	Chicago, IL	1913
Osborne	D. M. Osborne	Auburn, NY	1905
Osborne	Emerson-Brantingham Co.	Rockford, IL	1919
Osborne	International Harvester Co.	Chicago, IL	1909
Plano	International Harvester Co.	Chicago, IL	1905

Corn Cribs

W. J. Adam Co., Joliet, Ill.

Lest it be thought that the idea of a temporary corn crib was unique to 20th century thought, comes this Adam's Portable Corn Crib of 1894. The manufacturer, W.J. Adam, Joliet, Ill., received Patent No. 500,459 for his invention in June 1893. The patent covered the wire picket sections used in the crib, as well as a special access door when it came time to shell the corn. Scooping the corn over the top as shown, must have been a thrilling task!

Trade Names

Adam's	Adam's Steel & Wire Works	Joliet, IL	1905
Bloomer	R. H. Bloomer Mfg. Co.	Council Bluffs, IA	1905
Clippinger	A. B. Clippinger & Son	Kansas City, KS	1905
Columbia	Elliott & Reid Co.	Richmond, IN	1905
Denning	Denning Wire & Fence Co.	Ccedar Rapids, IA	1905
Oak	Elliott & Reid Co.	Richmond, IN	1905
Western	Western Mfg. Co.	Kansas City, MO	1905

Corn Crushers & Slicers

By the 1880s, farmers were deluged with new ideas, inventions and concepts. Researchers were finding new ways to make livestock-raising more efficient. Great efforts were made to make livestock feed more palatable. This included a variety of corn cutters, crushers and slicers. Undoubtedly, there were hundreds of different machines produced for this purpose, many of them having a localized sale. Others were offered by major manufacturers, which likely sold many thousands of their machines. With the passage of time, new and better ways of handling ear corn were developed. Ear-corn cutters slowly faded from the scene, almost completely disappearing by 1940. Early machines have a certain nostalgic value, ranging from $20 to $25 for one in poor condition to $100 or more for one in good condition.

Sandwich Enterprise Co., Sandwich, Ill.

The Dean Patent Ear Corn Cutter was built by Sandwich Enterprise Co., Sandwich, Ill. Patented under No. 309,773, 1884, this machine was developed earlier by George B. Dean and Jeremiah Y. Burnett of Lamoille, Ill. By the time this 1887 advetisement appeared, Sandwich Enterprise Co., was already a major manufacturer of windmills, pumps, planters, cultivators, feed grinders and many other implements.

Barnes Manufacturing Co., Freeport, Ill.

Barnes Manufacturing Co., Freeport, Ill., advertised this National Ear Corn Cutter in 1887. As noted in the engraving, two vertical tubes were used to feed corn into the machine; each ear had to be fed individually from the side-mounted storage box. No particulars have been found concerning the operating mechanism of this machine.

J. S. Bloom, Independence, Iowa

J.S. Bloom, Independence, Iowa, developed his ear corn cutter and crusher sometime prior to 1915; by that time, his company was building thousands of them for sale to farmers everywhere. The machine shown here could handle 100 to 250 bushels per hour, probably depending on the stamina of the operator.

Enterprise Engine Works, Independence, Iowa

The concept of the Bloom ear corn cutter and crusher came to J.S. Bloom in 1899, resulting from his efforts to secure more palatable feed for his livestock. By 1915, the company was offering numerous sizes and styles, including this large machine with its own gasoline engine. Curiously, the engine is marked "The Bloom," but, in fact, it is from Enterprise Engine Works, also in Independence, Iowa.

Appleton Manufacturing Co., Batavia, Ill.

Appleton Manufacturing Co., Batavia, Ill., offered its own version of a corn slicer in its 1917 catalog. This one used a pair of 6-inch knives attached to heavy cast arms. This heavy casting also served as a flywheel. When operated by hand, the cutters made two revolutions to every turn of the crank. Eventually, the need for corn slicers faded, as farmers turned to labor-saving grinders that could handle a combination of tasks.

Trade Names

American	Appleton Mfg. Co.	Batavia, IL	1892
B&G	Bristol and Gale Co.	Chicago, IL	1909
Blue Valley	Blue Valley Mfg. Co.	Manhattan, KS	1905
Boss	Woodcock Feed Mill	Chillicothe, OH	1905
Bowsher's Combination	N. P. Bowsher Co.	South Bend, IN	1905
Bowsher's Sweep	N. P. Bowsher Co.	South Bend, IN	1905
Buckeye	Buckeye Feed Mill Co.	Springfield, OH	1905
Buckeye	Victor Feed Mill Co.	Springfield, OH	1905
Carr	Carr & Co. New York	NY	1892
Challenge	Challenge Windmill & Feedmill Co.	Batavia, IL	1892
Dain's	Dain Mfg. Co.	Ottumwa, IA	1905

Trade Names (cont...)

Dean	Enterprise Windmill Co.	Sandwich, IL	1913
Diamond	New Winona Mfg. Co.	Winona, MN	1905
Eagle	Eagle Machine Co.	Lancaster, OH	1909
Eureka	Eureka Bark Mill Co.	Lancaster, PA	1905
Fleetwood	Fleetwood Foundry & Mach. Works	Fleetwood, PA	1905
Globe Sweep	N. P. Bowsher Co.	South Bend, IN	1905
Grain King	Marseilles Mfg. Co.	Marseilles, IL	1905
Heebner	Heebner & Sons	Lansdale, PA	1905
Hoosier	Nordyke & Marmon Co.	Indianapolis, IN	1892
Hustler	Monarch Grubber Co.	Lone Tree, IA	1905
Ideal	Stover Mfg. Co.	Freeport, IL	1892
Ideal Duplex	Stover Mfg. Co.	Freeport, IL	1905
Iowa	Bovee Grinder & Furnace Works	Waterloo, IA	1905
Kelly	O. S. Kelly Western Mfg. Co.	Iowa City, IA	1905
Keystone-Monarch	Keystone Farm Machine Co.	York, PA	1905
Kingsland	Kingsland Mfg. Co.	St. Louis, MO	1892
Little Giant	Bettendorf Axle Co.	Davenport, IA	1913
Little Giant	Kaestner & Co.	Chicago, IL	1905
Little Giant	Voss Bros. Mfg. Co.	Davenport, IA	1909
Marseilles	Marseilles Mfg. Co.	Marseilles, IL	1905
Maud S.	Union Foundry & Machine Works	Mansfield, OH	1905
Modern Hero	Appleton Mfg. Co.	Batavia, IL	1905
Mogul	Bovee Grinder & Furnace Works	Waterloo, IA	1905
Monarch	Sprout, Waldron & Co.	Muncy, PA	1905
Munson	Munson Bros. Co.	Utica, NY	1905
New Holland	New Holland Machine Works	New Holland, PA	1905
Nonpareil	L. J. Miller	Cincinnati, OH	1892
Noye	John T. Noye Mfg. Co.	Buffalo, NY	1892
Osage	New Winona Mfg. Co.	Winona, MN	1905
Perfection	Leonard D. Harrison	New Haven, CT	1892
Perkins	Perkins Wind Mill Co.	Mishawaka, IN	1905
Porter's	Whitman Agricultural Co.	St. Louis, MO	1905
Quaker City	A. W. Straub Co.	Philadelphia, PA	1905
Richmond	Richmond City Mill Works	Richmond, IN	1892
Scientific	Foos Mfg. Co.	Springfield, OH	1905
Smalley	Smalley Mfg. Co.	Manitowoc, WI	1905
Star	Star Mfg. Co.	New Lexington, OH	1905
Staver-Buckeye	Buckeye Feed Mill Co.	Springfield, OH	1905
Sterling	Sterling Mfg. Co.	Sterling, IL	1905
Stover	Stover Mfg. Co.	Freeport, IL	1905
Success	Hercules Mfg. Co.	Centerville, IA	1905
Triumph	C. O. Bartlett & Snow Co.	Cleveland, OH	1892
Triumph	Kaestner & Co.	Chicago, IL	1905
Victor	Victor Feed Mill Co.	Springfield, OH	1905
Victory	Thomas Roberts	Springfield, OH	1905
Whitman	Young America Whitman Agricultural Co.	St. Louis,, MO	1905
Whitman's Monarch	Whitman Agricultural Co.	St. Louis, MO	1905
Wilder	Wilder-Strong Implement Cco.	Monroe, MI	1905
Young America	A. B. Farquhar Co.	York, PA	1905

Corn Dryers

World War II is the great dividing line between the old and the new. Many of the time-honored farming practices of the pre-war years were replaced with new ideas and new methods after 1945. Grain farming was becoming more popular; with it came a bad growing season in 1947. This resulted in millions of bushels of soft corn. Storing this high moisture ear corn in large cribs would have been disastrous. Extra air ventilators and many other ideas were used in an effort to save as much of the crop as possible. Thus came the crop dryer, now widely used in most of the corn belt, as well as for other crops.

Peirson-Moore Co., Lexington, Ky

In 1947, Peirson-Moore Co., Lexington, Ky., was one of the firms offering an all-purpose farm dryer. It was equipped with a 5-horsepower electric motor and used a large oil burner for heat. It is shown here, ducted into a steel bin. The warm air was ducted below the grain; as the warm air circulated upward, it carried with it the excess moisture. Within a short time, there were numerous companies offering grain dryers in various sizes and styles. Virtually all grain-dryer designs use propane gas for fuel, although a few operate on alternative fuels.

Corn Graders

Until farmers began using hybrid corn varieties in the 1930s, most farmers used open pollinated corn. When harvesting corn, the best ears were selected and carefully dried for next year's seed. After shelling, it was also advantageous to grade the corn so that a uniform kernel size was planted in every hill. To that end, many companies manufactured seed-corn graders suitable for every farm. Oftentimes, a group of farmers would buy a grader together, each using it in turn for the new seed crop. Seldom seen today, a corn grader in nice shape will bring $100 or more.

Did You Know?

Ox-yokes sometimes bring $100 or more; excellent examples might bring several times that figure.

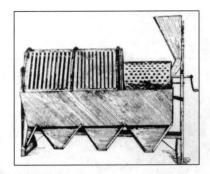

Nora Springs Manufacturing Co., Nora Springs, Iowa

Nora Springs Manufacturing Co., Nora Springs, Iowa, advertised its corn graders at the 1908 National Corn Exposition in Omaha, Neb. Shelled corn was fed into the hopper and traveled through a series of revolving screens. Three separate discharge spouts were provided for large, medium and small-sized kernels.

Meadows Manufacturing Co., Meadows, Ill.

Meadows Manufacturing Co., Meadows, Ill., built various farm implements, including elevators and hoists. In 1910, it offered The Improved Peoria seed corn grader, noting that it delivered four different grades of seed; besides that, it was "Indorsed by the State University." Also of note is the complete lack of guards around the open gears. In those days it was generally presumed that the operator had sense enough to keep fingers and other body parts away from the gears!

Universal Hoist & Manufacturing Co., Cedar Falls, Iowa

More than 40 years ago, the author salvaged a More Corn No. 2 seed corn grader from an attic. It had resided there for many years and was one of many sold in Central Iowa. This machine was made by the Universal Hoist & Manufacturing Co., Cedar Falls, Iowa. The company made an all-out effort to market these corn graders for several years and met with good success. However, the coming of hybrid corn obviated any further need for these machines, so the company entered and left the market within two or three decades.

Trade Names

Avery	Avery Co.	Peoria, IL	1915
Chatham	Manson Campbell Co.	Detroit, MI	1909
Clipper	A. T. Ferrell & Co.	Saginaw, MI	1915
Detroit	Detroit Grader Co.	West Detroit, MI	1909
Dickey	A. P. Dickey Mfg. Co.	Racine, WI	1922
Duplex	Kretchmer Mfg. Co.	Council Bluffs, IA	1915
Expert	Cleland Mfg. Co.	Minneapolis, MN	1909
Hero	Twin City Separator Co.	Minneapolis, MN	1909
Hudson	Hudson Mfg. Co.	Minneapolis, MN	1929
Improved Iowa	A. M. Baumgartner Co.	Manchester, IA	1922
Iowa	Kretchmer Mfg. Co.	Council Bluffs, IA	1915
Leader	Leader Mfg. Co.	Carthage, IL	1909
Ludwig	Nora Springs Mfg. Co.	Nora Springs, IA	1909
Maplebay	Maplebay Mfg. Co.	Crookston, MN	1909
Morecorn	Standard Mfg. Co.	Cedar Falls, IA	1917
Morecorn	Universal Hoist & Mfg. Co.	Cedar Falls, IA	1915
Noxall	Noxall Mfg. Co.	Seward, NE	1915
Owens	J. L. Owens Co.	Minneapolis, MN	1909
Peoria	Meadows Mfg. Co.	Meadows, IL	1909
Perfection	Chas. Hunnicutt Co.	Wilmington, OH	1909
Racine	Johnson & Field Co.	Racine, WI	1915
Rainbow	M. Rumely Co.	LaPorte, IN	1915
Star	Iowa Wind Mill & Pump Co.	Cedar Rapids, IA	1922
Trojan	Standard Mfg. Co.	Cedar Falls, IA	1917
Universal	Dreadnought Co.	Cedar Falls, IA	1922
Vaughn	Vaughn Products Co.	LaCrosse, WI	1929
Victory	Sperry Mfg. Co.	Owatonna, MN	1909
Webber	Hirsch Bros.	Milwaukee, WI	1915
Winner	American Grain Separator Co.	Minneapolis, MN	1915

Corn Harvesters

Corn harvesters are generally considered to be those machines that cut the corn slightly above ground level. Afterward, it was stood up into shocks for curing and later use. Many different companies built corn harvesters, particularly in the late 1880s and into the 1890s. With the coming of the corn binder during the 1890s, this task was mechanized, quickly relegating the corn harvester to obsolescence.

I. Z. Merriam, Whitewater, Wis.

The 1892 advertisement for the Badger Corn Harvester noted that "with it one man can cut and shock from three to five acres of corn in a day." One can only imagine what it was like using this strap-on device with a knife mounted near the ground. It was offered for sale by I.Z. Merriam, Whitewater, Wis., and was patented under No. 471,881. The patent was granted to James W. Parker at Viola, Ill.

Clipper Plow Co., Defiance, Ohio

Clipper Plow Co., Defiance, Ohio, advertised its Defiance Sulky Corn Cutter in 1889. At the time, this was one of the few corn harvesters built on a wheeled frame. Two men stood back-to-back on the harvester, catching the stalks of corn as they were cut. When enough had been gathered for a bundle, they were tied and dropped in the field. Later, the individual bundles were stood up in a stook or shock, bound into place and remained there to dry.

Standard Harrow Co., Utica, N.Y.

Standard Harrow Co., Utica, N.Y., offered its Peterson Corn Harvester to the trade in 1895, continuing with the same machine for several years. The hinged steel wings carried the cutting knives. With both wings down, two rows could be cut at a time; but in case there was only one man available, one wing was folded out of position for a single-row machine. This machine was built under the Peterson patent, No. 443,055 of Dec. 16, 1890.

A. W. Butt Implement Co., Springfield, Ohio

The Daisy Corn Harvester was similar to its contemporaries in that it utilized side-mounted and hinged knives. An 1895 advertisement noted that the machine had already been on the market for six years. The company rated this machine as being capable of cutting eight to 10 acres per day, and a strong sales point was the value of corn fodder as compared to hay, especially when the hay crop was short. This machine was made by the A.W. Butt Implement Co., Springfield, Ohio.

Foos Manufacturing Co., Springfield, Ohio

Licensed by the American Corn Harvester Co., the Foos Scientific Steel Corn Harvester was yet another approach to easy harvesting of standing corn. A substantial seat mounting permitted two men to sit back-to-back while catching the stalks as they were cut. When not in use, the side wings could be folded up out of the way. The Scientific used an all-steel frame, but Foos also offered a wood-frame machine called the Buckeye. Both came from Foos Manufacturing Co., Springfield, Ohio. The machine shown here is from an 1895 advertisement.

Dain Manufacturing Co., Ottumwa, Iowa

Dain Manufacturing Co., Ottumwa, Iowa, eventually became a part of Deere & Co. Originally established at Carrollton, Mo., this

firm came out with many innovative machines, including this all-steel Dain Steel Corn Cutter in 1895. The Dain used a somewhat different design, mounting the cutting knives farther back on the frame than its contemporaries. By 1895, the days of the corn harvester were approaching their end, since the corn binder would mechanize this laborious job.

Superior Hay Stacker Co., Linneus, Mo.

Superior Hay Stacker Co., Linneus, Mo., offered this automatic corn harvester in 1915. It was marketed by Parlin & Orendorff Plow Co., and Rock Island Implement Co., through its branch houses. Advertising of the time indicated that as this machine cut the stalks, they were held in an upright position and, when a sufficient number were gathered, the bundle of corn could then be removed to a shock or to a wagon, as desired. Outside of this 1915 advertisement, little more is known of the Superior Automatic Corn Harvester.

Eagle Manufacturing Co., Kansas City, Mo.

A specialized device was this Eagle Kaffir Corn Header, offered in 1905 by Eagle Manufacturing Co., Kansas City. At the time, the company claimed that this was "the only machine made that will successfully head and elevate kaffir corn." As shown here, the device was mounted on the side of a wagon and as it passed alongside the row, the heads were cut and elevated directly to the wagon box.

Trade Names			
Akron	Akron Cultivator Co.	Akron, OH	1913
Automatic	Automatic Mower & Mfg. Co.	Harvey, IL	1892
Bennett	H. L. Bennett & Co.	Westerville, OH	1905
Blue Valley	Blue Valley Mfg. Co.	Manhattan, KS	1905
Buckeye	Bauer Bros. Co.	Springfield, OH	1913
Buckeye	Foos Mfg. Co.	Springfield, OH	1905
Cyclone	Jeschke Mfg. Co.	Bellevue, OH	1909
Dain's	Dain Mfg. Co.	Ottumwa, IA	1905
Daisy	Springfield Implement Co.	Springfield, OH	1892

Trade Names (cont...)

Defiance	Clipper Plow Cco.	Defiance, OH	1905
Eagle	Eagle Mfg. Co.	Kansas City, MO	1913
Eureka	Dain Mfg. Co.	Carrollton, MO	1892
Fleming	Fleming and Sons Mfg. Co.	Huntsville, MO	1913
Hapgood	Hapgood Plow Co.	Alton, IL	1892
Havana	Havana Metal Wheel Co.	Havana, IL	1915
Jayhawk	F. Wyatt Mfg. Co.	Salina, KS	1915
Keyes	Keyes Corn Harvester & Mfg. Co.	Littleton, CO	1892
Lundgreen	St. Joseph Plow Co.	St. Joseph, MO	1892
Magic City	Wellbaum Bros.	Defiance, OH	1905
Monarch	Standard Harrow Co.	Utica, NY	1905
National	Shunk Plow Co.	Bucyrus, OH	1913
Neer	Neer Mfg. Co.	St. Paris, OH	1905
Peoria	Peoria Pump & Implement Co.	Peoria, IL	1892
Perfect	A. B. Clippinger & Bro.	Centralia, KS	1892
Perfect	Love Mfg. Co.	Lincoln, IL	1922
Scientific	Foos Mfg. Co.	Springfield, OH	1905
Scientific	Shunk Plow Co.	Bucyrus, OH	1913
Standard	Standard Harrow Co.	Utica, NY	1905
Superior	Superior Hay Stacker Mfg. Co.	Linneus, MO	1913
Western	Western Mfg. Co.	Kansas City, MO	1905
Ziegler	New Process Mfg. Co.	Lincoln, KS	1905

Corn Huskers & Shredders

Farmers of the 1890s were looking at corn fodder as an alternative to feeding hay. Poor hay crops were always a risk for the livestock farmer; shredded corn fodder was an excellent alternative. Thus came the husker-shredder in the 1890s. The standing corn was harvested just as the leaves started to turn brown or just before full maturity. With favorable fall weather, the corn was placed into shocks for drying and subsequent winter use. Initially, harvesting was achieved with the Corn Harvester by the late 1890s with a corn binder (see previous section on corn binders).

Some companies offered corn shredders with no husker mechanism. A few offered corn huskers that had no shredder. The great majority were combination machines, embodying both mechanisms. The cured corn stalks were fed into the machine where snapping rolls delivered the ear corn one direction and delivered the shredded corn stover in another. Many of these machines, especially the early designs, were extremely dangerous. This was because it was relatively easy for those feeding the shredder to become entangled in the mechanism and be drawn into the snapping rolls. Numerous farmers lost a hand, an arm or even their life while operating one of these machines. Later models were modified so that it was much more difficult to become caught in the mechanism.

Husker-shredders were fairly popular for some years, but were coming to an end in the 1930s. By that time, ensilage cutters were well established and the mechanical corn picker was becoming a reality, rather than a dream.

St. Albans Foundry Co., St. Albans, Vt.

This St. Albans Shredder of 1898 was, as the name implies, strictly a shredder, having no husking attachment. The St. Albans is shown to the left, with the end-product being illustrated as it drops to the floor. St. Albans also produced a smaller unit, The Leslie, shown to the right. It was designed for smaller requirements and required less power to operate. Both were built by St. Albans Foundry Co., St. Albans, Vt.

Crown Point Manufacturing Co. Crown Point, Ind.

Crown Point Manufacturing Co., Crown Point, Ind., announced this combination husker-shredder in 1897. A self-feed mechanism was used, with the manufacturer noting that "there is positively no danger of losing the hands." The snapped ears of corn dropped to a table below and were carried by elevator to a waiting wagon. The shredded fodder was moved by a large elevator to a stack or to a waiting wagon.

Keystone Manufacturing Co., Sterling, Ill.

Improved for 1895, the Keystone Corn Husker and Fodder Shredder had been on the market for a short time prior to this advertisement. This engraving shows the shredder placed near the barn so that the shredded fodder could be kept dry. Keystone offered this machine in three sizes; No. 1 for threshermen or large farms; No. 2 for medium farms or neighbors; and; No. 3 for small farms. It was built by Keystone Manufacturing Co., Sterling, Ill. This firm was eventually purchased by International Harvester Co.

DeSoto Agricultural Implement Manufacturing Co., DeSoto, Mo.

Manufacturers, large and small, attempted to capitalize on the burgeoning market in husker-shredders. This 1898 advertisement represents the Carrey Perfect Corn Shredder by DeSoto Agricultural Implement Manufacturing Co., DeSoto, Mo. Made in four sizes, the company represented its machines as having greater capacity than any other shredder made. Instead of an elevator for the shredded fodder, this machine used a pneumatic blower.

Safety Shredder Co., New Castle, Ind.

Safety Shredder Co., New Castle, Ind., used a completely automatic feeder to keep the operator's hands away from the shredder's mechanism. Its 1903 advertising noted, "No More Loss of Hands!" and, with this machine, to quote its advertising, "You put the corn on the feeder and the machine does the rest." Undoubtedly, the fear that many farmers had of injury while feeding a shredder was sufficient cause to take a serious look at buying the Safety shredder instead of another make.

E. A. Porter & Brox., Bowling Green, Ky.

Another approach to husker-shredder design was this 1895 model from E.A. Porter & Bros., Bowling Green, Ky. Billed as the Porter Corn Thresher, the engraving here illustrates the method

of feeding the corn into the machine, with the fodder emerging from the rear. After snapping the ears from the stalks, this machine shelled the corn, cleaned it and delivered it from a small side elevator.

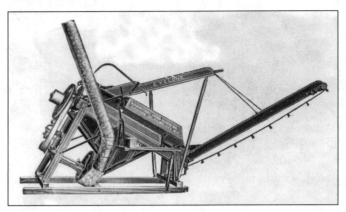

Rosenthal Corn Husker Co., Milwaukee, Wis.

Rosenthal Corn Husker Co., Milwaukee, was a pioneer firm in this field, having begun with this machine in 1896. It was extremely simple, and the company opted to specialize in husker-shredders. Instead of manufacturing a broad line of implements, Rosenthal made husker-shredders and ensilage cutters for many years.

Rosenthal Corn Husker Co., Milwaukee, Wis.

By 1908, the Rosenthal husker-shredder had taken on a new appearance over the 1896 model. Sold as the Big Cyclone, this machine had great capacity and used a pneumatic stacker to deposit the shredded fodder in a barn or shed. Meanwhile, the ear corn was elevated to a waiting wagon.

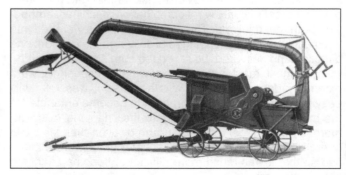

Rosenthal Corn Husker Co., Milwaukee, Wis.

Following the evolution of the Rosenthal husker-shredder, this Special 4 machine was offered in 1924. It was smaller and lighter than its ancestors, yet offered great capacity. It also had the advantage of requiring small power; most farm tractors could operate the Special 4. However, by 1930, the husker-shredder was losing in popularity and slowly faded from the scene.

Port Huron Engine & Thresher Co., Port Huron, Mich.

The Port Huron husker-shredder of 1903 was billed as being the only one made with a full-fledged band cutter and feeder. At the time, it was also the only shredder on the market with an all-steel design. Port Huron Engine & Thresher Co., was a major manufacturer of steam-traction engines and threshers and was located in Port Huron, Mich.

Milwaukee Hay Tool Co., Milwaukee, Wis.

Milwaukee Hay Tool Co., Milwaukee, offered this small husker-shredder in 1893. Regarding the husker itself, Milwaukee claimed its machine would husk the smallest nubbins as well as the full-sized ears of corn. This company went on to expand its line of shredders in the following years.

Milwaukee Hay Tool Co., Milwaukee, Wis.

The Milwaukee husker-shredder of 1895 was much more sophisticated than the original 1893 machine. This one had a somewhat larger husking and cleaning section for the ear corn and even included a cleaning screen beneath. Depending on the available power and other conditions, the feeder speed could be varied by the use of interchangeable feed gears. This machine was made by Milwaukee Hay Tool Co., Milwaukee, Wis.

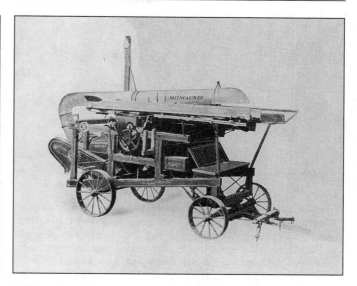

Milwaukee Hay Tool Co., Milwaukee, Wis.

By 1898, the Milwaukee husker-shredder had taken on the same general design, as is shown with this 1904 model. A pneumatic blower was used for the fodder, and the corn husker had been greatly improved. Note the substantial foot board beneath the feeder. With most of these machines it was necessary to feed the stalks into the throat of the husker by hand.

American Shredder Co., Madison, Wis.

American Shredder Co., Madison, Wis., announced this husker-shredder in 1903, having been in the business since before 1880. It was designed with the J.J. Power Automatic Corn Self Feeder. With this system, all danger was removed, as its 1903 advertising noted, "[it] leaves no cripples."

A. W. Stevens Co., Auburn, N.Y.

The A.W. Stevens Co. announced its new and improved Big 4 corn husker to the 1903 market. Stevens was an old company, first operating at Auburn, N.Y., and later removing to Marinette, Wis. The Stevens machine followed the same general lines as its contemporaries, although this machine shelled the corn and cleaned it.

Janney Manufacturing Co., Ottumwa, Iowa

Janney Manufacturing Co., Ottumwa, Iowa, was an early entrant in the husker-shredder business; shown here is its 1899 model. This was a small hand-fed machine and was distinctive for its all-steel construction. At the time, the majority of these machines were built on a wooden frame and utilized mainly wood construction.

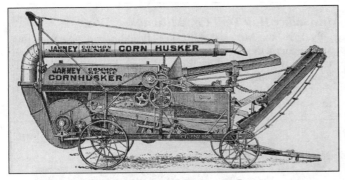

Janney Manufacturing Co., Ottumwa, Iowa

Janney Manufacturing Co., remained in the husker-shredder business for several years, with this 1903 model being substantially larger and more refined than its 1899 version. At this point, the feeder mechanism was much better than before, plus the machine could also shell the snapped corn, clean it and deliver it to a waiting wagon. Oftentimes, shredded corn fodder was referred to as corn hay.

U.S. Wind Engine & Pump Co., Batavia, Ill.

U.S. Wind Engine & Pump Co., Batavia, Ill., offered its U.S. Standard Husker at least into the 1920s. All of its machines built after 1915 could be retrofitted with a special silo-filling attachment. With this system, the corn could be husked and the stalks cut into 1/2-inch pieces for storage in a silo. This company also built husker-shredders. The machine shown here is of 1920 vintage.

J. I. Case Thresing Machine Co., Racine, Wis.

In 1905, the J.I. Case Threshing Machine Co., offered its Case Husker-Shredder. This machine embodied some of the same features found in its threshing machines and demonstrated the same rugged design. This company, located in Racine, Wis., continued producing husker-shredders until about 1920.

Appleton Manufacturing Co., Batavia, Ill.

Appleton Manufacturing Co., Batavia, Ill., was established in 1872. This company had a long history in the husker-shredder business and refined its 1917 line to include several innovative machines. Shown here is the No. 14 Appleton Corn Snapper. This machine was designed to snap the ears from the stalks, dropping them to the elevator below, meanwhile shredding or cutting the stalks as desired and blowing this material to a stack or into a barn.

Appleton Manufacturing Co., Batavia, Ill.

The Appleton Snapped Corn Husker of 1917 was a stationary machine used only for husking corn that had been snapped by a shredder. In other words, this machine was essentially a husking bed. The husks and debris left via the elevator to the left, while the clean ear corn was carried up the elevator to the right.

Appleton Manufacturing Co., Batavia, Ill.

Appleton's four-roll corn husker of 1917 was one of several sizes available at the time. This machine used both a cutter head and the shredding saws commonly found on most of these machines. Of all-steel construction, the Appleton was widely sold and used.

Parsons Band Cutter & Self Feeder Co., Newton, Iowa

Success husker-shredders were built by Parsons Band Cutter & Self Feeder Co., Newton, Iowa. Of wooden construction, this machine was available for several years; this particular machine was illustrated in its 1910 catalog. The Success followed many of the design features common to husker-shredders, including the pneumatic stacker that permitted blowing the shredded fodder directly into a barn.

McCormick Harvesting Machine Co., Chicago, Ill.

A 1900 catalog of McCormick Harvesting Machine Co., Chicago, illustrates its husker-shredder in operation. The man at the left is feeding the stalks into the machine, while the two men on the right are getting material up to the feeder. At the rear, another man can be seen stacking the shredded fodder.

International Harvester Co., Chicago, Ill.

International Harvester Co., continued building husker-shredders up to about 1940. However, production had dropped to very low levels. The onset of World War II ended it completely. By the time production ended, these machines were somewhat more sophisticated than their ancestors, including shellers, cleaners and other devices.

New Idea Co., Coldwater, Ohio

New Idea Co., Coldwater, Ohio, offered this six-roll husker shredder in 1927, continuing production for a few years. These machines were usually classed as two-roll, four-roll, six-roll and so on. This indicated the number of snapping rolls in the machine and was a general guide to its capacity.

Advance-Rumely Thresher Co., Kenton, Ohio

Many of the major farm equipment manufacturers offered husker-shredders up to about 1920. Included was the Advance-Rumely Thresher Co., LaPorte, Ind. While each company pronounced its machine to be the best on the market, all of them had good features, along with some that weren't so good. Much of the final decision rested on product loyalty and for those enamored of the Advance-Rumely line, this machine was undoubtedly their choice.

Daniel Engineering Co., Kenton, Ohio

In 1923, E.H. Daniel, designer of the London Motor Plow, announced plans to build the Mota-Husker. As shown in this photograph, the idea was to husk corn from a standing shock. The husked corn was delivered to a waiting wagon, while the fodder was deposited separately. This machine was built by the Daniel Engineering Co., Kenton, Ohio.

Schuman Corn Handling Machinery Co., Indianapolis, Ind.

One of the most unusual machines associated with the husker-shredder business was the Parsons-Schuman shock loader. With this device, the farmer could mechanically load up to six shocks of corn and bring them to a waiting shredder for processing. This machine was designed in 1909 by the Schuman Corn Handling Machinery Co., Indianapolis. In 1910, Maytag Co., Newton, Iowa, announced the machine under the Parsons-Schuman trade name. Little more is known of it after the 1910 introduction.

Trade Names

Advance	Advance Thresher Co.	Battle Creek, MI	1905
Advance	M. Rumely Co.	LaPorte, IN	1913
Appleton	Appleton Mfg. Co.	Batavia, IL	1905
Armsaver	Double Power Mill Co.	Appleton, WI	1905
Armsaver	Hayton Pump & Blower Co.	Appleton, WI	1924
Armsaver	Killen-Walsh Mfg. Co.	Appleton, WI	1922
Big Cyclone	Rosenthal Corn Husker Co.	Milwaukee, WI	1913
Big Four	A. W. Stevens Co.	Marinette, WI	1909
Carrey Perfect	Matt Sprout	Sparta, IL	1909
Case	J. I. Case Threshing Machine Co.	Racine, WI	1905
Cayuga Chief	Quick & Thomas Co.	Auburn, NY	1929
Chicopee	Chicopee Corn Husker Co.	Chicopee Falls, MA	1929

Trade Names (cont...)

Chicopee	Fred H. Bateman Co.	Grenloch, NJ	1924
Common Sense	Caldwell Mfg. Co.	Columbus, IN	1922
Corn Belt	Corn Belt Shredder Co.	Beatrice, NE	1909
Corn King	Corn King Husker Co.	Rochester, IN	1905
Deere	Deere & Mansur Co.	Moline, IL	1905
Deering	International Harvester Co.	Chicago, IL	1905
Dick's Blizzard	Joseph Dick Mfg. Co.	Canton, OH	1922
Dues	J. J. Dues Machine Co.	Minster, OH	1929
Fort Plain	Stewart & Bergen Co.	Fort Plain, NY	1929
Fox	Fox River Tractor Co.	Appleton, WI	1936
Gem	Taylor Husker & Shredder Co.	Joliet, IL	1905
Goodhue	Ohio Cultivator Co.	Bellevue, OH	1905
Gruendler	Gruendler Crusher Co.	St. Louis, MO	1936
Janney	Janney Mfg. Co.	Ottumwa, IA	1905
Janney	Kenny Machinery Co.	Indianapolis, IN	1922
Jenney	Hall Mfg. Co.	Cedar Rapids, IA	1929
Keystone	Keystone Co.	Sterling, IL	1892
Koger	Koger Pea & Bean Thresher Co.	Morristown, TN	1929
Kolling	Kolling Husker & Shredder Works	Arlington Heights, IL	1905
Kolling	Kolling Husker & Shredder Co.	Arlington Heights, IL	1922
Little Giant	International Harvester Co.	Chicago, IL	1913
McCormick	Internationa Harvester Co.	Chicago, IL	1905
Milwaukee	Milwaukee Hay Tool Co.	Milwaukee, WI	1892
Monarch	Morton Mfg. Co.	Muskegon Hts., MI	1892
New Idea	New Idea Spreader Co.	Coldwater, OH	1929
Plano	International Harvester Co.	Chicago, IL	1905
Port Huron	Port Huron Engine & Thresher Co.	Port Huron, MI	1905
Rosenthal	Rosenthal Corn Husker Co.	Milwaukee, WI	1905
Rumely-Watts	M. Rumely Co.	LaPorte, IN	1913
Safety	Safety Shredder Co.	New Castle, IN	1905
Safety	Safety Shredder Co.	New Castle, IN	1913
Slinger	Standard Machinery Co.	Schlesingerville, WI	1922
Smalley	Smalley Mfg. Co.	Manitowoc, WI	1909
Stevens Big Four	A. W. Stevens Co.	Marinette, WI	1905
Success	Maytag Co.	Newton, IA	1913
Success	Parsons Band Cutter & S. F. Co.	Newton, IA	1905
Taylor	W. H. Van Schalk	Walworth, WI	1905
U. S. Standard	U. S. Wind Engine & Pump Co.	Batavia, IL	1915
Victor	Foster & Williams Mfg. Co.	Racine, WI	1892
Walker	Walker Mfg. Co.	Council Bluffs, IA	1913

Corn Pickers

In the 1930s, the corn picker was finally perfected. With its coming ended the annual "battle of the bangboards," as well as the "school holiday" while rural kids helped bring in the crop. Beginning about 1900, there were numerous attempts to build and market a corn picker. McCormick even attempted to market one in 1904, but it was not successful.

A 1908 article in *Farm Machinery* discussed the efforts of Monroe Glick at Metcalf, Ill. He designed a machine that was to pick three rows at a time. Weighing more than two tons, it was equipped with a big 35-horsepower engine. Plans were to dispense with the horses needed to pull the machine, once the mechanism was perfected, leading to a self-propelled corn picker. Despite the publicity at the time, this attempt to build a commercially successful corn picker eluded Glick, as well as thousands of other inventors. Another early corn picker was developed by Appleton Manufacturing Co., Batavia, Ill. The firm brought a machine to the market in 1917, noting that it had been working on its design since about 1904. Like many others that showed some promise by 1917, the Appleton was another that beat a hasty retreat from the market.

International Harvester Co., poured huge sums of money into corn picker development, seeing the corn picker as the last major piece of farm mechanization, outside of the cotton picker. For the company coming out with a machine acceptable to the farmer, there was a huge bonanza waiting to be had. Thus, of all the major companies, International Harvester undoubtedly expended more research and development money than any other. Its work paid off, for, in the 1920s, Harvester made major strides in corn picker development. The company built on its experience derived over various corn picker models built in the 1904-1920 period. Although the early machines eliminated hand picking and did a reasonably good job of plucking the ears from the stalks, they also dropped most of the shucks and some of the stalks into the wagon. Farmers were most unhappy with this prospect, since hand-picked corn was not thus disadvantaged.

Goodhue Manufacturing Co., St. Charles, Ill., made a valiant effort to perfect a corn picker, offering what it considered to be a practical machine in 1908. As with others attempting to achieve this goal, success was elusive. During the 1930s, major strides were made, particularly with the concept of a tractor-mounted corn picker. By the late 1930s, the majority of ear corn was picked by machine instead of by hand. Progress continued apace until temporarily slowed by World War II. After its end, corn picker design renewed itself with a fury, continuing into the 1960s. However, the corn picker, like many other farm machines, had enjoyed its supremacy. The corn combine was on the way.

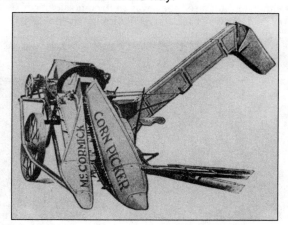

International Harvester Co., Chicago, Ill.

International Harvester marketed its first corn picker in 1904. It was driven through gearing from a large drive wheel and re-

quired four or five horses to pull the machine and operate the mechanism. A wagon was driven alongside the picker to receive the newly harvested corn. One farmer happily reported that he had picked 25 bushels of corn in 23 minutes with this machine. Considering that 100 bushels per day picking by hand was a high average, this was indeed something to gloat about.

Jesse H. Johnson, New Paris, Ohio

In 1906, Jesse H. Johnson of New Paris, Ohio, gained considerable attention with his new corn picker design. This one cut the stalks at the desired height, after which the ears and stalks were fed through combination snapping and husking rolls. Beyond this announcement, little more was heard of the Johnson machine.

Appleton Manufacturing Co., Batavia, Ill.

Appleton Manufacturing Co., Batavia, Ill., began corn picker development as early as 1904. After years of research, this machine appeared in 1917. Weighing more than 3,000 pounds, it was equipped with a ground-drive system for the mechanism, but could also be furnished with an auxiliary engine drive. The company noted that three horses were needed when the engine was used, but for the ground drive it took five horses. The 1917 Appleton could also be furnished with a tractor hitch, if desired.

Advance-Rumely Thresher Co., LaPorte, Ind.

Advance-Rumely Thresher Co., LaPorte, Ind., was a well-known engine and thresher builder. It also gained world-wide recognition for the inimitable OilPull tractors. In the 1920s, this firm attempted to build and market a corn picker, a prototype of which is shown here. Beyond this effort, little else is known of Rumely's venture.

Belle City Manufacturing Co., Racine, Wis.

In 1928, Belle City Manufacturing Co., Racine, Wis., offered its Continental mounted corn picker. With this one-row machine, Belle City claimed that a farmer could pick anywhere from six to 10 acres per day. This machine was moderately successful, with a very few early mounted corn pickers appearing at vintage tractor meets. This one is mounted on a McCormick-Deering tractor, although mounting equipment was available for the Fordson and a few other tractor makes.

John Deere Plow Works, Moline, Ill.

John Deere Plow Co., entered the corn picker market in the 1920s, with this horse-drawn one-row model being available in 1928. It

could be operated with ground power, auxiliary engine or from a tractor PTO shaft, as desired. Deere went on to develop an extensive corn picker line, both in pull-type and tractor-mounted models.

Nichols & Shepard Co., Battle Creek, Mich.

Nichols & Shepard advertised its mounted corn picker in 1928, noting that a farmer could pick his corn for a cost of 6 cents to 8 cents per bushel. Like most pickers of the time, it was necessary to synchronize a wagon beneath the corn spout, as the picker made its way through the field. Nichols & Shepard later joined with other partners to form Oliver Farm Equipment Co.

International Harvester Co., Chicago, Ill.

Of all the early corn picker designs, International Harvester was a genuine pioneer. The company had already spent more than a quarter-century searching for a practical corn picker when this pull-type machine came out in 1931. It also had the advantage of an overhead storage tank for dumping directly into a wagon; this eliminated the need for a wagon to come alongside as the picker made its way back and forth through the field.

J. I. Case Co., Racine, Wis.

J.I. Case Co., came along with its new corn harvester, a two-row machine, in 1931. This one was a companion to its one-row model. The Case model was designed for a one-man operation. It utilized a side-mounted wagon hitch, enabling the wagon to travel with the picker.

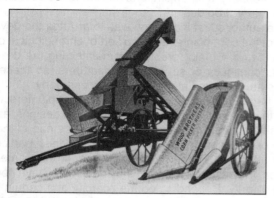

Wood Bros., Des Moines, Iowa

Wood Bros., at Des Moines, Iowa, attempted to diversify in the 1930s. Prior to that time, it had concentrated on the steam engine and thresher business. Its corn picker of the 1930s was light in weight and included a rear-mounted corn elevator and wagon hitch. Eventually, all corn pickers would follow this idea.

Oliver Farm Equipment Co., Chicago, Ill.

In 1935, Oliver Corp., came out with its Corn Master corn pickers. Undoubtedly, the company built on the ideas pioneered with the earlier Nichols & Shepard corn picker. A major feature was the use of rubber tires and the light weight of the machine; the Oliver Corn Master weighed less than 3,000 pounds.

New Idea Spreader Co., Coldwater, Ohio

In this overhead view, an Allis-Chalmers tractor is coupled to a New Idea picker of the 1930s. While the earliest New Idea design used steel wheels, the company quickly changed over to pneumatic tires to lessen the draft. The overhead view illustrates the unique side-hitch used by New Idea. A simple chain attachment was hooked to the wagon tongue. It engaged a dog in the side-hitch.

Through a control rope, the operator could shift the wagon forward or back, relative to the spout, thus filling the wagon from front to back without leaving the driver's seat.

New Idea Spreader Co., Coldwater, Ohio

This 1941 illustration shows the New Idea one-row model. This one used a rear-mounted elevator and embodied many features that remained in the New Idea corn picker line throughout a long production run. While some farmers preferred the one-row design, the vast majority opted for a two-row picker.

McGrath Manufacturing Co., Omaha, Neb.

The Sargent corn harvester was a fully mounted machine that emerged in 1947. With this unique design, the stalk was cut at the ground and cutting continued until the ear was cut from the stalk. Sargent even equipped this machine with a removable husking bed for picking sweet corn. It was built by McGrath Manufacturing Co., Omaha, Neb.

Trade Names			
Allis-Chalmers	Allis-Chalmers Mfg. Co.	Milwaukee, WI	1945
Appleton	Appleton Mfg. Co.	Batavia, IL	1929
Baird	Baird Harvester Co.	Decatur, IL	1919
Belle City	Belle City Mfg. Co.	Racine, WI	1929
Case	J. I. Case Co.	Racine, WI	1932
Continental	Belle City Mfg. Co.	Racine, WI	1936
Corn Belt	Miller Products Co.	Waterloo, IA	1932
Corn Master	Oliver Farm Equipment Co.	Chicago, IL	1939
Deere	Deere & Mansur Co.	Moline, IL	1909
Deering	International Harvester Co.	Chicago, IL	1905
Farm Aide	Geo. B. Miller & Son Co.	Waterloo, IA	1929
Goodhue	Appleton Mfg. Co.	Batavia, IL	1909
Huskor	Minneapolis-Moline Co.	Minneapolis, MN	1939
John Deere	John Deere Harvester Works	Moline, IL	1929
Kuhlman	Geo. B. Miller & Son Co.	Waterloo, IA	1929
Kuhlman	Gilderbloom Mfg. Co.	Oskaloosa, IA	1932

Trade Names (cont...)

Kurtz	Deere & Co.	Moline, IL	1936
McCormick	International Harvester Co.	Chicago, IL	1905
McCormick-Deering	International Harvester Co.	Chicago, IL	1929
Minneapolis-Moline	Minneapolis-Moline Co.	Minneapolis, MN	1936
New Idea	New Idea Spreader Co.	Coldwater, OH	1929
Port Huron	Port Huron Engine & Thresher Co.	Port Huron, MI	1913
Red River Special	Nichols & Shepard Co.	Battle Creek, MI	1929
Soilfitter	General Implement Co.	Cleveland, OH	1939
Steiner	August Steiner	Homewood, IL	1915
Taylor	Taylor Husker & Shredder Co.	Joliet, IL	1905
Wood Bros.	Harry Ferguson Inc.	Dearborn, MI	1945

Corn Planters

Corn cultivation has been pursued for centuries. Until the late 19th century, corn was planted with a hoe, with seeds being dropped into each hill by hand. This was a very laborious task and thousands of inventors were at work trying to perfect a machine that would plant corn. To cultivate the crop, it was planted in rows; during the 1850s, the idea of planting in check rows developed (the field could be cultivated lengthwise and crosswise to minimize weed infestations).

A few planters appeared in the 1840s, but, in the 1850s, real progress appeared. The George W. Brown patent (No. 9893) of 1853 was the first major development in corn planters. Brown set up a factory at Galesburg, Ill., and began building his new invention. This was the first planter to use runners to open the furrow and press wheels to firm the seed in the row. To plant the seed in check rows, it was first necessary to mark the field. This was achieved with a specially built marker that was pulled across the field, first lengthwise and then crosswise to mark the exact location for each hill of corn. The planter had two seats, one for the driver and one for the dropper. The latter operated a hand-lever each time he reached the intersection of the lines. Corn planters continued to be built under this pattern for a number of years, although there were many attempts to build an automatic check-row planter.

Guide markers first appeared in the late 1850s. Galt & Tracy, later Keystone Manufacturing Co., Sterling, Ill., made major improvements, introducing the open-heel runner, which permitted the kernels to drop inside the open heel, after which they were covered. Deere & Mansur were instrumental in developing the rotary-drop system, using rotating plates in the bottom of the seed canisters. Numerous other developments came along, but there still was not a successful automatic check-row planter.

Already, in the 1850s, attempts were made to check automatically, using a chain with buttons spaced periodically. Others attempted using rope with knots at the appropriate spacing, but none of these plans were entirely satisfactory. The initial success with a check-row planter is generally ascribed to G.D. Haworth. During the 1870s, Haworth made considerable progress, and, with the development of steel

wire suitable for the purpose, the check-row planter became a reality. Once this happened, improvements were needed in the dropping mechanism, and this led to the development of the rotary-drop design.

The author's first inclination was to arrange the development of the corn planter in some sort of chronological order. This created a major problem in maintaining the developmental continuity of several manufacturers, so these machines are arranged alphabetically, by company.

Of further interest, some of the early corn planters, especially those prior to the automatic check-row designs, are essentially museum pieces. If available, they can command $500 or perhaps much more. Later models, particularly those after 1930, often have little value. In this same connection, the cast-iron lids from the seed boxes have now become a rarity. Depending on the scarcity of a certain style, these can be valuable but, on average, bring $20 to $30 in good condition.

American Seeding Machine Co., Springfield, Ohio

This Evans Simplex corn planter of 1903 was equipped with disc openers instead of the usual planter runners. A.C. Evans Manufacturing Co., Springfield had long been established with its Buckeye grain drills and other farm implements. In 1903, Evans joined with several other firms to incorporate the American Seeding Machine Co., headquartered at Springfield, but maintaining the factories of most partners to the reorganized firm.

Avery Planter Co., Galesburg, Ill.

Avery Planter Co., was organized at Galesburg, Ill., in 1874. Robert Avery had developed some ideas about corn planters in the 1860s, an example of which is shown here. Eventually, he and his brother Cyrus M. Avery organized a company to manufacture the planters. In 1884, the company relocated to Peoria, Ill., all the while expanding its implement line. In 1891, the company began building steam engines and threshing machines. Eventually, the company opted for this endeavor, gradually going out of the implement business.

Avery Planter Co., Peoria, Ill.

From its humble beginnings in the corn planter business, Avery eventually grew to be an industry leader, manufacturing engines, tractors, and threshers. By the early 1920s, through difficulties not entirely of its own, Avery essentially was bankrupt. Reorganized as Avery Power Machinery Co., it never again rose to prominence due to market saturation, overproduction, and a failure to develop new machines to meet with ever-changing power farming requirements.

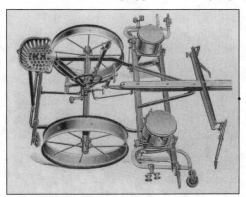

By 1899, Avery Co. had developed its Corn King and Corn Queen planters; the latter style is shown here. By this time, the company offered several different types of furrow openers as well as other options. For instance, the press wheels could be flat, concave or open design, as desired. Avery continued to build this planter at least until about 1910.

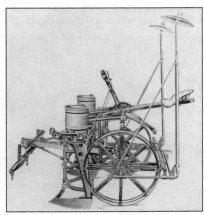

In 1908, Avery Co. announced its new Perfection planter. Options included three styles of press wheels and pointed, sled or disc run-

ners. The Avery Perfection used an automatic self-lift device and the guide markers were automatic in their operation. By 1912, Avery was opting out of the farm implement market in favor of its growing tractor and thresher business.

B.F. Avery & Sons, Louisville, Ky.

B.F. Avery began making plows at Louisville in 1845. The company grew and diversified, but we have established no precise date for the introduction of the Avery corn planters. Its 1916 line included the Avery Sure Drop planter, an all-steel unit that was ordinarily furnished with open press wheels as show. Like other planters of the period, this one featured an adjustable row width for various crop requirements.

The Avery Plainsman lister of 1916 was but one item in the extensive B.F. Avery line. The lister or lister-planter was developed about 1880, with most of the credit going to William Parlin of Parlin & Orendorff Co., Canton, Ill. From his efforts, came the majority of lister design as used for many years to follow. However, each manufacturer had its own designs and the Avery, like the others, had its own salient features. This company had no connection or relation to Avery Co., Peoria, Ill.

Beedle & Kelly Co., Troy, Ohio

By the 1880s, there were literally hundreds of companies attempting to build corn planters. Due to the great demand, there was room for everyone for a time, but as the market became saturated, many of the smaller firms were forced out of business. One small firm was Beedle & Kelly Co., Troy, Ohio. Shown here is its 1898 version of the ideal corn planter. Except for this advertisement, little else is known of the firm.

Belcher & Taylor Agricultural Tool Co., Chicopee Falls, Mass.

In 1903, Belcher & Taylor advertised this Eclipse Two-Row Two-Horse Corn Planter, claiming it to have all the good features of the Eclipse one-row model. Also included was a dry fertilizer attachment; it banded soil nutrients either into or beside the row. This firm was a well-known manufacturer of farm implements for many years.

Briggs & Enoch Manufacturing Co., Rockford, Ill.

Virtually nothing is known of Briggs & Enoch outside of this 1898 advertisement for its Rockford corn planter. Although this planter is obviously equipped as an automatic check-row machine, it also appears that it could be operated as formerly, using a separate person to work the valve lever and drop the corn into the row manually.

Geo. W. Brown & Co., Galesburg, Ill.

This artist's conception shows the Brown corn planter of the 1850s. One of the earliest to demonstrate any success, the Brown required two men, one to drive the team and the other to work the drop lever. The work of the dropper was exacting and very tiring for it required the accurate working of the valve lever each time the planter crossed one of the marks previously made in the seedbed. George W. Brown received many corn planter patents beginning in the 1850s.

An 1887 magazine article on corn planters noted that this Excelsior corn planter from Geo. W. Brown & Co., had been on the market for some years. It was equipped with Brown's Universal Checkrower, this company's solution to getting automatic check-rows. As with virtually all check-row machines, the check-row wire was stretched across the field and held at each end by steel stakes. As the planter traversed the field, the wire ran through the device pictured here. The buttons secured to the wire tripped a device to drop corn kernels precisely as desired.

An 1899 showing from Geo. W. Brown & Co., illustrates its Admiral Dewey corn planter. This machine was somewhat improved over the earlier Excelsior model. The check-row wire was stored on the reel as shown. Once a suitable wire was found, it could be used for several years before replacement was necessary.

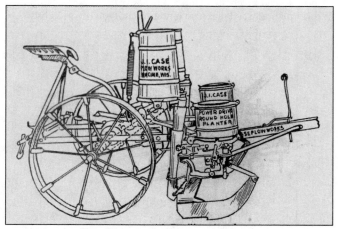

J.I. Case Plow Works, Racine, Wisc.

A relative latecomer to the corn planter business, J.I. Case Plow Works offered this Round Hole Plate Planter in 1908. This referred to the company's method of metering the seed. Cast iron disks or plates were placed beneath the seed boxes. In this instance, the plates were designed with holes around their periphery. The plates revolved beneath the seed boxes, thus picking up two, three or four kernels as desired for each hill of corn.

In 1912, Case announced its Power Drive planters with three exclusive features. These included, 1) no clutch on the drill shaft, the latter often being a troublesome feature on other planters; 2) round hole plates which Case claimed were more accurate than the common edge drop plates and 3) the Case accurate and positive Changeable Drop permitted the dropping of 2, 3 or 4 kernels in a hill in different parts of the field, at the will of the driver.

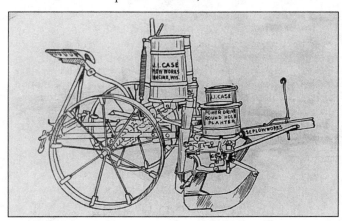

By 1920, the Case Power Drive Planter had changed very little from the 1912 model. This model could drill or check corn as

desired and this was a valuable feature when a farmer wished to plant beans, peas or other drilled crops. The planter shown here is equipped with an optional dry fertilizer attachment.

Challenge Corn Planter Co., Grand Haven, Mich.

An 1887 advertisement from Challenge Corn Planter Co. noted that at the time, there were over 30,000 Challenge corn planters in use. This was the planter that created a furor, finally being settled in the 1888 term of the United States Supreme Court. Farmer's Friend Manufacturing Co., at Dayton, Ohio, sued Challenge for infringement of certain patent rights. After years of litigation the Supreme Court ruled that the original patent claims of No. 231,104 of 1880 were valid, but that a subsequent reissue, two years later, did nothing but further broaden the original patent. Therefore, the court ruled in favor of Challenge. For many years this was referred to in legal circles as the Corn Planter Case.

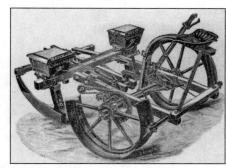

In 1890, the Challenge Leader Planter was introduced. It featured the Leader Drill Attachment, along with the Improved Wonder Check Rower Attachment. The company began manufacturing farm implements in 1872, but after the 1890 advertising, little more can be found concerning Challenge Corn Planter Co.

For small fields and very small farms, Challenge offered its one-row, one-horse drill and check planter in 1890. By this time, the open heel runner was in wide use. As the runner moved through the soil the seedbed was opened, with the kernels dropping through a boot and the open heal directly to their proper placement. As the soil dropped back behind the runner, a press wheel firmed the soil around the seed. This one-row planter was also available with the fertilizing attachment shown here.

Chambers, Bering, Quinlan Co., Decatur, Ill.

An 1890 advertisement of Chambers, Bering, Quinlan, manufacturers of the "CB&Q" line, noted that the company had been building corn planters for five years. Of course, the company hailed its machine as the "most compact, substantial, best working, easiest planters to operate made." With this machine it was possible to drill or plant in check-rows, as desired. The company appears in product listings as late as 1909, but was later acquired by International Harvester Co. Product listings show Harvester as building the CB&Q planters in 1914.

Cockshutt Plow Co., Ltd., Brantford, Ontario

Cockshutt Plow Co., began making plows and other farm implements in the 1870s. This company remained in place until merging with others into White Farm Equipment Co., in the 1960s. The Cockshutt corn planter of 1910 was a very modern machine using all-steel construction. It also featured a frame drilled so that the farmer could change the planting width anywhere from 28 to 44 inches, as desired.

Columbia Drill Co., Liberty, Ind.

Columbia Drill Co., announced its new line of corn drills in 1894. This single-row style was known as the "Duke" and dis-

played some interesting features. It did not use the open heel runner as most of its contemporaries, but instead used an open runner with the seed boot directly behind. Curved sweeps behind the seed mechanism tended to squeeze the soil around the newly planted seed and also tended to hill the rows slightly.

The Paragon Double Corn Drill was offered by Columbia Drill Co., in 1894. It was designed somewhat on the same principles as the smaller one-row unit. Planting depth was regulated by the hand levers shown here; they also were used to raise and lower the planting units, as well as to throw the planting mechanism out of gear. No further information has been found on Columbia Drill Co.

Common Sense Engine Co., Muncie, Ind.

A flurry of manufacturing activity was evident in the corn planter business during the 1890s. Farmers hurried to buy corn planters and oftentimes had to buy what was available rather than having a significant choice in the matter. The 1893 Common Sense Champion planter was made by Common Sense Engine Co., Muncie, Ind. This was the first planter with a steel frame and was patented by G. Campbell Janney, Springfield, Ohio. Unfortunately, the company went into receivership in 1893.

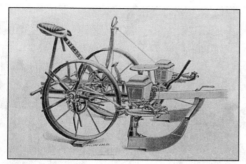

Deere & Co., Moline, Ill.

Deere & Mansur Co. was established by the Deere interests in 1877 to build corn planters. Twenty years later the company advertised this all-steel planter that came to a dominant position in the corn planter trade. Deere had numerous branch houses throughout the United States and this gave the company a marketing ability far beyond most of the competitors. The quality of the design and considerable product loyalty to John Deere implements all helped to propel this planter to its leading position in the industry.

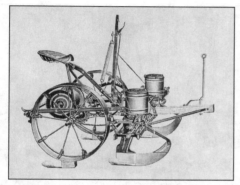

By 1906, the No. 9 planter was being offered by Deere & Mansur. This planter would be the direct ancestor of John Deere planter design for decades to come. Special attention was paid to getting an accurate drop and in this regard the No. 9 was eminently successful.

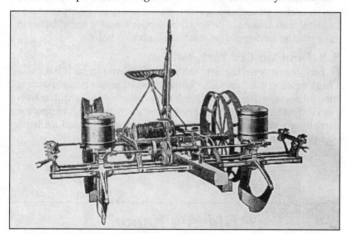

Deere & Mansur was merged into Deere & Co., 1911. Its No. 999 corn planter emerged about 1912 and was a great advance over the earlier No. 9 planter. With the No. 999 the farmer could plant various kinds of kernels, using different planter plates. The company also supplied plates for kaffir corn, sorghum, milo, maize, beans, peas and other row crops. With the variable drop feature, seed could be placed anywhere from 6-1/2 to 24 inches in the row. This planter remained on the market for many years, finally being replaced with

planters redesigned for use with tractors; this resulted in the famous 290 and 490 John Deere tractor planters.

H.P. Deuscher Co., Hamilton, Ohio

H.P. Deuscher Co. was organized in 1878, incorporating 10 years later. In 1892 A. J. Welliver became general manager; he had many years of experience in the farm implement business. The Hamilton corn planter of 1887 was a hand-operated checkrower and the identical engraving advertises this planter in 1898. A special feature was the clod fenders each side of the runners; thus the corn was covered only with loose soil.

In 1900, Deuscher advertised "The Excelsior" corn drill as part of its extensive implement line. Included at the time were disc and drag harrow, corn planters, cultivators and other items. This interesting design even included a guide marker, something unique to the majority of corn drills.

In 1906, Deuscher, advertised its Ideal corn planter. This design was a "Combined Hand Dropper, Driller and Check-Rower Planter." For reasons unknown the company still retained the hand-dropper portion of the design and probably was one of the last to do so. The company still appears in the 1909 implement directories but fell out of sight shortly afterward.

Emerson-Brantingham Co., Rockford, Ill.

Emerson-Brantingham Co., was founded in 1852 and was acquired by J.I. Case in 1928. The No. 25 Emerson Edge Drop Planter shown here was on the market in 1907, and the company continued building corn planters until being absorbed by J.I. Case. In fact, this No. 25 was eventually replaced by the No. 26; but except for a few improvements, it was essentially of the same design. E-B implements were very popular and thousands of these planters were sold.

A 1907 Emerson catalog illustrates its No. 4 Foot-Lift 4-Wheel Lister. This rather sophisticated design utilized the Emerson concept of "foot-lift" implements designed for easy manipulation by the driver. In certain areas of the South and West, the lister was an ideal method of planting corn and other crops. Advertising of the time noted that this machine would "take care of itself."

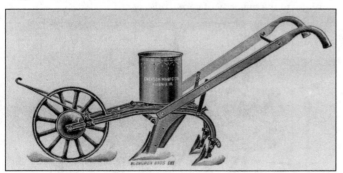

The No. B 19 combined corn and cotton planters were another new innovation for the 1907 market. This planter was designed especially for cotton growers, but could also used to plant corn, if so desired. Production of this and similar models continued until Emerson-Brantingham became a part of J.I. Case Co., 1928.

Farmer's Friend Manufacturing Co., Dayton, Ohio

The Farmer's Friend corn planter of 1887 was a hand dropper, as noted by the small seat located over the runners, plus the hand-lever that operated the slide valve. As noted previously under the Challenge Corn Planter Co., section, Farmer's Friend attempted to sue Challenge for infringement of its patents, taking its case all the way to the U.S. Supreme Court in 1888. Farmer's Friend lost the case.

By 1892, Farmer's Friend had come out with an entirely new automatic check-row planter. It was built along the same lines as its earlier planter and even retained the hand dropper mechanism, if so desired. The special dropper's seat is noted beneath the planter and could be attached with two bolts.

A.B. Farquhar Co., York, Pa.

Farquhar entered the farm implement business in the 1850s, making threshing machines. The firm prospered and expanded during the following years; by the 1890s, it was offering the Farquhar Keystone Planter. This simple device was intended for acreages too small for a larger two-row planter and was widely used for truck gardening, and for planting sweet corn.

Did You Know?

Today, vintage flour mills often sell at a considerable figure; a nicely restored small mill might bring up to $1,000. However, a mill with a poor framework or a broken stone will bring but a fraction of that figure.

The Farquhar Star two-row planter of the 1920s had several unique features, one of them being the single center-mounted guide marker. It also used disc closers instead of press wheels; thus its exceptionally wide footprint. Farquhar was acquired by Oliver Corp., in 1952.

Fuller & Johnson Manufacturing Co., Madison, Wisc.

Fuller & Johnson entered the corn planter business in the 1880s, using the design of Nils O. Starks, a former school teacher. This resulted in the Starks Force Drop Steel Corn Planter, with an 1895 example shown here. The company was overwhelmed with orders, selling everything it could produce. This advertisement is from the German-language edition of the famous *American Agriculturist Magazine*.

W.N. Harrison & Son, Sterling, Ill.

Hand corn planters were, of course, developed prior to the larger models. Even after the advent of the corn planter, the hand planters were often used for garden and truck farm work. In addition, they were used to "plug" corn where it was missing in the row. Oftentimes, farmers would walk the field as the corn

was emerging, looking for missing hills of their new crop. Pushing the Empire Rotary Hand Planter into the soil and squeezing the levers together dropped seed into the ground; as the farmer walked away, he packed the soil with his heel.

Haworth & Sons Manufacturing Co., Decatur, Ill.

The Haworth corn planter was the first successful check-row machine. George D. Haworth began perfecting this machine in the 1850s, building a successful one-row planter in 1859 and following with a two-row planter shortly after. In the late 1860s, the check-row design was fully developed; from it came most of the later developments along these lines. This 1896 model was typical of the Haworth design for many years and was the first four-wheel planter on the market. For reasons unknown, the Haworth dropped from view in the early 1900s.

Hayes Pump & Planter Co., Galva, Ill.

Eugenio K. Hayes set up his business at Galva, Ill., in 1886, having first begun at Kewanee. In 1887, the E.K. Hayes' Check-Row Planter appeared. It featured the patented Hayes wire reel for rolling and unrolling the check wire. It also featured the Hayes four-wheel press wheel design; the latter feature predominated the Hayes planter line from that time forward. The 1887 planter is shown here.

Did You Know?

Old feed grinders have appreciated in value considerably over the years. Sometimes, a rare or popular model will bring well more than $100.

By the 1890s, the Hayes planters were well known and were widely sold as "The Original 4-Wheel Planter." After building 10 planters in 1887, production increased 10-fold the following year. In 1892, the company made 2,500 planters, doubling this figure in 1894 and planning for sales of some 7,000 planters in 1895. This Hayes planter was equipped with solid press wheels, instead of the usual four-wheel pattern that characterized the Hayes' design.

By 1902, the Hayes 4-Wheel planter had again been modified to include an all-steel design. By that time, the company had sold more than 40,000 of its planters, and production continued at high levels for years to come. This 1915 model has all the salient features found in the 1902 version, except of course, for a few incidental refinements.

In the face of many company mergers, Hayes and three other firms reorganized in 1930 to form Farm Tools, Inc. The latter firm was in a better sales position, due to the merger, and production continued, despite the Great Depression. This No. 44 Hayes planter of the 1930s

typified the line at that time and was, in fact, little different from the 1902 model. Eventually, though, Farm Tools, Inc., also withered away, bringing an end to the Hayes planters. By the mid-1950s, only repair parts were available from the Farm Tools, Inc., Division of Pittsburgh Forgings Co., Coraopolis, Pa.

Hench & Dromgold Co., York, Pa.

By 1908, perhaps earlier, Hench & Dromgold Co., was offering this single-row corn planter. Designed for small acreages, this planter featured the round-plate design instead of the more common edge-drop pattern. This unit is also equipped with an optional fertilizer box. The company never opted into the two-row planter market and continued to offer this unit at least into the 1920s.

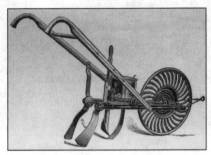

Hoosier Drill Co., Richmond, Ind.

During the 1890s, Hoosier Drill Co., perfected its one- and two-horse corn drills; the single-row model is shown here. Hoosier also perfected a conventional two-row corn planter about 1895. By this time, Hoosier had a wide reputation for the most extensive line of grain drills in the industry. However, in 1903, Hoosier joined numerous other firms to form the American Seeding Machine Co. The latter consolidated with additional companies to form Oliver Farm Equipment Co., in 1929.

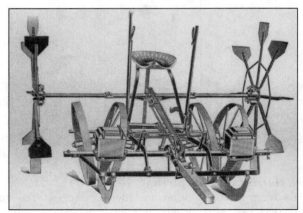

Implement Manufacturing Co., Davenport, Iowa

Implement Manufacturing Co., was organized in 1899 (perhaps a year earlier) to manufacture the unique Davenport Wireless Check Rower and Planter. Instead of the usual guide marker, this planter was equipped with the two large spade wheels shown in the engraving; they were mounted flexibly to accommodate variations encountered through the field. Although the company and its new planter received considerable attention for a short time, the Davenport planter soon faded from the scene.

International Harvester Co., Chicago, Ill.

International Harvester Co. acquired a corn planter line with its 1904 acquisition of Keystone Manufacturing Co. This was further enhanced with the later acquisition of Chambers, Bering, Quinlan Co. In 1919, IHC bought out P&O Plow Co., at Canton, Ill., and again, gained a corn planter line. Representative samples of these early IHC planters will be found under those respective headings. The IHC No. 1 planter shown here was built in the 1911-25 period. It was essentially the same as the CB&Q planter that preceded it. The company followed in 1926 with the No. 102 planter, its last horse-drawn model. Production of this style continued until 1946. Early IHC tractor planters included the No. 112. It was essentially a pair of No. 102 planters adapted to a tractor hitch. The IHC tractor planter developments are covered extensively in the author's book *150 Years of International Harvester* (Crestline/Motorbooks, 1981).

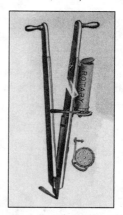

Keeney & Harrison Co., Rock Falls, Ill.

Hand corn planters remained popular, despite the introduction of two-row check-row planters. This 1887 version of the Keeney & Harrison rotary-drop hand corn planter was one of many different hand corn planters available over the years. With this one, as with most hand planters, the point was pushed into the ground, the levers were brought together and the seeds dropped into the ground at the proper planting depth. Today, hand corn planters are often sought as a collectible farm antique. Prices range from $10 to $30, depending on the age and the condition of the planter.

Keystone Manufacturing Co., Rock Falls, Ill.

In the 1860s, the firm of Galt & Tracy was organized at Rock Falls, Ill., to build farm implements; in 1880, the firm was reorganized as Keystone Manufacturing Co. Already in 1867 Galt & Tracy was building Keystone corn planters. The popularity of this machine led to the selection of "Keystone Manufacturing Co.," when the company was reorganized. The Galt Rotary Planter, as advertised in 1887, was a hand dropper; this engraving illustrates how the rows were marked out before planting with a marking sled or, in its absence, a bob sled. The driver attempted to drive a straight line while the "dropper" worked the hand lever at each intersecting line.

While Keystone still offered a hand dropper planter in 1887, the company had also introduced its automatic check-row design. This new feature, plus the use of a guide marker, eliminated the need to mark the field in advance, as well as eliminating the need for a "dropper" to work the slide valve as the planter traversed the field.

Keystone planters were very popular, as was the entire Keystone implement line. This humorous photograph relates that, "This corn was grown on ground prepared by a Keystone Disc Harrow, was planted by a Keystone Corn Planter, husked and shredded by a Giant Keystone Shredder and will be shelled by a Keystone Sheller that will be driven by a Keystone Horse Power. If the farmer determines to bale the fodder we hope to sell him a Keystone Baler." In reality, this 1903 advertisement was quite prophetic—within a year, Keystone Manufacturing Co., would come under the umbrella of International Harvester Co., and would be the foundation for its corn planter line.

Madison Plow Co., Madison, Wisc.

Madison Plow Co. went back to about 1880. At that time, it was merged into what became Fuller & Johnson Manufacturing Co., also at Madison. The Madison Plow name virtually disappeared until Fuller & Johnson sold out its farm implement line in 1911 to concentrate on manufacturing gasoline engines. At that point, Madison Plow reappeared, continuing in the implement business for some years. The Madison Variable Drop Disc Planter pictured here is of about 1917 vintage and likely is a direct descendant of Stark's planter, introduced some years earlier by Fuller & Johnson.

Moline Plow Co., Moline, Ill.

Moline Plow Co. began building tillage implements in 1865 and was a pioneer in the corn planter business. Moline introduced the concept of gearing the planter mechanism to the wheels. When it was desired to drill the corn or other seeds, the check-rower was not used and the drill delivered one seed at a time. Moline offered a wide variety of planters; this 1903 advertisement shows its Gretchen planter.

In 1904, Moline Plow Co. announced this lister planter, designed especially for cotton growers. Since the draft of the lister moldboard could be considerable in heavy soil, this unit was designed sufficiently heavy that four horses could be used. With the passage of time, Moline offered many sizes and styles of lister planters for both the cotton and the corn crops.

By 1908, Moline Plow Co. was offering its new Gilt Edge planter. Its simple drive mechanism continued on the Moline planter line for many years. In addition, the all-steel frame permitted adjustment of the planting width to suit various crops, growing practices or personal preference. The Moline planters were quite popular with farmers and many thousands were sold.

During the 1920s, Moline Plow Co., like its competitors, continued the development of new designs. This four-row planter was one such development. An interesting feature was the use of very small press wheels, compared to press wheels at least twice as large on many of the competing machines of the day. In 1929, Moline Plow Co. merged with two other firms to form the Minneapolis-Moline Power Implement Co. The latter continued to market Moline planters, using many of the design features pioneered by Moline Plow Co.

Monmouth Plow Co., Monmouth, Ill.

Boyd planters were first made by Galva Heater Co., Galva, Ill., about 1900. About 1918, Hayes Pump & Planter Co., also of Galva, bought out Galva Heater Co. Since the Boyd planter was quite similar to the Hayes, the latter sold out the patents, patterns and inventory of the Boyd planter to Monmouth Plow Co. However, Monmouth's career in the planter business did not long prevail; by 1924, parts only were available for the Boyd planter and the place to go was Galva Heater Co.

Ohio Cultivator Co., Bellevue, Ohio

Black Hawk corn planters were pioneered by D.M. Sechler Implement & Carriage Co., Moline, Ill. After Sechler went out of business, sometime in the 1920s, the Black Hawk planter line was acquired by Ohio Cultivator Co., which continued to build these planters for several years. Shown here is a 1927 model.

Ohio Rake Co., Dayton, Ohio

Ohio Rake acquired the Sure Drop Planter from Gale Manufacturing Co., Albion, Mich., about 1920. Ohio Rake developed an extensive implement line by this time, concentrating on various types of rakes and a wide variety of spring-tooth and spike-tooth harrows. While the Sure Drop had its own distinctive features, most planters of 1920 had resolved themselves into the same general designs.

Parlin & Orendorff Co., Canton, Ill.

Parlin & Orendorff Co. was established by Wm. Parlin in 1842. Plows, cultivators and other implements were available from P&O in the 1860s; about 1869, the company marketed the first lister. Shown here is a Canton lister, as built in the 1890s, although it differed little from the one introduced some 30 years earlier.

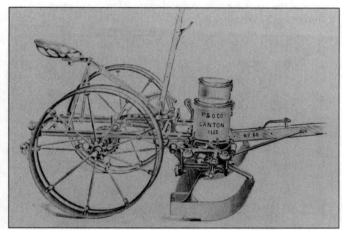

The ever-expanding P&O line included corn planters at least by 1900, perhaps earlier. This No. 66 combined check-row and drill planter was offered in 1912. The planter shown here was equipped with runner openers, but disc openers were also available. Another option was a dry fertilizer attachment; it could accurately sow anywhere from 40 to 500 pounds of fertilizer per acre, as desired.

When International Harvester purchased P&O in 1919, it acquired the No. 1 Tip-Top cotton and corn planter developed by P&O. Designed especially for the cotton grower, this planter could also be used for planting corn or other crops, as desired. IHC continued with the P&O line, expanding it and using it as a foundation for entirely new planters and related equipment.

The No. 71 variable edge-drop planter from P&O immediately became part of the IHC line upon its 1919 acquisition of the P&O factories. Except for changing the paint color and the stencils on the seed boxes, the No. 71 was amalgamated into the IHC line and was the basis for future developments in the planter line of International Harvester Co.

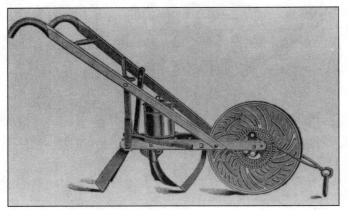

Pekin Plow Co., Pekin, Ill.

Numerous companies built and marketed corn drills; this 1887 offering of the Pekin Plow Co., was part of the chorus. Like many corn drills, it used a knife opener and a unique seed shoe with a front-mounted shovel. The seed dropped into the furrow directly behind the shovel and was covered by the knives to the rear. Little information has been found concerning this company.

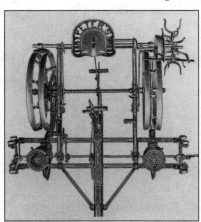

Peter's Pump Co., Galva, Ill.

A 1903 advertisement lists this company at Kewanee, Ill. Curiously, a substantial number of corn planter manufacturers were located in Illinois, perhaps more than in any other state. Its 1903 line includ-

ed the Peter's Ratchet Drop Planter, and the company claimed it to have fewer wearing parts than any other planter. Peter's was fortunate in having branch houses in several Midwestern cities; this helped immensely in marketing its products.

The Peter's Force Feed Planter of 1906 was built along somewhat the same lines as the 1903 Ratchet Drop design. By this time, though, the company was advocating its Force Feed Shuttle that represented substantial improvements to the dropping device over the competing brands. In addition to corn planters, the company also built a wide variety of pumps and other equipment.

Peter's 1907 Kewanee planter evolved from the earlier designs and included certain improvements, even though the basic machine was the same as before. The Peter's planters were available at least into the 1920s, with repair parts still being available from the company into the late 1930s.

Leoa Pratt, Amhurst, N.H.

From the May 3, 1851, issue of the *Boston Cultivator* comes this engraving of Pratt's Patent Seed Sower and Corn Planter. Patent No. 3562 was issued to Leoa Pratt on April 25, 1844, for this little planter, with the accompanying article noting that the machine had been on the market for the past five years. This is the earliest graphic record we have found concerning a corn planter.

Randall & Jones, Rockton, Ill.

During the 1850s, considerable interest was shown in the corn planter. Initially this included various kinds of hand corn planters; it probably seemed incredulous that a mechanical corn planter could ever be perfected. Thus came the Randall and Jones two-row hand-operated planter. It was patented by S.G. Randall and J.H. Jones of Rockton, Ill., in 1855, bearing Patent No. 13,401. Perhaps this was an improvement over planting a single row at a time, but surely it must have been back-breaking work going up and down the field with this device. Incredibly, this was a very popular unit at the time.

Rock Island Plow Co., Rock Island, Ill.

By the time this 1898 Rock Island planter appeared, Rock Island Plow Co. was a major manufacturer of plows and other implements. The planter shown here was of the four-wheel design, using a flexible joint between each pair of press wheels. Rock Island called this "the best selling corn planter on the market," and, while this claim would be hard to substantiate, there's no doubt that it was a strong competitor.

By 1903, the Rock Island planter line had assumed essentially the form it would follow for some years to come. Rock Island noted that by simplifying the construction of this machine, it weighed some 200 pounds less than many of its competitors. The Balance Frame design was also an advantage as it took most of the weight off the horses. Rock Island Plow Co. was acquired by J.I. Case in 1937.

Racine-Sattley Co., Springfield, Ill.

Sattley was an early plow manufacturer; over the years, the company expanded its line of tillage implements. By 1900, the company was manufacturing corn planters, with the style shown here being advertised in 1903. These planters were available with many different options, including open wheels, concave wheels or flat wheels.

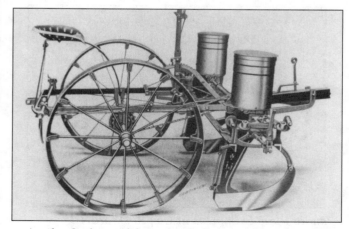

Another Sattley model was the No. 7 planter shown here. This was a two-row combined cotton and corn planter; this was especially convenient for farmers growing both crops, since they could plant either crop with the same planter. It was a combination planter, that is, it was equipped with the check-rower and could also be used for drilling, when so desired.

About 1907, Sattley merged with Racine Wagon Co. to form the Racine-Sattley Co. One of its offerings was the New Way Corn Planter, a redesigned machine from the earlier models. Racine-Sattley eventually took a contract with Montgomery Ward & Co., with the latter marketing the Sattley implement line. In 1916, Montgomery-Ward purchased part of the company, including the Sattley engine plant at Jackson, Mich.

D.M. Sechler Carriage Co., Moline, Ill.

In 1908, Sechler offered its No. 3 Black Hawk planter. This unit was an updated version of earlier designs and featured an all-steel frame. For reasons unknown, D.M. Sechler Carriage Co., eventually quit business, with the implement line being acquired by Ohio Cultivator Co. Its version of the Black Hawk planter is shown under that section.

Skandia Plow & Implement Co., Rockford, Ill.

Skandia offered this corn planter and check-rower in 1887. Little information has been found on Skandia, either regarding its

earlier development of the corn planter or its subsequent activities. This design carried the check wire (or perhaps knotted rope) over a pulley, across the frame of the planter and exiting on the opposite side.

F.B. Tait Manufacturing Co., Decatur, Ill.

For 1899, F.B. Tait Manufacturing Co. offered its New Decatur planter; it featured an all-steel design. This planter was obviously a check-rower and the flat-face press wheels were probably optional, with concave or open wheels being other possibilities. Outside of this 1899 advertisement, little else has been found concerning the New Decatur planters.

Vandiver Corn Planter Co., Quincy, Ill.

Many people considered the Barlow check-row planter to be the first successful check-rower on the market, although this was a point of hot contention at the time. An 1887 advertisement claimed however, the Barlow to be "The Best Corn Planter and Check Rower in the World." This may or may not have been true, but it is a certainty that the Barlow planter was very popular upon its introduction.

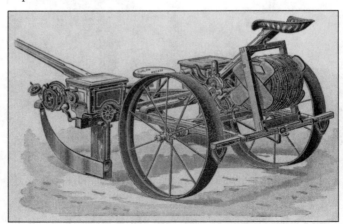

J.C. Barlow made numerous improvements to the original Vandiver corn planter; the latter dated back to 1863. However, at some point after this 1887 model appeared, Barlow went on his own to form the Barlow Corn Planter Co. Little is known of this venture. The 1887 Barlow planter from Vandiver illustrates the plan for carrying the check wire. Unrolling it when entering a field was fairly simple, but putting it back on the reel upon completion of the job was sometimes a different story, since the wire had to be threaded evenly across the reel if one was to plan on wrapping 80 rods of wire on a single spool.

Wistrand Manufacturing Co., Galva, Ill.

By 1907, perhaps earlier, Wistrand was offering its Blue Star planters. The company was a major pump manufacturer and apparently diversified for a time into the corn planter business. The company remained in the planter business for some years; by the late 1930s, repair parts only were available from Blue Star Manufacturing Co., Galva, Ill.

Trade Names

A1	Moline Plow Co.	Moline, IL	1922
Acme	McCalmont & Co.	Bellefonte, PA	1892
Advance	Hearst, Dunn & Co.	Peoria, IL	1892
Advance	Hearst, Dunn & Co.	Peoria, IL	1892
Armbuster's	Wytheville Foundry & Machine Co.	Wytheville, VA	1892
Arnold	Southern Mfg. Co.	Eddyville, KY	1892
Aspinwall	Aspinwall Mfg. Co.	Three Rivers, MI	1892
Avery	Avery Company	Peoria, IL	1922
Avery	B. F. Avery & Sons	Louisville, KY	1913
Balance Frame	Rock Island Plow Co	Rock Island, IL	1905
Barlow	Barlow Corn Planter Co.	Quincy, IL	1892
Barlow	Barlow Corn Planter Co.	Quincy, IL	1892
Barlow	Quincy Corn Planter Co.	Quincy, IL	1905
Barnes'	Chambers, Bering & Quinlan Co.	Decatur, IL	1892
Billings	Ames Plow Co.	Boston, MA	1892
Black Eagle	D. M. Sechler Carriage Co.	Moline, IL	1915
Black Hawk	D. M. Sechler Carriage Co.	Moline, IL	1905
Blue Star	Wistrand Mfg. Co.	Galva, IL	1905
Bob White	Ohio Rake Co.	Dayton, OH	1905
Boston	Ames Plow Co.	Boston, MA	1892
Boyd	Galva Heater Co.	Galva, IL	1915
Boyd	Mulford Heater Co.	Galva, IL	1905
Bradford	Decker Mfg. Co.	Brockport, NY	1919
Bradley	David Bradley Mfg. Co.	Bradley, IL	1905
Brown's Universal	Geo. W. Brown & Co.	Galesburg, IL	1892
Bull's Eye	Ohio Rake Co.	Dayton, OH	1905
Bull's Head	Ohio Rake Co.	Dayton, OH	1917
C. B. & Q.	Chambers, Bering & Quinlan Co.	Decatur, IL	1892
C. B. & Q.	International Harvester Co.	Chicago, IL	1913
Cadet	Rock Island Plow Co.	Rock Island, IL	1905

Trade Names (cont...)

Caledonian	Caledonia Bean Harvester Works	Caledonia, NY	1917
Campbell	James Campbell	Harrison, OH	1892
Canton Junior	Parlin & Orendorff Co.	Canton, IL	1905
Canton Senior	Parlin & Orendorff Co.	Canton, IL	1905
Cardwell	Cardwell Machine Co.	Richmond, VA	1892
Case	J. I. Case Co.	Racine, WI	1932
Case Edge Drop	J. I. Case Plow Works	Racine, WI	1905
Centennial	C. Billups, Son & Co.	Norfolk, VA	1892
Centennial	H. M. Smith & Co.	Richmond, VA	1892
Century	Thompson Plow & Engine Works	Beloit, WI	1919
Challenge	Challenge Corn Planter Co.	Grand Haven, MI	1892
Challenge	Pattee Plow Co.	Monmouth, IL	1892
Challenge Leader	Challenge Corn Planter Co.	Grand Haven, MI	1892
Champion	Caldwell Mfg. Co.	Columbus, IN	1909
Champion	Common Sense Engine Co.	Springfield, OH	1892
Champion	Moline Plow Co.	Moline, IL	1909
Chief	D. M. Sechler Carriage Co.	Moline, IL	1919
Collins	Collins Plow Co.	Quincy, IL	1909
Colton	G. D. Colton Co.	Galesburg, IL	1892
Common Sense	Common Sense Engine Co.	Springfield, OH	1892
Common Sense	Janney Mfg. Co.	Ottumwa, IA	1905
Conde	Peru Plow & Wheel Co.	Peru, IL	1905
Corn Belt	Rhea-Thielens Implement Co.	Peoria IL	1905
Corn King	Avery Company	Peoria, IL	1905
Corn Queen	Avery Company	Peoria, IL	1905
Crackajack	Moline Plow Co.	Moline, IL	1905
Daisy	Gale Mfg. Co.	Albion, MI	1905
Dakin	John H. Dakin	Schenectady, NY	1892
Davison	Eureka Mower Co.	Utica, NY	1905
Decatur	Chambers, Bering & Quinlan Co.	Decatur, IL	1905
Deere	Deere & Mansur Co.	Moline, IL	1892
Derby	Brinly-Hardy Co.	Louisville, KY	1915
Diamond	Parlin & Orendorff Co.	Canton, IL	1905
Disk-Dandy	F. B Tait & Co.	Decatur, IL	1892
Eagle	Eagle Machine Co.	Lancaster, OH	1892
Eastern Threeinone	Moline Plow Co.	Moline, IL	1905
Echo	Lehr Agricultural Co.	Fremont, OH	1892
Eclipse	Belcher & Taylor Agricultural Tool Co	Chicopee Falls, MA	1905
Eclipse	Chambers, Bering & Quinlan Co.	Decatur, IL	1905
Eclipse	Eclipse Corn Planter Co.	Enfield, NH	1892
Eclipse	Hayes Pump & Planter Co.	Galva, IL	1905
Eclipse	Jas. Selby & Co.	Peoria, IL	1892
Eclipse	Ohio Cultivator Co.	Bellevue, OH	1892
Electric	Edward Sellers	Oak Hall, PA	1905
Eli	H. H. Perkins Mfg. Co.	Kewanee, IL	1892
Emerson	Emerson-Brantingham Co.	Rockford, IL	1913
Emerson	Emerson Mfg. Co.	Rockford, IL	1905
Eureka	Cardwell Machine Co.	Richmond, VA	1892
Eureka	Eureka Mower Co.	Utica, NY	1905
Eureka	H. M. Smith & Co.	Richmond, VA	1892
Eureka	S. R. White & Bro.	Norfolk, VA	1892

Trade Names (cont...)

Trade Name	Company	Location	Year
Eureka Jr.	Eureka Mower Co.	Utica, NY	1905
Evans	A. C. Evans Mfg. Co.	Springfield, OH	1892
Evans	Superior Drill Co.	Springfield, OH	1905
Excelsior	Geo. W. Brown & Co.	Galesburg, IL	1892
F & J	Madison Plow Co.	Madison, WI	1913
Farmer's Choice	Skandia Plow Co.	Rockford, IL	1892
Farmers Friend	Farmers Friend Mfg. Co.	Dayton, OH	1892
Farquhar Keystone	A. B. Farquhar Co.	York, PA	1892
Flying Dutchman	Moline Plow Co.	Moline, IL	1915
Fowler	Harriman Mfg. Co.	Harriman, TN	1917
Fuller & Johnson	Fuller & Johnson Mfg. Co.	Madison, WI	1905
Galt	Keystone Mfg. Co.	Sterling, IL	1892
Genii	Lehr Agricultural Co.	Fremont, OH	1892
Giant	Jas. Selby & Co.	Peoria, IL	1892
Gilt Edge	Moline Plow Co.	Moline, IL	1909
Grand Detour	Grand Detour Plow Co.	Dixon, IL	1913
Gretchen	Moline Plow Co.	Moline, IL	1905
Hamilton	H. P. Deuscher Co.	Hamilton, OH	1892
Haworth	Haworth & Sons	Decatur, IL	1892
Haworth's	Haworth & Sons	Decatur, IL	1892
Hayes	Hayes Pump & Planter Co.	Galva, IL	1892
Hench & Dromgold	Hench & Dromgold Co.	York, PA	1892
Holt	Holt & Pitts	Harrison, ME	1892
Hoosier	Hoosier Drill Co.	Richmond, IN	1905
Hoosier	International Harvester Co.	Chicago, IL	1913
I. H. C.	International Harvester	Chicago, IL	1913+Co.
Ideal	Chambers, Bering & Quinlan Co.	Decatur, IL	1909
Ideal	H. P. Deuscher Co.	Hamilton, OH	1892
Imperial	Rockford Mfg. Co.	Rockford, IL	1892
Iron-Dandy	F. B Tait & Co.	Decatur, IL	1892
Ives	S. R. White's Sons	Norfolk, VA	1917
J. I. Case	J. I. Case Plow Works	Racine, WI	1913
Janesville	Janesville Machine Co.	Janesville, WI	1905
Janesville	Samson Tractor Co.	Janesville, WI	1924
Jim-Dandy	F. B Tait & Co.	Decatur, IL	1892
Jo-Dandy	F. B Tait & Co.	Decatur, IL	1892
Junior	Hayes Pump & Planter Co.	Galva, IL	1905
Junior	Keystone Mfg. Co.	Sterling, IL	1892
Kaar	Nebraska Mfg. Co.	Lincoln, NE	1913
Kentucky	American Seeding Machine Co.	Richmond, IN	1913
Kentucky	International Harvester Co.	Chicago, IL	1915
Kewanee	Hayes Pump & Planter Co.	Galva, IL	1892
Kewanee	Peters Pump Co.	Kewanee, IL	1913
Keystone	Keystone Company	Sterling, IL	1892
Keystone	Keystone Farm Machine Co.	York, PA	1915
King of the Corn Field	Belcher & Taylor Agricultural Tool Co	Chicopee Falls, MA	1905
King of the Corn Field	Whitman Agricultural Works	Auburn, ME	1892
Kingman	Kingman Plow Co.	Peoria, IL	1905
Ledbetter	Southern Plow Co.	Dallas, TX	1915
Lester	Gale Mfg. Co.	Albion, MI	1905
Lone Star	J. I. Case Plow Works	Racine, WI	1913

Trade Names (cont...)

Trade Name	Company	Location	Year
Louisville	B. F. Avery & Sons	Louisville, KY	1892
Luthy	Peru Plow & Wheel Co.	Peru, IL	1905
Madison	Madison Plow Co.	Madison, WI	1917
Mansur	Deere & Mansur Co.	Moline, IL	1909
Marietta	Marietta Mfg. Co.	Marietta, PA	1892
Massey-Harris	Massey-Harris Co.	Racine, WI	1929
McCormick-Deering	International Harvester Co.	Chicago, IL	1929
Memphis	B. F. Avery & Sons	Louisville, KY	1917
Mexican Senior	Parlin & Orendorff Co.	Canton, IL	1905
Minneapolis-Moline	Minneapolis-Moline Co.	Minneapolis, MN	1936
Miss Dixie	B. F. Avery & Sons	Louisville, KY	1917
Moline Champion	Moline Plow Co.	Moline, IL	1892
Monarch	Avery Planter Co.	Peoria, IL	1892
Moon	G. A. Kelly Mfg. Co.	Kellyville, TX	1892
Mr. Bill	B. F. Avery & Sons	Louisville, KY	1917
New Avery	Avery Planter Co.	Peoria, IL	1892
New Avery Special	Avery Planter Co.	Peoria, IL	1892
New Century	J. Thompson & Sons Mfg. Co.	Beloit, WI	1905
New Deere	Deere & Mansur Co.	Moline, IL	1905
New Model	A. McKenney	Rock, MA	1892
New Union	B. F. Avery & Sons	Louisville, KY	1917
New Way	Racine-Sattley Co.	Springfield, IL	1913
No. 99	Deere & Mansur Co.	Moline, IL	1913
Ohio	Ohio Cultivator Co.	Bellevue, OH	1892
Oliver	Oliver Chilled Plow Works	South Bend, IN	1917
Oliver Superior	Oliver Farm Equipment Co.	Chicago, IL	1936
On Time	Moline Plow Co.	Moline, IL	1905
Paragon	Kent Mfg. Co.	Fort Atkinson, WI	1913
Parlin	Parlin & Orendorff Co.	Canton, IL	1905
Perfection	Avery Company	Peoria, IL	1909
Peru	Peru Plow & Wheel Co.	Peru, IL	1905
Peter's	Peters Pump Co.	Kewanee, IL	1905
Peter's Kewanee	Peters Pump Co.	Kewanee, IL	1905
Play Ball	Moline Plow Co.	Moline, IL	1905
Porter	J. E. Porter Co.	Ottawa, IL	1905
Queen of the West	Caldwell Mfg. Co.	Columbus, IN	1909
Quincy	Barlow Corn Planter Co.	Quincy, IL	1892
Quincy Queen	Collins Plow Co.	Quincy, IL	1922
Reliable	Madison Plow Co.	Madison, WI	1913
Rich Valley	Look & Lincoln	Marion, VA	1892
Richmond Champion	Wayne Works	Richmond, IN	1905
Rock Island	Rock Island Plow Co	Rock Island, IL	1905
Rockford Pickup	H. D. Busing & Co.	Rockford, IL	1892
Samson	Samson Tractor Co.	Janesville, WI	1924
Sattley	Racine-Sattley Co.	Springfield, IL	1905
Scheurenberg	F. W. Scheurenberg	Brenham, TX	1892
Shawnee Jr.	B. F. Avery & Sons	Louisville, KY	1917
Simplex	American Seeding Machine Co.	Springfield, OH	1909
Sinclair	C. Billups, Son & Co.	Norfolk, VA	1892
Sinclair	S. R. White & Bro.	Norfolk, VA	1892
Skandia	Skandia Plow Co.	Rockford, IL	1892
Smith's Centennial	Cardwell Machine Co.	Richmond, VA	1905
Spangler	Spangler Mfg. Co.	York, PA	1892
Square Deal	Chambers, Bering & Quinlan Co.	Decatur, IL	1909
Standard	Emerson-Brantingham Co.	Rockford, IL	1913

Trade Names (cont...)

Standard	Emerson, Talcott & Co.	Rockford, IL	1892
Standard	Emerson, Talcott & Co.	Rockford, IL	1892
Standard	Standard Harrow Co.	Utica, NY	1905
Star	Ames Plow Co.	Boston, MA	1905
Star Billings	Ames Plow Co.	Boston, MA	1905
Stark's	Fuller & Johnson Mfg. Co.	Madison, WI	1892
Steel Centennial	Cardwell Machine Co.	Richmond, VA	1917
Sterling	Sterling Mfg. Co.	Sterling, IL	1905
Streiwig	A. B. Farquhar Co.	York, PA	1913
Sure-Drop	Gale Mfg. Co.	Albion, MI	1905
Tait's	F. B. Tait & Co.	Decatur, IL	1892
Threeinone	Moline Plow Co.	Moline, IL	1905
Tiger	Stoddard Mfg. Co.	Dayton, OH	1905
Tracy	Keystone Mfg. Co.	Sterling, IL	1892
Troy	Common Sense Engine Co.	Springfield, OH	1892
True Blue	Blount Plow Works	Evansville, IN	1939
Twin Drive	B. F. Avery & Sons	Louisville, KY	1929
U. S.	Chambers, Bering & Quinlan Co.	Decatur, IL	1892
U. S. Junior	Chambers, Bering & Quinlan Co.	Decatur, IL	1905
U. S. Steel	Chambers, Bering & Quinlan Co.	Decatur, IL	1905
Uncle Sam	B. F. Avery & Sons	Louisville, KY	1917
Unicorn	Fort Madison Plow Co.	Fort Madison, IA	1913
Union	Jas. Selby & Co.	Peoria, IL	1892
Union	Jas. Selby & Co.	Peoria, IL	1892
Union	B. F. Avery & Sons	Louisville, KY	1917
Union Victor	Ohio Rake Co.	Dayton, OH	1905
Universal	Deere & Mansur Co.	Moline, IL	1892
Van Wye	Z. P. Dederick	Sherman, TX	1892
Vandiver-Barlow	Quincy Corn Planter Co.	Quincy, IL	1905
Vandiver-Barlow	Barlow Corn Planter Co.	Quincy, IL	1892
Victor	Fuller & Johnson Mfg. Co.	Madison, WI	1905
Victor	Madison Plow Co.	Madison, WI	1913
Virginia	H. M. Smith & Co.	Richmond, VA	1892
Vulcan	Vulcan Plow Co.	Evansville, IN	1929
Western	Jas. Selby & Co.	Peoria, IL	1892
Western Champion	Moline Plow Co.	Moline, IL	1892
Western Rotary	Jas. Selby & Co.	Peoria, IL	1892
White's Centennial	S. R. White & Bro.	Norfolk, VA	1892
Wiard	Wiard Plow Co.	Batavia, NY	1913
York	Hench & Dromgold Co.	York, PA	1917

Corn Shellers

In 1850, the corn sheller was virtually unknown, but during that decade various ideas were tried, a few having some success. Until that time, corn was shelled by hand. The recognized founder of the corn sheller industry was Augustus Adams at Sandwich, Ill. He perfected the original spring sheller. During the 1850s, progress was also made on the cylinder sheller, with several designs showing some promise. Of the sheller designers, Thomas A. Galt at Sterling, Ill., was a moving force; his efforts culminated in the Keystone Manufacturing Co., Sterling. The latter, like Sandwich Manufacturing Co., Sandwich, Ill., predominated the corn sheller market for many years.

At Ottawa, Ill., the firm of King & Hamilton began building cylinder shellers in the 1860s; the latter firm continued in this business for many years. Another important maker was Joliet Manufacturing Co., Joliet, Ill. This firm owed much of its inventive genius to A.H. Shreffler. Yet, another Illinois firm was Marseilles Manufacturing Co., Marseilles. The latter was also very well known for its corn shellers.

Eventually, the major farm equipment builders got into the corn sheller business. International Harvester acquired the Keystone Manufacturing Co., and John Deere ended up with the Marseilles line. Yet, the corn sheller business was not to endure. The coming of the corn combine in the 1950s signaled the end for the harvesting of ear corn, precluding the need for corn shellers.

Today, antique corn shellers are a popular farm collectible. Small one-hole and two-hole designs usually bring $50 or more, depending on age, condition and various other factors. Larger four-hole and six-hole spring shellers usually command a higher price because they are much more difficult to find; a nice four-hole spring sheller might fetch $250 to $500 today. Cylinder shellers are still used to some extent and their price varies considerably, depending on mechanical condition, the local market and other factors.

Advance-Rumely Thresher Co., LaPorte, Ind.

The M. Rumely Co., acquired many product lines in the 1910-12 period. Included was the Rumely-Watts sheller, although research has failed to determine the "Watts" portion of the title. The Rumely-Watts shellers were of the cylinder type and were capable of far more capacity than competing spring shellers.

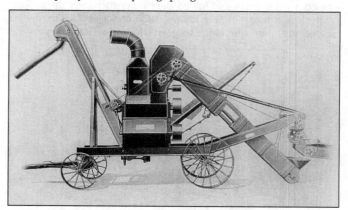

The No. 6 Rumely was a double-cylinder sheller; this represented a rather unusual design. In principle, most cylinder shellers operated by feeding the ear corn into one end of a closed cylinder, whose periphery consisted of round steel bars. Inside the cylinder a revolving shaft carried numerous heavy iron paddles. By the time the corn and cobs made their way through the iron grates, the kernels were shelled away. With suitable screens, the cobs went one direction, while the shelled corn was cleaned and elevated to a waiting wagon.

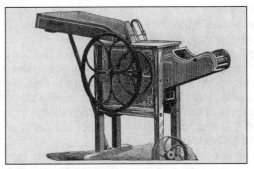

American Well Works, Aurora, Ill.

American Well Works offered its American Improved Corn Sheller No. 2, in 1887; from all indications, the company had been making shellers for a few years prior to this time. American Well Works was a large company that had made a great name for itself with its well drilling equipment; this, too, was an essential part of the developing Midwestern farm lands.

Appleton Manufacturing Co., Batavia, Ill.

By 1905, Appleton was offering its New Hero corn sheller; the unit shown here being a two-hole design. Spring shellers used a force-feed system to push the ears of corn into the shelling mechanism. It consisted of picker wheels having countless nibs protruding from their sides. Rag irons above them were held by heavy steel springs that forced the ears of corn over the picker wheels and removing the kernels from the cobs. This model is especially interesting, since it is geared for use with a horsepower.

In addition to power shellers Appleton offered various small corn shellers. The Royal was a one-hole design that was fed by hand and one ear at a time. The shelled corn dropped out of the bottom of the sheller while the cobs were spit out of the opening at the back of the machine. This was strictly a hand-operated machine.

Badger two-hole spring shellers could be furnished for hand or power operation. The belt pulley was standard equipment. When used with power, the hand-crank was removed. Two sets of picker wheels made this a two-hole sheller; due to its greater capacity, a small cob elevator was furnished. This one also included a small cleaning fan.

Appleton's New Hero 6-hole Force Feed Corn Sheller of 1917 used an all-steel design, compared to the wooden construction of earlier years. The feeder was arranged with separate feed chains having special lugs spaced about a foot apart. As they traveled upward to the sheller, the ears of corn arranged themselves in the slots and were fed into the separate holes of the sheller. Six-hole shellers were common, although a few companies made eight-hole shellers and a very few were even larger.

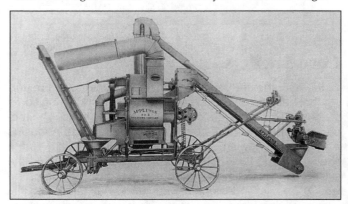

Cylinder shellers had much more capacity than the spring shellers and had much less mechanism than the latter. By the time this 1917 Appleton No. 2 Cylinder Sheller appeared, the cylinder sheller was becoming immensely popular. The cleaning system had been greatly improved. Now the corn shucks were blown away by a large fan, the cobs were elevated to a waiting wagon and the shelled corn to another.

F.C. Austin Manufacturing Co., Chicago, Ill.

This company was famous for its well drilling equipment. Its product line included many other farm items, including ensilage cutters and corn shellers. This Austin Sheller of 1889 was typical of the time; one person cranked the sheller while another fed the ears of corn one at a time. Shelled corn dropped into the basket below, while the cobs made their exit from the rear of the machine. Note the ornate striping evident on this sheller. This was common for many machines of the period.

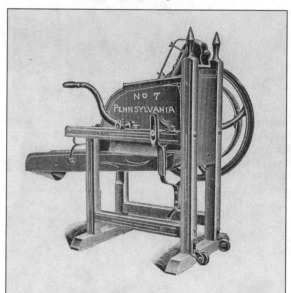

A. Buch's Sons, Elizabethtown, Pa.

The No. 7 Pennsylvania corn sheller of 1899 featured a shaker-screen system for cleaning the shelled corn. Also of interest are the two small casters at the bottom of the frame, permitting the machine to be moved about like a small cart. Although this firm was actively manufacturing numerous farm machines and implements at the time, few specifics have been found of its activities.

Challenge Co., Batavia, Ill.

Challenge was building windmills already in the 1890s, although it is unknown when the company began making corn shellers. This 1910 model of its Dandy one-hole sheller is shown with an optional cleaning fan for 80 cents. An optional feed table also shown here was priced at 40 cents. With a base price of $8, this brought the total list price to $9.20.

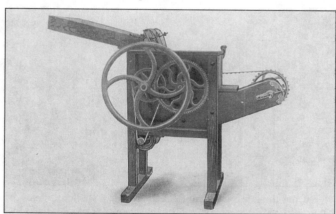

The Challenge Dandy two-hole corn sheller of 1910 weighed 300 pounds, required one or two horsepower and could shell 35 bushels per hour. The complete unit shown here was priced at $23 for 1910. Although it could be operated by hand, a pulley was ordinarily furnished for use with a gas engine or perhaps a sweep power.

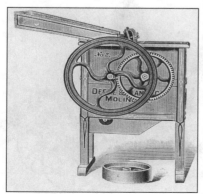

Deere & Co., Moline, Ill.

Deere & Co. (or properly, John Deere Plow Co.), marketed this No. 2 Deere & Mansur sheller in 1908 and probably for some years before and after this time. Deere & Mansur was essentially a part of the Plow Co., prior to all the various companies coming together in one unit during 1911.

Deere & Co., marketed many corn shellers, especially those made by Marseilles Manufacturing Co., Marseilles, Ill. The latter was founded already in 1859 and had a long career in the farm implement business. At an early date, the company developed an excellent corn sheller line; in 1911, Deere & Co., gained stock control of Marseilles, thus bringing it into the fold.

During the late 1930s, the John Deere No. 6 sheller appeared; it would soon become one of the most popular models used by custom corn shellers. Its foundations began already in the 1920s with this 1925 Deere cylinder sheller. While somewhat smaller than the famous No. 6, this 1925 model had tremendous capacity and made short work of the corn shelling job.

Dickey Manufacturing Co., Racine, Wisc.

In 1901, Dickey was offering its Racine corn sheller. Billed as "A marvel of perfection," the Racine shown here was equipped with a pulley drive suitable for operation with a gas engine, steam engine or a tractor. Outside of this 1901 advertisement, little else can be found concerning the Racine corn sheller line.

A.B. Farquhar Co., Ltd., York, Pa.

Into the early 1900s, Farquhar continued to offer the Smith's Patent or Cannon corn sheller. This design was one of the earliest cylinder shellers, apparently resulting from the efforts of J.P. Smith, Hummelstown, Pa. The latter received numerous corn sheller patents in the 1853-1869 period.

Rugged and plain, the Lancaster corn sheller from A.B. Farquhar was built for many years. Its makers claimed it to be capable of 200 bushels per day, but that undoubtedly took a great many turns of the hand-crank. Farquhar continued to build similar shellers at least into the 1920s.

While Farquhar's Lancaster sheller was a one-hole design, the Daisy was a two-hole machine. Many of the early corn shellers were just that, a plain sheller with no frills of any kind. Farquhar offered the Daisy in this manner, leaving the cleaning fan as an option. After a long and illustrious career in the implement and machinery business, Farquhar was bought out by Oliver Corp., in 1952.

Foos Manufacturing Co., Springfield, Ohio

By 1888, Foos Manufacturing Co., had emerged with its Foos Scientific corn sheller. This one differed from anything on the market; the entire case was made of cast iron, as compared to the wooden construction of virtually all others of the time. This one is shown complete with the feed table, cleaning fan and the cob elevator.

The Foos Scientific corn sheller of 1888 was available in various forms, with this one including a sacking elevator. Although a hand-crank is shown, the extension of the picker wheel shaft indicates that it was possible to add a belt-pulley for power operation. Foos eventually left the implement business to concentrate on its line of gasoline engines.

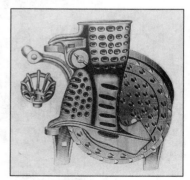

Hartman Co., Chicago, Ill.

Hartman Co., was a large mail-order house, offering virtually everything for the farm and home. Included was the Majestic Square Frame Corn Sheller. These small table-top shellers were often used for shelling ear corn that had previously been selected for next year's

seed. Thus, Hartman included a "butting and tipping attachment." It enabled the farmer to remove undesirable kernels from the butts and tips of the ears prior to shelling the remainder for seed.

Hocking Valley Manufacturing Co., Lancaster, Ohio

This Hocking Valley self-feed sheller was offered in 1890; apparently, the firm had been building shellers for some years prior to this time. The design was essentially the same that the company continued to use for many years to come; Hocking Valley appears in the various implement directories as late as 1948, but dropped from sight by the 1950s. The author restored a Hocking Valley sheller similar to this one some years ago.

Hocking Valley single-hole shellers were priced at $8.40, plus freight, in 1904. When the optional cleaning fan was included the price came to $9.15. Very few ads appear for the Hocking Valley shellers and implements. Despite more than a quarter of century researching the history of farm implement manufacturers, the author has yet to see a single piece of literature from this company.

Hutchinson Manufacturing Co., Port Huron, Mich.

In 1899, the Hutchinson Dustless Sheller was advertised; it was a cylinder sheller and it was probably far from being dustless. Five feet long and three feet high, this was a stationary machine, probably intended for commercial use in grain elevators and similar locations. Very little is known of the company or its manufacturing activities.

Joliet Manufacturing Co., Joliet, Ill.

In 1910, Joliet advertised its Eureka Ironsides shellers in two-, four- and six-hole sizes. However, these outfits were also available with a self-contained two-cylinder engine mounted as shown beneath the sheller frame. Joliet shellers owed much of its design to A.H. Shreffler, who was associated with the company for some years.

The Joliet spring shellers were offered in various sizes; a four-hole model is shown here. This one was complete with a cob stacker and a shelled corn elevator. While the company offered this machine for belt power, it could also be equipped as shown with the necessary gearing and tumbling rods for use with a horse power, sometimes called a sweep power.

For many years, Joliet offered its Rural Hand Feed Sheller. It was a two-hole spring sheller; the company claimed it capable of shelling anywhere from 25 to 50 bushels of corn per hour. As shown, it is equipped with a cleaning fan and the requisite belt pulley. Corn shellers in particular were usually highly adorned with fancy pin-striping and lettering. This was all done by hand and added to the cost of the machine. By the end of World War I, most machinery was using very little of the ornate pin-striping of earlier years.

By World War I, Joliet was offering its No. 2 Dustless Cylinder Corn Sheller to the market. Shown here in transport position, it could be easily pulled from farm to farm by a team. When setting up, two or three men set the cob stacker in place, along with setting the drag feeder in place alongside the corn crib. The corn combine ended the great need for corn shellers, beginning in the late 1950s.

Keystone Manufacturing Co., Sterling, Ill.

Keystone Manufacturing Co. began with Thomas A. Galt, who established a shop at Sterling in 1857, forming the firm of Galt & Tracy in 1863. Its development of the Keystone corn shellers took place subsequently. When the firm was incorporated as Keystone Manufacturing Co., in 1870, it was thus named because of the eminently successful Keystone shellers. This 1905 advertisement illustrates the Keystone sheller and is representative of its design for some years before this time. In 1905, Keystone came under ownership of International Harvester Co. Thomas A. Galt died in 1912.

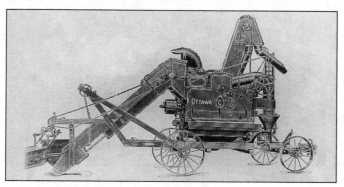

King & Hamilton, Ottawa, Ill.

King & Hamilton was an early contender in the corn sheller business, aiming primarily at the development of the cylinder sheller. Its Ottawa "C" Dustless Cylinder Sheller of the 1920s typified the line at the time, with this big machine capable of anywhere from 4,000 to 8,000 bushels per day. Ottawa shellers remained on the market for many years, being available at least into the 1950s.

Often billed as, "The best sheller on earth," the Ottawa was offered in various models, but the "C" and the "F" shellers seem to have been very popular over a long production run. This Ottawa "F" sheller is shown ready for the road; the shuck stacker is folded in its saddle atop the machine, the cob stacker is secured and the corn drag, partially visible here, is loaded and ready for the next job.

Marseilles Manufacturing Co., Marseilles, Ill.

By 1887, Marseilles was offering its Cyclone self-feed corn sheller. This two-hole spring sheller was available with numer-

ous options; the machine shown here was equipped with a cob stacker and a shelled corn elevator. Also obvious is the special gearing required for operation with a horse power. Thus equipped, it could likely shell 200 to 300 bushels per day.

Marseilles offered its New Process Dustless Cylinder Corn Sheller already in 1895. At this time, though, the New Process was not equipped with the necessary mechanism for drag feeders to pull corn into the large ear corn elevator. However, it was equipped with the other features salient to the cylinder sheller; these included the cleaning fan, shuck fan, cob stacker and shelled corn elevator.

For 1895, the Marseilles line included three sizes of shuck corn shellers of the spring sheller design. These were made in three different sizes and could be mounted as shown or could be supplied "down," that is to say, in a stationary design. At the purchaser's wish, these machines could be operated with either steam- or horse power. In 1895, Marseilles claimed to offer the largest line of corn shellers in the country.

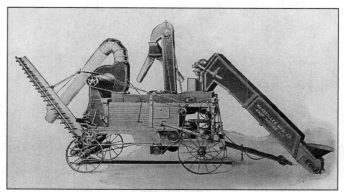

Marseilles was founded in 1859, coming under stock control of Deere & Co., in 1911. That year, the company offered its shuck corn shellers in three sizes. The acquisition of this company by John Deere led directly to the latter's own innovations in corn sheller design. In fact, the Deere corn shellers of the 1920s still had a strong resemblance to the original Marseilles designs.

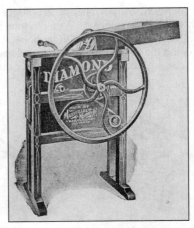

In addition to large corn shellers, Marseilles sold thousands of its small one-hole Diamond spring shellers. This small, hand-operated sheller weighed about 135 pounds, as did most of its competitors. After the 1911 Deere takeover, Diamond shellers continued on the market for some years to come.

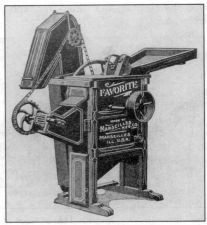

Favorite spring-type corn shellers from Marseilles were offered in one- and two-hole models. Some were even equipped with the optional sacking elevator for the shelled corn. A very simple design, it could be operated with a small engine or, in lieu of that, could be cranked by hand. When cranking by hand, the ideal speed was to crank at about 80 to 100 revolutions per minute.

Offered for many years, the Farmer spring sheller from Marseilles was strictly a power machine. Although it was a hand-feed model, the Farmer was ordinarily furnished with a sacking

elevator, along with a much larger cleaning fan than found on lighter and smaller models. This two-hole model weighed nearly 500 pounds.

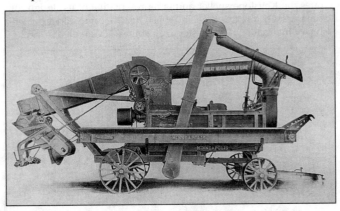

Minneapolis Threshing Machine Co., Hopkins, Minn.

Minneapolis entered the corn sheller business about 1910 with its big No. 2 cylinder sheller. This machine is shown with a section of the drag feeder mounted for transport. Several men picked it up and placed it in position for attachment to the boot of the ear corn elevator (at the left of the illustration). The No. 2 led to many other Minneapolis corn sheller designs. When the firm entered the 1929 merger that formed Minneapolis-Moline, the corn sheller line was enhanced considerably. M-M corn shellers were probably the strongest competitors with the John Deere cylinder shellers of the 1930-1950 period.

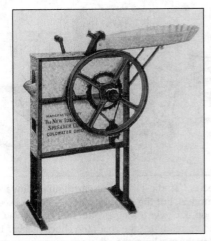

New Idea Manufacturing Co., Coldwater, Ohio

In the early 1930s, New Idea bought out Sandwich Manufacturing Co., Sandwich, Ill. Subsequently, New Idea continued making corn shellers for a number of years. Included was this attractive all-steel design. It was a one-hole spring sheller and could be operated with a hand-crank or could be powered, as desired. These small shellers were popular because they enabled the farmer to shell a small quantity of corn when hiring a large custom-sheller was impractical.

Sandwich-New Idea spring shellers of the 1930s were of an all-steel design, representing a bold move forward from time-honored wooden construction. The same held true for this all-steel cylinder sheller of the 1930s. It was a small machine, large enough for small- to medium-sized farms, but probably too small and too slow for custom operators. Apparently, this machine was only built for a few years.

Geo. K. Oyler Manufacturing Co., St. Louis, Mo.

An 1884 advertisement in the *Industrial Gazette*, published in St. Louis, illustrates the Oyler corn sheller of the time, complete with the horsepower and speed-jack required for power operation. Oyler was an early corn sheller manufacturer in the St. Louis area.

The Peony sheller from Geo. K. Oyler was typical for spring shellers of the day. This one was, of course, of wooden construction,

with iron castings used as necessary. When it is considered that corn shellers of any form were a rarity in 1860, farmers of 20 years later probably considered this hand-operated machine to be a real treat.

For 1887, Geo. K. Oyler offered its Peerless self-feeding power corn sheller. This one was a major step forward, but required either a horsepower or a steam engine for its operation; successful gas engines were a bit of a rarity in 1887. After considerable advertising in the 1880s, Oyler essentially drops from sight, probably being bought out or taken over by a successor firm.

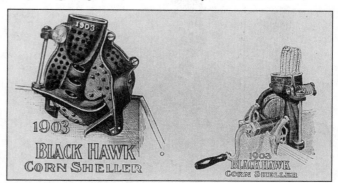

A.H. Patch, Clarksville, Tenn.

In 1875, A.H. Patch began manufacturing farm machines at Clarksville. Subsequently, came the Black Hawk corn sheller, with the 1903 pattern shown here. The Black Hawk brought both fame and fortune to Patch, who died in 1909 at the age of 84. Thousands of Black Hawk shellers were sold; undoubtedly a substantial number still exist.

Pease Manufacturing Co., Racine, Wisc.

Outside of this 1896 announcement, virtually nothing is known of the Racine corn sheller from Pease Manufacturing Co. It is obviously a spring sheller, probably a four-hole design. This one was equipped so that it could be operated either from a belt pulley or by a horsepower, as desired.

Port Huron Engine & Thresher Co., Port Huron, Mich.

In the late 1890s, Port Huron made a brief excursion into the corn sheller business, offering this Type B machine in 1899. The company claimed it to be capable of 200 to 800 bushels per hour, with a further claim that it was "the most substantial, finest finished steam sheller made." Apparently, this machine was intended to be a companion to the Port Huron steam-traction engines; the latter had already found great favor among threshermen.

Red Chief Manufacturing Co., Louisville, Ky.

The Red Chief corn sheller was another of those table top shellers with a certain market and, indeed, a market largely established by A.H. Patch. In 1918, this small sheller was priced at $2.25. Note how the sheller is mounted on a heavy wooden box. The shelled corn dropped into the box and the cobs were ejected from the side.

Red Cross Manufacturing Co., Bluffton, Ind.

The Cross cylinder sheller shown here was new in 1940. It was intended for the small farm at which a large sheller was impractical and afforded the farmer an inexpensive method of shelling small quantities of corn without hiring a custom operator. The Cross cylinder shellers were listed in various product directories as late as 1958.

Reeves & Co., Columbus, Ind.

In 1908, Reeves & Co., announced its Illinois Special Corn Sheller. This was a big cylinder sheller intended for use with Reeves or other steam engines. The company noted that this sheller worked equally well with shucked corn as with corn that was cleanly husked. This was a problem with some shellers, especially spring shellers. Within a few years, Reeves would come under control of Emerson-Brantingham Co., and that was the end of the Reeves corn shellers.

J.C. Richards, Lafayette, Ind.

The Richards' corn sheller was patented in 1860. Despite its crudeness, in comparison to later machines, the Richards' sheller established some of the principles involved in cylinder-type corn shellers. Apparently, this machine was made in Chicago for a number of years subsequent to 1860, but little is known of it outside of an occasional illustration.

Roberts, Throp & Co., Three Rivers, Mich.

This firm began in 1848 as Cox & Roberts and specialized in threshing machines. The firm started at Belleville, Ill., but moved to Three Rivers in 1855, finally becoming incorporated in 1875. Cyrus Roberts was the inventive force at the company, with this corn sheller of 1885 being named in his honor. Other products included its Invincible threshing machines and the Happy Thought potato diggers. The company also manufactured railroad specialties.

Root-Heath Manufacturing Co., Plymouth, Ohio

By 1914, Root-Heath was offering numerous styles of small hand shellers, including the Little Giant and the R&H styles shown here. The company also made Gem and Never Fail hand shellers. Note the special mountings permitting the R&H sheller to be clamped to a large barrel for the shelled corn.

Sandwich Manufacturing Co., Sandwich, Ill.

Augustus Adams set up a small foundry at Elgin, Ill., in 1840; this was the first iron foundry west of the Mississippi River. In 1857, he moved his business to Sandwich, Ill., initially under the title of A. Adams & Sons. From this, Sandwich Manufacturing Co., was organized in 1867. About this time, Adams removed himself from the business and became associated with Marseilles Manufacturing Co., Marseilles, Ill. Sandwich Manufacturing was an early manufacturer of corn shellers, with this 1890 Sandwich Rustler sheller being an example. This one is shown with a horsepower, also made by Sandwich.

The 1894 Sandwich corn sheller line included many models designed for steam- or horse-power. The Sandwich shown here is equipped for the latter, with the tumbling rod being plainly evident. Since horse power was readily available, this was a viable option for many farmers of the time.

In 1908, Sandwich Manufacturing was not yet building its own gas engines, but for this Sandwich-Stover Combination, the Stover engine was chosen as the power. By this time, Sandwich was building a complete line of spring and cylinder shellers, the largest having a capacity of 120 bushels per hour. A Sandwich spring sheller is shown here.

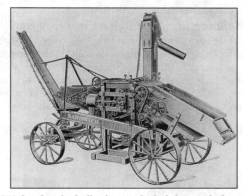

The 1910 Sandwich sheller line included this six-hole model, set up for operation with a steam engine or perhaps a gas engine. Although cylinder shellers had much more capacity, the spring sheller remained fairly popular into the 1920s, with the small one-hole models remaining with some manufacturers into the 1940s. Sandwich Manufacturing Co., was absorbed by New Idea in the 1930s.

Sidney Grain Machinery Co., Sidney, Ohio

Sidney offered an extensive range of mounted and stationary cylinder shellers; this one of 1919 was called its new one-farm size machine. Various product listings show the company as being in operation into the late 1940s, but little other information has surfaced on either the company or its corn shellers.

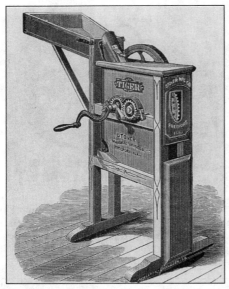

Stover Manufacturing & Engine Co., Freeport, Ill.

An 1889 advertisement illustrates the Tiger one-hole corn sheller, as built by Stover Manufacturing Co., the company title at the time. In another decade, the company would be building gas engines, later changing to the heading as shown. In addition to a rather extensive line of windmills and other farm products, the company was also a pioneer in small corn shellers.

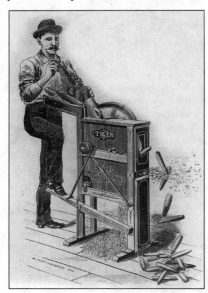

One of the most innovative ideas for a one-hole corn sheller comes from this 1890 advertisement for the Stover Tiger. Instead of the usual hand-crank, this sheller was set up with a foot-treadle arrangement, permitting the operator to feed corn with both hands and treadle with a spare foot.

Stover continued manufacturing corn shellers at least into the 1930s; the company ceased all operations in 1942. Already in the 1920s Stover was offering its No. 1 cylinder sheller, a small machine intended for the small farmer or for occasional shelling of small lots. These shellers were surprisingly popular for many years.

Tiffin Wagon Co., Tiffin, Ohio

Tiffin Wagon Co., was well known for its wagons, but less well known for its small corn shellers. This 1906 advertisement illustrates the two-hole Tiffin and the two-hole Favorite shellers. The company also built Challenge shellers in one-hole and two-hole versions. Little else is known of Tiffin's efforts in the corn sheller business.

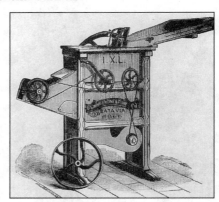

U.S. Wind Engine & Pump Co., Batavia, Ill.

U.S. Wind Engine & Pump Co., took its first step into fame with the renowned Halladay windmill. Subsequently, the company manufactured numerous farm implements and appliances, including this IXL corn sheller, shown here in an 1888 version. This two-hole sheller is shown with a hand-crank, but the furnished pulley meant that it could be converted to power.

Union Iron Works, Decatur, Ill.

By 1890, Union Iron Works was advertising its Western corn sheller; this was a cylinder sheller. Even at this early date, the Western was being advertised as a portable machine, capable of moving from one farm to another. By this time, and for the history of the corn sheller, large jobs were generally delegated to a custom corn sheller; very few farmers owned their own machine. Small quantities were handled on the farm with a spring sheller or a small cylinder sheller.

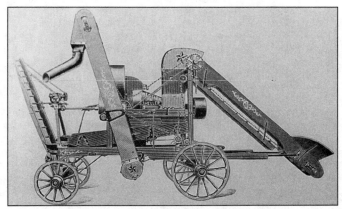

Particularly in shucked corn and the attendant amount of debris, cylinder shellers had the disadvantage of clogging the screens with this material until the 1896 Western patents. At this time, Union Iron Works patented a method of keeping the screen clear of this debris, thus giving much greater capacity to its machines.

By 1908, Western Field portable corn shellers were built in three sizes ranging from 500 to 2,000 bushels per hour. Production of the Western Field shellers appears to have continued at least into the 1940s, with repair parts still being available from Union Iron Works in the late 1950s. However, particulars regarding this company are lacking, as is specific product information outside of collected advertisements.

Whitman Agricultural Co., St. Louis, Mo.

Whitman was one of the early agricultural equipment manufacturers at St. Louis, with the St. Louis corn sheller shown here being of 1887 vintage. It is shown complete with a sacking elevator, together with a small horsepower for an elimination of the hand-cranking job. Due to the great difficulty of shelling corn by hand methods, the corn sheller was an essential part of bringing the corn crop to its position of dominance. Once the corn picker provided mechanical harvesting of the crop, corn assumed a role as a worldwide source of food and energy.

Trade Names

A.B.F.	A. B. Farquhar Co.	York, PA	1905
A. B. C.	Tiffin Wagon Co.	Tiffin, OH	1909
Aermotor	Aermotor Co.	Chicago, IL	1905
Appleton	Appleton Mfg. Co.	Batavia, IL	1913
Argentine	A. B. Farquhar Co.	York, PA	1905
Austin	F. C. Austin Mfg. Co.	Chicago, IL	1892
B & G	Bristol & Gale Co.	Chicago, IL	1915
B. M. Root	Hench & Dromgold Co.	York, PA	1905
Baby	Keystone Farm Machine Co.	York, PA	1905
Badger	Appleton Mfg. Co.	Batavia, IL	1892
Bayley	William Bayley Co.	Springfield, OH	1905
Belle	Pennslvania Electric Co.	Marietta, PA	1905
Big 4	Joliet Mfg. Co.	Joliet, IL	1909
Billups	C. Billups, Son & Co.	Norfolk, VA	1905
Billups Improved	C. Billups, Son & Co.	Norfolk, VA	1892
Black Eagle	Heath Foundry & Mfg. Co.	Plymouth, OH	1913
Black Hawk	A. H. Patch	Clarksville, TN	1905
Boss	Mountville Mfg. Co.	Mountville, PA	1909
Boston	A. B. Farquhar Co.	York, PA	1905
Boston	Ames Plow Co.	Boston, MA	1892
Buch	A. Buch's Sons Co.	Elizabethtown, PA	1909
Buckeye	S. R. White & Bro.	Norfolk, VA	1909
Buckeye	Staver & Abbott Mfg. Co.	Chicago, IL	189
Burrall	A. B. Farquhar Co.	York, PA	1892
Burrall	Messinger Mfg. Co.	Tatamy, PA	1905
Burrall	Munnsville Plow Co.	Munnsville, NY	1905
Burrall	H. N. Hubbard	New York, NY	1892
Burrall	Standard Harrow Co.	Utica, NY	1905
Burrall Improved	Gleason & Bailey Mfg. Co.	Seneca Falls, NY	1892
Burrall Improved	Goulds Mfg. Co.	Seneca Falls, NY	1892
Cannon	Ellis Keystone Agricultural Works	Pottstown, PA	1913
Challenge	Challenge Wind Mill & Feed Mill Co.	Batavia, IL	1892
Challenge	Tiffin Wagon Co.	Tiffin, OH	1905

Trade Names (cont...)

Champion	Forest City Machine Works	Cleveland, OH	1892
Champion	Mountville Mfg. Co.	Mountville, PA	1909
Champion	R. H. McGrath	LaFayette, IN	1892
Chicopee	Belcher & Taylor Agricultural Co.	Chicopee Falls, MA	1917
Chief	Marseilles Mfg. Co.	Marseilles, IL	1905
Clean Cob	W. Eddy Plow Co.	Greenwich, NY	1913
Climax	Thomas Peppler	Hightstown, NJ	1892
Clinton	A. B. Farquhar Co.	York, PA	1905
Clinton	Carr & Co.	New York, NY	1892
Clinton	H. N. Hubbard	New York, NY	1892
Clipper	Keystone Farm Machine Co.	York, PA	1905
Codorus	Keystone Farm Machine Co.	York, PA	1905
Corn King	Sandwich Mfg. Co.	Sandwich, IL	1892
Cow Boy	Mundie Mfg. Co.	Peru, IL	1924
Crescent	New Winona Mfg. Co.	Winona, MN	1905
Cumberland Valley	Keystone Farm Machine Co.	York, PA	1905
Custom	Appleton Mfg. Co.	Batavia, IL	1917
Cyclone	Foos Mfg. Co.	Springfield, OH	1905
Cyclone	Garry Iron & Steel Roofing Co.	Cleveland, OH	1892
Cyclone Junior	Marseilles Mfg. Co.	Marseilles, IL	1905
Cyclone Senior	Marseilles Mfg. Co.	Marseilles, IL	1905
Cyrus Roberts	Roberts, Throp & Co.	Three Rivers, MI	1892
Dain	Dain Mfg. Co.	Ottumwa, IA	1905
Daisy	Newark Machine Co.	Columbus, OH	1892
Daisy	Sutton Bros. & Bell	Indianapolis, PA	1892
Dandy	Challenge Wind Mill & Feed Mill Co.	Batavia, IL	1909
Deere	Deere & Mansur Co.	Moline, IL	1905
Deere Junior	Deere & Mansur Co.	Moline, IL	1905
Deere Senior	Deere & Mansur Co.	Moline, IL	1905
Defender	S. R. White & Bro.	Norfolk, VA	1905
Defiance	Western Mfg. Co.	Lincoln, NE	1892
Dexter	Brennan & Co.	Louisville, KY	1892
Dexter	American Seeding Machine Co.	Richmond, IN	1909
Diamond	Marseilles Mfg. Co.	Marseilles, IL	1892
Diamond	New Winona Mfg. Co.	Winona, MN	1905
Diamond	Straub Machinery Co.	Cincinnati, OH	1892
Diamond	Wilder-Strong Implement Co.	Monroe, MI	1905
Ditto	G. M. Ditto Mfg. Co.	Joliet, IL	1922
Dixie	Keystone Farm Machine Co.	York, PA	1905
Dow	B. F. Dow & Co.	Peru, IN	1892
Dude	Keystone Co.	Sterling, IL	1892
Eagle	A. B. Farquhar Co.	York, PA	1905
Eagle	Eagle Machine Co.	Lancaster, OH	1892
Eagle	Eagle Machine Co.	Lancaster, OH	1905
Eagle	Keystone Farm Machine Co.	York, PA	1905
Eagle	H. N. Hubbard	New York, NY	1892
Eagle	Taylor & Gale	Chicopee Falls, MA	1892
Eclipse	A. B. Farquhar Co.	York, PA	1905
Economy	Keystone Farm Machine Co.	York, PA	1905
Empire	Messinger Mfg. Co.	Tatamy, PA	1905
Eureka	Henry H. Lovejoy	Cambridge, NY	1892
Eureka Ironsides	Joliet Mfg. Co.	Joliet, IL	1905
F. & W.	Flint & Walling Mfg. Co.	Kendallville, IN	1913

Trade Names (cont...)

Fairbanks-Morse	Fairbanks, Morse & Co.	Chicago, IL	1892
Farmer	Marseilles Mfg. Co.	Marseilles, IL	1905
Favorite	Duplex Mfg. Co.	Superior, WI	1913
Favorite	Marseilles Mfg. Co.	Marseilles, IL	1892
Favorite	Nordyke & Marmon Co.	Indianapolis IN	1913
Favorite	S. R. White & Bro.	Norfolk, VA	1909
Favorite	Tiffin Agricultural Works	Tiffin, OH	1892
Favorite	Tiffin Wagon Co.	Tiffin, OH	1905
Favorite	Wilder-Strong Implement Co.	Monroe, MI	1905
Fawn	Deere & Mansur Co.	Moline, IL	1905
Fleetwood	Fleetwood Foundry & Mach. Works	Fleetwood, PA	1905
Freeman	S. Freeman & Sons Mfg. Co.	Racine, WI	1905
Gem Iron	Root-Heath Mfg. Co.	Plymouth, OH	1922
Genesee	Genesee Valley Mfg. Co.	Mt. Morris, NY	1892
Gilman	King & Hamilton Co.	Ottawa, IL	1892
Graham	Graham Foundry & Machine Co.	Graham, VA	1892
Great Western	Great Western Mfg. Co.	Leavenworth, KS	1936
Grier	Geo. L. Grier & Son	Milford, DE	1892
H. N. H.	H. N. Hubbard	New York, NY	1892
Harrison	Leonard D. Harrison	New Haven, CT	1892
Heebner	Heebner & Sons	Lansdale, PA	1892
Hocking Valley	Hocking Valley Mfg. Co.	Lancaster, OH	1892
Home	Eagle Machine Co.	Lancaster, OH	1905
Homeworth	Pilmer Bros.	Homeworth, OH	1892
Howell	R. R. Howell & Co.	Minneapolis, MN	1909
Hulshizer	Daniel Hulshizer	Doylestown, PA	1892
Hummer	New Winona Mfg. Co.	Winona, MN	1905
Hummer	Sandwich Mfg. Co.	Sandwich, IL	1913
I. X. L.	Taylor & Gale	Chicopee Falls, MA	1892
I. X. L.	U. S. Wind Engine & Pump Co.	Batavia, IL	1892
Ideal	Stover Mfg Co.	Freeport, IL	1892
Imperial	Keystone Farm Machine Co.	York, PA	1905
Improved Root	A. Buch's Sons Co.	Elizabethtown, PA	1892
Invincible	Keystone Farm Machine Co	York, PA	1905
Iron Star	Star Mfg. Co.	New Lexington, OH	1892
Ithaca	Treman, Waterman & Co.	Ithaca, NY	1892
Jewel	Whitman Agricultural Co.	St. Louis, MO	1905
John Deere	John Deere Spreader Works	East Moline, IL	1929
Joliet	Joliet Mfg. Co.	Joliet, IL	1905
Junior	Sandwich Mfg. Co.	Sandwich, IL	1913
Jupiter	Mountville Mfg. Co.	Mountville, PA	1909
Keck-Gonnerman	Keck-Gonnerman Co.	Mt. Vernon, IN	1922
Kelly-Duplex	Duplex Mill & Mfg. Co.	Springfield, OH	1915
Kentucky	Brennan & Co.	Louisville, KY	1892
Keynote	International Harvester Co.	Chicago, IL	1913
Keynote	Keystone Co.	Sterling, IL	1905
Keystone	A. Buch's Sons Co.	Elizabethtown, PA	1905
Keystone	Keystone Co.	Sterling, IL	1892
Keystone	Keystone Farm Machine Co.	York, PA	1905

Trade Names (cont...)

Keystone-Burrall	Keystone Farm Machine Co.	York, PA	1905
Keystone-Clinton	Keystone Farm Machine Co.	York, PA	1905
Keystone Lightning	Keystone Farm Machine Co.	York, PA	1905
Kid	Ames Plow Co.	Boston, MA	1905
King	Whitman Agricultural Co.	St. Louis, MO	1905
King	Whitman Agricultural Co.	St. Louis, MO	1913
Kingsland	Kingsland Mfg. Co.	St. Louis, MO	1905
Klauer	Klauer Mfg. Co.	Dubuque, IA	1922
Knox	Geo. W. Brown & Co.	Galesburg, IL	1892
Lancaster	A. B. Farquhar Co.	York, PA	1905
Leader	Marseilles Mfg. Co.	Marseilles, IL	1905
Lightning	Kansas City Hay Press Co.	Kansas City, MO	1913
Lightning	Keystone Farm Machine Co.	York, PA	1919
Lightning	Keystone Farm Machine Co.	York, PA	1909
Lion	A. B. Farquhar Co.	York, PA	1905
Lion	Belcher & Taylor Agricultural Co.	Chicopee Falls, MA	1892
Lion	Belcher & Taylor Agricultural Co.	Chicopee Falls, MA	1905
Lion	Keystone Farm Machine Co.	York, PA	1905
Little Better	Double Power Mil Co.	Appleton, WI	1913
Little Giant	Ohio Rake Co.	Dayton, OH	1892
Maine	Mountville Mfg. Co.	Mountville, PA	1909
Marseilles-Adams	Marseilles Mfg. Co.	Marseilles, IL	1892
McCormick-Deering	International Harvester Co.	Chicago, IL	1936
Minneapolis	Minneapolis Threshing Machine Co.	Hopkins, MN	1909
Mississippi Valley	Whitman Agricultural Co.	St. Louis, MO	1905
Modoc	Hudson Mfg. Co.	Minneapolis, MN	1924
Monarch	Sprout, Waldron & Co.	Muncy, PA	1905
Monitor	Enterprise Foundry Co.	Allegheny, PA	1892
Moore	Moore Plow & Implement Co.	Greenville, MI	1909
National	Carr & Co.	New York, NY	1892
Never Fail	Heath Foundry & Mfg. Co.	Plymouth, OH	1913
Never-Fail	Root-Heath Mfg. Co.	Plymouth, OH	1922
New Derby	Whitman Agricultural Co.	St. Louis, MO	1905
New Era	C. Billups, Son & Co.	Norfolk, VA	1892
New Hero	Appleton Mfg. Co.	Batavia, IL	1905
New Holland	New Holland New Macho\ine Co.	Holland, PA	1945
New Idea	New Idea Spreader Co.	Coldwater, OH	1936
New Kiger	James Thornton	Philadelphia, PA	1892
New Marseilles	Marseilles Mfg. Co.	Marseilles, IL	1909
New Process	Marseilles Mfg. Co.	Marseilles, IL	1905
New Process	Marseilles Mfg. Co.	Marseilles, IL	1909
New Queen	Whitman Agricultural Co.	St. Louis, MO	1905
Niagara	John T. Noye Mfg. Co.	Buffalo, NY	1892
Nordyke & Marmon	Nordyke & Marmon Co.	Indianapolis, IN	1892

Trade Names (cont...)

North Star	R. R. Howell & Co.	Minneapolis, MN	1913
Noxall	Keystone Farm Machine Co.	York, PA	1905
O. K.	Tiffin Agricultural Works	Tiffin, OH	1892
O. K.	Tiffin Wagon Co.	Tiffin, OH	1905
Opal	Ann Arbor Agricultural Co.	Ann Arbor, MI	1892
Ottawa	King & Hamilton Co.	Ottawa, IL	1905
Our Baby	Keystone Farm Machine Co.	York, PA	1905
Our Best	W. Eddy Plow Co.	Greenwich, NY	1913
Oyler	Geo. K. Oyler & Co.	St. Louis, MO	1892
Oyler's Pearl	Geo. K. Oyler & Co.	St. Louis, MO	1892
Patch's Blackhawk	A. H. Patch	Clarksville, TN	1892
Patch's Patent	A. H. Patch	Clarksville, TN	1905
Pearl	Marseilles Mfg. Co.	Marseilles, IL	1905
Pearl	Tiffin Agricultural Works	Tiffin, OH	1892
Peerless	B. Gill & Son	Trenton, NJ	1892
Pennsylvania	A. Buch's Sons Co.	Elizabethtown, PA	1905
Peony	Geo. K. Oyler & Co.	St. Louis, MO	1892
Peppler	Thomas Peppler	Hightstown, NJ	1905
Pet	Keystone Co.	Sterling, IL	1892
Pony	A. H. Patch	Clarksville, TN	1905
Pony	International Harvester Co	Chicago, IL	1909
Pony	Keystone Co.	Sterling, IL	1892
Pony	Mountville Mfg. Co.	Mountville, PA	1909
Port Huron	Port Huron Engine & Thresher Co.	Port Huron, MI	1905
Pottstown	Ellis Keystone Agricultural Works	Pottstown, PA	1909
Pottstown	Ellis Keystone Agricultural Works	Pottstown, PA	1909
Prairie	Pearl River Foundry & Agric. Works	Jackson, MS	1892
Premium	Belcher & Taylor Agricultural Co.	Chicopee Falls, MA	1892
President	Carr & Co.	New York, NY	1892
Prince	Whitman Agricultural Co.	St. Louis, MO	1905
Prize Yankee	Whitman Agricultural Co.	Auburn, ME	1892
R & H	Root-Heath Mfg. Co.	Plymouth, OH	1922
Racine	S. Freeman & Sons Mfg. Co.	Racine, WI	1909
Raisin Valley	Wilder-Strong Implement Co.	Monroe, MI	1905
Reading	Brennan & Co.	Louisville, KY	1892
Reading	Sandusky Mach. & Agric. Works	Sandusky, OH	1892
Red Chief	Brinly-Hardy Co.	Louisville, KY	1905
Reeves	Reeves & Co.	Columbus, IN	1905
Reliance	Keystone Farm Machine Co.	York, PA	1905
Reliance	S. R. White & Bro.	Norfolk, VA	1892
Root	A. B. Farquhar Co.	York, PA	1905
Root	Keystone Farm Machine Co.	York, PA	1905
Root	Lessig & Bro. Agricultural Works	Reading, PA	1892
Rover	Mountville Mfg. Co.	Mountville, PA	1909
Royal	Appleton Mfg. Co.	Batavia, IL	1892
Rumely-Watts	M. Rumely Co.	LaPorte, IN	1913
Rumsey	Rumsey & Co.	Seneca Falls, NY	1892

Trade Names (cont...)

Rural	Geo. K. Oyler & Co.	St. Louis, MO	1892
Rural	Joliet Mfg. Co.	Joliet, IL	1909
Rural Ironsides	Joliet Mfg. Co.	Joliet, IL	1905
Rustic	Geo. K. Oyler & Co.	St. Louis, MO	1892
Sandwich	Sandwich Mfg. Co.	Sandwich, IL	1892
Sandwich Jr.	Sandwich Mfg. Co.	Sandwich, IL	1905
Sattley	Racine-Sattley Co.	Springfield, IL	1913
Scientific	Foos Mfg. Co.	Springfield, OH	1892
Sheldon	Sheldon Engine & Sales Co.	Waterloo, IA	1924
Shenendoah Valley	S. R. White & Bro.	Norfolk, VA	1905
Shreffler's Ironsides	Joliet Mfg. Co.	Joliet, IL	1905
Sidney	Philip Smith Mfg. Co.	Sidney, OH	1922
Smalley	Smalley Mfg. Co.	Manitowoc, WI	1905
Smith	Oliver A. Smith	Clarkston, MI	1892
Smith's Cannon	Hiram Deats Jr.	Pittstown, NJ	1892
Smith's Cannon	F. F. Drinkhouse	Phillipsburg, NJ	1913
Southern	A. B. Farquhar Co.	York, PA	1905
Southern	Ames Plow Co.	Boston, MA	1892
Southern	Keystone Farm Machine Co.	York, PA	1905
Southern	H. N. Hubbard	New York, NY	1892
Southern Cross	Keystone Farm Machine Co.	York, PA	1905
Spangler	Spangler Mfg. Co.	York, PA	1892
Spring Valley	Donaldson Bros.	Mt. Clemens, MI	1905
St. Louis	Whitman Agricultural Co.	St. Louis, MO	1905
Standard	Joliet Mfg. Co.	Joliet, IL	1892
Star	A. Blaker & Co.	Newtown, PA	1892
Star	C. Billups, Son & Co.	Norfolk, VA	1892
Star	C. Billups Son & Co.	Norfolk, VA	1905
Star	J. A. Field Mfg. Co.	St. Louis, MO	1892
Stevens	A. W. Stevens & Son	Auburn, NY	1892
Stover	Stover Mfg. & Engine Co.	Freeport, IL	1922
Susquehanna	Keystone Farm Machine Co.	Yorkm, PA	1905
Sweepstakes	Smalley Mfg. Co.	Manitowoc, WI	1905
Syracuse Clinton	Syracuse Chilled Plow Co.	Syracuse, NY	1909
Syracuse Clinton	Syracuse Chilled Plow Co.	Syracuse, NY	1909
Ten-Broeck	Brennan & Co.	Louisville, KY	1892
Thompson	C. M. Thompson	Lexington, NC	1892
Tiffin	Tiffin Agricultural Works	Tiffin, OH	1892
Tiffin	Tiffin Wagon Co.	Tiffin, OH	1905
Tiger	Keystone Farm Machine Co.	York, PA	1905
Tiger	Stover Mfg Co.	Freeport, IL	1892
Tony	Abram Ellwood	Sycamore, IL	1892
Tony	Tiffin Agricultural Works	Tiffin, OH	1892
Tornado	W. R. Harrison & Co.	Massillon, OH	1905
Tracy	A. J. Tracy Co.	New York, NY	1892
U. S.	U. S. Wind Engine & Pump Co.	Batavia, IL	1905
Valley Chief	S. R. White & Bro.	Norfolk, VA	1905
Veteran	Sandwich Mfg. Co.	Sandwich, IL	1892
Vibrator	Kingsland & Douglas Mfg. Co.	St. Louis, MO	1892
Victor	H. N. Hubbard	New York, NY	1892
Virginia	Brennan & Co.	Louisville, KY	1892

Trade Names (cont...)

Western	Ames Plow Co.	Boston, MA	1892
Western	Union Iron Works	Decatur, IL	1892
Western	Union Iron Works	Decatur, IL	1909
White's Buckeye	S. R. White & Bro.	Norfolk, VA	1905
White's Favorite	S. R. White & Bro.	Norfolk, VA	1905
Wisconsin	Berres-Gehl Mfg. Co.	West Bend, WI	1905
Wisconsin	Silberzahn Mfg. Co.	West Bend, WI	1892
Wisconsin Valley	Bristol & Gale Co.	Chicago, IL	1915
Wrenn & Whitehurst & Co.	Wrenn, Whitehurst	Norfolk, VA	1892
X L	International Harvester Co.	Chicago, IL	1913
X. L.	Keystone Co.	Sterling, IL	1892
Yankee	Ames Plow Co.	Boston, MA	1892
Yankee	Carr & Co.	New York, NY	1892
Ypsilanti	Ypsilanti Machine Works	Ypsilanti, MI	1892

Cotton Pickers

Mechanizing the cotton harvest was a goal long sought for, but evaded reality until the 1940s. Prior to that time, there had been some meager success, particularly in the 1930s. However, efforts to build a successful cotton picker began already in the 1860s. Each new invention came out with high hopes and each failed to be commercially successful. One such invention was that of C.B. Sheehan of Springfield, Ill. His 1908 cotton picker was known as the Peerless and was designed to work by suction, actually sucking the cotton bolls from the stems. However, like all the rest, the Peerless never gained commercial status.

Along with many small manufacturers, John Deere and International Harvester spent considerable money developing a successful machine, ultimately achieving success. Due to a lack of suitable photographs, none have been included in this section. However, the cotton picker developments of the 1940s finally mechanized a job that was notoriously labor intensive and was the last major crop to be mechanized.

Trade Names			
Cunningham	J. I. Case Threshing Machine Co.	Racine, WI	1892

Cotton Planters

Due to the great similarity between cotton planters and corn planters (and because the same planter was generally used for both crops), a few examples of cotton planters will be found under the Corn Planter section of this book.

Cream Separators

For the farm wife, the invention of the cream separator was as great as the invention of the reaper was to the husband. Until the 1870s, there was little activity regarding the mechanical separation of cream from the milk; some experiments by German engineers led to partial success, but they failed to follow with additional research. In 1875, the Lefeldt separator was built at Kiel, Germany, and the company began marketing them by 1877. The following year came the famous DeLaval cream separator, followed the next year by the Nielsen-Petersen machine. All these machines were of European design.

In the early 1880s, W.W. Marsh, president of the Iowa Dairy Separator Co., began marketing the first American-made machine. This was the beginning of the famous "curved-disc" design; Iowa Dairy Separator Co., soon became the company to emulate. By 1915, here were more than two million cream separators in daily use, with continuing sales of more than 200,000 per year. Industry records show that in 1917, there were some 30 American manufacturers of cream separators.

Apparently, the first American-built cream separator was the Sharples, first built in 1881 or 1882. This company remained in the cream separator business for many years.

Old cream separators are highly sought after by a specialized group of collectors. Despite their relative scarcity today, vintage cream separators usually do not fetch high figures on auction, with rather nice ones sometimes selling for less than $100. On the other hand, rare models, especially in good condition, can bring several times that figure. Since relatively few appear, it is difficult to establish a pricing system for these interesting farm antiques.

D.H. Burrell & Co., Little Falls, N.Y.

A 1910 advertisement shows the Simplex Link-Blade separator from D.H. Burrell & Co. The machine apparently gained some status, since it was offered for sale by the large jobbing house of Baker & Hamilton in San Francisco. Little else is known of this machine.

Anker-Holth Manufacturing Co., Port Huron, Mich.

The Anker-Holth separators were well known in the United States. This 1917 version was the typical hand-cranked model; most models required the operator to turn the crank at 50 to 55 rpm. Whole milk was poured into the large bowl on top and as it fed through the centrifuge, cream came out of one spout and skim milk from the other.

Iowa Dairy Separator Co., Waterloo, Iowa

Iowa Dairy Separator Co. was among the first American manufacturers of cream separators. Beginning in the early 1880s, the company first offered large separators for use primarily in creameries. Eventually, the company began offering small units for home use.

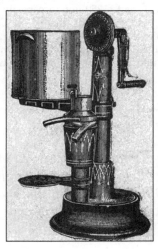

About 1910, Iowa Dairy Separator Co. became part of Associated Manufacturers at Waterloo, Iowa. The latter had recently developed its own gas-engine line, but continued making cream separators for years to come. This 1917 model is a hand-cranked machine. The number of Iowa cream separators leaving the Waterloo factory numbered into the hundreds of thousands.

B.F. Avery Co., Louisville, Ky.

As part of its overall farm line, B.F. Avery offered this ball-bearing cream separator in its 1916 general catalog. While it differed somewhat in general design from its contemporaries, nevertheless, its principle of operation was the same. Adding ball bearings was helpful because it reduced the effort necessary to crank the machine.

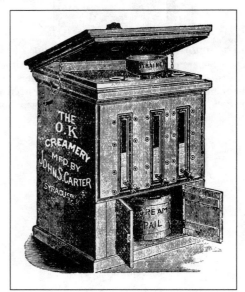

John S. Carter, Syracuse, N.Y.

Prior to the days of centrifugal cream separators, various means of separating cream from milk were used. Many of these units depended primarily on the natural forces that caused the cream to rise to the top, where it was carefully skimmed. Examples of the O.K. Creamery shown here and others of similar design, are very scarce at present.

Champion Blower & Forge Co., Lancaster, Pa.

Champion Blower & Forge Co., was apparently a late entry into the cream separator business, arriving about 1920. Shown here is its No. 70 Champion cream separator. It had a 700-pound capacity, about the average farm size. This meant that it was capable of handling the milk from up to 14 cows.

For the small farmer, Champion offered this little bench-type cream separator, it had a 250-pound capacity (or up to three cows). Weighing but 85 pounds, the No. 25 Champion bench separator was securely fastened to a heavy bench or table. The crank is stamped "60 turns per minute," and a small bell mounted on the crank handle helped the operator keep time.

Did You Know?

Today, vintage flour mills often sell at a considerable figure; a nicely restored small mill might bring up to $1,000. However, a mill with a poor framework or a broken stone will bring but a fraction of that figure.

Cockshutt Plow Co., Ltd., Brantford, Ontario

In 1910, Cockshutt Plow Co. offered the Lacta cream separator, primarily to its customers in Canada. This one was hailed because of its oiling system that kept all the gears and bearings bathed in a constant flow of oil. This was especially important for the high-speed spindle gears and bearings. By the late 1930s, the Lacta is shown as being built by Rite-Way Products at Chicago.

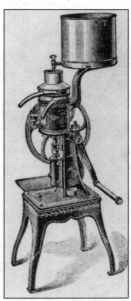

DeLaval Separator Co., New York, N.Y.

The DeLaval cream separator was among the earliest on the market. First built only in Europe, the company eventually began manufacturing them in the United States. This 1899 example demonstrates the utter simplicity of the DeLaval machine. Even though it took some time to crank the night and morning milking through the cream separator, this was still far preferable to skimming by hand.

A 1907 advertisement for the DeLaval cream separators notes that by that time, the company had sold more than 750,000 of them worldwide. The company began making cream separators in 1882, with the DeLaval rising to the top in a superior position, one that it held for decades.

By 1920, the DeLaval had taken on a modern appearance, especially when compared to the 1899 model. A great many cream separators of this time were also equipped with the necessary countershaft, enabling the machine to be operated with a gasoline engine or an electric motor.

Wm. Galloway Co., Waterloo, Iowa

The famous catalog house of Bill Galloway was offering cream separators even before this 1910 advertisement. Galloway's catalogs illustrated the newest things on the market, often phrasing the sales pitch to cash-minded farmers. This advertisement for instance, notes that "[the dairy] is the only department on the farm which brings in a pay check every week of the year."

Toward the end of the cream separator business, Galloway Co. offered this ultra-modern design, operated by a concealed electric motor. By this time, the design had been greatly simplified to minimize replacement of parts. With great joy, the author recalls junking the old hand-cranked Galloway in favor of this new one during the winter of 1947.

Did You Know?

Today, vintage flour mills often sell at a considerable figure; a nicely restored small mill might bring up to $1,000. However, a mill with a poor framework or a broken stone will bring but a fraction of that figure.

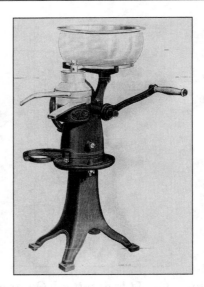

Hartman Co., Chicago, Ill.

Hartman Co., offered this style of its Majestic cream separator in the 1920s. It was offered in four different sizes, from 375 to 1,000 pounds per hour. The company recommended its 500-pound machine for the average farm, albeit this was probably a size smaller than desirable. The 500-pound separator sold for $62.

Hydraulic Cream Separator Co., Centerville, Iowa

An 1899 advertisement indicates that this machine was built and/or sold by Lourie Implement Co., Keokuk, Iowa. Billed as a Hydraulic Cream Separator, it claimed to do just as good a job as a $125 centrifugal machine, but at a fraction of the cost. But farmers weren't buying the argument, sales were brisk for the centrifugal machines, but languished for hydraulic separators.

International Harvester Co., Chicago, Ill.

By 1910, IHC was offering a series of cream separators as part of its extensive farm equipment line. A 1912 offering was its No. 1 Dairymaid cream separator with a capacity of 350 pounds of milk per hour. This one is shown belted to an IHC 1-horsepower Famous engine, obviating the need to crank the separator by hand.

International Harvester was a major player in the dairy equipment business for many years. Its Primrose cream separator pictured here was a popular machine that was sold by the thousands. International Harvester had a strong dealer organization, with stores in many small towns. Parts and service in those days were always important; that helped sell a lot of IHC products.

King Drill Manufacturing Co., Nebraska City, Neb.

The cream separator was a well established fact of life by 1900. Despite this, a few farmers still preferred the old-style natural separator as shown from King Drill Co.. However, the days were numbered for this method; farmers everywhere were flocking to town to get a new centrifugal machine.

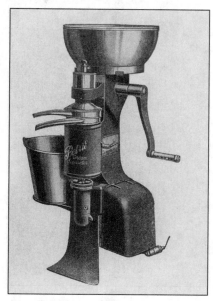

R.A. Lister Co., Ltd., Toronto, Ontario

A 1922 advertisement shows the Petrie cream separator; it was an all-electric machine that could be furnished with an AC or DC motor. By the 1930s, R.A. Lister appears as the manufacturer of this separator; unfortunately, we have found nothing further on the ancestry of the Petrie machine.

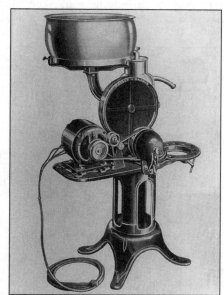

Massey-Harris Co., Toronto, Ontario

Massey-Harris was a major player in the farm equipment business, particularly in Canada. Its complete product line included cream separators for many years, with this example dating from the 1930s. M-H claimed that its machine would separate even the tiniest globules of butterfat from the milk. However, when correctly adjusted, so would virtually every other centrifugal separator.

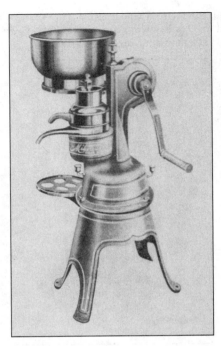

Milwaukee Separator Manufacturing Co., Milwaukee, Wisc.

In 1918, the Milwaukee Sanitary separator took on the form shown here, with the company remaining in the cream separator business a few more years. About this time, cream separator manufacturing reached its peak, with the majority of farms now owning a machine. Subsequently, the market consisted of those relatively few who didn't yet own a separator or those seeking a replacement.

Mosely & Pritchard Manufacturing Co., Clinton, Iowa

A 1901 advertisement illustrates Mosely's hydraulic cream separator. Established in 1885, this company continued to promote its design despite the withering competition of the centrifugal designs. Outside of this 1901 advertisement, nothing had been found of Mosely's separator.

Omega Separator Co., Lansing, Mich.

Omega appeared in 1906 with its concept of the ideal cream separator. For reasons unknown, the company survived for only a few years, probably unable to face the tremendous competition in the marketplace. The same scenario was replayed many times in the farm equipment business and sometimes high quality designs went to defeat simply because of a poor marketing strategy.

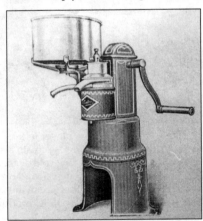

Peerless Cream Separator Co., Waterloo, Iowa

Outside of a 1909 advertisement, little is known of this Waterloo firm. Peerless was in strong competition from the start with Iowa Dairy Separator Co., one of the oldest American separator manufacturers. Eventually, the company was taken over by Associated Manufacturers at Waterloo, the successor to Iowa Dairy Separator Co.

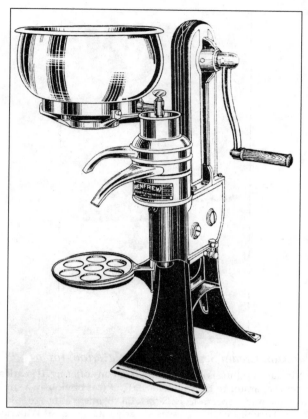

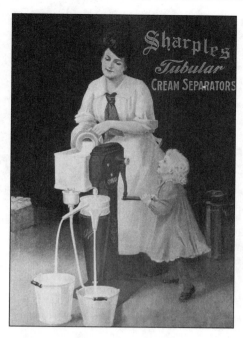

Renfrew Machinery Co., Milwaukee. Wisc.

Although a 1917 advertisement shows this company as located in Milwaukee, the parent company was actually located in Renfrew, Ontario, Canada. Little else has been found on the Renfrew, except that by the late 1930s, repair parts were available from a firm in Nebraska; no further reference to the company at Renfrew has been found.

Sharples Separator Co., West Chester, Pa.

A 1905 advertisement paints an idealistic scene of separating cream from milk. However, the Sharples dated back to the early 1880s and was, in truth, one of the very first American-made cream separators. Its "Tubular" design became quite popular and remained so for decades.

Rock Island Plow Co., Rock Island, Ill.

Originally built and sold by Smith Manufacturing Co., Chicago, the Great Western line was eventually bought out by Rock Island Plow Co. The latter continued to manufacture Great Western cream separators for many years. Shown here is a Great Western cream separator of the 1920s belted to a Rock Island gasoline engine.

By the late 1930s, repairs for the Sharples cream separators were available from United Dairy Equipment Co., West Chester, Pa. This 1925 advertisement illustrates essentially the same machine as was made in 1905. Two sizes were available, the 700-pound capacity, suitable for the average farmer and the big 1,650-pound separator for sizable dairy operations.

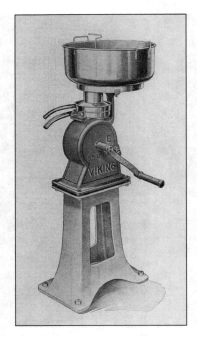

Swedish Separator Co., Chicago, Ill.

By about 1910, the Swedish Separator Co. was established as an American manufacturing branch of the Swedish design. Its Viking separators were very popular. The Viking retained its own market niche for some years, eventually coming into the fold of the United Engine Co., Lansing, Mich.

Vermont Farm Machine Co., Bellows Falls, Vt.

By 1905, the United States Cream Separator was being offered by Vermont Farm Machine Co. This machine remained on the market for decades and repair parts were still available into the late 1930s. Nothing further is known of this company or its U.S. cream separator.

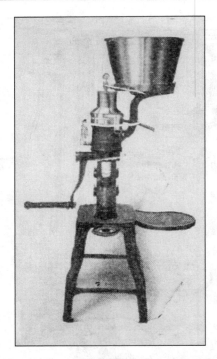

Waterloo Cream Separator Co., Waterloo, Iowa

Virtually nothing is known of this company offering its Peerless cream separator to the public in 1907. It was obviously a small machine and appears to have been a distinctive design. Since Iowa Dairy Separator Co., was already established at Waterloo for the same purpose, it would seem that the two companies might have joined forces. Eventually, they did, since for some years, parts for the Peerless were available from Associated Manufacturers at Waterloo.

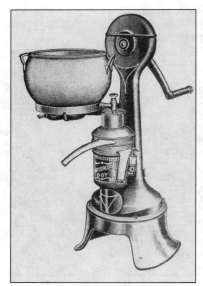

Waterloo Gasoline Engine Co., Waterloo, Iowa

In 1912, Waterloo Gasoline Engine Co. purchased the cream separator plant of Lisle Manufacturing Co., Clarinda, Iowa. The manufacturing equipment was moved to Waterloo; instantly, the company was in the cream separator business. Waterloo Gasoline Engine Co., continued with the line at least until the 1918 takeover by Deere & Co.; the latter continued to sell parts for the Waterloo Boy cream separators for some years.

Trade Names

Acme	De Laval Cream Separator Co.	New York, NY	1905
All-Electric	Galloway Co.	Waterloo, IA	1945
Alpha	De Laval Cream Separator Co.	New York, NY	1905
American	American Separator Co.	Bainbridge, NY	1905
Anderson	Westerfield Motor Co.	Anderson, IN	1922
Anker-Holth	Anker-Holth Mfg. Co.	Port Huron, MI	1915
Automatic	Standard Separator Co.	Milwaukee, WI	1913
Babson	Babson Bros.	Chicago, IL	1929
Baby	De Laval Cream Separator Co.	New York, NY	1892
Badger	Standard Separator Co.	Milwaukee, WI	1922
Baltic	Empire Cream Separator Co.	Bloomfield, NJ	1922
Beatrice	Beatrice Creamery Co.	Chicago, IL	1915
Bluebell	International Harvester Co.	Chicago, IL	1909
Bowman	William Galloway Co.	Waterloo, IA	1924
Boyd	John Boyd	Chicago, IL	1892
Burrell	Cherry-Burrell Corp.	Cedar Rapids, IA	1932
Burrell	D. H. Burrell Co.	Little Falls, NY	1929
Burton-Page	Burton-Page Co.	Chicago, IL	1936
Buttercup	Deere & Co.	Moline, IL	1924
Butterfly	Albaugh-Dover Co.	Chicago, IK	1936
Champion	Standard Separator Co.	Milwaukee, WI	1909
Clarinda	Clarinda Cream Separator Co.	Clarinda, IA	1929
Cleveland	Cleveland Cream Separator Co.	Cleveland, OH	1909
Creamaster	Galloway Co.	Waterloo, IA	1945
Dairy Queen	Dairy Queen Mfg. Co.	Flora, IN	1905
Dairy Queen	Dairy Cream Separator Co.	Lebanon, IN	1913
Dairymaid	International Harvester Co.	Chicago, IL	1909
Daisy	De Laval Cream Separator Co.	New York, NY	1905
Davis	Davis Cream Separator Co.	Chicago, IL	1905
Davis & Rankin	Davis & Rankin	Chicago, IL	1892
DeLaval	De Laval Cream Separator Co.	New York, NY	1909
Diabolo	United Engine Co.	Lansing, MI	1915
Economy	Sears, Roebuck & Co.	Chicago, IL	1924
Elgin	Elgin Cream Separator Co.	Chicago, IL	1913
Empire	Empire Cream Separator Co.	Bloomfield, NJ	1905
E-Z Challenger	American Separator Co.	Bainbridge, NY	1945
Galloway	William Galloway Co.	Waterloo, IA	1924
Gold Medal	Associated Manufacturers	Waterloo, IA	1929
Golden Harvest	Montgomery Ward & Co.	Chicago, IL	1929
Golden Rod	Golden Rod Separator Co.	Oxford, PA	1922
Great Western	Smith Mfg. Co.	Chicago, IL	1909
Great Western	Rock Island Plow Co.	Rock island, IL	1913
Harp	Harp Separator Co.	Minneapolis, MN	1929

Trade Names (cont...)

Hartman	Hartman Cream Separator Co.	Lansing, MI	1909
Hawkeye	Associated Manufacturers	Waterloo, IA	1913
Hawthorne	Montgomery Ward & Co.	Chicago, IL	1924
Hercules	Hercules Corporation	Evansville, IN	1924
Hummer	Hummer Plow Works	Springfield, IL	1929
Humming Bird	De Laval Cream Separator Co.	New York, NY	1905
Illinois Dairy	American Hardware Mfg. Co.	Ottawa, IL	1905
Improved Belt	P. M. Sharples	West Chester, PA	1892
International	International Cream Separator Co.	Lancaster, PA	1905
International	M. W. Savage Factories+	Minneapolis, MN	1929
Iowa	Associated Manufacturers	Waterloo, IA	1915
Iowa	Associated Manufacturers	Waterloo, IA	1929
Iowa Dairy	Iowa Dairy Separator Co.	Waterloo, IA	1905
Jersey	Sharples Separator Co.	West Chester, PA	1909
Justrite	Smith Mfg. Co.	Chicago, IL	1909
Lacta	Lacta Separator Co.	Chicago, IL	1929
Lily	International Harvester Co.	Chicago, IL	1913
Massey-Harris	Massey-Harris Harvester Co.	Batavia, NY	1924
Masterpiece	Galloway Co.	Waterloo, IA	1945
Maynard	Charles Williams Stores	Brooklyn, NY	1924
McCormick-Deering	International Harvester Co.	Chicago, IL	1929
McDermaid	J. McDermaid	Rockford, IL	1892
Melotte	Melotte Separator Co.	Chicago, IL	1924
Melotte	Pine Tree Milking Machine Co.	Chicago, IL	1929
Merit	Merit Separator Co.	Oxford, PA	1909
Miele	Miele Separator Co.	St. Louis, MO	1929
Milka	Lacta Separator Co.	Chicago, IL	1929
Monarch	Lisle Mfg. Co.	Clarinda, IA	1909
National	National Dairy Machine Co.	Newark, NJ	1905
National	National Dairy Machine Co.	Goshen, IN	1913
New Prosperity	William Galloway Co.	Waterloo, IA	1913
New Sandow	Interstate Engine & Tractor Co.	Waterloo, IA	1917
New Tubular	Sharples Separator Co.	West Chester, PA	1909
N-P	Bath Mfg. & Sales Co.	Bath, NY	1929
Official	Official Separator Co.	LaCrosse, WI	1929
Olds	M. Rumely Co.	LaPorte, IN	1913
Olive	Buckeye Cream Separator Co.	Oberlin, OH	1913
Omega	Omega Separator Co.	Lansing, MI	1905
Ottawa Chief	Montgomery Ward & Co.	Chicago, IL	1929
Papec	Papec Machine Co.	Lima, NY	1905
Peerless	Peerless Cream Separator Co.	Waterloo, IA	1909

Trade Names

Peerless	Waterloo Cream Separator Co.	Waterloo, IA	1905
Perfection	Perfection Milker Co.	Minneapolis, MN	1936
Phoenix	United Engine Co.	Lansing, MI	1924
Primrose	International Harvester Co.	Chicago, IL	1915
Primus	Buckeye Churn Co.	Sidney, OH	1913
Reid	A. H. Reid Creamery & Dairy Supply	Philadelphia, PA	1905
Reliance	Hummer Plow Works	Springfield, IL	1929
Reliance	Hummer Plow Works	Springfield, IL	1929
Renfrew	Renfrew Machinery Co.	Milwaukee, WI	1915
Robby Scientific	Harris Bros. Co.	Chicago, IL	1929
Rock Island	Rock Island Plow Co.	Rock island, IL	1936
Roe	D. H. Roe & Co.	Chicago, IL	1892
Rumely Automatic	M. Rumely Co.	LaPorte, IN	1913
Russian Dairy	P. M. Sharples	West Chester, PA	1892
Sandow	Interstate Engine & Tractor Co.	Waterloo, IA	1917
Sandow	Sandy McManus Inc.	Waterloo, IA	1915
Sandow	Waterloo Gasoline Engine Co.	Waterloo, IA	1924
Sanitary Milwaukee	Milwaukee Separator Co.	Milwaukee, WI	1917
Sattley	Hummer Plow Works	Springfield, IL	1929
Sharples	Sharples Separator Co.	West Chester, PA	1905
Sheldon's	Sheldon Engine & Sales Co.	Waterloo, IA	1917
Simplex	Cherry-Burrell Corp.	Cedar Rapids, IA	1932
Simplex	D. H. Burrell Co.	Little Falls, NY	1905
Skimmaster	American Separator Co.	Bainbridge, NY	1945
Springer	Valley Wind Engine & Iron Co.	Bay City, MI	1905
Standard	De Laval Cream Separator Co.	New York, NY	1905
Standard	Standard Separator Co.	Milwaukee, WI	1909
Standard Imperial	P. M. Sharples	West Chester, PA	1892
Success	Hummer Plow Works	Springfield, IL	1929
Supreme	Omega Separator Co.	Lansing, MI	1915
Sweden's Pride	Sheldon Engine & Sales Co.	Waterloo, IA	1922
Swedish Queen	Banner Engine Co.	Lansing, MI	1936
Tor	Northwestern Supply Co.	New York, NY	1924
Tubular	Sharples Separator Co.	West Chester, PA	1909
U. S.	Vermont Farm Machine Co.	Bellows Falls, VT	1892
United States	Vermont Farm Machine Co.	Bellows Falls, VT	1915
Upsala	Northwestern Supply Co.	New York, NY	1924
Van Duzen-Roys	Waterloo Gasoline Engine Co.	Waterloo, IA	1924
Vega	Vega Separator Co.	Fostoria, OH	1915
V-F-M	Vermont Farm Machine Co.	Bellows Falls, VT	1915
Victoria	Dairymen's Supply Co.	Philadelphia, PA	1892
Victory Gearless	Starch Bros. Co.	LaCrosse, WI	1913
Viking	Swedish Separator Co.	Chicago, IL	1915
Wasa	Northwestern Supply Co.	New York, NY	1924

Trade Names

Waterloo Boy	Waterloo Gasoline Engine Co.	Waterloo, IA	1915
Westfalia	Westfalia Separator Co.	Bloomfield, NJ	1939
Wheeler	Wheeler Mfg. Co.	Syracuse, NY	1913
Wilson	H. McK. Wilson & Co.	St. Louis, MO	1892
Wisconsin Dairy	Starch Bros. Co.	LaCrosse, WI	1913

Cultivators

Although row-crop cultivators are the general theme of this section, also included are some miscellaneous cultivators, weeders and the like. The term "field cultivator" as we know it today did not come into general use until after World War II. To reiterate, World War II is the great dividing line between horse-powered agriculture and mechanized agriculture. Granted, major strides toward farm mechanization were made in the 1930s, but these were considerably stifled by the Great Depression. Under the extreme circumstances of those years, farmers were forced to get by as economically as possible; there simply was very little money for anything but dire necessities. On its heels came World War II and the demands of war put an effective end to most farm machinery production for several years. After hostilities ended in 1945, it took a couple of years before farm machinery production could again resume. When it did, many of the small manufacturers were gone, never to return. Of those remaining, some continued producing horse-drawn machinery until about 1950.

Cultivators of some sort have roots in antiquity, dating back to the earliest of farm implements. In modern times, meaning in the period from 1850 onward, the cultivator received major attention. A study of U.S. Patents reveals literally thousands of patents granted for cultivators and their attachments.

Manufacturers abounded, with many of them being small shops that produced a few hundred units per year, while others produced cultivators by the thousands. Ohio Cultivator Co., found in this section, was one of the first to build a riding cultivator. Many farmers held it in disdain for some years, contending that the horses had enough to do with pulling the cultivator, much less giving the operator a ride.

There were tongueless cultivators and those with tongues, walking cultivators and riding cultivators, one-row and two-row styles, shovel cultivators and surface cultivators. By the 1920s, the motor cultivator appeared, although this machine is generally conceded to be a part of the tractor scene. With the wide acceptance of row-crop tractors by 1930, farmers got their first taste of tractor-mounted cultivators. The latter also marked the end for horse-drawn cultivators.

Of the hundreds, perhaps thousands of cultivator manufacturers, this section includes some of the most popular and a fair number of obscure makes. To include every cultivator from every company would be a book in itself; to avoid tedium and deny space for other parts of the farm equipment in a broad sense, this section is somewhat limited in scope.

Old cultivators have become a desirable collectible, although the market values still are very low. Oftentimes, an old rusty cultivator in a fence row or a grove can be purchased for scrap price, while nicely restored ones, especially those which are fairly rare, can command $100 to $200 or even more.

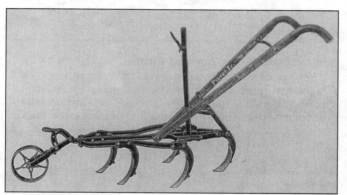

S.L. Allen & Co., Philadelphia, Pa.

This company was very active in the 1890s, continuing in the cultivator business for many years. Its specialty was in small cultivators suitable for truck farming. Shown here is its popular No. 101 Planet Jr., Plain Cultivator. The lever expander was an easy way to change the cultivating width.

The Planet Jr., line included a wide variety of small cultivators and implements. Among them was the No. 25 Planet Jr., Combined Hill and Drill Seeder, Double and Single Wheel Hoe, Cultivator and Plow. In other words, this single unit was recognized by satisfied users as a "Complete Gardener."

In the early 1900s, S.L. Allen & Co., began offering its No. 72G two-row cultivator. This one differed greatly from most two-row

units because it carried the extra shovels outside of the wheels. Instead of the usual wooden shear pins, this cultivator was equipped with spring-trip shanks.

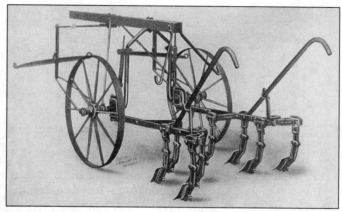

American Harrow Co., Detroit, Mich.

American Harrow Co., of the 1890s claimed to have the largest factory in the world, selling all its farm implements direct from the factory to the farmer. One example was this small one-row walking cultivator, available at a cash price of $14.75.

American Seeding Machine Co., Springfield, Ohio

The 1903 formation of American Seeding Machine Co., brought together a number of substantial implement manufacturers; this resulted in the new company having a line of cultivators and other implements. For 1915, the line included this Buckeye No. 157 Pivot Axle Riding Cultivator. Buckeye cultivators were made in numerous sizes and with a variety of attachments.

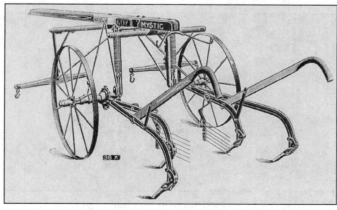

Avery Co., Peoria, Ill.

Originally organized as Avery Planter Co., this firm was building a variety of cultivators, planters and other equipment in the 1880s. By the 1890s, the company had diversified into threshers and steam-traction engines, but continued the implement line for some time after. Shown here is the Avery Mystic cultivator of 1903.

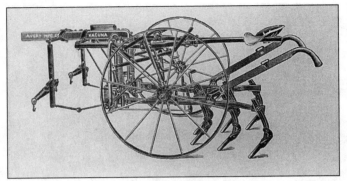

The 1906 Avery cultivator line included the Vacuna combined riding/walking cultivator. These combined units were expressly for farmers who shunned the notion of riding to give their feet a rest and, for them, walking behind was the preferred method.

B.F. Avery Co., Louisville, Ky.

B.F. Avery had a long history in the cultivator business, finally selling out to Minneapolis-Moline in 1951. Its 1916 cultivator line included this Avery Jack Rabbit model. It featured pipe-beam gangs and spring-trip shanks. Numerous other styles were also available.

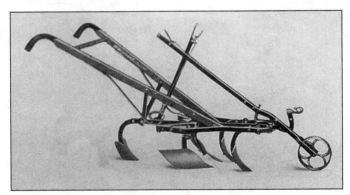

A. Belanger Ltd., Montmagny, Quebec

Although it greatly resembles the Planet Jr., cultivators from S.L. Allen & Co., this 1910 offering was called the Belanger Steel Scuffler. Weighing but 85 pounds, it could be adjusted to vary the cultivating width. A. Belanger Ltd. was established in 1867.

Pipe Frame   Channel Frame

Benicia Iron Works, Benicia, Calif.

Designed especially for use in groves and vineyards, the Benicia rotary harrows were ideal for cultivation in these situations. It could be made to run in either direction, with instructions to the operator that the slow side should run closest to the vines.

Blount Plow Works, Evansville, Ind.

A 1923 advertisement illustrates this company's Pilot Disc Cultivator. It could be adjusted so as to bar-off and throw dirt to the plants in a single operation. Numerous other attachments were available. The company also built a wide variety of harrows and planters.

David Bradley Manufacturing Co., Chicago, Ill.

Already in 1888, David Bradley was offering this riding-disc cultivator. The discs were adjustable so as to throw dirt toward the row or away from it. At the time, David Bradley also offered a walking-disc cultivator, along with a wide variety of shovel cultivators.

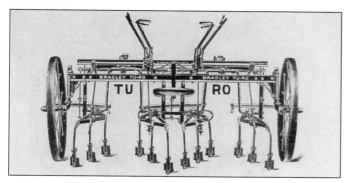

The Bradley Tu-Ro cultivator was announced to the trade in 1907. The operator guided the cultivator gangs with foot stirrups. Especially when plowing crosswise in checked corn, it required constant vigilance to avoid plowing out any of the growing crop. Woe to those who did!

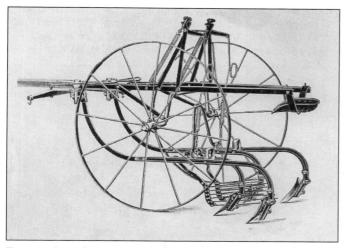

Brown, Lynch, Scott Co., Monmouth, Ill.

The Illinois Hammock Seat Riding Cultivator was announced by this firm in 1895. The hammock seat design was occasionally used, and as shown two extending irons carry the seat on a cross-piece, much like the old-fashioned hammock. Little is known of this company.

Brown Manufacturing Co., Zanesville, Ohio

Not to be confused with Geo. W. Brown Co., Galesburg, Ill., this firm was a pioneer in building cultivators. Its 1895 offerings included the Zanesville Brown, a small tongueless walking cultivator. Numerous options were available, including break-pin or spring-trip shanks, spring-tooth and surface gangs and much more.

In 1919, the Brown cultivator line included this Pivot Pole Disc Rider model, with the company noting that it was the result of 40 years' experience in the cultivator business. That would put the beginning of the Brown cultivators back to about 1880. Eventually, this company merged into Brown-Manly Plow Co., Malta, Ohio.

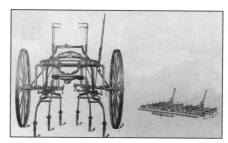

Brown-Manly Plow Co., Malta, Ohio

The history of Brown-Manly is presently unclear; our research found nothing except for a few advertisements. This 1911 advertisement illustrates its New Pivot Riding Cultivator. The company noted that it was a balanced frame design; this was important, since farmers complained of implements that placed a lot of weight on the horse's necks. If a horse got a sore neck, it was out to pasture until it healed.

J.I. Case Co., Racine, Wisc.

J.I. Case essentially stayed out of the implement business, concentrating on its steam engines, threshing machines and tractors until the 1920s. With its 1919 purchase of Grand Detour Plow Co., and the 1928 purchase of Emerson-Brantingham, the company was fully into tillage implements. With its introduction of row-crop tractors, Case offered this 1933 version of a listed crop cultivator.

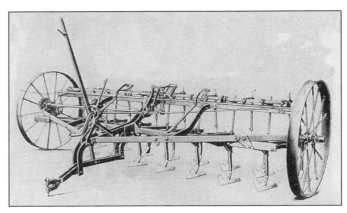

In 1928, Case offered its new Case Field Tiller. In today's terminology, it is an early form of field cultivator, not intended to cultivate crops, but to stir every square foot in a field. Eventually, the field cultivator would become an important part of minimum tillage farming.

J.I. Case Plow Works, Racine, Wisc.

Totally unconnected with the J.I. Case Threshing Machine Co., also in Racine, the Plow Works began serious efforts in the tillage equipment business in 1878. By the time this 1897 advertisement appeared, the Plow Works had an extensive line of cultivators, including the Dodger Disc Cultivator shown here. The disks were adjustable and could throw more or less soil into the row, as desired.

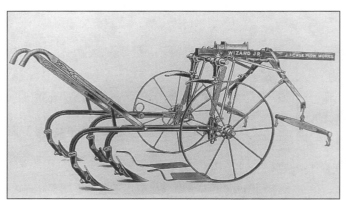

The Wizard Jr., was a walking cultivator that remained in the Case line for many years. Heavy springs helped the operator control the depth of the gangs. This 1897 example is but one of an astounding variety of cultivators offered the J.I. Case Plow Works.

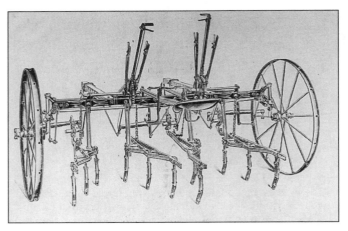

For 1908, Case offered its "Twin" two-row cultivator. Like most two-row cultivators, it required three horses, but could cut the time to cultivate a field in half over that required for a single-row cultivator. Numerous attachments were available. The Case Plow Works sold out to Massey-Harris in 1928; the latter then sold all rights to the Case name back to J.I. Case Threshing Machine Co.

Chase Plow Co., Lincoln, Neb.

In the 1920s, Chase Plow Co., offered this two-row cultivator; it differed from many of the competitors by using a set of front trucks to carry the weight of the cultivator. However, the coming of the row-crop tractor about 1930 soon put an end to many of the horse-drawn cultivators; many farmers could hardly wait to get a new row-crop tractor and a mounted cultivator.

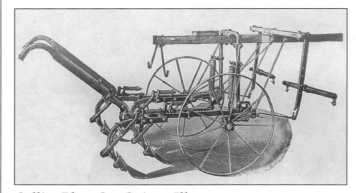

Collins Plow Co., Quincy, Ill.

For 1910, Collins Plow Co., offered this Balance Frame walking cultivator as part of its overall line. Various options were available; the company also made plows, harrows and hay presses. Collins

Plow appears in various trade directories as late as 1939, but nothing can be found regarding the company subsequent to World War II.

Deere & Co., Moline, Ill.

By the time this Peerless cultivator appeared in an 1878 catalog, John Deere had been in the plow business for some 40 years. This early design employed a wooden frame, as was customary at the time, but the Peerless was also unique in that it was a riding cultivator, unusual for an 1878 design.

The New Deere Walking Cultivator was introduced in the early 1900s and remained in the line for decades to come. This small cultivator was lightweight, simple and still quite an effective cultivator. Antique farm equipment buffs are often drawn to John Deere products; this walking cultivator is always popular among collectors.

Deere & Co., like most other cultivator makers, offered a huge line to accommodate virtually every cropping practice or local need. In addition, there were various options for each cultivator, with this one using pipe beams. The latter permitted easy adjust-

ment of the shovels to suit specific conditions. Deere Royal Combined Riding and Walking Cultivators were, as the title implies, capable of being used either way; one could either ride or walk.

Especially on larger farms, the two-row cultivator enjoyed a certain popularity. Conversely, many farmers preferred a single-row cultivator because they thought it would do a better job in eliminating every single weed in a field. This two-row model was offered in a 1905 advertisement, although the company sold two-row models for many years to come.

In 1928, Deere & Co., offered this three-row cultivator that was designed for mounting on the John Deere GP tractor. The tractor was designed with an arched front axle to permit driving over growing crops without damage and the company also pioneered the use of a three-row planter and other equipment suited to this cropping method. However, the three-row system didn't catch on very well with farmers; in the 1930s, Deere switched to the more common two-row design using a row-crop tractor.

Emerson-Brantingham Co., Rockford, Ill.

Emerson-Brantingham had roots going back to 1852, eventually operating as Emerson Manufacturing Co., and taking the E-

B name in 1909. By the time its 1907 catalog appeared, Emerson was a well-established firm in the tillage implement business; the Emerson Standard Cultivator shown here had already been on the market for several years.

Emerson's 1907 line included its No. 29 Hammock Seat Cultivator, shown here in a rear view. It was designed so that the operator had full control of the cultivator gangs with his feet in the iron stirrups. A convenient hand lever raised and lowered the cultivator gangs. This one is shown with the Emerson Gopher attachment, essentially a surface cultivator with rear-mounted sweeps.

The Emerson line for 1919 continued to include a huge variety of cultivators, including this Standard Walking Cultivator. Despite the popularity of riding cultivators, some farmers refused to use them, opting instead to walk behind their team.

Emerson-Brantingham was innovative in offering specialized implements for specialized purposes. Included was this 1919 model of its No. 1 Beet Cultivator, a unit designed especially for the purpose. It was intended to cultivate four rows at a time. E-B also built a few copies of a motor cultivator. Before it had fully

developed a tractor-mounted design, the company was bought out by J.I. Case Co., in 1928.

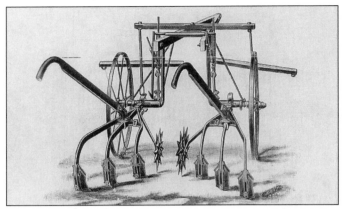

A.B. Farquhar Co., Ltd., York, Pa.

Farquhar was an old established machinery builder; at the turn of the century, it was offering its Pennsylvania Steel Walking Cultivator as part of an extensive line. Various styles and options were available; the rolling shield is an innovative feature.

Frost & Wood Co., Ltd., Smiths Falls, Ontario

Already in 1910, Frost & Wood was offering its Champion Cultivator for tractor power. It was essentially a field cultivator, although that specific term was not much used at the time. This one could be furnished with various kinds of teeth and was ordinarily furnished with 17 shanks.

Hartman Manufacturing Co., Vincennes, Ind.

The Pilot Disc Cultivator was available from Hartman in this 1907 advertisement. Although it was designed as a disc cultivator, the latter could be replaced with shovels, if so desired, thus making it a conventional cultivator. Little else is known of the company outside of this 1907 advertisement.

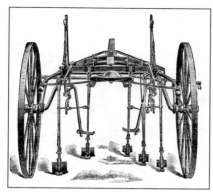

Hayes Pump & Planter Co., Galva, Ill.

Hayes, like many other implement manufacturers, advertised in German-language journals, such as the German edition of the *American Agriculturist*. An 1895 advertisement in the latter illustrates Hayes Perfect Balance Cultivator. This was an all-steel design. Note that it could be furnished with four or six shovels, as desired; the left gang has a pair, with three shovels on the right gang.

Hayes was a well-known planter manufacturer and also gained considerable fame with its cultivators. The Hayes Leila walking cultivator pictured here was a popular model that featured steel and malleable iron construction. The small tool box mounted on the tongue carried a couple of wrenches furnished specifically for this cultivator. This was a common practice at the time; usually these wrenches had the name of the manufacturer cast in place.

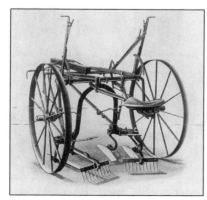

In addition to the usual line of shovel cultivators, Hayes also offered surface cultivators. As illustrated here, the sharpened steel blades ran just below the surface of the ground, cutting off

the weeds with minimum disturbance of the soil. Small rakes behind them leveled the ground. Hayes eventually merged with others to form Farm Tools, Inc.

Hench & Dromgold, York, Pa.

According to the company's own 1889 advertising, Hench's Riding or Walking Steel Cultivator had already been on the market for a decade. As pointed out various times in this section, it was important for manufacturers to give farmers the option to walk or ride, since many farmers thought that to ride was "the mark of a lazy man," and further, that to ride was to "kill the horses."

International Harvester Co., Chicago, Ill.

International Harvester did little in the way of making cultivators until about 1915. However, its International No. 9 walking cultivator shown here was an ultra-modern style for its time, with pipe beams, four shovels and spring-trip shanks.

Much of the early IHC cultivator line was a carryover from the Osborne line that Harvester had purchased earlier and then later divested. The International No. 4 pivot-axle cultivator shown here was billed as being "the most popular riding cultivator made." While the contention was probably impossible to prove (or disprove), there is not a doubt that IHC cultivators were well known and accepted.

Janesville Machine Co., Janesville, Wisc.

In 1887, Janesville Machine Co., was offering this riding-disc cultivator. It was entirely of wooden construction; even the beams were made of wood. Eventually, this firm was taken over by the Samson Tractor Co., also of Janesville; the latter was a part of Bill Durant's automotive empire known as General Motors.

L.H. Katelman Co., Council Bluffs, Iowa

Katelman offered this new-style cultivator with 50-inch wheels in 1930. Designed as the ultimate in one-row cultivators, the EM-7 Badger model was ordinarily furnished with break-pin shanks as shown and could also be furnished with spring shanks if so desired. Parts for these cultivators could be furnished direct from Katelman at least as late as 1948.

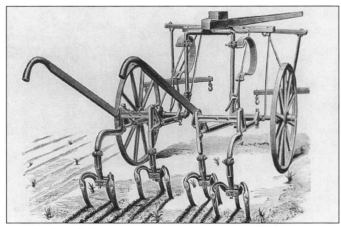

Kimberlin Manufacturing Co., Indianapolis, Ind.

Kimberlin offered this walking cultivator in 1887, noting that it was made under the Davis patent. Possibly, this referred to the

unique spring-design used to carry the weight of the cultivator gangs. Virtually nothing further is known of the company, apart from this 1887 advertisement.

Kingman Plow Co., Peoria, Ill.

In 1907, Kingman offered its Heretis cultivator as part of a somewhat larger line. This was a combination machine that permitted the farmer to walk or ride, as desired. Kingman eventually went out of business, but, into the 1920s at least, parts for the Heretis were available from the firm of Martin & Kennedy, Kansas City.

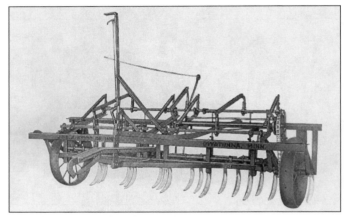

Joseph J. Kovar Co., Inc., Owatonna, Minn.

In the 1930s, Kovar perfected a field cultivator design that became quite popular. The Model C pictured here was 9-feet wide and carried 18 teeth. Since tractor hydraulics were essentially unknown in the 1930s, a power lift system was required and can be seen in the illustration.

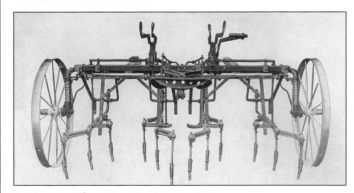

LaCrosse Plow Co., LaCrosse, Wisc.

This well-known company carved its own niche in the plow and tillage implement business, with its two-row cultivator being a part of the line. Although the basic design differed little from its contemporaries, the LaCrosse still had its own distinctive features. La-Crosse was taken over by Allis-Chalmers in 1929, forming the basis for the Allis-Chalmers tillage implement line.

Long & Alstatter Co., Hamilton, Ohio

Long & Alstatter was a pioneer in the tillage implement business, offering this adjustable arch cultivator in 1887. This was known as a bar-share cultivator. The huge dimensions of the beams are because they were made of wood.

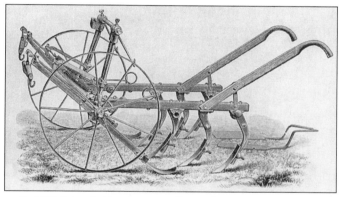

By 1899, Long & Alstatter was offering the Hamilton tongueless cultivator shown here along with numerous other styles. Some farmers preferred the tongueless design, although the majority of one-row cultivators were built with a tongue. Apparently, this style was produced at least into the mid-1920s.

Madison Plow Co., Madison, Wisc.

Madison Plow Co., was a successor to the tillage implement line, formerly made by Fuller & Johnson Co., also of Madison. This 1910 scene depicts what it was really like to cultivate corn one row at a time with a team. On close inspection, you can see the driver on the right has done the usual deed of tying the lines in a knot, putting them around his back and having both hands free to steer the plow beams.

Massey-Harris Co., Ltd., Toronto, Ontario

While the Massey-Harris line for the 1920s was especially popular in Canada, it was also sold to some extent in areas of the United States. After the company bought out J.I. Case Plow Works in Racine, Wis., in 1928, the company had a major base of operations in the United States; this two-horse combined cultivator was but one of many different designs offered by the company.

P.P. Mast & Co., Springfield, Ohio

For 1890, P.P. Mast offered its Sunbeam cultivators in various styles, including the New No. 4 Buckeye Sunbeam walking model shown here. By tying the lines around his shoulders the farmer could twist left or right to steer the team, meanwhile having both hands free to manipulate the cultivator gangs.

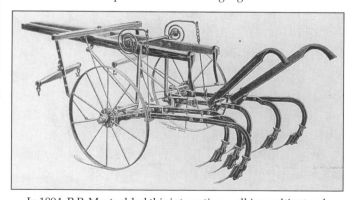

In 1894, P.P. Mast added this interesting walking cultivator design to the lineup. It used unique flat-coil springs on each side to help carry the weight of the cultivator beams. It also used a pair of wooden beams that tapered together at the end of the tongue; these carried the individual beams. Eventually, the Buckeye cultivators disappeared from the scene, but parts for the

Buckeye Sunbeam line were available from Oliver Corp., into the 1930s. P.P. Mast was part of the 1903 merger that formed American Seeding Machine Co.; the latter was part of the Oliver merger of 1929.

Mishawaka Plow Co., Mishawaka, Ind.

An 1887 advertisement claimed that the Indiana Wood Beam Tongueless Cultivator pictured here to be "the best wood beam cultivator in the world!" The high arch permitted cultivation even when corn was 2- to 3-feet high, just the time when many farmers wanted to "lay by" the crop until harvest. Apart from this advertisement, little is known of the company.

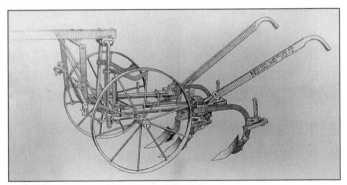

Moline Plow Co., Moline, Ill.

Moline Plow Co., was an immensely large manufacturer of plows and tillage implements. Its variety of cultivators was among the largest in the industry and included the Moline Strong Boy Cultivator No. 3, a walking model that was marketed at least into the 1920s. Moline Plow was a part of the 1929 merger that formed Minneapolis-Moline.

National Drill Co., Dublin, Ind.

Successful weed control was and is, imperative to a successful crop. Numerous cultivating methods were used. In 1903, National Drill Co., introduced this riding weeder. It was intended to destroy all the weeds in its path and was something akin to a field cultivator, but much less severe in its action.

New Process Manufacturing Co., Lincoln, Kan.

In 1905, New Process offered its Long Knife Cultivator; it was intended for listed corn and the company claimed that it made and sold more of these units than all other manufacturers of cultivators for listed corn. The unit as shown, carried a price of $8, plus shipping.

Ohio Cultivator Co., Bellevue, Ohio

In 1878, Harlow C. Stahl built his first double-gang cultivator with control of the gangs by the feet. His design was immensely successful. By the time this 1890 advertisement appeared for Ohio Cultivator Co., it was a widely recognized cultivator manufacturer. The firm remained in the market for decades to come.

Oliver Chilled Plow Works, South Bend, Ind.

From its humble beginnings, Oliver grew to be one of the world's largest plow makers, eventually merging with others to form Oliver Farm Equipment Co., 1929. Particularly in the 1930s,

Oliver began working with other manufacturers to develop cultivators, among them being a front-mounted design for the Cletrac from Cleveland Tractor Co. Despite the popularity of the Cletrac for other purposes, it met with a lukewarm reception as a cultivating tractor.

O'Neil Implement Co., Marseilles, Ill.

Little is known about this company, save for an early catalog (one that the author retrieved from Grandpa's attic nearly 50 years ago). The Flying Swede Terror was designed to weed and hill the growing plants. The company also built other implements in the Flying Swede line; by 1931, perhaps earlier, parts only were available from Wm. H. Rollo at Marseilles, Ill. Further details are unknown.

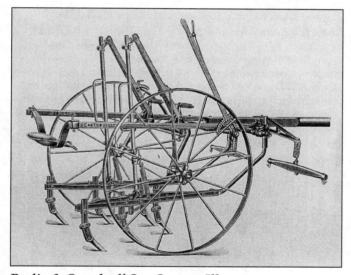

Parlin & Orendorff Co., Canton, Ill.

As noted in this book, P&O was a famous American plow maker. By the turn of the century, the company had developed its P&O Canton Line of implements, with this 1906 advertisement showing its Jewel Hammock cultivator. It was but one of a wide range of cultivators in one- and two-row styles.

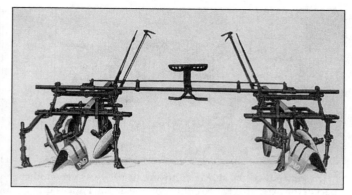

Already in 1909, P&O had contracted with International Harvester for the latter to sell the P&O line in Canada. This greatly stabilized the company's business, since IHC could be counted on to do an excellent marketing job in that country. Ten years later, in 1919, IHC bought out P&O, thus putting the company firmly into an established line of tillage implements. One example is the P&O No. 28 two-row lister cultivator shown here; it is of 1920 vintage.

Pattee Plow Co., Monmouth, Ill.

Pattee Plow Co., was an important part of the tillage implement line for many years, although this firm was not nearly so large as some of its competitors. A 1911 catalog illustration depicts its New Departure walking plow with wood-beam gangs. This was a tongueless design.

A very popular cultivator was the Jenny Lind, shown here from a 1911 Pattee catalog. Jenny Lind (1820-1887) was a very popular Swedish soprano who spent a great deal of time in the United States. Naming a cultivator after her undoubtedly gained a lot of attention at the time.

The Pattee two-row shovel cultivator of 1911 was yet another part of the extensive Pattee cultivator line. Many Pattee cultivators were built for decades; the Jenny Lind for example, was shown in the implement directories into the 1940s; but by this time the era of horse-drawn equipment was rapidly coming to a close.

D.C. & H.C. Reed, Kalamazoo, Mich.

This firm saw first light in the 1870s as the first manufacturer of a successful spring-tooth harrow. Its crowning success led to other tillage implements, including a line of cultivators. Shown here is an 1890 example of Reeds' No. 10 riding cultivator; this one is equipped with special spring-tooth shovels secured to wooden beams.

Rock Island Plow Co., Rock Island, Ill.

Rock Island Plow Co., had roots going back to 1855 as the firm of Tate & Buford. By 1887, the company was advertising its Rock Island Tongueless cultivator as part of the tillage equipment line. This one utilized wooden beams, plus cast-iron wheels cast in place over steel spokes.

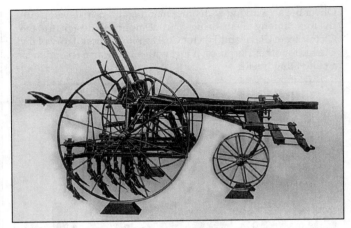

The Rock Island cultivator line was so extensive that several pages of this book could be devoted solely to its various cultivators. Shown here is its No. 112 two-row cultivator of the 1920s. It was equipped with front truck to carry the weight of the cultivator rather than transfer it to the horse's necks. Rock Island was sold to J.I. Case Co., in 1937.

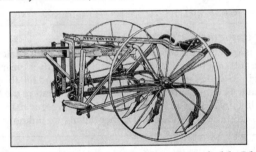

Roderick Lean Manufacturing Co., Mansfield, Ohio

Roderick Lean was the name of the man who founded this company in 1870. Among its extensive line of tillage implements was its New Century cultivator, said to be the original leverless cultivator. This one was perhaps the most popular of the line and remained in production even after Roderick Lean merged with others in 1930 to form Farm Tools, Inc.

Rude Bros., Manufacturing Co., Liberty, Ind.

The early adventures of Rude Bros., Manufacturing Co., are unknown. By 1894, the company was offering an extensive line of cultivators, including the Indiana wood-beam tongueless cultivator, shown here. The firm claimed it to be the "Best Wood Beam Cultivator in the World." Eventually, the company got into the manufacture of manure spreaders, concentrating its efforts on this endeavor, plus grain drills and other equipment.

Racine-Sattley Co., Springfield, Ill.

Like many other cultivator builders, Sattley was wont to use interesting trade names for its products. The Corker Walking Cultivator of 1910 was one such example. Other walking cultivators of that time included the Monarch Southern, Winner and Sattley models. All of these were walking cultivators. Sattley's riding cultivators of 1910 included the Happy Thought, Noxall and Texas Special.

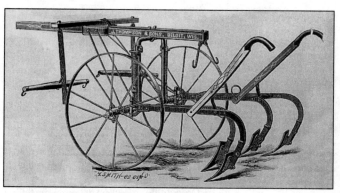

J. Thompson & Sons, Beloit, Wisc.

This firm had become an important implement manufacturer by the time this 1887 advertisement appeared. It pictures the Ole Olson Tongueless Sulky Plow, but one of the many different cultivators available at the time from Thompson. For a cultivator of 1887, this one was innovative because it used steel beams at a time when wood beams were far more common. Thompson remained in the implement business for some years; by 1910, the company appears to have concentrated most of its efforts on manufacturing gasoline engines.

J.D. Tower & Sons Co., Mendota, Ill.

Tower pioneered a system of surface cultivation for corn. A study of this 1912 illustration demonstrates the unique knives that served

to skim beneath the surface of the soil, effectively cutting off weeds beneath the ground, while loosening the top soil. Nothing can be found concerning this firm after the late 1920s.

Weir Plow Co., Monmouth, Ill.

An unidentified photograph in the authors collection illustrates a very early example of a Weir cultivator (in this case, the printer even misspelled the name). The beams could pivot on their standards, thus permitting the driver to dodge the corn as necessary. This illustration is probably from the 1860s.

By 1887, the Weir Plow Co., was making an extensive line of cultivators, including this "Iron Beam Spring Cultivator." The flat steel springs mounted to the arch were adjustable and made it easy for the driver to keep the gangs at the proper cultivating depth. No further information has been found on this company.

Trade Names

Acme	Geo. W. Brown Co.	Galesburg, IL	1892
Acme	Hartman Mfg. Co.	Vincennes, IN	1892
Acme	Hartman Mfg. Co.	Vincennes, IN	1905
Adams	Marseilles Mfg. Co.	Marseilles, IL	1892
Admiral	J. I. Case Plow Works	Racine, WI	1905
Admiral	Morrison Mfg Co.	Fort Madison, IA	1905
Ajax	Avery Company	Peoria, IL	1905
Ajax	E. Bement's Sons	Lansing, MI	1905
Ajax	Rock Island Plow Co.	Rock Island, IL	1892
Akron	Akron Tool Co.	Akron, OH	1892
Albion	Gale Mfg. Co.	Albion, MI	1905
Albright	J. H. Albright & Son	Millersburg, PA	1905
All-Steel	Toledo Plow Co.	Toledo, OH	1905
America	Sattley Mfg. Co.	Springfield, IL	1892
American	American Harrow Co.	Detroit, MI	1905
American	American Plow Co.	Madison, WI	1905
American Junior	American Harrow Co.	Detroit, MI	1905
American Special	American Harrow Co.	Detroit, MI	1905

Trade Names (cont...)

Antelope	Deere & Co.	Moline, IL	1892
Arion	Rock Island Plow Co.	Rock Island, IL	1892
Arnold	G. W. Arnold & Son	Ionia, MI	1892
Atchison Dandy	Bailor Plow Co.	Atchison, KS	1915
Atlanta	Atlanta Agricultural Works	Atlanta, GA	1905
Atwood	Rock Island Plow Co.	Rock Island, IL	1905
Auto	Emerson-Brantingham Co.	Rockford. IL	1913
Autocrat	Rock Island Plow Co.	Rock Island. IL	1905
Automatic Lift	J. I. Case Plow Works	Racine. WI	1913
Avery	B. F. Avery & Sons	Louisville. KY	1905
Avery's Comet	B. F. Avery & Sons	Louisville. KY	1905
Avery's Zebra	B. F. Avery & Sons	Louisville. KY	1905
Axtell	Rockford Mfg. Co.	Rockford. IL	1892
B. I. W.	Chase-Tinsman Plow Co.	Lincoln, NE	1922
Babcock	Babcock Mfg. Co.	Leonardsville, NY	1929
Badger	E. Children's Sons Co.	East Dubuque, IL	1892
Badger	Eagle Mfg. Co.	Kansas City, MO	1905
Baker-Shevlin	Baker & Shevlin	Schuylerville, NY	1892
Balance All	Gale Mfg. Co.	Albion, MI	1905
Bald Eagle	Eagle Mfg. Co.	Davenport, IA	1892
Baldwin's American	Donaldson Bros.	Mt. Clemens, MI	1909
Banner	Brown-Manly Plow Co.	Malta, OH	1905
Banner	Racine-Sattley Co.	Springfield, IL	1905
Banner	Sattley Mfg. Co.	Springfield, IL	1892
Beatrice	Chase-Tinsman Plow Co.	Lincoln, NE	1922
Beaver	J. S. Rowell Mfg. Co.	Beaver Dam, WI	1909
Bellevue	Ohio Cultivator Co.	Bellevue, OH	1905
Beloit	Pattee Plow Co.	Monmouth, IL	1909
Bement	E. Bement's Sons	Lansing, MI	1905
Bement Peerless	E. Bement's Sons	Lansing, MI	1905
Bement Texas	E. Bement's Sons	Lansing, MI	1905
Ben Hur	Kingman Plow Co.	Peoria, IL	1909
Best	Clipper Plow Co.	Defiance, OH	1905
Best	Marseilles Mfg. Co.	Marseilles, IL	1892
Best Girl	Morrison Mfg. Co.	Fort Madison, IA	1905
Best Yet	Moline Plow Co.	Moline, IL	1905
Black Hawk	D. M. Sechler Carriage Co.	Moline, IL	1905
Blount's True Blue	Henry F. Blount	Evansville, IN	1905
Blue Bird	Grand Detour Plow Co.	Dixon, IL	1905
Blue Grass	Brown Mfg. Co.	Zanesville, OH	1905
Blue Ribbon	Rock Island Plow Co.	Rock Island, IL	1905
Blue Valley	Blue Valley Foundry Co.	Manhattan, KS	1892
Bob Tail	Gale Mfg. Co.	Albion, MI	1915
Bobolink	Janesville Machine Co.	Janesville, WI	1905
Bonanza	Fuller & Johnson Mfg. Co.	Madison, WI	1905
Bonanza	Madison Plow Co.	Madison, WI	1913
Boss	D. O. Everest Co.	Pine Grove Mills, MI	1892
Boss	LaCrosse Plow Co.	LaCrosse, WI	1905
Bower City	Janesville Machine Co.	Janesville, WI	1905
Boys	Hapgood Plow Co.	Alton, IL	1892
Bradley	David Bradley Mfg. Co.	Bradley, IL	1892
Bradley Vulcan	David Bradley Mfg. Co.	Bradley, IL	1892
Brigadier	Moline Plow Co.	Moline, IL	1892
Briggs	Burton Handle Co.	Burton, OH	1892
Brown	Brown Mfg. Co.	Zanesville, OH	1905
Buckeye	P. P. Mast Co.	Springfield, OH	1905
Buckeye Sunbeam	P. P. Mast Co.	Springfield, OH	1905

Trade Names (cont...)

Buford	Rock Island Plow Co.	Rock Island, IL	1892
Bully Boy	Rock Island Plow Co.	Rock Island, IL	1905
Burnham	Charles City Mfg. Co.	Charles City, IA	1892
Busy Bee	Pattee Plow Co.	Monmouth, IL	1905
Busy Bee	Pattee Plow Co.	Monmouth, IL	1915
C. H. D.	Deere & Co.	Moline, IL	1905
C. T.	Greenville Implement Co.	Greenville, MI	1905
Cahill	L. Cahill & Co.	Kalamazoo, MI	1892
Canton	Parlin & Orendorff Co.	Canton, IL	1905
Captain	Brown Mfg. Co.	Zanesville, OH	1919
Carpo	Akron Cultivator Co.	Akron, OH	1905
Casaday	South Bend Chilled Plow Co.	South Bend, IN	1909
Case	J. I. Case Co.	Racine, WI	1929
Case Easy	J. I. Case Plow Works	Racine, WI	1905
Castile	Castile Chilled Plow Co.	Castile, NY	1905
Centennial	Hussey Plow Co.	North Berwick, ME	1905
Centerfield	Pekin Plow Co.	Pekin, IL	1905
Challenge	South Bend Chilled Plow Co.	South Bend, IN	1905
Champion	Hench & Dromgold Co.	York, PA	1905
Chancellor	Kingman Plow Co.	Peoria, IL	1905
Climax	Sandwich Enterprise Co.	Sandwich, IL	1892
Climax	Thomas Peppler	Hightstown, NJ	1892
Clipper	Clipper Chilled Plow Co.	Elmira, NY	1892
Clipper	Clipper Plow Co.	Defiance, OH	1905
Clipper	Janesville Machine Co.	Janesville, WI	1905
Clipper	Kingman Plow Co.	Peoria, IL	1905
Clipper Jr.	Parlin & Orendorff Co.	Canton, IL	1892
Clipper Sr.	Parlin & Orendorff Co.	Canton, IL	1892
Collins	Collins Plow Co.	Quincy, IL	1892
Colonel	Grand Detour Plow Co.	Dixon, IL	1913
Columbia	Deere & Co.	Moline, IL	1892
Combined Jr.	Kingman Plow Co.	Peoria, IL	1905
Combined Sr.	Kingman Plow Co.	Peoria, IL	1905
Comet	B. F. Avery & Sons	Louisville, KY	1905
Commander	Moline Plow Co.	Moline, IL	1905
Common Sense	Brown-Manly Plow Co.	Malta, OH	1905
Common Sense	David Bradley Mfg. Co.	Bradley, IL	1905
Competitor	Collins Plow Co.	Quincy, IL	1915
Conqueror	LaCrosse Plow Co.	LaCrosse, WI	1905
Corker	Grand Detour Plow Co.	Dixon, IL	1905
Corker	Racine-Sattley Co.	Springfield, IL	1905
Corn Dodger	Moline Plow Co.	Moline, IL	1905
Corn King	Marseilles Mfg. Co.	Marseilles, IL	1892
Corn Maker	LaCrosse Plow Co.	LaCrosse, WI	1905
Corn Palace	Sioux City Plow Co.	Sioux City, IA	1892
Corn Queen	Grand Detour Plow Co.	Dixon, IL	1905
Crown	Janesville Machine Co.	Janesville, WI	1905
Curry	Curry Mfg. Co.	Florence, AL	1892
Cutaway	Cutaway Harrow Co.	Higganum, CT	1892
Cyclone	Kingman Plow Co.	Peoria, IL	1905

Trade Names (cont...)

Cyclone	Sattley Mfg. Co.	Springfield, IL	1892
Czar	Hayes Pump & Planter Co.	Galva, IL	1905
Czar	Hayes Pump & Planter Co.	Galva, IL	1909
Daisy	Gale Mfg. Co.	Albion, MI	1905
Daisy	S. R. White & Bro.	Norfolk, VA	1905
Dakota	Beaver Dam Mfg. Co.	Beaver Dam, WI	1922
Dan Webster	R. C. Buckley	Peoria, IL	1892
Dandy	F. B. Tait & Co.	Decatur, IL	1892
Dandy	Mishawaka Plow Co.	Mishawaka, IN	1905
Dandy	Moline Plow Co.	Moline, IL	1905
Daniel Boone	B. F. Avery & Sons	Louisville, KY	1909
Dauntless	Collins Plow Co.	Quincy, IL	1905
Davis	Evan Davis & Son	Butler, MD	1892
Dayton	Ohio Rake Co.	Dayton, OH	1909
Dead Easy	Texas Implement & Machine Co.	Dallas, TX	1909
Deere	Deere & Co.	Moline, IL	1905
Deere	Deere & Co.	Moline, IL	1905
Deere	Deere & Mansur Co.	Moline, IL	1905
Deere Crescent	Deere & Mansur Co.	Moline, IL	1905
Deere World	Deere & Co.	Moline, IL	1905
Delight	Charles City Mfg. Co.	Charles City, IA	1892
Dempster	Dempster Mill Mfg. Co.	Beatrice, NE	1905
Dempster	Dempster Mill Mfg. Co.	Beatrice, NE	1909
Detroit	American Harrow Co.	Detroit, MI	1905
Dew Drop	J. I. Case Plow Works	Racine, WI	1905
Dewey	Brown Mfg. Co.	Zanesville, OH	1905
Dewey	Hayes Pump & Planter Co.	Galva, IL	1905
Dewey	Rockford Mfg. Co.	Rockford, IL	1905
Diamond	Standard Harrow Co.	Utica, NY	1905
Diamond	Superior Land Roller Co.	Gouverneur, NY	1892
Dictator	Rock Island Plow Co.	Rock Island, IL	1905
Dirigo	F. C. Merrill	South Paris, ME	1892
Dixie	Gale Mfg. Co.	Albion, MI	1905
Dodger	Grand Detour Plow Co.	Dixon, IL	1905
Dolphin	David Bradley Mfg. Co.	Bradley, IL	1905
Dolphin Jr.	David Bradley Mfg. Co.	Bradley, IL	1905
Duckfoot	Benicia Agricultural Works	Benicia, CA	1892
Dude	Hapgood Plow Co.	Alton, IL	1892
Duke	Hayes Pump & Planter Co.	Galva, IL	1905
Duplex	David Bradley Mfg. Co.	Bradley, IL	1892
Dutch Twins	Moline Plow Co.	Moline, IL	1905
Dutch Uncle	Moline Plow Co.	Moline, IL	1905
Eagle	Eagle Mfg. Co.	Kansas City, MO	1905
Eagle	Mishawaka Plow Co.	Mishawaka, IN	1905
Eagle Hammock	Eagle Mfg. Co.	Kansas City, MO	1905
Eastern Dandy	Moline Plow Co.	Moline, IL	1922
Easy	Avery Company	Peoria, IL	1905
Easy Buckeye	P. P. Mast Co.	Springfield, OH	1905
Easy Shift	Brown Mfg. Co.	Zanesville, OH	1922
Easy Way	Racine-Sattley Co.	Springfield, IL	1909
E-B	Emerson-Brantingham Co.	Rockford, IL	1922

Trade Names (cont...)

Eclipse	J. I. Case Plow Works	Racine, WI	1905
Edwards	Peru Plow & Wheel Co.	Peru, IL	1905
Ellwood	Abram Ellwood	Sycamore, IL	1892
Elmwood	Hench & Dromgold Co.	York, PA	1919
Emerson	Emerson Mfg. Co.	Rockford, IL	1905
Emerson Diamond	Emerson Mfg. Co.	Rockford, IL	1905
Emerson Standard	Emerson Mfg. Co.	Rockford, IL	1905
Empire	Empire Mfg. Co.	Keokuk, IA	1892
Empire	Empire Plow Co.	Cleveland, OH	1905
Empire	South Bend Chilled Plow Co.	South Bend, IN	1905
Empress	Gale Mfg. Co.	Albion, MI	1905
Enterprise	Sandwich Enterprise Co.	Sandwich, IL	1892
Eureka	Eureka Mower Co.	Utica, NY	1905
Eureka	Wm. M. Johnston	Wilmot, OH	1892
Evolution	Roderick Lean Mfg. Co.	Mansfield, OH	1913
Excelsior	Belcher & Taylor Agricultural Tool Co.	Chicopee Falls, MA	1905
F. A. H.	Rock Island Plow Co.	Rock Island, IL	1909
Famous	Brown Mfg. Co.	Zanesville, OH	1892
Famous Ohio	Ohio Cultivator Co.	Bellevue, OH	1905
Farmer	J. I. Case Plow Works	Racine, WI	1905
Farmer Boy	Beatrice Iron Works	Beatrice, NE	1915
Farmer's Delight	B. F. Avery & Sons	Louisville, KY	1892
Farmers Delight	Hartman Mfg. Co.	Vincennes, IN	1905
Farmer's Favorite	Brown Mfg. Co.	Zanesville, OH	1905
Farmers Friend	C. Sommars	Boone, IA	1892
Farquhar	A. B. Farquhar Co.	York, PA	1905
Fast Mail	Pattee Plow Co.	Monmouth, IL	1905
Favorite	Standard Harrow Co.	Utica, NY	1905
Fawn Jr.	Deere & Co.	Moline, IL	1905
Forkner	Light Draft Harrow Co.	Marshalltown, IA	1922
Fort Madison	Morrison Mfg. Co.	Fort Madison, IA	1905
Fosmir's Economy	Fosmir Iron Works	Los Angeles, CA	1892
Fountain	Charles Hutchinson	Ceresco, MI	1892
Fountain City	American Seeding Machine Co.	Springfield, OH	1913
Fowler	Harriman Mfg. Co.	Harriman, TN	1922
Front Rank	Rude Bros. Mfg. Co.	Liberty, IN	1905
Frye's	John J. Frye	Portland, ME	1892
Frye	John J. Frye	Portland, ME	1905
Fuller & Johnson	Fuller & Johnson Mfg. Co.	Madison, WI	1905
Fuller & Johnson	Fuller & Johnson Mfg. Co.	Madison, WI	1905
Gale	Gale Mfg. Co.	Albion, MI	1892
Gazelle	Mishawaka Plow Co.	Mishawaka, IN	1905
Genuine Brown	Brown Mfg. Co.	Zanesville, OH	1905
Gesley	Gesley Mfg. Co.	Beloit, WI	1892
Giant	Donaldson Bros.	Mt. Clemens, MI	1905
Globe	Skandia Plow Co.	Rockford, IL	1892
Go Easy	LaCrosse Plow Co.	LaCrosse, WI	1905
Gohn	Brown Mfg. Co.	Zanesville, OH	1905
Golden Eagle	Eagle Mfg. Co.	Davenport, IA	1892
Golden Eagle	Eagle Mfg. Co.	Kansas City, MO	1905
Golden Rule	Moline Plow Co.	Moline, IL	1905
Gowanda	Gowanda Agricultural Works	Gowanda, NY	1905
Grand Detour	Grand Detour Plow Co.	Dixon, IL	1892
Gray Eagle	Eagle Mfg. Co.	Davenport, IA	1892
Great West	Gale Mfg. Co.	Albion, MI	1915

Trade Names (cont...)

Greentown	Greentown Foundry Co.	Greentown, OH	1892
H & D	Hench & Dromgold Co.	York, PA	1905
Hamilton	Long & Alstatter Co.	Hamilton, OH	1905
Hammock Jr.	Kingman Plow Co.	Peoria, IL	1905
Hammock King	Fuller & Johnson Mfg. Co.	Madison, WI	1905
Hammock King	Ohio Rake Co.	Dayton, OH	1905
Hammock Sr.	Kingman Plow Co.	Peoria, IL	1905
Handy Brown	Brown Mfg. Co.	Zanesville, OH	1905
Handy Buckeye	P. P. Mast Co.	Springfield, OH	1905
Happy Thought	Racine-Sattley Co.	Springfield, IL	1913
Hartford	Hartford Plow Works	Hartford, WI	1905
Hartman	Hartman Mfg. Co.	Vincennes, IN	1905
Hawkeye	Morrison Mfg. Co.	Fort Madison, IA	1905
Hawkins	Hartman Mfg. Co.	Vincennes, IN	1913
Hayes Combined	Hayes Pump & Planter Co.	Galva, IL	1905
Hayes Hammock	Hayes Pump & Planter Co.	Galva, IL	1905
Hench's 20th Century	Hench & Dromgold Co.	York, PA	1905
Hench's Improved	Hench & Dromgold Co.	York, PA	1905
Hench's Junior	Hench & Dromgold Co.	York, PA	1905
Herendeen	Herendeen Mfg. Co.	Geneva, NY	1892
Heretis	King & Hamilton	Ottawa, IL	1909
Hero	Hayes Pump & Planter Co.	Galva, IL	1905
Hero	Rock Island Plow Co.	Rock Island, IL	1892
Higganum	Cutaway Harrow Co.	Higganum, CT	1892
High Ball	David Bradley Mfg. Co.	Bradley, IL	1905
Hiram	Rockford Mfg. Co.	Rockford, IL	1905
Hobo	Lehr Agricultural Co.	Fremont, OH	1905
Hoke	Hoke Mfg. Co.	Frankfort, IN	1909
Holt	Hartman Mfg. Co.	Vincennes, IN	1913
Hoosier Belle	Mishawaka Plow Co.	Mishawaka, IN	1905
Hoosier Belle	St. Joseph Mfg. Co.	Mishawaka, IN	1892
Hoosier Boy	Reeves & Co.	Columbus, IN	1892
Hoosier Boy	St. Joseph Mfg. Co.	Mishawaka, IN	1892
Hudson Bicycle	Riverhead Agricultural Works	Riverhead, NY	1892
Hummer	Racine-Sattley Co.	Springfield, IL	1915
Hurrah	David Bradley Mfg. Co.	Bradley, IL	1905
I. A. Special	S. R. White & Bro.	Norfolk, VA	1905
I. H. C.	International Harvester Co.	Chicago, IL	1913
I. X. L.	Rude Bros. Mfg. Co.	Liberty, IN	1892
Ideal	Bucher & Gibbs Plow Co.	Canton, OH	1905
Ideal	H. P. Deuscher Co.	Hamilton, OH	1905
Ideal	J. I. Case Plow Works	Racine, WI	1905
Ideal	Rock Island Plow Co.	Rock Island, IL	1905
Illanoy	Collins Plow Co.	Quincy, IL	1905
Illinois	Kingman Plow Co.	Peoria, IL	1905
Illinois	Rhea-Thielens Implement Co.	Peoria, IL	1905
Imperial	Sattley Mfg. Co.	Springfield, IL	1892
Independent	Independent Harvester Co.	Plano, IL	1922
Independent	J. S. Rowell Mfg. Co.	Beaver Dam, WI	1909
Indiana	Mishawaka Plow Co.	Mishawaka, IN	1905
International	International Harvester Co.	Chicago, IL	1915

Trade Names (cont...)

Invigorator	Whipple Harrow Co.	St. John's, MI	1892
Invincible	Parlin & Orendorff Co.	Canton, IL	1905
Iowa	Collins Plow Co.	Quincy, IL	1905
Iron Age	Bateman Mfg. Co.	Grenloch, NJ	1905
Iron Age	E. S. & F. Bateman	Grenloch, NJ	1892
Iron King	Abram Ellwood	Sycamore, IL	1892
J. B. M.	Morrison Mfg Co.	Fort Madison, IA	1905
J. H. B.	David Bradley Mfg. Co.	Bradley, IL	1905
J. H. B.	David Bradley Mfg. Co.	Bradley, IL	1909
J. W. B.	Collins Plow Co.	Quincy, IL	1905
Janesville	Janesville Machine Co.	Janesville, WI	1905
Jap	Lehr Agricultural Co.	Fremont, OH	1909
Jap	Lehr Agricultural Co.	Fremont, OH	1913
Jay Bird	Grand Detour Plow Co.	Dixon, IL	1905
Jay Eye See	J. I. Case Plow Works	Racine, WI	1915
Jenny Lind	Pattee Plow Co.	Monmouth, IL	1905
Jewel	Parlin & Orendorff Co.	Canton, IL	1905
Johnson	Belcher & Taylor Agricultural Tool Co.	Chicopee Falls, MA	1913
Johnston Continental	Johnston Harvester Co.	Batavia, NY	1905
Joker	Moline Plow Co.	Moline, IL	1892
Joy Rider	B. F. Avery & Sons	Louisville, KY	1915
Jubilee	Brown-Manly Plow Co.	Malta, OH	1905
Kalamazoo	D. C. & H. C. Reed & Co.	Kalamazoo, MI	1892
Kansas Mystic Jr.	Avery Company	Peoria, IL	1905
Katy Flyer	Eagle Mfg. Co.	Muskogee, OK	1915
Katydid	J. I. Case Plow Works	Racine, WI	1905
Kelly	G. A. Kelly Plow Co.	Longview, TX	1919
Kellyvator	G. A. Kelly Plow Co.	Longview, TX	1929
Keystone	Keystone Farm Machine Co.	York, PA	1905
Killefer	Killefer Mfg. Co.	Los Angeles, CA	1924
King	Donaldson Bros.	Mt. Clemens, MI	1892
King	Parlin & Orendorff Co.	Canton, IL	1905
King Bee	E. Bement's Sons	Lansing, MI	1905
King of All	Taylor & Henry	Kalamazoo, MI	1892
Kingman Jr.	Kingman Plow Co.	Peoria, IL	1905
Kingman Sr.	Kingman Plow Co.	Peoria, IL	1905
Klondike	David Bradley Mfg. Co.	Bradley, IL	1905
Klondike Jr.	David Bradley Mfg. Co.	Bradley, IL	1905
Knowlton	Skandia Plow Co.	Rockford, IL	1892
Korn King	Gale Mfg. Co.	Albion, MI	1905
Korn Koaxer	Peru Plow & Wheel Co.	Peru, IL	1909
Kovar	Joseph J. Kovar	Owatonna, MN	1924
Kraus	Akron Cultivator Co.	Akron, OH	1905
Kraus Junior	Akron Cultivator Co.	Akron, OH	1905
Lancaster	Frank Maute	Lancaster, NY	1892
Lansing	E. Bement's Sons	Lansing, MI	1892
Laurel	Thomas Meikle & Co.	Louisville, KY	1892
Lawrence	Lawrence & Chapin Co.	Kalamazoo, MI	1892
Leader	Hayes Pump & Planter Co.	Galva, IL	1905
Leho	Lehr Agricultural Co.	Fremont, OH	1919
Lehr	Lehr Agricultural Co.	Fremont, OH	1905
Leila	Hayes Pump & Planter Co.	Galva, IL	1905
LeRoy	LeRoy Plow Co.	LeRoy, NY	1924
Lester	Gale Mfg. Co.	Albion, MI	1905
Little Bee	E. Bement's Sons	Lansing, MI	1905

Trade Names (cont...)

Little Boy	King & Hamilton	Ottawa, IL	1905
Little Darling	Rude Bros. Mfg. Co.	Liberty, IN	1905
Little Giant	Howland Mfg. Co.	Pontiac, MI	1905
Little Giant	Ohio Cultivator Co.	Bellevue, OH	1905
Little John	Brown Mfg. Co.	Zanesville, OH	1915
Little Joker	Moline Plow Co.	Moline, IL	1905
Lone Star	Rock Island Plow Co.	Rock Island, IL	1905
Lucky Jim	B. F. Avery & Sons	Louisville, KY	1909
M. B. & B.	Mast, Buford & Burwell Co.	St. Paul, MN	1892
M. K. & T.	Eagle Mfg. Co.	Kansas City, MO	1905
Madison	Madison Plow Co.	Madison, WI	1915
Magnolia	Rock Island Plow Co.	Rock Island, IL	1905
Maiden	Grand Detour Plow Co.	Dixon, IL	1905
Majestic	J. S. Rowell Mfg. Co.	Beaver Dam, WI	1905
Major	Blount Plow Works	Evansville, IN	1915
Malta	Brown-Manly Plow Co.	Malta, OH	1909
Maltonian	Brown-Manly Plow Co.	Malta, OH	1905
Man-Weight	Prairie Mfg. Co.	Indianapolis, IN	1913
Marvel	Rude Bros. Mfg. Co.	Liberty, IN	1892
Mascot	Pekin Plow Co.	Pekin, IL	1905
Mascot	Rock Island Plow Co.	Rock Island, IL	1905
Massey-Harris	Massey-Harris Harvester Co.	Batavia, NY	1919
Maud S.	Peru Plow & Wheel Co.	Peru, IL	1892
Mayflower	Thomas Meikle & Co.	Louisville, KY	1892
McCormick	International Harvester Co.	Chicago, IL	1913
McCormick-Deering	International Harvester Co.	Chicago, IL	1924
McKinney	McKinney Traction Cultivator Co.	St. Louis, MO	1913
Midland	Midland Mfg. Co.	Tarkio, MO	1905
Miller's	F. W. Miller	Caledonia, NY	1892
Mishawaka	Mishawaka Plow Co.	Mishawaka, IN	1913
Mitchell	Rock Island Plow Co.	Rock Island, IL	1909
Moline	Moline Plow Co.	Moline, IL	1922
Monarch	Dowagiac Mfg. Co.	Dowagiac, MI	1892
Monarch	J. Thompson & Sons Mfg. Co.	Beloit, WI	1905
Monarch	Mishawaka Plow Co.	Mishawaka, IN	1905
Monarch	Ohio Rake Co.	Dayton, OH	1905
Monarch Southern	Racine-Sattley Co.	Springfield, IL	1905
Monitor	Brown-Manly Plow Co.	Malta, OH	1905
Monitor	Minneapolis Plow Works	Minneapolis, MN	1905
Monitor	Monitor Drill Co.	Minneapolis, MN	1913
Monitor	Star Mfg. Co.	Carpentersville, IL	1892
Moore	Moore Plow & Implement Co.	Greenville, MI	1905
Morrison	H. L. Miller	Morris, IL	1892
Morrison	Morrison Mfg Co.	Fort Madison, IA	1892
Morrow	R. F. Gaston	Woodward, OK	1922
Morse	Robt. E. Morse	Auburn, IL	1892
Munnsville	Munnsville Plow Co.	Munnsville, NY	1905
Munson	Okmulgee Implement & Mfg. Co.	Okmulgee, OK	1922
Mystic	Avery Company	Peoria, IL	1905
Mystic Jr.	Avery Company	Peoria, IL	1905
N. C. Thompson	H. B. Busing & Co.	Rockford, IL	1892

Trade Names (cont...)

Nachusa	Grand Detour Plow Co.	Dixon, IL	1905
National	National Drill Co.	Cambridge City, IN	1905
New Acme	Hartman Mfg. Co.	Vincennes, IN	1905
New Age	Ruos, Mills & Co.	Doylestown, PA	1905
New American	American Harrow Co.	Detroit, MI	1892
New Arrival	Morrison Mfg Co.	Fort Madison, IA	1905
New Badger	E. Children's Sons Co.	Council Bluffs, IA	1905
New Balance	Brown-Manly Plow Co.	Malta, OH	1905
New Bradley	David Bradley Mfg. Co.	Bradley, IL	1905
New Brown	Brown Mfg. Co.	Zanesville, OH	1905
New Buckeye	P. P. Mast Co.	Springfield, OH	1905
New Burch	Burch Plow Works Co.	Crestline, OH	1905
New Captain Kidd	Moline Plow Co.	Moline, IL	1905
New Century	Brown Mfg. Co.	Zanesville, OH	1905
New Century	Morrison Mfg Co.	Fort Madison, IA	1905
New Deere	Deere & Co.	Moline, IL	1905
New Departure	Pattee Plow Co.	Monmouth, IL	1892
New Eagle	Eagle Mfg. Co.	Kansas City, MO	1905
New Elk	Deere & Co.	Moline, IL	1905
New England	Belcher & Taylor Agricultural Tool Co.	Chicopee Falls, MA	1905
New Fremont	Lehr Agricultural Co.	Fremont, OH	1905
New Iowa	Collins Plow Co.	Quincy, IL	1905
New Iowa	Morrison Mfg Co.	Fort Madison, IA	1905
New Malta	Brown-Manly Plow Co.	Malta, OH	1905
New Market	South Bend Chilled Plow Co.	South Bend, IN	1892
New Market	Sparta Plow Works	Sparta, IL	1905
New Milford	Wells Cultivator Co.	Milford, MI	1892
New Model	Timothy B. Hussey	North Bewick, ME	1892
New Ohio	Ohio Cultivator Co.	Bellevue, OH	1905
New Sames	Peter Sames	Rockford, IL	1892
New Schofield	Gale Mfg. Co.	Albion, MI	1905
New South	B. F. Avery & Sons	Louisville, KY	1905
New Universal	Ames Plow Co.	Boston, MA	1905
New Western	Moline Plow Co.	Moline, IL	1892
New Western	Moline Plow Co.	Moline, IL	1905
Newago	Avery Company	Peoria, IL	1905
Ninety-Nine	Keystone Farm Machine Co.	York, PA	1909
No Name	Moline Plow Co.	Moline, IL	1905
Nome	J. I. Case Plow Works	Racine, WI	1905
Norman Junior	Rockford Mfg. Co.	Rockford, IL	1905
Normandie	J. Thompson & Sons Mfg. Co.	Beloit, WI	1905
Norwegian	J. Thompson & Sons Mfg. Co.	Beloit, WI	1905
Norwegian	Norwegian Plow Co.	Dubuque, IA	1892
Noxall	Racine-Sattley Co.	Springfield, IL	1905
O. K.	J. Thompson & Sons Mfg. Co.	Beloit, WI	1905
O. K.	LaCrosse Plow Co.	LaCrosse, WI	1905
Ohio	Brown-Manly Plow Co.	Malta, OH	1905
Ohio	Ohio Cultivator Co.	Bellevue, OH	1905
Ohio	Ohio Rake Co.	Dayton, OH	1905
Oklahoma	Swanson Mfg. Co.	Shenendoah, IA	1909
Old Pal	Roderick Lean Mfg. Co.	Mansfield, OH	1915
Old Reliable	Peter Sames	Rockford, IL	1892

Trade Names (cont...)

Oliver	Oliver Chilled Plow Works	South Bend, IN	1909
Only Way	Racine-Sattley Co.	Springfield, IL	1913
Orchard	Matteson & Williams Mfg. Co.	Stockton, CA	1892
Osborne	D. S. Osborne	Auburn, NY	1905
Osborne	International Harvester Co.	Chicago, IL	1913
Otsego	Babcock Mfg. Co.	Leonardsville, NY	1905
Ottawa	King & Hamilton	Ottawa, IL	1892
Overland	Pattee Plow Co.	Monmouth, IL	1913
P & O	Parlin & Orendorff Co.	Canton, IL	1915
Parlin	Parlin & Orendorff Co.	Canton, IL	1892
Pattee	Pattee Plow Co.	Monmouth, IL	1905
Peacock	Rock Island Plow Co.	Rock Island, IL	1905
Pearce's Patent	Grand Rapids Mfg. & Implement Co.	Grand Rapids, MI	1892
Pedro	Grand Detour Plow Co.	Dixon, IL	1905
Peerless	Rock Island Plow Co.	Rock Island, IL	1905
Pekin	Pekin Plow Co.	Pekin, IL	1892
Pennington	Towers & Sullivan Mfg. Co.	Rome, GA	1892
Pennsylvania	A. B. Farquhar Co.	York, PA	1905
Peoria	Millikin, Cisle & Co.	Peoria, IL	1892
Perfection	Stringer, Dexter & Coe	Munnsville, NY	1892
Perfecto	Parlin & Orendorff Co.	Canton, IL	1919
Peru	Peru Plow & Wheel Co.	Peru, IL	1905
Peterson	Mid-West Mfg. Co.	Cedar Falls, IA	1932
Pfeifer	Morrison Mfg Co.	Fort Madison, IA	1905
Pilot	Hartman Mfg. Co.	Vincennes, IN	1905
Ping Pong	Morrison Mfg Co.	Fort Madison, IA	1905
Pioneer	Peru Plow & Wheel Co.	Peru, IL	1905
Planet Jr.	S.L. Allen & Co.	Philadelphia, PA	1905
Planter's Pride	L. C. Lull & Co.	Kalamazoo, MI	1892
Planter's Pride	Ohio Rake Co.	Dayton, OH	1905
Plow Boy	Rock Island Plow Co.	Rock Island, IL	1909
Pontiac	Howland Mfg. Co.	Pontiac, MI	1905
Premier	Brown-Manly Plow Co.	Malta, OH	1905
Premium	Fort Madison Plow Co.	Fort Madison, IA	1913
Prime	Racine-Sattley Co.	Springfield, IL	1905
Princess	Mishawaka Plow Co.	Mishawaka, IN	1905
Princess	St. Joseph Mfg. Co.	Mishawaka, IN	1892
Prize	Kingman Plow Co.	Peoria, IL	1913
Q. I. C.	Rude Bros. Mfg. Co.	Liberty, IN	1905
Quail	Ohio Rake Co.	Dayton, OH	1905
Queen	Parlin & Orendorff Co.	Canton, IL	1905
Queen Anne	Moline Plow Co.	Moline, IL	1905
Queen Bee	E. Bement's Sons	Lansing, MI	1905
Quincy	Collins Plow Co.	Quincy, IL	1905
Racine	J. I. Case Plow Works	Racine, WI	1905
Rambler	Brown Mfg. Co.	Zanesville, OH	1919
Red Eagle	Eagle Mfg. Co.	Kansas City, MO	1905
Red Rider	David Bradley Mfg. Co.	Bradley, IL	1909
Reed	Reed Mfg. Co.	Kalamazoo, MI	1905
Reindeer	Deere & Co.	Moline, IL	1892

Trade Names (cont...)

Reliance	Brown-Manly Plow Co.	Malta, OH	1905
Revolution	B. F. Avery & Sons	Louisville, KY	1905
Rex	E. Bement's Sons	Lansing, MI	1905
Rex Hammock	Hayes Pump & Planter Co.	Galva, IL	1905
Rexford	George H. Rexford	Frankfort, KS	1892
Rival	Rude Bros. Mfg. Co.	Liberty, IN	1892
Rock Island	Rock Island Plow Co.	Rock Island, IL	1905
Rockford Tiger	Rockford Well Drill Co.	Rockford, IL	1909
Roderick Lean	Roderick Lean Mfg. Co.	Mansfield, OH	1905
Roderick Lean National	Roderick Lean Mfg. Co.	Mansfield, OH	1905
Rowell	I. B. Rowell Co.	Menomonee Falls, WI	1905
Rowell	J. S. Rowell Mfg. Co.	Beaver Dam, WI	1905
Royal	Deere & Co.	Moline, IL	1905
Royal	Gale Mfg. Co.	Albion, MI	1905
Royal	Peru Plow & Wheel Co.	Peru, IL	1905
Royal	Skandia Plow Co.	Rockford, IL	1892
Ruby	J. I. Case Plow Works	Racine, WI	1905
Sam Houston	G. A. Kelly Plow Co.	Longview, TX	1915
Sampson	Hayes Pump & Planter Co.	Galva, IL	1905
Samson	Hayes Pump & Planter Co.	Galva, IL	1909
San Jose	San Jose Agricultural Works	San Jose, CA	1892
Sangamo	Racine-Sattley Co.	Springfield, IL	1905
Sargent '76	S. R. Sargent & Son	Castleton, VT	1905
Sattley	Racine-Sattley Co.	Springfield, IL	1905
Schofield	Gale Mfg. Co.	Albion, MI	1905
Seatshift	Rock Island Plow Co.	Rock Island, IL	1922
See Saw	Moline Plow Co.	Moline, IL	1915
Seventy-Seven	Keystone Farm Machine Co.	York, PA	1909
Shallow-Cut	LaCrosse Plow Co.	LaCrosse, WI	1905
Shanghai Kid	Moline Plow Co.	Moline, IL	1905
She	Rock Island Plow Co.	Rock Island, IL	1892
Shew	Matt Shew	Cambridge City, IN	1905
Simplex	Lehr Agricultural Co.	Fremont, OH	1905
Skupemall	J. Thompson & Sons Mfg. Co.	Beloit, WI	1913
Slick	Hayes Pump & Planter Co.	Galva, IL	1905
South Bend	South Bend Chilled Plow Co.	South Bend, IN	1905
Southern	Kingman Plow Co.	Peoria, IL	1905
Southern Combined	Kingman Plow Co.	Peoria, IL	1905
Southern Kidd	Moline Plow Co.	Moline, IL	1905
Speechless	Avery Company	Peoria, IL	1892
Spring Beauty	Thomas Meikle & Co.	Louisville, KY	1892
St. Joseph	St. Joseph Plow Co.	St. Joseph, MO	1905
St. Joseph	St. Joseph Plow Co.	St. Joseph, MO	1905
Standard	A. C. Bruce	Lapeer, MI	1892
Standard	Emerson, Talcott & Co.	Rockford, IL	1892
Standard	Standard Harrow Co.	Utica, NY	1905
Standard	Taylor & Henry	Kalamazoo, MI	1892
Stapler	W. T. Stapler	Harmony Grove, GA	1892
Star	Carver Mfg. Co.	Carver, MN	1892
Star	Gale Mfg. Co.	Albion, MI	1905

Trade Names (cont...)

Star	Star Drill Co.	Rushville, IN	1892
Steel Age	Benicia Agricultural Works	Benicia, CA	1892
Steel King	Brown-Manly Plow Co.	Malta, OH	1905
Steel King	Donaldson Bros.	Mt. Clemens, MI	1905
Steel King	Lehr Agricultural Co.	Fremont, OH	1905
Steel King	Messinger Mfg. Co.	Tatamy, PA	1905
Steel Queen	Phelps Chilled Plow Works	Phelps, NY	1892
Stem Winder	David Bradley Mfg. Co.	Bradley, IL	1905
Sturgis	W. B. Sturgis	Shelbyville, IL	1892
Successor	Rude Bros. Mfg. Co.	Liberty, IN	1905
Sunshine	LaCrosse Plow Co.	LaCrosse, WI	1905
Superior	Fuller & Johnson Mfg. Co.	Madison, WI	1905
Superior	Rock Island Plow Co.	Rock Island, IL	1892
Superior	Stringer, Dexter & Coe	Munnsville, NY	1892
Superior	West & Townsend	Martinsville, OH	1905
Syracuse	Syracuse Chilled Plow Co.	Syracuse, NY	1905
Tango	Avery Company	Peoria, IL	1915
Tecumseh	Hartman Mfg. Co.	Vincennes, IN	1922
Teddy	Morrison Mfg Co.	Fort Madison, IA	1905
Teeter Totter	Kirlin Cultivator Co.	Kansas City, MO	1915
Terrell	Macon Agricultural Works	Macon, GA	1892
Texas Case	J. I. Case Plow Works	Racine, WI	1905
Texas Case Jr.	J. I. Case Plow Works	Racine, WI	1905
Texas Dandy	Moline Plow Co.	Moline, IL	1905
Texas New Brown	Brown Mfg. Co.	Zanesville, OH	1905
Thompson	J. Thompson & Sons Mfg. Co.	Beloit, WI	1905
Thompson	Rockford Implement Co.	Rockford, IL	1905
Thompson Hammock	J. Thompson & Sons Mfg. Co.	Beloit, WI	1905
Tiger	Rockford Mfg. Co.	Rockford, IL	1905
Tiger	Rockford Well Drill Co.	Rockford, IL	1905
Tiger	Stoddard Mfg. Co.	Dayton, OH	1905
Tip Top	Fuller & Johnson Mfg. Co.	Madison, WI	1905
Togo	Avery Company	Peoria, IL	1913
Toledo	Toledo Plow Co.	Toledo, OH	1905
Tongueless	Cass & McArthur	Harlan, IA	1892
Tower	J. D. Tower & Sons Co.	Mendota, IL	1892
Trojan	David Bradley Mfg. Co.	Bradley, IL	1905
Twin Badger	American Harrow Co.	Detroit, MI	1905
U. S.	J. I. Case Plow Works	Racine, WI	1905
U. T. K.	Chas. H. Childs & Co.	Utica, NY	1905
Umpire	Pekin Plow Co.	Pekin, IL	1905
Universal	Fuller & Johnson Mfg. Co.	Madison, WI	1905
Up-to-Date	Hapgood Plow Co.	Alton, IL	1913
Vacuna	Avery Company	Peoria, IL	1905
Van Brunt	Van Brunt Mfg. Co.	Horicon, WI	1905
Verybest	Kingman Plow Co.	Peoria, IL	1913
Veteran	Rock Island Plow Co.	Rock Island, IL	1905

Trade Names (cont...)

Vibert	F. C. Vibert	Hockanum, CT	1892
Victor	E. Bement's Sons	Lansing, MI	1905
Victor	Hayes Pump & Planter Co.	Galva, IL	1905
Victor	International Harvester Co.	Chicago, IL	1922
Victor	Sattley Mfg. Co.	Springfield, IL	1892
Victor Jr.	Parlin & Orendorff Co.	Canton, IL	1905
Volunteer	Parlin & Orendorff Co.	Canton, IL	1892
Wapello Chief	Fair, Williams & Co.	Ottumwa, IA	1892
Warsaw	Cress Bros. & Co.	Warsaw, IL	1892
Washtenaw	Ann Arbor Agricultural Co.	Ann Arbor, MI	1892
Washtenaw	Donaldson Bros.	Mt. Clemens, MI	1905
Webster	Charles City Mfg. Co.	Charles City, IA	1892
Weir	Kingman Plow Co.	Peoria, IL	1905
Weir	Weir Plow Co.	Monmouth, IL	1892
West Superior	Mast, Buford & Burwell Co.	St. Paul, MN	1892
Western	B. F. Avery & Sons	Louisville, KY	1905
Western King	Peru Plow & Wheel Co.	Peru, IL	1905
Whitehall	Whitehall Cultivator Mfg. Co.	Covington, IN	1892
Wide Spread	Fort Madison Plow Co.	Fort Madison, IA	1915
Wiggletail	International Harvester Co.	Chicago, IL	1922
Wilder	J. K. Wilder & Son	Monroe, MI	1892
Winner	Fuller & Johnson Mfg. Co.	Madison, WI	1905
Winner	Racine-Sattley Co.	Springfield, IL	1905
Wizard Jr.	J. I. Case Plow Works	Racine, WI	1905
Wolverine	Rock Island Plow Co.	Rock Island, IL	1915
Yankee Boy	Grand Detour Plow Co.	Dixon, IL	1905
Yankee Doodle	Grand Detour Plow Co.	Dixon, IL	1905
Yankee Girl	Grand Detour Plow Co.	Dixon, IL	1905
Yankee Maid	Grand Detour Plow Co.	Dixon, IL	1915
Yellow Kid	Pattee Plow Co.	Monmouth, IL	1905
Zebra	B. F. Avery & Sons	Louisville, KY	1915

Anyone having additional materials and resources relating to American farm implements is invited to contact C.H. Wendel, in care of Krause Publications, 700 E. State St., Iola, WI 54990-0001.

D

Dairy Equipment

Under this general heading will be found various items used in a dairy. Included are churns, butter workers and other items. Further information will be found under *Churns, Cream Separators* and various other headings.

By the 1880s, dairying had become a well-established industry in the United States. Prior to that, commercial dairying was practiced around the larger cities, with daily deliveries of fresh milk. Many people in small towns had a cow of their own or shared milk from a neighbor's cow. As pointed out in the *Churns* section, some of the old butter churns, particularly the square-box variety, can easily fetch $500 or more in good condition. Butter workers, butter paddles and similar items also can be quite expensive. A decent butter worker might bring $200 to $300 or more; butter paddles in nice condition often retail for $20 or more. Old cream cans, sometimes known as shipping cans, can often bring $20 to $40 or much more for an unusual or unique design. Establishing anything more than general guidelines for this equipment is very difficult, due to an ever changing market, uniqueness of the item, condition and local demand.

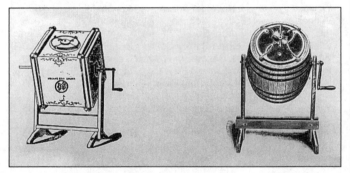

A 1910 Baker & Hamilton hardware catalog illustrates the two most common barrel and box churns. Both styles shown here were available in several sizes, ranging from a small 7-gallon model up to a big 60-gallon churn. At the time, the smaller ones sold for $5.50 to $8; the largest models sold for $26 to $28.

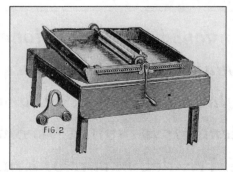

For quality butter, a butter worker was a necessity. It took much of the labor out of working the butter by hand to remove all traces of the buttermilk and bringing the butter to an even consistency. This one is from a 1910 Baker & Hamilton hardware catalog, although there were many others available.

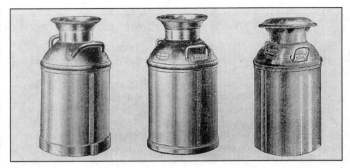

Cream cans, also known as shipping cans, were available in many different styles, sizes and patterns. Shown here from a 1910 Baker & Hamilton hardware catalog are the Ohio Pattern, Pioneer Pattern and Texas Pattern. There were many others. All had the purpose of providing a sanitary leak-proof container with which to haul milk or cream from the farm to a local dairy. Oftentimes, the product was hauled to the local railroad depot and picked up by a passing train and off-loaded at a nearby town.

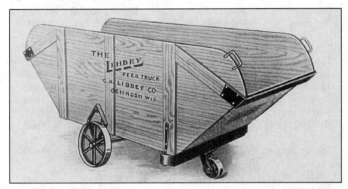

Within a dairy was also the need for equipment to feed the milk cows. To minimize the hand labor, modern barns of the 1920s had concrete floors throughout. This permitted the use of feed trucks like the one shown here. It was made by C.A. Libbey Co., Oshkosh, Wisconsin.

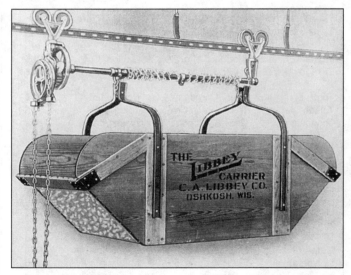

By the 1920s, there were numerous dairy barns equipped with a track system for delivering feed and grain to the livestock. This one, from C.A. Libbey Co., Oshkosh, Wis., had a simple lift system to enable the farmer to raise and lower the carrier at will. Compared to earlier hand methods, these appliances greatly reduced the hand work of an earlier time.

Disc Harrows

Although some development work was done in the 1850s, it was not until the 1870s that the disc harrow became a reality; generalized manufacturing of disc harrows only began in the 1880s. As with other implements, there were generalities and there were specialties. In general, the disc harrow consisted of a series of curved blades. When set on an angle to the direction of travel, the rolling blades sheared and crumbled the soil over which they passed, doing so in a much more aggressive manner than anything previously invented. Specialties were various types of blades, all intended to the same duty of pulverizing the soil. Then there were disc harrows that threw all the soil one way, there were tandem disc harrows and a variety of other designs. Coincidentally, some manufacturers used "di<u>sk</u> harrow" as the proper term, but most companies used "di<u>sc</u> harrow."

Curiously, the disc harrow underwent such major developments over the years that eventually it all but replaced the mold-board plows. Beginning with the first hydraulically controlled models of the 1940s, the disc harrow has undergone a continuing transformation into a primary tillage implement, a role once reserved solely for the plow.

Much of the development work on disk harrows came from small manufacturers, notable exceptions being Deere and the P&O line. Deere began as a plow maker, so the disk harrow fit into its plans; likewise, for P&O. Oliver Chilled Plow Works also was an early entrant into the disc harrow business. International Harvester was not formed until the turn of the century; some of its early tillage implements had been developed by Osborne, with the line taking on major dimensions with the purchase of P&O. J.I. Case was primarily a tractor and threshing machine builder, so it did not get into tillage implements for some years. Allis-Chalmers sold the LaCrosse line for a time, finally buying the company. Thus it is seen that much of the developmental work was carried on by smaller firms that eventually came into the fold of the developing major companies.

Regarding the antique value to collectors of old farm machinery, disc harrows generally are not a highly prized item, so their value is not usually much more than their scrap value. Restored and repainted examples, however, might bring $200 to $300.

The entire unit was carried on its own chassis. This rear view shows the action of the blades when encountering a stump as shown to the right. No further information has been found concerning this unique design.

B.F. Avery & Sons, Louisville, Ky.

B.F. Avery was a longtime manufacturer of tillage implements; its 1916 catalog illustrates the Avery Volcano and Volcano Jr., Disc Harrows. Shown here in transport position, the two gangs could be angled as desired by use of the hand levers. B.F. Avery & Sons had no connection with Avery Co., Peoria, Ill.

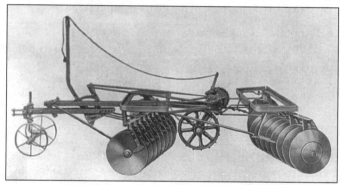

By 1916, B.F. Avery had developed a line of tractor disc harrows, noting that its disc was the only one that had a ground-driven power mechanism to change the gangs from transport to working position. No sooner had manufacturers begun perfecting the disc harrow for use with horse power than the coming of the small tractor necessitated a complete redesign for use with the farm tractor.

American Seeding Machine Co., Springfield, Ohio

In 1903, American Seeding Machine Co. offered this interesting disc harrow with individually controlled spring-loaded blades.

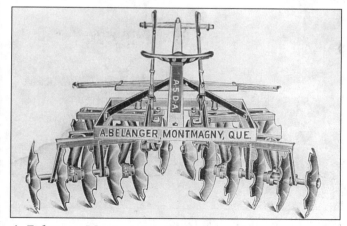

A. Belanger, Montmagny, Quebec

About 1910, Belanger was offering this interesting disc harrow with notched blades, the latter making the disc much more aggressive. In a curious aside, the Belanger was designed for two, three or four horses and could also be furnished with a tractor hitch. In most instances, though, the horse-drawn disc and the tractor disc were separate entities.

Belle City Manufacturing Co., Racine, Wisc.

By 1903, Belle City was offering its version of the ultimate disc harrow, with the engraving showing its extreme flexibility, even under the most adverse circumstances. Eventually, Belle City concentrated its efforts on threshing machines and other farm equipment, but opted out of the tillage equipment lines.

Brown Manufacturing Co., Zanesville, Ohio

Brown was a well-known manufacturer of hay loaders and other hay equipment; the company also had an extensive line of cultivators and tillage equipment. For 1928, the firm offered this tractor disc harrow; shortly after, trade directories note that parts for the Brown equipment line were available from Brown-Manly Plow Co., Malta, Ohio.

Bryan Plow Co., Bryan, Ohio

Little is known of Bryan Plow Co., outside of this 1893 advertisement of "Drader's New Reversible and Adjustable Harrow." This one was designed to be very aggressive in its work; it also featured changeable gangs so that it could be used as a cultivator. Bryan Plow Co., disappeared from the trade directories in the 1920s.

Bucher & Gibbs Plow Co., Canton, Ohio

A 1908 advertisement called this the Imperial Foretruck Double Disc Harrow. The notched blades were quite effective in pulverizing the soil; anything escaping the first gangs was certain to be encountered by the rear gangs. Bucher & Gibbs appears in the implement directories at least into the late 1950s, but no specific information has been found.

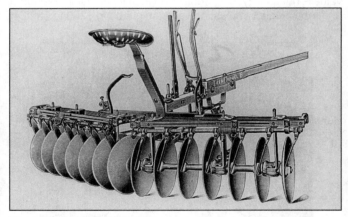

Cutaway Harrow Co., Higganum, Conn.

By 1903, Clark's Cutaway Harrow had already made a name for itself as a bush plow. The original design was intended for the heavy work required in uprooting heavy brush and grasses. This 1920 photograph shows a tandem harrow or as the company termed it, a Double Action Tractor Harrow. This one is being pulled in conjunction with a Cletrac crawler from Cleveland Tractor Co.

Deere & Co., Moline, Ill.

Deere was a major developer of the disc harrow; by the time this 1908 advertisement appeared, the company had made major strides toward perfection of this very important tillage implement. Shown here is its popular Model B Disk Harrow, available in 7- and 8-foot sizes. An important feature was the oscillating scraper system that enabled the driver to scrape the disc blades clean with a simple foot lever.

By 1935, the Deere line included several different tractor disc harrows; the unique design shown here could be used with only the front gang, since the rear gang could be easily disconnected. At this point in time, the tractor disc harrow was assuming a prominent role, while the sales of horse-drawn models languished, all but ending with the coming of World War II.

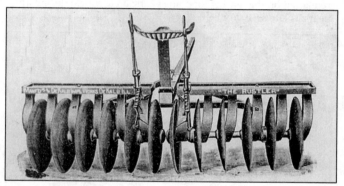

De Kalb Implement Works, De Kalb, Ill.

Virtually nothing is known of this company except for this 1895 illustration of the Rustler Disc Harrow. The company made plows and various kinds of harrows, claiming that its Rustler design "has no competitor."

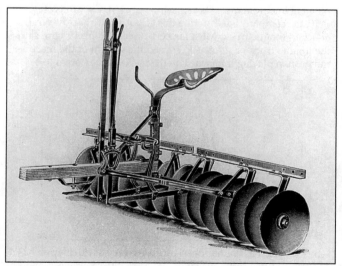

Emerson-Brantingham Co., Rockford, Ill.

Although the earliest products of Emerson consisted mainly of mowers and haying equipment, the 1907 line included an extensive offering of tillage implements. Included was The New Emerson disc harrow, available in 6-, 7- and 8-foot sizes and available with blades having a diameter of 16-, 18- or 20-inches.

The latter was unique at the time, since the majority of disc harrow in 1907 used 16-inch or smaller blades.

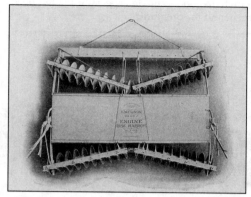

A 1919 catalog from Emerson-Brantingham shows a top view of its No. 60C tractor disc harrow. Emerson-Brantingham was an industry leader in designing farm equipment specifically for tractor power; many competing companies attempted to adapt its horse-drawn designs to tractor power, but with poor results much of the time. J.I. Case bought the company in 1928.

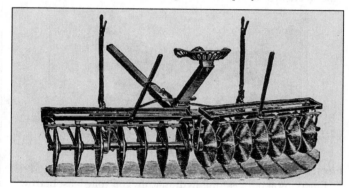

Empire Manufacturing Co., Rock Falls, Ill.

From the 1895 edition of the *Germania Kalendar* comes this advertisement for the Empire Steel Frame Disc Harrow. Outside of this advertisement, nothing whatever is known of Empire Manufacturing Co.

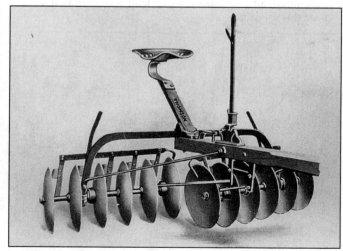

A.C. Evans Co., Springfield, Ohio

By the time this 1905 advertisement appeared, Evans was actually a part of American Seeding Machine Co., but is shown separately since the company had developed an extensive line of tillage implements prior to the merger. Evidence of the numerous options in disc harrows is shown by this extension-reversible orchard model, made especially for the needs of the nurseryman and the orchardist.

The 1905 Evans disc harrow line included its well-known Thomson In-Throw Disc Harrow. While most disc harrows threw the soil outward, this design was especially useful for certain farming practices. Note how the gangs are offset to permit the soil to be thrown inward.

Farm Tools, Inc., Mansfield, Ohio

Emerging about 1940, this hydraulically controlled disc harrow was an exclusive from Farm Tools, Inc. With this, the farmer could simply raise and lower the disc with a hand lever while turning at the ends of the field or for moving down the road to the next field. It is unlikely that anyone at the time fully grasped the idea that this would be the design to emulate; within a few years, almost all companies were making disc harrows that followed this concept.

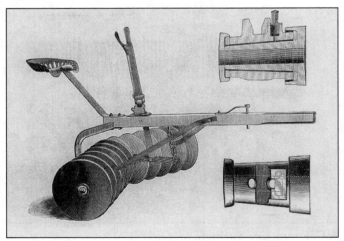

A.B. Farquhar Co., York, Pa.

Farquhar was an early entrant into the tillage equipment business, with its Pennsylvania Agricultural Works. Shown here is

an early example, probably from the 1890s. The company would later change its emphasis to include various other farm equipment, with sawmills and stationary steam engines always being a particular favorite.

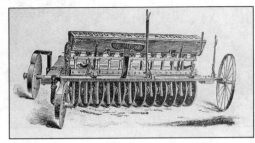

Hapgood Plow Co., Alton, Ill.

About 1887, Hapgood announced this new disc harrow, complete with a drill attachment. It offered several unique features, among them being the ability to carry the entire unit on wheels for transport or for turning at the ends of the field. This design remained on the market for some years; an identical design appears as late as 1906.

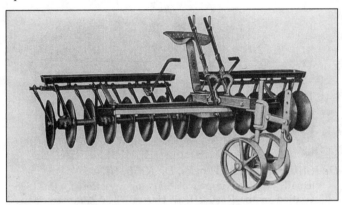

International Harvester Co., Chicago, Ill.

International Harvester initially gained much of its tillage implement line from the 1905 acquisition of D.M. Osborne & Co. By 1910, the company was offering this Osborne disc harrow with an attached tongue truck. Most farmers preferred this design, since the tongue truck or foretruck, carried the weight of the machine rather than placing it forward on the necks of the horses.

By 1920, the IHC line had been greatly enhanced with the purchase of Parlin & Orendorff. The latter was a greatly experienced manufacturer of tillage implements and had a very good reputation with farmers. Shown here is an International 8-foot disc harrow. IHC was developing a row-crop tractor at the time, ultimately coming out with the famous Farmall in a few short years. At the same time, the company was developing an entirely new series of implements designed specifically for tractor power.

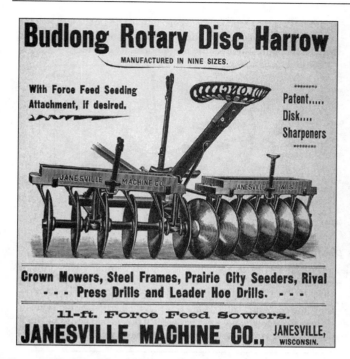

Janesville Machine Co., Janesville, Wisconsin

By the early 1890s, J. J. Budlong Company, Aurora, Illinois, had become a part of the Janesville Machine Co., Janesville, Wisconsin. The 1892 Budlong disc harrow was manufactured in nine sizes. Note the cast iron seat on this model. Janesville was bought out by Samson Tractor Co., a subsidiary of General Motors, about 1920.

Keystone Manufacturing Co., Sterling, Ill.

Keystone Manufacturing Co., became a part of International Harvester Co., in 1905. This well-known company had an established line of tillage implements, plus many other farm equipment items. An 1887 illustration depicts the Keystone Combined Disk Harrow and Seed Sower. Note the unique drive for the drill mechanism from the disc shaft.

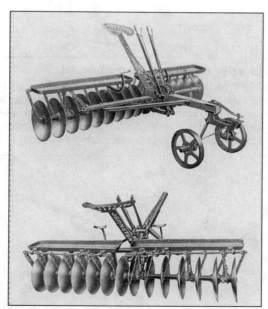

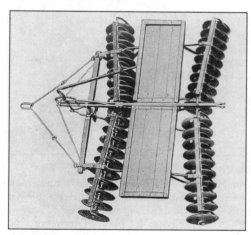

Johnston Harvester Co., Batavia, N.Y.

Johnston Harvester Co., began already in 1847 as a manufacturer of harvesting machines. Subsequently, the company expanded the line to include tillage implements. This advertisement of about 1910 shows the Johnston Continental disc harrow in two different views. Johnston came under stock control of Massey-Harris in 1910 and became a direct subsidiary in 1917.

LaCrosse Plow Co., LaCrosse, Wisc.

LaCrosse became a part of Allis-Chalmers in 1929, forming the basis of the Allis-Chalmers tillage equipment line. In the 1920s, LaCrosse was offering this impressive tractor disc harrow as one of many different styles and sizes. This model was furnished with a heavy platform that could be used as a weight box to provide better penetration of the disc blades.

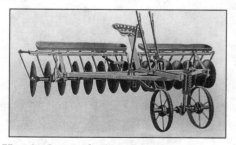

Massey-Harris Co., Ltd., Toronto, Ontario

Massey-Harris was originally a Canadian company but established a major manufacturing base in the United States with its 1910 stock control of Johnston Harvester Co., Batavia, N.Y. Included in the extensive Massey-Harris line was this No. 28 disc harrow, a horse-drawn model of the 1920s. The 8-foot model is shown here, but it was also available in 4-, 5-, 6-, 9- and 10-foot sizes.

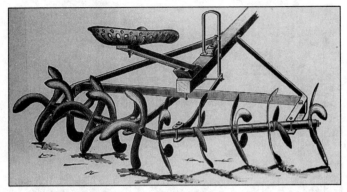

D.S. Morgan & Co., Brockport, N.Y.

D.S. Morgan & Co., was an early manufacturer of reapers, but eventually its line was diversified to include numerous tillage implements. An 1890 advertisement shows its rather unusual disc harrow; it appears to have been designed for a spading action, compared to the pulverizing action of most disc harrows.

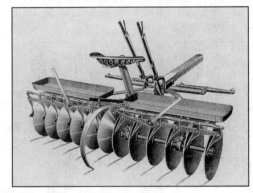

D.M. Osborne Co., Auburn, N.Y.

When established in 1856, Osborne manufactured mowers and other harvesting machines. In the 1880s, tillage implements were added to the line, with this Osborne Rival Disc Harrow appearing by 1900. Osborne became a part of International Harvester Co., in 1905.

Geo. K. Oyler Manufacturing Co., St. Louis, Mo.

Although this company manufactured an extensive line of implements, by the time of the 1887 disc harrow pictured here, the

company disappeared from advertising in the 1890s, for reasons now unknown. Its 1887 model featured a unique leveling disc behind the gangs to level the ridge normally created.

Parlin & Orendorff Co., Canton, Ill.

The history of P&O is well known; this company was a major manufacturer of tillage implements, as well as other machines. In 1919, P&O came under ownership of International Harvester. In 1887, the company offered the Rose Disc Harrow shown here. In evidence are the heavy wooden weight boxes that could be filled with dirt, rocks or iron to provide greater penetration of the soil.

Racine-Sattley Company, Springfield, Ill.

About 1907, Sattley Mfg. Co. of Springfield, Illinois, merged with Racine Wagon Co., Racine, Wisconsin. This circa-1910 engraving shows the Sattley Harrow Transporter. The harrow gangs were lifted over the standards of this device. The ironclad runners provided a long working life on a device rarely found today.

S.G. Randall, Providence, R.I.

S.G. Randall was the first to receive a patent for a combined grain seeder and disc harrow. When this patent was issued in 1859, Randall was shown residing at New Braintree, Mass. An 1874 illustration shows the Randall Pulverizing Harrow, as built at that time. Despite the qualities of this machine, compared to its peers, little reference can be found to Randall or his subsequent developments.

Roderick Lean Co., Springfield, Ohio

Roderick Lean established a tillage implement factory at Springfield in about 1865. The company thrived and sold all it wanted to, not seeming to be especially interested in growing beyond a certain point. The quality of the Roderick Lean line was undisputed. In 1930, this company joined with others to form Farm Tools, Inc. Shown here is a 1917 example of the New Century "H" Series disc harrow.

Stoddard Manufacturing Co., Dayton, Ohio

By 1887, Stoddard was offering its Climax pulverizing disc harrow. At the time, wood engraving had developed into a major art form; curiously, most engravers depicted light boned, rather fancy horses pulling one machine or another. In contrast, draft horses, as generally used, were heavy boned and not nearly so concerned with high stepping as with exerting power enough to do the job at hand.

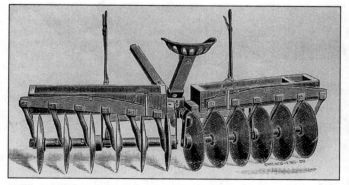

Zeller, Phelps & Swift, Rock Falls, Ill.

An 1887 advertisement illustrates the Empire Disc Harrow from the company. This one used a wooden framework with built-in weight boxes for better penetration of the disc blades. Beyond this illustration, nothing at all has been found regarding this company.

Trade Names			
Albion	Gale Mfg Co.	Albion, MI	1905
American	American Plow Co.	Madison, WI	1905
Anderson	E. Bement's Sons	Lansing, MI	1905
Ann Arbor	Ann Arbor Machine Co.	Ann Arbor, MI	1917
Avery's Tornado	B. F. Avery & Sons	Louisville, KY	1905
Bell	Ohio Rake Co.	Dayton, OH	1905
Bellevue	Ohio Cultivator Co.	Bellevue, OH	1905
Bonanza	Rock Island Plow Co.	Rock Island, IL	1905
Bradley Jr.	David Bradley Mfg. Co.	Bradley, IL	1905
Brown	Galesburg-Coulter Disc Co.	Galesburg, IL	1905
Bryan	Bryan Plow Co.	Bryan, OH	1905
Budlong	Janesville Machine Co.	Janesville, WI	1905
Canton	Parlin & Orendorff Co.	Canton, IL	1905
Case	J. I. Case Threshing Machine Co.	Racine, WI	1917
Clark's	Cutaway Harrow Co.	Higganum, CT	1892
Columbia	Ohio Cultivator Co.	Bellevue, OH	1905
Corbin	Matteson & Williamson Mfg. Co.	Stockton, CA	1892
Daley	M. H. Daley	Charles City, IA	1905
Dandy	Ohio Rake Co.	Dayton, OH	1905
Deere	Deere & Mansur Co.	Moline, IL	1905
Deere Junior	Deere & Mansur Co.	Moline, IL	1905
Deere Model B	Deere & Mansur Co.	Moline, IL	1905
Deere Universal	Deere & Mansur Co.	Moline, IL	1905
Defiance	Rock Island Plow Co.	Rock Island, IL	1905
Eagle	Eagle Mfg. Co.	Kansas City, MO	1905
Eclipse	J. Thompson & Sons Mfg. Co.	Beloit, WI	1905
Economy	Moline Plow Co.	Moline, IL	1906
Emerson	Emerson Mfg. Co.	Rockford, IL	1905
Empire	Empire Mfg. Co.	Keokuk, IA	1892
Evans	Evans Mfg. Co.	Hammond, NY	1905
Excello	McSherry Mfg. Co.	Middletown, OH	1905
Gale	Gale Mfg. Co.	Albion, MI	1905
Governor	Racine-Sattley Co.	Springfield, IL	1905
Grand Detour	Grand Detour Plow Co.	Dixon, IL	1905
Great Western Cutaway	Cutaway Harrow Co.	Higganum, CT	1905
Hamilton	H. P. Deuscher Co.	Hamilton, OH	1905
Hamilton	Long & Alstatter Co.	Hamilton, OH	1905
Hero	Sterling Mfg. Co.	Sterling, IL	1905
Holstein	Meilli-Blumberg Co.	New Holstein, WI	1917
Houser & Haines	Houser & Haines Mfg. Co.	Stockton, CA	1905
Ideal	David Bradley Mfg. Co.	Bradley, IL	1905
Imperial Perfect	Bucher & Gibbs Plow Co.	Canton, OH	1905
International	International Harvester Co.	Chicago, IL	1919
Iron Age	Bateman Mfg. Co.	Grenloch, NJ	1919
J. I. Case	J. I. Case Plow Works	Racine, WI	1905
Janesville	Janesville Machine Co.	Janesville, WI	1905
Johnston Continental	Johnston Harvester Co.	Batavia, NY	1905

Trade Names (cont...)

Kalamazoo	Kalamazoo Tank & Silo Co.	Kalamazoo, MI	1919
Kelley	John G. Kelley	Waukesha, WI	1917
Keystone	Keystone Co.	Sterling, IL	1905
Kingman	Kingman Plow Co.	Peoria, IL	1905
LaCrosse	LaCrosse Plow Co.	LaCrosse, WI	1905
Lansing Jr.	E. Bement's Sons	Lansing, MI	1905
Lehr	Lehr Agricultural Co.	Fremont, OH	1905
Little Bonanza	Rock Island Plow Co.	Rock Island, IL	1905
Michigan	E. Bement's Sons	Lansing, MI	1905
Monarch	Ohio Rake Co.	Dayton, OH	1905
Monitor	Fuller & Johnson Mfg. Co.	Madison, WI	1905
Morrison	Morrison Mfg. Co.	Fort Madison, IA	1905
New American	American Harrow Co.	Detroit, MI	1905
New Grand Detour	Grand Detour Plow Co.	Dixon, IL	1905
New Standard	Sterling Mfg. Co.	Sterling, IL	1905
New Yorker	Chapinville Wheel Co.	Poughkeepsie, NY	1905
O. K.	Joseph Wodsedalek	Algoma, WI	1919
Ohio	Ohio Mfg. Co.	Upper Sandusky, OH	1905
Osborne Rival	D. M. Osborne	Auburn, NY	1905
Our Dandy	F. B. Tait & Co.	Decatur, IL	1892
Pekin	Pekin Plow Co.	Pekin, IL	1905
Pennsylvania	A. B. Farquhar Co.	York, PA	1905
Peru	Peru Plow & Wheel Co.	Peru, IL	1905
Pioneer	McSherry Mfg. Co.	Middletown, OH	1905
Rock Island	Rock Island Plow Co.	Rock Island, IL	1892
Rockford	Rockford Mfg. Co.	Rockford, IL	1905
Roderick Lean	Roderick Lean Mfg. Co.	Mansfield, OH	1905
Rosenthal	Rosenthal Corn Husker Co.	Milwaukee, WI	1917
Rustler	Daley Mfg. Co.	DeKalb, IL	1892
Safety	Ohio Rake Co.	Dayton, OH	1905
Sandow	Emerson Mfg. Co.	Rockford, IL	1905
Shaw's	H. C. Shaw Plow Works	Stockton, CA	1892
Silage King	Silo Specialty Mfg. Co.	Clinton, IA	1917
Silver's	Silver Mfg. Co.	Salem, OH	1919
Spear Head	McSherry Mfg. Co.	Middletown, OH	1905
St. Joseph	St. Joseph Plow Co.	St. Joseph, MO	1905
Standard	Sterling Mfg. Co.	Sterling, IL	1905
Standard Model B	Standard Harrow Co.	Utica, NY	1905
Star	Ohio Cultivator Co.	Bellevue, OH	1905
Star	Wiard Plow Co.	Batavia, NY	1905
Steel King	Belle City Mfg. Co.	Racine, WI	1919
Stockton	H. C. Shaw Co.	Stockton, CA	1905
Sucker State	Hayes Pump & Planter Co.	Galva, IL	1905
Syracuse	Syracuse Chilled Plow Co.	Syracuse, NY	1905
Thomas	Thomas Mfg. Co.	Springfield, OH	1905
Thomson	Evans Mfg. Co.	Hammond, NY	1905
Tiger	Stoddard Mfg. Co.	Dayton, OH	1905
Toledo	Toledo Plow Co.	Toledo, OH	1905
Triumph	Dayton Farm Implement Co.	Dayton, OH	1892
United	United Engine Co.	Lansing, MI	1919
Vibert	F. C. Vibert	Hockanum, CT	1892
Walton	Walton Plow Co.	Bloomington, IL	1892

Trade Names (cont...)

Western	Rockford Mfg. Co.	Rockford, IL	1905
Western Cutaway	Cutaway Harrow Co.	Higganum, CT	1905
Wiard	Wiard Plow Co.	Batavia, NY	1905
Yankee	Belcher & Taylor Agricultural Tool Co.	Chicopee Falls, MA	1905

Disc Plows

The disc plow is a comparatively recent development; the classic title *American Agricultural Implements* by R.L. Ardrey and first published in 1894, makes no mention of the disc plow. *Farm Machinery & Farm Motors* written by Chase and Davidson in 1915, makes scant mention of the disc plow, noting that they were an alternative to the mold-board plow in very sticky soil or in soils that were too hard for mold-board plowing. Thus, the disc plow, while important in certain areas, has not generally been used in vast portions of the United States; Midwestern farmers, for example, have little knowledge of this important farm implement.

One example of a disc plow is that built by Emerson Manufacturing Co., Rockford, Ill., in 1907. Its New Model was available with one, two or three discs, with the No. 1 Single shown here. Emerson designed the frame so that right hand turns were possible without the front wheel running interference with the disc.

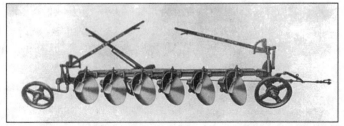

Available in lever or power-lift styles, the Avery Multiple Disc Plow as shown was listed in the company's 1916 catalog. Since Avery was located in Louisville, the company was much closer to Texas and other areas having a need for this type of plow. When set to turn 9 inches, this six-disc model plowed 54 inches at each pass.

LaCrosse Plow Co., LaCrosse, Wis., offered a variety of disc plows by the 1920s, including this Montana Disc Plow, an obvious reference for its intended area of use. By the 1920s, most of the major plow makers were offering at least a limited number of disc plows; for most, however, their major manufacturing efforts were still aimed at the time-honored moldboard plow.

Trade Names

Avery	Avery Company	Peoria, IL	1916
LaCrosse	LaCrosse Plow Company	LaCrosse, WI	1920
New Model	Emerson Mfg. Co.	Rockford, IL	1907

Ditching Machines

While technically, at least, not a farm implement, a great many ditching machines were used on farms. Usually, such a machine was owned by someone in a neighborhood, the latter then doing custom work for local farmers. All styles, sizes and designs appeared. Some were small horse-drawn affairs, while others required a sizable steam-traction engine or tractor.

H. W. Beldsmeyer & Co., St. Louis, Mo.

An 1887 advertisement illustrates Beldsmeyer's Patent Ditching Machine. This rather simple design plowed up the earth, with the loose soil being carried by elevator buckets up to a cross conveyor. The latter then dropped the soil off to one side of the machine. The advertising claimed that this machine could move 1,000 cubic yards of earth in 10 hours.

Standard Ditching Machine Co., St. Louis, Mo.

This 1892 Mogul Grader and Dieter claimed it could move up to 1,000 cubic yards of earth in a 10-hour day. Although it could be pulled by a sizable number of horses, probably 12 or more, it could also be pulled by a steam-traction engine, since, by 1892, there were a few of these capable of heavy traction work.

Owensboro Ditcher & Grader Co., Owensboro, Kty.

By the 1920s, this company was offering a variety of ditching machines. The Martin All-Steel Ditcher shown here was a small outfit designed to build ditches, particularly on farms and on rural roads. The company also made road graders and other earth-moving equipment.

Trade Names

Beldsmeyer	H.W. Beldsmeyer and Co.	St. Louis, MO	1887
Martin	Owensboro Ditcher & Grader Co.	Owensboro, KY	1920
Mogul	Standard Ditching Machine Co.	St. Louis, MO	1892

E

Earth Moving Equipment

Like the Ditching Machines section previous, earth-moving equipment is not technically related to the farm machinery business. Yet, numerous kinds of earth-moving devices made their way to the farm. Early on, it was the drag scraper or the fresno; with the coming of tractor power came all kinds of devices intended to move small quantities of dirt on the farm.

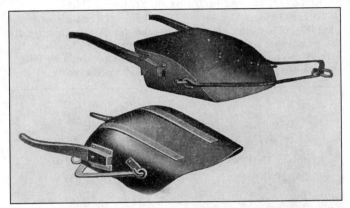

One of the most popular methods of moving dirt for the small farm was with a drag scraper, sometimes called a slip scraper. Pulled with a team, the slip scraper could be filled with relative ease; when pulled to the final location, the operator raised the handles to upset the load.

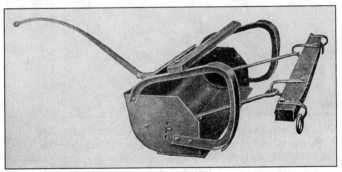

Another style of scraper was the Fresno or Buck Scraper. This one was somewhat larger than the slip scraper and was available in sizes up to 5-feet wide from P&O Plow Co., Canton, Ill. Some companies also made wheeled Fresno scrapers as yet another alternative.

The Albrecht Excavator was a curious machine announced in 1913. It was developed by John Albrecht of Madison, Wis. B.B. Clarke, founder of *American Thresherman* magazine was financially interested and closed a deal with Avery Co., Peoria, Ill., to build and market the machine. The slip scraper dumped into a hopper and the latter then dropped the load of dirt onto a waiting wagon. Little more is known of this design, outside of a 1913 announcement.

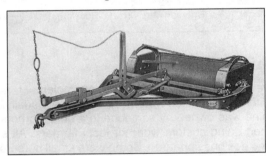

Popular during the 1930-1950 period was the Groundhog Scraper, also known as a "tumblebug." This simple little scraper was pulled by a tractor and is shown here in the loading position. When the load arrived at its destination, pulling a trip rope permitted the entire scraper box to revolve, discharging the load. This one was built by Roderick Lean Manufacturing Co., and later by Farm Tools, Inc.

Another style of rotary scraper was the K-S model built by Central Manufacturing Co., Omaha, Neb. A 1946 advertisement noted that this machine was again available; undoubtedly, production had been halted because of World War II. Eventually, the rotary scraper or tumblebug, was supplanted by other designs. After World War II, many styles of tractor-mounted scrapers and dozers appeared.

Elevators

Portable elevators and wagon dumps started gaining popularity in the 1890s. By 1905, several companies were building elevators, particularly in Illinois. The notion that ear corn and small grains had to be shoveled by hand quickly came to an end when the first elevator appeared in the neighborhood. While the farmer stood and watched the corn going into the crib with very little work on his part, envious neighbors soon made a trip to town and got one of their own. Numerous companies have built grain elevators over the years, but constraints of space have limited this section to a few of the notable examples.

Camp Bros., & Co., Metamora, Ill.

Among early trade journals, Camp Bros., was generally accepted as the first company to offer a portable elevator to the farmer. By mounting it on wheels, a single elevator could fill any number of cribs. This 1907 model is shown with a wagon dump, also made by Camp Bros. This eliminated much of the hard work for the farmer.

By 1915, Camp Bros. was offering a stationary cup elevator. It was intended for built-in use in a large crib. By this time, many cribs were also built with overhead grain storage for oats and other small grains. The Camp elevator could handle any of these jobs with ease.

Deere & Co., Moline, Ill.

A typical John Deere elevator set-up might have included the various items shown here. A small sweep power operates the elevator and the wagon dump. To avoid an excessively long elevator, a secondary elevator was used to carry grain to the cupola of the crib. From there, distributor spouts could deliver the crop wherever wanted. Deere continued manufacturing grain elevators for many years.

J.A. Engel & Co., Peoria, Ill.

No elevator set-up would have been complete without an automatic grain dump. Virtually all of these consisted of a mechanism to raise the front of the wagon, allowing the grain to exit by gravity. Engel's Ideal elevator was one of the earliest on the market, but, for reasons unknown, the company quickly blends into obscurity.

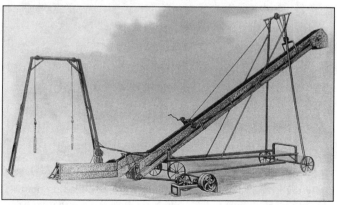

Kewanee Machinery & Conveyor Co., Kewanee, Ill.

This Kewanee Outfit No. 126 of the 1920s included a 26-foot elevator, hopper and the wagon dump or derrick, plus a speed jack to run everything at the proper speed. By this time, Kewanee was prepared to offer its all-steel design in sizes anywhere from 20 to 50 feet.

Kewanee was a major manufacturer of indoor or stationary elevators. These were usually built-to-order for each corn crib, shipped from the company and assembled on-site by a competent machine man. Once erected, many of these elevators operated for decades with little or no attention to repairs or replacement parts.

King & Hamilton Co., Ottawa, Ill.

By the 1920s, King & Hamilton had become a leading manufacturer of stationary cup elevators. A cutaway view of this large corn crib illustrates how the loaded wagon was driven over the dump, trussed to the lift chains and unloaded with almost no effort on the part of the farmer.

King & Hamilton excelled with its indoor cup elevators and also built an extensive line of portable elevators (as shown). This one was of all-steel design, although there were numerous makes still using wood for at least part of the construction.

A close-up view shows the American Dump, as built by King & Hamilton. The wagon was driven over the dump with the front wheels resting between the bottom irons. A simple gear clutch mechanism raised the wagon. The American was but one of probably hundreds of different designs. With the coming of tractor hydraulics and self-contained hydraulic wagon hoists, mechanically operated wagon dumps soon came to an end.

Luthy & Co., Peoria, Ill.

The Ideal elevator, as made by Luthy & Co., is shown in a 1908 magazine illustration. This one was an all-wood design, even the wagon derrick is made of wood. Since many grain elevators spent their lives outdoors, wooden construction was undesirable because of its short life when exposed to the elements.

Maroa Manufacturing Co., Maroa, Ill.

Little is known of Maroa Manufacturing, except for this 1908 illustration of its elevator. Various trade directories do not list this company by 1914. Perhaps the company sold out to another; the firm went into another endeavor; or, equally possible, it simply went out of business.

Marseilles Manufacturing Co., Marseilles, Ill.

Undoubtedly, the Marseilles elevator line was a major influence on the Deere elevator line; the latter bought out Marseilles in 1911. Shown here is a 1907 example of the Marseilles elevator; its heavy construction endeared it to many farmers.

Meadows Manufacturing Co., Pontiac, Ill.

In 1906, Meadows advertised its Improved Rocke grain elevators, small and light-weight when compared to many competing designs. The success of this small elevator led the company into a full-fledged business and an excellent reputation in the grain elevator business.

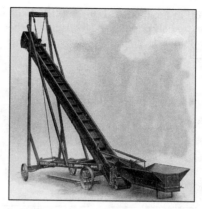

Following the Improved Rocke design, Meadows built this impressive all-wood elevator at least into the 1920s. It was available in sizes from 24 to 50 feet. Operating at its rated speed, the manufacturer claimed it could move 40 bushels of corn per minute from wagon to crib.

Meadows was offering an extensive line of portable and stationary grain elevators by 1912. As shown here, the elevator could be operated by a gasoline engine or with a small sweep power. To the right is shown a cutaway of an inside crib design; Meadows marketed thousands of these elevators. Sometime during the 1930s, Meadows became a part of Farm Tools, Inc., gradually disappearing from the scene.

A.F. Meyers Manufacturing Co., Morton, Ill.

By 1915, Meyers was offering its inside elevators to the market. The Meyers design shown here was typical for the period; in fact, this design changed little for many years. The elevator cups traveled along the bottom of the hopper, carrying their load of grain, dropping it off at the top and returning for another load. The Meyers was extremely popular and thousands of them were sold, with many still in use.

O'Neil Implement Co., Marseilles, Ill.

From about 1910 comes this illustration of the O'Neil grain elevator. This was an all-steel design that included an optional gasoline engine; it appears to be a Sandow two-cycle model from Detroit Motor Car Supply Co., Detroit. Presumably the O'Neil elevator line was available in varying lengths; the style shown here is probably a demonstrator model used for fairs and dealer exhibits.

Portable Elevator Manufacturing Co., Bloomington, Ill.

By 1908, The Little Giant elevators were available with a traveling cross conveyor as shown. With this unit permanently mounted beneath the crib roof, it was possible to elevate grain to any position within the structure.

The Little Giant Wagon Dump of 1909 was essentially the same unit as the company continued to make for decades. It was a very simple design, connected to the elevator with a tumbling shaft. Some farmers placed wooden guards over the tumbling shafts. Others didn't and many communities reported instances of farmers getting their pant legs caught in the rotating shaft, sometimes with injury.

Little Giant portable elevators of 1940 were of the latest all-steel design; this one is 46-feet long and a spare tractor is used to operate the speed jack. Oftentimes, a small gasoline engine was used. For those fortunate enough to have "high line" electricity by 1940, an electric motor became a reality.

Rumely Products Co., La Porte, Ind.

In 1913, Rumely announced its inclusion of the Swanson elevators into its product line. Apparently, it was the product of Swanson-St. Joseph Plow Co., St. Joseph, Mo. Outside of a few advertisements, little more is known of this excursion of Rumely into the farm elevator business.

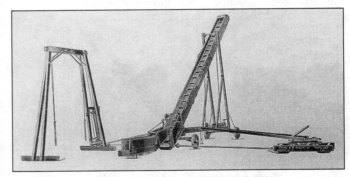

Sandwich Manufacturing Co., Sandwich, Ill.

A 1908 advertisement for the Sandwich elevator notes that "a few were sold in 1906, hundreds in 1907 and twice as many will be sold in 1908 as in this past season." The Sandwich farm machinery line was very popular, so its portable grain elevators gained rapid acceptance and considerable sales.

In the early 1930s, Sandwich Manufacturing Co. was bought out by New Idea Spreader Co., Coldwater, Ohio. The latter continued to market the Sandwich-New Idea line for several years. One example is this all-steel elevator, complete with speed jack, wagon dump and a Sandwich gasoline engine. Eventually, New Idea redesigned the elevators, continuing to market its own designs for decades after.

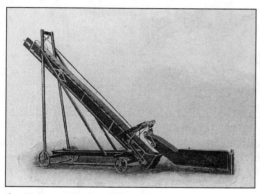

Schroeder Bros., Minier, Ill.

For reasons unknown, construction of portable and stationary grain elevators was centered in Illinois for decades. One example is the Schroeder elevator, shown here in a 1907 advertisement. This one was of all-wood construction, still preferred by many farmers and manufacturers over the "new-fangled" all-steel designs.

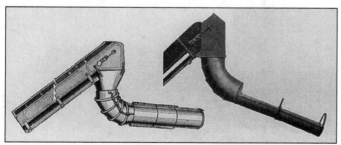

Once the grain or corn was elevated to the top of the crib, it was necessary to distribute it where it was wanted. To this end, most companies offered flexible spouts of various designs. Beyond this, companies like Baier Bros., Manufacturing Co., Cissna Park, Ill., offered a flexible spout that could be fitted to any elevator; it is shown on the left of this illustration. On the right is a flexible Schroeder spout made by Schroeder Bros.

Trade Names			
Camp Bros.	Camp Bros.	Metamora, IL	1907
Engel	J.A. Engel & Co.	Peoria, IL	1905
Ideal	Luthy and Co.	Peoria, IL	1920
John Deere	Deere and Co.	Moline, IL	1915
Kewanee	Kewanee Machy. & Conveyor Co.	Kewanee, IL	1920
Little Giant	Portable Elevator Mfg. Co.	Bloomington, IL	1908
Maroa	Maroa Mfg. Co.	Maroa, IL	1914
Marseilles	Marseilles Mfg. Co.	Marseilles, IL	1907
Meadows	Meadows Mfg. Co.	Pontiac, IL	1906
Meyers	A.F. Meyers Mfg. Co.	Morton, IL	1915
New Idea	New Idea Spreader Co.	Coldwater, OH	1931
O'Neill	O'Neill Implement Co.	Marseilles, IL	1910
Ottawa	King and Hamilton	Ottawa, IL	1920
Sandwich	Sandwich Mfg. Co.	Sandwich, IL	1908
Schroeder	Schroeder Brothers	Minier, IL	1907
Swanson	Rumely Products Inc.	LaPorte, IN	1913

Engines

While the reaper, the plow, the threshing machine and many other implements served to mechanize agriculture, the gasoline engine also had a dramatic effect on mechanization. With the introduction of the Otto Silent gas engine in 1876 came virtually all of today's internal combustion engines.

The heavy stationary engines that began to appear from 1900 onward soon made their way to almost every farm. By the thousands they made their way from factories to the wash house, the corn crib and the granary. We would be remiss in not making mention of the gasoline engine, but it has been covered extensively in our book *American Gas Engines Since 1872* (Crestline/Motorbooks: 1983). Its 584 pages represent the most comprehensive pictorial history ever published on gas and gasoline engines. Thus, we felt that to include engines in this book would only serve to exclude other significant developments in the farm equipment scene. Occasional references are made within this book to the gas engine, but for detailed information, the reader is referred to the above title.

Ensilage Cutters

Ensilage, that is, the process of putting a crop into a silo for storage, didn't begin in the United States until the late 1870s. At first, it was thought necessary to fill the silo then weight it down with stones, earth or whatever was available. In a short time, it was discovered that the weight of the material itself was enough to exclude the air, so that spoilage occurred only on the top. By the 1880s, ensilage was becoming a popular method of feed storage, especially with standing corn.

Prior to the coming of ensilage and ensilage cutters, numerous companies made feed cutters and/or fodder cutters. For a time, there were combination feed cutters/ensilage cutters. A few even tied back to the corn husker-shredder. Thus the reader is advised to look in the various sections of this book for relevant items, especially under Feed & Fodder Cutters, Corn Husker-Shredders, Feed Mills and Grinding Mills.

Ensilage cutters were very popular and there were a few in almost every farming community, most of them being owned by a group of farmers or perhaps by one or two farmers, who then filled silos on a custom basis. These machines maintained their popularity into the 1940s, but the coming of the field harvester brought a quick end to these machines, along with the corn binder. With the field harvester or field cutter, a farmer could cut and chop the corn or hay and blow it into a towed wagon. When full, the wagon went to the silo, its automatic unloading system was engaged and the material went via a blower into the silo. This system still prevails today.

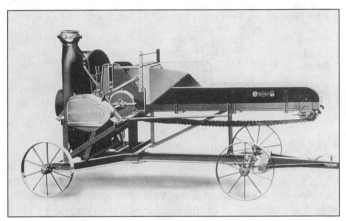

Advance-Rumely Thresher Co., LaPorte, Ind.

Rumely was offering ensilage cutters as early as 1912; in 1923, it announced this new No. 16 Silo Filler. It was a flywheel cutter, meaning that the cutter knives were mounted on what were also the fan blades to convey the cut material into the silo. The stalks of corn were fed onto the conveyor table by hand.

American Harvester Co., Minneapolis, Minn.

Heralding a revolutionary change, the Ronning field harvester was developed in the 1920s. It used an engine of 15 or 20 horsepower, mounted directly on the machine. A tractor towed the cutter through the field, delivering ensilage into a wagon alongside. Despite its obvious advantages, it took some years before the Ronning gained real success.

American Harvester also offered this semi-portable ensilage cutter, noting that it was the only one on the market that could be converted to a field harvester. The idea was that a farmer could buy this unit one year and buy the remaining parts a year or two later to make the conversion to a full-fledged field cutter.

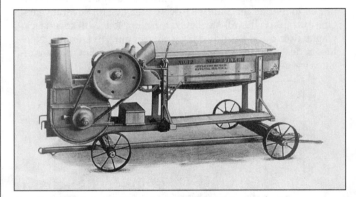

Appleton Manufacturing Co., Batavia, Ill.

Appleton had its No. 12D Silo Filler (pictured here) on the market by 1917. Depending on the wishes of the farmer, most cutters could be set for a cut of 5/16- to 2-1/2 inches. Ordinarily, it would be set somewhere between 1/2-inch and 1-inch. Many threshermen owned an ensilage cutter or silo filler; this gave them extra autumn work after the threshing season was past.

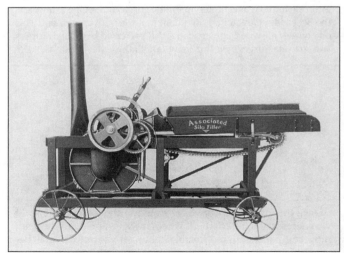

Associated Manufacturers, Waterloo, Iowa

In the 1910-20 period, the demand for ensilage cutters was stronger than at any other time. Up to 1910, many farmers had yet to be convinced of the need for a silo. In the decade that followed, the demand for silos and silo fillers was insatiable. Shown here is an Associated Silo Filler of 1917.

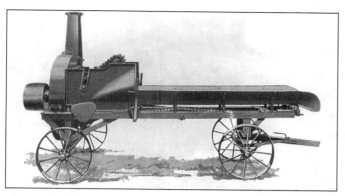

Avery Co., Peoria, Ill.

For a time in the early 1920s, Avery offered its version of the silo filler. Like most machines, it was a flywheel cutter, with the knives mounted together with the fan blades on a single hub. Since it was necessary to keep the knives sharp, a special grinding attachment was usually built integral with the machine.

Belcher & Taylor Agricultural Works, Chicopee Falls, Mass.

As pointed out in the introduction to this section, some companies advertised a combination ensilage and fodder cutter, precisely as advertised in this 1903 machine from Belcher & Taylor. Before pneumatic blowers came into general use, a few enterprising companies used an elevator to carry the cut material into the silo.

Belle City Manufacturing Co., Racine, Wisc.

By 1908, Belle City was offering several different styles of ensilage cutters, with its A-2 model shown here. This one weighed about 1,600 pounds on the four-wheel trucks; the latter was an option, if it was desired to have a stationary machine.

J.I. Case Co., Racine, Wisc.

J.I. Case introduced this Model B silo filler to the market in 1928. It was a flywheel cutter design, similar to others on the market. About this same time, J.I. Case began to greatly expand its product line; by the 1930s, Case offered one of the largest implement lines in the entire industry.

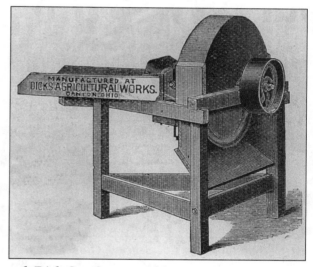

Joseph Dick Co., Canton, Ohio

In 1887, Dick's Agricultural Works offered its Famous Patent Feed Cutter, noting that it was "for hay, straw, corn stalks and ensilage. Adapted for hand, horse, steam or wind power." At the time, the terms "silo filler" and "ensilage cutter" hadn't yet come into vogue; in reality, they all meant the same thing as the term "feed cutter."

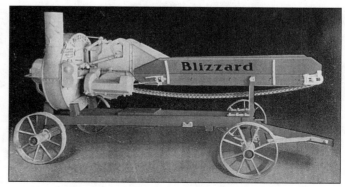

By the 1920s, Joseph Dick Co., had become a well established manufacturer of ensilage cutters. Shown here is its No. 400 machine; the company had sometime previously adopted the "Blizzard" trade name to its cutters. At some point, apparently in the 1930s, the company took the name of Blizzard Manufacturing Co.

Eagle Manufacturing Co., Appleton, Wisc.

Eagle Manufacturing Co. was an important source for ensilage cutters, feed grinders, gasoline engines, tractors and other equipment. Shown here is its 1907 model of the Eagle Self-Feed Ensilage and Fodder Cutter. Note that even at this time Eagle was speaking of a combination "ensilage and fodder" machine; the line of separation was indeed still present, but was slowly fading.

Farmers Manufacturing Co., Sebring, Ohio

In 1903, Farmers Manufacturing Co., offered its Cyclone Blowers and Carriers, along with its own feed or ensilage cutters. These were optional attachments; the plain machine simply dropped the cut material on the ground. Likewise, the semi-automatic feeder was an option that eliminated the tedium of feeding two or three stalks of corn at a time.

Gehl Bros., Manufacturing Co., West Bend, Wisc.

By 1912, Gehl was offering this style of the Silberzahn ensilage cutter. It was very popular, particularly in its native state of Wisconsin, as well as in other regions. This 1912 advertisement notes that "Our business is growing wonderfully in the West." Obviously the company was making sales inroads into various areas.

The Silberzahn ensilage cutter from Gehl Bros. took on an entirely new look by 1916. Here was an all-steel design that was fully portable. The cutter head was of the "lawn-mower" type—that is, the knives were mounted on a revolving drum. The cut material then dropped into a separate blower; in turn, it lifted the silage into the silo. Gehl was a pioneer in building field harvesters and was very successful in this endeavor.

W.R. Harrison & Co., Massillon, Ohio

By 1905, Harrison was offering its Celebrated Tornado Feed and Ensilage Cutter. The optional blower was named the "Tornado Pneumatic Elevator." Harrison also builds silos, steel field rollers, corn shellers and wheelbarrows. The company is listed as late as 1931; by 1939, repairs only could be secured from Massillon Bolt & Rivet Co., Massillon, Ohio.

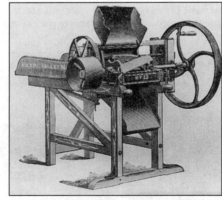

Hocking Valley Manufacturing Co., Lancaster, Ohio

Hocking Valley was a well-known firm that made corn shellers, feed cutters and other farm machines. Shown here is its No. 13 Feed Cutter. While this one was hand-fed and dropped the cut material out of a bottom chute, it probably could have been adapted to various attachments, if desired. This model is shown in a 1904 catalog.

Did You Know?

An ancient box or barrel churn can bring $500 or more on the antique market.

International Harvester Co., Chicago, Ill.

The International Type A ensilage cutter was built from 1912 to 1940. During that time, thousands of these immensely popular cutters were manufactured. The company built many other styles through the years, even selling the Belle City ensilage cutter line up to about 1917.

Kalamazoo Tank & Silo Co., Kalamazoo, Mich.

For 1920, Kalamazoo offered this all-steel machine. While no details of the company's origins have been found, it appears that the Kalamazoo ensilage cutter was available at least into the late 1930s. Parts were available at least into the late 1940s.

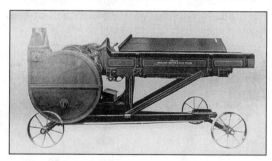

Maytag Co., Newton, Iowa

Today, Maytag Co. is best known for its home appliances. For many years, though, the company was an important manufacturer of farm machinery. Its 1914 offering included the Iowa Ensilage Cutter, an impressive machine with a large feed table and a heavy hard-maple frame. Eventually, Maytag opted out of the farm equipment business to build its washing machines and became a leader in that industry.

Papec Machine Co., Shortsville, N.Y.

When this 1905 advertisement appeared, Papec was located in Lima in Livingston County, N.Y. Subsequently, the company moved to Shortsville, operating there for many years. The Model D cutter shown here was claimed to be "The Strongest and best Ensilage Cutter on earth." Undoubtedly, this machine had some excellent qualities, since the Papec machines were very popular.

Pictured here is a 1927 scene depicting a farmer feeding stalks of corn into a Papec cutter. In reality, it usually demanded one person to stand by the feeder and help things along, all the while keeping those on the wagon from feeding in too much corn and plugging the machine from stem to stern.

A 1931 photograph illustrates a Papec ensilage cutter chopping dry hay and blowing it into a barn. An unusual feature was the installation of a large electric motor on the cutter; only those near a major power line could take advantage of this power source. Coincidentally, dry chopped hay was especially prone to spontaneous combustion, causing many barn fires as a result.

Plymouth Foundry & Machine Co., Plymouth, Wisc.

By 1915, the Plymouth Self-Feed Cutter had become very popular; in fact, Fairbanks, Morse & Co., had become distributing agents for the Plymouth line. At the time, Fairbanks-Morse was expanding greatly into the farm machinery market, although it withdrew somewhat in the 1920s. Plymouth is listed as a manufacturer at least into the late 1950s.

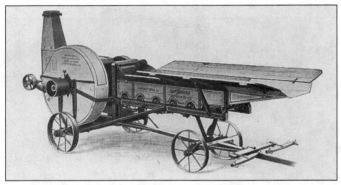

Rosenthal Corn Husker Co., Milwaukee, Wisc.

Rosenthal is perhaps best known for its corn huskers and shredders. By the 1920s, the company was offering a series of ensilage cutters. Included was its Big 21 Ensilage Cutter and Silo Filler. The company claimed it could cut and deliver anywhere from 15 to 30 tons of silage per hour. To do so required a sizable labor force, just to get the loads of corn up to the machine.

E.W. Ross Co., Springfield, Ohio

Ross was an early entrant in the feed cutter business, offering this Little Giant No. 11A feed cutter in 1887. As can be noted here, this cutter could be run by belt power, but could also be operated by hand-crank if necessary. The entire unit was built of heavy wood and ample iron castings.

For 1910, Ross was offering this feed cutter, although it had the blower for elevating the cut feed into a silo. As noted elsewhere, some companies preferred the title of "feed cutter," some used "ensilage cutter," and others preferred "silo filler." Parts for these machines were available as late as the 1940s from Ross Equipment Co.

I.B. Rowell Co., Waukesha, Wisc.

Rowell offered its Safety-Automatic ensilage cutter to the trade in the 1920s. Outside of a single 1920 advertisement, little is known of company activities, but the company is still listed as a manufacturer of ensilage cutters as late as 1948.

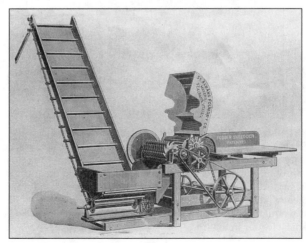

St. Albans Foundry Co., St. Albans, Vt.

In 1895, St. Albans was building this rather large corn fodder shredder; it did not have a husker, but shredded everything fed into it. An elevator carried the shredded material to a waiting wagon or perhaps a bin. For corn that had cured in a shock, the shredder was a better choice than a feed cutter. Mansur & Tebbetts Implement Co., St. Louis, was a distributor for the St. Albans line. St. Albans began building fodder shredders already in 1883.

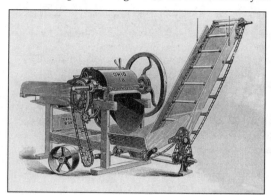

Silver Manufacturing Co., Salem, Ohio

An 1895 offering was the Ohio Standard Ensilage and Feed Cutter from Silver Manufacturing Co. The machine shown here was offered in four different sizes, this one being the No. 18. Silver also was building numerous other styles and sizes of cutters at the time. The company is listed as a manufacturer at least into the late 1940s.

Smalley Manufacturing Co., Manitowoc, Wisc.

In 1904, Smalley offered its Modern Silo Filler, with this one being the New Smalley Special 18 model. The blower was mounted down low, so as to pick up the cut material from the knives. To effectuate this design, a right-angle gear drive operated the blower shaft. This required an unusual belting arrangement.

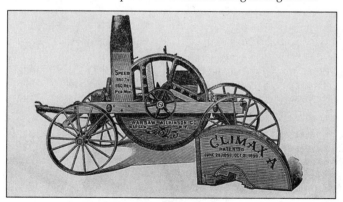

Warsaw-Wilkinson Co., Warsaw, N.Y.

An early entrant into the ensilage cutter business was the Climax from Warsaw-Wilkinson. This one was offered in three siz-

es: the smallest one selling for $190 and the big 23-inch model selling for $225. This price included a mounted self-feed table. With the cover removed, the cutter knives are plainly visible on the flywheel.

Wilder-Strong Implement Co., Monroe, Wisc.

This model of Wilder's Whirlwind was offered in 1905. It was billed as a feed cutter or fodder cutter, but the head-on view shown here offers little in the way of description. Obvious, though, is the unique folding feed carrier that permitted easy moving from one farm to another. Virtually no information has been located on this firm.

Trade Names			
Acme	Daniels Machine Co.	Woodstock, VT	1905
Adams	Adams Co.	Marysville, OH	1922
Advance	Rous, Mills & Co.	Doylestown, PA	1905
Advance-Leader	Doylestown Agricultural Works	Doylestown, PA	1924
Advance-Rumely	Advance-Rumely Thresher Co.	LaPorte, IN	1924
Aermotor	Aermotor Co.	Chicago, IL	1905
Alpine	Joseph Dick Agricultural Works	Canton, OH	1922
American	Wilder-Strong Implement Co.	Monroe, MI	1922
Ann Arbor	Ann Arbor Machine Co.	Ann Arbor, MI	1922
Apex	Joseph Dick Agricultural Works	Canton, OH	1922
Appleton	Appleton Mfg. Co.	Batavia, IL	1922
Armsaver	Killen-Strait Mfg. Co.	Appleton, WI	1922
Avery	Avery Co.	Peoria, IL	1922
Batavia	Climax Co.	Batavia, NY	1924
Belle City	Belle City Mfg. Co.	Racine Junction, WI	1905
Berres Gehl	Berres-Gehl Mfg. Co.	West Bend, WI	1905
Blizzard	Joseph Dick Agricultural Works	Canton, OH	1905
Boss	Hocking Valley Mfg. Co.	Lancaster, OH	1922
Brasher	P.E. Kennehan's Son & Co.	Brasher Falls, NY	1929

Trade Names (cont...)

Buckeye	Eagle Machine Co.	Lancaster, OH	1922
Case	J.I. Case Threshing Machine Co.	Racine, WI	1917
Challenge	Challenge Wind Mill & Feedmill Co.	Batavia, IL	1905
Clean Cut	Silver Mfg. Co.	Salem, OH	1924
Climax	Climax Co.	Batavia, NY	1922
Climax	Warsaw-Wilkinson Co.	Warsaw, NY	1905
Crown	W.R. Harrison & Co.	Massillon, OH	1922
Cummings	Ann Arbor Machine Co.	Ann Arbor, MI	1905
Cummings	Ann Arbor Machine Co.	Ann Arbor, MI	1922
Cyclone	Hartford Plow Works	Hartford, WI	1905
Daisy	Orangeville Agricultural Works	Orangeville, PA	1905
Dandy	Challenge Wind Mill & Feedmill Co.	Batavia, IL	1922
Dellinger-Mountville	Dellinger Mfg. Co.	Lancaster, PA	1936
Dixie	Letz Mfg. Co.	Crown Point, IN	1932
Dr. Bailey	Ames Plow Co.	Boston, MA	1905
Eagle	Eagle Machine Co.	Lancaster, OH	1905
Eagle	Eagle Mfg. Co.	Appleton, WI	1922
Electric	Silver Mfg. Co.	Salem, OH	1922
Empire	Messinger Mfg. Co.	Tatamy, PA	1905
Empire State	Climax Co.	Batavia, NY	1922
Fairbanks-Morse	Fairbanks, Morse & Co.	Chicago, IL	1922
Famous	Joseph Dick Agricultural Works	Canton, OH	1922
Fox	Fox River Tractor Co.	Appleton, WI	1924
Freeman	S. Freeman & Sons Mfg. Co.	Racine, WI	1905
Frenzel	Wausau Foundry & Machine Co.	Wausau, WI	1922
Gale-Baldwin	Belcher & Taylor Agricultural Tool Co.	Chicopee Falls, MA	1905
Gehl-Silberzahn	Gehl Bros. Mfg. Co.	West Bend, WI	1922
Geneva	Hocking Valley Mfg. Co.	Lancaster, OH	1922
Giant	Frank Hamachek	Kewaunee, WI	1905
Globe	Globe Foundry & Machine Co.	Sheboygan, WI	1905
Gray Fox	Fox River Tractor Co.	Appleton, WI	1929
Gray's	A.W. Gray's Sons	Middletown Springs, VT	1905
Hocking Valley	Hocking Valley Mfg. Co.	Lancaster, OH	1905
Holstein	John Lauson Mfg. Co.	New Holstein, WI	1922
Holstein	Meili-Blumberg Co.	New Holstein, WI	1917
Hummer	Rous-Meehan Foundry Co.	Chattanooga, TN	1905
Illinois	Illinois Tractor Co.	Bloomington, IL	1922
International	International Harvester Co.	Chicago, IL	1922
Invincible	Automatic Trip Carrier Co.	Rice Lake, WI	1922
Iowa	Gould Balance Valve Co.	Kellogg, IA	1922
Iron Age	Bateman Mfg. Co.	Grenloch, NJ	1922
Kalamazoo	Kalamazoo Tank & Silo Co.	Kalamazoo, MI	1922
Kelley	John G. Kelley	Waukesha, WI	1917
Kendrick	G.J. Emery	Fulton, NY	1922

Trade Names (cont...)

Keystone	Ellis Keystone Agricultural Works	Pottstown, PA	1905
Kinney's	Belcher & Taylor Agricultural Tool Co.	Chicopee Falls, MA	1905
Leader	Joseph Dick Agricultural Works	Canton, OH	1905
Leslie	St. Albans Foundry	St. Albans, VT	1905
Letz	Letz Mfg. Co.	Crown Point, IN	1924
Little Better	Double Power Mill Co.	Appleton, WI	1922
Little Giant	E.W. Ross Co.	Springfield, OH	1905
Mammoth Tornado	W.R. Harrison & Co.	Massillon, OH	1905
Massey-Harris	Massey-Harris Co.	Racine, WI	1929
M-B	Meili-Blumberg Co.	New Holstein, WI	1932
McCormick-Deering	International Harvester Co.	Chicago, IL	1924
Monarch	Lehr Agricultural Co.	Fremont, OH	1922
Mountville Clean-Cut	Mountville Mfg. Co.	Mountville, PA	192
New Hero	Appleton Mfg. Co.	Batavia, IL	1905
New Jenney	Hall Mfg. Co.	Cedar Rapids, IA	1932
Ohio	Silver Mfg. Co.	Salem, OH	1905
Owatonna	Owatonna Fanning Mill Co.	Owatonna, MN	1922
Papec	Papec Machine Co.	Lima, NY	1905
Pilgrim	Plymouth Foundry & Machine Co.	Plymouth, WI	1932
Pilot	Joseph Dick Agricultural Works	Canton, OH	1922
Plantation	Silver Mfg. Co.	Salem, OH	1922
Plymouth	Plymouth Foundry & Machine Co.	Plymouth, WI	1922
Porter's	Whitman Agricultural Co.	St. Louis, MO	1905
Randolph	Sargent, Osgood & Roundy	Randolph, VT	1922
Red Fox	Fox River Tractor Co.	Appleton, WI	1929
Richmond Champion	Wayne Works	Richmond, IN	1922
Robinson	Swayne, Robinson & Co.	Richmond, IN	1922
Rosenthal	Rosenthal Corn Husker Co.	Milwaukee, WI	1922
Ross	E.W. Ross Co.	Springfield, OH	1905
Rowell	I.B. Rowell Co.	Menomonee Falls, WI	1905
Rumely	M. Rumely Co.	LaPorte, IN	1915
Safe Lion	Geo. S. Comstock	Mechan-micsburg, PA	1909
Sandow	Sandy McManus Inc.	Waterloo, IA	1915
Silage King	Silo Specialty Mfg. Co.	Clinton, IA	1917
Silver's	Silver Mfg. Co.	Salem, OH	1922
Smalley	Smalley Mfg. Co.	Manitowoc, WI	1905
Speedway	Keystone Farm Machine Co.	York, PA	1905
Star	Star Mfg. Co.	Carpentersville, IL	1922
Steel King	Belle City Mfg. Co.	Racine, WI	1922
Stover	Stover Mfg. Co.	Freeport, IL	1922
Superior	Joseph Dick Agricultural Works	Canton, OH	1922
Swiss	Wilder-Strong Implement Co.	Monroe, MI	1905
Telegraph	F.F. Drinkhouse	Philipsburg, NJ	1905
Tornado	W.R. Harrison & Co.	Massillon, OH	1922

Anyone having additional materials and resources relating to American farm implements is invited to contact C.H. Wendel, in care of Krause Publications, 700 E. State St., Iola, WI 54990-0001.

F

Fanning Mills

Whether called a fanning mill or a grain cleaner is mostly a matter of semantics; both terms mean essentially the same thing. With the coming of intensive agriculture, farmers wanted to plant clean grain without replanting weeds harvested with the previous crop-there were enough of those already. Thus, there were many companies offering grain cleaners or fanning mills by the 1880s; this industry saw its peak in the 1920s. By that time, the market was fairly saturated and most of these little machines were so well built that it was nearly impossible to wear them out. In fact, a great many fanning mills used today saw first light in the 1920s or even earlier. Despite their age, they are used every season for cleaning oats and other grains.

Usually, a fanning mill will have a reasonable market value; it is not uncommon for a good machine to bring $100 or perhaps much more, depending on age and condition. Quite often, they are purchased for farm use, rather than as a farm antique.

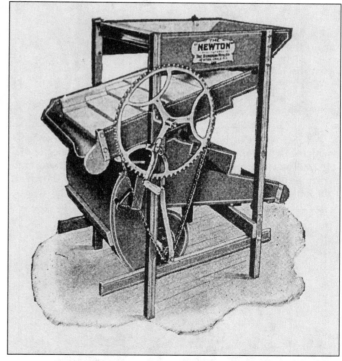

Bergman Manufacturing Co., Newton, Iowa, offered its Newton Grain Grader and Cleaner in this form for 1913. It was built for several years. Although there were probably other models designed for belt power, this one was purely a hand-powered outfit, as evidenced in the illustration.

Clipper Grain Cleaners from A.T. Ferrell & Co., Saginaw, Mich., were and remain the most popular of all fanning mills. Its fanning mills, such as this No. 1-B of the 1920s, were sold by the thousands and many are still in use. This one could be operated by hand power or could be belted. In the 1920s, this one was priced at $35.

A.T. Ferrell & Co., built several styles of Clipper bean sorters, with the two examples shown here coming from a catalog of the 1920s. They were specialized machines designed for picking and sorting edible beans, as well as soybeans. The Clipper shown at the left sold for $9.

Fosston Manufacturing Co., St. Paul, Minn., offered its Fosston Automatic No. 24 in 1910, shown here. This one was somewhat larger than the ordinary, even including a sacking elevator.

A large commercial warehouse fanning mill was offered by Grant-Ferris & Co., Troy, N.Y. at the turn of the century. Despite its size, this one was a hand-powered outfit, although it seems that a unit of this size might have been capable of belt power.

An 1897 catalog from Grant-Ferris & Co., illustrates its double-blast fanning mill of the time. As with most such mills, it not only cleaned the grain but also graded it so that small or broken seeds were discarded and only the best seed was saved for planting the new crop.

From 1909 comes this illustration of the Handicap Seed Cleaner and Grain Separator. It was built by the firm of Gunther & Lyman,

Wapakoneta, Ohio. Various companies entered this business in the early 1900s, but most of them only continued for a few years.

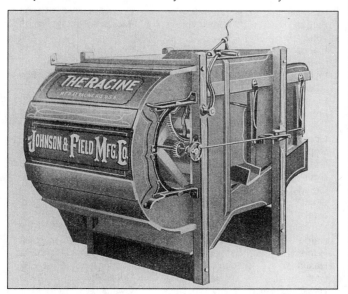

A very popular and widely advertised fanning mill came from Johnson & Field Manufacturing Co., Racine, Wis. This hand-powered outfit was even available with a separate sacking elevator, enabling the farmer to sack the cleaned grain for the new crop. Oftentimes, the grain cleaning was done in the winter, so cranking the mill probably wasn't a bad job after all-at least one could keep warm! Shown here is the No. 1 Racine Farm Mill of 1915.

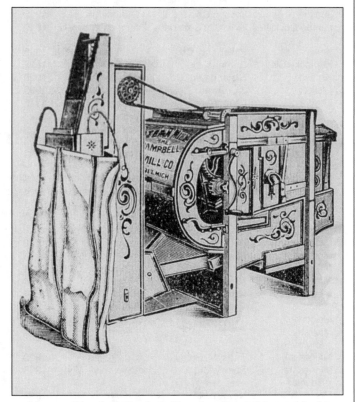

Manson Campbell Co., Ltd., Detroit, offered this model of its Chatham Fanning Mill in 1904. It is shown with its patented sacking attachment. For reasons unknown, fanning mills were usually decorated with extensive pin-striping, plus stencils or decals, even when most farm machinery was losing that special appearance.

About 1910, One Minute Manufacturing Co., Newton, Iowa, offered its One Minute Grain Grader and Seed Cleaner. Its Model No. 1 shown here is equipped with a hand-crank, but it was removable and the machine could be powered with a special drive attachment as shown in this engraving.

J.L. Owens Co., Minneapolis, specialized in large grain cleaners for elevators and mills, but also offered its New Superior Fanning Mills. Built in two different sizes for farm use, they could be powered by hand or belt and could be furnished with or without a bagging elevator. This one is of about 1910 vintage.

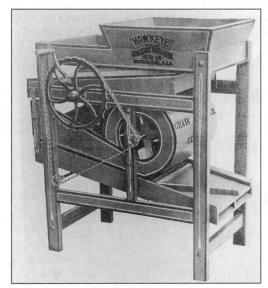

For a time, this Hawkeye Grain Grader was offered by Parsons-Hawkeye Co., Newton, Iowa. Eventually, the same machine appears under the auspices of Maytag Co., Newton. The Hawkeye carried as its slogan the Biblical expression, "Whatsoever a man soweth, that shall he also reap."

Trade Names

Trade Name	Company	Location	Year
Advance	J.L. Owens Co.	Minneapolis, MN	1905
Aul	Henry Aul & Son	Lyons, NY	1905
Aul	Wm. C. Aul	Lyons, NY	1924
B & G	Bristl & Gale Co.	Chicago, IL	1915
Badger State	Foster & Williams Mfg. Co.	Racine, WI	1892
Beeman	Beeman Grain Cleaner Co.	Minneapolis, MN	1892
Belle City	Racine Implement Co.	Racine, WI	1892
Bennett	L.H. Bennett	Plymouth, MI	1905
Blake	S. Howes Co., Johnson & Field Div.	Silver Creek, NY	1929
Bonanza	Twin City Separator Co.	Minneapolis, MN	1905
Bradford	Bradford Mill Co.	Cincinnati, OH	1892
Bradley	Johnson & Field Mfg. Co.	Racine, WI	1909
Bryan	W.A. Mallery	Hillsdale, NY	1892
Buckeye	John Hosford	Monroeville, OH	1892
Bull Dog	Colfax Mfg. Co.	Minneapolis, MN	1915
Calkins	Calkins Mfg. Co.	Spokane, WA	1929
Campbell	Schoharie Agricultural Works	Central Bridge, NY	1892
Canadian	Kink Mfg. Co.	Kansas City, MO	1929
Canton	Johnson & Field Mfg. Co.	Racine, WI	1909
Carter	Carter-Mayhew Co.	Minneapolis, MN	1924
Centennial	S. Freeman & Sons Mfg. Co.	Racine, WI	1892
Champion	J.L. Owens Co.	Minneapolis, MN	1909
Champion	Solar Mfg. Co.	Kaukauna, WI	1905
Chatham	Manson Campbell Co.	Detroit, MI	1905
Chatham	Manson Campbell Co.	Detroit, MI	1913
Cleland	A.V. Cleland	Minneapolis, MN	1905
Climax	Brennan & Co.	Louisville, KY	1892
Climax	Jerry Bros.	West Chazy, NY	1892
Clipper	A.T. Ferrell & Co.	Saginaw, MI	1913
Clipper	J.E. Smith	Shiloh, OH	1892
Colfax	Colfax Mfg. Co.	Minneapolis, MN	1929
Cutts	H.D. Nash Co.	Sacramento, CA	1892
Dakota	Dakota Mfg. Co.	Scotland, SD	1892
Daniel Best	Daniel Best Agricultural Works	San Leandro, CA	1892
Daniel Bull	Johnson & Field Mfg. Co.	Racine, WI	1924
Detroit	Detroit Grader Co.	Detroit, MI	1913
Dickey	A.P. Dickey Mfg. Co.	Racine, WI	1905
Dixie	Brennan & Co.	Louisville, KY	1892
Dual	J.L. Owens Co.	Minneapolis, MN	1924
Eagle	Eagle Mfg. Co.	Decatur, IL	1892
Eclipse	Eclipse Mfg. Co.	Middlebury, IN	1892
Emerson	Hart-Carter Co.	Minneapolis, MN	1932
Eureka	A.N. Durling	Detroit, MI	1905
Excelsior	C. Altringer	Racine, WI	1892
Excelsior	Johnson & Field Mfg. Co.	Racine, WI	1913
Expert	A.V. Cleland	Minneapolis, MN	1905
Famous	S. Howes Co., Johnson & Field Div.	Silver Creek, NY	1929
Farmer's Favorite	Johnson & Field Mfg. Co.	Racine, WI	1913
Farmer's Friend	Montgomery Ward Co.	Chicago, IL	1924

Trade Names (cont...)

Trade Name	Company	Location	Year
Fearless	Harder Mfg. Co.	Cobleskill, NY	1905
Fergus	M. Grollimund	Fergus Falls, MN	1905
Fleetwood	Fleetwood Foundry & Mach. Works	Fleetwood, PA	1905
Flying Dutchman	Johnson & Field Mfg. Co.	Racine, WI	1924
Fosston	Fosston Mfg. Co.	St. Paul, MN	1909
Freeman	S. Freeman & Sons Mfg. Co.	Racine, WI	1905
Ghent	Ghent Mfg. Co.	Ghent, MN	1932
Gopher	Gopher Machine Co.	New Prague, MN	1924
Grader	L.M. Crosby & Son	Ashtabula, OH	1892
Grain King	Vaughn Products Co.	LaCrosse, WI	1929
Granger	J.A. Bradmon	Lansing, MI	1892
Grant's	Ames Plow Co.	Boston, MA	1892
Haaky	Haaky Mfg. Co.	St. Paul, MN	1932
Handicap	Gunther & Lyman	Wapakoneta, OH	1909
Harder	Minard Harder	Cobleskill, NY	1892
Harrison	Leonard D. Harrison	New Haven, CT	1892
Hastings	John Lucas	Hastings, MN	1892
Hatfield	J.F. Hatfield	Dublin, IN	1892
Hawkeye Hustler	Sperry Mfg. Co.	Owatonna, MN	1905
Hero	Twin City Separator Co.	Minneapolis, MN	1905
Huntley	Huntley Mfg. Co.	Silver Creek, NY	1905
Ideal	Ideal Seed & Grain Separator Co.	Indianapolis, IN	1922
International	Burch Plow Works	Crestline, OH	1924
Johnson	Belcher & Taylor Agricultural Tool Co.	Chicopee Falls, MA	1905
Judson	Judson Co.	Detroit, MI	1932
Jumbo Cockle	Twin City Separator Co.	Minneapolis, MN	1909
Keller	Keller Mfg. Co.	Sauk Center, MN	1892
Kentucky Cief	Brennan & Co.	Louisville, KY	1892
Krussow	Cleland Mfg. Co.	Minneapolis, MN	1929
Leader	J.L. Owens Co.	Minneapolis, MN	1909
Leader	Leader Mfg. Co.	Carthage, IL	1913
Lightning	Kansas City Hay Press Co.	Kansas City, MO	1924
Little Barefoot	Miller Bros. Mfg. Co.	Alexandria, IN	1905
Little Chief	E.P. Dickey Racine Fanning Mill Co	Racine, WI	1892
Little Giant	A.P. Dickey Mfg. Co.	Racine, WI	1905
Little Star	Iowa Wind Mill & Pump Co.	Cedar Rapids, IA	1924
Lyons	C.H. Putney	Lyons, NY	1892
Lyons	Nagley Mfg. Co.	Lyons, NY	1913
Lyons Improved	Henry Aul & Son	Lyons, NY	1892
Maplebay	Maplebay Mfg. Co.	Crookston, MN	1913
Marquis	J.L. Owens Co.	Minneapolis, MN	1924
Maytag	Maytag Co.	Newton, IA	1924
Merryfield	Cedar Rapids Foundry & Mach. Co.	Cedar Rapids, IA	1924
Mexican	J.L. Owens Co.	Minneapolis, MN	1909
Michael Improved	E.F. Michael Co.	Laporte, IN	1892
Midget	Thos. M. Bales	Dublin, IN	1892
Minnesota Special	Sperry Mfg. Co.	Owatonna, MN	1905
Monarch	Newark Machine Co.	Columbus, OH	1892
Mt. Hood	Johnson & Field Mfg. Co.	Racine, WI	1913
New Eclipse	Johnson & Field Mfg. Co.	Racine, WI	1909

Trade Names (cont...)			
New Era	New Era Fanning Mill Co.	Minneapolis, MN	1924
New Martin	Johnson & Field Mfg. Co.	Racine, WI	1909
New Michael	C.H. Michael Mfg. Co.	Laporte, IN	1905
New Superior	J.L. Owens Co.	Minneapolis, MN	1909
New Victory	Sperry Mfg. Co.	Owatonna, MN	1905
New Victory	Sperry Mfg. Co.	Owatonna, MN	1909
Newark	Newark Machine Co.	Newark, OH	1905
Northwestern	J.L. Owens Co.	Minneapolis, MN	1905
Nu-Day	Fountain City Novelty Works	Fountain City, IN	1936
O.K.	C.D. Edwards	Albert Lea, MN	1892
One Minute	One Minute Mfg. Co.	Newton, IA	1924
Owatonna	Owatonna Fanning Mill Co.	Owatonna, MN	1892
Owens	Griffith & Turner Co.	Baltimore, MD	1913
Owens Advance	J.L. Owens Co.	Minneapolis, MN	1892
Owens End Shake	J.L. Owens Co.	Minneapolis, MN	1905
Owens Leader	J.L. Owens Co.	Minneapolis, MN	1905
Pease	E.H. Pease Mfg. Co.	Racine, WI	1892
Pease	Marseilles Mfg. Co.	Marseilles, IL	1905
Peerless	Johnson & Field Mfg. Co.	Racine, WI	1909
Pennsylvania	A. Buch's Sons Co.	Elizabethtown, PA	1913
Peoria	Kingman & Co.	Peoria, IL	1892
Plymouth	L.H. Bennett	Plymouth, MI	1892
Poyneer	P. Poyneer	Kalamazoo, MI	1892
Queen of the Harvest	Jerry Bros.	West Chazy, NY	1892
Queen of the West	Chas. H. Trappe	Mascoutah, IL	1892
Racine	Johnson & Field Mfg. Co.	Racine, WI	1892
Red Cross	Red Cross Mfg. Co.	Bluffton, IN	1924
Reist	J.B. Reist & Son	Harrisburg, PA	1905
Reschke	Reschke Machine Works	Wichita, KS	1929
Rock Island	Rock Island Plow Co.	Rock Island, MN	1913
Rowell	J.S. Rowell Mfg. Co.	Beaver Dam, WI	1892
S & H	Fosston Mfg. Co.	St. Paul, MN	1909
Star	Iowa Wind Mill & Pump Co.	Cedar Rapids, IA	1922
Success	Twin City Separator Co.	Minneapolis, MN	1909
Superior	J.L. Owens Co.	Minneapolis, MN	1905
Underwood	Farm Fanning Mill Co.	Minneapolis, MN	1929
Vaughn	Vaughn Mfg. Co.	Minneapolis, MN	1915
Viall	Grant Fanning Mill & Cradle Co.	Melrose, NY	1892
Victory	Sperry Mfg. Co.	Owatonna, MN	1905
Vindicator	Vindicator Fanning Mill Co.	Holland, MI	1892
Webber	Hirsch Bros.	Milwaukee, WI	1905
Webber	Knipscheid Bros.	Rockton, IL	1922
Webber	Webber Mfg. Co.	Rockton, IL	1915
Weed	D.T. Weed	Lanark, IL	1892
Western	JL. Owens Co.	Minneapolis, MN	1909
Whitman	Whitman Agricultural Works	Auburn, ME	1892
Worcester	Ames Plow Co.	Boston, MA	1909
X-L-All	Sears, Roebuck & Co.	Chicago, IL	1924
Young Giant	A.P. Dickey Mfg. Co.	Racine, WI	1892

Farmstead Tools & Equipment

Under this heading one could (and we probably will) write a complete book. The variety of farm tools and appliances is simply amazing. While the frontiersmen had little more than a plow, a spade and an ax, farmers of 1900 were equipping themselves with numerous tools and gadgets to make their work easier. For the purposes of this book, it has seemed the better course to provide a brief outline of farmstead tools and equipment rather than give the impression they were not an important part of the scene. Yet, to provide a comprehensive display would minimize other important areas of discussion.

By the 1880s, many farmers were convinced that cooked feed was more nutritious and more palatable than uncooked. Numerous companies sprang forth with feed cooking apparatus; some, like this one from Goulds & Austin, could be used for almost anything requiring hot water or steam

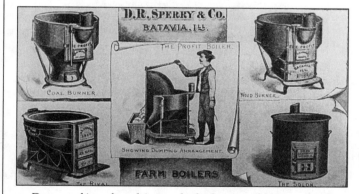

Dozens of iron foundries made the huge cauldrons or kettles as shown here from D.R. Sperry & Co. The company called them farm boilers, as compared to steam boilers. In other words, the farm boiler was capable of boiling water, as in a kettle, but could not generate steam. Large iron cauldrons as shown often bring $100 or more.

Feed cookers or farm boilers were often built on a regional basis, coming from iron foundries in a certain area, rather than being shipped hundreds of miles (with additional freight costs). Such was the case with Swift's Feed Cooker, made in sizes from 20 to 60 gallons. Swift Manufacturing Co., Waterloo, Iowa, offered this one in 1907; the company also made carts, feed grinders and other equipment.

Farm boilers, such as this one from F. Thurman & Co., Plymouth, Wis., were used for everything from cooking feed to scalding hogs or making soap. Sometimes, they were simply used for boiling large quantities of water. As noted, large cast-iron cauldrons like this one often bring $100 or more.

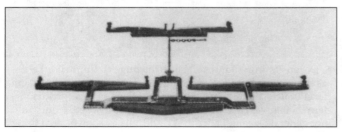

Heider Manufacturing Co., Carroll, Iowa, was a major manufacturer of eveners as shown. In fact, this illustration shows but one of its line, since the company made literally dozens of different styles. Today, wooden eveners sell sometimes for very little, while in other instances, they may bring $30 to $50.

Heider Manufacturing Co. also made various sorts of single-trees, each for a specific purpose. For those unfamiliar with the terminology, eveners were used to hitch a specific number of horses to, for instance, a plow. If the evener was for four horses, then four singletrees as shown, were needed, one for each horse. Singletrees today sell for anywhere from $5 to $20.

In cold weather climates, keeping a water supply available to livestock necessitated the use of a tank heater. These were usually of cast iron, heavy enough to sink to the bottom by their own weight. In cold weather it was necessary to tend the fire on a regular basis, usually several times every day. This one was made by Stover Manufacturing Co., Freeport, Ill.

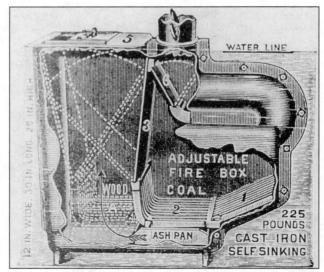

A very popular tank heater was the Cow Boy from Wills Manufacturing Co., Mendota, Ill. This sectional view shows the inside construction, particularly demonstrating the adaptability of this unit to either wood or coal. While this advertisement is from 1914, the company made the Cow Boy Tank Heater for many years.

Dayton-Dowd Co., Quincy, Ill., made the Economy tank heaters for a number of years. The Economy of the late 1920s was offered in three sizes (as shown in the specifications). The largest unit sold for $23.

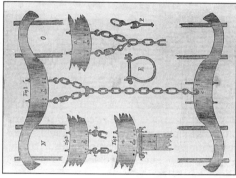

The early settlers used oxen as draft animals; doing so required that the farmer have an ox-yoke. For the benefit of blacksmiths and enterprising farmers, the Feb. 22, 1851, *Boston Cultivator* ran this engraving and description of a new ox-yoke design. Although a few ox-yokes were "factory-made," the great majority were the product of localized blacksmith or millwright shops. Ox-yokes sometimes bring $100 or more; excellent examples might bring several times that figure.

Most farmers had a small box on their corn wagon; when they came across an extra nice ear of corn, it was saved to be used for

next year's seed. These ears were carefully dried and many different kinds of drying racks were devised. This one of 1923 is from Bain Bros. Manufacturing Co., Cedar Rapids, Iowa. It would hold from 625 to 700 ears of corn.

Once the seed corn was dried and shelled, it was time to see how well it would germinate. To this end, many companies sold special corn testers. Bain Bros. Manufacturing Co., Cedar Rapids, Iowa, offered this Ideal Corn Tester in the 1920s. Samples were placed in individual cells; with the use of artificial heat from a kerosene lamp, the seed would germinate in a few days.

While coaster wagons may not have been essential to getting the farm work accomplished, they filled an important role for the youngsters. Having one of these 1907 Star Coaster Wagons must have indeed been a thrill in a day when toys were the exception rather than the rule. This line came from Hunt, Helm, Ferris & Co., Harvard, Ill.

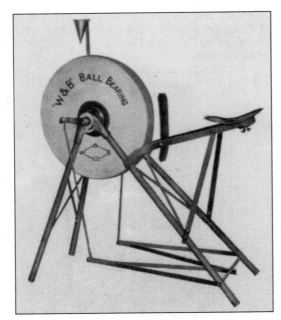

One of the necessities on a farm was the grindstone. Treadle units like this one from Whitman & Barnes Manufacturing Co., Akron, Ohio, were sold by the thousands. A small vessel above the stone kept it wet while the farmer sharpened the scythe, ax or other cutlery. Curiously, most old grindstones have a relatively low antique value.

In 1915, Peerless Machine Works at Freeport, Ill., offered its No. 1 Peerless grinder. Instead of the old-fashioned sandstone wheel, this one used a vitrified wheel that was easily replaceable and was much more aggressive than earlier designs. The grinding wheel is shown on one end of the spindle, while the other end could be fitted with a polishing wheel.

Old sickle grinders sometimes have a substantial antique value, occasionally selling for $50 or more. Shown here is the Star Sickle

Grinder of 1898; unfortunately, the magazine article does not give the name of the manufacturer, nor have we found it in subsequent research. Numerous companies made sickle grinders; oftentimes, they were made by the firms making the mowers or grain binders.

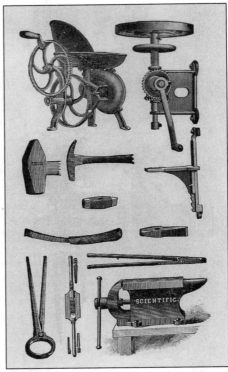

By the 1880s, enterprising farmers could buy a complete shop outfit from Foos Manufacturing Co., Springfield, Ohio. This 1888 catalog illustration displays the complete outfit for home blacksmithing and horse shoeing. Each of the items shown here is now in the antique tool category.

Did You Know?

Antique corn shellers are a popular farm collectible; small one- and two-hole designs usually bring $50 or more, while larger four- and six-hole versions fall in the $250 to $500 range.

Did You Know?

Old cream separators are highly sought after by a specialized group of collectors, but the separators usually do not fetch high figures on auction (less than $100).

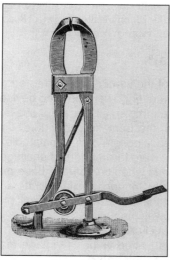

An early advertisement from The New London Vise Works gives the post office box number but fails to give the city and state where the company was located. However, a copy of this unique horse shoer's foot vise would likely be a highly prized item for tool collectors. Its action is easily seen in the engraving. This interesting vise sold for $15.

When this advertisement appeared in 1903, very few farmers or blacksmiths, had a lathe of any kind. Many were overjoyed to have a simple foot-operated lathe like this one from W.F. & John Barnes Co., Rockford, Ill. This 7-inch lathe sold for $40; today, its value as a collectible could be 10 times that figure.

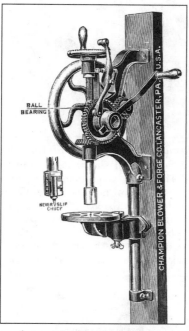

By 1920, many farmers had equipped themselves with a post drill. This was usually their first introduction to a machine that permitted them to drill a hole through a piece of iron; without it, the only choices were to journey to a local blacksmith or to heat the iron and punch a hole through the steel. This one is from Champion Blower & Forge Co., Lancaster, Pa.

An 1887 advertisement from A.S. Todd, Sterling, Ill., shows its Dandy Barrel Cart, a great labor-saver on the farm. This particular style involved fitting the hardware to a wooden barrel in a permanent manner. Dozens of companies made barrel carts.

Did You Know?

Workable grain binders are becoming a scarcity today; thus a grain binder in excellent operating condition may bring $200 to $300 or more.

One of the major implement manufacturers to include hand carts in its line was Roderick Lean Manufacturing Co., Mansfield, Ohio. Its Butler hand carts could be fitted with a barrel, a box or for whatever purpose might be desired.

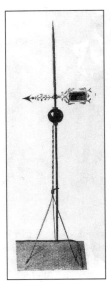

By the early 1900s, farmers in many areas were anxious to install lightning rod equipment. Few things were as devastating to a farmer as the loss of a barn, a crib or even the home to fire, and many of these fires were caused by lightning. Usually, the lightning rods were installed by people qualified in this business; the 1903 list of manufacturers included The Martin Co., Sac City, Iowa.

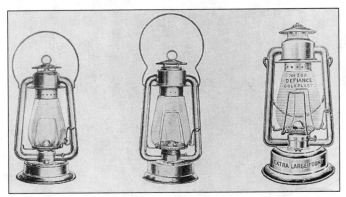

Almost every farm had a lantern or two on hand. These so-called Cold Blast lanterns could be safely used in the barn and could also light up a dark night. Numerous styles were made by several different companies, with three different sizes shown here. Pricing varies; the reader is directed to various antique price guides for further information.

For the farmer of 1900 and before, a macadam road was a rarity and paved roads didn't exist. Farmers in each township often band-

ed together to look after their own roads. To this end, Pitts Thresher Works at Marseilles, Ill., offered its Pitts Patent Road Worker in 1889. The complete outfit shown here sold for $95.

Feed Cutters

By the turn of the century, the term "feed cutters" generally implied a hand or power-operated device that would cut corn, hay or straw into small pieces for use as livestock feed. By comparison, the term "feed grinders" usually implied a machine for reducing grain to a palatable feed. Many of these machines were forerunners of ensilage cutters and an overlap is obvious when comparing these machines to feed cutters. Generally, though, ensilage cutters were machines designed to cut the forage crop into small pieces and either elevate it or blow it into a silo.

Today, relatively few feed cutters exist. Even so, they seem to have a limited value to vintage machinery collectors. Quite often they can be secured for a relatively low price of less than $50. As with all vintage equipment, the condition and the rarity of the particular item have a dramatic effect on the value.

Appleton Manufacturing Co., Appleton, Wisc.

This 1888 advertisement shows Peck's Improved Shelling, Cleaning and Threshing Attachment on an Appleton Fodder Cutter. All this is somehow tied together as Goddard's Process with a patent date of Dec. 18, 1883. Little is known of this unusual machine; although the side of the machine plainly states the address at Appleton, Wis., the accompanying article notes that the company is at Chicago. Is this the same Appleton Manufacturing Co., as at Batavia, Ill.? Our research has not indicated the answer.

Appleton Manufacturing Co., Batavia, Ill.

A 1917 catalog from Appleton Manufacturing Co., illustrates various of its fodder cutters, although the term might also be feed cutters. This one is shown with a hand-crank and one can only imagine the work it was to keep this machine in operation. Presumably, it could also be fitted with a belt pulley.

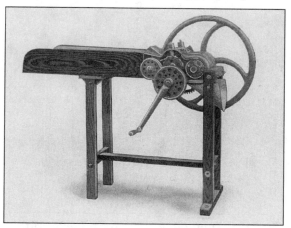

Challenge Co., Batavia, Ill.

Several different styles of fodder cutters are shown in the 1910 catalog of Challenge Co., Batavia, Ill. This small machine is a hand-cranked style, and the company has added substantial cast-iron guards over the open gears. As with most of these machines, the framework is entirely of hardwood.

A.B. Farquhar Co., Limited, York, Pa.

Another approach to the feed cutter was the hand-lever style. With this device, the feed was advanced on the table and the curved knife was brought down. The inherent dangers of this machine are hard to describe. In those days, however, owners of machinery were presumed to know better than to get fingers or other body parts in the way.

G.S. Garth, Mill Hall, Pa.

In 1887, Garth's Jumbo and Try Me feed cutters were available to the farmer. They were built along the same pattern, with the

Jumbo being substantially heavier and larger. Aside from this early illustration, nothing further is known of the firm.

W.R. Harrison & Co., Canton, Ohio

When this 1888 advertisement appeared, W.R. Harrison & Co., was located in Canton, Ohio. Shown here is its Tornado Feed Cutter No. 18. This unit was large for its time and was strictly a belt-powered machine. Although the elevator was probably optional, it would have been nearly imperative for a machine of this size.

At some point, now unknown, W.R. Harrison & Co., moved from Canton to Massillon, Ohio. A 1919 advertisement shows its Tornado Feed Cutter; it varied little from the one built at Canton back in 1888. While this one is shown with a hand-crank, it seems likely that a belt pulley was another option.

Hartman Co., Chicago, Ill.

Hartman Co., was a large catalog mail-order house that thrived into the 1930s. During the 1920s, the company offered its Majestic feed cutter, noting that it was made with a heavy hardwood frame. Hartman likely contracted with another manufacturer for this machine—the actual builder is now unknown.

Hocking Valley Manufacturing Co., Lancaster, Ohio

Hocking Valley was a leader in manufacturing various kinds of feed mills, corn shellers and other farm equipment. Its designs were always very substantial, as is evident on this 1890 version of the Improved Giant Feed Mill. Due to the size of the machine, it was furnished with a belt pulley; in the absence of a motive power, the hand-crank is obvious on the large flywheel.

Long, Black & Alstatter, Hamilton, Ohio

With a patent date of Nov. 2, 1858, this small feed cutter ranks among the earliest designs. This unique cutter used a v-shaped trough to feed material under the knife. Presumably, it could have been operated by one person, although one to feed and one to cut would have been a more likely scenario.

From the turn of the century comes an advertisement for the Hamilton Hay, Straw and Fodder Cutter from Long, Black & Alstatter. This one was equipped with a belt pulley, and, in case power was available, the hand-crank was easily removed. With the coming of small gasoline engines, mainly after 1910, farmers quickly added one of these to their farm power arsenal.

Did You Know?

The Appleton No. 19 Cyclone Corn and Cob Breaker sold for $25 in 1917.

Geo. K. Oyler Manufacturing Co., St. Louis, Mo.

When this 1884 advertisement appeared, Geo. K. Oyler's company was building a wide range of farm equipment. Its Feed & Straw Cutter shown here was of heavy all-wood construction. Little is known of this firm after the 1880s.

Plymouth Foundry & Machine Co., Plymouth, Wisc.

About 1910, Plymouth was offering its Emperor Cylinder Feed Cutter (this one has an unusual power-jack attachment). By its use, the cutter could be coupled through tumbling rods to a horsepower. For farmers without a gas engine or other power, this left the horse do the work while the farmer fed roughage into the cutter.

Did You Know?

Since so few threshing machines remain, especially the early wooden designs, they have now acquired collector status. Late model, all-steel machines of the 1920s and later, often bring $500 or more in good condition and some of the earliest wooden designs have acquired museum status.

Silver Manufacturing Co., Salem, Ohio

An 1888 advertisement notes the name of Silver & Deming on this No. 24 Ohio Special Ensilage Cutter. An 1892 advertisement notes Silver Manufacturing Co., and also refers to the Ohio Special as a feed cutter. The size of this machine precluded it from hand operation; a belt pulley is obvious on the far side of the main shaft.

Smalley Manufacturing Co., Manitowoc, Wisc.

From 1888 comes this advertisement for a big Smalley feed cutter. As shown here, farmers are taking baled hay or straw and converting it to fodder through the cutter; the latter is being operated by a portable steam engine. Smalley also built numerous other farm machines.

By 1915, Smalley was offering this No. 10 Force Feed Cutter and Blower. This small outfit was capable of blowing the cut

material to a barn or a small silo. While not intended to compete with the big silo fillers on the market, this small machine found its niche with the small farmer.

Stover Manufacturing Co., Freeport, Ill.

Long before Stover became famous for its gasoline engines, the company was building windmills, feed grinders and many other farm implements. From 1887 comes this illustration of a Stover Ideal Feed Mill. The protective cover is removed from the cutter, demonstrating an early version of the flywheel cutter design.

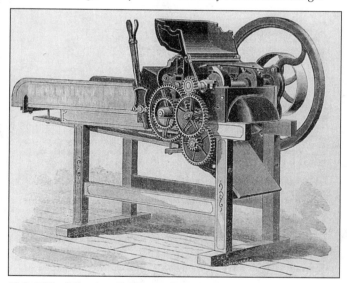

U.S. Wind Engine & Pump Co., Batavia, Ill.

This firm, well known among farmers for its windmills and its other equipment, met with a good reception on the farm. In 1887, the company offered this IXL Feed Cutter, a large machine designed for power use. This one was extraordinary for its time because it included a power-feed mechanism and other advanced features.

Did You Know?

Antique corn shellers are a popular farm collectible; small one- and two-hole designs usually bring $50 or more, while larger four- and six-hole versions fall in the $250 to $500 range.

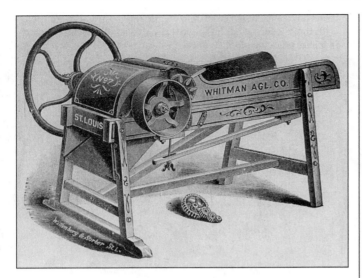

Whitman Agricultural Co., St. Louis, Mo.

For 1887, Whitman offered this heavy feed cutter to the farmer. It included a power-feed mechanism and the length of cut could be varied by substituting various change gears (as shown beneath the machine). Whitman was a well-known and respected manufacturer for many years.

Trade Names

Aermotor	Aermotor Co.	Chicago, IL	1905
Alligator	Keystone Farm Machine Co.	York, PA	1905
Alpine	Joseph Dick Agricultural Works	Canton, OH	1905
Ames	Ames Plow Co.	Boston, MA	1905
Appleton	Appleton Mfg. Co.	Batavia, IL	1909
B & G	Bristol & Gale Co.	Chicago, IL	1915
Baldwin	Belcher & Taylor Agricultural Tool Co.	Chicopee Falls, MA	1905
Belle City	Belle City Mfg. Co.	Racine Junction, WI	1905
Berres-Gehl	Berres-Gehl Mfg. Co.	West Bend, WI	1905
Boss	Edward Sellers	Oak Hall, PA	1905
Boss	Hocking Valley Mfg. Co.	Lancaster, OH	1905
Buch	A. Buch's Sons Co.	Elizabethtown, PA	1909
Challenge	Challenge Wind Mill & Feedmill Co.	Batavia, IL	1905
Chicken	Belcher & Taylor Agricultural Tool Co.	Chicopee Falls, MA	1909
Clipper	A.B. Farquhar	York, PA	1905
Columbia	W.R. Harrison & Co.	Massillon, OH	1905
Comet	Wilder-Strong Implement Co.	Monroe, MI	1905
Crown	W.R. Harrison & Co.	Massillon, OH	1905
Cumming	Ann Arbor Machine Co.	Ann Arbor, MI	1909
Cyclone Success	Ironwood Mfg. Co.	Bellefontaine, OH	1915
Daisy	Orangeville Agricultural Works	Orangeville, PA	1905
Dandy	Challenge Wind Mill & Feedmill Co.	Batavia, IL	1909
Dandy	E.W. Ross Co.	Springfield, OH	1905
Defender	S.R. White & Bro.	Norfolk, VA	1905
Defiance	Sidney Tool Co.	Sidney, OH	1905
Defiance Pony	Sidney Tool Co.	Sidney, OH	1905

Trade Names (cont...)

Dick's Famous	Joseph Dick Agricultural Works	Canton, OH	1905
Drinkhouse	F.F. Drinkhouse	Philipsburg, NJ	1905
Eagle	Eagle Machine Co.	Lancaster, OH	1905
Eagle	Eagle Mfg. Co.	Appleton, WI	1909
Easy	Edward Sellers	Oak Hall, PA	1905
Electric	Silver Mfg. Co.	Salem, OH	1905
Electric	Smalley Mfg. Co.	Manitowoc, WI	1905
Emperor	Plymouth Foundry & Machine Co.	Plymouth, WI	1915
Empire	Messinger Mfg. Co.	Tatamy, PA	1905
Empire State	Warsaw-Wilkinson Co.	Warsaw, NY	1909
Eureka	Eureka Mower Co.	Utica, NY	1905
Fischer	A.J. Fischer	Milwaukee, WI	1905
Freeman	S. Freeman & Sons Mfg. Co.	Racine, WI	1905
Frenzel	Wausau Foundry & Machine Co.	Wausau, WI	1905
Gale	Belcher & Taylor Agricultural Tool Co.	Chicopee Falls, MA	1905
Geneva	Hocking Valley Mfg. Co.	Lancaster, OH	1905
Giant	Frank Hamachek	Kewanee, WI	1905
Globe	Globe Foundry & Machine Co.	Sheboygan, WI	1905
Gowanda	Gowanda Agricultural Works	Gowanda, NY	1905
Hamilton	Long & Alstatter Co.	Hamilton, OH	1905
Handy	Fleetwood Foundry & Mach. Works	Fleetwood, PA	1905
Hide Roll	Ann Arbor Machine Co.	Ann Arbor, MI	1909
Hocking Valley	Hocking Valley Mfg. Co.	Lancaster, OH	1905
Holstein	John Lauson Mfg. Co.	New Holstein, WI	1922
Ideal	Frank Hamachek	Kewanee, WI	1905
Indiana	Indiana Foundry Co.	Indiana, PA	1905
Ithaca	Williams Bros.	Ithaca, NY	1905
Keystone	Ellis Keystone Agricultural Works	Pottstown, PA	1905
Keystone Tony	Ellis Keystone Agricultural Works	Pottstown, PA	1905
King	Donaldson Bros.	Mt. Clemens, MI	1905
Knox All	Keystone Farm Machine Co.	York, PA	1905
Kokosing	Hocking Valley Mfg. Co.	Lancaster, OH	1905
Lion	Belcher & Taylor Agricultural Tool Co.	Chicopee Falls, MA	1909
Little Giant	Spangler Mfg. Co.	York, PA	1905
Little York	Keystone Farm Machine Co.	York, PA	1905
Messinger	Messinger Mfg. Co.	Tatamy, PA	1905
Monarch	Lehr Agricultural Co.	Fremont, OH	1905
Moon's	Wayne Works	Richmond, IN	1905
Moore	Moore Plow & Implement Co.	Greenville, MI	1905
O.K.	Geo. S. Comstock	Mechanics-burg, PA	1905
Ohio	Silver Mfg. Co.	Salem, OH	1905
Otsego	Babcock Mfg. Co.	Leonardsville, NY	1905
Our Rapid	Keystone Farm Machine Co.	York, PA	1905
Papec	Papec Machine Co.	Shortsville, NY	1924

Trade Names (cont...)

Peerless	Hickox-Mull Mfg. Co.	Toledo, OH	1905
Pennsylvania	A. Buch's Sons Co.	Elizabethtown, PA	1905
Plantation	Silver Mfg. Co.	Salem, OH	1913
Plymouth	Plymouth Foundry & Machine Co.	Plymouth, WI	1915
Pony	Silver Mfg. Co.	Salem, OH	1909
Pony	Silver Mfg. Co.	Salem, OH	1909
Raisin Valley	Wilder-Strong Implement Co.	Monroe, MI	1905
Richmond Champion	Wayne Works	Richmond, IN	1905
Rich's	Ames Plow Co.	Boston, MA	1905
Ross	E.W. Ross Co.	Springfield, OH	1905
Sanford	Long & Alstatter Co.	Hamilton, OH	1913
Search	Search Mfg. Co.	Oshkosh, WI	1905
Self-Sharpener	Belcher & Taylor Agricultural Tool Co	Chicopee Falls, MA	1909
Sheldon's	Sheldon Engine & Sales Co.	Waterloo, IA	1924
Silberzahn	Gehl Bros. Mfg. Co.	West Bend, WI	1909
Smalley	Smalley Mfg. Co.	Manitowoc, WI	1905
Smith	Cardwell Machine Co.	Richmond, VA	1905
Smith	G.T. Glascock & Son	Greensboro, NC	1905
Smith	S.R. White & Bro.	Norfolk, VA	1905
Special	D.F. Tanner	Holland, NY	1913
Speedway	Keystone Farm Machine Co.	York, PA	1915
Star	Gowanda Agricultural Works	Gowanda, NY	1905
Star	Greenville Implement Co.	Greenville, MI	1905
Superior	Hench & Dromgold Co.	York, PA	1905
Swiss	Wilder-Strong Implement Co.	Monroe, MI	1905
Telegraph	F.F. Drinkhouse	Philipsburg, NJ	1913
Tornado	W.R. Harrison & Co.	Massillon, OH	1905
Triumph	Lyon Iron Works	Greene, NY	1909
U.T.K.	Chas. H. Childs & Co.	Utica, NY	1905
United	United Engine Co.	Lansing, MI	1924
Victor	Foster & Williams Mfg. Co.	Racine, WI	1909
Whirlwind	Wilder-Strong Implement Co.	Monroe, MI	1913
Wonder	E.W. Ross Co.	Springfield, OH	1905
Wyoming	Warsaw-Wilkinson Co.	Warsaw, NY	1913
Yankee	W. Eddy Plow Co.	Greenwich, NY	1913
Zilisch	A.T. Zilisch	Mayville, WI	1905

Feed Grinders

By the 1860s, farmers were aware of the benefits derived from grinding the grain fed to their livestock. It was more palatable and nutritious. But even better, livestock gained better with ground feed. Unfortunately, there were few farmers of the time who had a source of power to operate a grinder, except for those lucky enough to have a horsepower and willing horses.

Progress moved forward; by the 1880s, several companies made feed grinders with a built-in sweep so that one or two horses could walk in a circle around the mill, all the while grinding the feed. By the 1890s, steam power was available

to a few. Not until 1900 did the gasoline engine begin to make itself known to the average farmer. Combining all the factors, feed grinders gained great popularity by 1900. Within a few years, almost every farm had one.

Within this section are included feed grinders or burr grinders, along with the hammer mill. The latter did not gain popularity until the 1920s and subsequent. Many farmers opted for the hammermill in the 1930s—by then, tractor power was abundantly available. Eventually, the burr mill lost in the popularity contest, with the hammermill becoming the most widely used method of grinding feed. In this section, only a few examples are shown of what were literally thousands of different models from several hundred manufacturers. Also of note, a separate section entitled Grinding Mills is included. It includes primarily the stone buhr mill or flour mill. The latter was used primarily for grinding flour and other edibles, while the feed grinder, with its iron burrs, was limited mainly to use for livestock feed.

Old feed grinders have appreciated in value considerably over the years. Sometimes, a rare model, or one that is especially popular, will bring well more than $100, while one that is quite common might sell for $25 or less.

American Well Works, Aurora, Ill.

An 1887 catalog from American Well Works illustrates its IXL Iron Feed Grinder. It had been in use since the early 1870s and was made entirely of iron, except for the hopper. The IXL on the left is set up for use with a horsepower, while the one on the right could be belted to a steam engine, gas engine, windmill, or water wheel.

Appleton Manufacturing Co., Batavia, Ill.

Appleton began building feed grinders in the 1880s, with its Appleton, Hero and American feed grinders gaining wide popularity. Shown here is its No. 22 Appleton General Purpose mill, a belt-powered model that was suitable for the average farm.

Appleton's No. 1 Special Grinder of 1917 was a small mill with a capacity of five to 12 bushels per hour. This one, like most burr grinders, used safety shear pins so that if a foreign object made its way between the burrs, the pin would break and prevent serious damage to the grinder. This one could be successfully operated with a gas engine of only 1 or 2 horsepower.

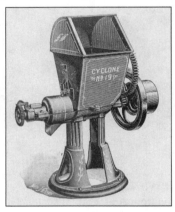

The Appleton No. 19 Cyclone Corn and Cob Breaker is shown here. It really wasn't a grinder but was designed specifically for breaking or crushing ear corn into small pieces. With a 6-horsepower engine, this machine could crush up to 15 bushels of corn per hour. In 1917, it sold for $25.

Associated Manufacturers, Waterloo, Iowa

Associated was a well-known engine manufacturer. It augmented its extensive engine line with various machines, including a series of grinders. Shown here is its 1917 version of the Amanco Feed Grinder.

The smaller No. 8 machine used 8-inch burrs; without a sacking elevator, it sold for $23. The larger No. 10 shown here, is equipped with a sacking elevator. This 10-inch grinder retailed at $45.

In addition to larger models, Associated also offered small mills. Its No. 18 (left) was a plain mill having 8-inch burrs and capable of 10 to 30 bushels per hour, depending on the fineness of the feed and the available power. To the right is the little No. 16 mill, a small bench-mounted grinder with 5-1/2 inch burrs. It weighed but 70 pounds.

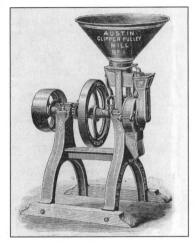

F.C. Austin Co., Chicago, Ill.

While this company would later become a well-known manufacturer of construction machinery, an 1889 advertisement illustrates its Austin Clipper Pulley Mill No. 1. Small mills like this abounded and a surprising number still exist, some of them coming from small manufacturers that are rarely known outside of their local area. Austin offered several sizes and styles of mills, with the largest being capable of 75 bushels per hour.

Bauer Bros. Co., Springfield, Ohio

At some point, now uncertain, Bauer Bros. took over the Feed Grinder Business Co., also of Springfield. This Scientific No. 1 Mill was extremely heavy, utilizing almost all cast iron except for the hopper and the sills. Although small and slow by contemporary standards, mills like this one were very popular in the 1900-1940 period.

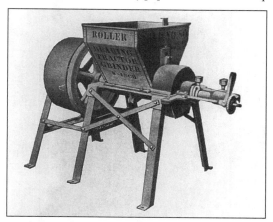

C.S. Bell Co., Hillsboro, Ohio

By the 1920s, several companies were offering mills designed especially for use with small tractors. Numerous feed grinders and other machines were "Designed Especially for the Fordson." Such was the case with the Bell No. 80 grinder. Bell called it "A Real Grain Grinder for Tractors."

Blue Valley Manufacturing Co., Manhattan, Kan.

Numerous companies were manufacturing feed mills in the 1890s, among them being the Blue Valley firm, as pictured in this 1898 advertisement. All that was needed was the mill; the horses were already on the farm and they provided the power. Nothing is known of this company.

N.P. Bowsher Co., South Bend, Ind.

This 1893 model of the Globe Feed Mill is listed in various implement directories as still being available from Bowsher as late as 1948. Like other sweep mills, it was very simple in design.

Bowsher also gained a high reputation for various other feed grinders offered during the years.

Bowsher's Combination Feed Mill of 1913 was a very popular model, with this one even including a sacking elevator. In addition to handling small grains, this model could also grind ear corn successfully. At the time, this was a major selling point since cattlemen, especially, saw the benefits of feeding ground ear corn to their livestock.

Carley Bros., Colfax, Wash.

In some areas of the country, barley was grown, at least occasionally, while for other areas it was an important annual crop. This roller machine, while technically not a feed grinder, was difficult to classify in any other section of the book; of interest is the legend on the sacking elevator denoting Carley's Roller Feed Mill. The concept of a roller mill as compared to the ordinary burr mill was dramatic indeed and gained rather poor acceptance for some years.

Cascaden Manufacturing Co., Waterloo, Iowa

In 1903, numerous advertisements appeared concerning Cascaden's Giant Killer Geared Grinder. Within a year or so, the identical mill is advertised by Davis Gasoline Engine Works Co., also of Waterloo, and also owned by Cascaden. Tangling things even further, see the Corn King Feed Mill Co. entry for a mill that is virtually identical. It likewise was made at Waterloo, Iowa.

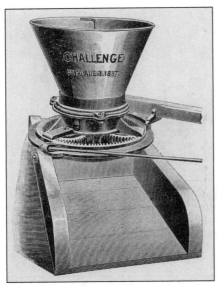

Challenge Wind Mill & Feed Mill Co., Batavia, Ill.

By 1899, Challenge was offering this example of a sweep mill. Patented in 1897, this was one of the first such mills in the Challenge line, but it remained for decades to come. Challenge was a well-known manufacturer of windmills, gasoline engines and other items.

A 1910 catalog illustrates the Challenge Belt Power Grinder. This small feed mill was made in three different sizes, all of the same pattern and differing mainly in physical size. Like most burr mills, this series was furnished with one set of coarse burrs and a set of fine burrs. Other styles were available for special purposes.

Shown here is the 1910 version of the Challenge No. 5 Grinder, complete with a sacking elevator. At the time, sacking was a preferred method of storage for many farmers, either because of personal preference or because that was the only method available on a given farm.

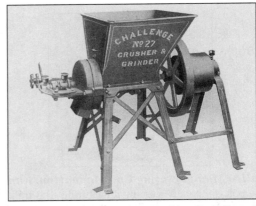

Initially, many burr mills were incapable of grinding ear corn; by 1910, the problem had been solved with the introduction of special crushing attachments built as a part of the mill. This No. 27 Challenge mill was furnished with 10-inch burrs.

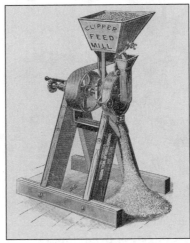

Chicago Tubular Well Works, Chicago, Ill.

An 1887 advertisement illustrates the Clipper Feed Mill from Chicago Tubular Well Works. The interesting company title resulted from its development of a well-drilling machine that used round steel casing to line the shaft. Very little is known of the company.

C.D. Colton & Co., Galesburg, Ill.

From 1906 comes this advertisement of the Corn Belt No. 5 Power Mill. Colton claimed this one would grind the corn and the cob, and this was indeed an important point for farmers wishing to feed ground ear corn. The extra set of burrs furnished with the grinder are shown on the sill in the foreground.

Common Sense Engine Co., Springfield, Ohio

In 1890, Common Sense Engine Co., offered its combination of a steam engine and the Common Sense grinder. In reality, the engine was probably belted to overhead line-shafting so that it could operate several different machines including the feed grinder.

Did You Know?

A nicely restored sleigh can bring more than $1,000.

Corn King Feed Mill Co., Waterloo, Iowa

Corn King mills were advertised in 1903 and were virtually identical to the Giant Killer mills from Cascaden Manufacturing Co., which is listed in this section. In the 1920s, repair parts for both were available from Swift Manufacturing Co., also at Waterloo. This Corn King advertisement notes that the company had sold more than 2,000 mills the previous season.

Dain Manufacturing Co., Ottumwa, Iowa

By 1900, Dain Manufacturing Co. was offering this Dain Double Geared Mill, a very popular design that remained on the market for some years. After Dain came into the fold of Deere & Co., the latter continued to build this mill. Very few sweep mills like this still remain, so they are now a scarce collector's item.

J.A. Field & Co., St. Louis, Mo.

Field's Favorite Corn Mill and Power Combine was the title of this attractive horse-powered outfit. Note also the unique system of using a tumbling rod to operate a small corn sheller. Nothing further is known of the company, save for this 1884 advertisement.

Foos Manufacturing Co., Springfield, Ohio

Foos began building its Scientific line of farm equipment at least by the mid-1880s. Its Scientific mill of 1888, as shown here, was virtually unchanged when an advertisement of 1900 appeared. Since the mill was built almost entirely of cast iron, there was little to wear out. Because of this, many of these mills were used for decades with almost nothing spent for repairs.

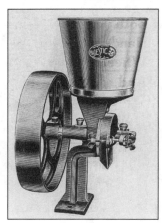

Hartman Co., Chicago, Ill.

Hartman Co. was a major mail-order house for the farmer of the 1920s. Its line of Majestic equipment included several different feed grinders. Among them was this small Majestic Power Mill, a little bench-top model intended for small farm or household needs.

Harvey Manufacturing Co., Racine, Wisc.

By the 1940s, the hammer mill had become an important equipment item for the livestock farmer. Newer and larger tractors were capable of the power needed for efficient operation. Numerous companies manufactured hammer mills, among them being the Harvey Red Hed line. This company also made Red Hed corn shellers.

Hocking Valley Manufacturing Co., Lancaster, Ohio

This interesting feed mill design was available from Hocking Valley in 1890. The special gearing is for direct attachment to the tumbling rod from a horsepower. Thus a farmer could hitch up a team to the power and grind feed with this Style B mill.

International Harvester Co., Chicago, Ill.

International Harvester Co. offered a wide variety of feed grinders to the farmer. One of its most popular mills up to the 1930s was this Type C grinder. These were sold by the thousands, along with several other IHC models. The Type C was very simple, being made entirely of steel and cast iron components.

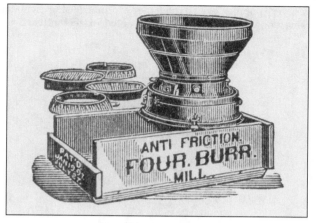

Iowa Grinder & Steamer Works, Waterloo, Iowa

From an 1898 advertisement comes this notice of the Four Burr Mill from Iowa Grinder & Steamer Works. With its two sets of burrs, this mill was claimed to have twice the capacity of its competitors. The company also made the Bovee Western Steamer, a device for cooking livestock feed.

Kelly & Taneyhill, Waterloo, Iowa

The Farmer's Friend Feed Grinder was a sweep grinder of somewhat the same design as its contemporaries. The company was one of several operating at Waterloo in 1898, all of them manufacturing feed grinders. Virtually nothing is known of the company's activities outside of this single illustration.

Lamb & Company, Freeport, Ill.

The business connection between Lamb & Co. and the Stover Mfg. Co., both of Freeport, Illinois, is unknown. At times, the two appear to be associated. In other instances, they appeared to compete. In the early 1890s, Lamb & Co. offered an extensive line of grinding mills. These included the buhr stone mills for edible flour and meal, along with the steel-plate burr mills used for grinding livestock feed.

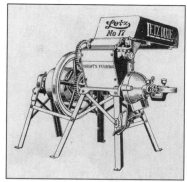

Letz Manufacturing Co., Crown Point, Ind.

In 1917, Letz promoted its Letz Dixie feed mills. The No. 77 used 8-inch burrs; the No. 88 had 10-inch burrs; and the big No. 22 had 12-inch burrs. The latter size required up to 30 horsepower for efficient operation. Letz claimed that this mill could "grind anything that's grindable."

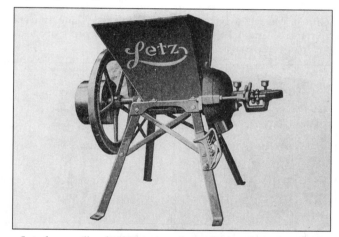

Letz burr mills of 1920 were an immediate success, being very popular with farmers. The design was simple, yet the mill was sturdy enough to stand up to heavy, daily usage. Steel and cast-iron components were used throughout.

By 1930, the Letz stationary burr mills had taken on the same general form they would follow throughout the remaining decades of production. Built in 8- or 10-inch sizes, the No. 80 was immensely popular, especially for grinding ear corn. A small tractor was sufficient to operate this mill.

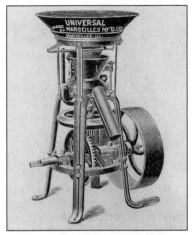

Marseilles Manufacturing Co., Marseilles, Ill.

An 1895 advertisement illustrates a rather unique feed grinder design from Marseilles Manufacturing Co. This Universal Feed Grinder was said to be capable of handling everything from ear corn to small grain. This one is furnished with the necessary gearing to operate from an overhead line-shaft.

Martin Manufacturing Co., Anoka, Minn.

The Martin grinders were small-sized units, with the two models shown here being of the bench-mounted type. The Junior B on the left used 4-1/2 inch grinding plates and only needed a 1 horsepower engine, while the No. 4 on the right used 5-1/4 inch plates and required about 2 horsepower.

New Holland Manufacturing Co., New Holland, Pa.

Feed grinders were often adorned with fancy striping and ornamentation; the New Holland was probably the epitome of this practice. Beyond its fancy appearance, the New Holland mills

were very popular, even though they continued using a wooden frame long after most companies had opted for steel and cast iron.

Nordyke & Marmon Co., Indianapolis, Ind.

While Nordyke & Marmon is perhaps better known for its stone buhr mills, the company produced a number of small feed grinders; this Diamond King Double Grinder is from an 1889 advertisement. Little else is known of this unique design, except that it weighed some 400 pounds.

An 1889 advertisement of Nordyke & Marmon illustrates its No. 8 Feed Grinder, a heavy machine capable of grinding 60 bushels per hour. This large grinder was probably better suited to a commercial elevator than to a farm of the time, since very few had any method of powering the machine.

Geo. K. Oyler Manufacturing Co., St. Louis, Mo.

During the 1880s, the sweep mill became very popular, with this Excelsior Mill from Geo. K. Oyler being an example. By the time this 1884 advertisement appeared, Oyler was offering feed mills, corn shellers, fanning mills and many other farm equipment from its St. Louis factory.

Papec Machine Co., Shortsville, N.Y.

Papec was a well-known manufacturer of feed grinders, ensilage cutters and other farm machinery. In 1930, the company offered this farm-type feed mixer. With the coming of feed concentrates and the need for feed additives, thorough mixing of the ground feed was virtually impossible, outside of a commercial establishment. The Papec unit sought to remedy this shortfall, but it would be another 20 years or more before the mobile grinder-mixer came to the farm.

Red Chief Manufacturing Co., Louisville, Kty.

In 1919, Red Chief offered this small hand mill, noting that it would meet the farmer's needs for grinding his own corn meal, graham flour, grits and other necessities. Red Chief also built several other sizes of hand- and power-operated mills.

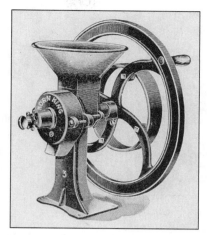

Root-Heath Manufacturing Co., Plymouth, Ohio

Root-Heath offered its small Korn King Grist Mills in several sizes for hand or power use. As noted in this 1915 engraving, the pulley could be easily added or detached with four small bolts. The company also made several styles of small corn shellers.

Racine-Sattley Co., Springfield, Ill.

For 1903, Sattley offered its Royal sweep mills; this one had an impressive and ornate iron base. In this engraving, the horses are shown with the mill in operation. Occasionally, one can see a mill like this at a thresher's show or vintage machinery exhibition.

J.B. Sedberry Inc., Utica, N.Y.

When the Jay Bee portable feed grinder appeared in the early 1930s, it created a sensation. Equipped with a large engine, the Jay Bee hammermill quickly converted grain to wholesome feed. A substantial number of custom operators thrived for some years, traveling from farm to farm, some having a regular "route" each week.

R. Sinclair Jr. & Co., Baltimore, Md.

An 1866 advertisement illustrates the Young American Corn and Cob Mill, also known as the R.F. Maynard Champion Mill. To the left is shown an extra set of burrs for this mill. If one is any judge at all of cast iron, the burrs must have been extremely heavy. Nothing at all is known of this firm, outside of the engraving shown here.

Springfield Engine & Thresher Co., Springfield, Ohio

An 1888 advertisement of the Kelly Duplex mill illustrates it in use. A caption with the engraving reads, "Kelly Duplex No. 2 Feed Mill in operation on the model farm of W.K. Thompson, near Springfield, Ohio." The mill is being operated by a Springfield engine.

From 1888 comes this illustration of the Kelly Duplex mill being driven by a stationary sawmill engine. This company later was renamed as O.S. Kelly Manufacturing Co., even moving for a

time to Iowa City, Iowa, and operating as O.S. Kelly Western Manufacturing Co.

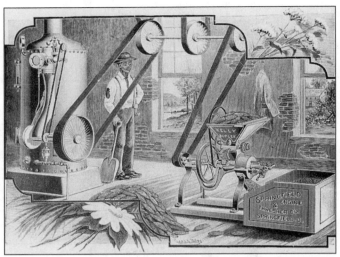

Springfield Engine & Thresher Co. was an early promoter of steam power for the farm, whether as a stationary engine pictured here or with its newly developed traction engine. The artist's conception illustrates the general form of a stationary setup, together with overhead line-shafting. Very few farms were thus equipped; it was an expensive proposition to set up a complete operation like this.

Star Manufacturing Co., New Lexington, Ohio

Star Manufacturing Co., advertised heavily in the *American Thresherman, Gas Review* and other titles that would be read by people interested in gas and steam power. For a time, the company even built its own gas engines to power its feed grinders. However, by the 1920s, parts only were available from Perry Manufacturing Co., at New Lexington. Eventually, the Star line faded from the scene.

Staver & Abbott Manufacturing Co., Chicago, Ill.

An 1894 advertisement illustrates the Buckeye Feed Mill, as built by Staver & Abbott. This one differed somewhat in its design, as can be seen by a comparison with others in this section. It also appears that the sweep power could be fitted with a tumbling rod and applied to other uses when not needed for grinding.

Stover Manufacturing Co., Freeport, Ill.

As early as 1887, perhaps before, the Stover Ideal Mill was available from Stover Manufacturing. The company advertised extensively in farm magazines such as the *American Agriculturist*. The latter was also published in a German-language edition; this 1895 illustration is from one of these magazines. Stover also built the Ideal Double Geared Sweep Mill for ear corn and shelled grain.

By 1889, Stover was offering its Ideal Duplex Grinding Mill in sizes ranging from 10 to 150 bushels per hour, requiring anywhere from 2 to 40 horsepower for efficient operation. Stover was already a famous name in the windmill business; within a few years, it would attain permanent fame as a gasoline engine manufacturer.

In addition to its Ideal grinding mills, Stover also offered a series of small, hand- or belt-powered grinders for bench or table mounting. These small mills were available until the company finally ceased business in 1942. Only the largest model to the far right of the illustration could be fitted for belt power the other three were hand-powered.

Numerous models of Stover feed grinders were built up to 1942. However, one of the most popular was the 40-series, including the No. 42 shown here. It could handle ear corn, small grain or almost anything grindable. Like the Stover engines, these mills were very popular with farmers.

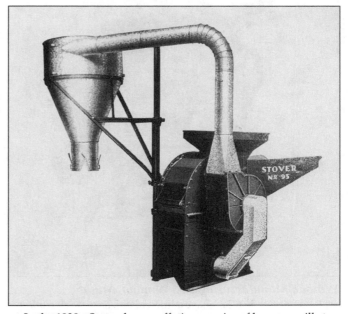

In the 1930s, Stover began offering a series of hammermills to take advantage of the available tractor power. The hammermill was becoming very popular by this time, and Stover was a leader in its design. Production of all Stover equipment ended when the factory closed in 1942.

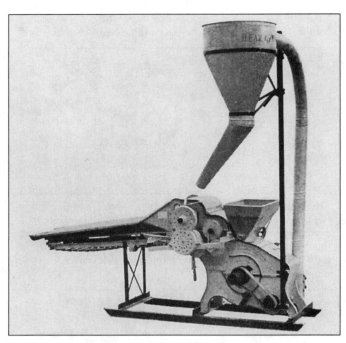

Western Land Roller Co., Hastings, Neb.

In the 1930s, the Western Bear-Cat hammermill became very popular. This heavy-duty mill used a frame of cast iron, the terminus of the feeder table was a cutter head for cutting up ear corn, grinding fodder and the like. A small hopper was furnished for adding small grain directly into the hammer chamber. These mills were very popular and enjoyed a long production run.

Winona Manufacturing Co., Winona, Minn.

From the German-language edition of the *American Agriculturist* comes this 1895 illustration of the Diamond Mill from Winona Manufacturing Co. The open gears are of massive size. The entire machine, except for the hopper, is made of cast iron. Virtually nothing is known of this company outside of the illustration shown here.

Trade Names

Acme	Acme Engine Co.	Lansing, MI	1915
Acme	Acme Wagon Co.	Emigsville, PA	1915
Acme	Blue Valley Mfg. Co.	Manhattan, KS	1909
Adams	Marseilles Mfg. Co.	Marseilles, IL	1892
Amanco	Associated Manufacturers	Waterloo, IA	1915
American	Appleton Mfg. Co.	Appleton, WI	1892
Appleton	Appleton Mfg. Co.	Appleton, WI	1913
Aurora	T.L. Phillups	Aurora, IL	1905
Austin	F.C. Austin Mfg. Co.	Chicago, IL	1892
B.E.S.	Shoudy Mfg. Co.	Rockford, IL	1892
Baker	Baker Mfg. Co.	Evansville, WI	1909
Barnard-Moline	Barnard & Leas Mfg. Co.	Moline, IL	1922
Bayley	Gray Iron Casting Co.	Springfield, OH	1913
Bercha	Dempster Mill Mfg. Co.	Beatrice, NE	1913
Bessemer	Bessemer Gas Engine Co.	Grove City, PA	1917
Best	Howe Scale Co.	Chicago, IL	1922
Big S	Buckeye Feed Mill Co.	Springfield, OH	1913
Blue Valley	Blue Valley Mfg. Co.	Manhattan, KS	1909
Boss	Boss Feed Mill Co.	Cherryvale, KS	1913
Boss	J.C. Woodcock Co.	Litchfield, IL	1909
Bowsher's	N.P. Bowsher	South Bend, IN	1905
Bradford	Nordyke & Marmon Co.	Indianapolis, IN	1913
Buckeye	Buckeye Feed Mill Co.	Springfield, OH	1909
Buckeye	Staver & Abbott Mfg. Co.	Chicago, IL	1892
Buckeye	Union Foundry & Machine Co.	Mansfield, OH	1909
Centennial	Elgin Wind Power & Pump Co.	Elgin, IL	1892
Challenge	Challenge Wind Mill & Feedmill Co.	Batavia, IL	1892
Champion	Victor Feed Mill Co.	Springfield, OH	1913
Chanticleer	Jacob Haisch Co.	DeKalb, IL	1915
Cherokee	Park Mfg. Co.	Cherokee, IA	1922
Cole	R.D. Cole Mfg. Co.	Newnan, GA	1892
Columbia	Wm. Fetzer Co.	Springfield, IL	1909
Concho	C.S. Bell Co.	Hillsboro, OH	1913
Corn Belt	Spartan Mfg. Co.	Galesburg, IL	1905
Cow Boy	Mundie Mfg. Co.	Peru, IL	1924
Cream City	Acme Wagon Co.	Emigsville, PA	1915
Crown Point	Letz Mfg. Co.	Crown Point, IN	1913
Cyclone	E.H. Stroud Co.	Chicago, IL	1915
Dain	Dain Mfg. Co.	Ottumwa, IA	1905
Daisy	Silver Mfg. Co.	Salem, OH	1913
Dandy	C.S. Bell Co.	Hillsboro, OH	1909
DeLoach	DeLoach Mill Mfg. Co.	Atlanta, GA	1892
Dempster-Bercha	Dempster Mill Mfg. Co.	Beatrice, NE	1917
Devore	Lamb & Co.	Freeport, IL	1892
Diamond	Fairbanks, Morse & Co.	Chicago, IL	1913
Diamond	New Winona Mfg. Co.	Winona, MN	1905
Ditto's	G.M. Ditto	Joliet, IL	1913
Dixie	Nordyke & Marmon Co.	Indianapolis, IN	1913
Duplex	Duplex Mill & Mfg. Co.	Springfield, OH	1909
Duplex	Fairbanks, Morse & Co.	Chicago, IL	1913

Trade Names (cont...)

Durham	Lamb & Co.	Freeport, IL	1892
Eagle	Eagle Machine Co.	Lancaster, OH	1905
Eagle	Eagle Mfg. Co.	Appleton, WI	1909
Eclipse	Fairbanks, Morse & Co.	Chicago, IL	1913
Elgin	Elgin Wind Power & Pump Co.	Elgin, IL	1913
Enterprise	Enterprise Wind Mill Co.	Sandwich, IL	1913
Eureka	Smith & Pomeroy Wind Mill Co.	Kalamazoo, MI	1915
Excel	Excel Mfg. Co.	Pottersville, NY	1913
Excelsior-Duplex	Excelsior Drill Co.	Springfield, OH	1917
Fairbanks-Morse	Fairbanks, Morse & Co.	Chicago, IL	1892
Famous	Sterling Mfg. Co.	Sterling, IL	1892
Farquhar	A.B. Farquhar	York, PA	1915
Freeman	S. Freeman & Sons Mfg. Co.	Racine, WI	1905
Garland	Valley Wind Engine & Iron Co.	Bay City, MI	1905
Gasoline Special	U.S. Wind Engine & Pump Co.	Batavia, IL	1917
Geiser Peerless	Emerson-Brantingham Co.	Rockford, IL	1913
Giant	Frank Hamachek	Kewaunee, WI	1913
Giant Killer	Cascaden Mfg. Co.	Waterloo, IA	1905
Gibson	Gibson Mfg. Co.	Waterloo, IA	1922
Gilson	Gilson Mfg. Co.	Port Washington, WI	1913
Globe	Globe Foundry & Machine Co.	Sheboygan, WI	1905
Goodhue	Goodhue Wind Engine Co.	St. Charles, IL	1892
Gopher	New Winona Mfg. Co.	Winona, MN	1915
Grain King	Litchfield Mfg. Co.	Waterloo, IA	1905
Handy	Havana Metal Wheel Co.	Havana, IL	1905
Harrison	Nordyke & Marmon Co.	Indianapolis, IN	1909
Hartford	Hartford Plow Works	Hartford, WI	1905
Hawkeye	E. Children's Sons Mfg. Co.	Council Bluffs, IA	1905
Heller	Heller-Aller Co.	Napoleon, OH	1913
Hercules	Leonard D. Harrison	New Haven, CT	1892
Hero	Appleton Mfg. Co.	Appleton, WI	1892
Holliday	Holliday Engineering Co.	Chicago, IL	1922
Hunt	Gilbert Hunt Co.	Walla Walla, WA	1913
Hustler	Monarch Grubber Co.	Lone Tree, IA	1905
I X L	Red Cross Mfg. Co.	Bluffton, IN	1913
I X L	U.S. Wind Engine & Pump Co.	Batavia, IL	1913
I.X.L.	U.S. Wind Engine & Pump Co.	Batavia, IL	1892
Ideal	Lennox Machine Co.	Marshalltown, IA	1913
Ideal	Stover Mfg. Co.	Freeport, IL	1892
Ideal	Stover Mfg. Co.	Freeport, IL	1905
Ingeco	Worthington Pump & Machy. Corp.	Cudahy, WI	1917
International	International Harvester Co.	Chicago, IL	1913
Invincible	Farm Tool Mfg. Co.	Carrollton, MO	1905
Iowa	Bovee Grinder & Furnace Works	Waterloo, IA	1909
Ironsides	Gilbert Hunt Co.	Walla Walla, WA	1913

Trade Names (cont...)

Jack's Friend	Fairbanks, Morse & Co.	Chicago, IL	1913
Jay Bee	Bossert Corp.	Utica, NY	1924
Jewel	Duplex Mill & Mfg. Co.	Superior, WI	1913
Jumbo	Nelson Bros.	Saginaw, MI	1915
Kaestner	Charles Kaestner & Co.	Chicago, IL	1892
Kelly Duplex	Duplex Mill & Mfg. Co.	Springfield, OH	1909
Kelly Duplex	O. S. Kelly Western Mfg. Co.	Iowa City, IA	1909
Keystone	Keystone Farm Machine Co.	York, PA	1905
Kid	New Winona Mfg. Co.	Winona, MN	1922
King	Gustav Wenzelmann	Missal, IL	1892
Kingsland	Kingsland Mfg. Co.	St. Louis, MO	1905
Lauson	John Lauson Mfg. Co.	New Holstein, WI	1917
Lay Porte	L. A. Young Industries	Detroit, MI	1919
Letz	Letz Mfg. Co.	Crown Point, IN	1913
Liberty	Liberty Mill Co.	Cedar Falls, IA	1922
Lightning	Fort Scott Mfg. Co.	Fort Scott, KS	1905
Lightning	L. B. McCargar Feed Mill Co.	St. Joseph, MO	1913
Litchfield	Litchfield Mfg. Co.	Waterloo, IA	1913
Little Better	Double Power Mill Co.	Appleton, WI	1913
Little Giant	C. S. Bell Co.	Hillsboro, OH	1909
Little Jumbo	Nelson Bros.	Saginaw, MI	1917
Magic	Whitman Agricultural Co.	St. Louis, MO	1915
Marseilles	Marseilles Mfg. Co.	Marseilles, IL	1905
Martin	Martin Mfg. Co.	St. Louis Park, MN	1913
Maud S.	Union Foundry & Machine Works	Mansfield, OH	1905
McCormick-Deering	International Harvester Co.	Chicago, IL	1924
McSherry	Wm. Fetzer Co.	Springfield, IL	1909
Meadows	International Harvester Co.	Chicago, IL	1913
Minneapolis	Minneapolis Separator Co.	Minneapolis, MN	1915
Model	C. S. Bell Co.	Hillsboro, OH	1915
Model	Nordyke & Marmon Co.	Indianapolis, IN	1915
Mogul	Bovee Grinder & Furnace Works	Waterloo, IA	1909
Monarch	Kirkwood, Miller & Co.	Peoria, IL	1892
Monarch	Smalley Mfg. Co.	Manitowoc, WI	1913
Monarch	Sprout, Waldron & Co.	Muncy, PA	1913
Monitor	Baker Mfg. Co.	Evansville, WI	1909
Monitor	Baker Mfg. Co.	Evansville, WI	1915
Monitor	C. S. Bell Co.	Hillsboro, OH	1909
Moore	Given Moore Co.	Spring Valley, IL	1915
Moore	Moore Plow & Implement Co.	Greenville, MI	1915
Morley	Morley Twine & Machinery Co.	Sioux City, IA	1913
National	National Tubular Axle Co.	Emigsville, PA	1915
New Century	Buckeye Feed Mill Co.	Springfield, OH	1913
New Era	Nordyke & Marmon Co.	Indianapolis, IN	1915
New Holland	New Holland Machine Co.	New Holland, PA	1909
New Prize	Appleton Mfg. Co.	Batavia, IL	1915
New Sandwich	Sandwich Mfg. Co.	Sandwich, IL	1913

Trade Names (cont...)

Newman Shear-Cut	Stanhope Mfg. Co.	Stanhope, IA	1929
Nonpareil	L.J. Miller	Cincinnati, OH	1909
Nordyke's	Nordyke & Marmon Co.	Indianapolis, IN	1892
North Star	R.R. Howell & Co.	Minneapolis, MN	1913
O.K.	Sandwich Mfg. Co.	Sandwich, IL	1892
Old Honesty	Wilhelm Mfg. Co.	Janesville, WI	1929
Olds	M. Rumely Co.	LaPorte, IN	1913
Omega	C.S. Bell Co.	Hillsboro, OH	1915
Oriole	Wilson Bros.	Easton, PA	1915
Osage	New Winona Mfg. Co.	Winona, MN	1909
Peerless	Joliet Strowbridge Co.	Joliet, IL	1892
Perfect	Macgowan & Finnigan Foundry Co.	St. Louis, MO	1913
Perfection	Leonard D. Harrison	New Haven, CT	1892
Perkins	Perkins Wind Mill Co.	Mishawaka, IN	1909
Planter's Pride	Richmond City Mill Works	Richmond, IN	1892
Plymouth	Wm. Fetzer Co.	Springfield, IL	1909
Porter	Whitman Agricultural Co.	St. Louis, MO	1909
Pride of Richmond	Richmond City Mill Works	Richmond, IN	1892
Prize	Appleton Mfg. Co.	Batavia, IL	1913
Quaker City	A.W. Straub Co.	Philadelphia, PA	1913
Rapid	C.S. Bell Co.	Hillsboro, OH	1909
Red Chief	Red Chief Mfg. Co.	Louisville, KY	1915
Reliance	Sandwich Mfg. Co.	Sandwich, IL	1905
Rowell	I.B. Rowell Co.	Waukesha, WI	1917
Royal	Woodcock Feed Mill Co.	Chillicothe, OH	1905
Royal Blue	New Winona Mfg. Co.	Winona, MN	1917
Royal Blue	U.S. Wind Engine & Pump Co.	Batavia, IL	1913
Rumely	M. Rumely Co.	LaPorte, IN	1913
S & P	Phelps & Bigelow Wind Mill Co.	Kalamazoo, MI	1913
Sandow	Sandy McManus Inc.	Waterloo, IA	1915
Scientific	Bauer Bros.	Springfield, OH	1913
Scientific	Foos Mfg. Co.	Springfield, OH	1905
Shelby	Shelbyville Foundry & Mach. Co.	Shelbyville, IN	1913
Sheldon	Sheldon Engine & Sales Co.	Waterloo, IA	1924
Silver	Silver Mfg. Co.	Salem, OH	1913
Simplicity	Turner Mfg. Co.	Port Washington, WI	1915
Smalley	Smalley Mfg. Co.	Manitowoc, WI	1913
Speed King	Chamberlain Machine Works	Waterloo, IA	1917
Standard	Leonard D. Harrison	New Haven, CT	1892
Standard	Ottumwa-Moline Eng. & Pump Co.	Ottumwa, IA	1913
Standard	U.S. Wind Engine & Pump Co.	Batavia, IL	1913
Star	Star Mfg. Co.	New Lexington, OH	1905
Staver-Buckeye	Buckeye Feed Mill Co.	Springfield, OH	1909
Steiner	M. Steiner & Co.	Dayton, OH	1917
Sterling	Sterling Mfg. Co.	Sterling, IL	1892
Stevens	Clark & Co.	Somonauk, IL	1892
Stover	Stover Mfg. Co.	Freeport, IL	1909
Stroud	E.H. Stroud Co.	Chicago, IL	1913

Trade Names (cont...)

Success	Hercules Mfg. Co.	Centerville, IA	1905
Success	Macgowan & Finnigan Foundry Co.	St. Louis, MO	1909
Success	Marseilles Mfg. Co.	Marseilles, IL	1892
Superior	Duplex Mill & Mfg. Co.	Superior, WI	1917
Swift's	Swift Mfg. Co.	Waterloo, IA	1905
Tornado	Appleton Mfg. Co.	Batavia, IL	1913
U.S.	U.S. Wind Engine & Pump Co.	Batavia, IL	1892
Ultimatum	U.S. Wind Engine & Pump Co.	Batavia, IL	1913
Union	Union Wind Mill Co.	Albion, MI	1892
United	United Engine Co.	Lansing, MI	1915
Universal	Marseilles Mfg. Co.	Marseilles, IL	1892
Up-to-Date	Up-to-Date Machine Co.	Green Bay, WI	1915
Utz	Scanland Mfg. Co.	Wichita, KS	1913
Victor	Victor Feed Mill Co.	Springfield, OH	1905
Victory	Thomas Roberts	Springfield, OH	1913
Watts	Watts Mfg. Co.	Jackson, MI	1913
Waupun	Althouse-Wheeler Co.	Waupun, WI	1913
Whiz Bang	Hocking Valley Mfg. Co.	Lancaster, OH	1929
Wilder	Wilder-Strong Implement Co.	Monroe, MI	1905
Williams	Williams Mill Co.	Ronda, NC	1915
Wilson	Wilson Bros.	Easton, PA	1909
Wilson-Wetterhold	Wilson-Wetterhold Gr. Mach. Co.	Wichita, KS	1922
Winger's New Royal	E.B. Winger	Chicago, IL	1892
Wolverene	Himes Mfg. Co.	Lansing, MI	1915
W-W	W-W Feed Grinder Co.	Wichita, KS	1924
X X	Sandwich Mfg. Co.	Sandwich, IL	1892
X X	Sandwich Mfg. Co.	Sandwich, IL	1915
York	Flinchbaugh Mfg. Co.	York, PA	1913
Young America	A.B. Farquhar	York, PA	1909

Did You Know?

Since so few threshing machines remain, especially the early wooden designs, they have now acquired collector status. Late model, all-steel machines of the 1920s and later, often bring $500 or more in good condition and some of the earliest wooden designs have acquired museum status.

Fence-Making Machinery

Up to about 1915, several companies offered fence-making machinery for use on the farm. Most of this equipment was intended for use right in the fence row; once the fence was completed, the equipment could be used on another fence in a different location.

During the years, though, various steel companies developed galvanized steel wire; a few, such as the Page Woven Wire Fence Co., Adrian, Mich., specialized in making woven wire. To this day, some farmers still speak of woven wire as "Page wire." The manufactured product was superior to the home-made styles, so the demand for on-the-farm fence making equipment vanished. Today, these machines are a rarity, but so few of them appear that there is no established market.

In 1887, M.C. Henley, Richmond, Ind., offered Henley's Monarch Fence Machine, a device obviously intended to manufacture picket fences. Outside of this illustration, nothing at all is known of the company or its activities.

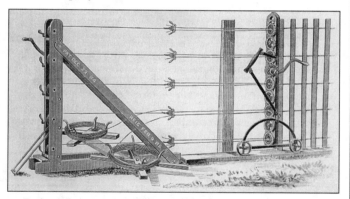

Perhaps by coincidence, the Richmond Check Rower Co., Richmond, Ind., offered its Little Giant Fence Loom in 1887, possibly in competition with the Henley machine, also made at Richmond. This one was patented in 1884, so it had been on the market for only a short time prior to this illustration. Presumably the company also made check-row corn planters, but nothing has been found regarding this endeavor.

Did You Know?

Vintage corn graders in nice shape are valued at $100 or more.

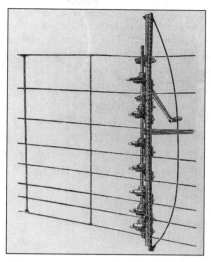

The Norwalk Lock Stay Fence Co., Norwalk, Ohio, offered this interesting fence-making machine in 1897. It claimed it would make anywhere from 50 to 65 rods of fence per day at a cost of only 16 to 24 cents per rod. It could use smooth or barbed wire; turning the crank twisted the stay cables from top to bottom, along with crimping the main wires. The latter was necessary to accommodate expansion and contraction of the fence with changing temperatures.

From an unknown source comes this 1914 illustration of the Empire Fence Building Machine. This engine-powered outfit was capable of building 200 different styles of fence and as shown is using barbed wire for the top and bottom. Unfortunately, we have found no address for this company, nor do we have any further information regarding the Empire fence machinery.

By 1900, thousands of miles of barbed wire were already in place. Recognizing the difficulty of rolling and unrolling barbed wire, the

Cosey Barb Wire Reel Co. was organized at Sterling, Ill., to mechanize the job. Shown here mounted to the back of a wagon, the Cosey Reel was an automatic outfit. This illustration goes back to 1905.

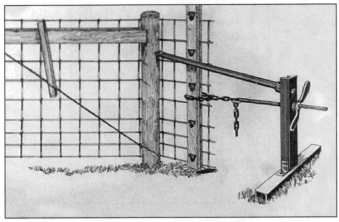

Various methods were developed for stretching barbed wire and woven wire, with the Matthews Woven Wire Fence Stretcher shown here. A wooden clamp was attached to the wire and, in this instance, a heavy screw did the job of stretching. This outfit was made by Bain Bros., Manufacturing Co., Cedar Rapids, Iowa, in the 1920s.

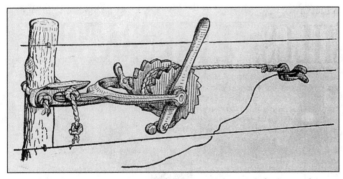

Already in 1887, a "comealong" was devised for stretching smooth or barbed-wire fencing. This one was made by Cortez V. Pugh at Bowling Green, Mo. Over the years, farmers used various methods, although a small tackle block with specially designed wire grips was probably the most common device.

Various devices were made to dig post holes; this one from 1914 ranks among the most unusual of the era. Built by Ohio Cultivator

Co., Bellevue, Ohio, the Cyclone auger used an anchor chain to automatically space the hole from the previous one. After the anchor chain was set, a 50-foot rope was wound at the top, the other end hitched to the horse, with the hole being dug in less than a minute. It should have been an interesting sight if the horse became frightened by the neighbor's dog!

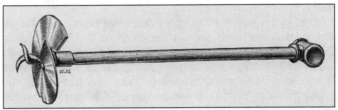

Looking somewhat like today's so-called "screw anchors" this device was actually Lee's Patent Post Hole Auger; it was patented in 1883. Shown here in an 1884 advertisement, this device was made by Branch, Crookes & Co., St. Louis.

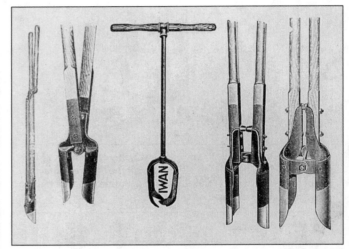

Among the tools in the farmer's arsenal were a variety of fence-making devices, most of them having to do with ways to dig a post hole. Some farmers preferred the Iawn auger in the center of this illustration, while other preferred the post hole diggers shown to the right. Late in the 1930s, a few companies began making some heavy and cumbersome augers for mounting on a tractor; until the 1950s, however, most post holes were dug with equipment similar to that shown here and available from numerous manufacturers.

Trade Names			
Advance	F. Van Doren	Adrian, MI	1892
American	F.A. Everett	Quincy, IL	1892
Amos	Charles Amos & Co.	Detroit, MI	1905
Ashland	Ashland Clover Huller Co.	Ashland, OH	1892
Automatic	Atomatic Fence Machine Co.	Lake Fork, OH	1892
Begole Lightning	Milan Agricultural Co.	Milan, MI	1892
Boss	W.B. Lehman & Co.	Goshen, IN	1892
Brown	John P. Brown	Rising Sun, IN	1892
Buckeye	Theodore B. Lecky	Holmesville, OH	1892
Carter	Carter Wire Fence Machine Co.	Mt. Sterling, OH	1905
Church	Church Bros.	Adrian, MI	1913
Columbia	Elliott & Reid Co.	Richmond, IN	1905
Combination	H.P. Deuscher Co.	Hamilton, OH	1892

Trade Names (cont...)

Cyclone	Cyclone Fence Co.	Waukegan, IL	1913
Cyclone	Cyclone Wire Fence Co.	Holly, MI	1905
Cyclone	Lane Bros.	Holly, MI	1892
Davis	R. Davis	Albion, MI	1905
Elliott & Reid	Elliott & Reid Co.	Richmond, IN	1909
Empire	Empire Machine Co.	Richmond, IN	1892
Eureka	Eureka Fence Machine Co.	New Paris, OH	1892
Eureka Jr.	Eureka Fence Mfg. Co.	Richmond, IN	1905
Eureka Sr.	Eureka Fence Mfg. Co.	Richmond, IN	1905
Everett's	F.A. Everett	Quincy, IL	1892
Farmer's Ideal	Elliott & Reid Co.	Richmond, IN	1892
Garrett	S.H. Garrett	Mansfield, OH	1892
Gem City	C. Wight & Son	Dayton, OH	1892
Hamilton	H.P. Deuscher Co.	Hamilton, OH	1905
Hoosier	Hoosier Drill Co.	Richmond, IN	1892
Hoover	Des Moines Fence Co.	Des Moines, IA	1892
Illinois	Illinois Wire & Mfg. Co.	Joliet, IL	1915
Illinois	International Steel Post Co.	St. Louis, MO	1905
Iron King	O.D. Reeves & Co.	Indianapolis, IN	1892
Kitselman	Kitselman Bros.	Ridgeville, IN	1892
Lafayette	Lafayette Fence & Machine Co.	Lafayette, IN	1913
Lansing	Lansing Wheelbarrow Co.	Lansing, MI	1892
Leader	Leader Fence Machine Mfg. Co.	St. Charles, IL	1905
Little Giant	Eureka Fence Mfg. Co.	Richmond, IN	1905
Little Giant Jr.	Richmond Check Rower Co.	Richmond, IN	1892
Louden's	L.C. Louden	Indianapolis, IN	1892
Mathews	Mathews Wire Fence Machine Co.	Sunbury, OH	1905
McCloskey	McCloskey Wire Fence Mach. Co.	Toledo, OH	1913
New American	Riter's Metallic Picket Fence Co.	Liberty, IN	1892
New Robinson	Eureka Fence Mfg. Co.	Richmond, IN	1905
Perfect	F.A. Everett	Quincy, IL	1892
Pope	Enterprise Wind Mill Co.	Sandwich, IL	1913
Richmond Champion	Wayne Works	Richmond, IN	1892
Rogers	Torrent Pump Co.	Sebring, OH	1905
Standard	Standard Mfg. Co.	Cincinnati, OH	1892
Standard	Standard Wire Fence Co.	Canandaigua, NY	1905
Steel Wonder	Goshen Fence Machine Co.	Goshen, IN	1892
Superior	Superior Fence Machine Co.	Detroit, MI	1892
Superior	Superior Mfg. Co.	Martinsville, OH	1905
Tom Thumb	Tom Thumb Machine Co.	Dublin, IN	1892
Triumph	C.O. Bartlett	Cleveland, OH	1892
Wide Awake	Thomas-Albright Co.	Goshen, IN	1892
Wise Patent	Wise Wagon Works	Buena Vista, VA	1892

Fertilizer Spreaders

This section only includes devices for spreading commercial fertilizers. Sometimes, in polite company, a manure spreader was referred to as a fertilizer distributor, but most commonly it was called what it was—a manure spreader. Thus there is a separate section for manure spreaders, as distinguished from the fertilizer spreader machines.

By the 1890s, commercial fertilizers were available on a limited basis, being primarily used by truck gardens and certain other crops. The average farmer of the 1890s did not use commercial fertilizer. Shown here is the 1892 version of the McSherry Dandy Fertilizer Distributor made by McSherry Manufacturing Co., Dayton, Ohio.

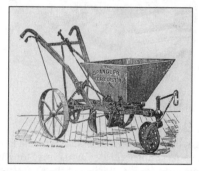

Truck gardeners, cotton and tobacco growers could purchase this model of the Spangler Fertilizer Distributor in 1892. The company also made other products at the time, including grain drills, corn planters, corn shellers, feed cutters and other items. Spangler Manufacturing Co. was located in York, Pa.

In the 1920s, the Nonpareil Lime & Fertilizer Sower, as shown, made its appearance. Nonpareil Manufacturing Co., Cochranton, Pa., was the manufacturer. By this time, many farmers were anxious to add lime to their fields as a means of controlling soil acidity. This popular line was taken over by Ohio Cultivator Co., Bellevue, Ohio, in 1927. Nonpareil spreaders were available in various forms at least into the 1940s.

A random photograph of the 1930s illustrates one of numerous special machines designed for truck gardeners. This special fertilizer distributor was designed especially for vegetables and featured variable row spacings and application rates. Unfortunately, this photograph gives no indication of the manufacturer.

By the 1930s, Portable Elevator Manufacturing Co., Bloomington, Ill., began marketing its Little Giant Lime Stone and Fertilizer Spreader. This little device attached to the rear of a wagon, with the farmer keeping the hopper filled as he went through the fields. This small spreader was very popular.

Late in the 1930s came Flink's Self-Feeding Spreader, made by The Flink Co., Streator, Ill. This was a truck-mounted unit that prac-

tically eliminated the hand work involved with previous devices. Eventually, lime and fertilizer spreading would become a mechanized process using specially designed trucks and equipment.

Trade Names			
Acme	A. McKenney	Rock, MA	1892
Acme	Moffatt Mfg. Co.	Chester, SC	1892
Aspinwall	Aspinwall Mfg. Co.	Three Rivers, MI	1892
Atlanta	Atlanta Agricultural Works	Atlanta, GA	1905
Ayers	J.R. Ayers	Petersburg, VA	1905
Collins	Griffin Agricultural Works	Griffin, GA	1892
Columbus	Southern Plow Co.	Columbus, GA	1905
Eclipse	Eclipse Corn Planter Co.	Enfield, NH	1892
Empire	Empire Drill Co.	Shortsville, NY	1905
Flink's	Flink Company	Streator, IL	1936
Hall	James H. Hall Plow Co.	Maysville, KY	1905
Hench & Dromgold	Hench & Dromgold Co.	York, PA	1905
Hubbard	H.N. Hubbard	New York, NY	1892
Keystone	Keystone Farm Machine Co.	York, PA	1905
Little Giant	Portable Elevator Mfg. Co.	Bloomington, IL	1930
McSherry Dandy	McSherry Mfg. Co.	Dayton, OH	1892
McWhorter	C. Billups, Son & Co.	Norfolk, VA	1892
McWhorter	McWhorter Mfg. Co.	Riverton, NJ	1905
Peerless	Moffatt Mfg. Co.	Chester, SC	1892
Perry	A.G. Perry	Coldwater, MS	1892
Philpot's	Longview-Kelly Plow Co.	Longview, TX	1892
Randolph's	P.F. Randolph	Bernardsville, NJ	1892
Spangler	Spangler Mfg. Co.	York, PA	1892
Vibert	F.C. Vibert	Hockanum, CT	1892
West	Sullivan Mfg. Co.	Anderson, SC	1892

Did You Know?

Challenge's 1910 model of its Dandy one-hole sheller had a base price of $8.

G

Garden Equipment

Over the years, garden tools have been manufactured by probably thousands of different companies. Garden hand tools—hoes, cultivators and other implements—were available almost everywhere and remain so today. On the other hand, wheeled implements, such as cultivators and special planters, have had their role largely usurped by small garden tractors; this began in earnest during the 1920s when many companies began building motorized units.

For the purposes of this book, a few wheeled garden tools are presented to provide a thumbnail sketch of activity in this field. While many of these implements were made by specialty companies, some of the major manufacturers also entered the field, at least for a few years. Antique garden cultivators have appreciated somewhat in value, especially those which are quite unusual in design.

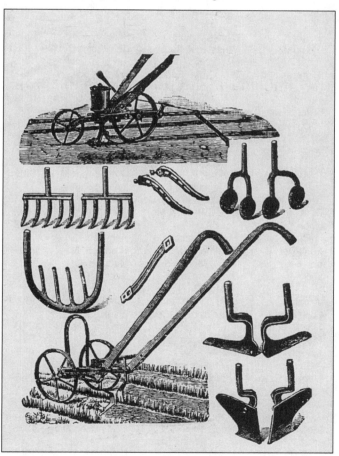

An 1889 advertisement in the *American Agriculturist* illustrates the new line of hand cultivators from Deere & Mansur at Moline, Ill. This was a combination sold as the McGee Cultivator. Included was a variety of attachments for cultivating almost any garden crop.

J.I. Case Plow Works at Racine, Wis., offered this combined garden seeder/cultivator in its 1897 catalog. More than likely, it had already been on the market for a time. Numerous attachments were included for every conceivable purpose; today, it is difficult to find a vintage cultivator like this with all its accessory parts.

One of the popular equipment lines for the truck farmer was the Iron Age from Bateman Manufacturing Co., Grenloch, N.J. This 1899 model is complete with planting attachment, row marker and a variety of cultivating tools. Bateman was eventually taken over by A.B. Farquhar Ltd., York, Pa.

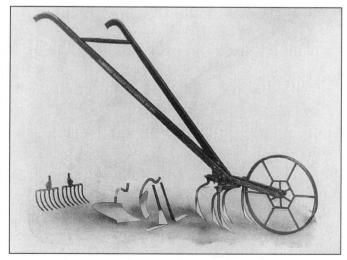

S.L. Allen & Co., Philadelphia, specialized in cultivators of all kinds. Shown here is a garden cultivator of 1900; this one was furnished with a variety of attachments. Some of these designs were built for decades without substantial changes.

Watson Disc Garden Plows were built by the Newton Disc Plow Co., Newton, Iowa. This one from 1910 was available through numerous hardware jobbers at the time. The heavy handles tend to indicate that it took a lot of strength to handle this outfit, although the company advertised it as "A Good Thing to Push."

Although motor-powered garden tractors are outside the scope of this book, a 1920 copy of the Beeman One-Horse Tractor is shown here to demonstrate the size and weight of early garden tractors. Despite this, truck gardeners welcomed machines like this because they tremendously cut down on the work force. This one was built by Beeman Garden Tractor Co., Minneapolis.

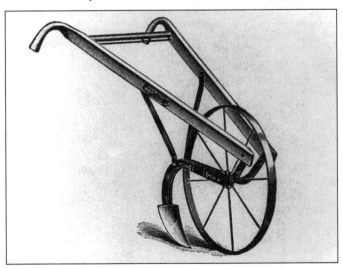

From 1932 comes this advertisement for an Arden cultivator from Brown-Manly Plow Co., Malta, Ohio. This one was a very

simple design with a single shovel, although it is likely that additional cultivating equipment was an option. Hand cultivators retained a major niche in the market until the advent of the modern small garden tractor in the 1950s.

Trade Names			
Apex	Brown-Manly Plow Co.	Malta, OH	1905
Avery	B.F. Avery & Sons	Louisville, KY	1892
Bacon	Bacon Mfg. Co.	Pontiac, MI	1905
Banner	F.C. Mason Co.	St. Johns, MI	1905
Banner	Greenville Implement Co.	Greenville, MI	1905
Bissell	T.M. Bissell Plow Co.	South Bend, IN	1892
Boyd's Bonanza	J.M. Boyd	Fond du Lac, WI	1892
Buckley	R.C. Buckley	Peoria, IL	1892
Canton Clipper	Parlin & Orendorff	Canton, IL	1892
Climax	Ohio Cultivator Co.	Bellevue, OH	1905
Clipper	Peru Plow & Wheel Co.	Peru, IL	1905
Cole's Improved	G.W. Cole	Canton, IL	1892
Columbia	Brinly-Hardy Co.	Louisville, KY	1905
Daisy	Daisy Implement Co.	Pleasant Lake, IN	1892
Decatur	Tenney & Sikkind Inc.	Decatur, IL	1905
Dexter	Motherwell Iron & Steel Co.	Logan, OH	1892
Dexter	Ohio Cultivator Co.	Bellevue, OH	1905
Diamond	Whitman & Barnes Mfg. Co.	Chicago, IL	1905
Everitt's	J.A. Everitt Seed Co.	Indianapolis, IN	1892
Fair	Brown-Manly Plow Co.	Malta, OH	1905
Fire Fly	S.L. Allen & Co.	Philadelphia, PA	1892
Fuller & Johnson	Fuller & Johnson Mfg. Co.	Madison, WI	1892
Gale	Gale Mfg. Co.	Albion, MI	1892
Garden King	Grand Rapids Mfg. & Implement Co.	Grand Rapids, MI	1892
Garden King	Greenville Implement Co.	Greenville, MI	1905
Garden King	Hickox-Mull Mfg. Co.	Toledo, OH	1905
Gem	E.S. & F. Bateman	Grenloch, NJ	1892
Hood	Josa A. Hood	Philadelphia, PA	1892
Ideal	H.P. Deuscher Co.	Hamilton, OH	1905
Iron Age	Bateman Mfg. Co.	Grenloch, NJ	1905
Iron King	W.H. Genung & Son	Madison, OH	1892
Jackson	Jackson-Crose Mfg. Co.	Denver, CO	1892
Jewel	E.S. & F. Bateman	Grenloch, NJ	1892
Lou Dillon	Schaible Mfg. Co.	Elyria, OH	1905
Man Weight	Prairie Mfg. Co.	Indianapolis, IN	1905
McGee	Deere & Mansur Co.	Moline, IL	1892
Moore's Gardener	Moore Plow & Implement Co.	Greenville, MI	1905
Moore's Gem	Moore Plow & Implement Co.	Greenville, MI	1905
Moore's Jr.	Moore Plow & Implement Co.	Greenville, MI	1905
Moore's Sr.	Moore Plow & Implement Co.	Greenville, MI	1905
New Universal	Ames Plow Co.	Boston, MA	1905
Peerless	Greenville Implement Co.	Greenville, MI	1905
Peru	Peru Plow & Wheel Co.	Peru, IL	1892
Queen of the Garden	George H. Black	Buchanan, MI	1892
Rival	Brown-Manly Plow Co.	Malta, OH	1905
Scott's	Weyburn Co.	Rockford, IL	1905

Trade Names (cont...)			
Star	Star Implement Co.	Flint, MI	1892
Success	Kirkwood, Miller & Co.	Peoria, IL	1892
Syracuse	Syracuse Chilled Plow Co.	Syracuse, NY	1892
Toledo	Hickox-Mull Mfg. Co.	Toledo, OH	1905
Vulcan	Heilman Plow Co.	Evansville, IN	1892
Wilder	Wilder Mfg. Co.	Monroe, MI	1892

Grain Binders

For the benefit of those unfamiliar with the terminology, *grain binders* refer to those machines that cut the standing grain and formed it into a sheaf, securing same with wire or twine. The wire binder came first, followed shortly after by the twine binder. *Harvesters* refer to those machines that cut the grain, elevating it to a table on which it was bound by hand, using wisps of straw. Reapers cut the grain, with the revolving rake pushing it off the table in small gavels, suitable for binding. This section deals with grain binders, also including the Marsh harvester. The latter was the springboard for the grain binder because the brothers Marsh developed some of the features essential to the successful grain binder.

Although there are dozens of grain binders illustrated in this section, there are many others for which we had no illustrations or, even worse, no history to work with, outside of a company name. As with other sections of this book, perhaps the author will be fortunate enough to receive additional materials for a future edition of this book.

Some historians say that huge factories—such as the Ford Motor Co., and its inimitable Model T automobile—heralded the beginning of mass-production techniques and interchangeability of parts. Yet, it would seem that these techniques were developed years before by the farm equipment industry. For example, McCormick Harvesting Machine Co., in 1860 was already a gigantic manufacturing concern, with its employees numbering into the thousands. It seems inconceivable to the author that the thousands of reapers and mowers leaving the McCormick factories did not have interchangeable parts. How many farmers would have bought a machine for which each part had to be hand-fitted by a company expert?

As the grain binder developed in the 1870s, the complicated knotter mechanism used precision parts, some of which were subject to wear or breakage. Imagine trying to sell a grain binder to a farmer, with the farmer knowing that in the busy harvest season he would have to telegraph the company and await the arrival of an expert machinist to fit a replacement. The fact is, repair parts were carried by local dealers; in case of breakage, the part could be replaced with little delay. In the author's opinion, interchangeability of parts was in full swing long before the automobile industry ever took its first breath.

With the coming of the combine, subsequent to 1915, the slow transition came to combine harvesting. Progress continued apace until the 1930s and the introduction of the All-Crop Combine from Allis-Chalmers. This small, light-weight machine probably did as much to convert small farmers to combines as any single make from any manufacturer. Production of grain binders slowed dramatically in the 1930s,

practically ending during World War II and resuming for a brief time after. Today, workable grain binders are becoming a scarcity. Oftentimes, the canvases are deteriorated beyond repair and it's an expensive proposition to have new ones custom-made. Thus, a grain binder in excellent operating condition may bring $200 to $300 or more, with a machine resting in a fence row barely bringing scrap price.

Acme Harvesting Machine Co., Peoria, Ill.

Acme Harvester Co. was often plagued by financial problems, going out of business at one point and resuming in 1903. The company specialized in grain binders, but this was a very competitive business, often characterized as the "Harvester Wars." The Acme of 1912 is shown here; it developed along the same lines as its competitors, but had important features, including an all-steel binding table.

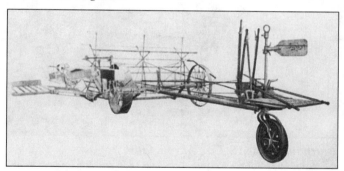

In some areas, the push binder was preferred over the conventional design. For 1903, Acme offered its Hodges Harvester King Combined Header-Binder. This one could operate as a push binder or could easily be converted to a grain header. This was preferable when little or no straw was wanted; the header cut the grain slightly below the heads rather than just above the ground.

Adriance, Platt & Co., Poughkeepsie, N.Y.

From a magazine of the 1880s comes this illustration of the Adriance Rear Discharge Binder. While the majority of grain binders, including most models of the Adriance, used elevator canvases to carry the grain to the table, this one was a low-profile outfit that was marketed for only a short time.

When this 1906 version of the Adriance grain binder appeared, the company was a well-established manufacturer of mowers, grain binders, hay rakes, harrows and other equipment. With the excellent reputation of Adriance farm equipment, little wonder is it that the company was bought out by Moline Plow Co., in 1912.

Aultman, Miller & Co., Akron, Ohio

Aultman, Miller & Co. went back to 1856 and the invention of the Buckeye mower by Lewis Miller. About 1883, the company launched its Banner Binder, but numerous improvements were made to this machine in subsequent years. Shown here is an 1888 version of the Buckeye Binder.

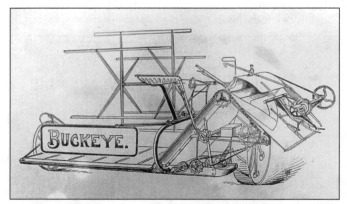

By 1900, the Buckeye line was one of the better known names in the harvester business. The company offered its catalogs in English, as well as in several foreign languages, to the benefit of immigrants. This company came under control of International Harvester Co., sometime in 1903.

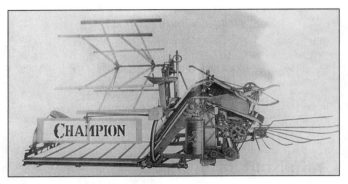

B.F. Avery & Sons, Louisville, Kty.

Shown here is the Champion Improved Binder, as sold by B.F. Avery in 1916. The Champion line was acquired after it was divested by International Harvester Co. In a court battle that went on for years, Harvester finally agreed to divest itself of certain companies if it was permitted to begin manufacturing plows. Thus, B.F. Avery acquired the Champion line and Harvester bought out P&O Plow Co.

Brown Straw Binder Co., Indianapolis, Ind.

In 1895, a man by the name of Brown came up with an idea for a grain binder that would use straw for binding instead of twine. After a few years, Brown sold out his ideas to Albert Izor of Indianapolis. Eventually, he sought the mechanical counsel of H.A. Hancock; together, they worked on the design. With this device, the grain came onto a grain table, as usual, but once a sufficient amount had accumulated, a twisting device formed a band for the sheaf, encircling it one and a half times. A "tucker" then pushed the twisted ends under the band. However, history repeated itself; despite considerable time and money spent in developing the straw binder, a commercially successful machine escaped the grasp of the inventors.

J.I. Case Co., Racine, Wisc.

In 1919, J.I. Case acquired the famous Osborne line from International Harvester Co. For some years after, the company built and sold the Case-Osborne line, including this grain binder of 1930. This one is shown with four horses providing the power.

J.I. Case Co., announced its new Case Power Binder in 1931. It was designed for tractor power and utilized the recently perfected PTO shaft to operate the binder mechanism. However, the combine was on the horizon; while a substantial number of power binders were sold, they were only produced until the early 1950s.

Craver & Steele Manufacturing Co., Harvey, Ill.

An 1887 advertisement shows this firm as Craver, Steele & Austin at Grinnell, Iowa. The company began building the Randolph Header pictured here at least by 1881, noting that it was "the [ideal] harvesting machine for timothy and flax." Nothing has been found concerning the company's activities in Grinnell, Iowa.

Sometime prior to 1894, this company relocated from Grinnell, Iowa, to Harvey, Ill. An 1894 advertisement illustrates Craver's Harvester King Header. It was actually a combination of a header and a push binder. Despite heavy advertising for a time, little else is known of the company.

Craver's Harvester Queen for 1894 was a conventional grain binder, albeit a small machine designed to be pulled by two horses. Chain drives were used extensively in lieu of gears and the machine shown here is not equipped with a bundle carrier. Despite the large number of grain binder manufacturers during the 1890s, the numbers diminished dramatically by 1910, when power was concentrated with a half dozen companies.

Davis Platform Binder, address unknown

In a magazine article of 1889, testimonials galore praised the merits of the Davis Platform Binder pictured here. This unusual design put the operator at the front of the machine instead of his usual perch at the rear. This one is a low-profile grain binder that attempted to eliminate the need for elevating the cut grain to the binding table. Unfortunately, the magazine article cited assumes that the reader knew the company name and address or, more likely, simply omitted them in error. No other information has been found.

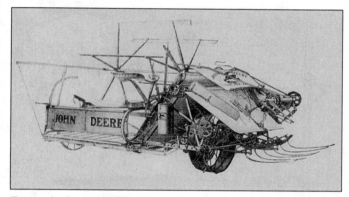

Deere & Co., Moline, Ill.

John Deere began making grain binders in 1910, going into full production for 1912. By this time, Deere had developed a large dealer organization. With the wide acceptance of the Deere line, the grain binder also became very popular. Shown here is a John Deere binder of 1918 vintage.

An advertising photograph from Deere & Co., 1927, illustrates The Light Running New John Deere at work. In some instances, three horses were used—sometimes it was four. Regardless, this new machine made extensive use of roller bearings and other features to minimize friction and reduce draft. Like other manufacturers, John Deere also recognized the coming of the combine, beginning developments of its own by the 1930s.

Deering Harvester Co., Chicago, Ill.

The history of the Deering grain binders goes back to the Marsh harvester of the 1850s. At various points, E.H. Gammon and J.D. Easter had a part in its commercial development, but it was Gammon's friend, Wm. Deering, who took hold in the 1870s. Shown here is Deerings Marsh Self-Binding Harvester of 1877; the engraving is from a German-language edition of an early Deering catalog. The binder shown here bound the sheaves with wire.

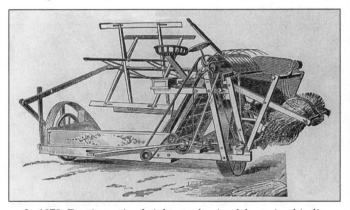

In 1878, Deering gained rights to the Appleby twine-binding apparatus and revolutionized the industry. Farmers complained about bits of wire being ingested by their livestock, to their detriment and the farmer's loss. The twine binder eliminated this problem completely. This Deering Draht (wire) binder is shown in an 1885 German-language edition of the company catalog.

For a number of years, Deering published its catalogs in several languages to the benefit of immigrant farmers. This 1885 German Edition illustrates the Standard Deering Schnur (twine) Binder using the Appleby knotter. With the advent of the grain binder, the reaper soon took a secondary role in the grain harvest.

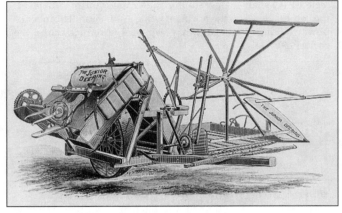

An 1885 edition of Deering's catalog illustrates the Junior Deering, a machine smaller than the Deering Standard. In 1880, the Deering factory employed about 800 people; this increased to 1,200 by 1885. Ten years later, the work force stood at 3,000; by 1898, the company employment more than doubled to 6,100.

By 1893, the Deering grain binder had been redesigned as the Deering Improved Steel Harvester and Binder. This reflected a major change from using mainly wood in the construction of the machine to an all-steel design with very few wood components. Deering also pioneered the use of ball and roller bearings in its machines to reduce draft.

An 1899 catalog illustration shows the Deering Ideal, sold as "the lightest draft binder ever built." This came about largely because the frame was redesigned and lightened with steel components, plus the company made extensive use of ball and roller bearings to reduce the draft. As shown here, the bundle carrier could carry four to six sheaves or bundles at a time, dropping them conveniently in rows to ease the work of the field workers.

Transporting the binder from one field to another was a problem with early machines because of their width. To overcome the problem, Deering devised a binder truck whereby the machine was put into a transport position as shown. The changeover was relatively easy and could be accomplished with one or two people. In 1902, Deering was a partner in the newly formed International Harvester Co., but the Deering line continued for some years within the Harvester organization.

Charles Denton, Peoria, Ill.

The July 30, 1853, issue of *Scientific American* illustrates Denton's Reaper and Self-Raker. This machine was far ahead of anything at the time and heralded the use of a platform canvas to carry the cut grain to the elevator canvases. The latter deposited the cut grain into a revolving box. When one section was full, it was tripped and the contents were discharged on the ground, ready for binding. Meanwhile, the next section of the box came into position for non-stop operation. Aside from this early article, nothing further is known of Denton's developments.

Emerson-Brantingham Co., Rockford, Ill.

Emerson-Brantingham had a long history in harvesting equipment; in 1918, it bought the Osborne implement line from International Harvester Co. Subsequently, it built and sold the E-B Osborne line, including the grain binder shown here. When J.I. Case took over E-B in 1928, the Case-Osborne implement line continued for a time.

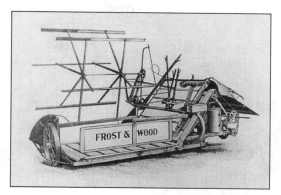

Frost & Wood Co., Ltd., Smiths Falls, Ontario

Frost & Wood was a major Canadian farm machinery builder, with its grain binders occupying a place of prominence in the line. This 1910 catalog illustration notes that its binders were made in 5-, 6-, 7- and 8-foot sizes. The 8-foot binder was ordinarily furnished with a tongue truck and equipment for a four-horse hitch. Shown here is a Frost & Wood No. 5 binder with a 6-foot cut.

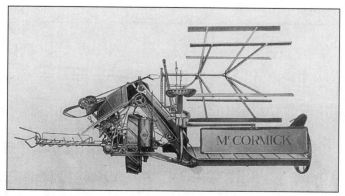

International Harvester Co., Chicago, Ill.

Shortly after organizing in 1902, International Harvester opted to build right-hand binders, in addition to the usual left-hand design. Shown here is one example, made with a 5-, 6- or 7-foot cut. When viewed from the rear as shown, the platform is to the right. Ordinarily it is to the left. A few companies made right-hand binders; some, such as International Harvester, offered both styles for a time.

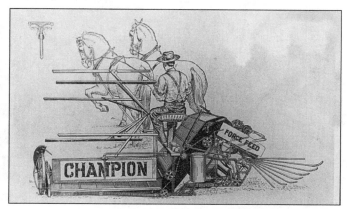

After the organization of International Harvester in 1902, the company continued many of the same product lines as previously, but operated them under the IHC corporate umbrella. The subsequent confusion plagued the industry for years. Shown here is a Champion Force Feed Binder of 1905; the latter had been developed by Warder, Bushnell & Glessner Co.

By 1920, the McCormick grain binders took the form shown here. It was often said that there were more McCormick grain binders in the field than any other make. Regardless of the precise figures, the McCormick was immensely popular; a great many of them can be found today. Of this number, however, a great many now reside in fence rows.

Recognizing the needs of certain crops and locales, Harvester offered various styles of headers and push binders at least into the 1940s. Shown here is a McCormick Header; it was made in 10-, 12- and 14-foot sizes.

Rice farmers needed special equipment for their crop; International Harvester responded with this special rice binder; the one shown here is of 1920 vintage. Although it was essentially the same as the ordinary grain binder, it was of heavier construction and the main wheel was covered to keep it from filling with mud.

International Harvester pioneered the use of the PTO drive, utilizing tractor power to operate machinery. In 1920, the company offered this tractor binder, shown with an 8-16 International tractor. While ahead of its time, it marked another epoch in the transition from horse power to tractor power.

Johnston Harvester Co., Batavia, N.Y.

Johnston Harvester Co. was incorporated in 1870 by Samuel Johnston, Byron E. Huntley and others. Johnston began making reapers already in 1862, organizing with Byron E. Huntley in 1868, under Johnston, Huntley & Co. Shown here is an 1878 version of the company's "string-binding reaper."

An 1892 illustration depicts Johnston's "Continental" steel binder. This machine, like many of its contemporaries, abandoned the almost exclusive use of wood for the framework of the machine in favor of light-weight steel components. This reduced the manufacturing cost, as well as lightening the weight of the binder.

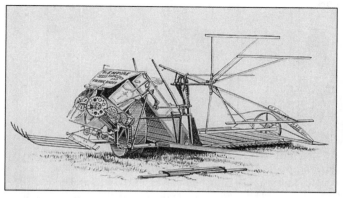

Johnston's grain binder line of 1892 also included the New Empire design. This was a light-weight machine that the company claimed was "the most economical binder in the use of twine ever manufactured." After the death of Byron E. Huntley in 1906, the company continued under Johnston's leadership until his death in 1911. The company was sold out to Massey-Harris Co. in 1917, which used it as a base for its expansion of sales into the United States.

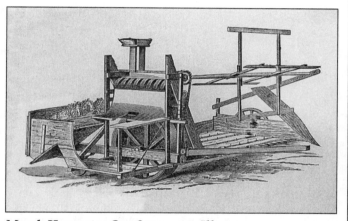

Marsh Harvester Co., Sycamore, Ill.

In 1869, the Marsh Harvester Co. was organized to continue building the designs perfected by C.W. and W.W. Marsh. Its 1858 design is shown here; it was the progenitor of the Deering harvester, illustrated under that heading. With the Marsh design, it was no longer necessary to gather the gavels of grain from the ground for binding. This was done by one or two men standing on the platform shown to the left of this illustration.

Massey-Harris Harvester Co., Batavia, N.Y.

The 1917 acquisition of Johnston Harvester Co. gave Massey-Harris a base of operations in the United States. The parent company was located in Toronto, Ontario, Canada. Its Massey-Harris No. 5 grain binder of 1923 was a takeoff from the earlier Johnston designs. In addition, Massey-Harris developed other product lines at the Batavia, N.Y., factory.

McCormick Harvesting Machine Co., Chicago, Ill.

By the 1870s, McCormick had become the undisputed leader in the reaper business. When the first wire binder and twine binder appeared, McCormick reacted slowly at first, apparently thinking that these new inventions would not prove themselves successful. Once it became apparent that the binder had come to stay, McCormick offered this "binding-reaper" to the trade in 1878. It was a wire-tie machine, with the wire reel plainly evident in the engraving. Also of note, grain binders at this time were largely of wood construction.

By 1893, McCormick had developed this open elevator grain binder. In most machines, the cut grain was conveyed by the platform canvas and between a pair of elevator canvases to the binding table. The open-elevator design attempted to eliminate the top elevator canvas, but the design only remained for a short time.

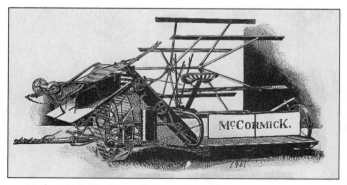

About 1895, McCormick decided to change to a right-hand binder instead of the usual left-hand design. As previously noted, a right-hand binder is as shown with the sickle and platform to the right of the operator. Whether it was a sales ploy or whether for some other reason, the change got a mediocre reception— after about a decade, the right-hand design fell from view.

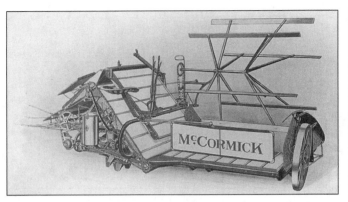

McCormick was early to develop a special rice binder. A close look at the illustration depicts the large lugs attached to the main wheel for needed traction. In addition the frame was heavier to accommodate the heavy draft encountered in wet or muddy fields. After the 1902 formation of International Harvester, the latter continued to build special rice binders for some years to come.

Milwaukee Harvester Co., Milwaukee, Wisc.

Milwaukee Harvester Co. was incorporated in 1884, although the company had a long history in the harvester business; its roots went all the way back to 1850. Building reapers and other equipment, the company entered the grain binder business in the 1870s, coming out with this attractive design about 1890. The windboard bearing the "Milwaukee" logo was used to keep the wind from disturbing the cut grain as it made its way to the binding table.

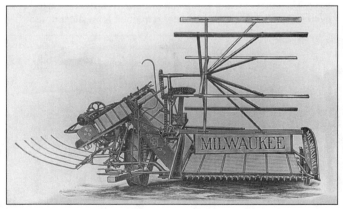

An 1899 illustration of the Milwaukee grain binder notes that this No. 10 model weighed 1,250 pounds and was available with a 5-, 6- or 7-foot cut. Although many grain binders of the 1890s were utilizing a steel frame, this 1899 model still retains major components of wood. The company merged with others to form International Harvester Co. in 1902.

Minneapolis Harvester Co., Minneapolis, Minn.

This Minneapolis grain binder was billed by its makers as "The Best Balanced Harvester and Binder ever Built." Apparently, the company gained in popularity, even with the competitive market that existed at the time. About 1894, the firm was reorganized as the Minnie Harvester Co.; in 1903, it came under control of International Harvester. An interesting note is that D.S. Morgan, the famous reaper manufacturer, had a financial interest in Minneapolis Harvester Co.

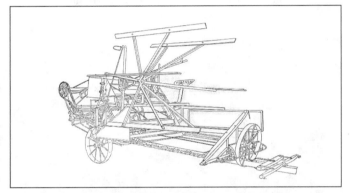

Minnesota Prison Industries, St. Paul, Minn.

In the 1930s, the Minnesota grain binders were available, gaining considerable attention in parts of the Midwest. The author recalls several Minnesota binders as a youth and, in fact, had one on the farm. Little information has been found on this enterprise.

Moline Plow Co., Moline, Ill.

With the advent of the Moline Universal tractor in 1917, the company came out with an entire series of implements designed for one-man operation. This tractor-binder combination is one such instance. In 1913, the company had acquired Adriance, Platt & Co.; this gave the firm a full line of harvesting equipment.

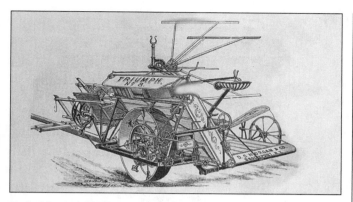

D.S. Morgan & Co., Brockport, N.Y.

This was the oldest reaper factory in the world. In fact, before Cyrus Hall McCormick moved to Chicago to establish his large factory, was of his reapers was built by Seymour & Morgan, an early title given to the business. Shown here is an 1890 version of the Triumph No. 8 Steel Frame Binder from Morgan.

D.M. Osborne & Co., Auburn, N.Y.

D.M. Osborne associated with W.A. Kirby in 1855; subsequently, they began building the Kirby mower. After various partnerships, D.M. Osborne & Co. was formed in 1862, after the company had been building reapers for almost five years. By 1878, this was the form of the Osborne Binding Reaper; this wire-tie binder first came on the market in 1876.

By 1900, the Osborne Columbia binder had become a very popular machine. In addition, Osborne had developed an extensive farm equipment line, gaining the notice of the competition. Thus, by 1903, International Harvester had gained stock control of the company, with complete ownership by 1905. Subsequently, the Osborne line was sold to Emerson-Brantingham; in 1928, the latter was purchased by J.I. Case Co.

Plano Harvester Co., Plano, Ill.

J.F. Steward associated with the Marsh brothers, who had earlier developed the Marsh Harvester. During 1864, Steward and Marsh put out 26 of its machines. William H. Jones had developed the Jones Lever Binder, and, in 1881, the Plano Manufacturing Co. shops were put to work building them. This binder was unique in offering an optional flywheel attachment as shown. This illustration is from the 1890s.

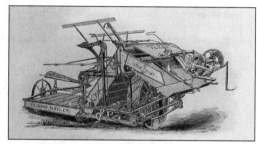

In 1898, Plano offered its New Steel-Frame Harvester and Binder. At the time, many manufacturers were reluctant to give up the term, "harvester," since it was already impressed on the mind of the farmer. However, it was only a few years until the semantics ceased, with "grain binder" even being replaced with the simple term of "binder." Plano Manufacturing Co. became a part of the 1902 merger that formed International Harvester Co.

Warder, Bushnell & Glessner Co., Springfield, Ohio

This famous company pioneered the harvesting equipment of Wm. H. Whitely and others. The company had a grand reputation and was a part of the 1902 merger forming International Harvester Co. The latter continued building Champion equipment for a time, but sold the Champion line to B.F. Avery Co., about 1918. Further details on this and other companies involved in the IHC merger of 1902 can refer to the author's *150 Years of International Harvester* (Crestline/Motorbooks 1981).

Walter A. Wood Mowing & Reaping Machine Co., Hoosick Falls, N.Y.

Walter A. Wood began building his first reapers in 1861, having been previously engaged in farm equipment manufacturing for at least a decade. Shown here is Wood's binding reaper of 1878; this machine tied the sheaves with wire. Instead of elevator canvases, as used later, this binder is equipped with a toothed rake to carry the grain up to the binding table.

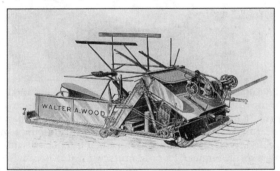

An 1887 advertisement shows the Walter F. Wood Iron Frame Binder. An important feature of this machine was the use of a bundle-carrier attachment. At the time, this was usually an optional feature; not having it would save a few dollars on the cost of the machine. However, dropping anywhere from three to five bundles in a group was a great help for the field workers sent there to put the grain into stooks or shocks.

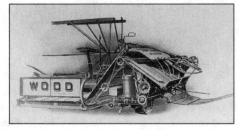

The New Century Grain Binder of 1906 was an impressive machine, neat in design and very popular with the farmer. The company continued apace in the farm equipment business; in the late 1930s, parts for Walter A. Wood implements were available from Hoosick Falls Implement Co., Hoosick Falls, N.Y.

Our North-Western Wheat Fields

From an 1889 issue of *American Agriculturist* comes this pictorial view of the grain crop from seeding to harvest: 1) shows the tillage process with several teams and plows doing their work; 2) several grain drills planting the crop; 3) shows the grain binder at work; 4) shows grain being brought to the thresher; 5) wagonload leaving the field; and 6) grain unloaded at the grain elevator. During this period, expert engravers were readily available. Their artistic talents have greatly enhanced this book.

Trade Names

Acme Queen	Acme Harvesting Machine Co.	Peoria, IL	1909
Adriance	Adriance, Platt & Co.	Poughkeepsie, NY	1905
Adriance Rear Discharge	Adriance, Platt & Co.	Poughkeepsie, NY	1892
Banner	Aultman, Miller & Co.	Akron, OH	1892
Bovee's	Bovee Harvesting Machine Co.	Tama, IA	1892
Buckeye	Aultman, Miller & Co.	Akron, OH	1905
Case (Osborne)	J.I. Case Threshing Machine Co.	Racine, WI	1929
Champion	B.F. Avery & Sons	Louisville, KY	1924
Champion	International Harvester Co.	Chicago, IL	1905
Champion	Warder, Bushnell & Glessner Co.	Springfield, OH	1892
Craver & Steele	Craver & Steele Mfg. Co.	Harvey, IL	1887
Daniel Best	Daniel Best Agricultural Works	San Leandro, CA	1892
Deere	Deere & Co.	Moline, IL	1915
Deering	International Harvester Co.	Chicago, IL	1905
Deering	William Deering & Co.	Chicago, IL	1892
Denton	Charles Denton	Peoria, IL	1853
E-B	Emerson-Brantingham Co.	Rockford, IL	1919
Empire	J.F. Seiberling & Co.	Akron, OH	1892
Empire	Seiberling & Miller Co.	Doylestown, OH	1892

Trade Names (cont...)

Esterly	Esterly Harvester Co.	Whitewater, WI	1892
Excelsior	Hoover & Gamble	Miamisburg, OH	1892
Hero	Sandusky Mach. & Agricultural Works	Sandusky, OH	1892
Hodges Queen	Acme Harvester Co.	Peoria, IL	1905
Independent	Independent Harvester Co.	Plano, IL	1915
Johnston Bonnie	Johnston Harvester Co.	Batavia, NY	1905
Johnston Continental	Johnston Harvester Co.	Batavia, NY	1905
Keystone	Keystone Co.	Sterling, IL	1905
Marsh	Marsh Harvester Co.	Sycamore, IL	1869
Massey-Harris	Johnston Harvester Co.	Batavia, NY	1915
McCormick	International Harvester Co.	Chicago, IL	1905
McCormick	McCormick Harvesting Machine Co.	Chicago, IL	1892
Milwaukee	International Harvester Co.	Chicago, IL	1905
Milwaukee	Milwaukee Harvester Co.	Milwaukee, WI	1892
Minneapolis	Minneapolis Harvester Works	Minneapolis, MN	1892
Minnie	Minnie Harvester Co.	St. Paul, MN	1905
Moline	Moline Plow Co.	Moline, IL	1918
New Century	Walter A. Wood M. & R. Mach. Co.	Hoosick Falls, NY	1905
New Ideal	International Harvester Co.	Chicago, IL	1913
Osborne Columbia	D.M. Osborne	Auburn, NY	1905
Osborne Steel Frame	D.M. Osborne	Auburn, NY	1892
Perry	Wyckoff & Co.	Perry, NY	1892
Plano	International Harvester Co.	Chicago, IL	1905
Plano	Plano Mfg. Co.	Chicago, IL	1892
Reliance	Sandwich Mfg. Co.	Sandwich, IL	1892
Triumph	D.S. Morgan & Co.	Brockport, NY	1892
Walter A. Wood	Walter A. Wood M. & R. Mach. Co.	Hoosick Falls, NY	1892
Whiteley	Amos Whiteley & Co.	Springfield, OH	1892

Grain Drills

The reaper and the grain drill follow each other in their development. On the one hand, the grain drill permitted the farmer to seed a larger acreage than before; this demanded more manpower or a mechanized machine to harvest the larger crop. On the other hand, the reaper permitted a farmer to harvest much larger acreages than was possible to seed-by-hand methods, so a machine was needed to accommodate the need.

Development went slowly in the 1850s, not really beginning to bud until after the Civil War ended in 1865. By then, several promising developments were coming to the market. Soon, there were many manufacturers offering grain drills to the farmer. Once the basic designs were worked out, the grain drill remained with little change into the 1930s. By that time, the advent of tractor power and higher field speeds de-

manded changes in design. Despite these changes, grain drill design changed little until recent years, when entirely new technologies emerged.

Today, old grain drills are becoming difficult to find. Many of the early ones have rotted away in a grove, to the point that the only thing of value is the fancy end-plates, some with particularly nice ornamentation cast in place. While we know of no established market for grain drills, grain drill end-plates often fetch as much (or more) as the lids of ancient corn planter boxes.

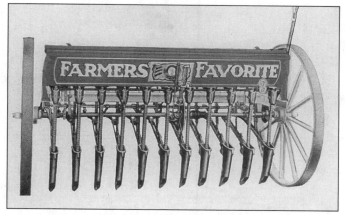

American Seeding Machine Co., Springfield, Ohio

A 1915 advertisement illustrates the Farmers' Favorite Drill as built by American Seeding Machine Co. The latter resulted from a 1903 merger of seven different grain drill and seeder manufacturers. This one is a single-disc fertilizer drill.

From 1903 comes this advertisement for the Superior line of seeding machines from American. This included single- and double-disc drills, hoe drills, shoe drills, beet drills and various kinds of seeders. American Seeding Machine Co. sold its Richmond, Ind., plant to International Harvester Co. in 1919.

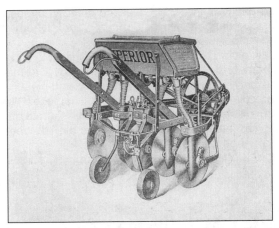

In 1912, Superior advertised this One-Horse Drill, a small machine suitable for grain and fertilizer. While the disc-drill model is shown here, it was also available as a hoe drill. Machines like this were well suited to small plots, truck farming and similar uses.

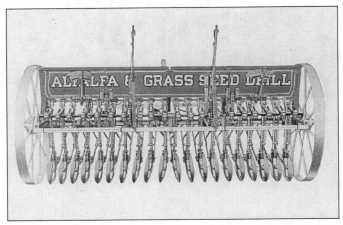

Recognizing the special needs of alfalfa and hay farming, Superior offered a special Alfalfa & Grass Seed Drill. With a combination drill, the coarse grain was planted behind the disc openers, with the hay seed dropping onto the surface through small flexible tubes. This special design permitted planting the tiny seeds at just the right depth. American merged with others to form Oliver Farm Equipment Co. in 1929.

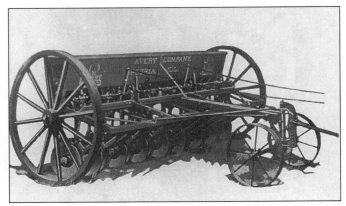

Avery Co., Peoria, Ill.

For a time in the 1920s, Avery offered this disc drill in two different sizes. It's possible the company had manufactured grain drills previously; however, after this 1923 announcement, it does not appear that Avery exerted further activity in this regard.

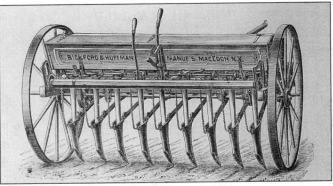

Bickford & Huffman Co., Macedon, N.Y.

Bickford & Huffman was one of the early manufacturers of grain drills, with an 1888 example shown here. Its Farmers' Favorite drills were very popular, with a hoe drill shown here. As the hoes moved forward through the soil, seed was dropped down through their hollow center. In 1903 Bickford & Huffman merged with others to form American Seeding Machine Co.

Brown, Adams & Co., Shortsville, N.Y.

An 1869 catalog illustrates the Empire Grass Seed Sower, as made by this firm. The company had acquired patents in 1861, 1862 and 1866, as well as winning premiums at several important fairs and expositions. Little else is known of the company or its activities.

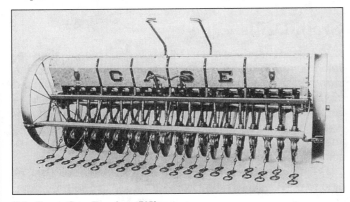

J.I. Case Co., Racine, Wisc.

After acquiring Emerson-Brantingham Co. in 1928, Case was endowed with an extensive line of grain drills previously developed by E-B. By the 1940s, Case came out with its new Seedmeter Grain Drill; this one was equipped with a horse hitch.

Chambers, Bering, Quinlan Co., Decatur, Ill.

In 1903, CB&Q advertised the Haworth grain drills; the name apparently reflected back to G.D. Haworth, a moving force behind the Haworth check-row corn planter. The Haworth drill only remained in production for a few years. By the early 1920s, only repair parts could be secured.

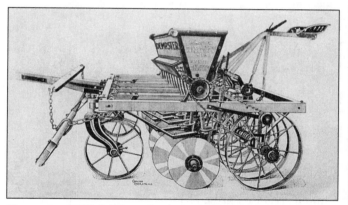

Dempster Mill & Manufacturing Co., Beatrice, Neb.

Recognizing the needs of the wheat farmer, Dempster offered this steel-frame grain drill as early as 1902. It was equipped with steel wheels, offset discs and iron press wheels. A special fore-carriage supports the front of the drill.

Dowagiac Manufacturing Co., Dowagiac, Mich.

An 1888 advertisement illustrated a single shoe of the Dowagiac Shoe Drill. As shown here, the shoe somewhat resembled the runner of a corn planter, dropping seed between the split sides of the shoe. A press wheel followed behind to firm the seed in the soil.

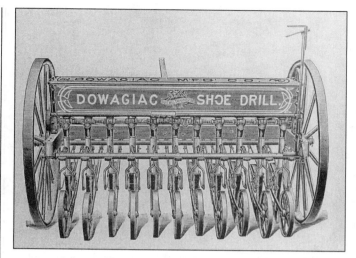

In 1895, Dowagiac was still offering its Shoe Drill, essentially unchanged from earlier years. In addition to this style, the company eventually offered disc drills and other models. By the early 1920s, the company had apparently left business.

Emerson-Brantingham Co., Rockford, Ill.

With its 1913 acquisition of American Drill Works at Marion, Ind., E-B was instantly into the grain drill business. The company capitalized on the line, expanded it and offered some excellent grain drills to the farmer. This one of 1919 typifies the line. E-B was bought out by J.I. Case in 1928.

Empire Drill Company, Shortsville, N.Y.

In the early 1890s, Empire offered an extensive line of grain drills. Plain drills could be substituted for the Combined Drill with a grass seeder attachment. The two-horse drill was the most common, but small one-horse drills were also available.

Farmer's Friend Manufacturing Co., Dayton, Ohio

An early entrant into the grain drill business was Farmer's Friend Manufacturing Co. Shown here is its 1878 copy of Kuhn's Grain Drill, apparently referring to the name of the patentee. At the time, of course, wooden construction was the only viable method of construction. This company disappeared from the scene in the early 1900s (perhaps earlier), but no information has been found.

A.B. Farquhar Co., Ltd., York, Pa.

In the 1890s, Farquhar offered its Pennsylvania Low Down Grain Drill to the farmer; the terminology referred to the low profile of the design, compared to many of the contemporaries. As with most grain drills of the time, there was no seat; the farmer walked behind the drill back and forth through the entire field.

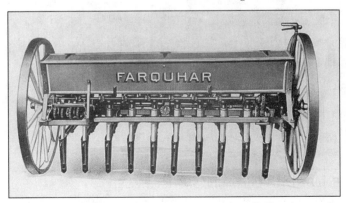

In the 1920s, Farquhar was offering this hoe drill with a steel frame, but still retaining the wooden wheels of an earlier time. A distinct advantage to this hoe drill was the addition of a spring-

trip drag bar. This kept from breaking the hoes if a rock or other obstruction was encountered in the field.

By the 1930s, Farquhar was offering the So-Rite fertilizer sower, a small one-man outfit. Its two drill tubes and a steel hopper were carried on a wheelbarrow frame; it is not known if this device could also be used as a seeder or if it was purely a fertilizer sower.

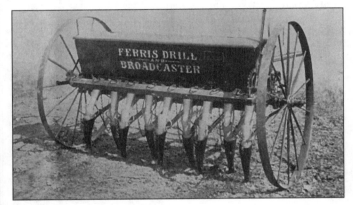

Grant-Ferris Co., Troy, N.Y.

An 1892 catalog from Grant-Ferris illustrates its Drill and Broadcast Seeder Combined; the company billed it as being "equivalent to two machines for the price of one." This unique machine featured steel wheels when they were not yet in vogue, along with largely steel construction.

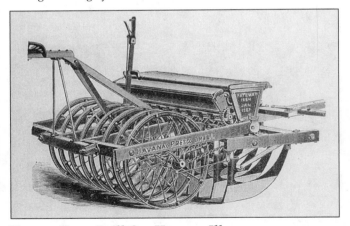

Havana Press Drill Co., Havana, Ill.

From 1888 comes this illustration of the Havana Press Drill, patented only a year before. This design was unique in its use of large iron press wheels behind the planting shoes; in addition, it was fitted with a seat for the driver. Eventually, this drill was built by the Ashurst Press Drill Co., also of Havana, but it also dropped from sight.

Hayes Pump & Planter Co., Galva, Ill.

Sometime after 1905, Hayes apparently acquired the Sucker State Drill Co. at Belleville, Ill. Subsequently, the company began manufacturing the Hayes Sucker State drills, continuing to do so until merging with others to form Farm Tools, Inc. in 1930.

In addition to its extensive line of grain drills, Hoosier also offered several styles of broadcast seeders as shown. This 1903 advertisement was just prior to the American Seeding Machine Co. merger. In 1919, American sold its Richmond plant to International Harvester Co.

Hoosier Drill Co., Richmond, Ind.

Hoosier Drill Co. began operations at Milton, Ind., sometime prior to 1873. That year, the company moved to Richmond, establishing a factory that grew to large size. This 1895 illustration shows a Hoosier Wheat Drill with a combined fertilizer attachment.

International Harvester Co., Chicago, Ill.

With the 1919 acquisition of the Hoosier Drill Co. plant from American Seeding Machine Co., IHC was in a better market position than before. Prior to 1919, IHC had contracted for the entire output of the Richmond factory, but now the Hoosier was purely its own line, as illustrated in this 1920 engraving.

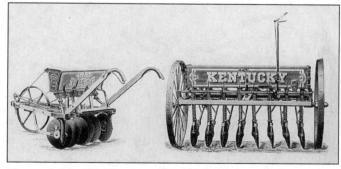

Kentucky Drill Co., Louisville, Kty.

About 1904, Kentucky Drill Co. was acquired by American Seeding Machine Co. American continued marketing the Kentucky line. In 1919, it sold this division (as well as the Hoosier Drill Co., Richmond, Ind.) to International Harvester Co.

An 1899 edition of the Hoosier line shows its Hoosier Disk Grain Drill, with disk openers. It was also equipped with a seat for the driver and employed a steel frame instead of the wooden style of earlier years. In 1903, Hoosier merged with others to form the American Seeding Machine Co.

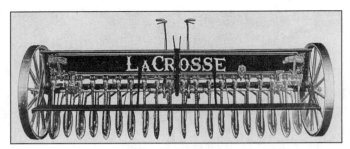

LaCrosse Plow Co., LaCrosse, Wisc.

Although LaCrosse Plow Co. was founded in 1865, information of its activity in the grain drill business is scarce. Shown here is a model from the 1920s. Although it uses a modern steel frame and other important features, this model retains the wooden wheels of earlier days. This model could be pulled by horses or a tractor. LaCrosse was purchased by Allis-Chalmers in 1929, forming the basis for its own line of drills and seeders.

Long, Black & Alstatter, Hamilton, Ohio

A wood engraving of about 1869 illustrates Page & Clary's Patent Seed Drill. It was priced at $60, half down and the balance by the following Jan. 1. The company gave a great sales pitch for the advantages of drilling over broadcast seeding; in the following decades, the same argument continued. In most instances, the choice boiled down to a matter of personal preference.

McSherry Manufacturing Co., Middletown, Ohio

McSherry grain drills were on the market at least by 1888, with this hoe drill typifying the line at that time. In a write-up about its features, the beauty, as well as the practicality of the design was cited. A fertilizer attachment was also available, but there is no indication of whether this drill could be equipped with a grass seeder.

By 1895, the McSherry grain drills were available from some major distributors, including the Parlin & Orendorff Co., warehouses at St. Louis and Kansas City. Subsequently, the company endured hard times, apparently going out of business sometime before 1920. In the 1920s, parts for the McSherry drills were available from Fetzer Co., Springfield, Ill.

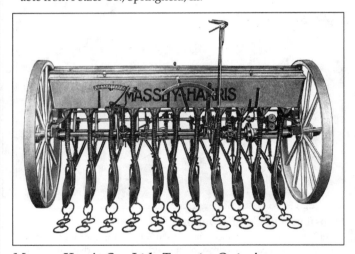

Massey-Harris Co., Ltd., Toronto, Ontario

Although Massey-Harris was a Canadian company, the firm moved into the U.S. market with its 1917 formation of Massey-Harris Co., Batavia, N.Y. Subsequently, the firm offered an extensive line of farm equipment, including this Combined Grain and Fertilizer Drill.

P.P. Mast & Co., Springfield, Ohio

Shown here is the 1890 version of the New Buckeye Low Down Shoe and Press Wheel Drill. This one was available in seven different sizes, from eight to 24 shoes. The "Low Down" of the title refers to the low profile of this drill compared to many others of the time.

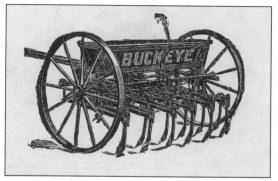

An 1895 advertisement in a German-language magazine portrays the Buckeye grain drill, telling of its qualities and suggesting that interested parties write to the company asking for more information. The company was established in 1854 and had a long career in the grain drill business. Thus, the Buckeye name carried with it a fine reputation in this business.

By 1903, the Mast drill had been redesigned to include an all-steel frame and spring pressure on each disc. The same year, P.P. Mast & Co. joined with others to form American Seeding Machine Co., with the Mast and Buckeye brand names remaining before the public for some time to come.

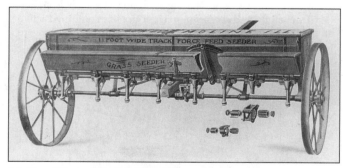

Moline Plow Co., Moline, Ill.

With the 1909 acquisition of Minneapolis-based Monitor Drill Co., Moline Plow Co. was firmly in the grain drill business. This illustration of about 1918 illustrates the company's Style E Seeder, a machine that broadcast the grain on top of the ground where it was harrowed to blend it with the soil. Moline was a major manufacturer of grain drills until the 1929 merger forming Minneapolis-Moline; the latter continued building drills until merging some years later into White Farm Equipment.

Few farm tractors gained the attention of farmers as did the Moline Universal. After it came onto the market in 1917, the company announced all kinds of machines to which it could be adapted, including the grain drill shown here. Fortunately, the attached implements did not necessarily have to be from Moline; almost any make could be converted. This is a Moline-Monitor beet drill attached to a Moline Universal tractor.

Ontario Drill Co., Despatch, N.Y.

For 1906, Ontario offered this grain drill as one of several different models in its line. The company eventually moved to Rochester, N.Y., but disappears from the trade directories by the late 1920s. As with many of the firms included in this book, very little information can be found outside of an occasional advertisement.

Peoria Drill & Seeder Co., Peoria, Ill.

The Illinois grain drills from Peoria Drill were very well known in Illinois and in surrounding states. In fact, the company utilized branch houses of several well-known companies over the years—this broadened its sales base considerably. The Illinois drill shown here was offered in 1903.

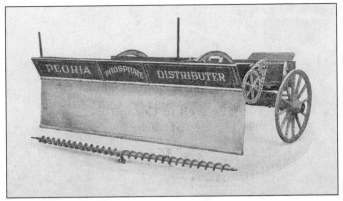

By the early 1900s, many farmers recognized the need for phosphate fertilizers; in 1908, Peoria responded with its Peoria Phosphate Machine. The unit was attached to the back of an ordinary farm wagon, with the drive coming from a rear wheel. The heavy canvas curtain was a wind guard to keep the phosphate on the ground rather than in the next county.

After the merger forming Farm Tools, Inc. in 1930, the latter continued making many of the Peoria implements virtually identical to those prior to that time. An example is the Peoria Hercules Wheel Seeder, advertised by Farm Tools, Inc. in 1938, but essentially the same machine as Peoria had been building for several years.

By the late 1930s, Farm Tools, Inc. came out with a New Peoria Grain Drill line, typified by the model shown here. It utilized galvanized steel wherever needed, plus steel components throughout. This modern machine was a takeoff of the earlier Peoria drill line. Eventually, Farm Tools, Inc. faded from view. There are indications that the New Peoria took residence with the Farm Implement Division of Ford Motor Co. sometime in the early 1950s.

Rentchler Drill Co., Belleville, Ill.

From 1884 comes this illustration of Rentchler's Improved Force Feed Drill. This is a hoe drill and the cover chains are placed on convenient hooks for transport. Rather than use any chains, this drill is geared directly from the wheels. A small grass seeder box is situated behind the grain box. Outside of this advertisement, virtually nothing else is known of the company.

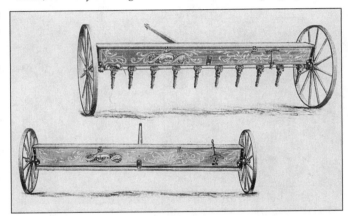

J.S. Rowell Manufacturing Co., Beaver Dam, Wisc.

Rowell had established a substantial factory by the 1880s; its products included hay rakes, cultivators and various kinds of grain drills and seeders. The Tiger Broadcast seeder is shown here from an 1894 advertisement. The Tiger line continued active at least to 1910, but a 1924 listing shows that repair parts were then available from Vim Tractor Co., Slinger, Wis.

Rude Bros., Manufacturing Co., Liberty, Ind.

Rude Bros. began building farm machines, wheat drills in particular, in 1868. Two years later, the company was established in Liberty, moving there from the farm blacksmith shop. The company was incorporated in 1881 to build farm equipment. By 1899 when this advertisement appeared, the Indiana grain drill line was known throughout the United States. Eventually, Rude Bros. opted for the manure spreader business, continuing in this for a number of years.

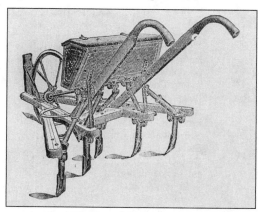

Spring Grain Drill Manufacturing Co., Peru, Ind.

From 1899 comes this engraving of the Spring Grain Drill, a small five-hoe drill with nothing more complicated than a pair of handles. The company apparently continued in business for some years, making various kinds of drills, but disappears from the trade directories by 1915.

Stoddard Manufacturing Co., Dayton, Ohio

The Tiger Combination Disk and Seeder is illustrated by Stoddard Manufacturing Co. in 1895. Stoddard was a leader in the development of disc harrows, offering either a curved blade Newton gang (as shown) or, in lieu of that, a spading gang with individual spading blades spread around the length of the axle. Units like this were intended for seeding and discing in a single operation.

Superior Drill Co., Springfield, Ohio

This company had roots going back to 1840 and was a principal partner in the 1903 merger forming American Seeding Machine

Co. This 1888 illustration shows its hoe drill of the time. One of its unusual features was a seat running the length of the machine. Its purpose was so that the farmer could slide to one end or the other to check the seed box while going across the field.

After the 1903 American Seeding Machine Co. merger, the Superior name continued to appear as it had in the past. The merger was beneficial for the partners in that it brought together a great number of patents under a single umbrella. This solved many of the infringement problems, since many of the patents overlapped one another. This 1907 model is an all-steel design with a convenient pressed-steel seat for the operator.

With the advent of tractor power, Superior responded with a tractor drill, probably sometime before this 1918 photograph. It shows a Case tractor pulling a Superior Grain Drill. In addition to having all the controls in easy reach of the driver, this model also used a power-lift attachment to raise and lower the mechanism.

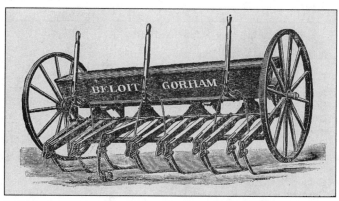

J. Thompson & Sons Manufacturing Co., Beloit, Wisc.

The Beloit Gorham Seeder, pictured here from an 1895 engraving, was unusual in its design. The seed dropped ahead of the shovels, from whence it was mixed with the soil for better germination. A special trip mechanism was employed so that if hitting a rock or other obstruction, the machine was not damaged. Very little is known of this machine aside from the illustration shown.

Van Brunt Manufacturing Co., Horicon, Wisc.

D.C. Van Brunt began building seeding machines as early as 1860. Various changes took place in the following years; as late as 1896, the company operated under the title of Van Brunt & Wilkins Manufacturing Co. A 1906 advertisement notes that "We will take back all Van Brunt Drills dealers take back that fail to do first-class work."

Among its wide range of grain drills and seeders, Van Brunt offered this Five-Disc Drill in a 1905 advertisement. The quality of the Van Brunt machines was undisputed. For several years, a major portion of the production was sold through the John Deere Branch Houses. Finally, the company was bought out by Deere in 1912.

Trade Names

Allis-Chalmers-LaCrosse	Allis-Chalmers Mfg. Co.	Milwaukee, WI	1932
American	American Drill Co.	Springfield, OH	1905
Ashurst	St. Joseph Plow Co.	St. Joseph, MO	1913
Beaver Dam	Beaver Dam Mfg. Co.	Beaver Dam, WI	1909
Blue	Geo. W. Blue	Bunker Hill, IN	1892
Buckeye	P. P. Mast & Co.	Springfield, OH	1892
Campbell	Moline Plow Co.	Moline, IL	1892
Canargua	C. W. Bradley & Co.	East Bloomfield, NY	1892
Carson	Moline Plow Co.	Moline, IL	1892
Case	J. I. Case Co.	Racine, WI	1936
Cassopolis	Cassopolis Mfg. Co.	Cassopolis, MI	1905
Champion	Champion Drill Co.	Avon, NY	1892
Clark	T. C. Clark	Russellville, KY	1892
Columbia	McSherry Mfg. Co.	Middletown, OH	1905
Columbia	Wm. Fetzer Co.	Springfield, IL	1909
Crown	C. W. Bradley & Co.	East Bloomfield, NY	1892

Trade Names (cont...)

Crown	Crown Mfg. Co.	Phelps, NY	1892
Davis	Wheel & Seeder Mfg. Co.	LaCrosse, WI	1892
Decatur	Chambers, Bering & Quinlan Co.	Decatur, IL	1905
Deere	Deere & Mansur Co.	Moline, IL	1892
Dempster	Dempster Mill Mfg. Co.	Beatrice, NE	1905
Dowagiac	Dowagiac Mfg. Co.	Dowagiac, MI	1892
Eagle	Eagle Mfg. Co.	Davenport, IA	1892
Emerson	Emerson-Brantingham Co.	Rockford, IL	1913
Empire	Empire Drill Co.	Shortsville, NY	1892
Empire	Geo. O. P. Turner	Churchville, NY	1892
Empire	Hagerstown Steam Engine & Mach.	Hagerstown, MD	1892
Empire	International Harvester Co.	Chicago, IL	1913
Empire	S. S. Messinger & Son	Tatamy, PA	1892
Farmer's Choice	W. A. Maloney	Telford, TN	1892
Farmer's Favorite	Bickford & Huffman	Macedon, NY	1892
Farmers Friend	Farmers Friend Mfg. Co.	Dayton, OH	1892
Ferguson	Harry Ferguson Inc.	Dearborn, MI	1945
Flying Dutchman	Minneapolis-Moline Co.	Minneapolis, MN	1932
Fountain City	American Seeding Machine Co.	Springfield, OH	1913
Fountain City	Wheel & Seeder Mfg. Co.	LaCrosse, WI	1892
Fuller-Lee	Genesee Valley Mfg. Co.	Mt. Morris, NY	1905
Glendale	Selby, Starr & Co.	Peoria, IL	1892
Gundlach's	P. M. Gundlach	Belleville, IL	1892
Hapgood	Hapgood Plow Co.	Alton, IL	1913
Havana	Stoddard Mfg. Co.	Dayton, OH	1892
Hawkeye	E. Children's Sons Mfg. Co.	Council Bluffs, IA	1905
Haworth	Chambers, Bering & Quinlan Co.	Decatur, IL	1909
Hocking Valley	Hocking Valley Mfg. Co.	Lancaster, OH	1892
Hoosier	Hoosier Drill Division	Richmond, IN	1905
Hoosier	International Harvester Co.	Chicago, IL	1913
Hoosier	Spicer Mfg. Co.	New Philadelphia, OH	1892
Ideal	Ideal Drill Co.	Albion, IN	1892
Illinois	Peoria Drill & Seeder Co.	Peoria, IL	1905
Imperial	LaCrosse Plow Co.	LaCrosse, WI	1909
Improved Empire	D. F. Hull & Son	Hagerstown, MD	1892
Independent	Ashurst Press Drill Co.	Havana, IL	1892
Independent	Independent Harvester Co.	Plano, IL	1922
Indiana	Rude Bros. Mfg. Co.	Liberty, IN	1905
Jewell	Rude Bros. Mfg. Co.	Liberty, IN	1892
John Deere-Van Brunt	Van Brunt Mfg. Co.	Horicon, WI	1929
Johnston	Johnston Harvester Co.	Batavia, NY	1915
Kentucky	Brennan & Co.	Louisville, KY	1892
Kentucky	Kentucky Drill Co. Division	Louisville, KY	1905
Keystone	Keystone Mfg. Co.	Sterling, IL	1892

Trade Names (cont...)

King	Bryan Plow Co.	Bryan, OH	1892
King	King Drill Mfg. Co.	Nebraska City, NE	1905
Kuhn's	Farmers Friend Mfg. Co.	Dayton, OH	1878
Leader	Janesville Machine Co.	Janesville, WI	1892
Little Giant	Lincoln Press Drill Co.	Lincoln, IL	1892
Magnet	Rude Bros. Mfg. Co.	Liberty, IN	1892
Malsbary	Houser & Haines Mfg. Co.	Stockton, CA	1913
Massey-Harris	Johnston Harvester Co.	Batavia, NY	1917
Massey-Harris	Massey-Harris Harvester Co.	Batavia, NY	1922
Master of All	Poirer Mfg. Co.	Gladstone, MN	1913
McCormick-Deering	International Harvester Co.	Chicago, IL	1929
McSherry	McSherry Mfg. Co.	Dayton, OH	1892
McSherry	Wm. Fetzer Co.	Springfield, IL	1909
Missouri	Genesee Valley Mfg. Co.	Mt. Morris, NY	1892
Moline	Deere & Mansur Co.	Moline, IL	1892
Moline	Moline Plow Co.	Moline, IL	1922
Moline-Monitor	Moline Plow Co.	Moline, IL	1919
Monarch	Farmers Friend Mfg. Co.	Dayton, OH	1892
Monarch	LaCrosse Plow Co.	LaCrosse, WI	1905
Monitor	Monitor Mfg. Co.	Minneapolis, MN	1892
National	National Drill Co.	Cambridge City, IN	1905
Needham-Crown	Crown Mfg. Co.	Phelps, NY	1932
New Casaday	South Bend Chilled Plow Co.	South Bend, IN	1913
New Cass	Dowagiac Mfg. Co.	Dowagiac, MI	1909
New Era	Dempster Mill Mfg. Co.	Beatrice, NE	1905
New Peoria	Peoria Drill & Seeder Co.	Peoria, IL	1909
New York Champion	Champion Drill Co.	Avon, NY	1913
Northern	Peoria Drill & Seeder Co.	Peoria, IL	1909
Oliver	Oliver Farm Equipment Co.	Chicago, IL	1932
Ontario	Ontario Drill Co.	Despatch, NY	1905
Ontario	Ontario Drill Co.	East Rochester, NY	1913
Owatonna	Owatonna Mfg. Co.	Owatonna, MN	1905
Owego	Champion Wagon Co.	Owego, NY	1915
Peerless	Peoria Drill & Seeder Co.	Peoria, IL	1909
Pennsylvania	A. B. Farquhar Co.	York, PA	1892
Peoria	Kingman & Co.	Peoria, IL	1892
Peoria	Peoria Drill & Seeder Co.	Peoria, IL	1905
Peoria Union	Peoria Drill & Seeder Co.	Peoria, IL	1909
Perfect	Moline Plow Co.	Moline, IL	1892
Poirer	Poirer Mfg. Co.	Gladstone, MN	1905
Rentchler's	Rentchler Drill Co.	Belleville, IL	1884
Richmond Champion	Wayne Works	Richmond, IN	1892
Rival	Janesville Machine Co.	Janesville, WI	1892
Rival	Samson Tractor Co.	Janesville, WI	1924
Rock Island	Rock Island Plow Co.	Rock Island, IL	1892

Trade Names (cont...)

Roderick Lean	Roderick Lean Mfg. Co.	Mansfield, OH	1905
Royal	Rude Bros. Mfg. Co.	Liberty, IN	1892
Rude	Rude Bros. Mfg. Co.	Liberty, IN	1909
Seymour	C. W. Bradley & Co.	East Bloomfield, NY	1892
Southern	Wm. Fetzer Co.	Springfield, IL	1909
Spangler	Spangler Mfg. Co.	York, PA	1892
Spring	Spring Grain Drill Mfg. Co.	Peru, IN	1905
St. Louis	St. Louis Drill Works	St. Louis, MO	1892
Star	Star Drill Co.	Rushville, IN	1892
Sterling	Sterling Mfg. Co.	Sterling, IL	1915
Strayer	Jacob Strayer & Co.	South Bend, IN	1892
Sucker State	Farm Tools Inc.	Galva, IL	1932
Sucker State	Hayes Pump & Planter Co.	Galva, IL	1905
Sucker State	Hayes Pump & Planter Co.	Galva, IL	1924
Sucker State	Sucker State Drill Co.	Belleville, IL	1892
Superior	Oliver Farm Equipment Co.	Chicago, IL	1932
Superior	Superior Drill Co.	Springfield, OH	1892
Thomas	Thomas Mfg. Co.	Springfield, OH	1905
Tiger	J. S. Rowell Mfg. Co.	Beaver Dam, WI	1892
Tiger	Vim Tractor Co.	Schleisingerville, WI	1922
Triumph	Stoddard Mfg. Co.	Dayton, OH	1905
Van Brunt	Deere & Co.	Moline, IL	1936
Van Brunt	Van Brunt & Wilkins Mfg. Co.	Horicon, WI	1892
Van Brunt	Van Brunt Mfg. Co.	Horicon, WI	1905
Victor	Ewald Over	Indianapolis, IN	1892
Victor	International Harvester Co.	Chicago, IL	1913
W. A. Lee	Western Mfg. Co.	Kansas City, MO	1905
Whitman's	Whitman Agricultural Co.	St. Louis, MO	1892
Wizard	Bickford & Huffman	Macedon, NY	1892
Yankee	Wheel & Seeder Mfg. Co.	LaCrosse, WI	1892
York	Hench & Dromgold Co.	York, PA	1909
Young Hoosier	J. F. Harcourt	Milroy, IN	1892

Grain Seeders

In the 1850s, there were already a few grass seeders on the market. However, it is well to remember that in 1850 there was not a noticeable transportation system in place and little in the way of communication outside of one's local area. Thus the majority of farm machines, those few that existed, were made locally. For a manufacturer to have a sales base of more than the surrounding counties was to be a major manufacturing concern in the farm equipment business. With the simultaneous development of the telegraph and the railroad, communication and transportation became possible. Looking at our history, much of our industrial development, particularly within the farm equipment industry, paralleled the building of the railroads. These factors played a role in the seeder business, as well as for reapers, grain drills and other developing machines. As the transportation system, postal system and the telegraph (and later on, the telephone) developed, so did the mass production of farm machinery. All were interdependent on one another.

Grain seeders or grass seeders were an inexpensive alternative to the grain drill. Many farmers preferred to sow the tiny clover or timothy seeds on top of soil, stirring dirt around them later with a harrow. Small hand seeders and wheelbarrow seeders retained a place in the market because they were especially suited to planting small fields that would otherwise be too difficult for a larger machine.

Today, small seeders, especially the wheelbarrow and "knapsack" seeders, have attained an antique value, often selling for more than $200, depending on condition. Various other styles sell anywhere from scrap value to $100 or more

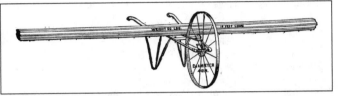

Crown Manufacturing Co., Phelps, N.Y.

An 1889 advertisement fully explains the features and the operation of the Crown Wheelbarrow Grass Seeder. The Crown was available with a 14- or 16-foot seed box; the company also made small grain drills. Crown Manufacturing Co. is listed in the trade directories at least into the late 1930s.

Cyclone Seeder Co., Urbana, Ind.

The Little Giant Seeder was already a popular hand seeder by the time this 1910 advertisement appeared. Ideal for seeding small areas, it simply required that one put the seeder over the shoulder and turn the crank. By the late 1950s, Cyclone had acquired several other product lines, including the Chicago, Combination, Fiddle Bow, Horn and Noc-Out.

Did You Know?

Workable grain binders are becoming a scarcity today; thus a grain binder in excellent operating condition may bring $200 to $300 or more.

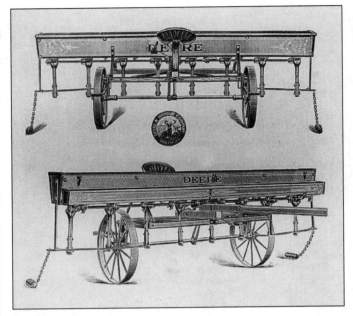

Deere & Co., Moline, Ill.

In its 1908 catalog, Deere offered this force-feed seeder through its Deere & Mansur organization. Drag markers were essential when planting and they are shown at each side of the seeder. The company marketed many kinds of drills and seeders, including the Advance end-gate seeder which eventually became the John Deere. (See also Sester Manufacturing Co. in this section.)

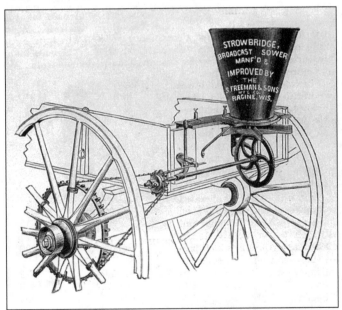

S. Freeman & Sons, Racine, Wisc.

The Strowbridge Broadcast Sower was offered by Freeman & Sons in 1887; the legend on the hopper notes that it had been improved by them. However, Strowbridge is also shown in this section and appears to have built the identical seeder at the same time. Further details are unknown. However, by 1909, the Strowbridge was being built by this firm, plus Foster & Williams Manufacturing Co. and Racine Implement Co., all of Racine, Wis. By the 1920s, repair parts only were available from Freeman.

Goodell Co., Antrim, N.H.

An 1861 article in *Boston Cultivator* demonstrates Cahoon's Broadcast Seeder. This paper had published an article on the Cahoon invention already in 1858, with one farmer stating that he had seeded his entire crop with this device. At the time, the Cahoon Seeder sold for $10.

A 1909 advertisement illustrates virtually the same hand seeder as Cahoon demonstrated in 1861. This probably proved the claim that this seeder "Lasts a Lifetime." The company remained in the trade directories at least into the late 1940s, but few other specifics have been found.

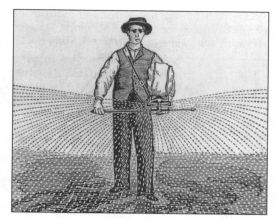

Goshen Sweeper & Wringer Co., Goshen, Ind.

From 1887 comes this engraving of the Goshen Broadcast Hand Seed Sower in use. This one operated with a "fiddlebow" that the farmer pulled back and forth to spin the fan. Outside of this display of the Goshen seeder, no other information has surfaced on the company.

Higganum Manufacturing Co., New York, N.Y.

At first glance, it would appear that Higganum made Pearce's Improved Cahoon's Broadcast Seed Sower. A look at the fine print of this 1889 advertisement indicates, however, that it was built and sold by Goodell Co., Antrim, N.H. The latter had developed the Cahoon seeder back in the 1850s. Further information on the connection between Higganum and Goodell is unknown.

F.F. Holbrook & Co., Boston, Mass.

During the 1850s, numerous companies began developing seed sowers of various kinds. One example was the Harrington, a small hand-powered device that placed seed in a row and even included a guide marker for even row placement. As with many of the very early companies, its history is virtually lost to time.

Hoosier Drill Co., Richmond, Ind.

Hoosier was selling this broadcast seeder in an 1899 advertisement and, as noted in the Grain Drills section, the company had been in the drill and seeder business for some years previously. As many implements of the day, this one was well adorned with ornamentation, even including a fancy decal in the center of the seed box.

In 1903, Hoosier became a part of American Seeding Machine Co.; the latter continued marketing the same Hoosier line until selling it to International Harvester Co. in 1919. The Hoosier End-Gate Seeder shown here was a simple device that was built on a wagon end-gate. To install it, all that was necessary was to take out the end-gate, set the seeder in place and run the drive chain onto the sprockets.

Janesville Machine Co., Janesville, Wisc.

Janesville's Prairie City Seeder is illustrated in this 1887 engraving. This one was part of an assortment of drills and seeders

offered by Janesville. Proof of its qualities is the fact that the Prairie City was offered yet in 1909, but eventually the company was taken over by the Samson Tractor Co. of Janesville; it continued to supply repair parts for a few years.

Peoria Drill & Seeder Co., Peoria, Ill.

Additional details of this company are found in the Grain Drills section of this book, but the illustration here from the 1930s shows the same Victor end gate seeder that Peoria had been building for many years. Peoria merged with others to form Farm Tools, Inc., in 1930. As evident in this illustration, a large open chain sprocket was attached to the left rear wagon wheel. These were available in various sizes, depending on the diameter of the wagon wheel and the desired speed of the seeder.

During the 1920s, the Peoria Poison Bran Sower was developed. The idea was to control grasshoppers or other insect infestations. Bran, water and a chemical such as Paris Green were mixed together. The poisonous mixture was then spread over the field. Aside from this special use, the machine shown here could also be used for broadcasting oats or fertilizer if so desired.

Sester Manufacturing Co., Peoria, Ill.

About 1908, the Advance Auger Force-Feed Sower came onto the market. It immediately became very popular and in 1911, the author's grandfather took one to the field. At the time, the grain drill was the only acceptable method in the area, so the entire neighborhood took notice. Within a few years, there were a number of Advance end-gate seeders in the area. Deere & Co. sold the Advance seeder for some years; by the late 1940s, Deere is listed as a parts source. The Advance and the John Deere end-gate seeders are identical.

Star Seeder Co., Shortsville, N.Y.

The origins of the Star Force Feed Wheelbarrow Grass Seeder are unknown. Subsequent to this 1897 illustration, the company continued to make the same seeders for at least another two decades. Also unknown is the extent of the Star seeder line; all that has been found is a trade listing of 1924 indicating that parts for this specific seeder were still available from Star.

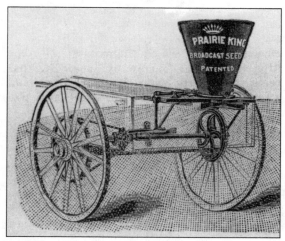

H.C. Staver Implement Co., Chicago, Ill.

Prairie King broadcast seeders were available from Staver in 1887. This one is a carbon copy of the Strowbridge seeder, as well as the Freeman article earlier in this section. The connection is now unknown; perhaps someone patented this seeder and then sold manufacturing rights to various companies. However, as with the Strowbridge, repair parts were later available from Freeman.

Joliet Strowbridge Co., Joliet, Ill.

The booming popularity of the end-gate seeder during the 1880s probably created plenty of marketing opportunities. For a time at

least, it gave plenty of manufacturing opportunities to satisfy the demand. As noted under the Freeman and Staver headings in this section, there were three different firms, including Strowbridge, all building the same end-gate seeder in 1887. Eventually, though, the Freeman interests came into control of the entire operation.

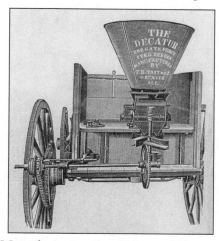

F.B. Tait Manufacturing Co., Decatur, Ill.

For 1899, Tait Manufacturing Co. displayed its Decatur end-gate seeder. This one differed slightly from the Strowbridge, but had the same physical appearance. A force-feed mechanism is evident, with a worm gear driving the feed system. For reasons unknown, the Decatur seeder slips from view by the early 1900s.

O.E. Thompson, Ypsilanti, Mich.

By 1908, Thompson's advertising noted that this wheelbarrow seeder had already been on the market for 30 years, with more than 150,000 sold. Like others in its class, the Thompson seeder was simple, sturdy and reliable. Wearing one out was almost impossible. Thompson seeders appear in various trade directories into the late 1940s, but the final disposition of the company is unknown.

Whitman Agricultural Co., St. Louis, Mo.

Details concerning the Pacific Broadcast Seed Sower are largely unknown outside of this 1887 advertisement. Instead of being an end-gate seeder, this one was mounted directly to the floor of the wagon box. Curiously, a 1924 trade listing shows that repair parts for the Pacific were still available from Solano Iron Works at Berkeley, Calif.

Trade Names

Acme	Racine Malleable & Wrought Iron Co.	Racine, WI	1905
Agitator	Peoria Drill & Seeder Co.	Peoria, IL	1905
Albion	Gale Mfg. Co.	Albion, MI	1892
Aremac	Aremac Mfg. Co.	Peoria, IL	1905
Badger	Appleton Mfg. Co.	Batavia, IL	1905
Beloit Gorham	J. Thompson & Sons Mfg. Co.	Beloit, WI	1905
Buckeye	P. P. Mast & Co.	Springfield, OH	1905
Burlington	Foster & Williams Mfg. Co.	Racine, WI	1905
Cahoon	Benicia Agricultural Works	Benicia, CA	1892
Cahoon	Goodell Company	Antrim, NH	1861
Cahoon	Whitman Agricultural Co.	St. Louis, MO	1905
Cahoon Improved	Higganum Mfg. Co.	New York, NY	1889
Carver	Carver Mfg. Co.	Carver, MN	1892
Champion	C. C. Carmien	Goshen, IN	1892
Champion	Joliet Strowbridge Co.	Joliet, IL	1892
Champion	Patten, Stafford & Myer	Canastota, NY	1892
Champion	S. Freeman & Sons Mfg. Co.	Racine, WI	1905
Climax	Joliet Strowbridge Co.	Joliet, IL	1892
Columbia	Peoria Drill & Seeder Co.	Peoria, IL	1905
Crown	Crown Mfg. Co.	Phelps, NY	1889
Cyclone	Selby, Starr & Co.	Peoria, IL	1892
Cyclone	Whitman Agricultural Co.	St. Louis, MO	1905
Deere	Deere and Mansur Co.	Moline, IL	1892
Dowagiac	Dowagiac Mfg. Co.	Dowagiac, MI	1905
Eagle	J. A. Engel & Co.	Peoria, IL	1905
Eclipse	S. Freeman & Sons Mfg. Co.	Racine, WI	1905
Eclipse	Staver & Abbott Mfg. Co.	Chicago, IL	1892
Empire Force-Feed	Empire Mfg. Co.	Keokuk, IA	1892
Farmer's Friend	S. Freeman & Sons Mfg. Co.	Racine, WI	1905
Foster's Force Feed	Foster & Williams Mfg. Co.	Racine, WI	1905
Foster's Perfect	Foster & Williams Mfg. Co.	Racine, WI	1905
Fountain City	P. P. Mast & Co.	Springfield, OH	1905
Freeman	S. Freeman & Sons Mfg. Co.	Racine, WI	1905
Freeman Force-Feed	S. Freeman & Sons Mfg. Co.	Racine, WI	1905

Trade Names (cont...)

Freeman Friction Drive	S. Freeman & Sons Mfg. Co.	Racine, WI	1905
Frisco	Whitman Agricultural Co.	St. Louis, MO	1905
Gem	Benicia Agricultural Works	Benicia, CA	1892
Genuine Gorham	Rockford Well Drill Co.	Rockford, IL	1905
Gray's Noiseless	Chambers, Bering & Quinlan Co.	Decatur, IL	1905
Glendale	Selby, Starr & Co.	Peoria, IL	1892
Gorham	Benicia Agricultural Works	Benicia, CA	1892
Goshen	Goshen Sweeper & Wringer Co.	Goshen, IN	1887
Great Western	H. N. Blatton & Co.	Franklin Grove, IL	1892
Harrington	F. F. Holbrook Co.	Boston, MA	1850
Hoosier	Hoosier Drill Co.	Richmond, IN	1905
Hurlbert	W. M . Hurlbert	Winona, MN	1892
Invigorator	Whipple Harrow Co.	St. John's, MI	1892
Keller	Keller Mfg. Co.	Sauk Center, MN	1892
Keystone	Keystone Co.	Sterling, IL	1905
Little Giant	Cyclone Seeder Co.	Urbana, IN	1910
Mann	Mann Mfg. Co.	Ogdensburg, NY	1892
McSherry	McSherry Mfg. Co.	Middletown, OH	1905
Moline	Deere & Mansur Co.	Moline, IL	1905
Monarch	Deere & Mansur Co.	Moline, IL	1905
Monarch	LaCrosse Plow Co.	LaCrosse, WI	1905
Monitor	Monitor Drill Co.	Minneapolis, MN	1905
New American	American Harrow Co.	Detroit, MI	1892
New Deere	Deere & Mansur Co.	Moline, IL	1905
New Departure	Rhea-Thielens Implement Co.	Peoria, IL	1905
New Leader	Janesville Machine Co.	Janesville, WI	1905
Niagara	Racine Malleable & Wrought Iron Co.	Racine, WI	1905
Owatonna	Owatonna Mfg. Co.	Owatonna, MN	1905
Pacific	Whitman Agricultural Co.	St. Louis, MO	1905
Peerless	Joliet Strowbridge Co.	Joliet, IL	1892
Peerless	Racine Implement Co.	Racine, WI	1905
Peoria	Foster & Williams Mfg. Co.	Racine, WI	1905
Peoria	Kingman & Co.	Peoria, IL	1892
Peoria City	Avery Planter Co.	Peoria, IL	1892
Prairie City	Janesville Machine Co.	Janesville, WI	1905
Prairie King	S. Freeman & Sons Mfg. Co.	Racine, WI	1905
Prairie King	Staver & Abbott Mfg. Co.	Chicago, IL	1892
Racine	Foster & Williams Mfg. Co.	Racine, WI	1905
Reed's	D. C. & H. C. Reed & Co.	Kalamazoo, MI	1892
Richmond Champion	Wayne Works	Richmond, IN	1905
Scandinaven	Foster & Williams Mfg. Co.	Racine, WI	1905

Trade Names (cont...)			
Stag	Deere & Mansur Co.	Moline, IL	1905
Star	Star Mfg. Co.	New Lexington, OH	1892
Sterling	Sterling Mfg. Co.	Sterling, IL	1905
Strowbridge	Foster & Williams Mfg. Co.	Racine, WI	1905
Strowbridge	Racine Implement Co.	Racine, WI	1905
Strowbridge	S. Freeman & Sons Mfg. Co.	Racine, WI	1905
Superior	Superior Drill Co.	Springfield, OH	1892
The Only	Rhea-Thielens Implement Co.	Peoria, IL	1895
The Only	Whitman Agricultural Co.	St. Louis, MO	1905
Tiger	Foster & Williams Mfg. Co.	Racine, WI	1905
Tiger	J. S. Rowell Mfg. Co.	Beaver Dam, WI	1905
Tornado	Whitman Agricultural Co.	St. Louis, MO	1905
Triumph	Dayton Farm Implement Co.	Dayton, OH	1892
Triumph	Stoddard Mfg. Co.	Dayton, OH	1905
Twentieth Century	E. F. Molck & Co.	Davenport, IA	1905
Union Jr.	Selby, Starr & Co.	Peoria, IL	1892
Wilder	Wilder Mfg. Co.	Monroe, MI	1892

Did You Know?

Hartman's Majestic cream separator in the 1920s was offered in four sizes, from 375 to 1,000 pounds per hour. The 500-pound separator originally sold for $62.

Grain Shockers

In the early 1900s, numerous inventors set about developing a machine that would mechanically shock the grain. Their vision was a machine attached to the grain binder that would automatically set the sheaves of grain in place, dropping the completed shock on the ground for curing and awaiting the coming of the threshing crew. The concept even caught the attention of some major farm equipment manufacturers, such as John Deere and International Harvester. Deere experimented with the Kellogg machine and IHC was confident in offering its grain shocker to the market about 1920.

Unfortunately, all these ideas failed. Part of the problem was the cost of the machine; another part was the lack of uniformity in the finished shocks; finally, most farmers simply weren't about to relinquish the art of shocking grain to a machine. By the late 1920s, the whole idea died for lack of interest—the combine was on the horizon.

Deere & Co., Moline, Ill.

In 1911, Deere & Co. took special notice of the Kellogg grain shocker; it was the product of one E. M. Kellogg. In the article accompanying this 1911 photograph, it was noted that Deere would build and sell the Kellogg shocker under a license it had secured from the inventor. Little more is known of this venture. From all appearances, this machine never reached the market. If it did, production was quite limited.

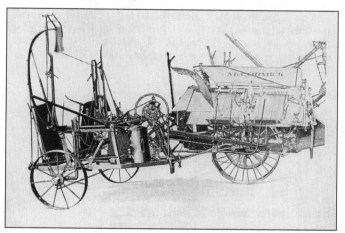

International Harvester Co., Chicago, Ill.

IHC included this International Grain Shocker in its 1920 General Line catalog. The company noted that it had placed a few of these machines in the field for the 1914 harvest, with additional ones during 1915 and 1916. The following year, 1917, the company placed this machine on the market, apparently selling a few along the way. However, the idea languished, with production apparently ending in the 1920s.

Grinding Mills

Stone grinding mills are a tradition that goes back centuries; from the earliest times, grain was reduced to flour between a pair of stones. The rotary mills in this section, likewise, have a long history; it is rather common to see old millstones at a historic site, both in the United States, as well as abroad. During the 1880s, there was an impetus to develop small stone buhr mills. While many used special imported French stone deemed the best for flour grinding, some used certain forms of granite found in the United States. Regardless, a number of companies offered small mills for the benefit of farmers and small grain millers. A few examples are shown in this section. Unfortunately, many of the flour mill manufacturers did not advertise in the farm journals because their trade was with bona fide flour millers rather than farmers.

Today, vintage flour mills often sell at a considerable figure; a nicely restored small mill might bring up to $1,000. However, a mill with a poor framework or a broken stone will bring but a fraction of that figure.

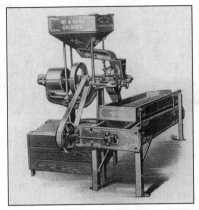

Appleton Manufacturing Co., Batavia, Ill.

Most folks preferred their corn meal and flour to be ground in a stone mill; a small burr grinder could leave the taste of iron in the finished product and that was undesirable. Even so, Appleton offered this small grinder in 1917, and it was equipped with the shaker or bolter to screen the finished meal. This model is its No. 4 Hero Pulley Grinder.

Foos Manufacturing Co., Springfield, Ohio

There is no certainty that Foos built stone buhr mills, but its 1888 catalog includes the Scientific Corn Meal Bolter, a device for screening the ground mill. The larger particles remained on the top screen, finally going to an offal pile, while the fine-grade corn meal dropped through the screen to a waiting basket.

Freeport Machine Co., Freeport, Ill.

This 1884 illustration shows the Freeport stone buhr mill of the day. There are indications that Freeport Machine Co. was somehow associated with Stover Manufacturing Co. or other manu-

facturing interests of D.C. Stover. Outside of this engraving, little more is known of the Freeport mill.

Meadows Mill Co., North Wilkesboro, N.C.

Meadows mills were very popular, being offered in various sizes and directed to the farm trade. For some years, the Meadows mills were sold through International Harvester dealers; this probably accounts for the substantial number of Meadows mills still in existence. This advertisement of the 1920s shows many of the operating parts of the mill.

Munson Bros., Utica, N.Y.

Stone buhr mills were used primarily for the reduction of corn to corn meal and wheat to flour, but, as noted in this 1884 Munson Bros. advertisement, it could also be used for grinding spices, cement and other materials. Stone buhr mills like this one were used into the 1880s, when the roller mill was developed by Edward P. Allis & Co. Subsequently, the roller mill became the predominant method of flour milling and the stone buhr mill lost most of its dominance in the industry.

Nordyke & Marmon Co., Indianapolis, Ind.

The Nordyke & Marmon mills had their beginnings during the 1850s, eventually becoming a predominant force in the milling industry. In addition to its large commercial mills and flour milling machinery, Nordyke & Marmon offered its Farm and Plantation Mill for decades. Built in 14- and 18-inch sizes, this small mill used a cast-iron housing for the stones; a small 14-inch model could provide sufficient corn meal for several families in a very short time. In 1927, the company was purchased by Allis-Chalmers Manufacturing Co.

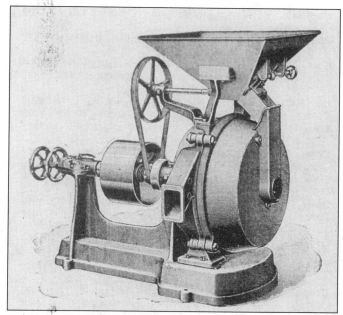

Richmond City Mill Works, Richmond, Ind.

Outside of this 1901 advertisement, virtually nothing is known of Richmond City Mill Works. Apparently, the company had already been in operation for a time; nothing has been found relating to its subsequent activities. The Planter's Pride Mill shown here featured a cast-iron casing, along with a massive cast-iron base plate.

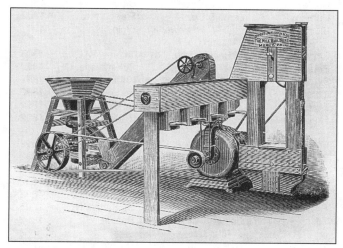

Sprout, Waldron & Co., Muncy, Pa.

From the 1890s comes this engraving of the Monarch Mill Outfit. At the far left is a corn crusher for reducing ear corn to small pieces. The material is conveyed to the stone buhr mill beneath; an elevator takes the ground material to a sacking stand. The company noted that in addition to its utility for grinding livestock feed, the same mill would make an excellent grade of corn meal or graham flour. Sprout, Waldron & Co., was primarily involved in making commercial mills.

A.W. Stevens & Son, Auburn, N.Y.

This well-known manufacturer of grain threshers and steam-traction engines also built Stevens French Buhr Stone Feed Mills for some years; this one is from the 1890s. The grain left the hopper dropping through the eye of the fast (stationary) stone, making its way between the fast and the runner stones and finally emerging from the periphery as ground meal. An interesting sidelight is that millstones were dressed in many different ways; hundreds of patents were issued on this point.

Stover Manufacturing Co., Freeport, Ill.

In 1912, Stover announced its new Stone Buhr Mill. This one was entirely of cast iron. As can be seen here, the runner (revolving) stone was forced against the stationary stone by an adjustable thrust bearing at the outer end of the shaft. Millers were very careful not to permit the stones to rub against each other, lest damage result. For reasons unknown, Stover built these mills for only a short time, probably less than two years.

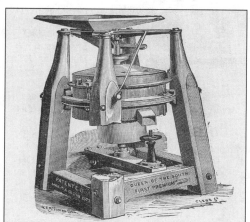

Straub Machinery Co., Cincinnati, Ohio.

An 1887 advertisement illustrates the Queen of the South Mill, as made by Straub Machinery Co. This was a typical vertical design, with the casing being carried by four large posts; the latter terminated as supports for the grain hopper. Patented already in the 1870s, this mill gained a wide reputation in its class.

By 1888, Straub was offering the horizontal version of its flour mill, calling it the "Gem of the South." This one used a cast-iron casing for the grinding stones, as well as a substantial cast-iron base to maintain shaft alignment. Its advertising noted that the stones were "of Solid French Burr." This material was deemed the best for flour grinding and could be found only in France.

Trade Names

Adams	Marseilles Mfg. Co.	Marseilles, IL	1892
American	Appleton Mfg. Co.	Appleton, WI	1892
American	Appleton Mfg. Co.	Appleton, WI	1892
Austin	F. C. Austin Mfg. Co.	Chicago, IL	1892
B. E. S.	Shoudy Mfg. Co.	Rockford, IL	1892
Baker	Baker Mfg. Co.	Evansville, WI	1905
Banner	St. Johns Foundry Co.	St. Johns, MI	1909
Bercha	Dempster Mill Mfg. Co.	Beatrice, NE	1909
Big "S"	Buckeye Feed Mill Co.	Springfield, OH	1905
Big Giant	J. A. Field Mfg. Co.	St. Louis, MO	1892
Blocki's	F. Blocki	Sheboygan, WI	1892
Blue Valley	Blue Valley Foundry Co.	Manhattan, KS	1892
Boss	Ohio Thresher & Engine Co.	Upper Dandusky, OH	1892
Boss	Woodstock Feed Mill Co.	Chillicothe, OH	1905
Bowsher's Combination	N. P. Bowsher	South Bend, IN	1892
Bradford	Bradford Mill Co.	Cincinnati, OH	1892
Bradford	Nordyke & Marmon Co.	Indianapolis, IN	1892
Buckeye	Buckeye Feed Mill Co.	Springfield, OH	1905
Buckeye	J. H. McLain Machine Co.	Canton, OH	1892
Buckeye	Staver & Abbott Mfg. Co.	Chicago, IL	1892

Trade Names (cont...)

Caldwell	Caldwell Mfg. Co.	Columbus, IN	1909
Cascaden's	Thos. Cascaden Jr.	Waterloo, IA	1892
Centennial	Elgin Wind Power & Pump Co.	Elgin, IL	1892
Challenge	Challenge Wind Mill & Feedmill Co.	Batavia, IL	1892
Champion	Forest City Machine Works	Cleveland, OH	1892
Champion	Kohler, Hayssen & Stehn Mfg. Co.	Sheboygan, WI	1892
Cole	R. D. Cole Mfg. Co.	Newnan, GA	1902
Common Sense	Common Sense Engine Co.	Springfield, OH	1892
Corn Belt	Spartan Mfg. Co.	Galesburg, IL	1905
Cornell	Cornell Mfg. Co.	Louisville, KY	1892
Crescent	Blue Valley Foundry Co.	Manhattan, KS	1909
Cutler	Cutler Co.	N. Wilbraham, MA	1892
Cyclone	R. R. Howell & Co.	Minneapolis, MN	1905
Cyclone	R. R. Howell & Co.	Minneapolis, MN	1909
D & S	Duisdieker & Smith	Pekin, IL	1892
Daisy	Lamb & Co.	Freeport, IL	1892
Dandy	Winchester & Partridge Mfg. Co.	Whitewater, WI	1892
DeLoach	DeLoach Mill Mfg. Co.	Atlanta, GA	1892
Dempster	Dempster Mill Mfg. Co.	Beatrice, NE	1909
Devore	Lamb & Co.	Freeport, IL	1892
Diamond	New Winona Mfg. Co.	Winona, MN	1905
Diamond Kid	New Winona Mfg. Co.	Winona, MN	1905
Diamond King	New Winona Mfg. Co.	Winona, MN	1905
Diamond Pony	New Winona Mfg. Co.	Winona, MN	1905
Diamond Queen	New Winona Mfg. Co.	Winona, MN	1905
Diamond Standard	New Winona Mfg. Co.	Winona, MN	1905
Dixie	Nordyke & Marmon Co.	Indianapolis, IN	1892
Duplex	Duplex Wind Mill Co.	Brooklyn, WI	1892
Durham	Lamb & Co.	Freeport, IL	1892
Elgin	Elgin Wind Power & Pump Co.	Elgin, IL	1905
Empire	Messinger Mfg. Co.	Tatamy, PA	1905
Enterprise	Enterprise Mfg. Co.	Columbiana, OH	1892
Eureka	Smith & Pomeroy	Kalamazoo, MI	1892
Excelsior	Geo. K. Oyler & Co.	St. Louis, MO	1892
Excelsior	Jas. L. Haven & Co.	Cincinnati, OH	1892
Fairbanks-Morse	Fairbanks, Morse & Co.	Chicago, IL	1892
Famous	Sterling Mfg. Co.	Sterling, IL	1892
Farm & Ranch	Rogers Iron Co.	Springfield, OH	1892
Farmer's Choice	Star Mfg. Co.	New Lexington, OH	1892
Farquhar	A. B. Farquhar Co.	York, PA	1892
Field Favorite	J. A. Field Mfg. Co.	St. Louis, MO	1892
Fosston	Fosston Mfg. Co.	St. Paul, MN	1905
Foster & Williams	Foster & Williams Mfg. Co.	Racine, WI	1892
Freeman	S. Freeman & Sons Mfg. Co.	Racine, WI	1892
Gasoline Special	Goodhue Rotary Grinder Co.	St. Charles, IL	1905
Gasoline Standard	Goodhue Rotary Grinder Co.	St. Charles, IL	1905
Gem of the South	Straub Machinery Co.	Cincinnati, OH	1892
Giant	Frank Hamachek	Kewaunee, WI	1909
Giant Killer	Thos. Cascaden Jr.	Waterloo, IA	1892
Gilbert Hunt	Gilbert Hunt Co.	Walla Walla, WA	1905

Trade Names (cont...)

Globe	Globe Foundry & Machine Co.	Sheboygan, WI	1905
Goodhue	Goodhue Wind Engine Co.	St. Charles, IL	1892
Graham	Graham Foundry & Machine Co.	Graham, VA	1892
Groton	Groton Bridge & Mfg. Co.	Groton, NY	1892
Harrison	Nordyke & Marmon Co.	Indianapolis, IN	1909
Hartford	Hartford Plow Works	Hartford, WI	1892
Havana	Havana Metal Wheel Co.	Havana, IL	1905
Haw Patch	Caldwell Mfg. Co.	Columbus, IN	1909
Heebner	Heebner & Sons	Lansdale, PA	1892
Hercules	Leonard D. Harrison	New Haven, CT	1892
Hero	Appleton Mfg. Co.	Appleton, WI	1892
Hero	Appleton Mfg. Co.	Appleton, WI	1892
Hobson	Hobson & Co.	Tatamy, PA	1892
Hocking Valley	Hocking Valley Mfg. Co.	Lancaster, OH	1892
Howell	R. R. Howell & Co.	Minneapolis, MN	1892
Howland's	B. Gill & Son	Trenton, NJ	1892
Hubbard's	H. N. Hubbard	New York , NY	1892
Hummer	Buckeye Engine & Foundry Co.	Havana, IL	1905
Ideal	Stover Mfg. Co.	Freeport, IL	1892
International	International Harvester Co.	Chicago, IL	1909
Iron King	Valley Iron Works Mfg. Co.	Appleton, WI	1892
IXL	Phelps & Bigelow Windmill Co.	Kalamazoo, MI	1905
IXL	U. S. Wind Engine & Pump Co.	Batavia, IL	1892
Jack's Friend	Fairbanks, Morse & Co.	Chicago, IL	1909
Jewel	Duplex Mfg. Co.	Superior, WI	1905
K. M. & Co.	Kirkwood, Miller & Co.	Peoria, IL	1892
Kaestner	Charles Kaestner & Co.	Chicago, IL	1892
Kelly Duplex	O. S. Kelly Co.	Springfield, OH	1892
Keystone	Ellis Keystone Agricultural Works	Pottstown, PA	1892
Keystone	Enterprise Foundry Co.	Allegheny, PA	1892
Keystone	J. E. Armour	Philadelphia, PA	1892
King	Gustav Wenzelman	Missal, IL	1892
Kingsland	Kingsland Mfg. Co.	St. Louis, MO	1905
L & S	Leonard & Silliman	Bridgeport, CT	1892
Lamson	L. J. Lamson	Cato, NY	1905
Lansing	Lansing Motor & Pump Co.	Lansing, MI	1905
Lightning	Kansas City Hay Press Co.	Kansas City, MO	1909
Litchfield	Litchfield Mfg. Co.	Waterloo, IA	1905
Little Better	Double Power Mill Co.	Appleton, WI	1905
Little Giant	Little Giant Power Converter Co.	Cincinnati, OH	1892
Little Giant Improved	J. A. Field Mfg. Co.	St. Louis, MO	1892
Little Victor	Carpenter & Genung	Independence, IA	1892
Lombard	Geo. R. Lombard & Co.	Augusta, GA	1892

Trade Names (cont...)

Magic	Whitman Agricultural Co.	St. Louis, MO	1905
Maple Leaf	Valley Wind Engine & Iron Co.	Bay City, MI	1905
Martin	M. R. Martin	St. Louis Park, MN	1909
Mascotte	Union Foundry & Machine Works	Mansfield, OH	1905
Menasha	D. T. H. MacKinnon	Menasha, WI	1892
Meyer & Schrage	Meyer & Schrage	Sheboygan, WI	1892
Model	Nordyke & Marmon Co.	Indianapolis, IN	1909
Modern Hero	Appleton Mfg. Co.	Appleton, WI	1892
Monarch	Kirkwood, Miller & Co.	Peoria, IL	1892
Monarch	Logan & Strobridge Iron Co.	New Brighton, PA	1892
Monarch	Smalley Mfg. Co.	Manitowoc, WI	1905
Monarch	Sprout, Waldron & Co.	Muncy, PA	1905
Monitor	Baker Mfg. Co.	Evansville, WI	1892
Moore	Moore Plow & Implement Co.	Greenville, MI	1909
Morley	Morley Self-Feeder Co.	Sioux City, IA	1905
Mound City	J. A. Field Mfg. Co.	St. Louis, MO	1892
Munson	Munson Bros.	Utica, NY	1892
Nelson	N. O. Nelson Mfg. Co.	St. Louis, MO	1892
New Era	Nordyke & Marmon Co.	Indianapolis, IN	1909
New Giant	J. A. Field Mfg. Co.	St. Louis, MO	1892
New Holland	New Holland Machine Works	New Holland, PA	1905
New Prize	Appleton Mfg. Co.	Batavia, IL	1909
Newell Universal	Newell Universal Mill Co.	New York, NY	1892
Nichols	Ames Plow Co.	Boston, MA	1892
Nonpareil	L. J. Miller	Cincinnati, OH	1892
Nordyke's	Nordyke & Marmon Co.	Indianapolis, IN	1892
North Star	L. J. Miller	Cincinnati, OH	1909
O. K.	Sandwich Mfg. Co.	Sandwich, IL	1892
Omega	C. S. Bell Co.	Hillsboro, OH	1909
Oriole	Wilson Bros.	Easton, PA	1905
Osage	Winchester & Partridge Mfg. Co.	Whitewater, WI	1892
Over's	Ewald Over	Indianapolis, IN	1892
Peerless	Geo. K. Oyler & Co.	St. Louis, MO	1892
Peerless	Joliet Strowbridge Co.	Joliet, IL	1892
Perfect	Macgowan & Finigan Foundry Co.	St. Louis, MO	1909
Perfection	Leonard D. Harrison	New Haven, CT	1892
Perkins	Perkins Wind Mill Co.	Mishawaka, IN	1905
Philips	C. C. Philips	Philadelphia, PA	1892
Phoenix	B. H. & J. Sanford	Sheboygan Falls, WI	1892
Pioneer	Silberzahn Mfg. Co.	West Bend, WI	1892
Plantation	John T. Noye Mfg. Co.	Buffalo, NY	1892
Planter's Pride	Richmond City Mill Works	Richmond, IN	1892
Pride of Richmond	Richmond City Mill Works	Richmond, IN	1892

Trade Names (cont...)			
Quaker City	A. W. Straub & Co.	Philadelphia, PA	1892
Quaker City	Springfield Implement Co.	Springfield, OH	1892
Queen of the South	Straub Machinery Co.	Cincinnati, OH	1892
Rogers	William Bayley Co.	Springfield, OH	1905
Royal Blue	U. S. Wind Engine & Pump Co.	Batavia, IL	1909
S & P	Smith & Pomeroy Wind Mill Co.	Kalamazoo, MI	1909
Sandwich-Reliance	Sandwich Mfg. Co.	Sandwich, IL	1909
Scientific	Foos Mfg. Co.	Springfield, OH	1905
Smalley	Smalley Mfg. Co.	Manitowoc, WI	1905
Special	Moline Pump Co.	Moline, IL	1905
Standard	Ajax Mfg. Co.	Pittsburg, PA	1892
Standard	Enterprise Foundry Co.	Allegheny, PA	1892
Standard	Leonard D. Harrison	New Haven, CT	1892
Standard	Moline Pump Co.	Moline, IL	1905
Star	Lamb & Co.	Freeport, IL	1892
Star	Star Mfg. Co.	New Lexington, OH	1892
Sterling	Sterling Mfg. Co.	Sterling, IL	1892
Stevens	A. W. Stevens & Son	Auburn, NY	1892
Stevens	Clark & Co.	Somonauk, IL	1892
Stover	Stover Mfg. Co.	Freeport, IL	1892
Straub	Nordyke & Marmon Co.	Indianapolis, IN	1892
Strayer's	Lewis Strayer	York, PA	1892
Success	Macgowan & Finigan Foundry Co.	St. Louis, MO	1909
Success	Marseilles Mfg. Co.	Marseilles, IL	1892
Superior	Duplex Mfg. Co.	Superior, WI	1909
Swift's	Swift Mfg. Co.	Waterloo, IA	1905
Texas	Chatham Machinery Co.	Bryan, TX	1892
Tornado	Appleton Mfg. Co.	Appleton, WI	1892
Two A	Eclipse Wind Engine Co.	Beloit, WI	1892
U. S.	U. S. Wind Engine & Pump Co.	Batavia, IL	1892
Undulatory	Kingsland & Douglas Mfg. Co.	St. Louis, MO	1892
Union	Lamb & Co.	Freeport, IL	1892
Union	Union Wind Mill & Mfg. Co.	Albion, MI	1892
Universal	Marseilles Mfg. Co.	Marseilles, IL	1892
Victor	J. H. McLain Machine Co.	Canton, OH	1892
Victory	Thomas Roberts	Springfield, OH	1892
Victor	Victor Feed Mill Co.	Springfield, OH	1892
Waupun	Althouse-Wheeler Co.	Waupun, WI	1892
Wilder	Wilder-Strong Implement Co.	Monroe, MI	1905
Wilder's Universal	Wilder-Strong Implement Co.	Monroe, MI	1905
Wilson	J. K. Wilder & Son	Monroe, MI	1892
Wilson's	Wilson Bros.	Easton, PA	1892
Winger's New Royal	E. B. Winger	Chicago, IL	1892
Woodmanse	Woodmanse & Hewitt Mfg. Co.	Freeport, IL	1892
X X	Sandwich Mfg. Co.	Sandwich, IL	1892
Young America	Enterprise Mfg. Co.	Columbiana, OH	1892

H

Hammermills

In the 1920s, hammermills gained attention as an alternative to the time-honored burr mills or feed grinders. The hammermill was faster and had no problem in reducing small grains to the finest consistency. By comparison, running the burrs tight enough to do this job caused excessive wear and frequent replacement of the grinding plates on the burr mill. A few hammermills are found in the Feed Grinders section of this book; this section includes a couple of representative examples, although there were numerous manufacturers emerging in the 1930s. With the practically complete cessation of farm equipment production during World War II, the hammermills built after the war reflected new ideas and new technologies during the production furlough. Due partially to a lack of space for this edition, it is hoped that additional items in this category can be included in subsequent editions.

J.I. Case Co., Racine, Wis.

Reflecting this company's entry into all phases of the farm equipment business, Case offered this huge hammermill in 1929; the mill shown here was equipped with the company's new Case LE engine. This same engine powered its newly designed Model L farm tractor. With its traveling feed table, this machine was capable of grinding virtually anything grindable, including various forage crops.

Stover Manufacturing Co., Freeport, Ill.

In 1931, Stover announced its new No. 91 hammermill. This one replaced some of the company's earlier models introduced in the 1920s and earlier. Stover actively pursued this line of business, despite the difficult times of the 1930s. However, the Great Depression had its effects; Stover closed its doors in 1942.

Trade Names

Ajacs	A. E. Jacobson Machine Works	Minneaapolis, MN	1931
American	Mid-West Steel Products	Kansas City, MO	1936
Aristocrat	Gruendler Crusher & Pulverizer Co.	St. Louis, MO	1939
Badger	Badger Body Mfg. Co.	Omaha, NE	1936
Baker Impact	Dellinger Mfg. Co.	Lancaster, PA	1945
Bear Cat	Western Land Roller Co.	Hastings, NE	1931
Bell	C. S. Bell Co.	Hillsboro, OH	1936
Blue Streak	Prater Pulverizer Co.	Chicago, IL	1929
Bossert	Bossert Corp.	Utica, NY	1924
Brower	Brower Mfg. Co.	Quincy, IL	1945
Bull Dog	Reschke Machine Works	Wichita, KS	1931
Case	J. I. Case Co.	Racine, WI	1931
Crackerjack	J. B. Sedberry Co.	Utica, NY	1931
Deere	Deere and Co.	Moline, IL	1939
Dellinger	A. M. Dellinger Co.	Lancaster, PA	1929
Diamond	Diamond Huller Co.	Winona, MN	1936
Dick	Joseph Dick Mfg. Co.	Canton, OH	1929
Duplex	Duplex Mill and Mfg. Co.	Springfield , OH	1929
Easy	Easy Mfg. Co.	Lincoln, NE	1929
Eclipse	Reschke Machine Works	Wichita, KS	1931
Electric	Viking Mfg. Co.	Jackson, MI	1939
Fairbanks-Morse	Fairbanks, Morse and Co.	Chicago, IL	1929
Fords	Myers-Sherman Co.	Chicago, IL	1936
Gately	Gately Mfg. Co.	Syracuse, NE	1945
Gately	Western Land Roller Co.	Hastings , NE	1929
Gehl	Gehl Bros. Mfg. Co.	West Bend, WI	1931
Gleaco	Gleaner Harvester Corp.	Independence, MO	1929

Trade Names (cont...)

Gleaner	Gleaner Harvester Corp.	Independence, MO	1931
Gold Medal	Meadow Mills Co.	No. Wilkesboro, NC	1945
Grain Buster	Link Mfg. Co.	Fargo, ND	1936
Greyhound	I. B. Rowell Co.	Waukesha, WI	1929
Gruendler	Gruendler Crusher & Pulverizer Co.	St. Louis, MO	1924
H. V.	Hocking Valley Mfg. Co.	Lancaster, OH	1929
Hesse	Hesse Mfg. Co.	Leavenworth, KS	1936
Heywood Probert	Heywood Probert Co.	Jackson, MI	1945
Hogmoe	Hogmoe Mfg. Co.	Minneapolis, MN	1936
Humdinger	J. B. Sedberry Co.	Utica , NY	1929
Hummer	Hummer Plow Works	Springfield, IL	1931
Iowa	Hay Tool Mfg. Co.	Council Bluffs, IA	1936
Iowa	Iowa Portable Mill Co.	Oelwein, IA	1945
Jay Bee	J. B. Sedberry Co.	Utica , NY	1929
Kentucky Special	Kentucky Wagon Mfg. Co.	Louisville, KY	1931
Knoc-Out Special	Hocking Valley Mfg. Co.	Lancaster, OH	1936
Marshalltown All-Crop	Farm Machinery Mfg. Co.	Marshalltown, IA	1945
Massey-Harris	Massey-Harris Co.	Racine, WI	1936
Mastiff	I. B. Rowell Co.	Waukesha, WI	1929
McCormick-Deering	International Harvester Co.	Chicago, IL	1924
Meadows	Meadows Mill Co.	No. Wilkesboro, NC	1939
Miller	Miller Mfg. Co.	Modesto, CA	1945
Miller	Miller Mfg. Co.	Stratton, NE	1936
Minneapolis-Moline	Minneapolis-Moline Co.	Minneapolis, MN	1936
Mooers	Mooers Machine Works	Windom, MN	1945
Myers-Sherman	Myers-Sherman Co.	Chicago, IL	1931
New Holland	New Holland Machine Co.	New Holland, PA	1929
O. B. Wise	O. B. Wise Pulverizer Co.	Knoxville, TN	1929
O. K.	Algoma Foundry & Machine Co.	Algoma, WI	1929
Papec	Papec Machine Co.	Shortsville, NY	1929
Port Huron	Port Huron Machinery Co.	Des Moines, IA	1939
Prater	Prater Pulverizer Co.	Chicago, IL	1929
Quaker City	A. W. Straub Co.	Philadelphia, PA	1936
Rex	Ideal Mfg. Co.	Denver, CO	1931
Roberts	Roberts Mill & Machinery Co.	Denver, CO	1936
Rowell	I. B. Rowell Co.	Waukesha, WI	1929
Sedberry	J. B. Sedberry Co.	Utica, NY	1929
Speedy	A. E. Jacobson Machine Works	Minneapolis, MN	1931
Standard	Standard Steel Co.	Kansas City, MO	1936
Stover	Stover Mfg. Co.	Freeport , IL	1931
Stroud	W. H. Stroud & Co.	Chicago, IL	1924
Swifton	Swifton Mfg. Co.	Milwaukee, WI	1929
Universal	Universal Crusher Co.	Cedar Rapids, IA	1929
W & F	W & F Machine Works	Norfolk, NE	1945
Western	Western Machinery Co.	Wichita, KS	1924
Western	Western Machinery Co.	Wichita, KS	1929
Wetmore Clipper	Wetmore Pulverizer & Machy. Co.	Tonkawa, OK	1939

Harrows

From time immemorial, man has used a harrow of some sort for leveling and smoothing the soil. Tradition has it that a small tree was often used for the purpose. During the 1800s, the Geddes harrow appeared; its distinctive triangular frame was fitted with steel spikes. Genuine progress in harrow design occurred simultaneously with the development of most other planting equipment; the high point being the 1870-1900 period. Today, a few ancient harrows have a minimal value. For the most part, an old harrow has little value, even to the seasoned collector of agricultural implements.

B.F. Avery & Sons, Louisville, Kty.

From a 1916 Avery catalog comes the Avery Staytite Harrow. Its design was such that the teeth were securely fastened to the frame, so much so that they would not be lost while in operation. Thus came the "Staytite" trade name for this model. Avery produced a wide range of harrows over its long history in the farm equipment business.

E.S. & F. Bateman, Spring Mills, N.J.

Later located at Grenloch, N.J., this company was already making an extensive line of implements by 1889. To the left of this advertisement is shown one of its Gem wheel hoes; this is somewhat of a combination between a harrow and a field cultivator. To the right is illustrated a small one-row planter.

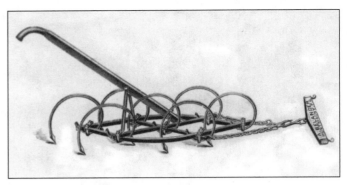

A. Belanger, Montmagny, Quebec

For 1910, Belanger advertised this Special Stumpy Land Spring Tooth Harrow. With seven teeth, it weighed only 65 pounds. As the descriptive title implies, this unit was designed especially for stumpy or stony ground, being built heavy enough to stand the abuse encountered when striking a stone or a tree root.

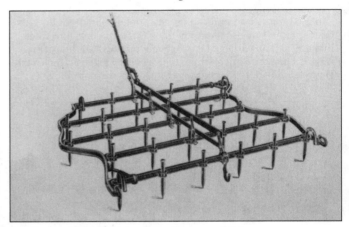

Bucher & Gibbs Plow Co., Canton, Ohio

By 1908, Bucher & Gibbs had developed several styles of spike-tooth harrows, most of them having a lever to control the pitch of the teeth. For aggressive work, the teeth were stood in a vertical position; for smoothing, they were laid down nearly flat.

David Bradley Manufacturing Co., Bradley, Ill.

By the early 1900s, several companies were offering a harrow cart, sometimes called a harrow sulky. The long arms reached forward over the harrow sections and was attached to the harrow draw-bar. The axle pivoted with the frame for turning. Most farmers welcomed this little device, but some preferred to walk behind the harrow as they had always done.

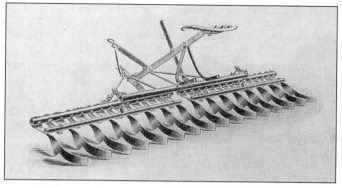

Deere & Co., Moline, Ill.

For 1913, John Deere Plow Co., offered the Acme Pulverizing Harrow to its customers. At the time, Deere did not manufacture all the implements it sold; the company marketed numerous other machines through its branch houses. This harrow was actually built by Duane H. Nash Inc., Millington, N.J.

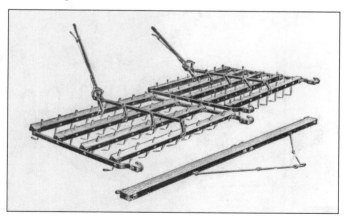

During the 1930s, the changeover from horse power to tractor power was virtually completed. Horses were rapidly becoming the minority choice for farm power. At the time, and even into the 1940s, farmers still saw a place for horses on the farm, but no one dreamed the change would be so rapid or so totally complete. Shown here is a John Deere tractor and harrow at work in a typical setting of the 1940s.

Emerson-Brantingham Co., Rockford, Ill.

The all-steel harrow became a reality during the 1890s, but wood frame harrows were still marketed at least into the 1920s. At the time, it was considered by many that the wooden beams were better able to hold the harrow spikes in place, since many designs were prone to losing them in the field. This is a 1907 example from Emerson.

Many companies were offering a Harrow Cart by the early 1900s, including this Emerson design. In those days, even a simple contrivance like this came as a blessing to the farmer. Most were tired of walking behind a harrow and welcomed this development. Others saw it as a sign of laziness, further contending that the additional load would "kill the horses."

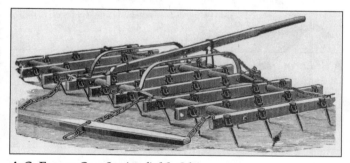

A.C. Evans Co., Springfield, Ohio

An 1887 engraving shows the Evans Triple Harrow with reversible teeth. The latter referred to a design permitting the farmer to turn the teeth half-way around for even wear and longer life. Note also the early approach to a lever design for variable pitch of the harrow teeth.

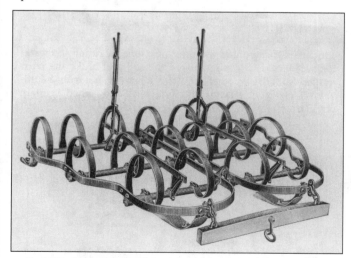

By 1900, the spring-tooth harrow was well known. This design was perfect for certain soil conditions and was also ideal for ground heavy with roots or stones. When it is considered that there were few means of removing either, except with horses and manpower, the heavy work of clearing land becomes much more apparent.

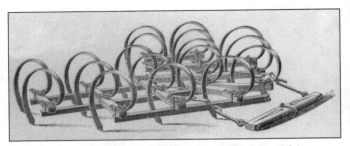

Farmer's Friend Manufacturing Co., Dayton, Ohio

For 1887, Farmer's Friend offered its UTK Spring Tooth Harrow; at this point in time, there is no clue for the meaning of the UTK initials. This one used all-wood construction with the individual teeth being mounted on diagonal wooden bars. Farmer's Friend Manufacturing Co., disappears from the scene by 1900.

A.B. Farquhar Co., Ltd., York, Pa.

Farquhar had a history of making farm implements going back to 1856. By the time this Wood Frame Spring Tooth Harrow came on the market, the company had already been in business for some 40 years. The company also built a variety of wood- and steel-frame spike-tooth harrows.

In the 1920s, Farquhar was offering a series of riding and walking weeders. This design stirred the soil and broke the crust formed from dry weather. Not truly a harrow, not truly a cultivator, the weeder was an entity unto itself and gained a certain popularity for a few years.

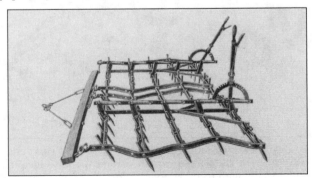

Hench & Dromgold Co., York, Pa.

This company had roots going well back into the 1800s; in 1908, it announced a new Spring Trip Spike Tooth Harrow.

This design featured a spring-trip mechanism that released the teeth to their flat or transport position if a foreign object was encountered. At the time, this was the only harrow of its kind on the market.

Herendeen Co., Geneva, N.Y.

No information can be located on this company or its Thomas Smoothing Harrow of 1889. Billed as its Improved Reversible Harrow, it was part of a line that also included spring-tooth harrows. The company does not appear in trade directories of the early 1900s.

John I. Hoke & Company, South Bend, Ind.

In 1890, John I. Hoke & Company offered their Spring Tooth Harrow with two, three, or four dictions, as desired. We have been unable to determine if the company noted here was the same as the one that later got into the tractor business.

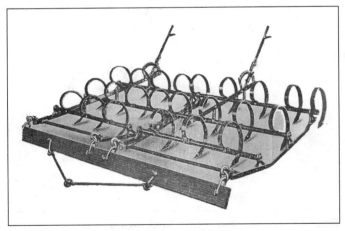

Joseph J. Kovar Co., Owatonna, Minn.

For 1918, Kovar announced its combination spring-tooth harrow, alfalfa cultivator and quack grass killer. This company continued manufacturing various kinds of harrows at least into the 1930s; Kovar came out in the late 1930s with a mounted machine that well might be considered a forerunner to today's field cultivators.

E.M. Kramer Co., Paxton, Ill.

Kramer announced its new Rotary Harrow in 1907. This small device was intended to pulverize the freshly turned soil before the sun had the chance to burn it into hard clods. It also saved the farmer a trip over the field with a disc harrow. Despite the early promotions of this device, it does not appear to have gained great popularity, since it probably required an additional horse at the head of the plow.

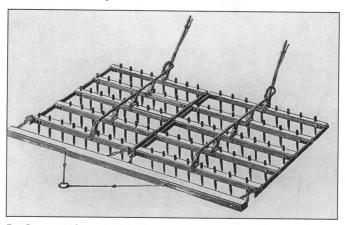

LaCrosse Plow Co., LaCrosse, Wis.

With its beginnings going back to 1865, LaCrosse had a well established line of tillage implements long before 1900. Even into the 1920s, LaCrosse continued to offer a wood-bar lever harrow to its customers, although the all-steel design had long since been on the market. LaCrosse eventually was purchased by Allis-Chalmers.

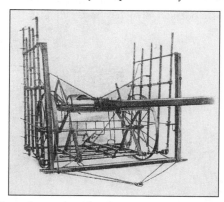

Maroa Manufacturing Co., Maroa, Ill.

Since information on this company has been impossible to locate, outside of this 1912 advertisement, it is the present assumption that the Maroa Riding Harrow pictured here was a product of short duration. This unique design permitted the farmer to

leave the harrow assembled, simply swinging up the side-wings to move to the next field.

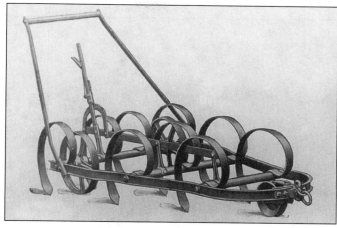

Moline Plow Co., Moline, Ill.

While it would have been possible to illustrate some of the common harrow varieties built by Moline, this small one-horse vineyard harrow represents an unusual design of about 1915. Moline Plow Co., offered an extensive harrow line with virtually every possible option.

Duane H. Nash, Millington, N.J.

An 1889 advertisement in the *American Agriculturist* illustrates the Acme Pulverizing Harrow, Clod Crusher and Leveler. This design was made in sizes from 3- to 12-feet wide. As noted in the Deere & Co., section above, this same harrow from Nash was sold by the Deere organization as late as 1912.

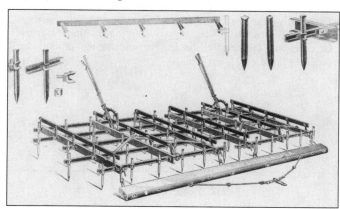

D.M. Osborne & Co., Auburn, N.Y.

Osborne is best known for its extensive line of harvesting equipment, although the company also manufactured many tillage implements. Shown here is the Osborne Junior Peg-Tooth Harrow of 1900. Eventually, the company was purchased by International Harvester Co.

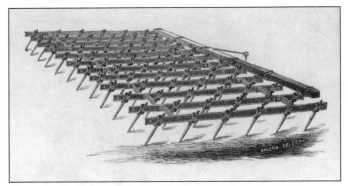

Geo. K. Oyler Manufacturing Co., St. Louis, Mo.

For 1887, Oyler offered its Steel Frame Reversible Smoothing Harrow. This design was a leverless design; the teeth were pitched for smoothing and could not be altered. A distinct advantage was the reversible feature, whereby the teeth could be turned every few years for even wear and longer life. Many of these harrows were used season after season for decades.

D.C. & H.C. Reed Co., Kalamazoo, Mich.

This company was the premiere manufacturer of the spring-tooth harrow, beginning in the early 1870s under the Garver patent. This detailed engraving of 1890 demonstrates the Reed Spring Tooth Harrow at work, with the farmer following behind. Eventually, the patent litigation on spring-tooth harrows brought about a manufacturing trust known as National Harrow Co., with the members all having manufacturing rights under patents placed into the trust.

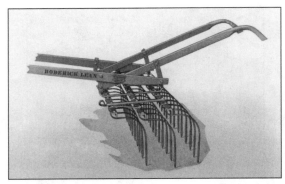

Roderick Lean Manufacturing Co., Mansfield, Ohio

Among its extensive line of tillage implements, Roderick Lean offered this Walking Weeder that was somewhat like a spring-tooth harrow, but wasn't. Weeders gained some slight popularity in the 1920s and less in the 1930s. However, Farm Tools Inc., the successor to Roderick Lean, continued to offer them as late as 1939.

Smalley Bros. & Company, Bay City, Mich.

For 1890, little known Smalley Bros. offered an interesting all-steel sulky harrow. The design apparently gained little interest for at least another 40 years. Many farmers preferred to walk behind their harrow and deemed the sulky a lazy man's approach that only served to put more work onto the horses pulling it.

Did You Know?

The Amanco concrete mixer sold for $115 when introduced.

Did You Know?

Hartman's Majestic cream separator in the 1920s was offered in four sizes, from 375 to 1,000 pounds per hour. The 500-pound separator originally sold for $62.

Trade Names

"I. A." Special	S. R. White & Bro.	Norfolk, VA	1905
Acme	Duane H. Nash	Millington, NJ	1892
Adriance	Adriance, Platt & Co.	Poughkeepsie, NY	1905
Advance	Western Mfg. Co.	Lincoln, NE	1892
Ajax	Deere and Co.	Moline, IL	1913
Ajax	E. Bement's Sons	Lansing, MI	1905
Albion	Gale Mfg. Co.	Albion , MI	1913
Allis-Chalmers	Allis-Chalmers Mfg. Co.	Milwaukee, WI	1939
American	American Plow Co.	Madison, WI	1905
Arkansas	Atlanta Agricultural Works	Atlanta, GA	1905
Arkansas Traveler	Southern Plow Co.	Columbus, GA	1905
Atlanta	Atlanta Agricultural Works	Atlanta, GA	1905
Avery	B. F. Avery and Sons	Louisville, KY	1892
Avery	B. F. Avery and Sons	Louisville, KY	1922
Bement	E. Bement's Sons	Lansing, MI	1905
Benicia	Benicia Agricultural Works	Benicia, CA	1892
Best	Hartman Mfg. Co.	Vincennes, IN	1909
Bird	Star Mfg. Co.	Carpentersville, IL	1892
Blaine	Blaine Harrow Mfg. Co.	Piqua, OH	1905
Blaine	Galena Harrow Co.	Galena, KS	1909
Bloom	Bloom Mfg. Co.	Nashua, IA	1909
Blount	Blount Plow Works	Evansville, IN	1922
Boss	International Harvester Co.	Chicago, IL	1922
Boss	St. Paul Plow Works	St. Paul, MN	1892
Bradley	David Bradley Mfg. Co.	Bradley, IL	1905
Breeding	Woodard, Hey & Co.	Sterling, IL	1892
Brinly	Brinly, Miles & Hardy Co.	Louisville, KY	1892
Brown	Brown Mfg. Co.	Zanesville, OH	1905
Buckley	R. C. Buckley	Peoria, IL	1892
Buffalo Bill	Gale Mfg. Co.	Albion, MI	1909
Buffalo Pitts	Pitts Agricultural	Buffalo, NY	1892
Burch	Burch Plow Works Co.	Crestline, OH	1909
Busing	H. B. Busing & Co.	Rockford, IL	1892
Canton	Parlin & Orendorff Co.	Canton, IL	1892
Carstensen	Carstensen Bros. & Co.	Walnut, IA	1892
Case	J. I. Case Co.	Racine, WI	1936
Case	J. I. Case Plow Works	Racine, WI	1892
Caterpillar	Roderick Lean Mfg. Co.	Mansfield, OH	1917
Champion	J. Thompson & Sons Mfg. Co.	Beloit, WI	1905
Clipper	Northwestern Steel & Iron Works	Eau Claire, WI	1909
Clore	W. H. Clore Mfg. Co.	Washington, IN	1922
Collins	Collins Plow Co.	Quincy, IL	1917
Columbian	Brown-Manly Plow Co.	Malta, OH	1905

Trade Names (cont...)

Common Sense	F. B. Ogden	Republic, OH	1892
Common Sense	Gilbert Hunt Co.	Walla Walla, WA	1905
Common Sense	Marseilles Harrow Mfg. Co.	Marseilles, IL	1922
Corbin	Superior Land Roller Co.	Gouveneur, NY	1892
Cotton King	International Harvester Co.	Chicago , IL	1913
Crescent	Standard Harrow Co.	Utica, NY	1905
Critic	J. I. Case Plow Works	Racine, WI	1905
Daley	M. H. Daley	Charles City, IA	1905
Dayton	Ohio Rake Co.	Dayton, OH	1905
Deere	Deere and Co.	Moline, IL	1915
Deere	Deere & Mansur	Moline, IL	1892
Deering	International Harvester Co.	Chicago, IL	1909
Dirigo	F. C. Merrill	South Paris, ME	1892
Dixie	International Harvester Co.	Chicago, IL	1922
Donaldson	Donaldson Bros.	Mt. Clemens, MI	1905
Dugaw	J. J. Morse	Weston, MI	1892
Eagle	Eagle Mfg. Co.	Davenport, IA	1892
Eagle	Eagle Mfg. Co.	Kansas City, MO	1905
Eagle	Smalley Bros. & Co.	Bay City, MI	1892
Eaton's	E. C. Eaton	Pinckneyville, IL	1892
Eclipse	David Bradley Mfg. Co.	Bradley, IL	1892
Ellwood	Abram Ellwood	Sycamore, IL	1892
Emerson	Emerson Mfg. Co.	Rockford, IL	1905
Emerson	Emerson-Brantingham Co.	Rockford, IL	1913
Empire	Empire Plow Co.	Ensley, AL	1905
Empire	Empire Plow Co.	Cleveland, OH	1905
End Rail	Gale Mfg. Co.	Albion, MI	1913
Eureka	Eureka Mower Co.	Utica, NY	1905
Everlasting	Austin Plow and Harrow Works	Austin, MN	1922
Everlasting	Johnson & Smith	Austin, MN	1892
Excelsior	Brown Mfg. Co.	Zaneville, OH	1922
F & J	Madison Plow Co.	Madison, WI	1913
Fairfield	Fairfield Plow Works	Fairfield, OH	1922
Famous Ohio	Ohio Cultivator Co.	Bellevue, OH	1922
Fargo	Monitor Mfg. Co.	Auburn Junction, IN	1892
Favorite	Parlin & Orendorff Co.	Canton, IL	1905
Fort Madison	Fort Madison Plow Co.	Fort Madison, IA	1913
Fuller & Johnson	Fuller & Johnson Mfg. Co.	Madison, WI	1905
Furfly	Brown-Manly Plow Co.	Malta, OH	1922
Gale	Gale Mfg. Co.	Albion, MI	1905
Gale	Moline-Hooper Co.	Memphis, TN	1936
Galloway	Galloway Co.	Waterloo, IA	1945
Gardener's Friend	Brown Mfg. Co.	Zanesville, OH	1905
Geddes	Ames Plow Co.	Boston, MA	1892
Genuine Brown	Brown Mfg. Co.	Zanesville, OH	1905
Glendale	Peoria Drill & Seeder Co.	Peoria, IL	1905
Glendale	Selby, Starr & Co.	Peoria, IL	1892

Trade Names (cont...)

Glidden	Deere and Co.	Moline, IL	1929
Gopher	Carver Mfg. Co.	Carver, MN	1892
Grain King	Grain King Mfg. Co.	St. Paul, MN	1936
Grand Detour	Grand Detour Plow Co.	Dixon, IL	1905
Guard	International Harvester Co.	Chicago, IL	1922
Guard	Parin and Orendorff Co.	Canton, IL	1917
Hamilton	H. P. Deuscher Co.	Hamilton, OH	1905
Hartford	Hartford Plow Works	Hartford, WI	1905
Hawkeye	Norwegian Plow Co.	Dubuque, IA	1892
Hayes	Hayes Pump & Planter Co.	Galva, IL	1905
Hazen	W. S. Hazen	Ripon, WI	1905
Hench & Dromgold	Hench & Dromgold Co.	York, PA	1905
Hoke's	John I. Hoke & Co.	South Bend, IN	1892
Houser & Haines	Houser & Haines Mfg. Co.	Stockton, CA	1905
Hustler	Daley Mfg. Co.	DeKalb, IL	1892
Ideal	Beaver Dam Mfg. Co.	Beaver Dam, WI	1922
Imperial	Bucher & Gibbs Plow Co.	Canton, OH	1905
Iron Age	Bateman Mfg. Co.	Grenloch, NJ	1905
J. I. Case Co.	J. I. Case Plow Works	Racine, WI	1909
Jackson	Gilbert Hunt Co.	Walla Walla, WA	1905
Janesville	Janesville Machine Co.	Janesville, WI	1905
John Deere	Deere and Co.	Moline, IL	1909
Johnson	J. S. Johnson	Waukon, IA	1892
Johnston	Johnston Harvester Co.	Batavia, NY	1913
Kalamazoo	D. C. & H. C. Reed Co.	Kalamazoo, MI	1892
Kelly	G. A. Kelly Plow Co.	Longview, TX	1917
Keystone	International Harvester Co.	Chicago, IL	1913
Keystone	Keystone Farm Machine Co.	York, PA	1905
Kingman	Kingman Plow Co	Peoria, IL	1905
Knox	Geo. W. Brown & Co.	Galesburg, IL	1892
Kynett	H. P. Kynett	Lisbon, IA	1892
LaCrosse	LaCrosse Plow Co.	LaCrosse, WI	1905
Lance	Robert Sleeth	Fargo, MI	1892
Ledbetter	Southern Plow Co.	Longview, TX	1929
Lehr	Lehr Agricultural Co.	Fremont, OH	1905
Lenhart	Lenhart Wagon Co.	Minneapolis, MN	1939
LeRoy	LeRoy Plow Co.	LeRoy, NY	1929
Little Giant	Ohio Cultivator Co.	Bellevue, OH	1905
Little Joe	Atlanta Agricultural Works	Atlanta, GA	1905
M. & F.	Macgowan & Finnigan Foundry	St. Louis, MO	1905
Madison	Madison Plow Co.	Madison, WI	1917
Malta	Brown-Manly Plow Co.	Malta, OH	1892
Maroa	Maroa Mfg. Co.	Maroa, WI	1922
Massey-Harris	Massey-Harris Harvester Co.	Batavia, NY	1922
McCormick	International Harvester Co.	Chicago, IL	1909
McCormick-Deering	International Harvester Co.	Chicago, IL	1924

Trade Names (cont...)

Meeker	C. O. Jelliff Mfg. Co.	Southport, CT	1922
Model	Bloom Mfg. Co.	Nashua, IA	1922
Moline	Minneapolis-Moline Co.	Minneapolis, MN	1936
Moline	Moline Plow Co.	Moline, IL	1892
Monarch	L. C. Lull & Co.	Kalamazoo, MI	1892
Monitor	Ohio Cultivator Co.	Bellevue, OH	1905
Moore	Moore Plow & Implement Co.	Greenville, MI	1905
Morrison	Morrison Mfg. Co.	Fort Madison, IA	1892
Morsman's	J. A. Morsman & Co.	Mapleton, KS	1892
Munnsville	Munnsville Plow Co.	Munnsville, NY	1905
Naylor	Naylor Mfg. Co.	LaGrange, IL	1909
Neosho	Neosho Foundry & Plow Works	Neosho, MO	1945
New Burch	Burch Plow Works Co.	Crestline, OH	1905
New Idea	California Garden Tool Co.	Ferndale, CA	1892
New Market	South Bend Chilled Plow Co.	South Bend, IN	1905
New Universal	Ames Plow Co.	Boston, MA	1905
Norwegian	Norwegian Plow Co.	Dubuque, IA	1892
Ohio	Ohio Cultivator Co.	Bellevue, OH	1905
Osborne	D. M. Osborne	Auburn, NY	1905
Osborne	International Harvester Co.	Chicago, IL	1909
Osborne	International Harvester Co.	Chicago, IL	1913
Oscillator	Rhea-Thielens Implement Co.	Peoria, IL	1905
Otsego	Babcock Mfg. Co.	Leonardsville, NY	1905
Our Dandy	F. B. Tait & Co.	Decatur, IL	1892
Palm	A. Palm	Lawrence, KS	1892
Paragon	McCalmont & Co.	Bellefonte, PA	1892
Pekin	Pekin Plow Co.	Pekin, IL	1892
Pennington	Towers & Sullivan Mfg. Co.	Rome, GA	1905
Pennsylvania	A. B. Farquhar Co.	York, PA	1913
Peoria	Kingman & Co.	Peoria, IL	1892
Perfect	A. B. Clippinger & Bro.	Centralia, KS	1892
Perfect	V. S. Barker Mfg. Co.	Ebensburg, PA	1892
Peru	Peru Plow & Wheel Co.	Peru, IL	1892
Planter's Pride	Ohio Cultivator Co.	Bellevue, OH	1905
Plattner	Plattner Implement Co.	Denver, CO	1909
Quail	Ohio Rake Co.	Dayton, OH	1905
Queen Anne	Moline Plow Co.	Moline, IL	1905
Quincy	Collins Plow Co.	Quincy, IL	1905
Reed	Reed Mfg. Co.	Kalamazoo, MI	1905
Rock Island	Rock Island Plow Co.	Rock Island, IL	1892
Rockford	Rockford Mfg. Co.	Rockford, IL	1905
Roderick Lean	Roderick Lean Mfg. Co.	Mansfield, OH	1905
Round Bar	Parlin & Orendorff Co.	Canton, IL	1909
Sargent	S. R. Sargent & Son	Castleton, VT	1905
Sattley	Sattley Mfg. Co.	Springfield, IL	1892
Scotch	David Bradley Mfg. Co.	Bradley, IL	1892

Trade Names (cont...)

Shanghai	LaCrosse Plow Co.	LaCrosse, WI	1909
Skandia	Skandia Plow Co.	Rockford, IL	1892
South Bend	South Bend Chilled Plow Co.	South Bend, IN	1905
Sparta	Sparta Plow Works	Sparta, IL	1905
Square	H. N. Hubbard	New York, NY	1892
St. Joseph	St. Joseph Plow Co.	St. Joseph, MO	1905
Standard	Brown-Manly Plow Co.	Malta, OH	1905
Standard	J. Thompson & Sons Mfg. Co.	Beloit, WI	1892
Standard	Standard Harrow Co.	Utica, NY	1905
Standard	Taylor & Henry	Kalamazoo, MI	1892
Star	Gale Mfg. Co.	Albion, MI	1905
Steel Age	Keystone Farm Machine Co.	York, PA	1905
Sterling	Sterling Mfg. Co.	Sterling, IL	1892
Sterling	Sterling Mfg. Co.	Sterling, IL	1905
Sturgis	W. B. Sturgis	Shelbyville, IL	1892
Syracuse	Syracuse Chilled Plow Co.	Syracuse, NY	1905
Thomas	Herendeen Mfg. Co.	Geneva, NY	1892
Thornburgh	Thornburgh Mfg. Co.	Bowling Green, OH	1922
Tiger	Lawrence & Chapin Co.	Kalamazoo, MI	1892
Togo	Racine-Sattley Co.	Springfield, IL	1909
Toledo	Toledo Plow Co.	Toledo, OH	1905
Ulsh Champion	Blake & Elliott	Racine, WI	1892
Universal	Deere and Co.	Moline, IL	1922
Vaughn	Vaughn Mfg. Co.	Jefferson, WI	1922
Victor	Fair, Williams & Co.	Ottumwa, IA	1892
Victor	P. H. Wilms	Holland, MI	1892
Walker	Walker Mfg. Co.	Morasvia, NY	1892
Walton	Walton Plow Co.	Bloomington, IL	1892
Ware's	Hackney Mfg. Co.	St. Paul, MN	1913
Ware's	Law Mfg. Co.	St. Paul, MN	1905
Warner	Dowagiac Mfg. Co.	Dowagiac, MI	1892
Watertown	Lee Bros.	Watertown, SD	1892
Weir	Weir Plow Co.	Monmouth, IL	1892
Whitman's	Whitman Agricultural Co.	St. Louis, MO	1892
Wilcox	A. Wilcox Co.	Cedar Rapids, IA	1892
Wild Cat	Lehr Agricultural Co.	Fremont, OH	1922
World Beater	World Beater Harrow Co.	Boonville, MO	1922
Zig Zag	David Bradley Mfg. Co.	Bradley, IL	1892
Zigzag	Bucher and Gibbs Plow Co.	Canton, OH	1913
Zilisch	A. T. Zilisch	Mayville, WI	1905

Hay Loaders

Until the 1880s, most hay that was loaded onto a wagon was loaded by hand, just as it had been done for centuries. In fact, from 1870 to the close of the 19th century, farmers saw more mechanization than at any other period in recorded history. The hay loader came as another of the great labor-saving inventions, remaining at the forefront of the hay crop until the hay baler became the dominant method in the 1950s.

Shown in this section are representative examples of the hay loader in its various forms. As with other sections of this book, no attempt is made to display every model from every company. Little is known of market values for vintage hay loaders. They are seldom seen today; most of them have gone under the cutter's torch long ago or have rotted away along a fence row. Several hay loaders not pictured in this section will be found in the color section of this book.

B.F. Avery & Sons, Louisville, Ky.

A 1916 catalog from B.F. Avery shows its cylinder hay loader. It straddled the windrow, effectively picking up all the hay in its path, carrying it over the top and onto the hay wagon ahead. One or two men were needed to "make the load." Loading hay was an acquired art; some farmers were very good at it, while others never got the knack of making a straight, square load of hay.

Chambers, Bering, Quinlan Co., Decatur, Ill.

By 1907, the CB&Q line included the Hawkeye hay loader. Like all hay loaders, it followed behind the hay rack, carrying the windrow up to the back of the wagon for those who were loading. Loading hay was a hot and dusty job, but was accepted as part of farm life. A mechanical loader, even a poorly made one, was much better than the alternative of loading the hay by hand.

Did You Know?

A small single-drum cider mill might sell from $50 to $100 today.

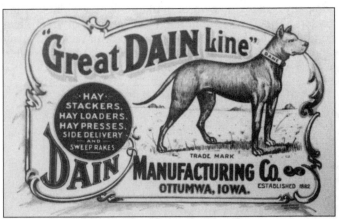

Dain Manufacturing Co., Ottumwa, Iowa

A Dain hay loader is shown in the color section of this book. As might have been expected, the Dain; trademark was none other than a Great Dane this trademark was introduced in 1903. The company was established in 1882 at Carrollton, Mo. Eventually, it was acquired by Deere & Co.

Deere & Co., Moline, Ill.

A 1908 Deere catalog illustrates its New Deere Cylinder Hay Loader. Numerous hay loader designs emerged, each having its protagonists. The double-cylinder style shown here was considered to be one of the best on the market, although some farmers complained that the extra mechanism increased the draft considerably. This one does not have the forecarriage used by numerous other styles. The Deere hay loader line was dominated by the Dain loaders, as noted previously.

Deere & Mansur Company, Moline, Illinois

Deere hay loaders of 1890 would change very little over another 30 years. The hay loader was an important labor-saving device that rapidly gained in popularity during the 1890s. Prior to that time, hay was loaded and unloaded for storage at the barn with pitchforks.

The combination of the hay loader in the field and the automatic hay carrier in the barn mechanized the hay harvest to some extent.

Keystone Manufacturing Co., Sterling, Ill.

By 1887, the Keystone Rotary Hay Loader had emerged; this was one of the earliest cylinder loaders on the market. Shown here in operation, one man is loading while the other is driving. However, most hay racks were equipped with a ladder on the front. The lines were tied off to the ladder and the front man loaded the front part of the load, while the man to the back bucked all the hay from the loader and loaded the back part of the load.

Lasack Bros., & Co., Oxford Junction, Iowa

In 1914, the Oxford Hay Loader and Hay Rake Combined was offered to the farmer. This was a rake-bar loader that could load dry hay directly from the swath without raking, if so desired. Although this loader was claimed by its makers to have many and distinct advantages, little information is available on this machine outside of a few advertisements.

Massey-Harris Harvester Co., Batavia, N.Y.

Subsequent to its 1917 purchase of Johnston Harvester Co., Batavia, Massey-Harris continued the hay loader line, augmenting it with some new models under the M-H trademark. Shown here is its popular No. 4 Cylinder Hay Loader. The model shown here is equipped with an adjustable loading deck, preferred by many farmers.

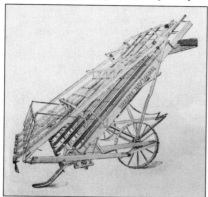

Moline Plow Co., Moline, Ill.

The extensive Moline implement line of 1918 included several styles of hay loaders; this Moline Gearless Hay Loader No. 1 was one such design. The raker bars picked up hay from the windrow or swath and the hinged rake teeth propelled the hay upward by their reciprocating action.

New Idea Inc., Coldwater, Ohio

New Idea Spreader Co. expanded its line considerably in the 1930s with the acquisition of Sandwich Manufacturing Co., Sandwich, Ill. From the late 1930s comes this all-steel design. These loaders were much lighter in weight and far more durable than their all-wood ancestors. This one is even equipped with a loading deck for the benefit of the farmer bucking hay on the wagon.

Ohio Rake Co., Dayton, Ohio

An early entrant into the hay loader business was Ohio Rake Co. with its Ohio Hay Loader. This rake-bar design was typical

for hay loaders of its time. Several large implement distributors handled the Ohio line, including Avery Planter Co. and the J.I. Case Implement Co. warehouses.

Parlin & Orendorff Co., Canton, Ill.

Best known as a plow maker, P&O also ventured into other farm equipment lines, including its Canton Hay Loader of 1888. Of the ordinary raker design, this loader was of wooden construction, but thoroughly braced for a long life in the field. Eventually, P&O would become a part of International Harvester Co.

Sandwich Manufacturing Co., Sandwich, Ill.

This 1901 illustration of the Sandwich Clean Sweep Hay Loader is virtually identical to the engraving of 1894; thus the design changed little for several years. With this design, hay could be loaded directly from the swath, leaving no need for raking the hay as a separate operation. This idea took hold with some farmers, although most preferred to rake the hay into windrows.

By 1915, Sandwich was offering its Easyway Hay Loader; it had been introduced already in 1912 and remained in the line virtually until it was acquired by New Idea about 1930. A small bottom cylinder picked the hay from the ground, transferring it to the raker bars.

Wixcel Manufacturing Co., Marcus, Iowa

In an attempt to further mechanize the loading of hay, Wixcel announced this automatic loader in 1912. It was designed so that a minimum of work was needed in making the load from front to back. Apparently, the company had been building these loaders for a few years prior to this illustration, but no substantial information has been found regarding the company or this interesting design.

Trade Names

Acme	Acme Harvesting Machine Co.	Peoria, IL	1915
Canton	Ohio Rake Co.	Dayton, OH	1915
Champion	Sterling Mfg. Co.	Sterling, IL	1915
Cherokee	Cherokee Mfg. Co.	Cherokee, IA	1915
Clean Sweep	Sandwich Mfg. Co.	Sandwich, IL	1905
Cooper	E. Cooper	Theresa, NY	1892
Dain	Dain Mfg. Co.	Carrollton, MO	1892
Dain	Dain Mfg. Co.	Ottumwa, IA	1905
Daisy	Gilliland, Jackson & Co.	Monroe City, MO	1892
Dayton	Ohio Rake Co.	Dayton, OH	1915
Deere	Deere & Mansur	Moline, IL	1905
Deering	International Harvester Co.	Chicago, IL	1913
Easyway	Sandwich Mfg. Co.	Sandwich, IL	1915
Emerson Gearless	Emerson-Brantingham Co.	Rockford, IL	1913
Favorite	Sterling Mfg. Co.	Sterling, IL	1915
Flying Dutchman	Minneapolis-Moline Co.	Minneapolis, MN	1936
Flying Dutchman	Moline Plow Co.	Moline, IL	1915
Gearless	Johnston Harvester Co.	Batavia, NY	1913
Gem	Sterling Mfg. Co.	Sterling, IL	1915
Giant	Imperial Machinery Co.	Minneapolis, MN	1913
H. V.	Hocking Valley Mfg. Co.	Lancaster, OH	1913
Hainke	Hainke Foundry	Kensington, KS	1945
Harris	Harris Mfg. Co.	Stockton, CA	1929
Hawkeye	Chambers, Bering & Quinlan Co.	Decatur, IL	1905
Hocking Valley	Hocking Valley Mfg. Co.	Lancaster, OH	1905
International	International Harvester Co.	Chicago, IL	1913
Jewett	Jewett Hay Loader Co.	Sand Springs, IA	1892
Johnston	Johnston Harvester Co.	Batavia, NY	1915

Trade Names (cont...)

Keystone	International Harvester Co.	Chicago, IL	1913
Keystone	Keystone Co.	Sterling, IL	1905
Lightning	Kansas City Hay Press Co.	Kansas City, MO	1892
Louden's Economy	Louden Machinery Co.	Fairfield, IA	1892
Massey-Harris	Johnston Harvester Co.	Batavia, NY	1913
McCormick	International Harvester Co.	Chicago, IL	1913
Moline	Moline Plow Co.	Moline, IL	1917
New Deere	Deere and Co.	Moline, IL	1922
New Deere	Deere & Mansur	Moline, IL	1905
New Idea	New Idea Inc.	Coldwater, OH	1939
New Sandwich	Sandwich Mfg. Co.	Sandwich, IL	1913
Ohio	Ohio Rake Co.	Dayton, OH	1905
Ohio Valley	Thornburgh Mfg. Co.	Bowling Green, OH	1913
Oliver	Oliver Farm Equipment Co.	Chicago, IL	1939
Osborne	International Harvester Co.	Chicago, IL	1913
Oxford	Lasack Bros. and Co.	Oxford Junction, IA	1922
Peerless	Famous Mfg. Co.	Chicago, IL	1892
Peerless	Thornburgh Mfg. Co.	Bowling Green, OH	1913
Porter's	J. E. PorterOttawa	IL	1892
Reliable	Thomas Mfg. Co.	Springfield, OH	1913
Rock Island	Rock Island Plow Co.	Rock Island, IL	1905
Rock Island-Jewett	Rock Island Plow Co.	Rock Island, IL	1892
Sandwich	Sandwich Mfg. Co.	Sandwich, IL	1913
Sterling	Sterling Mfg. Co.	Sterling, IL	1905
Thomas	Thomas Mfg. Co.	Springfield, OH	1905
U. S.	U. S. Hay Press Supply Co.	Kansas City, MO	1892
Wixcel	Wixcel Mfg. Co.	Marcus, IA	1913

Hay Presses

As a matter of semantics, the term "hay press" was used well into the 1930s. Occasionally, the term, "baler" occurs prior to that time, but it is our opinion that the latter term usually refers to field machines that picked up hay from the windrow, vis-à-vis the portable and stationary models. Since this book has become far larger than originally anticipated, balers are given little attention in this section, particularly since they did not become widely accepted until after World War II. A few machines appeared in the 1930s, with the New Holland Automaton of the 1940s being one of the most influential machines in convincing farmers to bale their hay instead of putting it in the barn loose.

Regarding the New Holland Automaton, the Author well remembers one of these coming to the neighborhood about 1947. The fellow pulled it from farm to farm with a surplus Jeep from World War II. Farmers were lined up one after another waiting for the baler to come; in fact, one season, this baler used a semi-trailer load of New Holland twine! By the 1950s, the transformation was well under way, with loose hay and the hay loader quickly becoming history.

Hay presses were built prior to 1880, but they were seldom seen until after that time. Companies like Famous Manufacturing Co., Chicago, began building portable hay presses that could move from farm to farm; with the coming of the portable press, they were soon available in many neighborhoods. Usually a hay press was owned by a custom operator; often, a farmer would bale any hay remaining in the loft so there was room for the new crop. A common saying was that "You can never have enough hay!"

Several promising developments appeared over the years, but the fully automatic press did not appear until the 1940s. For example, in 1914, Elmer Curnutt of Garrett, Kan., developed what he hoped would be a practical self-tying baler. Despite the inventor's hopes, this early development gained little success.

Today, a few vintage hay presses survive. More often than not, they have deteriorated almost beyond repair. However, nicely restored presses can fetch $250 or more at an auction, and sometimes much more. Establishing market values on antique farm equipment is very difficult since there are numerous factors affecting their market value; the most important one being what the buyer will give and what the seller will take.

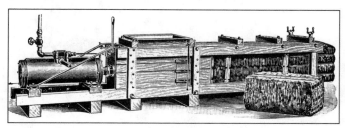

American Saw Mill Machinery Co., Hackettstown, N.J.

Completely out of the ordinary is this direct-acting steam baling press from American Saw Mill Machinery Co. Although the stationary style is shown here, it could also be mounted for portable use and could be connected to any high pressure boiler. No further information has been found on this unit outside of the 1902 advertisement given here.

Ann Arbor Agricultural Co., Ann Arbor, Mich.

By 1895, Ann Arbor was advertising its Columbia Hay Press, with this illustration coming from a copy of the *American Agri-*

culturist. Ann Arbor was a leader in hay press design, particularly the portable press as shown here. By 1895, the company had also developed an extensive line of feed and ensilage cutters, along with other equipment.

In 1910, Ann Arbor offered a truly portable hay press with its own gasoline engine; the one shown on this machine is an Olds from Olds Gas Engine Works. Once the baling job was done, a suitable mechanism was engaged and the press could move to the next job without the need of a team or a tractor. At the time, Ann Arbor advertised as having the "completest line of hay presses in the United States."

A 1932 announcement illustrated the Ann Arbor field baler at work baling oat straw behind a Caterpillar Thirty tractor. Ann Arbor pioneered the "pick-up" baler design and although it required two men to ride the machine for tying the wires, it was a major step forward in the hay harvest.

In 1941, Ann Arbor announced its new one-man pick-up baler. This machine featured automatic tying and eliminated the need for people to sit next to the bale chamber breathing huge quantities of dust while making the ties. In 1943, Oliver entered into a long-term lease agreement for the Ann Arbor plant, finally buying it and making it the basis for the Oliver hay balers.

David Bradley Manufacturing Co., Bradley, Ill.

By 1906, and probably earlier, David Bradley was offering this double-cam all-steel hay press to its customers. Small presses like this were operated by two horses turning the sweep arm, visible above the frame. As they walked around the pivot, a toggle linkage provided the power necessary for compressing the bale.

The Bradley Power Press was somewhat larger than the two-horse model shown in this heading and was available for a number of years. At the appropriate time, special separator blocks were dropped into the bale chamber. As they emerged behind the plunger, wires were pushed to the opposite side, fed across the bale and back through to the other side where they were then tied. This baler featured Bradley's own patented block-dropper mechanism.

Burkett Manufacturing Co., Columbus, Ohio

An illustration of the 1920s pictures the Burkett Motor Hay Press. This one was equipped with Burkett's own gasoline engine; it was easily removed for other purposes. Apparently, this company operated for only a few years; research has not found any existing presses; apparently, Burkett was acquired by K.C. Hay Press Co.

J.I. Case Co., Racine, Wis.

Case began marketing a field-type pick-up baler in the early 1930s, with this new model appearing in 1941; it is being pulled by a Case VC tractor. Three people were needed—one to drive the tractor and two more to place and tie the wires. The latter was often a very undesirable task; few people volunteered for it.

Collins Plow Co., Quincy, Ill.

A 1903 advertisement illustrates the Eli Hay Press, a portable machine that remained on the market for decades. This popular hay press featured an automatic bell that told the operator when to drop another separator block into the chamber. By this method, bale length was uniformly maintained.

Eli Baling Presses were offered in some 40 styles and sizes, giving Collins Plow Co. one of the largest selections in the industry. This small horse-powered model was fairly popular, especially for the average farmer or perhaps an association of farmers within a neighborhood. Shown here is a team hitched to the sweep arm of the press. Collins Plow Co. and the Eli hay presses remain in the trade listings at least until 1940, but the final disposition of the company is unknown.

Dain Manufacturing Co., Ottumwa, Iowa

A 1910 illustration shows the Dain Power Press, one of many models offered by this company. The Dain line of haying equipment had few rivals and much of the production was sold by Deere & Co. Eventually, the latter bought out Dain, forming the basis for Deere's line of hay presses and balers.

P.K. Dederick's Sons, Albany, N.Y.

Dederick's Hay Press was one of the first to appear on the market; patents by Dederick first appear in 1843. An early style is shown here; the fellow feeding the press had to ascend to his platform via a ladder. Purely a stationary unit, it heralded the beginning of a new industry.

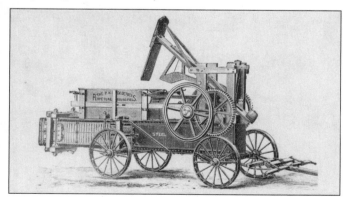

In an 1895 catalog, it was noted that "Dederick's Presses Never Bust, because they are made of steel." The company also claimed that theirs was the only all-steel press to appear for competitive testing at the Columbian World's Fair in Chicago during 1893. The company appears in product listings as late as 1910, but its final destiny is unknown.

DeLoach Mill Manufacturing Co., Chattanooga, Tenn.

A 1905 magazine article cites the new hay press from DeLoach. This company was a well-known manufacturer of sawmills, remaining in this business for many years. However, its hay press does not appear in any of the product listings which we researched for this book, thus any further data in this regard is currently unavailable. Presumably, this hay press was made for only a short time.

Devol-Livengood Manufacturing Co., Kansas City, Kan.

Fortunately, this 1893 engraving illustrates how the Farmers' Hay Press looked when at work and when on the road. This press was advertised for a few years in essentially the same form as shown here; in the early 1900s, it is shown under the heading of P.K. Dederick's Sons company at Albany, N.Y.

Eagle Machine Works, Indianapolis, Ind.

From 1888 comes this illustration of Johnson's Baling Press, a heavy stationary style. This one was made in two sizes; 16-by-18 or 20-by-30 inches, any length desired. The larger size used three wires to tie the completed bale. Aside from this illustration, no further history on the company has been found.

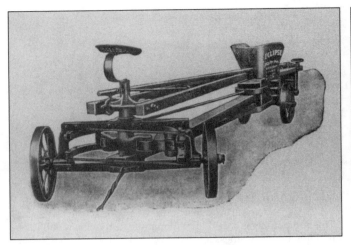

Eclipse Hay Press Co., Kansas City, Kan.

Eclipse hay presses were shown in this form for 1910, but little is known of the company's activities prior to that time. Above the front axle of the press is shown part of the toggle linkage operated by the revolving sweep. This greatly multiplied the force exerted by the horses, making it possible to manufacture tight bales with relative ease. Eventually, this company came under control of Kansas City Hay Press Co., also of Kansas City.

Emerson-Brantingham Co., Rockford, Ill.

Surprisingly, few details can be found regarding the E-B Baling Press, as shown from its 1919 catalog. This one was equipped with an E-B 6-horsepower gasoline engine and was arranged so that the tyer could return his own wires for tying. The low profile was a distinct advantage to feeding the machine.

Geo. Ertel Co., Quincy, Ill.

From 1908 comes this illustration of the Daisy Hay Press from Geo. Ertel Co. George Ertel had a long career in the hay press business, securing his first patent in 1867. The company continued making hay presses into the 1930s but disappears from view at that time; no further details have been found.

Famous Manufacturing Co., Chicago, Ill.

Famous Manufacturing Co. was an early entrant into building portable hay presses, doing so by the early 1880s. An 1895 advertisement illustrates some of its designs. The company remains in product listings until at least 1909; a few years later, the Champion hay presses appear under the heading of Sterling Manufacturing Co., Sterling, Ill.

A.B. Farquhar Co., Ltd., York, Pa.

In the late 1930s, Farquhar listed this pick-up baler in its catalogs, but little is known of its background. There is a great similarity to a machine from Ann Arbor Hay Press Co., although this might be coincidental. Farquhar's efforts in the hay baler business did not seem to make a major impact in the industry; in 1952 the company was absorbed by Oliver Corporation.

Geiser Manufacturing Co., Waynesboro, Pa.

In 1912, Emerson-Brantingham Co., at Rockford, Ill., purchased the Geiser Manufacturing Co. With this Peerless Hay Press of about 1910, E-B instantly acquired a machine that was already perfected. This Class B press was available in 14-by-18 and 17-by-22 inch sizes, with the length being optional.

Harrison Machine Works, Belleville, Ill.

Belleville Self-Feed Balers were available in two sizes; 16-by-18 and 17-by-22 inches. The self-feed design was a distinct improvement over the hand-fed models. In this design, the hay was fed onto the large table, being raked into the chamber by an automatic feed arm. The press shown here is from the company's 1924 catalog.

D.B. Hendricks & Co., Kingston, N.Y.

By 1895, Hendricks was offering this huge stationary hay press. This style placed five wires around the periphery of the bale, rather than the usual method of tying from end-to-end. The company appears in product listings until about 1910, but then disappears from view.

International Harvester Co., Chicago, Ill.

IHC was formed in 1902 and began building hay presses in 1907. Numerous styles and sizes followed, with this International Power Press of 1920 being a very popular model. This one is equipped with the company's own gasoline engine, although the machine could also be belt-powered from a tractor. IHC continued in the hay press business through the years, becoming one of the predominant manufacturers.

Kansas City Hay Press Co., Kansas City, Kan.

By 1887, Kansas City Hay Press Co. had become an established force in the hay press business. This Lighting Baling Press of 1887 is shown here in its working position; the truck wheels for portability are resting to one side. With a small press like this, a farmer could bale several tons of hay in a day's work.

Lightning Hay Press styles developed over the years; by 1897, the company was offering this portable model, with two horses supplying the power. As shown, one man is feeding hay into the press, another is getting it to the feeder and a third person is tying the bales. The person feeding the press had to be careful, lest his fork be in the bale chamber as the plunger moved forward. If this happened, all that was left was the handle—the rest of the fork was already squeezed into the bale!

Kansas City Hay Press Co., was early to develop a belt-powered press. Its K.C. Belt Press was on the market for years; it or its descendants were being marketed at least into the 1940s. Parts were available for many K.C. presses into the late 1950s, but subsequent company activities are unknown.

Kappe & Daab, Belleville, Ill.

Virtually nothing is known of Kappe & Daab, outside of this 1884 advertisement. Its Favorite Hay Press of that time was a rather unusual design, as noted from the peculiar bale form shown in the foreground. The latter was secured with three wires. Also of interest is the unique linkage from the sweep arm to the plunger.

James Kemp, Kempton, Ill.

The history of many early implement manufacturers has been obscured by time, and this repeats itself with the Double Cam Hay Press from James Kemp. Shown here in the transport position, this was a small two-horse press. The engraving is from its 1887 version. Further details are unknown.

Kinnard Press Co., Minneapolis, Minn.

One of the early manufacturers in the hay press business was O.B. Kinnard. By 1892, he had built several styles and his No. 7 press shown here could handle 15 to 25 tons of hay per day. Although it was ordinarily a belt-powered machine, this one was equipped with a special countershaft for attachment to a horse power. Kinnard later reorganized as Kinnard-Haines Co. and entered the tractor business for a number of years.

Did You Know?

As late as 1919, the Majestic Feed Cooker sold for $20.

Martin & Morrissey Manufacturing Co., Omaha, Neb.

Since this company appears in very few industry listings, it is assumed that its Omaha Hay Press of 1894 was a rather short-lived adventure. Shown here in the operating position, the press could be trucked for moving to another location. This was achieved with a pair of lifting jacks to raise one end. The wheels were then placed beneath the machine and secured.

F.X. Maurer Co., Spencer, Iowa

In 1905, Maurer announced its new Standard Belt Press. It included a patented feed box, as shown in the illustration. Maurer presses were advertised for a few years, but disappear from the product listings in the 1920s. No further information has been located.

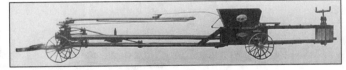

Maytag Co., Newton, Iowa

Maytag's Buffalo Hay Press, a two-horse model appeared about 1910, remaining on the market for about 10 years; subsequently the company offered repair parts at least into the 1930s. The Buffalo is shown here in the transport position, with the company claiming that it had developed a relatively easy system of setting it up in the working position.

Missouri Hay Press Co., Moberly, Mo.

In the early 1900s, the Missouri Hay Press appeared from this firm; the model shown here is of about 1920 vintage and is powered by a Stover gasoline engine. Many engine manufacturers built special hay press engines with suitable air-intake equipment to keep chaff out of the cylinder, along with an extended exhaust. Likewise, the water hopper was enclosed to keep out foreign materials. Missouri Hay Press Co. appears in the product listings at least into the late 1940s, but then disappears from view.

Monitor Hay Press Co., Kansas City, Kan.

An 1887 illustration of the Monitor Hay Press is identical to its Ironclad model of 1894. Shown here in the operating position, the farmer "dug in" the transport wheels to lower the machine for work; three people are at work operating the press. By the early 1900s, the Monitor disappears; no further information has been located.

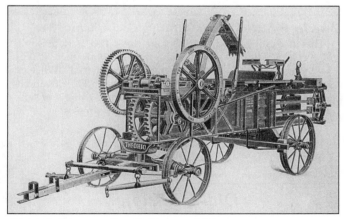

Ohio Cultivator Co., Bellevue, Ohio

The Ohio Cultivator Co. line was rather extensive, also including a series of hay presses. This model of 1910 typified the line

at that time, although the company also made a series of one- and two-horse presses. Ohio hay presses and balers remain in industry listings until the 1950s when repair parts became available from the American Baler Co., also at Bellevue.

J.E. Porter Co., Ottawa, Ill.

The *American Thresherman* of 1904 illustrated this model of Porter's Hay Press, a simple two-horse model. Porter was engaged in making various kinds of farm equipment, with the Porter hay carriers being well known. However, the company disappears from the product listings by 1910 and no information has surfaced regarding its subsequent activities.

Quincy Baling Press Co., Quincy, Ill.

An 1889 illustration of the Noxall Baling Press also refers to the Blank & Schwarzburg designs, apparently in reference to its inventors. This 1893 engraving notes the Noxall to be "the best 2-horse full circle press made." By the early 1900s, the Noxall drops out of sight.

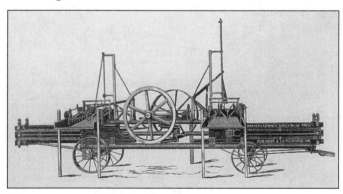

Robinson & Co., Richmond, Ind.

Apparently, Bricker's Automatic Baling Press as shown here in an 1897 engraving was built by Robinson for several years. By 1905, it was replaced with an improved design. This unusual hay press was called a duplex press since it utilized a plunger each side of the crank and made two bales simultaneously. It was also available in a single design, the latter then being marketed for several years. However, by the early 1920s, parts only were available from Swayne, Robinson & Co., also in Richmond.

Sandwich Manufacturing Co., Sandwich, Ill.

Sandwich was an early manufacturer of hay presses; this one of 1894 typified its two-horse design. This machine differed from most two-horse balers in that the sweep power was situated separately from the hay press, eliminating the need to dig the wheels in or remove them entirely for baling. A machine like this could bale from 12 to 16 tons in a good day.

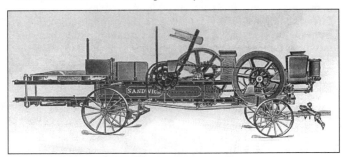

Sandwich Manufacturing Co. built a full line of power presses, such as this Solid Steel Motor Press of 1913. The company was early to adapt a gasoline engine to its presses and prior to making its own engines utilized those from Stover Manufacturing Co., in Freeport, or Appleton Manufacturing Co., in Batavia, Ill. Subsequently, the company used its own Sandwich engines on motor-equipped models. New Idea took over Sandwich about 1930, gaining from the latter's vast experience in the hay baler business.

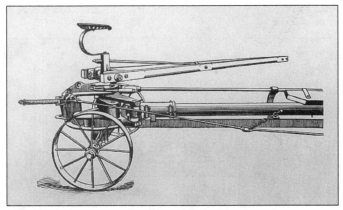

Scott Hay Press Co., Kansas City, Kan.

The Scott O.K. Hay Press of 1910 is shown here, but the precise origins of the company have not been ascertained. This cut shows the sweep arm and linkage mechanism used in the Scott press, giving it great squeezing power for making tight bales. The company appears to be active into the late 1920s; by the early 1930s, repair parts for Scott presses were available from Kansas City Hay Press Co.

J.A. Spencer, Dwight, Ill.

From an 1895 issue of *American Agriculturist* comes this illustration of the Alligator Hay Press. This one carries patents going back to 1882, but few details can be found regarding the company. Alligator two-horse presses were marketed into the 1920s, with repair parts still being available from Spencer Manufacturing Co. into the 1930s.

Square Deal Manufacturing Co., Delaware, Ohio

A 1910 advertisement illustrating the Square Deal Hay Press also notes that the company manufactured the famous Harrold Friction Drive Tractors in sizes up to 70 horsepower, having recently purchased the factory of Marion Manufacturing Co. at Marion, Ohio. However, the company disappears from the trade listings in a few years and no further traces have been found.

Wheeler & Melick Manufacturing Co., Albany, N.Y.

This interesting two-horse machine was billed as Robinson's Universal Baling Press, with the company noting that "it will bale more hay, straw or any other baleable material." Wheeler & Melick disappears from trade listings in the early 1900s and it is unknown whether the company left business entirely or simply sought other product lines aside from hay presses.

Did You Know?

A vintage broom-making machine might cost about $200 today.

Whitman Agricultural Co., St. Louis, Mo.

Introduced about 1880, Whitman's New Rebound Plunger Press soon made its record as a superior machine. In one test at the 1883 California State Fair, it even won over the Dederick, then considered to be the premier hay press or the one to beat. Whitman offered this hay press at least until 1900.

Early to recognize the advantages of steam power, Whitman offered this belt-powered hay press as early as 1887. A press like this had far greater capacity than the smaller horse-powered styles, usually requiring several men to tend to feeding, tying and carrying off the finished bales. By the 1920s, however, repair parts only were available for the Whitman presses and these were from Chattanooga Implement & Manufacturing Co., Chattanooga, Tenn.

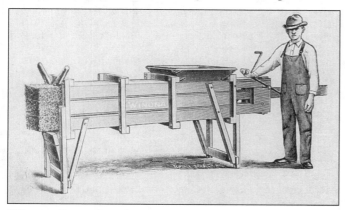

Winona Fence Co., Winona, Minn.

For those hardy souls wishing to "go it alone," Winona Fence Co., had the perfect solution with its 1901 edition of the Common Sense Hand Power Hay Baling Press. In addition to feeding the hay and tying the bales, one also had the chance to turn the crank. This small hay press was designed to utilize small quantities of hay scattered in the barn or left in the field. The company stated

that "two good-sized boys can bale three tons a day." Considering that hay averaged $1.75 a ton at the time, that came to more than $5 a day—pretty good wages for 1901.

Ypsilanti Hay Press Co., Ypsilanti, Mich.

In the early 1900s, the Wolverine Balers began to appear from Ypsilanti. Its 1910 offering included sizes of 14-by-18, 16-by-18, 17-by-22 and 18-by-22 inches. The length of the bales could be regulated by the operator. Ypsilanti specialized in belt-powered presses, but offered them with wood frames or steel construction to suit the purchaser. By the 1920s, the Wolverine balers were available from Banting Manufacturing Co., Toledo, Ohio; the latter continued to offer Wolverine parts at least into the late 1940s.

Trade Names			
Adco	Adco Mfg. Co.	Columbus, OH	1922
Admiral	Admiral Hay Press Co.	Kansas City, MO	1905
Admiral	Admiral Hay Press Co.	Kansas City, MO	1922
Advance	Ann Arbor Agricultural Co.	Ann Arbor, MI	1892
Ajax	Whitman Agricultural Co.	St. Louis, MO	1905
Alligator	J. A. Spencer	Dwight, IL	1892
American	Sandwich Mfg. Co.	Sandwich, IL	1905
Ann Arbor	Ann Arbor Machine Co.	Ann Arbor, MI	1913
Auto-Fedan	Auto-Fedan Hay Press Co.	Topeka, KS	1905
Automatic	Robinson and Co.	Richmond, IN	1909
Beckman	Beckman Bros. Co.	Des Moines, IA	1913
Belleville	Belleville Baler Co.	Belleville, IL	1913
Big Four	DeLoach Mill Mfg. Co.	Atlanta, GA	1905
Bradley	David Bradley Mfg. Co.	Bradley, IL	1905
Bricker	Robinson & Co.	Richmond, IN	1913
Buffalo	Maytag Company	Newton, IA	1913
Buffalo	Parsons Band Cutter & S. F. Co.	Newton, IA	1905
Burkett	Burkett Agricultural Works	Columbus, OH	1913

Trade Names (cont...)

C. P. Co.	Chattanooga Plow Co.	Chattanooga, TN	1913
Cascaden	Waterloo Threshing Machine Co.	Waterloo, IA	1905
Case	J. I. Case Threshing Machine Co.	Racine, WI	1915
Caswell	Caswell Mfg. Co.	Cherokee, IA	1913
Champion	Famous Mfg. Co.	Chicago, IL	1892
Chattanooga	Chattanooga Implement & Mfg. Co.	Chattanooga, TN	1905
Chattanooga	Chattanooga Plow Co.	Chattanooga, TN	1913
Collins	Collins Plow Co.	Quincy, IL	1913
Colonial	Whitman Agricultural Co.	St. Louis, MO	1905
Colt-Pull	Auto-Fedan Hay Press Co.	Kansas City, MO	1913
Columbia	Ann Arbor Machine Co.	Ann Arbor, MI	1905
Common Sense	McCall Mfg. Co.	Macon, MO	1909
Common Sense	Winona Fence Co.	Winona, MN	1901
Copeland	Roanoke Iron & Wood Works	Chattanooga, TN	1905
Cumming	Southern Plow Co.	Columbus, GA	1909
Curry	Curry Mfg. Co.	Florence, AL	1892
Cyclone	George Ertel & Co.	Quincy, IL	1913
Czar	Whitman Agricultural Co.	St. Louis, MO	1915
Dain	Dain Mfg. Co.	Ottumwa, IA	1905
Daisy	George Ertel & Co.	Quincy, IL	1913
David Bradley	David Bradley Mfg. Co.	Bradley, IL	1909
Dederick's	P. K. Dederick & Co.	Albany, NY	1892
Deitz Big Four	Deitz Hay Press Co.	Denver, CO	1892
DeLoach	DeLoach Mill Mfg. Co.	Chattanooga, TN	1905
Diamond	New Winona Mfg. Co.	Winona, MN	1905
Dixie	Wirtz & Hernlen	Augusta, GA	1913
Double Cam	James Kemp	Kempton, IL	1887
Duplex	Robinson & Co.	Richmond, IN	1913
Eagle	Eagle Mfg. Co.	Kansas City, MO	1905
Eclipse	Eclipse Hay Press Co.	Kansas City, MO	1913
Eclipse	Whitman Agricultural Co.	St. Louis, MO	1905
Economy	Chattanooga Implement & Mfg. Co.	Chattanooga, TN	1913
Economy	George Ertel & Co.	Quincy, IL	1892
Eli	Collins Plow Co.	Quincy, IL	1892
Elk	International Mfg. Co.	Omaha, NE	1905
Emmons	C. J. Hyde	Meridian, MS	1905
Emperor	Whitman Agricultural Co.	St. Louis, MO	1905
Ertel's Victor	George Ertel & Co.	Quincy, IL	1892
Eureka	Wirtz & Hernlen	Augusta, GA	1913
Farmer's	Devol-Livengood Mfg. Co.	Kansas City, KS	1893
Farmer's	P. K. Dederick & Co.	Albany, NY	1905
Farquhar-Seely	A. B. Farquhar Co.	York, PA	1892
Favorite	Kappe and Daab	Belleville, IL	1884
Flour City	Kinnard Press Co.	Minneapolis, MN	1892
Gardner	J. H. Gardner	Dalton, GA	1892
Geiser Peerless	Emerson-Brantingham	Rockford, IL	1913
Gem	George Ertel & Co.	Quincy, IL	1905

Trade Names (cont...)

Giant	Ford Giant Press Co.	Louisville, KY	1892
Globe	Barlow Corn Planter Co.	Quincy, IL	1892
Gregory	C. J. Hyde	Meridian, MS	1905
Greyhound Wolverine	Banting Mfg. Co.	Toledo, OH	1929
Handy	Little Giant Hay Press Co.	Dallas, TX	1905
Hay King	New Winona Mfg. Co.	Winona, MN	1905
Hendrick's	D. B. Hendricks	Kingston, NY	1892
Hercules	J. A. Spencer	Dwight, IL	1905
Hercules	Whitman Agricultural Co.	St. Louis, MO	1905
Hercules	Wirtz & Hernlen	Augusta, GA	1913
Hoosier	Flint & Walling Mfg. Co.	Kendallville, IN	1892
I. H. C.	International Harvester Co.	Chicago, IL	1913
Ideal	Progress Mfg. Co.	Meridian, MS	1892
International	International Harvester Co.	Chicago, IL	1913
Invincible	Whitman Agricultural Co.	St. Louis, MO	1905
Jackson	Jackson-Crose Mfg. Co.	Denver, CO	1892
John Deere Dain	Deere and Co.	Moline, IL	1939
Johnson	Indianapolis Excelsior Mfg. Co.	Indianapolis, IN	1892
Johnson's	Eagle Machine Works	Indianapolis, IN	1888
Jumbo	Collins Plow Co.	Quincy, IL	1913
Jumbo	David Bradley Mfg. Co.	Bradley, IL	1905
Kemp	Kemp's Mfg. Co.	Kankakee, IL	1905
Lauson Ann Arbor	John Lauson Mfg. Co.	New Holstein, WI	1922
Lightning	Kansas City Hay Press Co.	Kansas City, MO	1892
Lilliston	Lilliston Implement Co.	Albany , GA	1945
Little Giant	Little Giant Hay Press Co.	Dallas, TX	1905
Little Giant	Reed Mfg. Co.	Kalamazoo, MI	1913
Little Giant	S. E. Sprout & Son	Muncy, PA	1892
Little Giant	Wirtz & Hernlen	Augusta, GA	1913
Luebben	Beatrice Steel Tank Mfg. Co.	Beatrice, NE	1922
Luebben	Luebben Baler Co.	Beatrice, NE	1913
Maurer	Frank X. Maurer Co.	Spencer, IA	1892
McCormick-Deering	International Harvester Co.	Chicago, IL	1924
Mead	Mead Hay Press Co.	Pueblo, CO	1905
Mead	Port Huron Engine & Thresher Co.	Port Huron, MI	1905
Michigan Columbia	Ann Arbor Machine Co.	Ann Arbor, MI	1909
Midland	Midland Mfg. Co.	Tarkio, MO	1905
Miller Lightning	Stockton Combined Harvester Works	Stockton, CA	1892
Minnich	Watt Plow Co.	Richmond, VA	1892
Missouri	Missouri Hay Press Co.	Moberly, MO	1924
Mogul	Whitman Agricultural Co.	St. Louis, MO	1915
Monarch	Wrenn, Whitehurst & Co.	Norfolk, VA	1892

Colorful Memories

A Deering binder in action. Deering Harvester Co., Chicago, Ill.

A 1900 color catalog from Johnston. Johnston Harvester Co., Batavia, N.Y.

An image from the Minneapolis Threshing Machine Co., Minneapolis, Minn.

Cultivators

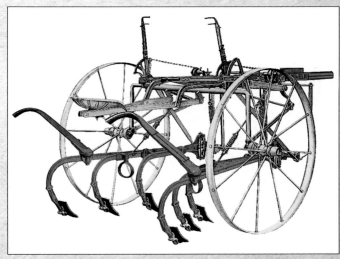

The John Deere New Elk Automatic Cultivator was a popular outfit for many years. This one dates from about 1907. Deere & Co., Moline, Ill.

Cultivators

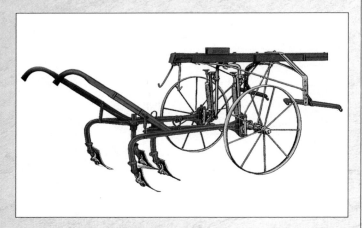

John Deere walking cultivators were extremely popular; a fair number still exist. Deere & Co., Moline, Ill.

In the early 1920s, Avery mechanized cultivation with its AveryMotor Cultivator. It would be replaced in a decade with the row-crop tractor. Avery Co., Peoria, Ill.

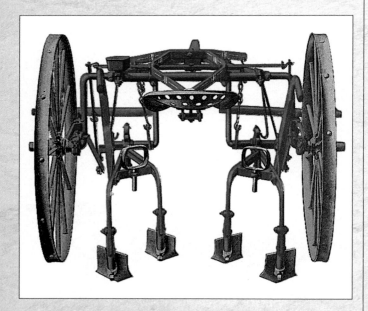

E-B had a huge range of implements, including this No. 45 Leverless Cultivator, illustrated in its 1923 catalog. Emerson-Brantingham Co., Rockford, Ill.

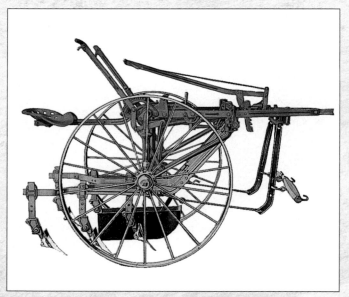

A 1920 catalog illustrates the IHC No. 4 Pivot Axle Cultivator. It ranked as one of the most popular cultivators of all time. International Harvester Co., Chicago, Ill.

Cultivators

Roderick Lean came out with its New Century in the early 1900s, claiming it to be the first "leverless" cultivator. Roderick Lean Mfg. Co., Mansfield, Ohio.

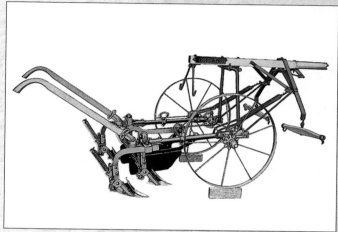

This ever-popular IHC No. 9 Walking Cultivator is illustrated in the company's 1920 General Line Catalog. International Harvester Co., Chicago, Ill.

Plows

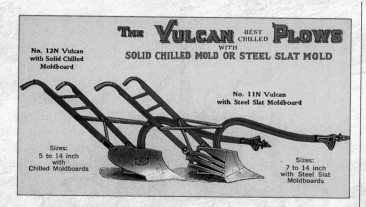

Vulcan was established in 1874, continuing until 1930, when it merged with others to form Farm Tools, Inc. Vulcan Plow Co., Evansville, Ind.

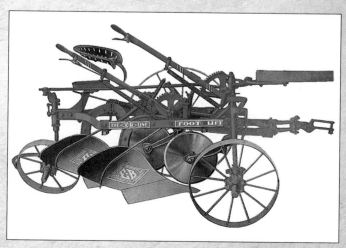

A wide range of plows was available from E-B, especially in the 1910-25 period. This Foot-Life plow was quite popular. Emerson-Brantingham Co., Rockford, Ill.

Plows

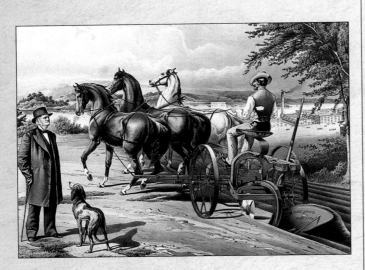

A 1920 catalog illustrates the IHC No. 4 Pivot Axle Cultivator. It ranked as one of the most popular cultivators of all time. International Harvester Co., Chicago, Ill.

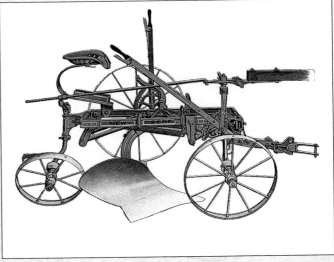

John Deere sulky plows were built for many years, until after World War II. This is an example from 1908. Deere & Co., Moline, Ill.

The Sattley plow line was quite popular, especially in certain areas. Shown here is its gang plow of the early 1900s. Racine-Sattley Co., Springfield, Ill.

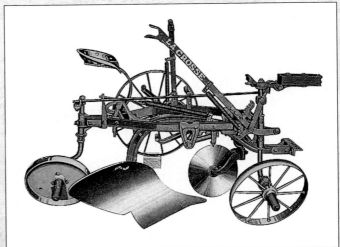

LaCrosse had a popular implement line that included an extensive variety of plows. The sulky plow shown here goes back to about 1920. LaCrosse Plow Co., LaCrosse, Wis.

Plows

After the 1919 purchase of P&O at Canton, Ill., IHC was able to fully pursue the tillage equipment business. This Little Genius plow was illustrated in the 1920 catalog. International Harvester Co., Chicago, Ill.

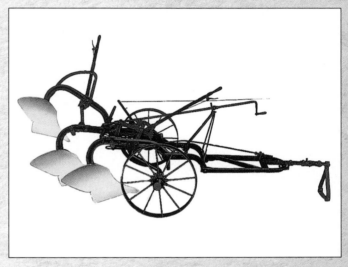

In 1919, Case acquired Grand Detour Plow Co., and this put the firm fully into the tillage equipment business. This was augmented by the 1928 purchase of the Emerson-Brantingham Co., with still more tillage equipment. J.I. Case Co., Racine, Wis.

Roderick Lean merged with others to form Farm Tools, Inc., in 1930. For some years prior to this time, Roderick Lean offered this FT-Series horse-drawn disc harrow. Roderick Lean Mfg. Co., Mansfield, Ohio.

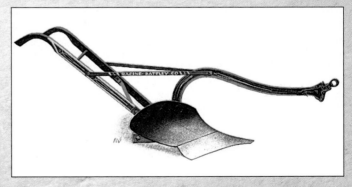

Racine-Sattley Company, Springfield, Illinois
By 1910 the Sattley line included this attractive model with a steel beam. For those who preferred a wood beam design, numerous styles also were available.

Plows

By 1920, IHC was well into the tillage equipment business. Shown here is its 8-foot horse-drawn disc with forecarriage. International Harvester Co., Chicago, Ill.

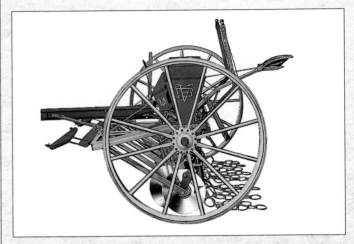

Van Brunt was founded in 1861. For a few years prior to the 1912 acquisition by Deere & Co., much of the production was sold through John Deere dealers. Van Brunt Mfg. Co., Horicon, Wis.

Seeders, Planters and Drills

An advertising postcard of the 1880s demonstrates the Budlong combination disc and seeder. J.J. Budlong & Co., Aurora, Ill.

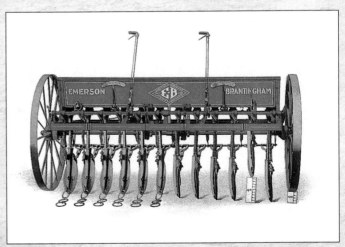

A 1923 E-B catalog illustrates one of its grain drills. At the time, E-B was manufacturing an extensive line of planting, harvesting, and tillage equipment. Emerson-Brantingham Co., Rockford, Ill.

Seeders, Planters and Drills

Avery was one of the earliest promoters of power farming. Its 1917 catalog illustrates an Avery tractor pulling a moldboard plow. Avery also produced some of the best catalog art of any farm equipment manufacturer. Avery Co., Peoria, Ill.

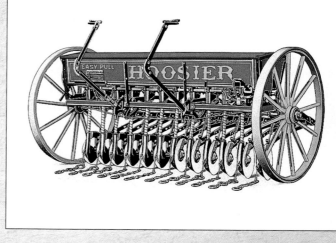

In 1912, IHC contracted to sell the entire output of Hoosier Drill, finally buying the firm outright in 1920. Hoosier Drill Co., Richmond, Ind.

Thompson's Wheelbarrow Seeder was marketed for decades through numerous equipment jobbers. Today, they are a desirable antique. O.E. Thompson & Sons, Ypsilanti, Mich.

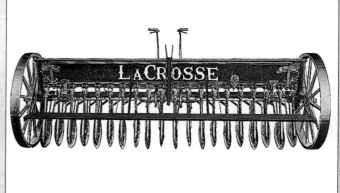

From the late 1920s comes this color illustration of the LaCrosse Drill. It was available for use with horses or a tractor. LaCrosse Plow Co., LaCrosse, Wis.

Seeders, Planters and Drills

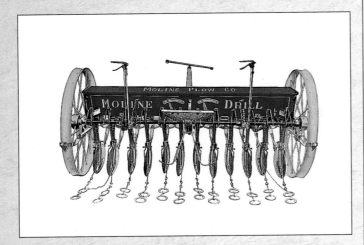

In 1909, Moline Plow Co. acquired the Monitor Drill Co. of Minneapolis. This was the basis of its grain drill business. Moline Plow Co., Moline, Ill.

A 1908 catalog from Deere illustrates its No. 9 corn planter. Subsequently came the No. 99 and then the inimitable No. 999. Deere & Co., Moline, Ill.

A catalog illustration of about 1912 portrays the bright red planter with green wheels, as built by Sattley, at the time. Racine-Sattley Co., Springfield, Ill.

An undated folder, probably from the 1890s, depicts a one-horse drill available at the time. Deere & Mansur Co., Moline, Ill.

Grinders

An advertisement of the 1930s shows the Letz No. 80 Series grinders vividly painted in orange and blue. Letz Mfg. Co., Crown Point, Ind.

A Corn Belt Mill of the 1920s is shown here. The company offered these in several sizes. Spartan Mfg. Co., Pontiac, Ill.

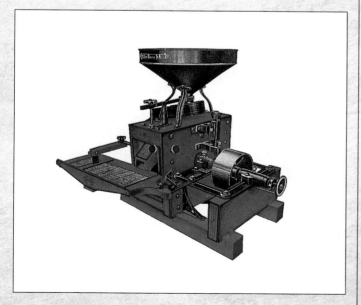

A Meadows stone buhr mill of the 1920s is shown here. This same mill was built for decades in several sizes. Meadows Mfg. Co., North Wilkesboro, N.C.

Creamer Separators and More...

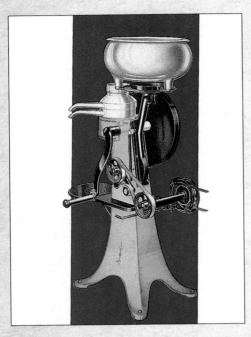

The ever-popular DeLaval cream separator was known throughout the world. This attractive model is from the 1920s. DeLaval Cream Separator Co., New York, N.Y.

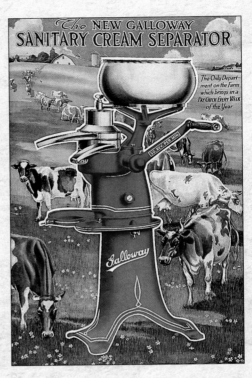

Galloway cream separators were well known by 1913, and a subsequent Galloway catalog devoted an entire page to its machine. Wm. Galloway Co., Waterloo, Iowa.

IHC was an early entrant into the cream separator business; its Primrose model of 1920 is shown here. International Harvester Co., Chicago, Ill.

Minneapolis offered this large cylinder sheller in a 1915 catalog. The company continued in the corn sheller business under the Minneapolis-Moline name for decades to come. Minneapolis Threshing Machine Co., Minneapolis, Minn.

Creamer Separators and More...

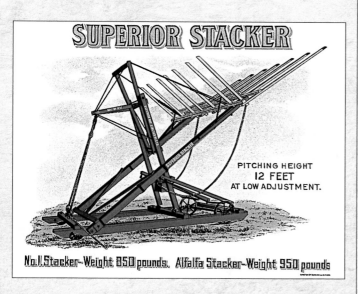

An advertisement of the 1920s shows the Superior stacker, a popular implement in some areas. Superior Hay Stacker Co., Linneus, Mo.

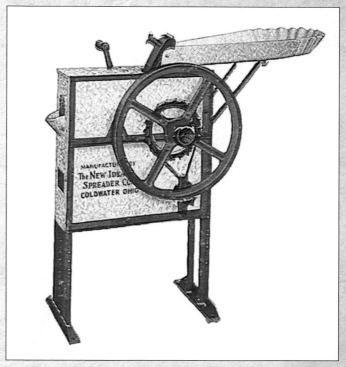

This small one-hole corn sheller was introduced in the early 1930s and thousands were sold. New Idea Spreader Co., Coldwater, Ohio.

When New Idea came out with this corn picker in the 1930s, mechanized corn harvesting had come to stay. New Idea Co., Coldwater, Ohio.

Mowers

A color catalog from Johnston illustrates its mower at work in the 1890s. Johnston Harvester Co., Batavia, N.Y.

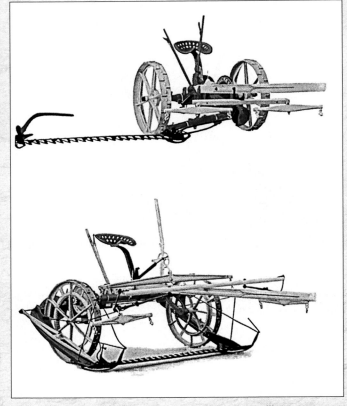

A German-language catalog of the 1880s illustrates two models of the Buckeye mowers available from Aultman, Miller & Co., Akron, Ohio.

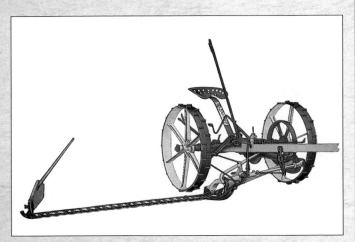

A 1920 catalog shows the Deering mower, much of the same as it had been built for the previous 20 years. International Harvester Co., Chicago, Ill.

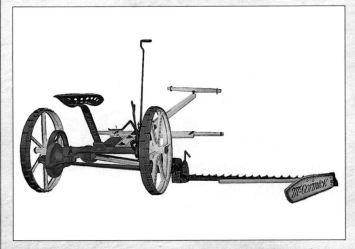

McCormick No. 6 mowers were very popular and were exported all over the world. This one is from 1920. International Harvester Co., Chicago, Ill.

Hay Loaders, Corn Binders and Grain Binders

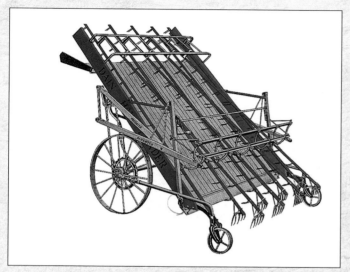

John Deere sold the Dain equipment line for several years before gaining stock control in 1911. The Dain Hay Loader was a popular item. Dain Mfg. Co., Ottumwa, Iowa.

Into the 1920s, E-B offered this Gearless Hay Loader, a simple raker design that brought loose hay from windrow to rack with ease. Emerson-Brantingham Co., Rockford Ill.

By the 1920s, Deere had come out with an all-steel hay loader design. This double-cylinder style was advertised at least into the 1930s. Deere & Co., Moline, Ill.

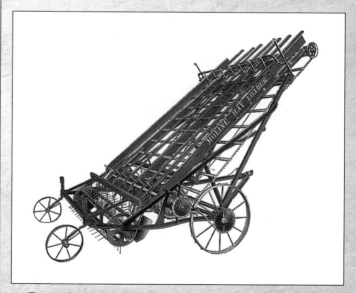

Even after the 1929 merger forming Minneapolis-Moline, the latter continued offering hay loaders much like this one of the 1920s. Moline Plow Co., Moline, Ill.

Hay Loaders, Corn Binders and Grain Binders

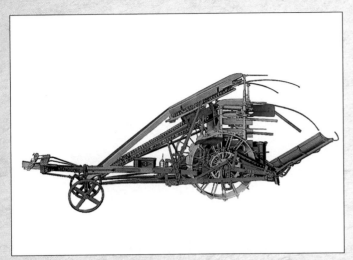

The 1923 E-B Osborne Corn Binder was essentially the same machine that had been developed some 20 years earlier by D.M. Osborne Co. Emerson-Brantingham Co., Rockford, Ill.

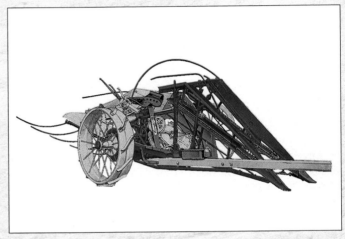

Deering's Corn Binder, as developed in the 1890s, used a different design than many of its competitors. This machine was built by IHC at least into the 1920s. International Harvester Co., Chicago, Ill.

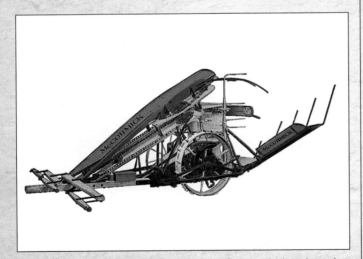

McCormick Harvesting Machine Co. had developed a corn binder in the late 1890s. This model of 1920 was essentially the same machine, although with some improvements. International Harvester Co., Chicago, Ill.

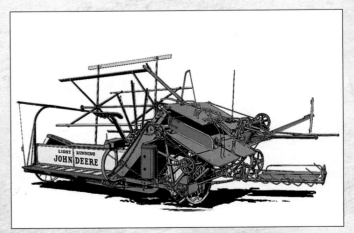

Deere got into the grain binder business about 1912. This attractive machine is from the 1930s. Deere & Co., Moline, Ill.

Hay Loaders, Corn Binders and Grain Binders

An advertising circular of the 1880s illustrates the Deering reaper of the day with its attractive combination of cream and vermilion color. Deering Harvester Co., Chicago, Ill.

With the invention of the McCormick reaper to its credit, this company went on to manufacture a popular line of grain binders. This one is from the 1890s. McCormick Harvesting Machine Co., Chicago, Ill.

Deering merged into International Harvester in 1902 after a very successful era in the grain binder business. This is a Deering grain binder of 1920. International Harvester Co., Chicago, Ill.

The McCormick grain binder of 1920 was essentially the same machine that the company began with when organized in 1902. International Harvester Co., Chicago, Ill.

Hay Loaders, Corn Binders and Grain Binders

Farm equipment catalogs of the 1890s were particularly colorful. Some, such as this cover from a McCormick catalog, were lithographic prints of exceptional clarity and beauty. McCormick Harvesting Machine Co., Chicago, Ill.

The 1912 acquisition of Adriance, Platt & Co., provided Moline with the backbone of its harvester line, as manifested with the binder of about 1918. Moline Plow Co., Moline, Ill.

Harvesting Grain

A catalog cover of the 1890s portrays how farmers once cut grain with a cradle, before the days of the reaper or grain binder. Minneapolis Harvester Co., Minneapolis, Minn.

With the catalog as its primary salesman, most farm equipment companies went all-out to portray their equipment in the best possible way. This is evident on the Johnston catalog cover of the 1890s. Johnston Harvester Co., Batavia, N.Y.

Manure Spreaders

In the 1920s, Miller offered the Robinson manure spreader. It had formerly been built at Vinton, Iowa. Geo. B. Miller & Son, Waterloo, Iowa.

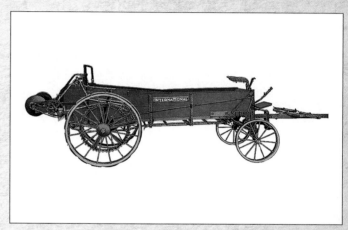

Already in 1906, IHC purchased a factory from J.S. Kemp Mfg. Co.. The latter was instrumental in development of this valuable farm machine. International Harvester Co., Chicago, Ill.

Geo. B. Miller & Son Company, Waterloo, Iowa
    The Robinson manure spreader was first built in Vinton, Iowa. Like many manufactures of the early 1900s, Robinson likely suffered from a perpetual lack of capital. Eventually, the firm was sold to Miller. The latter continued with the Robinson spreaders for a number of years.

About 1912, this model of the Bradley spreader was offered to the public. Eventually, the company came under control of Sears, Roebuck & Co. David Bradley Mfg. Co., Bradley, Ill.

Manure Spreaders

Moline was offering a manure spreader to the farmer by 1915 and perhaps earlier. This one is of about 1918 vintage. Moline Plow Co., Moline, Ill.

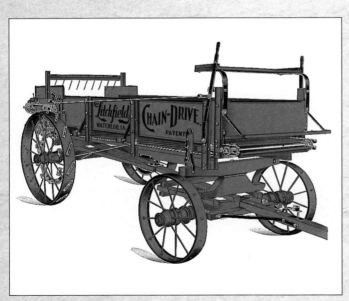

Sometime prior to 1920, Litchfield was offering this spreader, a chain-drive unit that could be placed on any available wagon gear. Litchfield Mfg. Co., Waterloo, Iowa.

From the 1930s comes this catalog illustration of the John Deere manure spreaders. This popular design was marketed for a number of years. Deere & Co., Moline, Ill.

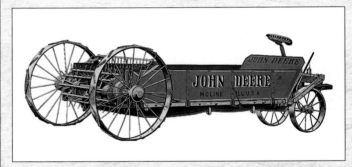

By about 1909, Deere & Co. had developed its manure spreader. Farmers were anxious for these machines because of the labor-savings that resulted. Deere & Co., Moline, Ill.

J.S. Kemp was instrumental in the development of the manure spreader, having built a sizable factory by that time. In 1906, International Harvester bought this factory. J.S. Kemp Mfg. Co., Newark Valley, N.Y.

Manure Spreaders

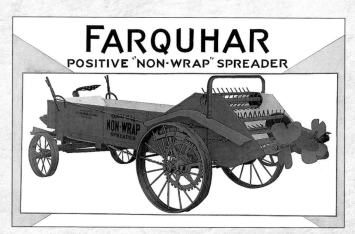

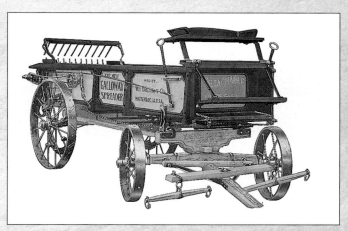

By the 1920s, New Idea had become an established manufacturer of manure spreaders. They gained great popularity; this one is from the 1930s. New Idea Spreader Co., Coldwater, Ohio.

In the 1930s, Farquhar offered its Non-Wrap Spreader, a small lightweight machine, compared to its ancestors. A.B. Farquhar Co., York, Pa.

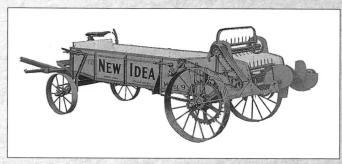

By 1912, Galloway was offering numerous styles of manure spreaders, including some models designed to fit on any available wagon gear. Galloway's spreaders were widely sold through his mail-order catalogs. Wm. Galloway Co., Waterloo, Iowa.

In 1910, IHC published this catalog of its Corn King manure spreaders. As noted elsewhere, the artistry of the day was designed to catch the eye of even the most jaded viewer. This catalog cover is a case-in-point. International Harvester Co., Chicago, Ill.

Threshers

A scene from the 1920s is displayed on a catalog cover from this firm. One of its OilPull tractors is operating a Rumely Ideal Thresher. Advance-Rumely Thresher Co., LaPorte, Ind.

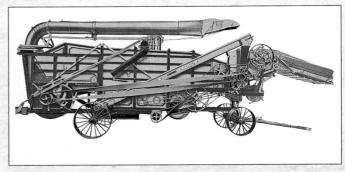

Avery Yellow Fellow Grain Threshers first appeared about 1900, remaining on the market into the early 1920s when they were replaced with all-steel designs. Avery Co., Peoria, Ill.

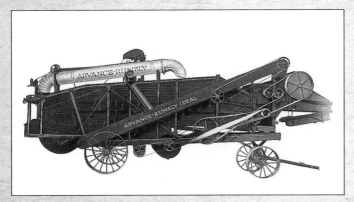

The Rumely Ideal was a popular design that emerged about 1905 and remained on the market until replaced with an all-steel machine in the late 1920s. Advance-Rumely Thresher Co., LaPorte, Ind.

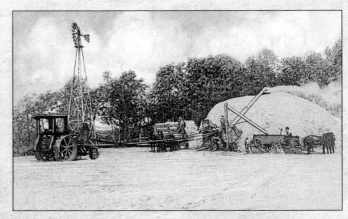

A typical threshing scene from the World War I era is depicted in this catalog illustration from Avery. Avery Co., Peoria, Ill.

Threshers

The Banting Greyhound threshers of the early 1920s featured an all-steel design. Banting was a small company that built an excellent grain thresher. Banting Mfg. Co., Toledo, Ohio.

This Cape New Model thresher appeared on the market in the 1920s. By the early 1930s, it disappeared from the industry listings. Cape Mfg. Co., Cape Girardeau, Mo.

This was the premiere American thresher builder. The Pitts brothers began making threshers in the 1830s. Buffalo Pitts Co., Buffalo, N.Y.

Case probably built more threshing machines than anyone and likely built more than any of several other companies combined. Case also pioneered the all-steel thresher. J.I. Case Co., Racine, Wis.

Threshers

This company offered numerous styles and sizes of grain threshers. The firm was acquired in the 1950s by Oliver Corporation. A.B. Farquhar Co., York, Pa.

Into the 1920s, the Gopher threshing machine was built in limited numbers. By 1930, the company was out of business. Gopher Machine Mfg. Co., New Prague, Minn.

Acquired by Rumely in 1912, Gaar-Scott had been in the thresher business for more than 60 years. Gaar, Scott & Co., Richmond, Ind.

This Canadian company was very popular in the provinces and also sold a sizable number of its threshing machines in the United States. Goodison Thresher Co., Ltd., Sarnia, Ontario, Canada.

Threshers

Until it began building all-steel machines sometime around 1920, Huber offered the contemporary wooden design as shown here. Huber Mfg. Co., Marion, Ohio.

Until sometime in the 1920s, IHC bought its threshing machines from other companies, notably Buffalo-Pitts and Belle City. This all-wood design is from 1920. International Harvester Co., Chicago, Ill.

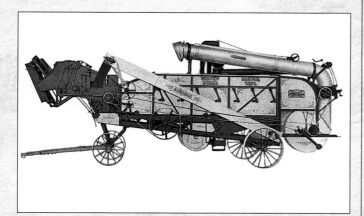

With the advent of its all-steel threshers, Huber continued in the grain thresher business for a number of years, along with its developing tractor business. This model is from the 1920s. Huber Mfg. Co., Marion, Ohio.

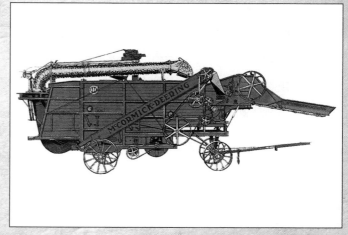

Into the 1920s, this all-wood separator was offered by IHC, albeit under the McCormick-Deering trade name. IHC eventually built its own all-steel machine. International Harvester Co., Chicago, Ill.

Threshers

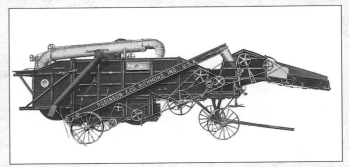

The Robinson Money-Maker threshers were marketed for decades; for a time, about 1916, Hart-Parr Co., at Charles City, Iowa sold them as the "Hart-Parr Money-Maker." Robinson & Co., Richmond, Ind.

By 1910, Minneapolis had all but finalized its thresher design with this all-wood example built in 1912. Eventually, the company began building all-steel designs. Minneapolis Thresher Co., Minneapolis, Minn.

This company sold manufacturing rights for its Farmer's Friend Windstackers. Shown here is a beautiful cover from its 1895 catalog. It portrays the famous Farmer's Friend trademark, known all over the world. Indiana Mfg. Co., Indianapolis, Ind.

In 1912, this company was purchased by Emerson-Brantingham Co. in Rockford, Ill. The thresher shown here is from a 1903 advertisement. Reeves & Co., Columbus, Ind.

Owens specialized in bean threshers. Most of its models were stationary, but the company offered this mounted style in the 1920s. J.L. Owens Co., Minneapolis, Minn.

Cutters, Hullers and Presses

Birdsell was the patriarch of the clover huller business. The Birdsell Hullers remained popular until the All-Crop combines from Allis-Chalmers brought the harvest to the field. The latter bought out Birdsell in 1931. Birdsell Mfg. Co., South Bend, Ind.

An ancient postcard of the 1890s depicts the Ross feed cutter as the centerpiece of goods offered for sale by S.E. Lincoln, a manufacturer's agent located at Rochester, N.Y. E.W. Ross Co., Springfield, Ohio.

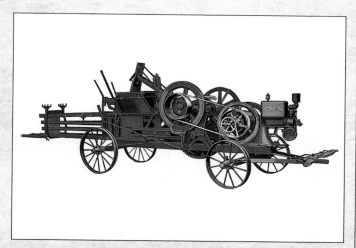

IHC offered numerous styles of hay presses during its long history, with this one being illustrated in its 1920 catalog. International Harvester Co., Chicago, Ill.

For 1920, IHC continued to offer its husker-shredder. These machines remained in the line at least into the 1930s. By then, the corn picker had come to stay. Meanwhile farmers opted for livestock feed other than shredded corn fodder. International Harvester Co., Chicago, Ill.

Cutters, Hullers and Presses

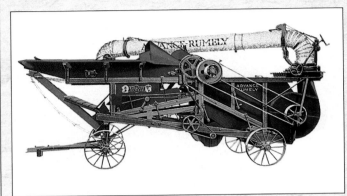

About 1912, Rumely began offering a husker-shredder to its customers, continuing with them until the early 1920s. Advance-Rumely Thresher Co., LaPorte, Ind.

Until the early 1920s, Burkett offered its motorized hay press, along with other models. The company eventually was bought out by Kansas City Hay Press Co. Burkett Mfg. Co., Columbus, Ohio.

Beginning about 1913, Rumely started offering ensilage cutters or silo fillers to its customers. This continued apparently into the early 1920s. Advance-Rumely Thresher Co., LaPorte, Ind.

By the 1920s, ensilage cutters were found in nearly every neighborhood. A great many of them were the IHC Type A cutter shown here. International Harvester Co., Chicago, Ill.

Dick's Blizzard Ensilage Cutter was one of the early models on the market, with the company continuing to build ensilage cutters at least into the late 1940s. Joseph Dick Mfg. Co., Canton, Ohio.

Wagons

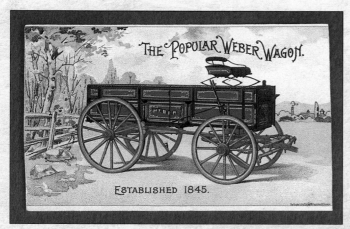

IHC acquired this company in 1904. Weber had been an established wagon builder for some years prior to this time. Weber Wagon Co., Chicago, Ill.

While Studebaker is probably better known for its fine carriages, the company also built high-quality farm wagons. Shown here is a fine example from about 1900. Studebaker Bros. Mfg. Co., South Bend, Ind.

This famous automobile maker started business making wagons and carriages. Shown here is its Village Market Wagon. Studebaker Bros. Mfg. Co., South Bend, Ind.

Many companies built wagons on a more-or-less localized basis. This company had various kinds of dirt scrapers as its main line, eventually dropping wagons altogether. Western Wheel Scraper Co., Mt. Pleasant, Iowa.

Wagons

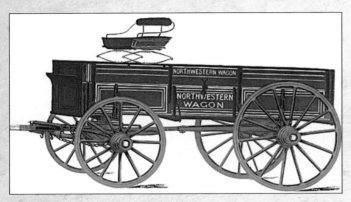

Northwestern Mfg. Company, Fort Atkinson, Wisconsin
This attractive wagon was offered in sizes 3 x 9, 3 1/4 x 10, and 3 1/2 x 11 feet. These figures refere to the inside demensions of the box.

Velie Carriage Company, Moline, Illinois
By the time their 1915 trade catalog appeared, the days of horse-drawn vehicles were rapidly coming to an end. The Velie line included this No. 604 Driving Wagon, shown here with a classic black body. And it could be furnished in green, maroon, or red.

Ohio Carriage Mfg. Company, Columbus, Ohio
Ohio Carriage Mfg. Co. was a mail-order concern that would ship this attractive runabout direct to your railway depot for $54. The company claimed this vehicle would easily sell for $75 or more at a local carriage dealer.

Ohio Carriage Mfg. Company, Columbus, Ohio
For the 1909 price of $73.75, one could purchase a copy of the Split Hickory Special Short Turn Buggy. Adding Goodyear solid rubber tires raised the price another $15. Heavy, dark blue wool broadcloth was used for the upholstery. Crated for shipment, this buggy weighed about 500 pounds.

Wagons

Ohio Carriage Mfg. Company, Columbus, Ohio

The Split Hickory Surrey shown here was priced at $87.50...a handsome price in 1909. This one had a black body with a Brewster Green running gear, and dark green wool upholstery. Brewster Green was a popular shade. Some vehicles were finished in austere Quaker Green, best described as greenish black.

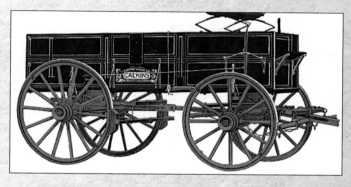

Electric Wheel Company, Quincy, Illinois

Although Electric Wheel Company was one of the preeminent builders of all-steel wagons. The Calkins Farm Wagon from EWC was available at least into the 1920s.

Deeds & Hirsig Mfg. Company, Nashville, Tennessee

In the 1890s, Deeds & Hirsig billed themselves as the "Largest Exclusive Vehicle House in the World." Despite this claim, we've found little information on the company. An ancient dealer catalog offers their attractive No. 6 buggy with a cash price of $100 for three buggies, crated and shipped to your depot.

David Bradley & Company, Council Bluffs, Iowa

This famous implement manufacturer operated a large vehicle and wagon warehouse at Council Bluffs, Iowa, for a number of years. An 1890s catalog notes their buying volume allowed them to secure their vehicles from manufacturers at a very low price. The company was buying 1,000 or more buggies per order. The vehicles were then sold under the David Bradley name and guarantee.

Wagons

Studebaker Bros. Mfg. Company, South Bend, Indiana
Studebaker was one of the largest wagon and vehicle manufacturers. A Studebaker catalog of the early 1900s notes their 65-acre lumber yard usually had over 700 million board feet of lumber, and the factories consumed some 250 million board feet per year.

In 1906 Moline acquired the Mandt Wagon Co., at Stoughton, Wis., following for decades to come with the Moline-Mandt line. Moline Plow Co., Moline, Ill.

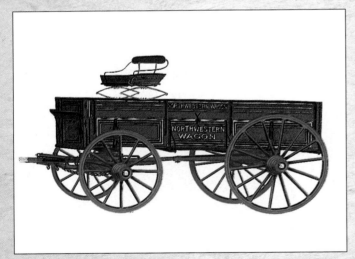

Northwestern wagons were well known, not only locally, but also in several surrounding states. The demand for wagons was insatiable, finally slowing to a trickle by World War II. Northwestern Mfg. Co., Fort Atkinson, Wis.

The original Mandt wagons differed slightly from those built later by Moline Plow Co., but had one thing in common with virtually all farm wagons; it was green. Mandt Wagon Co., Stoughton, Wis.

Wagons

The Troy Dump Wagon shown here was rarely seen on a farm, but was used mainly for building roads and other construction. Often, local farmers were hired when a road job or construction project came to the area. Troy Wagon Works Co., Troy, Ohio.

This company was well known for its carriages. Apparently the company made few, if any, wagons. However, a carriage was an essential part of rural life, as shown with this family on a Sunday outing. Velie Carriage Co., Moline,

In 1910, Deere acquired the Moline Wagon Co., at Moline, followed a year later by acquisition of Fort Smith Wagon Co., Ft. Smith, Ark. Shown here is a Deere Ironclad wagon of about 1912. Deere & Co., Moline, Ill.

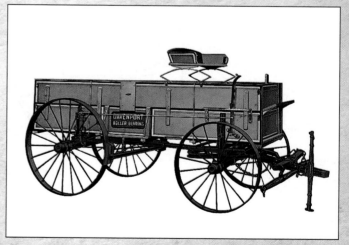

The John Deere line for 1912 included the Deere Davenport Wagon, apparently a product from its newly acquired Davenport Wagon Co., Davenport, Iowa. Deere & Co., Moline, Ill.

Wagons

Wagon manufacturers thrived until the coming of rubber-tired wagons and row-crop tractors. As the tractor retired the horse, so also did these new wagons retire the time-honored designs as shown in this attractive model from Miller Wagon Co., Edina, Mo.

Studebaker Bros. began building wagons and vehicles prior to the Civil War. By 1872, they proclaimed themselves to be the largest vehicle builders in the world.

Studebaker built farm wagons by the thousands but this only accounted for a small portion of the enterprise. For example, delivery wagons of many styles were mass-produced in the Studebaker factories.

Trade Names (cont...)

Money-Maker	Swayne, Robinson and Co.	Richmond, IN	1915
Monitor	Monitor Hay Press Co.	Kansas City, KS	1894
Monitor	U. S. Hay Press Supply Co.	Kansas City, MO	1892
National	H. N. Strait Mfg. Co.	Kansas City, KS	1905
New Century	Western Steel & Wire Co.	Kansas City, MO	1905
New Holland	New Holland Machine Co.	New Holland, PA	1945
New Model	Whitman Agricultural Co.	St. Louis, MO	1913
New South	Wirtz and Hernlen	Augusta, GA	1909
New Way	Sandwich Mfg. Co.	Sandwich, IL	1905
Noxall	Collins Plow Co.	Quincy, IL	1905
Noxall	Quincy Baling Press Co.	Quincy, IL	1892
O. K.	Scott Hay Press Co.	Kansas City, MO	1892
O. K.	Scott Hay Press Co.	Kansas City, MO	1913
Ohio	Ohio Cultivator Co.	Bellevue, OH	1905
Ohio	Ohio Mfg. Co.	Upper Sandusky, OH	1905
Oliver	Oliver Farm Equipment Co.	Chicago, IL	1945
Omaha	Martin and Morrissey Mfg. Co.	Omaha, NE	1894
Over	Ewald Over	Indianapolis, IN	1892
Paris	Paris Foundry & Machine Works	Paris, IL	1913
Peerless	Geiser Mfg. Co.	Waynesboro, PA	1913
Perpetual	J. A. Spencer	Dwight, IL	1905
Petaluma	Benicia Agricultural Works	Benicia, CA	1892
Petaluma	Truman, Hooker & Co.	San Francisco, CA	1892
Pony	Auto-Fedan Hay Press Co.	Kansas City, MO	1913
Port Huron	Port Huron Engine & Thresher Co.	Port Huron, MI	1909
Porter	J. E. Porter Co.	Ottawa, IL	1905
Rajah	Whitman Agricultural Co.	St. Louis, MO	1915
Rapid Fire	Williams Buggy Co.	Macon, GA	1905
Red Ripper	Whitman Agricultural Co.	St. Louis, MO	1905
Reed	Reed Mfg. Co.	Kalamazoo, MI	1913
Reeves	Emerson-Brantingham	Rockford, IL	1913
Reliance	Southern Plow Co.	Columbus, GA	1905
Roanoke	Henry Copeland	Chattanooga, TN	1892
Roanoke	Roanoke Iron & Wood Works	Chattanooga, TN	1905
Robinson	Robinson & Co.	Richmond, IN	1905
Robinson's Universal	Wheeler and Melick Mfg. Co.	Albany , NY	1900
Royal	Chattanooga Implement & Mfg. Co.	Chattanooga, TN	1913
Rumely	M. Rumely Co.	LaPorte, IN	1913
Rumely	Robinson & Co.	Richmond, IN	1913
Sandwich	Sandwich Mfg. Co.	Sandwich, IL	1905
Scott	Scott Hay Press Co.	Kansas City, MO	1915
Simplex	Little Giant Hay Press Co.	Dallas, TX	1905
Simplex	Reed Mfg. Co.	Kalamazoo, MI	1905
So-Ezy	Williams Buggy Co.	Macon, GA	1913
Southwick	Sandwich Mfg. Co.	Sandwich, IL	1892

Trade Names (cont...)

Square Deal	Ohio Tractor Mfg. Co.	Marion, OH	1913
Square Deal	Square Deal Mfg. Co.	Delaware, OH	1909
Standard	F. X. Maurer Co.	Spencer, IA	1913
Standard	Quincy Baling Press Co.	Quincy, IL	1892
Star	Geo. Ertel Co.	Quincy, IL	1913
Star	Star Pea Huller Co.	Chattanooga, TN	1913
Stearns	Stearns Mfg. Co.	Los Angeles, CA	1892
Steel Alligator	J. A. Spencer	Dwight, IL	1913
Steel Beauty	Whitman Agricultural Co.	St. Louis, MO	1905
Steel King	Whitman Agricultural Co.	St. Louis, MO	1905
Steel Perpetual	J. A. Spencer	Dwight, IL	1913
Success	Reed Mfg. Co.	Kalamazoo, MI	1909
Thunder	Kansas City Hay Press Co.	Kansas City, MO	1892
Tichenor's	Hercules Lever Jack Co.	Irvington, NJ	1892
Turner	Turner Mfg. Co.	Statesville, NC	1945
Uncle Tom	Orion Hay Press Co.	Orion, IL	1905
Universal	Whitman Agricultural Co.	St. Louis, MO	1905
Victor	George Ertel & Co.	Quincy, IL	1905
Wendy	Ann Arbor Machine Co.	Ann Arbor, MI	1913
Western	Sandwich Mfg. Co.	Sandwich, IL	1905
Western Chief	H. Clark	Cherokee, KS	1892
Whitman's	Whitman Agricultural Co.	St. Louis, MO	1892
Wolverine	Ypsilanti Hay Press Co.	Ypsilanti, MI	1913
Wonder	Geo. Ertel Co.	Quincy, IL	1913
Wood Alligator	J. A. Spencer	Dwight, IL	1913
Wood Perpetual	J. A. Spencer	Dwight, IL	1913
Woodruff	Woodruff Hardware Co.	Winder, GA	1905
Wygant	Hartman Mfg. Co.	Vincennes, IN	1915
X. L.	Scott Hay Press Co.	Kansas City, MO	1905
Ypsilanti	Ypsilanti Hay Press Co.	Ypsilanti, MI	1913

Hay Rakes

The coming of the mower brought with it a demand for a suitable rake. Early examples were the dump rake that gathered the dry hay from the swath and with a hand lever it was deposited into a windrow. Later, a power-lift device was included so that a simple trip lever could be used to raise the teeth.

During the 1880s, the side-delivery rake appeared infrequently, but was fairly well perfected by 1890; within a few years, it became the predominant method, with the dump rake enjoying only a fraction of its former popularity. Another device to make its appearance in the 1880s was the hay tedder, a device for lifting hay so that it would dry, but not leaving it in a windrow. A few companies built combination side-delivery rakes and hay tedders. By that time, however, the benefits of using a tedder were put to question, so the idea gained mediocre support.

Most companies building rakes also built other haying equipment, but a few early companies specialized in this line to the exclusion of all others. As with many other facets of the farm equipment business, companies came and companies fell, many of them leaving business entirely before 1920. Others merged to bolster their position and still others sold out, often at a great loss, to salvage a small return for their efforts.

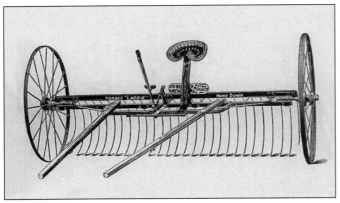

Acme Harvester Co., Pekin, Ill.

Shown here is an 1899 version of the Hodges "Laddie" Hand Dump Rake. Making straight windrows took constant vigilance as the driver traveled back and forth across the field. Acme Harvester Co., had beginnings going back to 1860.

Albion Manufacturing Co., Albion, Mich.

From 1887 comes this engraving of the Daisy Sulky Hay Rake from Albion Manufacturing Co. This one used a foot lever to raise the teeth as the farmer sat astride an iron seat. The Daisy was of wooden construction; even the bar supporting the teeth is a wooden beam, suitably fitted for the rake teeth.

Ames Plow Co., Boston, Mass.

The June 5, 1869, issue of the *Boston Cultivator* carried a front page article on Burt's Self-Adjusting Horse Hay Rake. The design was patented in 1867; the following year, 1,500 rakes were built

and sold. The editor of the *Boston Cultivator* commented: "Let those who toiled and sweat over hand-rakes during the last hay-season read the following significant TESTIMONIALS FROM HAYMAKERS." Then follows about a dozen glowing reports of the new rake.

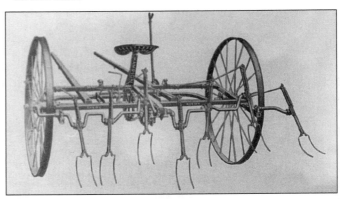

B.F. Avery & Sons, Louisville, Kty.

After Avery bought the Champion line from IHC, the company gained an already developed line of hay tools. Included was the Champion Hay Tedder. Advertising of the day claimed that hay in heavy swaths would not dry evenly, therefore the tedder was needed to stir the hay so that it would dry evenly. While there was a certain amount of validity in the claim, many farmers considered it not be worth the bother.

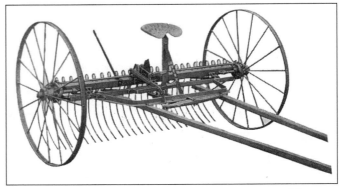

A 1916 catalog from B.F. Avery shows its Improved Dump Rake, with the most notable feature being a power-lift system that automatically lifted the tines just by pushing a foot pedal. This eased the work for the farmer considerably. While some farmers of this time still used a dump rake, most had opted for the side-delivery style.

Charles Carlisle, Hartford, Quechee Village, Vt.

From the Jan. 27, 1849, issue of the *Boston Cultivator* comes this front page illustration of Carlisle's Patent Improved Horse Rake.

Apparently, Carlisle had been having good success with his new design and it was awarded a First Premium by Vermont's Windsor County Agricultural Society. With this article, Carlisle was offering to sell manufacturing rights to those of other towns or counties who might be interested.

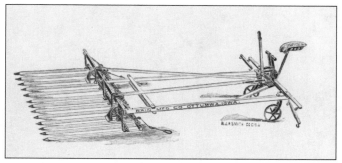

Dain Manufacturing Co., Ottumwa, Iowa

Dain began business in the 1880s at Carrollton, Mo., and eventually moved to Ottumwa. Various kinds of rakes were among the earliest developments, including the Dain Power Lift Hay Rake. This device was marketed for a number of years, with the example shown here coming from a 1900 advertisement.

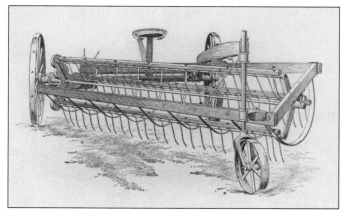

In addition to various kinds of dump rakes and sweep rakes, Dain also perfected a side delivery rake in the 1900s. This rake became very popular, partly because it was offered by the John Deere Plow Co., through its extensive dealer organization. Eventually, the Dain operation became a part of Deere & Co.

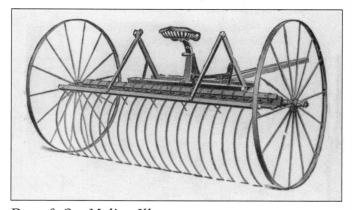

Deere & Co., Moline, Ill.

By 1895, Deere had an extensive line of haying tools: everything from hay tedders, hay forks, hay carriers, hay rakes, hay loaders, hay stackers, mowers, sickle grinders and more. Shown here is the Deere rake of 1895; it was available with either a steel or wood frame.

A 1908 John Deere catalog illustrates the company's New Deere Reversing Side Rake. This unusual design picked up the hay much like a hay loader, then carried it by a conveyor to one side, leaving it in a windrow. Aside from this catalog illustration, little more is found of this very interesting design.

Deering Harvester Co., Chicago, Ill.

Deering, like many other manufacturers, published its catalogs in several languages; this German-language edition of 1899 shows the Deere Automatic Dump Rake. It was offered in 8-1/2, 10-1/2 and 12-foot sizes. The larger sizes required two horses.

J. Dodds, Dayton, Ohio

The Hollingsworth rake was introduced by Dodds about 1875 and remained on the market for a few years. It featured an all-steel design and this was out of the ordinary for most farm equipment of the time. Outside of this illustration, virtually nothing is known of the company.

Emerson-Brantingham Co., Rockford, Ill.

In 1907, Emerson Manufacturing Co. offered its Alfalfa Champion Rake. At the time, alfalfa or lupine as it was sometimes called—it still is in Australia and some other parts of the world, was gaining greatly in popularity as a forage crop. Since alfalfa was a heavy crop, Emerson devised its own alfalfa rake with a heavier design than ordinary.

Sweep rakes were a popular implement in some areas. With this 1919 design, the horses pushed the rake ahead of themselves. Once the rake was loaded a lifting device raised the teeth off the ground and the load was taken to a convenient place for stacking.

Emerson-Brantingham developed its No. 166 Side-Delivery Rake sometime prior to this 1919 model. While many side rakes used a single tail wheel, this model featured two tail wheels for better stability on rough ground. With this design, one wheel could support the tail of the rake, thus keeping the rake teeth from digging into the ground.

Gale Manufacturing Co., Albion, Mich.

An 1889 advertisement illustrates Gale's Daisy Hay Rake. It appears to be a successor to the Daisy from Albion Manufacturing Co. see previous. Little history is known of Gale, but it seems to be a safe assumption that Albion was indeed a forerunner of the Gale line.

Gilliland, Jackson & Co., Monroe City, Mo.

Patented March 9, 1886, the Daisy Ricker and Rake are shown here. The ricker is pictured to the left as it transfers a load of hay to the stack. On the right is the rake, free from its burden and ready to return to the field for another load. These devices were very popular in certain areas where outdoor haystacks were built instead of storing the hay in a barn.

While the Daisy rake was a push rake, the Missouri Hay Rake of 1889 was pulled with the team forward. Apparently, the company was experiencing great success at the time, but future years leave no mark as to its activities. Possibly, the line was sold out to another manufacturer, but trade directories of the early 1900s show no listings for the Daisy or Missouri lines.

Grand Rapids Manufacturing & Implement Co., Grand Rapids, Mich.

An interesting study of gears and linkages is provided with the Grand Rapids Hay Tedder of 1895. By using a combination of tongue and shafts, this tedder could be used with one horse or two. The advertisement noted that the company had a few hundred machines on hand for immediate shipment. Beyond this notice, little else is known of the company.

Hay Tool Manufacturing Co., Council Bluffs, Iowa

From 1905 comes this advertisement of push rakes and sulky rakes in various styles. Apparently, the company had a sizable trade, since it engaged jobbing houses at St. Louis and Kansas City. However, the advertisement also notes that N.H. McCall was manager of the firm. It would appear that his subsequent activities were with McCall Manufacturing Co., which follows.

International Harvester Co., Chicago, Ill.

For 1920, IHC offered its combined side rake and tedder as part of an extensive line of haying tools. Of the original partners that formed IHC, Deering and McCormick both had well-developed hay tool lines and these were expanded in the following years. Eventually, the idea of a combined rake and tedder disappeared.

Into the 1920s, IHC continued to offer its International hay tedder; it was virtually identical to the McCormick hay tedder introduced some 30 years before. Some farmers saw the tedder as an essential part of their farm equipment, while others saw it as something nice to have. Others saw no use for it at all.

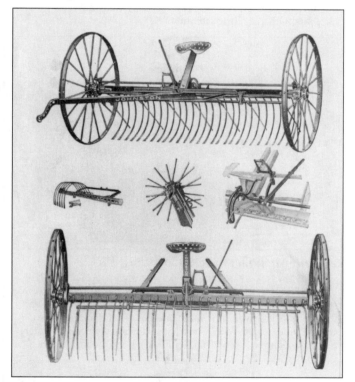

Johnston Harvester Co., Batavia, Ill.

With an implement such as the dump rake, there were few basic differences from one make to another. However, each manufacturer had a slightly different approach to the lifting system, wheel design or perhaps the curvature of the teeth. Shown here is the Johnston design, ca. 1910.

Did You Know?

Old cultivators are a desirable collectible, although the market values still are very low. Nicely restored ones can command $100 to $200 or more.

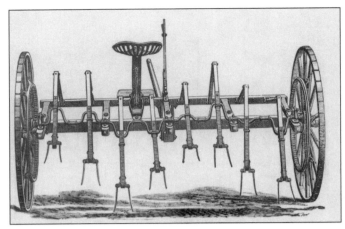

Johnston's Steel Hay Tedder, ca. 1910, was a rather heavy machine; a noticeable difference was the use of three-tine forks (most contemporaries used a two-tine fork). The entire design of the machine was such that it was almost impossible to wear out, especially if oil was kept on the moving parts. Most farmers used too much oil rather than too little, so these machines could run for years with very little attention.

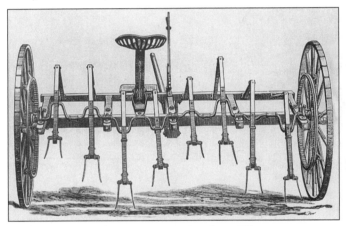

Keystone Manufacturing Co., Sterling, Ill.

During the 1880s, Keystone developed its hay tool line, including this Sterling Hay Tedder. This eight-fork machine was of wood construction. An interesting drive mechanism was used; the crankshaft for the forks is driven from large internal gears mounted on each wheel of the tedder. With its tedder, rake, mower and hay loader, Keystone claimed to have "The four best haying tools in America."

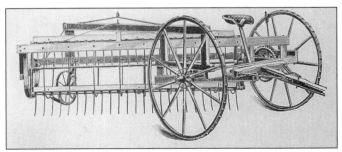

By 1894, Keystone had developed a side-delivery rake. This model was built entirely of wood; even the rake bars were of wood. An accompanying article explains to farmers that it was essential to rake the hay at the proper time and by delaying, "it will surely be sunburned on top while yet green and damp underneath." Keystone became a part of International Harvester in 1904.

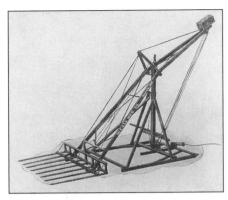

McCall Manufacturing Co., Macon, Mo.

A 1903 advertisement lists McCall Manufacturing Co., at Moberly, Mo. Then the Hay Tool Manufacturing Co. (see previous listing) appears with McCall as the General Manager. A 1908 advertisement shows McCall Manufacturing Co., at Macon, Mo. However, the McCall line attracted considerable attention since it was handled by most of the major machinery distributors in the Midwestern states.

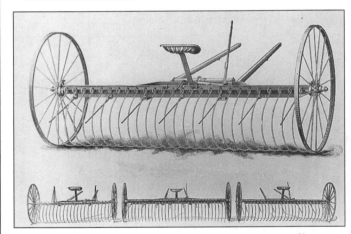

McCormick Harvesting Machine Co., Chicago, Ill.

About 1900, McCormick advertised its All-Steel Hay Rakes as "Kings of the Meadow." Indeed, this unit was available in three different sizes; the 8-foot with 20 or 26 teeth, the 10-foot with 26 or 32 teeth and the big 12-foot rake with 32 or 40 teeth. International Harvester Co., continued building virtually the same rake for years to come.

New Idea Spreader Co., Coldwater, Ohio

With its purchase of Sandwich Manufacturing Co., about 1930, New Idea gained a well-developed line of hay tools, including the Sandwich side-delivery rake. Building on this experience, New Idea offered hay rakes of various kinds, including this one of the late 1930s. The company continued with various side-delivery rakes for many years after.

D.M. Osborne & Co., Auburn, N.Y.

By the 1890s, the Osborne All-Steel Self-Dump Rake had taken the form shown here. An important feature was Osborne's early adoption of the self-lift design; this used power from the wheels to raise the tines, rather than requiring the farmer to raise and lower the rank with a hand lever with great frequency. This style was made in 8-, 10- and 12-foot sizes.

Like most companies of the time, Osborne considered the tedder to be an essential part of the hay tool arsenal. Its design shown here was somewhat different than its contemporaries. Each fork was equipped with a spring mechanism in case the forks hit an obstruction, preventing or minimizing breakage. The drive system for the tedder was at the center of the frame, rather than on the wheels; this kept hay from getting tangled in the gears and mechanism.

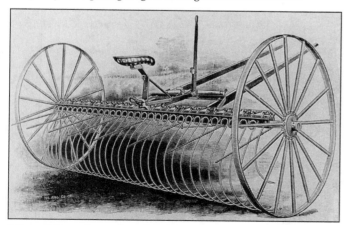

Plano Manufacturing Co., Plano, Ill.

Plano Manufacturing Co. had developed an excellent line of hay tools by 1900, including this combination hand-lift and self-lift rake. With this one major feature to its credit, the Plano looked much like its contemporaries. In 1902, Plano became a part of International Harvester Co. This illustration is from a German-language edition of the 1900 Plano catalog.

Rude Bros., Manufacturing Co., Liberty, Ind.

The Mascot Sulky Hay Rake was offered by Rude Bros., in 1887. At that time, the company was offering a wide range of "Indiana" implements, including wheat drills, corn drills and many other items. The dump rake shown here is of an all-wood design. Eventually, Rude Bros. began manufacturing manure spreaders. They were so successful that the company eventually built manure spreaders exclusively.

Sandwich Manufacturing Co., Sandwich, Ill.

Particularly in the Midwestern states, the Sandwich side-delivery rake was one of the most popular of its time. This model of 1903 underwent little change for several years; some of these early models were still in the field 40 years later. Eventually, tractor rakes designed for higher field speeds brought an end to their many years of service. The Sandwich line was the basis for the New Idea hay tool line; the latter bought out Sandwich about 1930.

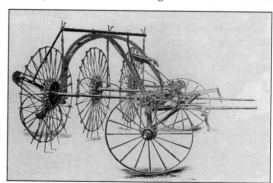

Stoddard Manufacturing Co., Dayton, Ohio

Perhaps the old adage that "history repeats itself" might be appropriate for the Beck side-delivery rake of the 1880s and 1890s. Over the years, various companies built "wheel rakes" somewhat in the form of the Beck; eventually the design was perfected. Today, the wheel rake is an important design. Unfortunately, it sold very poorly when it was first offered in 1887.

Thomas Manufacturing Co., Springfield, Ohio

Part of the 1887 Thomas hay tool line was its Royal Hay Rake, a hand-lift dump rake of all-wood construction. The simple lift mechanism with its linkages is quite evident in the engraving; one can only be amazed at the stamina required to work the lever up and down, almost constantly while raking a field of hay into windrows.

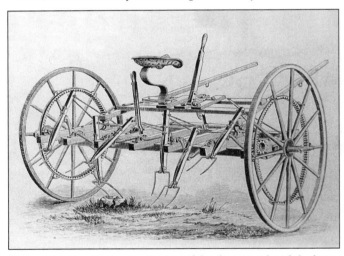

As noted, leading agriculturists of the day considered the hay tedder to be an essential part of the hay tool arsenal. The thinking was that leaving the hay in the swath to dry completely would sunburn the top while leaving the rest damp and uncured. Eventually, farmers quit buying into the argument, so the hay tedder fell into disuse. Shown here is the Thomas machine of 1887.

Trade Names

Acme	Acme Harvester Co.	Pekin, IL	1892
Acme	Acme Harvester Co.	Peoria, IL	1905
Acme	Byron Jackson Machine Works	San Francisco, CA	1892
Adriance	Adriance, Platt & Co.	Poughkeepsie, NY	1905
Advance	Farm Tool Mfg. Co.	Carrollton, MO	1905
Albion Champion	Gale Mfg. Co.	Albion, MI	1905
Alexander	Louden Machinery Co.	Fairfield, IA	1892
American	Ames Plow Co.	Boston, MA	1905
American	John Wolff	Albany, NY	1892
B. B.	Long & Alstatter Co.	Hamilton, OH	1905

Trade Names (cont...)

Belleville	Hayes Pump & Planter Co.	Galva, IL	1905
Belleville	Sucker State Drill Co.	Belleville, IL	1892
Beloit Champion	J. Thompson & Sons Mfg. Co.	Beloit, WI	1905
Bob White	Ohio Rake Co.	Dayton, OH	1905
Boss	Thos. K. Barley	Sedalia, MO	1905
C. B. & Q.	Chambers, Bering & Quinlan Co.	Decatur, IL	1905
Cascaden	Waterloo Threshing Machine Co.	Waterloo, IA	1905
Case	J. I. Case Threshing Machine Co.	Racine, WI	1929
Champion	International Harvester Co.	Chicago, IL	1905
Champion	Kansas City Hay Press Co.	Kansas City, MO	1905
Champion	Kirkwood, Miller & Co.	Peoria, IL	1892
Chaplin	A. H. Chaplin	Tecumseh, MI	1892
Chickasaw	Ohio Rake Co.	Dayton, OH	1892
Chieftain	Aultman, Miller & Co.	Akron, OH	1892
Chieftain	Western Machine Co.	Albia, IA	1905
Coates	A. W. Coates & Co.	Alliance, OH	1892
Columbian	Chariton Iron Works	Chariton, IA	1905
Constantine	George & Tweedale	Constantine, MI	1892
Crescent	Moline Plow Co.	Moline, IL	1913
Dain	Dain Mfg. Co.	Ottumwa, IA	1905
Daisy	Gale Mfg. Co.	Albion, MI	1905
Daisy	Gilliland, Jackson & Co.	Monroe City, MO	1892
Daisy	Riter's Metallic Picket Fence Co.	Liberty, IN	1892
Daley	Daley Mfg. Co.	DeKalb, IL	1892
Dayton	Ohio Rake Co.	Dayton, OH	1905
Deere	Deere & Mansur Co.	Moline, IL	1905
Deere	Deere & Mansur Co.	Moline, IL	1905
Deering	International Harvester Co.	Chicago, IL	1905
Denver	Plattner Implement Co.	Denver, CO	1909
Eagle	Eagle Mfg. Co.	Davenport, IA	1892
Eclipse	Eclipse Hay Press Co.	Kansas City, MO	1905
Eddy	W. Eddy Plow Co.	Greenwich, NY	1913
Ellwood	Rockford Mfg. Co.	Rockford, IL	1905
Emerson	Emerson Mfg. Co.	Rockford, IL	1909
Emerson	Emerson-Brantingham Co.	Rockford, IL	1915
Emperor	Wiard Plow Co.	Batavia, NY	1905
Excelsior	Alpheus Bailey	Sand Lake, NY	1892
Excelsior	Reed & Rogers Mfg. Co.	Vernon, IN	1892
F & J	Madison Plow Co.	Madison, WI	1913
F. & W.	Foster & Williams Mfg. Co.	Racine, WI	1905
Favorite	Farm Tool Mfg. Co.	Carrollton, MO	1905
Favorite	Sterling Mfg. Co.	Sterling, IL	1915
Fleming	Fleming & Sons Mfg. Co.	Huntsville, MO	1905
Flying Dutchman	Moline Plow Co.	Moline, IL	1915
Fuller & Johnson	Fuller & Johnson Mfg. Co.	Madison, WI	1905
Galena	Hughes & Smythe	Galena, OH	1892
Galena	Hughes & Smythe	Galena, OH	1905
Galt	Keystone Co.	Sterling, IL	1892

Trade Names (cont...)

Gazelle	Ohio Rake Co.	Dayton, OH	1905
Golden Farmer	Aultman, Miller & Co.	Akron, OH	1892
Grand Detour	Grand Detour Plow Co.	Dixon, IL	1905
H. V.	Hocking Valley Mfg. Co.	Lancaster, OH	1913
Hagerstown	D. F. Hull & Son	Hagerstown, MD	1892
Hamilton	Long & Alstatter Co.	Hamilton, OH	1905
Hay King	Tiffin Agricultural Works	Tiffin, OH	1892
Hayes-Dayton	Ohio Rake Co.	Dayton, OH	1915
Hocking Valley	Hocking Valley Mfg. Co.	Lancaster, OH	1905
Hocking Valley	Hocking Valley Mfg. Co.	Lancaster, OH	1905
Hodges	Acme Harvester Co.	Peoria, IL	1905
Hollingsworth	Hocking Valley Mfg. Co.	Lancaster, OH	1905
Hollingsworth	Ohio Rake Co.	Dayton, OH	1905
Hollingsworth	Stoddard Mfg. Co.	Dayton, OH	1905
Huber	Implement Mfg. Co.	Marion, OH	1905
Hummer	McCall Mfg. Co.	Macon, MO	1909
Imperial	Rockford Mfg. Co.	Rockford, IL	1892
Improved Western	Louden Machinery Co.	Fairfield, IA	1892
International	International Harvester Co.	Chicago, IL	1913
Iowa	Hay Tool Mfg. Co.	Council Bluffs, IA	1905
Iron Age	Bateman Mfg. Co.	Grenloch, NJ	1913
Ithaca	Williams Bros.	Ithaca, NY	1905
Jackson's Acme	Byron Jackson Machine Works	San Francisco, CA	1905
Jenkins	Jenkins Hay Rake & Stacker Co.	Browning, MO	1905
Johnston	Johnston Harvester Co.	Batavia, NY	1905
Jumbo	Thos. K. Barley	Sedalia, MO	1905
K. C.	Western Mfg. Co.	Kansas City, MO	1905
Keokuk	A. L. Courtright & Co.	Keokuk, IA	1892
Keystone	International Harvester Co.	Chicago, IL	1913
Keystone	Keystone Co.	Sterling, IL	1905
Lancaster	Hocking Valley Mfg. Co.	Lancaster, OH	1913
Lone Star	H. P. Deuscher Co.	Hamilton, OH	1905
Mascot	Rude Bros. Mfg. Co.	Liberty, IN	1892
Master	H. P. Deuscher Co.	Hamilton, OH	1905
McCormick	International Harvester Co.	Chicago, IL	1905
McCormick	International Harvester Co.	Chicago, IL	1913
Meadow Queen	Hannibal Hay Harvester Co.	Hannibal, MO	1892
Midland	Midland Mfg. Co.	Tarkio, MO	1905
Milwaukee	International Harvester Co.	Chicago, IL	1905
Milwaukee	International Harvester Co.	Chicago, IL	1913
Minneapolis	R. R. Howell Co.	Minneapolis, MN	1913
Minnie	Minnie Harvester Co.	St. Paul, MN	1905
Model	Roderick Lean Mfg. Co.	Mansfield, OH	1905
Moline	Minneapolis-Moline Co.	Minneapolis, MN	1936
Monarch	Acme Harvester Co.	Peoria, IL	1905

Trade Names (cont...)

Morgan	D. S. Morgan & Co.	Brockport, NY	1892
National	Belcher & Taylor Agricultural Co.	Chicopee Falls, MA	1905
New Deere	Deere & Mansur Co.	Moline, IL	1905
New Idea	New Idea Spreader Co.	Coldwater, OH	1931
New Meadow	E. Children's Sons Mfg. Co.	Council Bluffs, IA	1905
New York Champion	Patten & Stafford Co.	Canastota, NY	1905
New Yorker	Chapinville Wheel Co.	Poughkeepsie, NY	1905
Novelty	Geo. S. Comstock	Mechanicsburg, PA	1913
O. K.	Scott Hay Press Co.	Kansas City, MO	1905
Ohio	Ohio Rake Co.	Dayton, OH	1915
Ohio Champion	Ohio Rake Co.	Dayton, OH	1905
Oliver	Oliver Farm Equipment Co.	Chicago, IL	1936
Osborne	D. M. Osborne Co.	Auburn, NY	1905
Osborne	International Harvester Co.	Chicago, IL	1913
Ottumwa	LaCrosse Mfg. Co.	Ottumwa, IA	1909
Peerless	Famous Mfg. Co.	Chicago, IL	1892
Plano	International Harvester Co.	Chicago, IL	1905
Plano	International Harvester Co.	Chicago, IL	1913
Plano	J. R. Mears	Morrill, ME	1892
Plattner	Plattner Implement Co.	Denver, CO	1905
Prairie Queen	Kingman & Co.	Peoria, IL	1892
Progress	B. F. Avery & Sons Mfg. Co.	Louisville, KY	1913
Quail	Ohio Rake Co.	Dayton, OH	1905
Queen	David Bradley Mfg. Co.	Bradley, IL	1905
Rancher	E. Children's Sons Mfg. Co.	Council Bluffs, IA	1905
Red Bird	John Dodds Mfg. Co.	Dayton, OH	1892
Reliable	Thomas Mfg. Co.	Springfield, OH	1913
Richmond Champion	Wayne Works	Richmond, IN	1905
Risedorph	Risedorph Agricultural Works	Albany, NY	1905
Robison	Geo. E. Robison	Locke, NY	1905
Rock Island	Rock Island Plow Co.	Rock Island, IL	1922
Roderick Lean	Roderick Lean Mfg. Co.	Mansfield, OH	1905
Rowell	J. S. Rowell Mfg. Co.	Beaver Dam, WI	1905
Sandow	Emerson-Brantingham Co.	Rockford, IL	1913
Sandwich	Sandwich Mfg. Co.	Sandwich, IL	1905
Sattley	Racine-Sattley Co.	Moline, IL	1913
Stahl	Ohio Cultivator Co.	Bellevue, OH	1892
Standard Champion	Emerson Mfg. Co.	Rockford, IL	1905
Standard Sandow	Emerson Mfg. Co.	Rockford, IL	1905
Steel King	Messinger Mfg. Co.	Tatamy, PA	1905
Steel King	Ohio Rake Co.	Dayton, OH	1905
Steel Reliable	Thomas Mfg. Co.	Springfield, OH	1905
Steel Western	Thomas Mfg. Co.	Springfield, OH	1905
Sterling	Sterling Mfg. Co.	Sterling, IL	1905
Sterling	Sterling Mfg. Co.	Sterling, IL	1905
Strait's	Clipper Chilled Plow Co.	Elmira, NY	1905
Success	E. Children's Sons Mfg. Co.	Council Bluffs, IA	1905

Trade Names (cont...)

Sucker State	Hayes Pump & Planter Co.	Galva, IL	1905
Superior	Superior Hay Stacker Co.	Linneus, MO	1905
Surprise	Reed & Rogers Mfg. Co.	Vernon, IN	1905
Thomas	Thomas Mfg. Co.	Springfield, OH	1905
Thompson	H. D. Busing & Co.	Rockford, IL	1892
Thompson	J. Thompson & Sons Mfg. Co.	Beloit, WI	1913
Tiger	Stoddard Mfg. Co.	Dayton, OH	1905
Tommy Atkins	Acme Harvester Co.	Peoria, IL	1905
Triumph	Stoddard Mfg. Co.	Dayton, OH	1905
Union	Western Mfg. Co.	Lincoln, NE	1892
Veteran	Abram Ellwood	Sycamore, IL	1892
Victor	Hughes & Smythe	Galena, OH	1905
Walker	Walker Mfg. Co.	Council Bluffs, IA	1905
Walter A. Wood	Walter A. Wood Mowing & R. M. Co.	Hoosick Falls, NY	1905
Winnishiek	Cascaden Mfg. Co.	Waterloo, IA	1909
Wixcel	Wixcel Mfg. Co.	Marcus, IA	1913
Worcester	Richardson Mfg. Co.	Worcester, MA	1905
Wright	Wright Rake & Stacker Co.	Wheeling, MO	1909
Yankee	Chas. G. Allen Co.	Barre, MA	1929

Hay Stackers

In certain areas, the hay stacker developed as an important part of the hay harvest. Usually these areas stored hay in outdoor stacks rather than in barns. The hay stacker mechanized the process to some extent. A few of these stackers are also illustrated in the Hay Rakes section, especially because a few were intended as combination machines to rake and stack the hay crop.

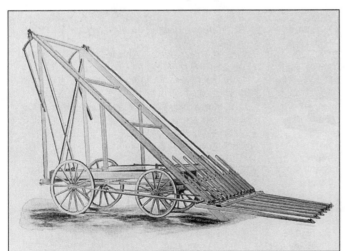

Dain Manufacturing Co., Ottumwa, Iowa

Joseph Dain began building hay equipment in Kansas City in 1882. The company moved to Carrollton, Mo., in 1889, remaining there until removing to Ottumwa in 1900. Eventually, the Dain plant came under ownership of Deere & Co. Shown here is the Dain Automatic Steel-Armed Hay Stacker of 1892; the stacker offered at Ottumwa in 1900 was virtually identical.

Famous Manufacturing Co., Chicago, Ill.

In 1884, Famous Manufacturing Co., illustrated its Peerless Combined Hay Stacker & Derrick, noting that it was the only such machine in existence. It was also claimed that the Peerless was the only machine to lift to the height of the stack, then allowing the hay to slide off the arms. Little else is known of this particular device.

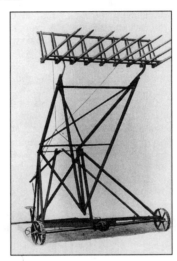

Wyatt Manufacturing Co., Salina, Kan.

From the 1930s comes this wood-frame stacker from Wyatt. Its Jayhawk line of stackers gained wide renown; there were Jayhawkers present almost everywhere stackers were used. The company modernized its machines in the 1940s and continued building them for some time after. Eventually, the hay baler took precedence and, when "big bales" came along, demand for the Jayhawk dwindled.

Trade Names

A. B. C.	A. B. Clippinger & Son Co.	Kansas City, KS	1909
Acme	Acme Harvester Co.	Peoria, IL	1892
Adjustable Arm	Jenkins Hay Rake & Stacker Co.	Chillicothe, MO	1913
Aerial	McCall Mfg. Co.	Macon, MO	1909
American	Farm Tool Mfg. Co.	Carrollton, MO	1905
Anderson	Anderson Co.	St. Paul, MN	1909
Barley	Thos. K. Barley	Sedalia, MO	1909
Bovee	Bovee Harvesting Machine Co.	Tama, IA	1892
Buchey	Midland Mfg. Co.	Tarkio, MO	1909
Cascaden	Waterloo Threshing Machine Co.	Waterloo, IA	1905

Trade Names (cont...)

Champion	International Harvester Co.	Chicago, IL	1905
Champion	Kansas City Hay Press Co.	Kansas City, MO	1892
Chieftain	Western Machine Co.	Albia, IA	1905
Climax	Jenkins Hay Rake & Stacker Co.	Browning, MO	1905
Columbian	Chariton Iron Works	Chariton, IA	1905
Cope	Dempster Mill Mfg. Co.	Beatrice, NE	1915
Cyclone	Ideal Pump & Mfg. Co.	Green City, MO	1909
Dain	Dain Mfg. Co.	Carrollton, MO	1892
Dain	Dain Mfg. Co.	Ottumwa, IA	1905
Daisy	Gilliland, Jackson & Co.	Monroe City, MO	1892
Danielson	Danielson Implement Co.	Independence, MO	1909
Deering	International Harvester Co.	Chicago, IL	1905
Eclipse	Byron Jackson	San Francisco, CA	1892
Eclipse	Eclipse Hay Press Co.	Kansas City, MO	1905
Emerson	Emerson-Brantinham Co.	Rockford, IL	1913
Fleming's U. S.	Fleming Mfg. Co.	Huntsville, MO	1892
Giant	Thos. K. Barley	Sedalia, MO	1905
Hannibal	Hannibal Hay Harvester Co.	Hannibal, MO	1892
Harris	Litchfield Mfg. Co.	Waterloo, IA	1909
Harris	Litchfield Mfg. Co.	Waterloo, IA	1913
Hawkeye	A. L. Courtright & Co.	Keokuk, IA	1892
Hodges	Acme Harvester Co.	Peoria, IL	1909
International	International Harvester Co.	Chicago, IL	1909
Iowa	Hay Tool Mfg. Co.	Council Bluffs, IA	1905
Jackson's	Byron Jackson Machine Works	San Francisco, CA	1909
Jayhawk	F. Wyatt Mfg. Co.	Salina, KS	1909
Jenkins	Jenkins Hay Rake & Stacker Co.	Browning, MO	1892
LaCrosse	LaCrosse Hay Tool Co.	Ottumwa, IA	1909
Lark	Thos. K. Barley	Sedalia, MO	1909
Law	Hackney Mfg. Co.	St. Paul, MN	1913
Lever Lift	Walker Mfg. Co.	Council Bluffs, IA	1905
Lightning	Kansas City Hay Press Co.	Kansas City, MO	1905
Louden's	Louden Machinery Co.	Fairfield, IA	1892
McCormick	International Harvester Co.	Chicago, IL	1905
McCormick-Deering	International Harvester Co.	Chicago, IL	1929
Meadow Lark	J. B. Barley, Bro. & Co.	Sedalia, MO	1892
Meadow Lark	Thos. K. Barley	Sedalia, MO	1905
Midland	Midland Mfg. Co.	Tarkio, MO	1909
New Century	Farm Tool Mfg. Co.	Carrollton, MO	1905
New Idea	Dain Mfg. Co.	Ottumwa, IA	1913
New Iowa	Hay Tool Mfg. Co.	Council Bluffs, IA	1913
New Meadow Queen	E. Children's Sons Mfg. Co.	Council Bluffs, IA	1905

Trade Names (cont...)

New Royal	Monarch Grubber Co.	Lone Tree, IA	1913
O. K.	Scott Hay Press Co.	Kansas City, MO	1905
Ottumwa	LaCrosse Hay Tool Co.	Ottumwa, IA	1909
Peerless	Famous Mfg. Co.	Chicago, IL	1892
Plattner	Plattner Implement Co.	Denver, CO	1905
Plattner-Yale	Yale & Hopewell Mfg. Co.	Lincoln, NE	1922
Rancher	E. Children's Sons Mfg. Co.	Council Bluffs, IA	1905
Rochester	Ricker & Montgomery	Rochester, NY	1892
Roseberry	O. F. Orndorff	Council Bluffs, IA	1915
Sampson	Thos. K. Barley	Sedalia, MO	1909
Stalcup	Stalcup Hay Stacker Co.	Unionville, MO	1905
Stearns	Stearns Mfg. Co.	Los Angeles, CA	1892
Sunflower	Sunflower Mfg. Co.	Manhattan, KS	1913
Superior	Superior Hay Stacker Co.	Linneus, MO	1905
Twentieth Century	Farm Tool Mfg. Co.	Carrollton, MO	1905
U. S.	U. S. Hay Press Supply Co.	Kansas City, MO	1892
Universal	Dain Mfg. Co.	Ottumwa, IA	1909
Western Epic	Western Land Roller Co.	Hastings, NE	1929
Will Jr.	Ideal Pump & Mfg. Co.	Green City, MO	1909
Wright	Wright Rake and Stacker Co.	Kansas City, MO	1913
Wright	Wright Rake and Stacker Co.	Wheeling, MO	1909

Hay Tools

Under this heading one could include a small book in itself, given the multitude of hay carriers, pulleys, hay forks, slings, pitch forks and other items incidental to the harvesting and handling of hay. Some of these items are already displayed in various guides to antiques and some will be found scattered in various sections of this book. Given the huge amount of material encompassed by this title, this section gives but a cameo view of the larger scene; for instance, in 1910, there were more than 50 different kinds of hay carriers offered to the farmer.

Some of the items shown here have come to the ranking of a collectible farm antique; very early wooden forks for instance, might bring $100 or perhaps even more, while common metal forks usually sell from $10 and upwards. An ordinary hay carrier might now bring $40 and various kinds of hay knives might sell from $15 to $35.

Readers should consult various pricing guides, since many hay tools are usually listed. Eventually, the author hopes to compile a guide to farmstead tools and equipment as a comprehensive treatment of the subject. Attempting this within the present volume would be to deny illustration of many other important pieces of farm equipment.

Fleming & Sons Manufacturing Co., Huntsville, Mo.

Numerous kinds of hay stackers, buck rakes, push rakes and related equipment emerged in the 1880s. These designs were well developed during the 1890s, with this offering from Fleming coming in 1899. Additional illustrations of this equipment can be found under Hay Stackers and other hay equipment sections within this book.

Hoth Hay Mower Co., Luana, Iowa

The origins of this company are unknown; in the 1930s, Hoth offered this belt-driven hoist specifically for raising hay into a barn. Through a rope system, the hoist could be operated directly from the load. Machines like this eliminated the need for a horse to pull hay into the barn; many "farm kids" got the chance to walk an old plow horse for this job. With hay-making in full swing, there were a lot of trips back and forth in a day's time.

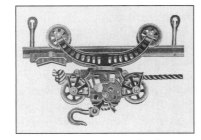

Hunt, Helm & Ferris Co., Harvard, Ill.

In 1904, this company offered two new hay carriers to the farmer, supplementing its already extensive line of Star hay tools. This one is shown with the track latch plainly visible to the left. As the carrier returned to the left, it engaged the latch, holding it firmly in position. A mechanism within the carrier tripped it from the latch after locking the load into the carrier for the lateral journey into the depths of the barn.

Louden Machinery Co., Fairfield, Iowa

By 1888, Louden had developed the hay sling for carrying hay into a barn. Usually two or three slings were placed in the load, one at the bottom, with one or two more being laid out as the load was built. At the barn, the farmer hooked the two ends of the sling into the pulleys as shown, thus carrying the loose hay into the barn. At the proper time, he pulled the trip rope, releasing one end of the sling and completing the process.

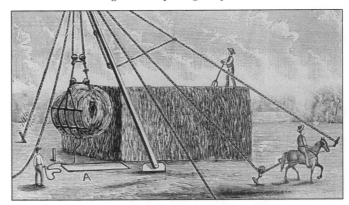

For outside stacking, Louden offered this design in 1888. With a unique arrangement of ropes and pulleys, a hay sling carries another load to the top of the stack. While this artist's conception of a hay stack goes to the extreme, building a straight and square hay stack was indeed an art, mastered by some and giving mediocre results for many others.

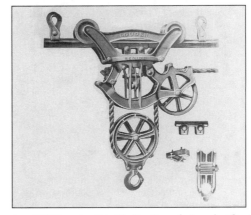

From about 1910 comes this illustration of a Louden Senior Fork Carrier. The continued building of large barns at the time demanded larger and heavier hay carriers, with this one featuring roller bearings and a swivel frame. Many hay carriers were operated for decades with little or no attention.

Mechanizing the hay harvest was important to the Louden operation; this illustration from about 1915 demonstrates the Louden Power Hoist, showing its operation. With an operator at the hoist, lifting the load was under complete control, as was the return of the carrier for the next load. The hoist is being operated by a Monitor engine from Baker Manufacturing Co., Evansville, Wis.

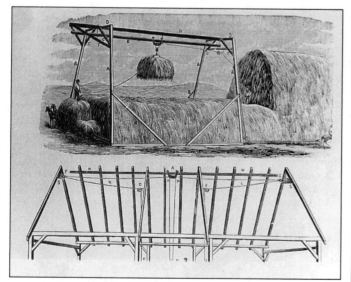

F.E. Myers & Bro., Ashland, Ohio

A pioneer in the development of hay tools, Myers offered this portable hay stacker in 1888. It was essentially a framework carrying the same kind of track as would have been used for unloading into a barn. The man with the trip rope could drop the load at any point; far to the back is another man ready to stack the coming load.

Did You Know?

The Red Chief table-top corn sheller was priced at $2.25 in 1918.

From 1890 comes this catalog illustration demonstrating the Myers system to prospective buyers. Many early barns had a drive-through area, since in earlier times the hay was pitched by hand into the barn for mowing. With this center-mounted carrier, hay could be carried to either end of the barn using a suitable and rather complicated pulley arrangement.

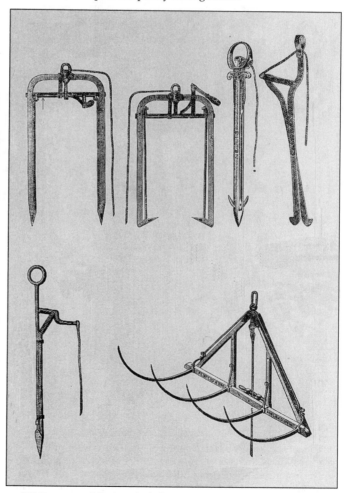

While some of the hay fork designs pictured here were unique to the Myers line, some were commonly used by almost every manufacturer. This illustration from an 1890 pictures the most commonly used styles of the time. Not shown is the hay sling, previously referred to in this section.

By 1890, Myers had developed its New Myers' Nickel Plate Hay Carrier for outside hay stacks. Its cable-track design was a new feature. Ordinarily, this unit was shipped without the support timbers; they could be secured locally, with the hardware fitted on-site. This design was fairly popular, especially when the hay crop was larger than the capacity of the barn.

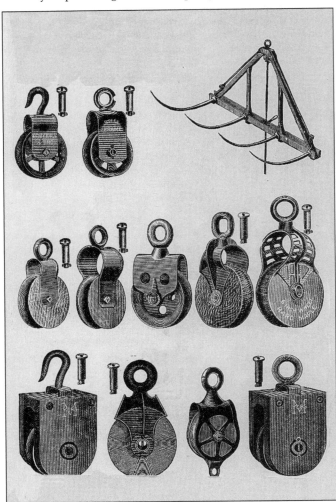

Today's collectors of farm antiques often encounter pulleys of various kinds. Indeed, there were a host of different styles. In most instances, a wooden pulley was preferred to one of iron, since it was considered that wood and rope got along better than rope and iron. While this selection of pulleys is from an 1890 Myers catalog, there were countless others from dozens of different companies.

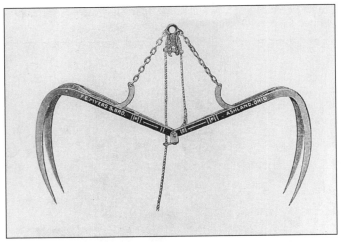

In 1909, Myers introduced its new Automatic Grapple Fork. This design was suitable for handling loose or baled hay. It was also easy to set and could handle long or short hay with ease. In contrast, the single- and double-harpoon designs were best suited to long material such as timothy. Within a few years, the grapple fork was adopted by most farmers; the hay sling, the harpoon fork and other designs now sat quietly in a corner.

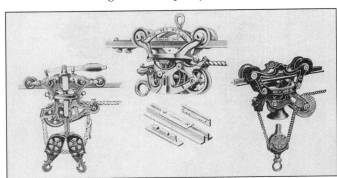

Ney Manufacturing Co., Canton, Ohio

A close competitor to the Myers line was the Ney; this company was well known for its hay tools. The size of its operation was such that it maintained branch houses at Minneapolis, Peoria, Ill., and Council Bluffs, Iowa. Ney hay tools were marketed for many years, with this 1904 illustration showing three of its hay carrier designs.

North River Agricultural Works, New York, N.Y.

An 1866 catalog of North River Agricultural Works illustrates Beardsley's Patent Hay Elevator or Horse Power Fork. It consisted of a so-called horse pitchfork, also shown in this heading, along with a suitable arrangement of ropes and pulleys. Despite the dearth of advanced features, this system still represented a major improvement over hand methods.

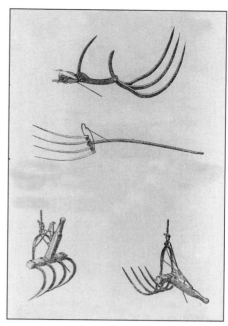

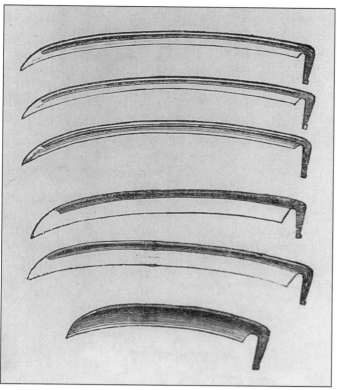

While the mowing machine was gaining favor by 1866, the scythe was still an important part of the farm tool arsenal. Shown here are various styles of the period, including from top to bottom, grass, lawn, grain and three styles of bramble or bush scythes. With the scythe, the farmer needed a grindstone for regrinding, plus a whetstone carried in the pocket, to maintain a razor-sharp edge.

Clement's Improved Horse Hay Fork is shown at the top of this 1866 illustration; below it is Clowe's Patent Straw and Barley Fork, another of the special designs developed for a special need. This one could be furnished with wood or steel tines, as desired. At the bottom of this illustration is Palmer's Excelsior Self-Sustaining Horse Pitchfork, another early design; the company claimed to have made 7,000 of these forks in 1863, with another 12,000 in 1864.

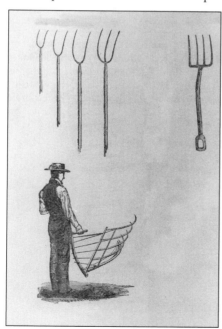

In its 1866 catalog, North River Agricultural Works offered numerous kinds of forks; four styles of hay forks or pitch forks are pictured to the left, and at the bottom is Grant's Patent Grain Cradle. Using one of these required a bit of dexterity and practice. To the right is a four-tine manure fork. In addition, North River offered other kinds of forks for special purposes.

J.E. Porter Co., Ottawa, Ill.

An early manufacturer of hay tools and equipment, Porter offered this hay-carrier design in 1905. Porter, among others, initially used a wooden track for the carrier instead of the steel design shown here. Large barns usually had the track and its mountings installed when the structure was built; doing so afterwards was a formidable project unless, of course, the barn was filled with hay.

Already in 1907, Porter offered its Nelson Friction Windlass that was patented a couple of years earlier. This engine-driven hoist mechanized the operation of getting hay into the barn and gained a certain popularity. Porter continued manufacturing hay tools into the 1930s, but a 1939 listing shows that repair parts for the Porter line were available from Louden Machinery Co., listed previously in this section.

Whitman & Barnes Manufacturing Co., Chicago, Ill.

Whitman & Barnes was famous for its Diamond line of hay tools. This illustration of the early 1900s shows a Diamond carrier installed in an early barn. The company gave instructions for mounting the track: "Scaffold by placing a rope from rafter to rafter, say six feet from the ridge pole or peak and about 10 feet apart. Then place an extension ladder across the ropes with a board to stand on. Now nail one rafter bracket at each end of the barn, draw a line from one end to the other and stretch it tight." Once this was completed, the same process continued, mounting each bracket to the line for perfect alignment of the finished track.

Did You Know?

Today, most farm wagons in reasonably good condition will bring $500 or more, while a good carriage will be much more expensive. Nicely restored carriages—especially one that is quite fancy and equipped with brass driving lights and other paraphernalia—can often bring $2,000 or more.

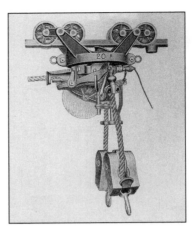

For 1908, Whitman & Barnes offered this heavy hay carrier utilizing a total of eight truck wheels to carry the load. Since wooden pulleys were preferred by some, the idler pulley at the bottom side of this carrier is made of wood, probably containing a hardened steel bearing at its center.

Some farmers and some manufacturers, for that matter, preferred a 4-by-4 inch wooden track to a steel track. One such design was offered by Whitman & Barnes in the early 1900s; this particular design was patented in 1907. Eventually, the wood-track design fell into disfavor with the steel track being found preferable.

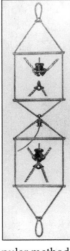

The hay sling was a popular method of lifting hay into a barn. Shown here is the Whitman & Barnes design of the early 1900s. One of these was placed on the floor of the hay rack, followed by one or two more as the layers of hay accumulated. After going into the barn, the load was dropped by pulling the trip rope shown at the center of the illustration. This released a latch, separating the two halves of the sling.

As noted earlier in this section, every supplier of hay tools offered a wide range of pulleys and sheaves to route the rope. The vast majority of these pulleys were of hard wood, carried by a steel or iron shackle. Some were bushed with steel and some with rawhide. Some had plain bearings and others had roller bearings. The different examples were almost without limits.

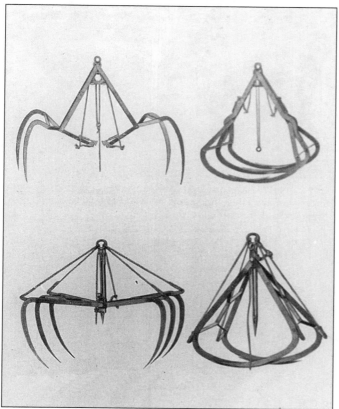

Grapple forks came into popularity during the early 1900s, eventually displacing the hay sling, the harpoon fork and other devices. Whitman & Barnes, like other companies, offered many styles and sizes of grapple forks. Some were of four-tine design and others used six tines. The Jackson fork and the California fork, both shown at the bottom of this illustration, eventually fell into disuse. After 1915, Whitman & Barnes disappeared from the scene.

Trade Names

Acme **Carriers**	J. E. Porter	Ottawa, IL	1905
Acme	Stowell Mfg. & Foundry Co.	South Milwaukee, WI	1905
Ajax	Stowell Mfg. & Foundry Co.	South Milwaukee, WI	1905
Apex	Stowell Mfg. & Foundry Co.	South Milwaukee, WI	1905
Argus	Stowell Mfg. & Foundry Co.	South Milwaukee, WI	1905
Arion	Stowell Mfg. & Foundry Co.	South Milwaukee, WI	1905
Atlas	Stowell Mfg. & Foundry Co.	South Milwaukee, WI	1905
Badger	Stowell Mfg. & Foundry Co.	South Milwaukee, WI	1905
Barnes	J. E. Porter	Ottawa, WI	1905
Boyd's	J. M. Boyd	Fond du Lac, WI	1892
Boyd's	Stowell Mfg. & Foundry Co.	South Milwaukee, WI	1905
Capital	Wheel & Seeder Mfg. Co.	LaCrosse, WI	1892
Chamberlin's	Chamberlin Mfg. Co.	Newton, NJ	1892
Champion	J. E. Porter	Ottawa, IL	1905
Champion	Star Seeder Co.	Shortsville, NY	1905
Church	Church Hay Tool Co.	Harvard, IL	1905
Church	E. L. Church	Harvard, IL	1892
Clark's	Eureka Mower Co.	Utica, NY	1905
Clark's	W. I. Scott	Bridgewater, NY	1892
Columbia	R. C. Jordan	Ottawa, IL	1905
Columbian	J. E. Porter	Ottawa, IL	1905
Cross	Fultonville Mfg. Co.	Fultonville, IL	1905
Diamond	Whitman & Barnes Mfg. Co.	Chicago, IL	1905
Eagle	Eagle Mfg. Co.	Appleton, WI	1892
Farrell's	John Farrell	Huntsville, NJ	1892
Fayette	Fayette Mfg. Co.	Fayette, OH	189
Fowler	Fowler & Farrington	Taughannock Falls, NY	1892
Genuine Ney	Ney Mfg. Co.	Canton, OH	1905
Giant	J. A. Cross	Fultonville, NY	1892
Hercules	Goshen Mfg. Co.	Goshen, IN	1892
Jewel	Louden Machinery Co.	Fairfield, IA	1905
Jordan	Jordan & Hamilton	Ottawa, IL	1892
Jordan	R. C. Jordan	Ottawa, IL	1905
Jumbo	Wisconsin Hay Tool Mfg. Co.	Ottawa, IL	1892
Kingman	Kingman & Co.	Peoria, IL	1892
King's Improved	Marion Jack & Hoist Co.	Marion, OH	1892
Law's	Law Mfg. Co.	St. Paul, MN	1905
Leader	Milwaukee Hay Tool Co.	Milwaukee, WI	1892
Louden	Louden Machinery Co.	Fairfield, IA	1892
Milwaukee	Milwaukee Hay Tool Co.	Milwaukee, WI	1892]
Myers'	F. E. Myers & Bro.	Ashland, OH	1892
Ney	Ney Mfg. Co.	Canton, OH	1892
Ney's Latest	V. L. Ney Co.	Canton, OH	1905

Trade Names (cont...)			
Oborn	Oborn Bros.	Marion, OH	1892
Ottawa	Jordan & Hamilton	Ottawa, IL	1892
Ottawa	R. C. Jordan	Ottawa, IL	1905
Palmyra	Geo. H. Rundle	Palmyra, WI	1892
Porter's	J. E. Porter	Ottawa, IL	1892
Ricker	Ricker Mfg. Co.	Rochester, NY	1905
Rochester	Ricker & Montgomery	Rochester, NY	1892
Royal	Louden Machinery Co.	Fairfield, IA	1905
South Western	South Western Supply Co.	St. Louis, MO	1892
Star	Hunt, Helm & Ferris Co.	Harvard, IL	1905
Strickler's	Janesville Hay Tool Co.	Janesville, WI	1892
Swift's	Swift & Monfort	Millbrook, NY	1892
Syracuse	Syracuse Chilled Plow Co.	Syracuse, NY	1905
Trackless	Trackless Hay Elevator Co.	Toledo, OH	1892
Victor	Louden Machinery Co.	Fairfield, IA	1905
Victor	Superior Mfg. Co.	Martinsville, OH	1892
Walker	Byron Jackson Machine Works	San Francisco, CA	1905
Wisconsin	Milwaukee Hay Tool Co.	Milwaukee, WI	1892

Hemp Mills

Hemp mills gained limited attention, particularly during the 1800s; after suitable treatment, the fibers were used for cordage. Of the farm equipment manufacturers, International Harvester and some of its predecessors were among the leaders, along with a few others. Interest in hemp waned until World War I. At that time, the scarcity of imported materials led to a renewal of domestic hemp production; this phenomenon repeated itself during World War II. Further information on hemp machines can be found in the author's *150 Years of International Harvester* (Crestline/Motorbooks, 1981).

An 1892 advertisement from C. Aultman & Co., Canton, Ohio. For a time, this company built the Shely Hemp and Fibre Brake. Chances are that production of this machine was very limited,

given the general lack of interest in this crop. A few other companies built this equipment and most of them have disappeared without a trace of their activities.

Hog Equipment

If there were room in this book, one could include literally dozens of hog oilers, hog waterers and related items, most made of cast iron. In recent years, hog oilers or hog greasers have become an important farm collectible, with some of these bringing considerable sums. This market seems to be quite volatile. While a farmer might sell an old abandoned oiler for $5 or $10, a collector might give $100 or even much more for a particularly desirable style. Since the collecting of hog oilers and hog waterers is a relatively new hobby, many of the current price guides to farm collectibles do not include any pricing for these items. Buyers and sellers alike are advised to familiarize themselves with these items at various shows, flea markets and the like to gain an idea of the values in their area.

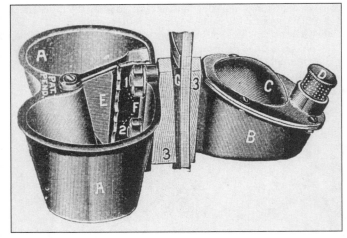

B-B Manufacturing Co., Davenport, Iowa

By the early 1900s, numerous companies were offering hog waterers similar to this one; it was mounted to a large barrel or a livestock tank for automatic watering.

Bain Bros., Manufacturing Co., Cedar Rapids, Iowa

Bain Bros. offered its Helm Sanitary Hog Fountain in 1923. This was a valveless and floatless design, totally automatic and used mainly for hog and sheep watering.

From a 1923 catalog comes this illustration of Bain's Faultless Hog Waterer, available in 55-gallon and 90-gallon sizes. This one also had a door in the side so that during cold weather a kerosene lamp could be placed beneath to prevent freezing. Refilling the lamps was a job that came along every couple of days. Most of the time, it seemed that the weather was at its worst during this task, whether it was rain, wind, snow or sub-zero temperatures.

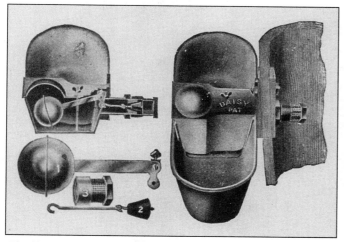

Challenge Co., Batavia, Ill.

With its large trade following, Challenge had no problem in selling its Daisy Hog Waterers. Thousands of these appeared all over the country and a fair number still appear today. As shown here, the Daisy was attached to the side of a barrel, giving the farmer a cheap and easy method of obtaining a self-waterer. This one had a 1910 price of $3.

Did You Know?

Antique corn shellers are a popular farm collectible; small one- and two-hole designs usually bring $50 or more, while larger four- and six-hole versions fall in the $250 to $500 range.

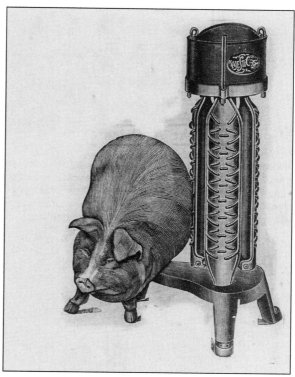

Hartman Co., Chicago, Ill.

Among its many products, the Hartman Co., catalog of 1920 offered the Majestic Valveless Hog Oiler, citing its benefits in improving the health of the animals, adding to their comfort and manifesting improved weight gains.

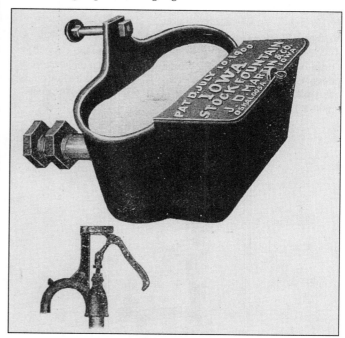

J.D. Martin & Co., Oskaloosa, Iowa

The Iowa Automatic Stock Fountain first appeared about 1900; this one did not use a float, but worked off of a spring mechanism. Also pictured in this 1909 illustration is a frost hydrant to provide water wherever wanted and at any time of year. In the early 1900s, farmers got their first taste of running water on the farm by digging in water pipes to the barn and other areas.

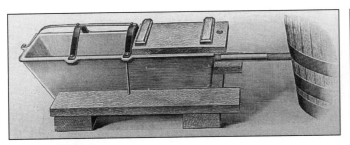

Maytag Co., Newton, Iowa

Hawkeye Automatic Hog Waterers were a 1910 product of Maytag Co. As shown here, the waterer was connected directly to a large barrel, but could also be fitted to a stock tank or even to a pressurized water pipe. Sometimes the whole affair was bolted to a wooden skid, making the outfit semi-portable.

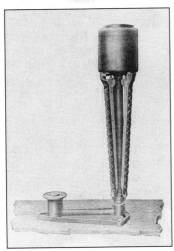

National Oiler Co., Richmond, Ind.

A 1914 advertisement illustrates the National Hog Oiler. The promotional material that accompanied this unit gave some very persuasive claims as to the benefits of these oilers. With hog oilers and related equipment, the relatively new livestock care industry gained new impetus.

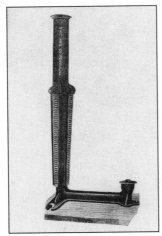

O.H.C. Manufacturing Co., Peoria, Ill.

Hog oilers took on virtually every shape and size imaginable. This interesting cast-iron design is from 1914. Each company tried to offer what it thought was the simplest, cheapest and best hog oiler on the market. Most designs lasted but a few years, to be replaced with still other designs

O'Neil Implement Co., Marseilles, Ill.

As part of its 1910 line, O'Neil offered this combination hog trough and twin oiler in one unit. A large unit is placed at one end, with a small unit at the other. Between them is a heavy cast-iron trough. This outfit sold for $15.

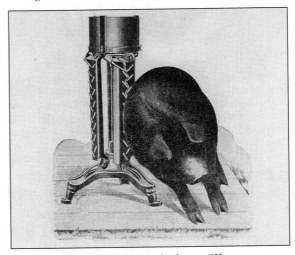

Rowe Manufacturing Co., Galesburg, Ill.

In 1914, Rowe offered its Row Rubbing Post, a design patented by Alvin V. Rowe. Presumably, the company also manufactured other items, but, as with many small companies, little or no history can be found.

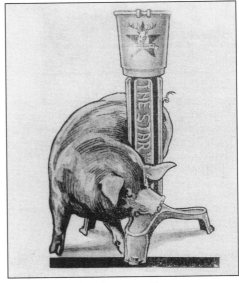

Illinois Implement Co., Peoria, Ill.

No information regarding this firm has been located outside of this 1914 advertisement. Featured was the Star hog oiler, another design competing with dozens of others for a share of the hog equipment market.

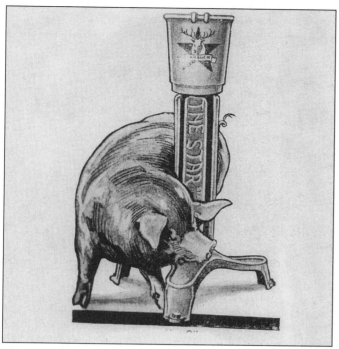

Starbuc Manufacturing Co., Peoria, Ill.

For reasons now obscured by time, Star hog oilers were advertised simultaneously by Illinois Implement Co. shown above and Starbuc Manufacturing Co., also of Peoria. The advertising is identical, even using the same engraving. Curiously, the same advertisements occur in the same issue of *Farm Machinery Magazine*.

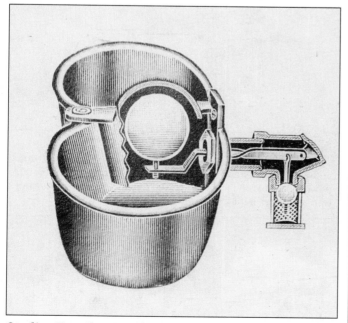

Sterling Foundry Co., Sterling, Ill.

For manufacturers up to the 1930s, iron castings were the preferred method of making an article. Small foundries were a frequent sight; many small towns were within 20 miles or less of a foundry. Thus hog waterers and similar items could be readily manufactured. The "Best" hog waterer from Sterling Foundry Co., was a 1915 creation.

Weldex Manufacturing Co., Richmond, Ind.

This 1914 design was called the Weldex Wonder Oiler; it was unique in its design, using welded steel components almost exclusively. A few manufacturers began using welded steel fabrication at this time, but progress was slow and many pieces of farm equipment into the 1930s still employed iron castings to a great extent.

Horse Powers

By the 1830s, the tread power shown in this section had become a practical machine. As shown in various illustrations in this section and scattered throughout this book, are various kinds of tread powers. The tread power consisted of a moving belt, usually constructed of heavy wooden slats connected at each end by an endless chain. While most of these were for horses, smaller ones were also made as dog powers or sheep powers. The tread power was also called a railway power; the two terms are synonymous.

Horse powers and sweep powers are the same thing; farmers sometimes simply called them "powers." These machines were of several varieties. First, the power was either a low- or high-speed power. The earliest designs were by the Pitts brothers, built by them subsequent to their development of the threshing machine in the 1830s. It is generally considered that the Pitts was the first successful sweep power. It was later modified and improved as the Pitts-Carey power.

Another important design was the Woodbury power; this one appeared in the early 1850s, but mechanical problems did not bring it to the forefront. Eventually, W.W. Dingee of J.I. Case Threshing Machine Co., modified the Woodbury power; from it came the best known of the later styles, the Dingee power. This model was built and sold in large numbers by J.I. Case.

Numerous other styles appeared and many were built under license from its respective patentees. Especially before 1910, many threshing machine companies also offered a sweep power. In most cases, the thresher manufacturer built the power, using the design perfected by others. Evidence of a changing source of power, is the fact, that in 1915 there were still more than 30 different companies making sweep powers, plus at least a dozen offering railway powers. By the 1930s, there were only a half-dozen companies offering powers. After World War II, the era ended altogether.

Small two- and four-horse powers are found occasionally and even one that is well rusted can bring $50 or more. The large powers are rarely found, so there is no established market. Tread power or railway powers are very scarce. Again, there seems to be no established market. Small dog powers for butter churns and the like can bring $500 or more.

Appleton Manufacturing Co., Batavia, Ill.

In 1917, this one-horse tread power sold for $90. This style was called a "down" power because it had no wheel mounting for portability. With most farm equipment of the time, a "down" machine was for floor mounting, while a "mounted" or "porta-ble" style was equipped with wheels. Depending on the walk of the horses, 32 to 36 rpm on the reel shaft, main shaft gave 96 to 108 rpm on the band wheel.

This four-horse down-power was dubbed the Modern Hero by Appleton in its 1917 catalogs. This power was geared to give 56 revolutions of the jack shaft for every round of the horses. By 1920, Appleton no longer manufactured powers, according to industry listings.

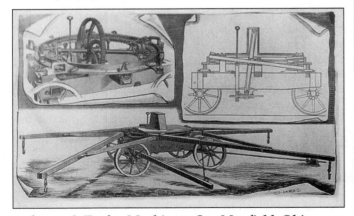

Aultman & Taylor Machinery Co., Manfield, Ohio

An 1890 catalog from Aultman & Taylor illustrates its sweep power as used with the Aultman & Taylor grain threshers. The

sweep power was a viable alternative to the steam engine, espe-cially when there were plenty of horses available. Eventually, though, the steam engine took precedence; it required no rest stops and far less work than handling eight, 10 or 12 horses.

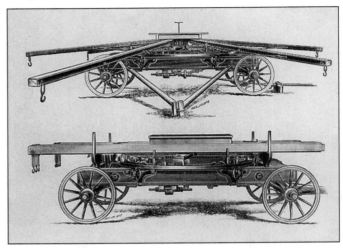

Buffalo-Pitts Co., Buffalo, N.Y.

The Pitts brothers began building threshers in the 1830s and developed the Pitts Power soon after. It was later modified as the Pitts-Carey power and remained on the market at least into the early 1900s. This example of 1895 shows the Pitts two-speed mounted power. Above it is shown ready for work; below it is ready to move to another job.

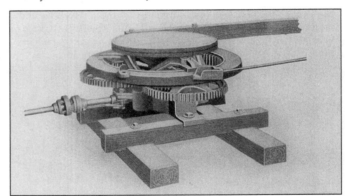

Challenge Co., Batavia, Ill.

Small horse powers were offered by Challenge into the 1920s. Shown here is a small unit made for two or four horses. Small powers like this one were often used for sawing wood, grinding feed and other light jobs around the farm.

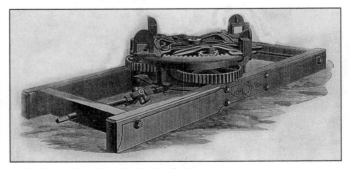

A.B. Farquhar Co. Ltd., York, Pa.

Into the 1890s, Farquhar came with its Climax Horse Power, suggesting it for threshing and other farm duties. This was a down-power and the engraving illustrates the rather complicated system of gearing required for these machines. The sweep arms were fitted into the square sockets noted at the top of the main drive casting.

Farquhar Railway Horse Powers were warranted to equal any tread power in use; this engraving of the early 1900s shows the small carrier wheels built into the track or tread of the machine. Also evident is the brake lever on the band wheel for stopping the machine.

Harrison Machine Works, Belleville, Ill.

For 1903, Harrison offered the Dingee-Woodbury power, essentially the same machine as that developed and built by J.I. Case Threshing Machine Co. The Dingee design emerged as probably the best of the sweep powers, although the steam-traction engine and eventually the tractor, took away the need for sweep powers.

Did You Know?

Bone cutters can now fetch $100 or more.

Heebner & Sons, Lansdale, Pa.

A 1910 listing shows Heebner's Double-Geared Level-Tread Power. This one-horse power was designed for small threshers, corn shellers and similar equipment. Heebner also built small threshers and various other farm equipment.

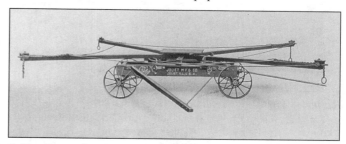

Joliet Manufacturing Co., Joliet, Ill.

Ostensibly built to operate its own corn shellers, as well as other equipment, the Joliet Pitts Power was built on the Pitts design, as compared to the Dingee design, previously noted in this section. This illustration goes back to about 1908. While Joliet continued making corn shellers for decades to come, little else is known of its Joliet-Pitts Power.

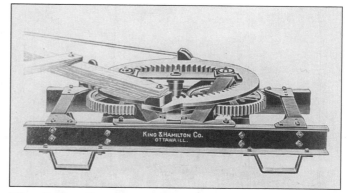

King & Hamilton Co., Ottawa, Ill.

This company manufactured many items of farm equipment, with this two-horse power being a later design, probably of the late 1920s. The all-steel frame lowered the power and lightened the weight; in addition, the power didn't rot away in a few years of being exposed to the weather. By 1940, less than half a dozen companies were making sweep powers.

Kingsland & Ferguson Manufacturing Co., St. Louis, Mo.

An 1884 advertisement from Kingsland & Ferguson illustrates its Carey Horse Power, staked and ready for operation. Mounted powers became very popular upon their release. A large down-power for eight or 12 horses would weigh at least half a ton. Since there was no means of lifting anything outside of the power provided by men and horses, a portable machine of any kind was always welcomed.

Roberts, Throp & Co., Three Rivers, Mich.

For 1882, this company offered the Improved Pitts Power, also known as the Carey Power. This heavy machine was mounted and featured a two-speed output, as is shown in the engraving. The speed jack is built into the system, utilizing a heavy casting that could be move-into or out of gear, as desired. With this power, the thresherman had the choice of 76, 79 or 103 revolutions of the output shaft to every round of the horses.

St. Albans Foundry Co., St. Albans, Vt.

From 1881 comes this illustration of the St. Albans one-horse power, a small unit for various farm jobs. The company suggest-
ed that this device could mechanize butter churning, grinding, sawing wood, cutting fodder and other uses. St. Albans manufactured a wide range of farm implements.

Sandwich Manufacturing Co., Sandwich, Ill.

Sandwich Manufacturing Co. was instrumental in the development of the spring-type corn sheller; this design gained great popularity in the 1880s. For a power source, Sandwich offered its Young Samson Eight-Horse Mounted Power. This design was intended to operate the largest Sandwich shellers and could also be used with threshers and other farm machines. After New Idea took over about 1930, the latter continued to offer small powers suitable for operating grain elevators into the late 1930s or perhaps slightly longer.

Trade Names			
Adams	E. H. Pease Mfg. Co.	Racine, WI	1892
Adams	Smith & Pomeroy	Kalamazoo, MI	1892
Advance	Advance Thresher Co.	Battle Creek, MI	1892
Advance	M. Rumely Co.	LaPorte, IN	1913
Advance Planet	Ann Arbor Machine Co.	Ann Arbor, MI	1905
American	R. R. Howell & Co.	Minneapolis, MN	1924
Andean	Hobson & Co.	New York, NY	1892
Appleton	Appleton Mfg. Co.	Appleton, WI	1892
Atlas	King & Hamilton	Ottawa, IL	1892
Aultman	Aultman & Taylor Machinery Co.	Mansfield, OH	1913
B. E. S.	Shoudy Mfg. Co.	Rockford, IL	1892
Bausman	D. H. Bausman	Bausman, PA	1892
Bell	Kohler, Hayssen & Stehn Mfg. Co.	Sheboygan, WI	1892
Belle City	Belle City Mfg. Co.	Racine, WI	1892
Benicia	Benicia Agricultural Works	Benicia, CA	1892
Berres-Gehl	Berres-Gehl Mfg. Co.	West Bend, WI	1905
Berres-Gehl Climax	Berres-Gehl Mfg. Co.	West Bend, WI	1905
Berres-Gehl Pitts	Berres-Gehl Mfg. Co.	West Bend, WI	1905
Big B	Warner Elevator Co.	Warner, IL	1909
Big B	Warner Elevator Mfg. Co.	Warner, IL	1909
Bignell	F. B. Bignell	Smyrna, MI	1892
Birdsall	Birdsall Co.	Auburn, NY	1892
Blake & Elliott	Blake & Elliott	Racine, WI	1892
Buckeye	Buckeye Feed Mill Co.	Springfield, OH	1905
Buckeye	Staver & Abbott Mfg. Co.	Chicago, IL	1892
Buffalo Pitts	Pitts Agricultural Works	Buffalo, NY	1892

Trade Names (cont...)

Butterworth	New Jersey Agricultural Works	Trenton, NJ	1892
C. C. G.	Cornish, Curtis & Greene	Ft. Atkinson, WI	1892
Camp	Camp Mfg. Co.	Washington, IL	1924
Cardwell's	Cardwell Machine Co.	Richmond, VA	1892
Carey	Ann Arbor Agricultural Co.	Ann Arbor, MI	1902
Carey	B. F. Dow & Co.	Peru, IN	1892
Carey	Cardwell Machine Co.	Richmond, VA	1892
Carey	Joliet Mfg. Co.	Joliet, IL	1913
Carey	Kingsland & Douglas Mfg. Co.	St. Louis, MO	1892
Challenge	Challenge Wind Mill & Feedmill Co.	Batavia, IL	1892
Champion	Forest City Machine Works	Cleveland, OH	1892
Champion	Kohler, Hayssen & Stehn Mfg. Co.	Sheboygan, WI	1892
Champion	Valley Iron Works Mfg. Co.	Appleton, WI	1892
Climax	A. B. Farquhar	York, PA	1892
Climax	I. B. Rowell & Co.	Menomonee Falls, WI	1892
Climax	King & Hamilton	Ottawa, IL	1892
Currier	H. A. Currier	Almont, MI	1892
Dairy Queen	F. W. Krogh & Co.	San Francisco, CA	1892
Davis	John S. Davis Sons	Davenport, IA	1892
Deere	Deere and Co.	Moline, IL	1929
Deere	Marseilles Mfg. Co.	Marseilles, IL	1909
Dempster	Dempster Mill Mfg. Co.	Beatrice, NE	1892
Diamond	Diamond Huller Co.	Winona, MN	1939
Diamond Winona	New Winona Mfg. Co.	Winona, MN	1909
Dingee-Woodbury	Advance Thresher Co.	Battle Creek, MI	1905
Dingee-Woodbury	Belleville Machine Works	Belleville, IL	1905
Dingee-Woodbury	Belleville Machine Works	Belleville, IL	1905
Dingee-Woodbury	C. Aultman & Co.	Canton, OH	1892
Dingee-Woodbury	Geiser Mfg. Co.	Waynesboro, PA	1905
Dingee-Woodbury	Harrison Machine Works	Belleville, IL	1892
Dingee-Woodbury	J. I. Case Threshing Machine Co.	Racine, WI	1892
Dingee-Woodbury	M. Rumely Co.	LaPorte, IN	1892
Dingee-Woodbury	Minneapolis Threshing Machine Co.	Hopkins, MN	1905
Dingee-Woodbury	Minnesota Thresher Mfg. Co.	Stillwater, MN	1892
Dingee-Woodbury	Northwest Thresher Co.	Stillwater, MN	1905
Dingee-Woodbury	Russell & Co.	Massillon, OH	1892
Duplex	Thos. Cascaden Jr.	Waterloo, IA	1892

Trade Names (cont...)

Eagle	Eagle Machine Co.	Lancaster, OH	1892
Eagle	F. W. Krogh & Co.	San Francisco, CA	1892
Eclipse	F. W. Krogh & Co.	San Francisco, CA	1892
Economy	F. W. Krogh & Co.	San Francisco, CA	1892
Edgecombe	Edgecombe Agricultural Works	Tarboro, NC	1892
Edinburgh	Edinburgh Agricultural Works	Edinburgh, VA	1892
Ellwood	Abram Ellwood	Sycamore, IL	1892
Empire	S. S. Messinger & Son	Tatamy, PA	1892
F & W	Flint & Walling Mfg. Co.	Kendallville, IN	1892
Fairbanks-Morse	Fairbanks, Morse & Co.	Chicago, IL	1892
Famous	Famous Mfg. Co.	East Chicago, IN	1905
Famous	Sterling Mfg. Co.	Sterling, IL	1892
Farquhar-Dingee	A. B. Farquhar Co.	York, PA	1905
Field	J. A. Field Mfg. Co.	St. Louis, MO	1892
Fleetwood	Fleetwood Foundry & Mach. Works	Fleetwood, OH	1905
Foster & Williams	Foster & Williams Mfg. Co.	Racine, WI	1892
Freed	Y. C. Freed & Co.	Royersford, PA	1892
Freeman	S. Freeman & Sons Mfg. Co.	Racine, WI	1892
Ft. Worth	Ft. Worth Machine & Foundry Co.	Ft. Worth, TX	1905
Geiser	Geiser Mfg. Co.	Waynesboro, PA	1905
Giant	Frank Hamachek	Kewaunee, WI	1909
Gilbert Hunt	Gilbert Hunt Co.	Walla Walla, WA	1913
Gillis Improved	Benicia Agricultural Works	Benicia, CA	1892
Globe	D. T. H. MacKinnon	Menasha, WI	1892
Globe	Globe Foundry & Machine Co.	Sheboygan, WI	1905
Grand Rapids	Grand Rapids Mfg. & Implement Co.	Grand Rapids, MI	1892
Greencastle	Greencastle Foundry & Machine Co.	Greencastle, IN	1892
Greenville	Greenville Implement Co.	Greenville, MI	1905
Grier	Geo. S. Grier & Son	Milford, DE	1892
Hamacek	A. Hamacek & Co.	Ahnapee, WI	1892
Harriman	Harriman Co.	Harriman, TN	1913
Harrison	Harrison Machine Works	Belleville, IL	1913
Hart	Hart Grain Weigher Co.	Peoria, IL	1913
Hartford	Hartford Plow Works	Hartford, WI	1892
Harvey	W. Harvey	Lock Haven, PA	1892
Hawkeye	E. Children's Sons Mfg. Co.	Council Bluffs, IA	1909
Hayes	Hayes Pump & Planter Co.	Galva, IL	1913
Heebner's	Heebner & Sons	Lansdale, PA	1892
Hercules	Collins Plow Co.	Quincy, IL	1905
Hercules	Marseilles Mfg. Co.	Marseilles, IL	1892
Hercules	W. R. Harrison & Co.	Canton, OH	1892
Hercules	Wilder-Strong Implement Co.	Monroe, MI	1905
Hildreth	Hildreth Bros.	Harvard, MA	1892

Trade Names (cont...)

Hocking Valley	Hocking Valley Mfg. Co.	Lancaster, OH	1892
Howell	R. R. Howell & Co.	Minneapolis, MN	1892
Huber	Huber Mfg. Co.	Marion, OH	1913
Hustler	Eagle Machine Works Co.	Indianapolis, IN	1892
Ideal	Frank Hamachek	Kewaunee, WI	1905
Ideal	Stover Mfg. Co.	Freeport, IL	1892
Imperial	Joliet Strowbridge Co.	Joliet, IL	1892
Improved	L. Spence & Son	Martin's Ferry, OH	1892
Iron King	Aaron Wissler	Brunnerville, PA	1892
Iron King	B. H. & J. Sanford	Sheboygan Falls, WI	1892
Iron King	Valley Iron Works Mfg. Co.	Appleton, WI	1892
Ithaca	Treman, Waterman & Co.	Ithaca, NY	1892
Jackson's High Speed	Byron Jackson	San Francisco, CA	1892
Johnson	J. S. Johnson	Waukon, IA	1892
Joliet	Joliet Mfg. Co.	Joliet, IL	1892
Joliet Pitts	Joliet Mfg. Co.	Joliet, IL	1905
Kelly	O. S. Kelly Co.	Springfield, OH	1892
Kelly & Taneyhill	Kelly & Taneyhill Co.	Waterloo, IA	1905
Kelly-Woodbury	L. Spence & Son	Martin's Ferry, OH	1892
Kentucky	Brennan & Co.	Louisville, KY	1892
Kewanee-Hart	Kewanee Implement Co.	Kewanee, IL	1924
Keystone	International Harvester Co.	Chicago, IL	1913
Keystone	Keystone Farm Machine Co.	York, PA	1905
Keystone	Keystone Mfg. Co.	Sterling, IL	1892
King	Gustav Wenzelmann	Missal, IL	1892
Krauss	Krauss Bros.	Geryville, PA	1892
Lehr	Lehr Agricultural Co.	Fremont, OH	1892
Lessig's	Lessig & Bro. Agricultural Works	Reading, PA	1892
Little Giant	Morgan, Kelly & Taneyhill	Waterloo, IA	1892
Little Giant	Portable Elevator Mfg. Co.	Bloomington, IL	1922
Marseilles	Marseilles Mfg. Co.	Marseilles, IL	1892
Marsh	E. B. Marsh & Bro.	Snydersville, PA	1892
Massillon	Russell and Co.	Massillon, OH	1913
Maurer's	F. X. Maurer Co.	Spencer, IA	1905
Meadows	Meadows Mfg. Co.	Pontiac, IL	1913
Meyer & Schrage	Meyer & Schrage	Sheboygan, WI	1892
Minneapolis	Minneapolis Threshing Machine Co.	Hopkins, MN	1913
Modern Hero	Appleton Mfg. Co.	Appleton, WI	1892
Mogul	Wenzelmann Mfg. Co.	Galesburg, IL	1909
Monitor	F. W. Krogh & Co.	San Francisco, CA	1892
Moritz	Wm. Moritz	Hastings, NE	1892

Trade Names (cont...)

Morton	Morton Mfg. Co.	Muskegon Heights, MI	1892
Myers	F. E. Myers & Bro.	Ashland, OH	1915
New Deere	Deere & Mansur	Moline, IL	1905
New Idea	New Idea Spreader Co.	Coldwater, OH	1932
New Prize	Appleton Mfg. Co.	Appleton, WI	1892
Nichols & Shepard	Nichols & Shepard Co.	Battle Creek, MI	1892
No. 6	G & D Mfg. Co.	Streator, IL	1929
North Star	R. R. Howell and Co.	Minneapolis, MN	1924
Novelty	Novelty Iron Works	Dubuque, IA	1892
Ohio	Ohio Cultivator Co.	Bellevue, OH	1913
Over	Ewald Over	Indianapolis, IN	1892
Owens	J. L. Owens & Co.	Minneapolis, MN	1892
Oyler's	Geo. K. Oyler	St. Louis, MO	1892
Pelton	Evan Davis & son	Butler, MD	1892
Pennsylvania	Hobson & Co.	New York, NY	1892
Phoenix	Appleton Mfg. Co.	Appleton, WI	1892
Pitts	Ann Arbor Agricultural Co.	Ann Arbor, MI	1892
Pitts	B. F. Dow & Co.	Peru, IN	1892
Pitts	Joliet Mfg. Co.	Joliet, IL	1913
Pitts	Kohler, Hayssen & Stehn Mfg. Co.	Sheboygan, WI	1892
Pitts	Silberzahn Mfg. Co.	West Bend, WI	1892
Pitts-Carey	Russell & Co.	Massillon, OH	1892
Pony	F. W. Krogh & Co.	San Francisco, CA	1892
Porter	E. A. Porter & Bros.	Bowling Green, KY	1892
Pottstown	Ellis Keystone Agricultural Works	Pottstown, PA	1909
Racine	Racine Implement Co.	Racine, WI	1892
Reliance	Minneapolis Threshing Machine Co.	Minneapolis, MN	1892
Richards	Richards' Iron Works	Manitowoc, WI	1892
Richmond	H. M. Smith & Co.	Richmond, VA	1892
Robison	J. Robison & Son	Curwensville, PA	1892
Rochester	Rochester Agricultural Works	Rochester, NY	1892
Rollins	B. F. Rollins	St. Johnsbury, VT	1892
Ross	E. W. Ross Co.	Springfield, OH	1905
S & P	Phelps & Bigelow Wind Mill Co.	Kalamazoo, MI	1913
Samson	Sandwich Mfg. Co.	Sandwich, IL	1892
Sandow	Wilder-Strong Implement Co.	Monroe, MI	1905
Schoepflin	Chas. Schoepflin & Bro.	Gardenville, NY	1892
Schroeder	H. V. Schroeder Co.	Minier, IL	1929
Scientific	Foos Mfg. Co.	Springfield, OH	1892
Sergeant	Sergeant Mfg. Co.	Greensboro, NC	1905
Seward	Seward Co.	Bloomington, IN	1892
Smalley	Smalley Mfg. Co.	Manitowoc, WI	1892
Sparta	Sparta Iron Works	Sparta, WI	1905
St. Albans	St. Albans Foundry & Impl. Co.	St. Albans, VT	1905

Trade Names (cont...)

St. Johnsville	St. Johnsville Agricultural Works	St. Johnsville, NY	1892
Star	Star Mfg. Co.	Carpentersville, IL	1892
Steel Frame	Nichols and Shepherd Co.	Battle Creek, MI	1913
Sterling	Sterling Mfg. Co.	Sterling, IL	1892
Sumner	Sumner Mfg. Co.	Hutchinson, MN	1892
Tally Ho	Hartford Plow Works	Hartford, WI	1905
Taylor Elevated	Bristol & Gale Co.	Chicago, IL	1892
Tornado	W. R. Harrison & Co.	Massillon, OH	1913
Totman's	Gowanda Agricultural Works	Gowanda, NY	1892
Triple Gear	Port Huron Engine & Thresher Co.	Port Huron, MI	1892
U. S.	U. S. Wind Engine & Pump Co.	Batavia, IL	1892
Veteran	Sandwich Mfg. Co.	Sandwich, IL	1909
Victor	Victor Feed Mill Co.	Springfield, OH	1905
Virginia	H. M. Smith & Co.	Richmond, VA	1892
Wachuset	Hobson & Co.	New York, NY	1892
Walburn-Swenson	Walburn-Swenson Mfg. Co.	Ft. Scott, KS	1892
Walker	E. W. Walker & Co.	Goshen, IN	1892
Wenzelmann	Wenzelmann Mfg. Co.	Galesburg, IL	1936
Western	R. R. Howell and Co.	Minneapolis, MN	1924
Westinghouse	Westinghouse Company	Schenectady, NY	1892
Wheelock	S. G. Cree	Wheelock, VT	1892
Whitman's	Whitman Agricultural Co. 1905	St. Louis, MO	1892
Whitman's	Whitman Agricultural Works	Auburn, ME	1892
Wilson	H. McK. Wilson & Co.	St. Louis, MO	1892
Wilson	Gilbert Hunt Co.	Walla Walla, WA	1905
Wissler	Aaron Wissler	Brunnerville, PA	1905
Winona	New Winona Mfg. Co.	Winona, MN	1913
Woodbury	B. F. Dow & Co.	Peru, IN	1892
Woodbury	King & Hamilton	Ottawa, IL	1892
Woodbury-Dingee	Aultman & Taylor Machinery Co.	Mansfield, OH	1905
Zilisch	A. T. Zilisch	Mayville, WI	1892

Household Equipment

This heading has been and continues to be the subject of numerous titles, antique price guides and nostalgia. The primary purpose of this section is to acknowledge, rather than ignore the role of the farm household in the overall picture. Even though the farmer of those bygone days spent many hard hours in the hot sun or the freezing cold, the housewife also did her share under the same conditions. Beyond the usual household duties, it usually fell to the housewife to look after the poultry, skim the cream, churn the butter, can the garden produce and other jobs too endless to name.

Various parts of the household activities will be found under headings such as Garden Equipment or Washing Machines. Some items presented here are found nowhere else in this book. For a value guide, the reader should consult any of many guides on the subject.

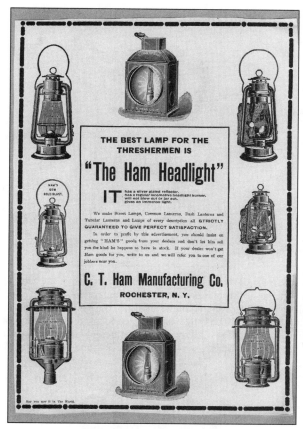

The kerosene lamp was an essential part of rural life until the coming of electric power. Various companies produced them, but one that gained attention from most farmers and threshermen was the line from C.T. Ham Manufacturing Co. Threshermen were familiar with the Ham Headlight for steam-traction engines; these are now a valuable collector's item, often in the $100-plus category. Other styles included the Cold Blast Lantern or the Globe Hanging Lamp. Fortunate indeed was the rural town with a few Ham Globe Street Lamps on its main street.

Few early farms had a lawn mower; cattle or sheep grazed near the house, with the garden being fenced and off-limits. However, an 1889 advertisement illustrates the New Model, being the latest lawn mower from Chadborn & Coldwell Manufacturing Co. Later on, Coldwell gained fame for its early power lawn mowers.

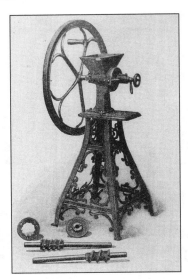

Grist mills of some sort were frequently found on the farm, although most rural folks preferred taking some of their grain to a local miller for conversion into household corn meal and flour. This unnamed mill, of about 1910, was designed to grind everything from nuts to corn meal, being supplied with different grinding plates for various commodities. The ornate iron-work is typical of the period.

Aside from the ordinary kraut cutters usually found in antique shops, some companies made larger units, such as the Buffalo Kraut Cutter of 1909. This one was produced by John E. Smith's Sons Co., Buffalo, N.Y. This company also made meat and vegetable cutters, potato chip cutters, horse radish graters and other equipment.

North River Agricultural Works at New York included this special sugar mill in its 1866 catalog. Its description notes that it was used by "country dealers for crushing and preparing sugar for use; by which process damp and hard portions are crushed and disintegrated and made to look light and uniform in appearance."

One Minute Manufacturing Co., Newton, Iowa, offered its Iceless Refrigerator about 1910. A pit was dug beneath the unit; by means of a self-contained winch, the refrigerator shelves were lowered into the cool ground. When anything was needed, the unit was hoisted to the top, appearing in the glass door, as shown.

In the 1890s, Zimmerman Fruit Dryer Co., Cincinnati, advertised its Fruit and Vegetable Dryer and Baker, with the No. 1 Small unit being pictured here. By this time, the company had sold more than 10,000 of these units. The shelves could be loaded with the desired fruits or vegetables and a small fire beneath the unit took care of dehydration. Dried apples for example, were a favorite treat among many rural families.

I

Ice Making Equipment

Rural life was a busy life; there was something to do in every season. The cover engraving for the January 1889 issue of *American Agriculturist* is titled, "The First Harvest of the Year." It fully depicts the typical scene of gathering ice for the coming year. An ice saw is used to cut out large blocks from a pond, with others pulling the blocks onto the ice and skating them across to a waiting wagon. In the background, is an ice house. Often, these consisted of a wooden framework covered with straw. To cut down on heat loss, a second roof is constructed over the straw; this also helped preserve the straw so that the ice house would last for several seasons. In the 1880s, my great-grandfather had an ice house on the family farm. Ice was cut and hauled from a pond about five miles distant and ice was sold in the neighborhood during the spring and summer months for the princely sum of 50 cents a block. This section could well have included various kinds of ice saws, picks, bars and other tools associated with the ice harvest, but, in my opinion, this engraving tells the whole story as well as it can be told to most of us who never experienced the task.

Incubators

Instead of trusting nature to take its course, farmers of the 1880s were becoming familiar with special incubators for hatching chickens, ducks and geese. By and large, early incubators were less than satisfactory, according to various trade reports as late as 1910. It was essential to maintain the proper temperature throughout the incubation period and accurately regulating the temperature was indeed difficult. Most early incubators used a kerosene burner of some description, but the problem was to maintain accurate heat regulation.

Eventually, electric models were developed, ending the need for kerosene-fired designs. By the early 1900s, commercial hatcheries were becoming well established. Many farm families preferred buying their baby chicks from one of these firms, since it eliminated yet another duty for the farm family.

Today, old incubators are hard to find. When they appear, those still complete can often bring $100 or more. Some were built with fine hardwood lumber and finished like a piece of furniture. These elaborate designs are far more desirable and much more expensive than ordinary styles made of common lumber.

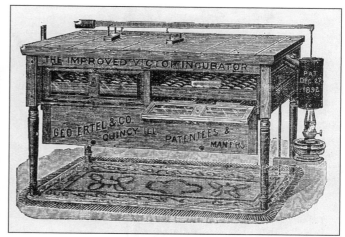

An early manufacturer of incubators was Geo. Ertel & Co., Quincy, Ill. Its Improved Victor design utilized an ordinary kerosene lamp as the heat source; this cut the first cost, since almost any lamp could be used. This one is highly finished with turned legs and other niceties.

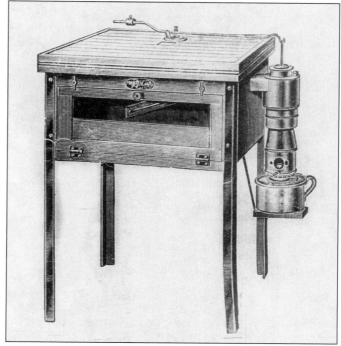

The Simplicity Incubators became popular for several years around 1918. Made at Indianapolis, this round design was built with no cold side walls and no cold corners. The external kerosene lamp is visible to the right of the illustration.

Hartman Co., Chicago, included Majestic incubators in its 1918 catalog. With this design, the kerosene lamp heated jacket water; in effect, hot water heat was supplied to this unit. The latter provided a much more even temperature, day and night, during the incubation period.

Trade Names

Automatic	Automatic Incubator Co.	Delaware, OH	1936
Brower	Brower Mfg. Co.	Quncy, IL	1939
Buckeye	Buckeye Incubator Co.	Springfield, OH	1939
Chatham	Manson Campbell Co.	Detroit, MI	1905
Close-to-Nature	Close-to-Nature Co.	Colfax, IA	1924
Cornell	Cornell Incubator Co.	Ithaca, NY	1909
Crescent	Des Moines Incubator Co.	Des Moines, IA	1905
Cyphers	Cyphers Incubator Co.	Buffalo, NY	1905
Dico	Delaware Industries	Delaware, OH	1936
Eclipse	Des Moines Incubator Co.	Des Moines, IA	1905
Electrobator	Cyphers Incubator Co.	Buffalo, NY	1922
Excelsior	Geo. H. Stahl	Quincy, IL	1905
Fairfield	Klondike Incubator Co.	Fairfield, NE	1909
Hawkeye	Hawkeye Incubator Co.	Newton, IA	1905
Honest Injun	Hiawatha Mfg. Co.	Hiawatha, KS	1915
Jamesway	James Mfg. Co.	Fort Atkinson, WI	1939
Klondike	Klondike Incubator Co.	Des Moines, IA	1905
Makomb	Globe American Corp.	Kokomo, IN	1936
Miller	J. W. Miller Co.	Freeport, IL	1913
New Excelsior	Geo. H. Stahl	Quincy, IL	1905
Oakes	Oakes Mfg. Co.	Tipton, IN	1939
Perfected Excelsior	Geo. H. Stahl	Quincy, IL	1905
Pineland	Pineland Incubator & Brooder Co.	Jamesburg, NJ	1905
Poor Man's Friend	Geo. Ertel Co.	Quincy, IL	1909
Prairie State	Prairie State Incubator Co.	Homer City, PA	1905
Queen	Queen Incubator Co.	Lincoln , NE	1929
Reliable	Reliable Incubator & Brooder Co.	Quincy, IL	1905
Royal	Royal Incubator Co.	Des Moines, IA	1905
Sherer	M. O. Sherer	Louisville, OH	1913
Simple Excelsior	Geo. H. Stahl	Quincy, IL	1905

Trade Names (cont...)

Standard Excelsior	Geo. H. Stahl	Quincy, IL	1905
Star	Star Incubator Co.	Boundbrook, NJ	1905
Successful	Des Moines Incubator Co.	Des Moines, IA	1905
Sure Hatch	Sure Hatch Incubator Co.	Clay Center, NE	1905
Victor	Geo. Ertel Co.	Quincy, IL	1905
Wooden Hen	Geo. H. Stahl	Quincy, IL	1905

Did You Know?

Large iron cauldrons, called farm boilers, often sell for $100 or more.

Did You Know?

A fanning mill will have a reasonable market value; it is not uncommon for a good machine to bring $100 or much more. Quite often, they are purchased for farm use, rather than as a farm antique.

L

Land Rollers

With the development of agriculture, the land roller became an important part of the tillage equipment. Land rollers have existed for centuries and once served as the primary method of leveling the seed bed. During the 1860s, the disc harrow came along, plus numerous other kinds of harrows and tillage machines. All of these pushed the smooth drum rollers of earlier days into a role of minor importance. Subsequently, came various kinds of clod crushers with a large number of wheels set on a common axle. Various kinds of these rollers are still used at the present time.

American Seeding Machine Co., Springfield, Ohio

In 1905, American Seeding Machine Co. continued to market this plain roller as formerly built by A.C. Evans Co. The latter was a partner in the earlier formation of American. Rollers like this were used for many years, but sticky soil was always a problem, as it adhered to the drum and usually had to be removed with a spade or shovel. A smooth drum also had a tendency to push the clods into the loose soil rather than breaking them up.

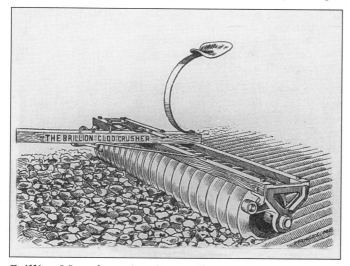

Brillion Manufacturing Co., Brillion, Wis.

Prior to 1908, Brillion had developed its clod crusher as an alternative to the land roller. As pictured here, a number of individual rolls moving through the soil helped break up the clods, leaving a smooth seed bed. This model was sold by John Deere Plow Co., through some of its branch warehouses in the 1908-10 period.

A. Buch's Sons Co., Elizabethtown, Pa.

The Pennsylvania roller had been on the market for some years prior to this 1903 advertisement. Like most pre-1900 rollers, this one had a smooth drum or, more precisely, three small drums mounted on a common shaft. The top-mounted weight box could be loaded for additional clod-busting power.

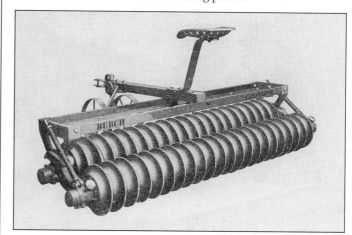

Burch Plow Works Co., Crestline, Ohio

For 1927, the Burch Pulverizer line included this tandem outfit. A special feature was the spring-loaded rear gang that placed downward pressure on the individual cast-iron wheels. A weight box was provided for the front gang.

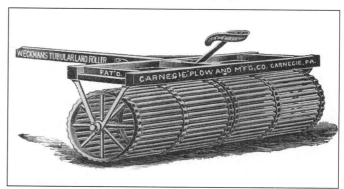

Carnegie Plow & Manufacturing Co., Carnegie, Pa.

A 1903 advertisement illustrates the Weckman Steel Tubular Pulverizer and Land Roller. This design was a step forward in land-roller design because the tubular steel perimeter permitted greater contact pressure. This resulted in improved clod-busting power. Carnegie claimed that there was no other made like it.

Castree & Shaw, Owosso, Mich.

Patented in 1895, the Star Steel Land Roller claimed its great advantage was the all-steel construction. The frame and the drums were all made of steel and this frame would not work loose or become weakened as was likely to happen with a wooden frame.

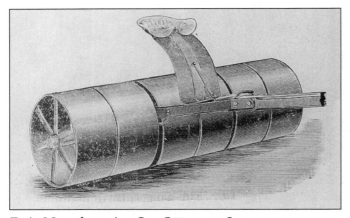

Dain Manufacturing Co., Ottumwa, Iowa

This 1887 version of the Dain Improved Land Roller was likely built in Kansas City or possibly at the Carrollton, Mo., factory—at least it was manufactured prior to the company's 1900 removal to Ottumwa, Iowa. The Dain design was a step in the right direction; it used six separate cast-iron rolls mounted on a common shaft.

H.P. Deuscher Co., Hamilton, Ohio

An 1892 advertisement illustrates the McColm Soil Pulverizer and Field Roller. This design was a great improvement in land

rollers, since each individual tooth had great clod-busting power compared to the smooth drum rollers of the day. Curiously, this early advertisement also includes Deuscher's Favorite Churn, demonstrating another part of the sizable Deuscher line.

J.W. Dunham & Son, Berea, Ohio

Dunham was offering various kinds of land rollers in the early 1900s and perhaps earlier; the company origins are presently unknown. By 1920, the company was offering its Dunham Culti-Packer, a tandem unit that was very effective when conditions demanded its use.

Emerson-Brantingham Co., Rockford, Ill.

For 1907, Emerson Manufacturing Co. offered its Flexible Roller Pulverizer, a new design that permitted the machine to follow the contours of the field rather than being obligated with a stiff axle its full length. The toothed design of the wheels was very popular, primarily because it was so effective in reducing a cloddy field to a fine seed bed.

Frost & Wood, Smiths Falls, Ontario

Frost & Wood advertised this "Champion" land roller as late as 1915. Despite the advantages of newer designs, some farmers resisted change, having used a smooth roller for decades and seeing no reason to adopt a new design. However, by 1915, the industry trend was toward units with individual wheels and a floating frame.

Grand Rapids Manufacturing Co., Grand Rapids, Mich.

In 1889, Grand Rapids announced its new flexible design. As shown here, each drum could oscillate on its axis. In addition, this roller used wood lagging over the drum heads, probably because mud or heavy soil would not stick so tightly to the wood as it did to cast iron.

Ohio Cultivator Co., Bellevue, Ohio

In a 1925 advertisement, Ohio Cultivator Co. predicted that "Thirty-five years from today there will be a double pulverizer on every good farm in the United States." Ironically, its prediction was fairly accurate—by 1960, there were many different kinds of soil pulverizers on the market. By then, the soil pulverizer had come under hydraulic control and enjoyed many revisions, but, in principle, it was still the same machine.

Ewald Over, Indianapolis, Ind.

An 1888 advertisement displays Over's 3-In-1 machine, a pulverizer, roller and stalk cutter. The tubular perimeter of the drum was a distinct advantage, as it was not so likely to pick up mud—if so, small quantities would drop away within a few rods of travel.

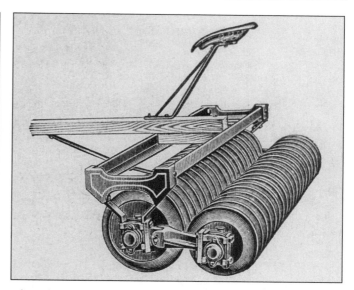

Thornburgh Manufacturing Co., Bowling Green, Ohio

In 1920, Thornburgh advertised its Tandem Disc Pulverizer in 7-, 8- and 10-foot sizes. This machine differed little from several others on the 1920 market, but a noticeable change is Thornburgh's method of attaching the rear gang to the front one. In case a single gang was wanted, the rear one could be detached simply by removing two pins.

Western Land Roller Co., Hastings, Neb.

By the 1930s, this three-gang roller from Western was being shipped to farms all over the United States, with heavy concentrations in the Midwestern states. Alternating toothed and smooth rollers characterized this design and thousands were used year after year. Reflecting on the popularity of this unit, a great many can still be found today, with some of them still in active service.

Trade Names			
Adriance	Adriance, Platt & Co.	Poughkeepsie, NY	1905
Albion	Gale Mfg. Co.	Albion, MI	1905
Allen	E. R. Allen & Co.	Whitesville, NY	1892
Ames	Ames Plow Co.	Boston, MA	1905
Ames	Ames Plow Co.	Boston, MA	1892
Anchor	Anchor Bolt and Nut Co.	Poughkeepsie, NY	1915
Arnold	G. W. Arnold's Son	Ionia, MI	1905
Arnold's	G. W. Arnold's Son	Ionia, MI	1892
Aurora	S. H. Peek	East Aurora, NY	1905
Austin	F. C. Austin Mfg. Co.	Chicago, IL	1892
Avery	B. F. Avery & Sons	Louisville, KY	1905
B. I. W.	Beatrice Iron Works	Beatrice, NE	1915

Trade Names (cont...)

Babcock	H. D. Babcock	Leonardsville, NY	1892
Barber	Geo. Sweet Mfg. Co.	Dansville, NY	1905
Barley	J. H. Barley, Bro. & Co.	Sedalia, MO	1892
Belcher & Taylor	Belcher & Taylor Agricultural Co.	Chicopee Falls, MA	1905
Berres-Gehl	Berres-Gehl Mfg. Co.	West Bend, WI	1905
Big Bill	Ohio Rake Co.	Dayton, OH	1909
Bignell	F. B. Bignell	Smyrna, MI	1892
Boss	A. Bostick	Millington, MI	1892
Boss	A. Bostick & Son	Lapeer, MI	1905
Boss	Jacob Bros.	Avoca, IA	1892
Boss	P. H. Wilms	Holland, MI	1892
Boy	E. R. Allen Foundry Co.	Corning, NY	1905
Brennan	Brennan & Co.	Louisville, KY	1892
Brillion	Brillion Pulverizer Co.	Brillion, WI	1936
Bromley	D. D. Bromley	Waterport, NY	1892
Buch	A. Buch's Sons Co.	Elizabethtown, PA	1909
Buckeye	Cental Implement Co.	Lansing, MI	1905
Buffalo Pitts	Buffalo Pitts Co.	Buffalo, NY	1905
Buffalo Pitts	Pitts Agricultural Works	Buffalo, NY	1892
Caledonian	Caledonian Bean Harvester Works	Caledonia, NY	1919
Cambridge	LeRoy Plow Co.	LeRoy, NY	1919
Canton	Bucher & Gibbs Plow Co.	Canton, OH	1892
Carter	H. Carter & Sons	Canisteo, NY	1892
Case	J. I. Case Co.	Racine, WI	1936
Cass City	Cass City Foundry & Machine Co.	Cass City, MI	1905
Castile	Castile Chilled Plow Co.	Castile, NY	1905
Champion	A. Buch's Sons	Elizabethtown, PA	1892
Champion	American Foundry & Machine Co.	Bowling Green, OH	1892
Champion	American Road Machine Co.	Kennett Square, PA	1892
Champion	Hickox-Mull Mfg. Co.	Toledo, OH	1905
Champion	Richford Foundry Co.	Richford, VT	1905
Chicopee	Belcher & Taylor Agricultural Co.	Chicopee Falls, MA	1919
Clark's	Cutaway Harrow Co.	Higganum, CT	1905
Clipper	Clipper Plow Co.	Defiance, OH	1905
Columbia	Wm. Fetzer Co.	Springfield, IL	1909
Combined	J. H. Yingling & Bro.	Seven Mile, OH	1892
Competitor	Dunham Co.	Berea, OH	1913
Comstock	Geo. S. Comstock	Mechanicsburg, PA	1905
Comstock	Geo. S. Comstock	Mechanicsburg, PA	1892
Corrugated	S. J. Fisher	Packerton, IN	1892
Currier's	Henry A. Currier	Almont, MI	1892
Curtis	Curtis Mfg. Co.	Albion, NY	1892
Dain	Dain Mfg. Co.	Carrollton, MO	1892
Daisy	F. J. Nickel & Son	Holt, MI	1905
Dandy	Durham Co.	Berea, OH	1913
Daniels	E. B. Daniels & Co.	Havana, NY	1892
Dansville	Geo. Sweet Mfg. Co.	Dansville, NY	1905
Deats	Hiram Deats Jr.	Pittstown, NJ	1892
Dew	Martin Dew	Cass City, MI	1892
Donaldson **1892**	Donaldson Bros.	Mt. Clemens, MI	1905
Douglass	John W. Douglass	New York, NY	1892
Doylestown	Daniel Hulshizer	Doylestown, PA	1892

Trade Names (cont...)

Dunham	J. W. Dunham & Son	Berea, OH	1892
Dunham	J. W. Dunham & Son	Berea, OH	1905
Eddy	W. Eddy & Sons	Greenwich, NY	1892
Edinburgh	Edinburgh Agricultural Works	Edinburgh, VA	1892
Empire	E. B. Marsh & Bro.	Snydersville, PA	1892
Empire	E. R. Allen Foundry Co.	Corning, NY	1905
Empire	Messinger Mfg. Co.	Tatamy, PA	1905
Eureka	Wilder-Strong Implement Co.	Monroe, MI	1913
Fair	G. Fair & Sons	Blaine, MI	1905
Fair	George Fair	Blaine, MI	1892
Farmer's Friend	Basil Foundry	Basil, OH	1892
Farquhar	A. B. Farquhar Co.	York, PA	1892
Fetzer	Wm. Fetzer Co.	Springfield, IL	1913
Flexible	J. J. Morse	Weston, MI	1892
Flexible King	Genesee Valley Mfg. Co.	Mt. Morris, NY	1905
Freed	Y. C. Freed & Co.	Royersford, PA	1892
Frost	C. S. Frost	Watkins, NY	1892
Fulton	Fulton Machine Co.	Canal Fulton, OH	1892
Gem	E. R. Allen Foundry Co.	Corning, NY	1905
Gem	Greenville Implement Co.	Greenville, MI	1905
Genesee	Genesee Valley Mfg. Co.	Mt. Morris, NY	1905
George & Tweedale	George & Tweedale	Constantine, MI	1892
Gold Medal	Dunham Co.	Berea, OH	1913
Gowanda	Gowanda Agricultural Works	Gowanda, NY	1905
Grand Rapids	Grand Rapids Mfg. & Implement Co.	Grand Rapids, MI	1892
Green's	Sam'l. Green	Florida, NY	1892
Grier	Geo. S. Grier & Son	Milford, DE	1892
Hamilton	H. P. Deuscher Co.	Hamilton, OH	1905
Harvey	W. I. Harvey	Lock Haven, PA	1892
Hazen	W. S. Hazen	Ripon, WI	1905
Heebner	Heebner & Sons	Lansdale, PA	1892
Herald	Watkins Chilled Plow Co.	Watkins, NY	1892
Hillsdale	Hillsdale Plow Co.	Hillsdale, NY	1905
Hillsdale	W. A. Mallery	Hillsdale, NY	1892
Holly	Patterson & Brown Bros. Mfg. Co.	Holly, MI	1905
Hubbard's	H. N. Hubbard	New York, NY	1892
Hunt's	Gilbert Hunt & Co.	Walla Walla, WA	1892
Ideal	Frank W. Weaver	New Oxford, PA	1909
Imboden	Imboden Harrow & Roller Co.	Cleona, PA	1909
Imperial	Bucher & Gibbs Plow Co.	Canton, OH	1905
Improved	Geo. O. P. Turner	Churchville, NY	1892
Ionia	Ionia Wagon Co.	Ionia, MI	1905
Iron Age	Bateman Mfg. Co.	Grenloch, NJ	1919
Jayhawk	F. Wyatt Mfg. Co.	Salina, KS	1915
Johnston	Johnston Harvester Co.	Batavia, NY	1915
Kemp's Frameless	Kemp's Mfg. Co.	Kankakee, IL	1905

Trade Names (cont...)

Keystone	Ellis Keystone Agricultural Works	Pottstown, PA	1892
Keystone	Keystone Farm Machine Co.	York, PA	1905
King	King Drill Mfg. Co.	Nebraska City, NE	1936
Lancaster	Frank Maute	Lancaster, NY	1892
Leader	Everts & Co.	Meridian, NY	1905
Lehr	Lehr Agricultural Co.	Fremont, OH	1909
LeRoy	LeRoy Plow Co.	LeRoy, NY	1915
Little	O. J. Little	Deckertown, NJ	1892
Lovejoy	Henry H. Lovejoy	Cambridge, NY	1892
Lyon	Lyon Iron Works	Greene, NY	1892
Malta	Brown-Manly Co.	Malta, OH	1909
Marseilles	Marseilles Mfg. Co.	Joliet, IL	1892
May	W. H. May & Son	Alexandria, VA	1892
McColm	H. P. Deuscher Co.	Hamilton, OH	1892
McGrath	R. H. McGrath	LaFayette, IN	1892
McSherry	Wm. Fetzer Co.	Springfield, IL	1909
Meridian	Everts Mfg. Co.	Meridian, NY	1909
Messinger	S. S. Messinger & Son	Tatamy, PA	1892
Miller's	F. W. Miller	Caledonia, NY	1892
Missouri	Genessee Valley Mfg. Co.	Mt. Morris, NY	1915
Mitts & Merrill	Mitts & Merrill	Saginaw, MI	1892
Mogul	Lehr Agricultural Co.	Fremont, OH	1915
Mogul	LeRoy Plow Co.	LeRoy, NY	1915
Monitor	Monitor Mfg. Co.	Minneapolis, MN	1892
Monroeton	Monroeton Mfg. Co.	Monroeton, PA	1892
Mt. Clemens	Donaldson Bros.	Mt. Clemens, MI	1905
Munnsville	Munnsville Plow Co.	Munnsville, NY	1905
National	Hickox-Mull Mfg. Co.	Toledo, OH	1905
Nelson	N. O. Nelson Mfg. Co.	St. Louis, MO	1892
New Idea	New Idea Spreader Co.	Coldwater, OH	1915
Newtown	A. Blaker & Co.	Newtown, PA	1892
Northville	American Bell & Foundry Co.	Northville, MI	1905
Ohio	Ohio Cultivator Co.	Bellevue, OH	1905
Oliver	Oliver Chilled Plow Works	South Bend, IN	1919
Over	Ewald Over	Indianapolis, IN	1892
Overland	L. H. Katelman	Council Bluffs, IA	1929
Palm Iron	A. Palm	Lawrence, KS	1892
Paris	Paris Foundry & Machine Works	Paris, IL	1936
Parnell	Geo. Parnell	Ontario, NY	1892
Parsons	Genesee Valley Mfg. Co.	Mt. Morris, NY	1905
Patten's	Patten, Stafford & Myer	Canastota, NY	1892
Patton	Sutton Bros. & Bell	Indianapolis, PA	1892
Peek's	Peek Bros.	East Aurora, NY	1892
Pennsylvania	A. Buch's Sons	Elizabethtown, PA	1905
Plymouth	Plymouth Foundry & Machine Co.	Plymouth, WI	1919
Pontiac	Howland Mfg. Co.	Pontiac, MI	1905
Progress	Progress Engine & Machine Works	Fredericksburg, VA	1892
Racine	Johnson & Field Mfg. Co.	Racine, WI	1892
Racine	Johnson & Field Mfg. Co.	Racine, WI	1905

Trade Names (cont...)

Rasmussen	R. N. Rasmussen	Randolph, WI	1892
Ripson	Wm. Ripson & Son	Youngstown, NY	1892
Robison	J. Robison & Son	Curwensville, PA	1892
Rock Island	Rock Island Plow Co.	Rock Island, IL	1892
Roderick Lean	Roderick Lean Mfg. Co.	Mansfield, OH	1905
Sandiford	W. Sandiford	Joliet, IL	1892
Seville	Seville Foundry & Machine Co.	Seville, OH	1892
Sheer	Eugene Sheer	Lincoln, IL	1905
Smith	Oliver A. Smith	Clarkston, MI	1892
South Bend	South Bend Chilled Plow Co.	South Bend, IN	1909
St. Louis	St. Louis Drill Works	St. Louis, MO	1892
Standard	E. R. Allen Foundry Co.	Corning, NY	1905
Standard	Kingman & Co.	Peoria, IL	1892
Standard	Otter Lake Iron Works	Otter Lake, MI	1892
Standard	Standard Harrow Co.	Utica, NY	1905
Star	Castree and Shaw	Owosso, MI	1895
Star	Central Implement Co.	Lansing, MI	1905
Star	F. B. Ogden	Republic, OH	1892
Star	Star Implement Co.	Flint, MI	1892
Stringer	Stringer, Dexter & Coe	Munnsville, NY	1892
Superior	Mountville Mfg. Co.	Mountville, PA	1905
Superior	Superior Land Roller Co.	Gouverneur, NY	1892
Toledo	Hickox-Mull Mfg. Co.	Toledo, OH	1905
Toledo	Toledo Plow Co.	Toledo, OH	1905
Tompkins	Watkins Chilled Plow Co.	Watkins, NY	1892
Tornado	W. R. Harrison & Co.	Massillon, OH	1905
Victor	Edward Sellers	Oak Hall, PA	1905
Wakefield	C. Wakefield & Son	Theresa, NY	1892
Walker	Geo. S. Cady Co.	Moravia, NY	1905
Walker	Walker Mfg. Co.	Moravia, NY	1892
Weckman Tubular	Carnegie Plow & Mfg. Co.	Carnegie, PA	1905
Western	J. D. Tower and Sons	Mendota, IL	1936
Western	Western Land Roller Co.	Hastings, NE	1936
Whirlwind	Wilder-Strong Implement Co.	Monroe, MI	1936
White's Improved	S. R. White & Bro.	Norfolk, VA	1892
Whitman's	Whitman Agricultural Co.	St. Louis, MO	1905
Wiard	Champion Drill Co.	Avon, NY	1892
Wilder's	Wilder Mfg. Co.	Monroe, MI	1892
Wilder's	Wilder-Strong Implement Co.	Monroe, MI	1905
Wilson	J. K. Wilder & Son	Monroe, MI	1892
Wooster	Wooster Machine Co.	Wooster, OH	1909
Wright	Wright Bros. Mfg. Co.	Monroe, MI	1892
Wyandot	Van Buren & Bitler	Carey, OH	1892
Yankee	Wheel & Seeder Mfg. Co.	LaCrosse, WI	1892
Ypsilanti	McCullough Bros.	Ypsilanti, MI	1892

Lighting Plants

In 1909, the *Farm Implement News Buyer's Guide* had no listings for Lighting Plants. Only a few companies were making home electric plants at the time; by 1912, the numbers began to swell, with this industry reaching its peak about 1920. As a sidebar to this section, a couple of acetylene gas lighting systems are included; they gained slight popularity in the early 1900s, but were troublesome to operate and were also dangerous if improperly used. When this happened, an explosion was entirely possible.

Home lighting plants were a major step forward for those in rural areas. During the 1920s and even before, numerous small towns erected their own electric generator plants and occasionally ran power lines to nearby farms. The changeover to the "high line" came during the 1930s with rural power becoming a reality. This ended the need for the home light plant.

Almost all home light plants used a bank of batteries to supply power for lighting and an occasional appliance. The generator was operated periodically to keep the batteries charged. In later designs, the generator started automatically whenever a light was turned on. The majority of the home light plants operated on 32 volts direct-current, but a few were designed for 110 volts direct-current.

This section gives but a sampling of electric lighting plants. A comprehensive view of these units and internal combustion engines of all kinds is given in the author's *American Gas Engines Since 1872* (Crestline/Motorbooks: 1983). Electric lighting plants often do not have the value of stationary engines, but prices of $300 to $600 are not uncommon.

Delco-Light Co., Dayton, Ohio

Of all home electric plants, the Delco was probably the best known and the most widely sold. Beginning about 1915, the Delco was a self-contained unit that required minimal attention. Shown here is a typical home lighting set-up; usually, the entire operation was in the basement of the house, since it stayed reasonably warm in winter and was easy to get at when the batteries needed recharging.

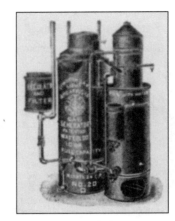

Epworth Gas Light & Heating Co., Waterloo, Iowa

In 1903, the Ideal Epworth Acetylene Generator was available for farm use. Due to the potential danger of explosion, this equipment was usually located outside of the home. The metered dropping of calcium carbide granules onto water creates acetylene gas and this was used for lighting and heating. However, acetylene gas becomes unstable above a certain pressure and this created the danger with these units.

Frost Engine Co., Evansville, Ind.

A few companies attempted to furnish a complete outfit that could be used for pumping water, generating electricity or for other duties. One of these is shown here in the 1912 offering from Frost Engine Co. Included is its Hustler engine, together with a well pump, plus a generator, switchboard and battery set.

Hanover Utilities Corporation, Hanover, Pa.

In 1921, Hanover advertised this 1-1/2 kilowatt home lighting plant. By this time, the majority of lighting plants were direct-connected, self-contained units. Earlier, many lighting plants consisted of an engine belted to a generator. Many of the home lighting plants utilized the generator as a motor for automatic engine that started off the battery set.

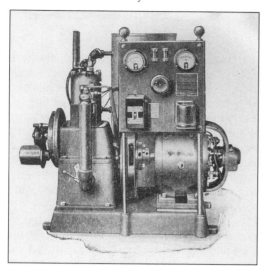

Mayhew Co., Milwaukee, Wisc.

A 1918 offering was this Type K Farm Lighting Plant from Mayhew Co. It included features like automatic starting off the battery set, plus an automatic shutdown when the batteries were fully charged. This unit consisted of the engine and generator mounted separately on a common base.

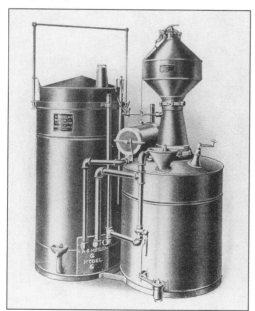

National Welding & Manufacturing Co., Buffalo, N.Y.

National offered its Model Generator in this 1909 advertisement. This unit consisted of the acetylene generator shown at right; it created acetylene gas by a controlled addition of calcium carbide granules to water in the bottom tank. With an increase in tank pressure the mechanism closed so that no more granules could be added. To the left is a storage tank for the acetylene gas. These systems were an alternative to rural areas where there was no natural gas. Due to the dangers of acetylene, the systems failed to become highly popular. This was also due to the fact that the electric lighting plants came along about the same time and soon dominated the market.

E.I. Pearson Corporation, Cincinnati, Ohio.

By the late 1920s, electric lighting plants were losing ground due to market saturation as well as to the coming of rural electric power. Despite this, Pearson offered this compact Cincinnati Lighting Plant in 1925. It consisted of a small air-cooled engine that was direct-coupled to a generator. Most of these systems included an automatic shutdown once the battery set was recharged.

Stearns Motor Manufacturing Co., Ludington, Mich.

The Stearns DeLuxe farm lighting plant was announced in 1922. It had a 1,500-watt capacity with the generator only or 2,000 watts with the generator and battery set. Advertising of the time noted that "this is considered ample capacity for electrical household appliances." Today, a single branch circuit in a home is on a 20-ampere fuse or circuit breaker.

Stover Manufacturing & Engine Co., Freeport, Ill.

Many engine manufacturers attempted to get into the farm light plant business using its own engine, plus a generator and battery set from another manufacturer. Such was the case with this 1923 offering from Stover. Shown here is a 1-1/2 horsepower Stover Type K engine connected to a 700-watt generator and control from Western Electric.

Universal Motor Co., Oshkosh, Wis.

Universal offered many different styles and sizes of home lighting plants, including this 1922 "Unimote" plant with a capacity of 2,000 watts. It was a self-contained unit using a small four-cylinder engine. A starter button motorized the generator using power from the battery set. When the batteries were recharged, the engine shut itself down automatically.

Wagner Electric Corporation, St. Louis, Mo.

Evidence of the changing scene on the farm was this 1928 offering of the Wagner Farm Handi-Motor. This mounted outfit consisted of the motor, a long cord, two different sizes of pulleys and a starting device that protected the motor from overloads or low-voltage problems. Motors like this were not a possibility with the home lighting plant, but became a reality with the coming of rural power lines.

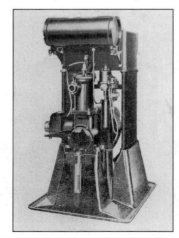

Waterman Motor Manufacturing Co., Detroit, Mich.

A 1916 offering from Waterman Motor Co. was its Uni-Lectric farm lighting plant. With the coming of electricity to the farm,

kerosene lamps were now used only when the batteries went dead. Running a pair of wires to the barn now permitted the farmer to finish his chores without having to use a kerosene lantern and its ever-present danger of a fire. With the coming of electricity to the farm, life would never be the same.

Listers

The lister was developed in the 1860s; history has it that the first lister ever marketed was built by Parlin & Orendorff Co., Canton, Ill. It was said to have been the invention of an unnamed blacksmith in Missouri. Subsequently, the lister was built and sold by most major plow manufacturers.

Listers are simply a double plow that throws a furrow both ways. The seed bed is at the bottom of this furrow; planting may be done at the time with an attached drill or may be finished later. The lister was designed for use in semi-arid regions with little rainfall. It was unsatisfactory on level ground, since water can collect in the ditches and drown the young crop. Likewise, it is not always ideal on hilly ground since heavy rains wash out the growing corn. Even in its prime, the lister gained attention only in those areas where it was used. The average Midwestern farmer knew little or nothing about it. Eventually, other tillage practices emerged so that the lister gains even less attention than formerly.

Parlin & Orendorff Co., Canton, Ill.

P&O developed the lister in the 1860s and eventually began building a sulky lister as shown. This offering of 1887 shows the Canton Sulky Lister and Dropper. The latter was a simple corn drill connected to the sulky wheel by a chain.

Rock Island Plow Co., Rock Island, Ill.

An 1887 engraving illustrates the Rock Island Lister and Drill. This style was ideal for small plots but, in most instances, farmers wanted a sulky lister, preferably a two-row model to hasten planting of the crop. The corn drill is operated by the dual star wheels attached behind the lister.

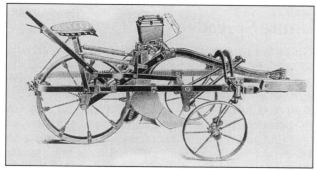

Rock Island's Injun Lister of 1900 was available in one-row and two-row models, with the single-row style shown here. This one threw up the furrows, planted the seed and firmed it in place with an ordinary press wheel. The two-row model was identical except in size.

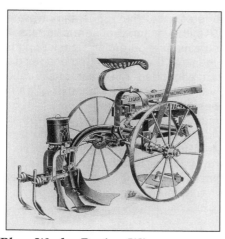

J.I. Case Plow Works, Racine, Wis.

An 1897 catalog illustrates the Juno Listing Plow from Case Plow Works. This one placed the lister behind the operator who sat well forward on the unit. The drill mechanism was operated through gears and a telescoping shaft from the sulky wheels. Also shown on this one are two small spear shovels to assist in providing a substantial seed bed.

Massey-Harris Co., Toronto, Ontario

From 1930 comes this illustration of the M-H No. 4 two-row power-lift lister. The power-lift mechanism is clearly visible; the same chain drive also operated the drill mechanism. Chances are that this design was developed from earlier work by J.I. Case Plow Works, Racine, Wis. Massey-Harris bought the latter in 1928.

Trade Names			
Big Four	Fort Madison Plow Co.	Fort Madison, IA	1915
Black Hawk	D. M. Sechler Carriage Co.	Moline, IL	1905
Boss	Peru Plow & Wheel Co.	Peru, IL	1905
Brown	Galesburg Coulter-Disc Co.	Galesburg, IL	1905
Canton	Parlin & Orendorff Co.	Canton, IL	1905
Cock of the Walk	Peru Plow & Wheel Co.	Peru, IL	1892
Combined	Weir Plow Co.	Monmouth, IL	1892
Craig's Canton	Parlin & Orendorff Co.	Canton, IL	1892
David Bradley	David Bradley Mfg. Co.	Chicago, IL	1892
Deere	Deere & Co.	Moline, IL	1892
Deere	Deere & Mansur Co.	Moline, IL	1892
Defiance	LaCrosse Plow Co.	LaCrosse, WI	1905
Eagle	Eagle Mfg. Co.	Davenport, IA	1892
Eagle	Eagle Mfg. Co.	Kansas City, MO	1905
Emerson	Emerson Mfg. Co.	Rockford, IL	1905
Emperor	Rock Island Plow Co.	Rock Island, IL	1905
Famous	St. Joseph Plow Co.	St. Joseph, MO	1892
Grand Detour	Grand Detour Plow Co.	Dixon, IL	1892
Hayes	Hayes Pump & Planter Co.	Galva, IL	1905
Improved Hapgood	Hapgood Plow Co.	Alton, IL	1892
J. I. Case	J. I. Case Plow Works	Racine, WI	1892
Janesville	Janesville Machine Co.	Janesville, WI	1905
Kingman	Kingman Plow Co.	Peoria, IL	1905
Kirlin	Kirlin Cultivator Co.	Kansas City, MO	1915
Knox Combined	Geo. W. Brown & Co.	Galesburg, IL	1892
LaCrosse	LaCrosse Plow Co.	LaCrosse, WI	1915
Little Duke	Peru Plow & Wheel Co.	Peru, IL	1905
Model	Peru Plow & Wheel Co.	Peru, IL	1905
Moline	Moline Plow Co.	Moline, IL	1892
Morrison	Morrison Mfg. Co.	Fort Madison, IA	1892
Norwegian	Norwegian Plow Co.	Dubuque, IA	1892
Norwegian	J. Thompson & Sons	Beloit, WI	1892
Ohio	Ohio Cultivator Co.	Bellevue, OH	1905
Old Reliable	Hapgood Plow Co.	Alton, IL	1892
P & O	Parlin and Orendorff Co.	Canton, IL	1915
Paragon	Kingman Plow Co.	Peoria, IL	1915
Perfection	Kingman Plow Co.	Peoria, IL	1915
Racine	J. I. Case Plow Works	Racine, WI	1905
Rock Island	Rock Island Plow Co.	Rock Island, IL	1892
Royal Jr.	J. I. Case Plow Works	Racine, WI	1905
Sattley	Racine-Sattley Co.	Springfield, IL	1905
Skandia	Skandia Plow Co.	Rockford, IL	1892
St. Joe	St. Joseph Plow Co.	St. Joseph, MO	1892

Trade Names			
Syracuse	Syracuse Chilled Plow Co.	Syracuse, NY	1905
Thompson	J. Thompson & Sons	Beloit, WI	1905
Tri Belle	Moline Plow Co.	Moline, IL	1905
Tricycle	Rock Island Plow Co.	Rock Island, IL	1905
Warner's	St. Paul Plow Works	St. Paul, MN	1892
Watson's	St. Joseph Plow Co.	St. Joseph, MO	1892
Western Belle	Moline Plow Co.	Moline, IL	1905

Did You Know?

In the 1890s, the American Harrow Co., sold its farm implements direct from the factory to the farmer. A small one-row walking cultivator was available for $14.75.

Anyone having additional materials and resources relating to American farm implements is invited to contact C.H. Wendel, in care of Krause Publications, 700 E. State St., Iola, WI 54990-0001.

M

Manure Spreaders

Only a few patents were issued for manure spreaders prior to 1875. Of these, none gained any importance. Subsequently, Joseph S. Kemp designed a spreader while residing at Waterloo, Ontario, Canada. His original 1875 design marked the beginning of a practical and successful manure spreader. By 1904, Kemp had accumulated nearly 15 different patents on manure spreaders, the first one coming in 1877.

Farmers were well aware of manure's value as a soil conditioner and fertilizer. Numerous agriculturists editorialized on the subject and several books were written on the subject. Despite this, the pre-spreader days saw an unpleasant task for every farmer, since the only alternative was to pile it up in the yard. When manure spreaders first came to the forefront in the 1880s, they were a welcome sight; by 1910 the majority of farms across the United States owned a manure spreader. Considering the number of farms at the time, there was a tremendous demand and manufacturers abounded. After market saturation, one after another left this business for another or perhaps abandoned business aspirations altogether.

Today, manure spreaders bear little resemblance to those early designs, yet the underlying purpose remains the same—fertilize the soil with animal manure. Occasionally, the term "fertilizer distributor" was used in the early days, but most farmers and most manufacturers called it what it was—a manure spreader.

Before the invention of the manure spreader, farmers loaded barnyard manure onto a wagon, then drove to the field and scattered it by hand. Leaving large clumps wouldn't work; later on it would plug up the plow. This is what it was like in the "good ol' days."

American Harrow Co., Detroit, Mich.

For 1905, this was the appearance of the New American manure spreader from American Harrow Co. It was typical of the time, using what was essentially a heavy wagon chassis to which was fitted the spreader box and mechanism.

American Seeding Machine Co., Springfield, Ohio

D.M. Sechler Carriage Co., Moline, Ill., developed the Black Hawk manure spreader in the early 1900s. Eventually, this firm went out of business, apparently being acquired by American Seeding Machine Co. The latter offered several styles in subsequent years, this one being the New Black Hawk No. 40A of 1927.

Appleton Manufacturing Co., Batavia, Ill.

Appleton offered this style of manure spreader in 1906. It was a heavy wooden design, but offered cut-under front wheels to permit the short turns required to back into a barn or shed for ease in loading. By 1906, the market was booming in the manure spreader business.

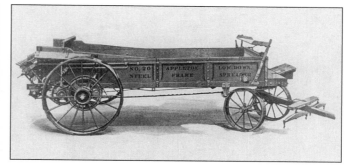

A radical departure from the high-profile spreader designs of earlier times was this low-down style offered by Appleton in 1917. Appleton began building spreaders in 1905 and this machine of 12 years later shows marked improvement, including the use of a steel frame.

Bloom Manufacturing Co., Nashua, Iowa

Two sizes of Bloom spreaders were available in 1910—the 65-bushel model and the larger 75-bushel spreader. Bloom's spreader evidenced the trend to a low-profile design; farmers disliked pitching manure by hand into a spreader nearly as tall as they were. Bloom apparently began building spreaders about 1906. Eventually, the company relocated to Independence, Iowa.

Cedar Rapids Implement Works, Cedar Rapids, Iowa

In 1906, the Up-2-Date Manure Spreader appeared from this firm; it was billed as being the most modern spreader of the time. This one, like many others, used a returnable apron instead of the continuous apron design. The latter was not held in high esteem at the time, but has since come to be the universal method of delivering material to the beaters. This operation lasted but a few years.

David Bradley Manufacturing Co., Bradley, Ill.

From about 1910 comes this illustration of the David Bradley Manure Spreader, which it claimed was the "strongest, simplest and most perfect working spreader made." An attractive feature of this lightweight spreader was that it carried a price of only $69.50.

Deere & Co., Moline, Ill.

An important design development was embodied in the John Deere manure spreader of 1924. As pictured here, the main beater was mounted directly over the drive axle. This permitted a low profile while providing beater teeth exactly where they were needed. Deere manure spreaders are also illustrated in the color section of this book.

Cockshutt Plow Co. Ltd., Brantford, Ontario

About 1914, the Cockshutt No. 3 Manure Spreader appeared; this one was fitted with Hyatt roller bearings for easier draft and longer life. This spreader typified the low-profile design to follow at least into the 1930s. It was simple and, best of all, it was low to the ground.

Emerson-Brantingham Co., Rockford, Ill.

Emerson-Brantingham built several sizes and styles of manure spreaders. Its 1919 offering included this one-man straw-spreader attachment. This device was primarily for hauling the remainder of a straw stack back to the field in spring to be used as fertilizer. The straw attachment is attached to the E-B No. 1 spreader.

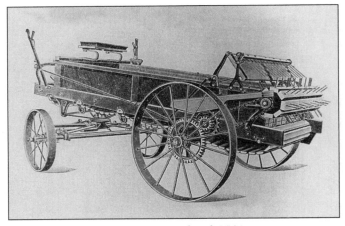

Cortland Implement Co., Cortland, N.Y.

A 1905 advertisement illustrates the Improved Advance spreader with an endless apron design. For the Midwest, J.I. Case Plow Works at Racine, Wis., functioned as agents and this likely improved the sales base considerably. Little is known of this company.

A.B. Farquhar Co. Ltd., York, Pa.

In the 1930s, Farquhar offered its Non-Wrap spreader. This referred to the beater design, intended to minimize wrapping of long straw around the beater blades. Farquhar spreaders were sold primarily in the Eastern states and were not as well known in the Midwest.

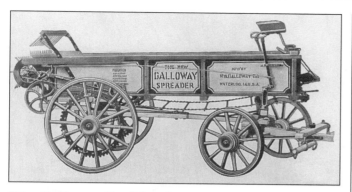

Wm. Galloway Co., Waterloo, Iowa

By 1912, the Galloway catalog was going to thousands of farmers and included items like this Wagon Box Spreader. For about $50, a farmer could buy one of these spreaders, attaching it to his own running gear and instantly having a manure spreader. This design was fairly popular, especially since the same running gear could be used for other purposes. Within a few years this style lost out to dedicated designs.

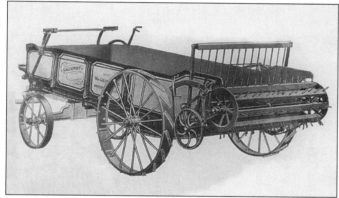

Galloway's catalog mail-order business included almost everything for the farm, including the 80-bushel Jumbo spreader, shown in its 1914 catalog. At the time, this was a huge spreader, particularly when most designs ranged from 50 to 65 bushels. This spreader retailed for $93.50.

Glen Wagon Co., Seneca Falls, N.Y.

The Johnson Star Manure Spreader is shown here from a 1909 advertisement. This model was sold through numerous jobbing houses, including Dain Manufacturing Co., Parlin & Orendorff, plus several others in the Midwest. However, nothing is known of the company or the spreader, aside from this advertisement.

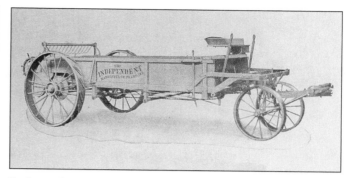

Independent Harvester Co., Plano, Ill.

By the time this 1917 promotion appeared, most companies had developed a low-profile design for its spreaders. For the Independent, this was achieved by using narrowed front wheels and a cut-under design to permit sharp turns, as when backing into a barn or shed.

International Harvester Co., Chicago, Ill.

Almost from its 1902 beginning, IHC sold Kemp spreaders through its dealer organization. Harvester bought the Kemp factory at Newark Valley, N.Y., in 1906, along with certain of the Kemp patents. In addition, Harvester leased the company's factory at Waterloo, Iowa, until 1908, but did not renew the lease after that time. Shown here is the IHC Corn King Spreader No. 2 of 1905.

A 1905 offering from IHC was its Cloverleaf Spreader No. 2. It was much like the competing Corn King model; one style was sold by Deering dealers and the other by McCormick dealers. Operating several different companies under a single corporate umbrella created many problems, including some interesting clashes between dealers in the same town.

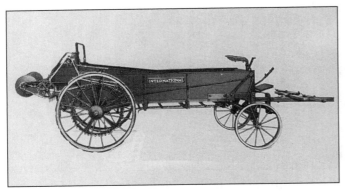

By 1920, the IHC manure spreader line included the International roller-bearing model with an auto-steer front axle, a tight bottom and a wide-spread attachment. Few farm machines saved as much labor for the farmer as did the manure spreader. While the tractor-mounted manure loader didn't become a practical reality until the 1930s and later, pitching the manure onto the spreader wasn't the worst job on the farm and was certainly better than having to pitch the same load off by hand once in the field.

Johnston Harvester Co., Batavia, N.Y.

In 1913, Johnston bought out the Richardson Manufacturing Co., of Worcester, Mass. The latter had been building the Worcester-Kemp spreaders for some years, with Johnston buying its spreaders from Richardson until the 1913 takeover. Subsequently, Johnston began manufacturing the "Easy Loader" spreaders at its own plant in Batavia. Johnston sold out to Massey-Harris in 1917.

J.S. Kemp Manufacturing Co., Newark Valley, N.Y.

In 1875, Joseph Kemp built the first successful manure spreader. At the time, Kemp was working in Waterloo, Ontario, Canada. This first machine carried about 25 bushels and was made at a cost of about $300. From this first design came a host of manufacturers looking for a share of the market by 1900.

By the beginning of 1900, Kemp had introduced its 20th Century manure spreaders. At this point, Kemp had already enlisted numerous branch houses and agents to distribute the new machine and set up a branch office at Cedar Rapids, Iowa. By the time this 1903 advertisement appeared, Kemp was selling spreaders to International Harvester Co.

In the early 1900s, Kemp set up a Midwestern factory at Waterloo, Iowa. IHC leased this factory for two years commencing in 1906 and ending in 1908. Subsequently, Kemp announced its new Kemp's Triumph spreader, a front-unloading design. Also known as The Federal Spreader Works, this 1908 company advertised heavily for a time that year; after that, no further trace has been found.

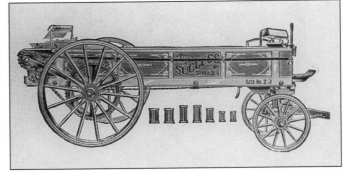

Kemp & Burpee Manufacturing Co., Syracuse, N.Y., apparently was operating in the early 1900s or perhaps before; meanwhile, the Newark Valley, N.Y., factory was also viable. By the 1920s, parts for the Original Kemp spreaders were available from Deere & Co.

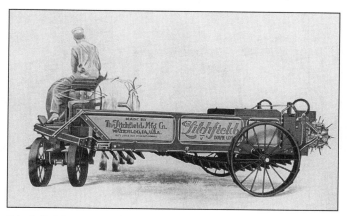

Litchfield Manufacturing Co., Waterloo, Iowa

Litchfield began manufacturing manure spreaders in the early 1900s, apparently continuing in this business approximately until World War II. This design of about 1915 was quite popular with Midwestern farmers and bore a striking resemblance to other low-down designs of the period. The company also made various other farm implements.

Massey-Harris Harvester Co., Batavia, N.Y.

With the 1917 purchase of Johnston Harvester Co., Massey-Harris acquired a fully developed line of manure spreaders. The 1920s included this No. 7 model, a modern looking outfit with a wide spread attachment. During the 1920s and 1930s, manure spreaders changed little, but, with the coming of small row crop tractors, farmers were soon looking for power-driven tractor manure spreaders.

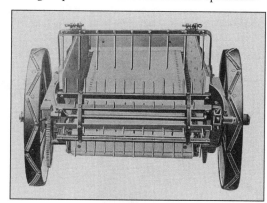

Geo. B. Miller & Son Manufacturing Co., Waterloo, Iowa

Numerous farm equipment manufacturers have been located at Waterloo, Iowa. One of these, Geo. B. Miller & Son, manufactured many items of farm equipment, electing to build the Robinson spreaders for a time in the 1920s. Shown here is the Robinson straight-beater design; the endless wooden apron is also evident.

To provide a wide-spread feature to the ordinary beater, the Robinson angle beater was used. This one used a rather complicated set of castings with interlocking teeth at the center. They permitted the beater to tear the straw apart at the rear of the machine, all the while casting it out in a wide pattern. The Robinson design came from the Robinson Spreader Co. noted below.

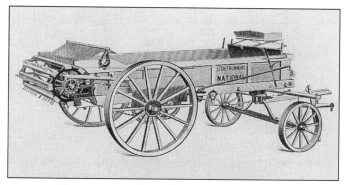

Moline Plow Co., Moline, Ill.

In 1906, Moline Plow Co. announced its National Light Running Manure Spreader. This one was built at the company's Mandt Wagon Co., in Stoughton, Wis. In a promotional piece, Moline gave more than 20 reasons why farmers should select its spreader above all others. A later style of the Moline spreader is pictured in the color section of this book.

New Idea Spreader Co., Maria Stein, Ohio

For 1905, New Idea offered their Acme Manure Spreader. At this time the company was situated at Maria Stein, Ohio, but later relocated to nearby Coldwater, Ohio.

Of all manure spreader manufacturers, New Idea was one of the most prolific, building numerous models and sizes over a long career in the business. Shown here is its original New Idea design; this spreader was built in the 1904-09 period.

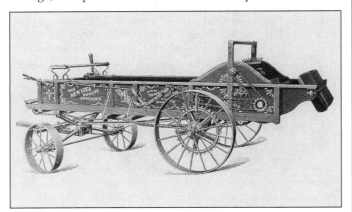

In the 1909-12 period, New Idea offered this new design; it had a 75-bushel capacity and also included a wide-spread attachment. In fact, New Idea claimed to be the original design with a wide-spread attachment.

By 1922, the New Idea line included this improved style, with a noticeably different wide-spread attachment. The latter would change but little for some years to come. The New Idea B-3 was a continuation of the Model B spreader of the 1912-14 period.

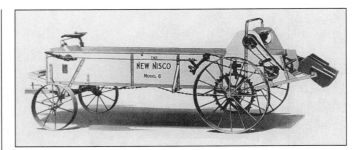

New Idea sold its spreaders under the NISCO trademark for a number of years, with this one being the New NISCO Model 6 of 1926. A New Idea parts book notes that this one was "painted red with black lettering."

In 1927, New Idea emerged with its No. 8 spreader; it had a 70-bushel capacity. Roller bearings were extensively used, along with 7-inch rear drive wheels. Company parts books note that this spreader "is painted a dark orange with green trimmings."

By 1940, New Idea was offering the farmer a new Model 12 tractor drawn spreader. This was a ground-driven model that gained tremendous popularity and enjoyed a long production run.

Newark Machine Co., Newark, Ohio

A 1908 advertisement noted that this spreader was "the result of twenty-five years of experience." That would mean that the

Miller spreader from Newark Machine Co., saw first light in 1883. Little else is known of the company aside from this illustration.

Ohio Cultivator Co., Bellevue, Ohio

Ohio Cultivator Co. apparently did not begin manufacturing its own manure spreaders until the early 1920s. However, the Ohio spreaders became fairly popular within a short time, partially due to the company's reputation with various other farm implements. In 1935, the company announced its new Famous Ohio spreader, an improved version with many of the modern features found on spreaders of its time.

Oliver Farm Equipment Co., Chicago, Ill.

In 1939, the Oliver Superior manure spreader line was augmented with the tractor spreader (in the bottom part of the illustration). It was a second choice over the conventional horse-drawn model shown at the top. The Oliver spreader line had the Superior spreader from American Seeding Machine Co. as its direct ancestor. The latter was one of the partners in the 1929 merger forming Oliver Farm Equipment Co.

Racine-Sattley Co., Kansas City, Kan.

For reasons now unknown, this spreader was manufactured by Racine-Sattley Co., of Kansas rather than at the main plant in Springfield, Ill. Another curiosity is that this Up-to-Date manure spreader reappears at Cedar Rapids Implement Co., a couple of years later. Further details are unknown.

Richardson Manufacturing Co., Worcester, Mass.

In 1903, Richardson Manufacturing Co. advertised this Worcester Kemp manure spreader; it was built under license of certain Kemp patents. Numerous jobbing houses handled the Worcester Kemp spreader, including several in the Midwestern states. Eventually, the line was bought out by Johnston Harvester Co., Batavia, N.Y.

Robinson Spreader Co., Vinton, Iowa

Apparently, beginning about 1906, Robinson offered this spreader to the farmer. The unique feature was a wide-spread beater unlike any other. Various claims were made for this design and the company continued building these spreaders for several years. Eventually, the Robinson factory closed, with Geo. B. Miller & Sons at Waterloo, Iowa, taking up the design and putting it on the market for a few more years.

Rock Island Plow Co., Rock Island, Ill.

Rock Island Plow Co., introduced the Model B spreader shown here in 1922. This design was fairly popular, although it continued to use a stiff front axle at a time when many companies were opting for the auto-steer front axle. The latter eventually became the norm, since it permitted sharp turns that were impossible for the design shown here. Rock Island began selling the Great Western spreaders from Smith Manufacturing Co. in 1911.

E. W. Ross Company, Springfield, Ohio

E. W. Ross had developed a sizable implement line by 1905, especially with ensilage cutters and feed cutters. The Ross Manure Spreader of the time was offered in 50, 70, and 100-bushel sizes. The largest model was indeed big. Few companies offered anything more than a 70-bushel size.

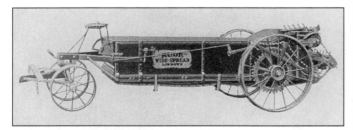

Rude Bros. Manufacturing Co., Liberty, Ind.

A product of the 1920s was this Rude manure spreader. As noted elsewhere, Rude had a long history in the farm equipment business, finally opting to concentrate all its efforts on manufacturing manure spreaders. Sometime in the 1930s, Rude became a part of General Implement Co.; in the 1940s, repair parts could be secured from B.F. Avery Co.

Did You Know?

A corn binder in good condition will fetch in excess of $200 today.

D.M. Sechler Carriage Co., Moline, Ill.

For 1906, the Black Hawk spreader from D.M. Sechler Carriage Co. took the same essential form as the Kemp spreaders of the same period. More than likely the design was built under license from Kemp. Sechler continued to build the Black Hawk for a number of years; eventually, parts for the Black Hawk could be secured from Oliver Farm Equipment Co.

Smith Manufacturing Co., Chicago, Ill.

By 1905, the farm implement line from Smith Manufacturing Co. was well known and was also very extensive. Its Great Western line included an endless apron manure spreader by 1905 and this continued for some years. In 1911, Smith made an agreement with Rock Island Plow Co. for the latter to handle its spreaders. Eventually, Rock Island came into control of the Great Western line.

Standard Harrow Co., Utica, N.Y.

Another of many early spreaders using the Kemp designs was the Standard shown in its 1904 edition. Farmers were anxious to buy manure spreaders because they saved a tremendous amount of work. Besides, taking another load to the field gave an opportunity for rest before pitching on another load.

Union Foundry & Machine Co., Ottawa, Kan.

In some areas, particularly the wheat-growing regions, there was always far more straw than could be used. Thus came the Perfection Straw Spreader in 1915. This $75 outfit attached to the rear of a hay rack, providing the means to evenly spread unused straw over the fields. The company also advertised this device as a manure spreader. But since it had no apron or unloading device, it is unlikely that this application was of any great value.

Trade Names

Acme	New Idea Spreader Co.	Maria Stein, OH	1905
Advance	Cortland Implement Co.	Cortland, NY	1905
Appleton	Appleton Mfg. Co.	Appleton, WI	1905
Arrow	Rock Island Plow Co.	Rock Island, IL	1913
Badger State	Davies Threshing Machine Co.	Oshkosh, WI	1913
Black Hawk	D. M. Sechler Carriage Co.	Moline, IL	1909
Black Hawk	Oliver Farm Equipment Co.	Chicago, IL	1936
Bloom	Bloom Mfg. Co.	Nashua, IA	1909
Bryan	Bryan Plow Co.	Bryan, OH	1915
Burch	Burch Plow Works	Crestline, OH	1917
Caldwell	Caldwell Mfg. Co.	Columbus, IN	1909
Case	J. I. Case Threshing Machine Co.	Racine, WI	1929
Chase	Chase Mfg. Co.	Mason City, IA	1915
Climax	Climax Corp.	Batavia, NY	1924
Cloverleaf	International Harvester Co.	Chicago, IL	1909
Coldwater	New Idea Spreader	Coldwater, OH	1915
Corn King	International Harvester Co.	Chicago, IL	1909
Curtis	Richardson Mfg. Co.	Worcester, MA	1915
Cyclone	G. G. Griswold Co.	Madison, OH	1913
Daniels	Sam Daniels Mfg. Co.	Hardwick, VT	1945
Easy Loader	Richardson Mfg. Co.	Worcester, MA	1913
Easy Loader	Johnston Harvester Co.	Batavia, NY	1913
Eckhardt	Eckhardt Mfg. Co.	St. Paul, MN	1932
Eclipse	Pana Enterprise Mfg. Co.	Pana, IL	1913
Emerson	Emerson-Brantingham Co.	Rockford, IL	1913
Empire	A. W. Hawks	Phoenix, NY	1892
Ertel	Geo. Ertel Co.	Quincy, IL	1922
E-Z	Bloom-Burns Mfg. Co.	Freeport, IL	1913

Trade Names (cont...)

Fearless	Harder Mfg. Co.	Cobleskill, NY	1909
Ferguson	Harry Ferguson Inc.	Dearborn, MI	1945
Field King	Litchfield Mfg. Co.	Waterloo, IA	1909
Flying Dutchman	Moline Plow Co.	Moline, IL	1915
Galloway	Wm. Galloway Co.	Waterloo, IA	1913
Garst	D. M. Sechler Carriage Co.	Moline, IL	1913
Gehl	Gehl Bros. Mfg. Co.	West Bend, WI	1922
Grand	Litchfield Mfg. Co.	Waterloo, IA	1924
Great Western	Rock Island Plow Co.	Rock Island, IL	1913
Great Western	Smith Mfg. Co.	Chicago, IL	1905
Hawkeye	Maytag Co.	Newton, IA	1913
Hayden	Geo. Ertel Co.	Quincy, IL	1909
Hercules	Caldwell Mfg. Co.	Columbus, IN	1909
Herron	Gus Pech Foundry and Mfg. Co.	LeMars, IA	1917
IHC	International Harvester Co.	Chicago, IL	1913
Independent	Independent Harvester Co.	Plano, IL	1915
IOA	Iowa Wagon Co.	Shenandoah, IA	1913
John Deere	Marseilles Mfg. Co.	Marseilles, IL	1913
Johnson Star	Glen Wagon Co.	Seneca Falls, NY	1909
Keller	Keller Mfg. Co.	Minneapolis, MN	1924
Kelly Standard	O. S. Kelly Western Mfg. Co.	Iowa City, IA	1909
Kemp	B. F. Rollins	St. Johnsbury, VT	1892
Kemp	Kemp & Burpee Mfg. Co.	Syracuse, NY	1892
Kemp	Richardson Mfg. Co.	Worcester, MA	1892
Kemp's 20th Century	International Harvester Co.	Chicago, IL	1913
Kemp's Climax	N. J. Kemp Co.	Batavia, NY	1919
Kentucky	Kentucky Wagon Mfg. Co.	Louisville, KY	1915
LaCrosse	Caldwell Mfg. Co.	Columbus, IN	1909
Leader	Oliver Chilled Plow Works	South Bend, IN	1922
Leader	Oliver Farm Equipment Co.	Chicago, IL	1936
LeRoy	LeRoy Plow Co.	LeRoy, NY	1929
Liberty	Liberty Cow Milker Co.	Hammond, IN	1910
Litchfield	Litchfield Mfg. Co.	Waterloo, IA	1905
Low Lift	International Harvester Co.	Chicago, IL	1913
Low Spread	International Harvester Co.	Chicgao, IL	1913
Lowest Low Down	New Idea Spreader Co.	Coldwater, OH	1915
Mandt	Mandt Wagon Co.	Stoughton, WI	1909
Mandt	Moline Plow Co.	Moline, IL	1909
Massey-Harris	Massey-Harris Harvester Co.	Batavia, NY	1919
McCormick-Deering	International Harvester Co.	Chicago, IL	1924
Miller	Geo. B. Miller and Son Inc.	Waterloo, IA	1929
Miller	Newark Machine Co.	Columbus, OH	1892
Midland	Midland Mfg. Co.	Tarkio, MO	1909
Moline	Minneapolis-Moline Co.	Minneapolis, MN	1936
Moline	Moline Plow Co.	Moline, IL	1915
Monarch	C. M. Parks	Manchester, OH	1915
National	Mandt Wagon Co.	Stoughton, WI	1909
National	Moline Plow Co.	Moline, IL	1909

Trade Names (cont...)

New American	American Harrow Co.	Detroit, MI	1905
New B. B.	Bloom-Burns Mfg. Co.	Freeport, IL	1913
New Idea	New Idea Spreader Co.	Coldwater, OH	1909
New Idea	New Idea Spreader Co.	Maria Stein, OH	1905
New Stoughton	Stoughton Wagon Co.	Stoughton, WI	1913
New Way	Robinson Spreader Co.	Vinton, IA	1909
Newlow	International Harvester Co.	Chicago, IL	1913
Newton	One Minute Mfg. Co.	Newton, IA	1924
Nisco	New Idea Spreader Co.	Coldwater, OH	1915
Ogburn	Ogburn Mfg. Co.	Newton, IA	1913
Old Hickory	Kentucky Wagon Mfg. Co.	Louisville, KY	1917
Only Simple	Corn Belt Mfg. Co.	Waterloo, IA	1913
Original Kemp	Deere and Co.	Moline, IL	1922
Peerless	Associated Manufacturers	Waterloo, IA	1913
Raber & Lang	Raber and Lang Mfg. Co.	Kendallville, IN	1919
Robinson	Corn Belt Mfg. Co.	Waterloo, IA	1936
Robinson	Robinson Spreader Co.	Vinton, IA	1909
Rock Island	Rock Island Plow Co.	Rock Island, IL	1909
Ross	E. W. Ross Co.	Springfield, OH	1905
Rude	Rude Bros. Mfg. Co.	Liberty, IN	1909
Sandow	Sandy McManus Inc.	Waterloo, IA	1915
Sandwich	Sandwich Mfg. Co.	Sandwich, IL	1919
Sandwich-New Idea	New Idea Spreader Co.	Coldwater, OH	1932
Sattley	Hummer Plow Works	Springfield, IL	1932
Standard	Standard Harrow Co.	Utica, NY	1905
Star	Adriance, Platt and Co.	Poughkeepsie, NY	1913
Success	Kemp & Burpee Mfg. Co.	Syracuse, NY	1905
Superior	New Idea Spreader Co.	Coldwater, OH	1913
Superior	New Idea Spreader Co.	Maria Stein, OH	1905
Superior	Oliver Farm Equipment Co.	Chicago, IL	1936
Twentieth Century	J. S. Kemp Mfg. Co.	Newark Valley, NY	1905
Twentieth Century	J. S. Kemp Mfg. Co.	Waterloo, IA	1905
United	Ohio Cultivator Co.	Bellevue, OH	1932
Up-to-Date	Cedar Rapids Implement Works	Cedar Rapids, IA	1905
Victory	Stoughton Wagon Co.	Stoughton, WI	1922
Waterloo	Iowa Spreader Mfg. Co.	Waterloo, IA	1909
Worcester-Kemp	Richardson Mfg. Co.	Worcester, MA	1905

Milking Machines

About 1910, the first practical milking machines appeared, but most of the early models remained on the market for a short time, then disappeared. Work continued, however, on milking machine designs; by the 1920s, there were some practical models available. Particularly in the

Midwestern states, dairy cows were a part of most farms. Some farmers had half a dozen cows or less, while others might milk 15 or 20 cows by hand, morning and night, every day of the year. Particularly to the latter group, the milking machine came as a great invention.

Conventional milkers, as shown in this section, flourished until the 1950s, when the coming of pipeline milkers and dairy parlors changed the methodology once again. An aside to the milking machines themselves were some of the peculiar devices used for the required vacuum system. Some companies made a specialty of these units, as is noted below. Other companies built milking machines that are not shown here, primarily due to a lack of illustrations for these machines. No particular antique value has been established for vintage milking machines.

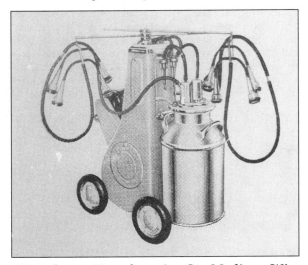

Ben H. Anderson Manufacturing Co., Madison, Wis.

Outside of this 1940 advertisement, nothing is known of the Clean Easy Portable Milker. This machine used an ordinary milk can as the storage receptacle, conveying milk directly from the cow to the can. When it was full, the can was hoisted into a large tank of chilled water for immediate cooling.

Babson Bros., Chicago, Ill.

In the late 1920s, the Surge milkers appeared from Babson Bros., at Chicago. With this design a long surcingle was placed over the cow's back, and the notched handle shown here was hooked into place. This eliminated the long tubes required of other designs. Surge milkers immediately became very popular and the Surge line is still well known among dairymen. This illustration dates to 1927.

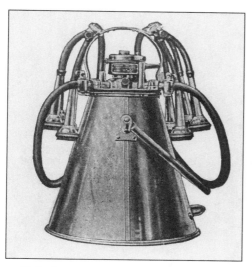

D.H. Burrell & Co., Little Falls, N.Y.

A 1910 offering was the Burrell-Lawrence-Kennedy Milking Machine, also known simply as the B-L-K milker. This one first came out in 1908 and remained on the market for several years.

DeLaval Separator Co., New York, N.Y.

DeLaval pioneered the development of the cream separator and was a leading force in the development of the milking machine. This 1928 illustration shows the Alpha-DeLaval engine to the right; it is belted to the vacuum-pump system. Two milkers are in place, with the farmer moving to another cow in the interim. Milking machines greatly lessened the time required for this twice-daily process.

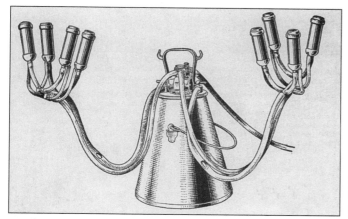

Empire Cream Separator Co., Bloomfield, N.J.

About 1917, Empire began offering milking machines to the farmer; the company had already made a name for itself with its cream separators. The Empire line proved to be quite popular, so much so, that in 1925, Rock Island Plow Co., took on the Empire milker line, offering it through its Rock Island implement dealer organization.

Globe Milker Inc., Des Moines, Iowa

In 1941, the Globe portable milker appeared. This design was a completely self-contained unit with its own vacuum pump built into the milker. Probably due to the onset of World War II, it does not appear that the Globe milker was marketed for any length of time, but additional information has not been located.

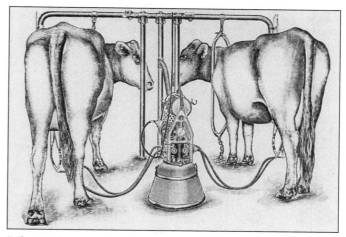

Liberty Cow Milker Co., Hammond, Ind.

For 1910, Liberty offered its cow-milker direct to the farmer, noting that there were "no jobbers, no catalogue houses and no trusts" to deal with. Aside from this advertisement, nothing more can be found on the company. Up to about 1915, these machines were usually billed as "cow milkers." The term "milking machine" came into vogue after that time.

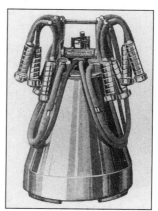

Perfection Manufacturing Co., Minneapolis, Minn.

Perfection milkers were well known by dairymen. The company developed this machine sometime before World War I and continued to build milkers for decades. Meanwhile, many other manufacturers entered the market and left again after only a short time in business.

Taylor Engine Co., Elgin, Ill.

By the early 1920s, the Taylor Vacuum engine appeared. This special design included a vacuum piston and cylinder cast in place directly behind the engine piston. Thus, the engine served as a vacuum pump and an engine within a single unit. Various other engine-vacuum pump combinations were built, but none compared to the Taylor design.

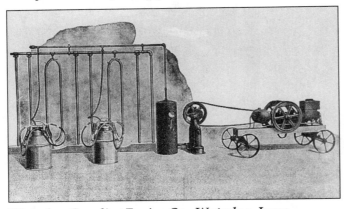

Waterloo Gasoline Engine Co., Waterloo, Iowa

In 1916, this company announced its Waterloo Boy Milker. To the right is the vacuum pump and storage tank. Belted to the pump is a Waterloo Boy gasoline engine; to the left are two milker units. Deere & Co., bought out Waterloo Gasoline Engine Co., in 1918, but nothing regarding the Waterloo Boy milker has been found in its literature.

Trade Names

Airliner	Myers-Sherman Co.	Streator, IL	1945
All-Rite	All-Rite Milker Co.	Milwaukee, WI	1924
Anderson	Anderson Milker Co.	Randolph, NY	1924
Anker-Holth	Anker-Holth Mfg. Co.	Port Huron, MI	1939
Blue Ribbon	Electric Milker Corp.	Chicago, IL	1922
Burrell	A. H. Barber Creamery Supply	Chicago, IL	1913
Burrell	Cherry–Burrell Co.	Cedar Rapids, IA	1932
Burrell	D. H. Burrell Co.	Little Falls, NY	1917
Burton-Page	Burton-Page Co.	Chicago, IL	1936
B-V	Geo. B. Miller Mfg. Co.	Waterloo, IA	1922
Calf-Way	Calf-Way Milker Co.	Chicago, IL	1917
Chore Boy	Hinman Milking Machine Co.	Oneida, NY	1939

Trade Names

Clean-Easy	Ben H. Anderson Mfg. Co.	Madison, WI	1929
Clean-Easy	Clean-Easy Milker Co.	Madison, WI	1924
Cloverleaf	Cloverleaf Milker Co.	Urbana, IN	1924
Dairy Maid	Aspinwall-Drew Co.	Jackson, MI	1922
DeLaval	DeLaval Separator Co.	New York, NY	
Empire	Empire Cream Separator Co.	Bloomfield, NJ	1917
Empire	Empire Cream Separator Co.	Bloomfield, NJ	1917
Fords	Myers-Sherman Co.	Chicago, IL	1929
Fort Atkinson	Fort Atkinson Mfg. Co.	Fort Atkinson, WI	1924
George	Geo. F. Worthington	Minneapolis, MN	1945
Harner	Harner-Jones Co.	Springfield, OH	1919
Hinman	Hinman Milking Machine Co.	Oneida, NY	1913
Hoover's	Universal Milking Machine Co.	Waukesha, WI	1932
Independent	Independent Silo Co.	St. Paul, MN	1919
Lactant	Buckwalter Supply Co.	Lancaster, PA	1919
Lay	L. A. Young Industries	Detroit, MI	1919
Litchfield	Litchfield Mfg. Co.	Waterloo, IA	1913
McAlpine	Factory Sales Co.	New York, NY	1919
McClure	McClure Co.	Saginaw, MI	1922
McCormick-Deering	International Harvester Co.	Chicago, IL	1939
McL. Twin	Excavating & Screening Machy. Co.	St. Paul, MN	1917
Magnetic	DeLaval Separator Co.	New York, NY	1939
Mehring	Wm. H. Mehring	Keymar, MD	1917
Milk-Master	Perfection Mfg. Co.	Minneapolis, MN	1917
Mullins	Mullins Mfg. Co.	Brillion, WI	1917
Nu-Way	Nu-Way Milker Co.	Syracuse, NY	1924
Official	Official Mfg. Co.	LaCrosse, WI	1917
Page	Pioneer Mfg. Co.	West Allis, WI	1939
Perfection	Perfection Mfg. Co.	Minneapolis, MN	1917
Pine Tree	Pine Tree Milking Machine Co.	Chicago, IL	1929
Q & E	Q & E Milker Co.	Minneapolis, MN	1919
Rite-Way	Rite-Way Products	Chicago, IL	1929
Sharples	Dairy Specialty Co.	West Chester, PA	1913
Sharples	Sharples Separator Co.	West Chester, PA	1913
Success	Success Milking Machine Co.	Milwaukee, WI	1917
Super Deluxe	National Milker Co.	Des Moines, IA	1945
Surge	Babson Mfg. Co.	Chicago, IL	1932
Surge	Pine Tree Milking Machine Co.	Chicago, IL	1929
Uebler	Geo. D. Pohl Mfg. Co.	Vernon, NY	1917
Universal	Universal Milking Machine Co.	Columbus, OH	1917
Upward Squeeze	Sharples Separator Co.	West Chester, PA	1917
Victory	Mullins Mfg. Co.	Brillion, WI	1919
Victory	Starch Bros.	LaCrosse, WI	1917
Waterloo Boy	Waterloo Gasoline Engine Co.	Waterloo, IA	1917
Western	Western Milking Machine Co.	Stevens Point, WI	1913

Mowers

When first developed in the 1850s, mowers were also known as mowing machines. The latter title stuck for 20 years or so, but eventually everyone—manufacturers and farmers alike—opted for the simpler term. "Mower" has been the term ever since.

In the author's *150 Years of International Harvester* (Crestline/Motorbooks: 1981), an outline is presented regarding the complex tangle of patents, infringement suits and the pandemonium created by a host of mower patents held or licensed by a host of manufacturers. Complicating matters further, some reapers were built as double-purpose machines, being a reaper or a mower. Although the idea didn't work very well, it still was better than having neither machine and resorting to hand methods once again.

This section illustrates many different mowers built at various stages of their development, being the products of many different manufacturers. Of those shown, many others were built but for which no illustrations were available as the book was assembled. Complicating the matter further, the same mower was sometimes built simultaneously by two or more companies.

Among collectors of vintage farm equipment, old mowing machines have acquired a market value that is quite variable. Very old machines often bring $250 or more, even in poor condition. Later machines, usually after 1920, can sometimes sell for $100 or more, but many of these can be bought for much less, especially those that have resided outdoors for half a century or more.

Acme Harvester Co., Peoria, Ill.

This 1899 advertisement for the Hodges Mower lists the company as Acme Harvesting Machine Co., Pekin, Ill. By 1903, Acme was listed at Peoria and building the New Hodges Mower, an improved design. Little of the history concerning Acme can presently be found.

Did You Know?

Disc harrows are generally not a highly prized item; restored and repainted examples, however, might bring $200 to $300.

Adriance, Platt & Co., Poughkeepsie, N.Y.

An 1895 advertisement illustrates the Adriance Buckeye Mower which they termed as being The Original Buckeye. Adriance, Platt & Co. had a long career in the mower business, but this ended when the company was bought out by Moline Plow Co. in 1912.

Aetna Manufacturing Co., Salem, Ohio

For 1869, Aetna offered its Mower and Reaper, built under the Amos Rank patents. Particularly during the 1860s and 1870s, mower patents abounded, with many of them overlapping to such a degree that patent suits were commonplace. In this engraving, the Aetna is shown "on the road." Little history of the firm can now be found.

Ames Plow Co., Boston, Mass.

During the 1850s, Ames Plow Co., emerged as a major Eastern manufacturer of plows and other implements. By the late 1860s, the company was offering the Perry Gold Medal mower as shown. This unusual design placed the mower bar within the center of the right-hand wheel, as shown in the engraving. By 1866, Ames Plow Co. had taken over Nourse & Mason Co. also of Boston; the latter had become well known for building the Kirby mowers.

C. Aultman & Co., Canton, Ohio

For 1868, Aultman offered this style of the Buckeye Mower & Reaper. Through a tangled series of takeovers, buyouts, reorganizations and mergers, Ball, Aultman & Co. appears in the mix, with Lewis Miller as the inventive force. Eventually, Miller came to own most of Ball, Aultman & Co.

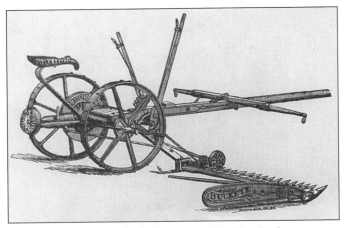

By 1878, Aultman & Co. had announced its New Buckeye mower; this hinged-bar design was due to the inventiveness of Lewis Miller. The latter is generally credited with inventing the hinged-bar design; in fact, once the Miller design was marketed, there were so many other "hinged-bar" patents that eventually they were combined in the Hinged Bar Pool so that participating manufacturers could build under license from the pool and avoid the constant tangle of infringement suits.

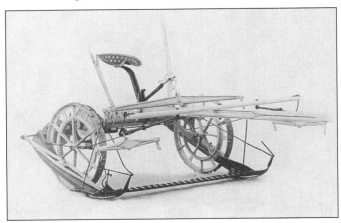

Aultman, Miller & Co., Akron, Ohio

Extensive research would be required to follow the development of the Buckeye mowers. Aultman, Miller & Co. appeared, apparently by the 1880s, as the successor to Ball, Aultman & Co. Its 1901 catalog illustrates this center-cut mower, a design still on the market, despite some 30 years of hinged-bar machines.

A 1901 Aultman-Miller catalog illustrates its hinged-bar mower of the day. By this time, mowing machines had been well perfected and would give the farmer day after day of trouble-free operation. Subsequently, Aultman, Miller & Co., came under stock control of International Harvester Co., in 1903. In 1905, the implement line was abandoned and the factory was converted to making twine and automobiles.

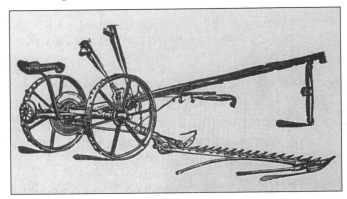

Koenig mowers appear in a 1907 advertisement, with the copy noting that "The Koenig Mower is an exact duplicate of the old Aultman, Miller & Co. Mower." This design was offered for sale by Weber Implement Co., St. Louis.

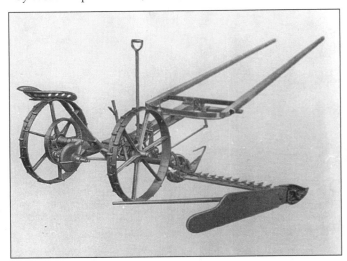

B.F. Avery & Sons, Louisville, Kty.

A 1916 catalog illustration shows the Avery Champion one-horse mower. This machine was made in two sizes—a 3-1/2 and a 4-foot model. This style was billed as being ideal for places where the ordinary two-horse model would be too large. If desired, the thills could be replaced with an ordinary tongue for use with two horses.

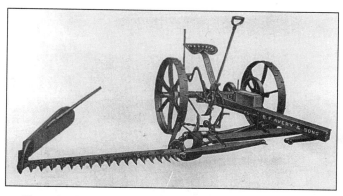

Champion Improved Mowers took the form shown here for the 1916 Avery catalog. By this time, most mowers had the same general form, featuring a hinged bar, foot-lift device and cast-iron wheels. The most noticeable differences were in the drive mechanism.

J.I. Case Co., Racine, Wis.

Case introduced its new Oil-Bath Mower in 1934. This model was a major leap forward because the drive gears were now enclosed in an oil-tight case. Aside from this feature, the mower was a continuation of the designs created by Emerson-Brantingham Co. J.I. Case purchased E-B in 1928.

Cayuga Chief Manufacturing Co., Auburn, N.Y.

The Cayuga Chief emerged in the 1860s as a leading design from Cyrenus Wheeler Jr. Major conflicts existed between Wheeler's patents and those of several others, especially Lewis Miller. Eventually, the contentions subsided; in 1874, the Cayuga Chief came under ownership of D.M. Osborne Co., also in Auburn.

Clipper Mower & Reaper Co., Yonkers, N.Y.

An engraving of 1870 shows the one-horse Clipper at work. This machine used a 3-1/2 foot cutter bar and weighed but 480 pounds. Clipper first marketed this machine in 1866, building 50 units that year. Two years later, the company made 580 machines, but could not fulfill all of its orders. Little else is known of the company outside of this illustration and accompanying data.

Corry Machine Co., Corry, Pa.

Outside of an 1869 engraving, nothing is known of the Climax Mower from Corry Machine Co. Numerous manufacturers built mowers for a time, particularly during the 1860s and 1870s. Usually these were built under license from another company or perhaps from the Hinged Bar Pool, a patent pool that operated for several years, ending in 1871.

Dain Manufacturing Co., Ottumwa, Iowa

Dain's early manufacturing efforts centered on haying equipment. This included the Dain Center-Draft Mower shown here in its 1894 version. Little is known of this early Dain design; in fact, when this mower was built, Dain was still operating his factory in Missouri. The company was founded in 1881 and came under control of Deere & Co., in 1911.

Deere & Co., marketed much of the Dain equipment line prior to gaining stock control of the Dain operation in 1911. A 1908 John Deere Plow Co. catalog illustrates the Dain Vertical Lift Mower; this model was made in 5- and 6-foot sizes.

Deere & Co., Moline, Ill.

In 1927, Deere offered this High-Lift Mower as part of its haying machine arsenal. The Deere mowers were direct descendants of the Dain mower, pioneered in the 1890s and sold by Deere for some years until a final takeover in 1911.

Deering Harvester Co., Chicago, Ill.

For 1885, Deering offered mowers in several styles, including the Deering Ideal Giant, its largest model. At this point in time, the principles of mower design were well established and Deering had a factory capable of building a top quality machine. In addition, Deering had already developed an extensive dealer organization.

Deering Ideal one-horse mowers for 1899 were offered in 3-1/2 and 4-foot sizes. This small mower was ideal for the small farmer and indeed, the "Ideal" trade name lent further credence to an excellent design.

By 1899, Deering had further developed the Ideal and Ideal Giant mowers of the 1880s, with these mowers continuing into the 1902 merger that formed International Harvester Co. Deering mowers continued in the IHC line into the 1920s.

Emerson-Brantingham Co., Rockford, Ill.

The Emerson line of mowers went back to the 1850s with the Manny reapers. Subsequently, the company built and sold numerous styles of mowing machines. This New Standard mower is of 1907 vintage. Essentially the same mower was built by Emerson-Brantingham until the company sold out to J.I. Case in 1928.

In 1919, Emerson-Brantingham acquired D.M. Osborne & Co. from International Harvester. Subsequently, the company offered E-B Osborne mowers in many styles and sizes. Shown here is its 1919 version of the No. 2 mower, a small model made in a 4-1/2 and a 5-foot cut.

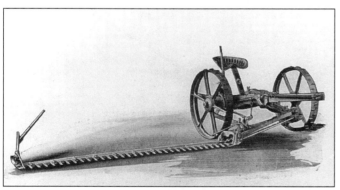

An unusual mower for 1919 was this E-B Standard 8-foot mower. While most horse mowers were of 5- or 6-foot design, a few were made in 7-foot sizes. Rare indeed was the 8-foot model, since most farmers considered it to be too heavy for a team, especially considering the side draft.

Frost & Wood Manufacturing Co. Ltd., Smiths Falls, Ontario

A 1910 offering of Frost & Wood was the Giant Mower. This Canadian company built several styles of mowers at the time, but little history of the firm has been located, aside from its 1910 catalog.

R.L. Howard, Buffalo, N.Y.

Sometime prior to 1860, R.L. Howard Co. acquired the interests of the Ketchum mower. The Ketchum design was one of the earliest successful mowing machines and Howard continued building it for some years; the style shown here graced the cover of its 1860 catalog. Eventually, Howard slips from view and no further information has been located.

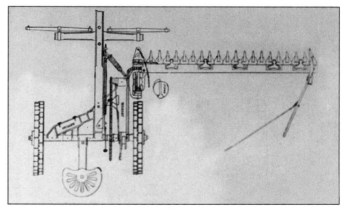

Hussey Mower & Implement Co., Knightstown, Ind.

A 1903 advertisement illustrates the Hussey No-Pitman Mower. This rather complicated design was intended to obviate the need for the usual mower pitman which sometimes caused problems. However, the advantages were probably offset by the complicated mechanism of the design. Aside from this 1903 illustration, nothing further is known of the company.

International Harvester Co., Chicago, Ill.

A 1920 catalog lists the McCormick No. 6 mower. This was essentially the same McCormick mower that the company had been building for years. By this time, McCormick mowers had been shipped all over the world, in addition to being a household term in the United States.

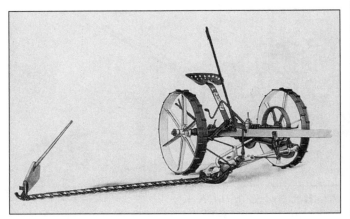

Deering mowers of 1920 were little different than those the company brought into the 1902 merger forming International Harvester Co. From the McCormick and the Deering designs, the company came out in the 1920s with a McCormick-Deering design that embodied all the best from both designs.

Johnston Harvester Co., Batavia, N.Y.

Johnston Harvester had roots going back to the 1840s, with the firm operating under the title of Johnston, Huntley & Co. for some years. During the 1860s, Johnston-Huntley sold its patented Cycloid mower as pictured here. Its success led to the subsequent development of improved designs.

Johnston's Wrought Iron Mower made its appearance in the 1870s. This design was unusual in its placement of the cutter bar; the latter pivoted in line with the main axle and was supported by offset bars extending from the machine frame.

By the 1890s, Johnston had developed an entirely new line of mowers and harvesting equipment under its Continental trade name. Shown here is the Continental Mower No. 6 of 1892. This machine featured a variable speed drive so that it could easily be adapted to various mowing conditions.

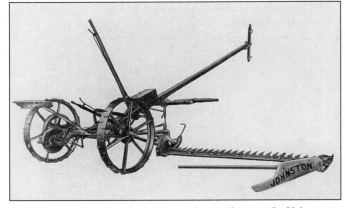

Johnston Harvester Co., came under stock control of Massey-Harris about 1910, with the latter acquiring the company outright in 1917. During the early 1900s, Johnston continued marketing new mower designs, with this one being known as the Johnston No. 10 Lever-Fold Mower.

McCormick Harvesting Machine Co., Chicago, Ill.

McCormick began building mowers in the 1860s, using its past experience in the reaper business to develop a unique and practical mower. In the years that followed, the McCormick remained a popular design, having developed to the style shown here for 1896.

One of the popular McCormick models was this No. 4 Steel Mower. Billed by McCormick as "the acknowledged king of grass cutters," the No. 4 embodied great strength and durability. With the extensive McCormick dealer organization, farmers also found it easy to secure repair parts when needed.

Massey-Harris Harvester Co., Batavia, N.Y.

With stock control of Johnston Harvester Co. in 1910, Massey-Harris broadened its sales base considerably. Massey-Harris was based at Toronto, Ontario, Canada, and the usual problems of shipping across national borders prompted the firm to expand with a factory in the United States. With this accomplished, the company bought out Johnston in 1917, continuing to market mowers such as this Massey-Harris No. 20 model.

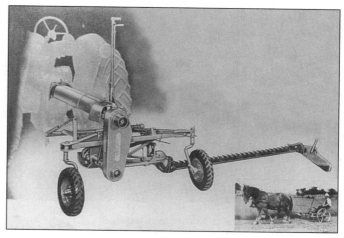

During the 1930s, many companies recognized the coming of tractor power to all phases of farming. Thus the company developed its No. 5 Semi-Mounted mower strictly for tractor use. Many other companies developed tractor mowers during the 1930s, bringing an end to horse-drawn mowers by the early 1950s.

Milwaukee Harvester Co., Milwaukee, Wisc.

Milwaukee Harvester Co. was a partner of the 1902 merger forming International Harvester Co. The roots of this company went back to the 1850s, with the Milwaukee Harvester name appearing first in 1884. Subsequent to the IHC merger, much of the Milwaukee line was phased out, with its factories being devoted to other manufacturing activities.

Moline Plow Co., Moline, Ill.

Moline Plow Co. made its first major entry into the mower business with its 1912 purchase of Adriance, Platt & Co., Poughkeepsie, N.Y. Subsequently, Moline built on this prior experience and marketed mowers of its own design, including the Moline No. 8 of 1919 vintage; it is shown here.

North River Agricultural Works, New York, N.Y.

An 1866 catalog from North River Agricultural Works illustrates Swift's Improved Lawn Mower, an interesting machine pulled by one horse and guided by hand. Decades have turned into centuries, so no other information has been located.

An 1869 pamphlet displays the Kirby mower in the transport position. This was a combination machine designed as a mower, a reaper and a self-raker. Changing from one machine to another was accomplished with relative ease, but the majority of farmers preferred dedicated machines that could mow or reap or rake, but not all in the same unit.

Nourse, Mason & Co., Boston, Mass.

The Davis Improved Mowing Machine was built under the Ketchum patents and marketed in this form for 1861. In 1866, the company came under control of Ames Plow Co., but subsequent developments have eluded the current research.

Osborne operated on its own until coming under control of International Harvester Co., about 1903, and coming to a close in 1905. Curiously, IHC continued to sell numerous items of the Osborne line for some years and under the Osborne trademark. Shown here is an Osborne Columbia mower of 1900.

D.M. Osborne & Co., Auburn, N.Y.

For 1866, Osborne offered Kirby's American Harvester shown here as a mower; this machine was convertible to a reaper. Osborne was an active participant in the development of the mowing machine and garnered a great many significant patents.

Plano Manufacturing Co., Plano, Ill.

Founded in 1881, Plano was offering the Jones Chain-Drive Mower shortly afterwards; it took the form shown here in 1889. The chain drive was simple and eliminated the need for noisy and troublesome gears, but it also had its disadvantages. A chain is no stronger than its weakest link and weak chain links certainly were cause for a farmer to have extras on hand.

A 1900 advertisement in the *American Agriculturist* shows the Jones mower at that time; it differs very little from its 1889 edition. Subsequently, the Plano line was merged into International Harvester when the latter was organized in 1902.

Sandwich Manufacturing Co., Sandwich, Ill.

This company, formed in 1867, was a well-known manufacturer of corn shellers. Several members of the Adams Family were involved in the company, among them being J. Phelps Adams, who devised a hinged-bar mower somewhat similar to that of Lewis Miller (see Aultman, Miller & Co. listing). In the 1880s, the Sandwich Chain Geared Mower appeared; it continued on the market for several years. The 1890 model is pictured here.

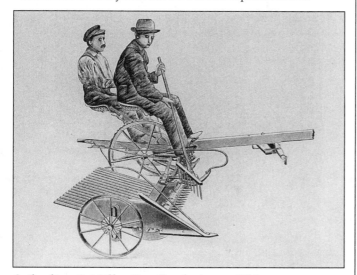

Seiberling & Miller Co., Doylestown, Ohio

An illustration of about 1900 shows the No. 3 Standard Senior Mower from Seiberling & Miller. It is equipped with a hand-operated dropper. With the dropper teeth raised as shown, hay or grain accumulated until the operator tripped the hand lever to leave behind gavels of grain suitable for hand binding. Little else is known of the company aside from this illustration.

James A. Smith & Co., Ancaster, Ontario

Wheeler's Combined Reaper & Mower is illustrated in this 1874 engraving. Obviously, it was being built under patents owned or controlled by Cyrenus Wheeler Jr. The latter was a major force in the American development of the mowing machine. The mower is shown here in its transport position.

Sprague Mowing Machine Co., Providence, R.I.

From 1872 comes this illustration of the Sprague mower. William Sprague was its president and had been involved in the design of mowing machines for some years. This model uses a hinged-bar design; the gearing is enclosed in a huge cast-iron case to keep out dust and dirt. With occasional oiling, gears and bearings in these early machines lasted far longer than might have been expected.

Syracuse Agricultural Works, Syracuse, N.Y.

An advertisement of the 1880s illustrates the new Hubbard mower from Syracuse Agricultural Works. Moses G. Hubbard was responsible for at least four different patents on mowing machines; in fact, when McCormick Harvesting Machine Co., entered the arena, its first mowers were built under license from Hubbard.

Warder, Bushnell & Glessner Co., Springfield, Ohio

Warder, Brokaw & Child at Springfield, Ohio included a sheet of instructions for its Champion Mowing Machine of 1855. Farmers were warned to "Follow the Directions or No Warranty." This early design preceded the hinged-bar mowers; the machine shown here had the cutter bar attached rigidly to the frame.

An 1892 advertisement displays the Whiteley's Champion mower of the time; this was a hinged bar machine that included all the latest developments of the Champion line. Ten years later, the Champion line would become a part of International Harvester Co.

Warrior Mower Co., Little Falls, N.Y.

From the June 6, 1874, issue of *Boston Cultivator* comes this engraving of the Warrior mower, a hinged-bar machine typical of its day. It is shown here with the farmer raising the lever to dodge a large stone. The Warrior was undoubtedly built under license from one or more patentees, but no further information on the firm has been located.

Wilber, Stevens & Co., Poughkeepsie, N.Y.

An advertisement of the 1880s shows this company's Eureka mower at work in the field. This was a center-cut design and, unlike most of these machines, the Eureka employed an unusual hitch that placed the horses outside of the cutting area.

No promotion would have been complete without this demonstration of the Eureka on the road. Since the farmer's coattails are flying, one gets the impression of a substantial road speed. J.D. Wilber acquired several mower patents in the 1860s and 1870s.

Walter A. Wood Mowing & Reaping Machine Co., Hoosick Falls, N.Y.

From 1887, this engraving illustrates the Wood Mowing Attachment as used on the company's reapers. Numerous companies offered these conversion units for a multiple-use or combination machine. Apparently, they met a mediocre reception, partially because of the work required to convert the machines back and forth for varying duties.

Organized already in the 1850s, the Wood operations continued under Walter A. Wood's leadership, until his death in 1892. The Wood design was the first to feature enclosed gearing; this was a distinct advantage in prolonging the life of the machine. Shown here is a Walter A. Wood mower of 1887.

In the 1890s, Walter A. Wood announced its new Tubular Steel Mower. This new design did away with much of the cast iron formerly used and simultaneously provided great strength. By the 1920s, repair parts for these mowers were still available from the company; this, too, came to an end about 1930.

Wm. Anson Wood, Albany, N.Y.

Current research has not determined the connection, if one existed, between this company and Walter A. Wood's Co., Hoosick Falls, N.Y. For 1878, William Anson Wood advertised the Eagle mower as shown here. Beyond the illustration, no further information can be located.

Miscellany

During more than a quarter century of research, the author has acquired many unidentified illustrations, with a few of them being pictured here. All of these machines display interesting designs and perhaps further research will determine the names of their respective manufacturers.

One-horse Kniffen, priced at $110.

Meadow King mower.

Granite Mowing Machine of 1866.

An 1884 engraving illustrates the Improved Seven-Foot Cut Smith Mower.

Trade Names

Acme	Acme Harvesting Machine Co.	Peoria, IL	1909
Admiral	Walter A. Wood Mowing & R.M. Co.	Hoosick Falls, NY	1909
Adriance	Adriance, Platt & Co.	Poughkeepsie, NY	1892
Adriance	Moline Plow Co.	Moline, IL	1915
Advance	Ann Arbor Agricultural Co.	Ann Arbor, MI	1892
Advance	Geo. Sweet Mfg. Co.	Dansville, NY	1892
Aetna	Aetna Mfg. Co.	Salem, OH	1869
Allis-Chalmers	Allis-Chalmers Mfg. Co.	Milwaukee, WI	1945
America	Richardson Mfg. Co.	Worcester, MA	1905
American	American Harvester Co.	Moline, IL	1905
Argentine	Sandwich Mfg. Co.	Sandwich, IL	1892
Bradley	Bradley & Co.	Syracuse, NY	1892
Buckeye	Aultman & Miller	Akron, OH	1905
Buckeye	C. Aultman & Co.	Canton, OH	1868
Buckeye	Richardson Mfg. Co.	Worcester, MA	1905
Capital	Western Mfg. Co.	Lincoln, NE	1892
Case (Osborne)	J. I. Case Co.	Racine, WI	1932
Cayuga Chief	Cayuga Chief Mfg. Co.	Auburn, NY	1865
Cayuga Chief	D. M. Osborne and Co.	Auburn, NY	1874
Champion	B. F. Avery and Sons	Louisville, KY	1919
Champion	International Harvester Co.	Chicago, IL	1905
Champion	Warder, Bushnell & Glessner Co.	Springfield, OH	1892
Climax	Corry Machine Co.	Corry, PA	1871
Clipper	Clipper Mower & Reaper Co.	Yonkers, NY	1870
Continental	Johnston Harvester Co.	Batavia, NY	1892
Crawford Improved	Haskins Mfg. Co.	Lake Geneva, WI	1892
Crown	Janesville Machine Co.	Janesville, WI	1892

Trade Names (cont...)

Crown	Janesville Machine Co.	Janesville, WI	1905
Curtis	Curtis Mfg. Co.	Albion, NY	1892
Dain	Dain Mfg. Co.	Ottumwa, IA	1905
Dain Center Draft	Dain Mfg. Co.	Carrollton, MO	1892
Davis	Nourse, Mason & Co.	Boston, MA	1866
Dayton	Stoddard Mfg. Co.	Dayton, OH	1892
Deere	Deere and Co.	Moline, IL	1917
Deering	International Harvester Co.	Chicago, IL	1905
Deering Giant	Wm. Deering & Co.	Chicago, IL	1892
Deering Junior Giant	Wm. Deering & Co.	Chicago, IL	1892
Denver	Plattner Implement Co.	Denver, CO	1909
Detroit	Detroit Harvester Co.	Detroit, MI	1945
Eagle	Wm. Anson Wood	Albany, NY	1878
E-B	Emerson-Brantingham Co.	Rockford, IL	1919
E-B Osborne	Emerson-Brantingham Co.	Rockford, IL	1905
Ellwood	Rockford Mfg. Co.	Rockford, IL	1905
Elward Center Draft	Winchester & Partridge Mfg. Co.	Whitewater, WI	1892
Emerson	Emerson Mfg. Co.	Rockford, IL	1909
Empire	J. F. Seiberling & Co.	Akron, OH	1892
Empire	J. F. Seiberling & Co.	Akron, OH	1909
Empire	Messinger Mfg. Co.	Tatamy, PA	1905
Empire	Seiberling & Miller Co.	Doyleston, OH	1905
Esterly	Esterly Harvesting Machine Co.	Whitewater, WI	1892
Eureka	Eureka Mower Co.	Utica, NY	1905
Eureka	Wilber, Stevens & Co.	Poughkeepsie, NY	1884
Evans	Beatrice Iron Works	Beatrice, NE,	1915
Excelsior	Hoover & Gamble	Miamisburg, OH	1892
Farmall	International Harvester Co.	Chicago, IL	1936
Ferguson	Harry Ferguson Inc.	Detroit, MI	1945
Flying Dutchman	Minneapolis-Moline Co.	Minneapolis, MN	1932
Frye's New Model	John J. Frye	Portland, ME	1892
Giant Admiral	Walter A. Wood Mowing & R. M. Co.	Hoosick Falls, NY	1909
Globe	Johnston Harvester Co.	Batavia, NY	1892
Granite State	Granite State Mowing Machine Co.	Hinsdale, NH	1892
Granite State	Newhall & Stebbins	Hinsdale, NH	1892
Hall	Hall Mowing Machine Co.	Portland, ME	1892
Homeworth	Pilmer Bros.	Homeworth, OH	1892
Hopkins Automatic	Automatic Mower & Mfg. Co.	Chicago, IL	1892
Horst	Horst Mfg. Co.	Detroit, MI	1945
Hubbard	Syracuse Agricultural Works	Syracuse, NY	1883
Hussey	Hussey Mower & Implement Co.	Knightstown, IN	1903
Imperial	Rockford Mfg. Co.	Rockford, IL	1905
Independent	Independent Harvester Co.	Plano, IL	1915
John Deere	Deere and Co.	Moline, IL	1919

Trade Names (cont...)

Johnston	Johnston Harvester Co.	Batavia, NY	1905
Jones Chain-Drive	Plano Mfg. Co.	Chicago, IL	1892
Judson	Judson Mfg. Co.	San Francisco, CA	1892
Kelly	Daniel T, Kelly	Portland, ME	1892
Ketchum	R. L. Howard	Buffalo, NY	1860
Keystone	Keystone Co.	Sterling, IL	1905
Kirby	D. M. Osborne and Co.	Auburn, NY	1866
Kirby	Nourse and Mason	Boston, MA	1855
Knowlton	Abram Ellwood	Sycamore, IL	1892
Lee's No. 2	Pilmer Bros.	Homeworth, OH	1892
Little Giant	Little Giant Products Corp.	Peoria, IL	1945
Massey-Harris	Johnston Harvester Co.	Batavia, NY	1917
Mayflower	Johnston Harvester Co.	Batavia, NY	1892
McCormick	International Harvester Co.	Chicago, IL	1905
McCormick	McCormick Harvesting Machine Co.	Chicago, IL	1892
McCormick-Deering	International Harvester Co.	Chicago, IL	1936
Meadow Fork	Gordon & DeGarmo	Rochester, NY	1892
Meadow King	Gregg & Co.	Trumansburg, NY	1892
Meadow Lark	Rochester Agricultural Works	Rochester, NY	1905
Milwaukee	International Harvester Co.	Chicago, IL	1909
Milwaukee Chain-Drive	Milwaukee Harvester Co.	Milwaukee, WI	1892
Minneapolis	Minneapolis Harvester Works	Minneapolis, MN	1892
Minnie	Minnie Harvester Works	St. Paul, MN	1905
Moline	Moline Plow Co.	Moline, IL	1919
Moline-Milwaukee	Minneapolis-Moline Co.	Minneapolis, MN	1936
Moline-Milwaukee	Moline Implement Co.	Moline, IL	1909
New Big Four	International Harvester Co.	Chicago, IL	1913
New Deering	Wm. Deering & Co.	Chicago, IL	1892
New Four	International Harvester Co.	Chicago, IL	1913
New Hodges	Acme Harvester Co.	Peoria, IL	1905
New Idea	New Idea Inc.	Coldwater, OH	1939
New Ideal	International Harvester Co.	Chicago, IL	1913
New Osborne	D. M. Osborne	Auburn, NY	1905
New Standard	Emerson Mfg. Co.	Rockford, IL	1905
New Standard	Emerson-Brantingham Co.	Rockford, IL	1913
Nisco	New Idea Spreader Co.	Coldwater, OH	1919
Oliver	Oliver Farm Equipment Co.	Chicago, IL	1936
Osborne	D. M. Osborne & Co.	Auburn, NY	1892
Osborne	International Harvester Co.	Chicago, IL	1909
Osborne Columbia	International Harvester Co.	Chicago, IL	1913

Trade Names (cont...)

Perry	Wyckoff & Co.	Perry, NY	1892
Perry Gold Medal	Ames Plow Co.	Boston, MA	1850
Plano	International Harvester Co.	Chicago, IL	1905
Plattner-Yale	Plattner-Yale Mfg. Co.	Lincoln, NE	1919
Red, White & Blue	Fuller & Johnson Mfg. Co.	Madison, WI	1892
Ross	A. M. Ross & Co.	Ilion, NY	1892
Sandwich	Sandwich Mfg. Co.	Sandwich, IL	1892
Screw	W. H. H. Heydrick	Philadelphia, PA	1892
Sprague	Sprague Mowing Machine Co.	Providence, RI	1872
Standard	Emerson Mfg. Co.	Rockford, IL	1905
Standard	Emerson, Talcott & Co.	Rockford, IL	1892
Standard	Emerson-Brantingham Co.	Rockford, IL	1913
Standard Senior	Sieberling and Miller Co.	Doylestown, OH	1900
Steele	Craver & Steele Mfg. Co.	Harvey, IL	1892
Swift's	North River Agricultural Works	New York, NY	1866
Thomas	Ohio Cultivator Co.	Bellevue, OH	1932
Thomas Crown	Thomas Mfg. Co.	Springfield, OH	1909
Tiger	Stoddard Mfg. Co.	Dayton, OH	1892
Triumph	D. S. Morgan & Co.	Brockport, NY	1892
Trojan	Troy Mowing Machine Co.	Troy, NY	1892
Victor	R. I. Schlabach	Nazareth, PA	1892
Walter A. Wood	Bateman Bros. Inc.	Philadelphia, PA	1929
Walter A. Wood	Walter A. Wood Mowing & R. M. Co.	Hoosick Falls, NY	1892
Warrior	Warrior Mower Co.	Little Falls, NY	1874
Whitely	Amos Whitely & Co.	Springfield, OH	1892
Whitely	Wm. N. Whitely Co.	Springfield, OH	1892
Whitewater	Winchester & Partridge Mfg. Co.	Whitewater, WI	1892
Worcester	Richardson Mfg. Co.	Worcester, MA	1905
Worcester Buckeye	Richardson Mfg. Co.	Worcester, MA	1909
Worcester Chain Gear	Richardson Mfg. Co.	Worcester, MA	1913

Did You Know?

A fanning mill will have a reasonable market value; it is not uncommon for a good machine to bring $100 or much more. Quite often, they are purchased for farm use, rather than as a farm antique.

O

Orchard Machinery

By the 1880s, several companies had developed equipment specific to orchard and vineyard requirements. This was in addition to the special implements needed for truck gardening and other applications. Various equipment is already included in this book under numerous headings. Since much of this equipment is simply a modified version of standard equipment, it would be redundant to include it again in this section. Also, much of this equipment is specifically designed for orchard and vineyard work and very little information on this type of equipment resides within our files.

Grand Rapids Manufacturing Co., Grand Rapids, Mich.
By 1889, Grand Rapids Manufacturing Co. was offering Pearce's Patent Orchard Gang Plow, a special design suited for orchards, vineyards and similar applications. The specialized nature of this equipment kept much of it apart from the standard line of implements, thus it is not illustrated in many cases; this was reserved for special orchard equipment catalogs.

With the coming of the tractor, many implements were designed for orchard work. In addition, tractors were designed with special fenders and hoods to permit working close to trees and vines without damaging either the growing crop or the tractor itself. This 1931 photograph shows the Oliver Hart-Parr Orchard Tractor at work. Especially during the 1930s, orchard tractors and orchard equipment gained greatly in its popularity with orchardists.

P

Peanut Machinery

Various kinds of equipment has been developed specific to the culture and harvesting of peanuts. Since this crop is regional in nature, few advertisements or other information reached the general agricultural press. Within this section are a number of items located in our research. It is to be assumed that there are numerous other items suitable for this heading.

Ferguson Manufacturing Co., Suffolk, Va.
A 1917 advertisement illustrates the New Ferguson Peanut Picker. This machine was designed to pick and stem the crop. Of all-wood construction, it typifies the construction of many farm machines of the day. No additional information has been found on this firm.

Williams Mill Manufacturing Co., Texarkana, Tex.
From about 1920 comes this illustration of the Williams peanut digger. This unit appears to be a modified form of the potato digger; the latter had been well developed by this time. A noticeable difference was the steel tines to the rear of the machine which left the vines in a windrow to the side of the furrow.

Williams offered its peanut thresher for some years, although little information has been found regarding this company. Once the peanuts were separated from the vines, the hay was conveyed to a stack. This peanut thresher was designed to "leave the hay in the best possible feeding condition."

Plows

From ancient times, the plow has been considered to be a primary tillage implement. Until recent years, the disc harrow and various other tillage devices have all been considered to be secondary tillage implements. With today's emphasis on minimum tillage or no-tillage farming, the plow has lost its dominant role, one that it held for centuries. Yet, without the plow, the vast plains of the United States and Canada would not have become productive farmland.

Until the 1820s, most plows used a wooden moldboard. About this time, the cast-iron plow appeared; by 1840, the majority of plows were made of cast iron. These plows were quite satisfactory in the Eastern states, but the heavy black soil of the Midwest was another matter. Cast-iron plows would not scour in these soils—this led to the development of the steel plow.

John Deere built his first steel plow in 1837. It proved to be very popular from the beginning. Within a few years, the John Deere plow was well known in the Midwestern and Southern states. Who actually built the first steel plow is a matter of conjecture, but, in 1833, John Lane of Chicago built a steel plow. His invention did not gain the attention that followed the Deere plow, but it was John Lane who conceived the idea of a three-layered moldboard, hard on its outer surfaces, but with a soft center. Eventually, the soft-center moldboard was built by virtually every steel plow manufacturer.

Other important developers of the steel plow were Major Andrus, Deere's early partner in the plow business. Andrus went on to form the Grand Detour Plow Co. Another important figure in the plow business was William Parlin, Canton, Ill. The firm of Parlin & Orendorff emerged as a major plow maker.

Recognizing the deficiencies of the cast-iron plow, many inventors attempted to devise a method of building one of chilled iron. In foundry parlance, a chill is a device—often of iron and sometimes water cooled—that is placed near the mold cavity. When iron is poured into the mold, the chill quickly absorbs heat from the iron, causing the outer surfaces to cool more quickly than the inner parts. This hardens or chills the outer surface, making it very hard and also capable of acquiring the "land polish" required for scouring in black, sticky soil. Several inventors achieved some degree of success, but James Oliver was by far the predominant force in the development of the chilled-iron plows. Thus came the Oliver Chilled Plow Works; this company was a leader in manufacturing plows of this type.

Already in the 1840s, there were thoughts of building a sulky plow, a design that carried the beam and moldboard on wheels. These made little progress into the 1860s, with some designs appearing at that time, but farmers were not flocking to buy them. For one thing, many farmers thought that the horses had enough work pulling the plow itself, without carrying along still more mechanism. Many others were barely able to afford a simple walking plow, much less the more expensive sulky plow. At this point, the idea of a riding sulky plow met with even less favor.

Numerous sulky plow designs came onto the market in the 1870s, but the Gilpin Moore Patent of 1875 finally brought a truly successful sulky plow to the market; this plow was manufactured by Deere & Co. A year later, W.L. Casaday received a patent on a sulky plow; this design was subsequently marketed by Oliver Chilled Plow Works. Moline Plow Co., began making sulky plows based on the patents of G.W. Hunt in 1884 and numerous others followed suit.

By definition, a sulky plow is a wheeled plow with one moldboard. A gang plow was usually considered to be a two-bottom wheeled plow, but this definition was later broadened to any plow with two or more moldboards. Jones Malone, a farmer near Orena, Ill., claimed to have made the first gang plow and also claimed that the patent was stolen from him. However, once the sulky plow came to success in the 1870s, the gang plow soon followed. Usually, farmers would pull a sulky plow with three horses and a gang plow with four or even five horses.

Sharpening the plow lays was an annual process. Most farmers kept an extra set of plow lays on hand in case one should be spoiled in an encounter with a rock. If the damage was not too severe, the local blacksmith could put it in the forge and draw the metal to a sharp edge once again. Every farmer had his favorite blacksmith. Undoubtedly, some were better at plow work than others. For those who were skilled in the art, a good income was assured, since the need to sharpen plow shares never ended.

By the 1890s, some attempts were being made to build large plows for use with steam-traction engines. These early attempts were largely unsuccessful, partially because the traction engines were not yet developed for the heavy work of plowing. By 1900, special engine gang plows were a reality and these were built and sold in limited numbers for about 20 years. By that time, the smaller tractor plows had been developed, having two, three or more bottoms. As a result, the huge engine gang plows faded from the scene. In addition, disc plows were coming into use in some areas, so the moldboard plow was not needed in those regions.

With the coming of minimum tillage and no-tillage farming, the time-honored moldboard plow faded from the scene in the 1960s and today is used only to a limited extent in most regions. However, it is of interest that in Great Britain and many other parts of the world, plowing still remains as the primary tillage method.

Allis-Chalmers Manufacturing Co., Milwaukee, Wisc.
(See LaCrosse Plow Co.)

American Plow Co., Madison, Wisc.

Aside from this 1905 advertisement, no information has come to light on the American Plow Co., or its line of plows, cultivators and other implements. Its interesting trademark leaves the impression that these plows were sold all over North and South America.

Ames Plow Co., Boston, Mass.

An article in the Feb. 17, 1872, issue of *Boston Cultivator*, delves at length into the success of Ames Plow Co. and illustrates its huge warehouse at the Faneuil Hall Market. At the time, Ames Plow Co. was a major supplier of almost every kind of farm implement on the market, but it eventually faded into obscurity.

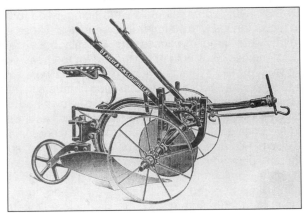

B.F. Avery & Sons, Louisville, Kty.

B.F. Avery & Sons Co., was incorporated in 1877 for $1.5 million. Benjamin Franklin Avery had founded the company in 1825

with $400 in capital. Over the years, the company built countless models of plows; this is a sulky model of 1917.

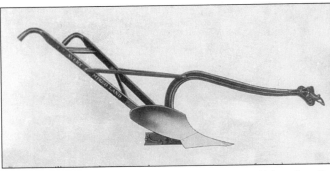

B.F. Avery offered this Mixed Land Plow in its 1916 catalog. It was designed to work well in varying soil conditions, thus the trade name. Avery was a long-standing builder of plows, beginning in the days of the cast-iron plow with a small factory in Clarksville, Va.

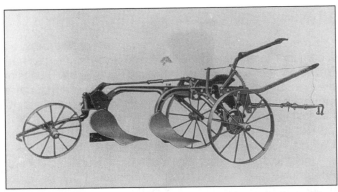

By 1916, B.F. Avery was offering a series of tractor plows. The continuing popularity of the Avery line prompted further expansion, including the acquisition of the Champion line of hay and harvest tools from International Harvester Co. After a long career in the farm equipment business, Avery merged into the Minneapolis-Moline Co., in 1951.

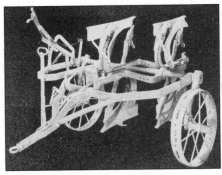

Boggs Manufacturing Co., Atlanta, N.Y.

Nothing at all is known of this firm aside from this 1928 illustration of its Neufang two-way tractor plow. The company had previously gained attention with its line of potato warehouse machinery, including graders, sorters and other equipment.

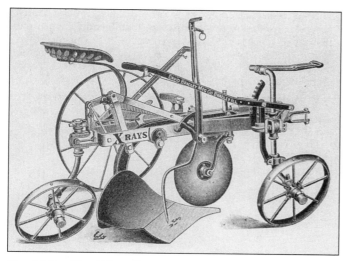

David Bradley Manufacturing Co., Bradley, Ill.

David Bradley had family roots in America traceable back to the 1630s. The family moved to Chicago in 1849, becoming involved in the retail seed and implement business in the 1860s. Through a series of events, the company eventually became David Bradley Manufacturing Co., in 1882. Shown here is the David Bradley X Rays Sulky Plow of 1897.

An 1897 advertisement calls this model the XX Rays Gang Plow. This model featured an improved hitch system. One of the major difficulties with sulky and gang plows was to achieve the correct hitch so that the plow would run easy and perform as it should. Some farmers achieved this skill. For others, setting up the hitch correctly was always a problem.

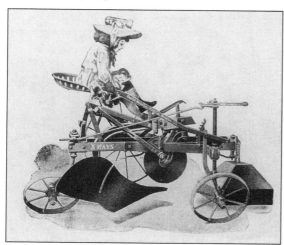

A 1903 advertisement of the X Rays sulky plow illustrates its unique lift system whereby "a little girl six years old can raise the

X Rays with 10,000 lbs. weight on the front end." David Bradley implements were marketed through Sears, Roebuck & Co. for some years, with the latter finally gaining control of the company.

Bryan Plow Company, Bryan, Ohio

It appears that in 1905, Bryan Plow Company specialized in walking plows and disc harrows. The company's 1905 steel-beam version is shown here. Little is known of this firm.

Bucher & Gibbs Plow Co., Canton, Ohio

Established in 1864, Bucher & Gibbs Plow Co., had its line of Imperial plows on the market during the 1880s. Shown here is the Imperial Prairie Plow, a wood-beam version designed especially for the black prairie land. It was also built in a steel-beam style.

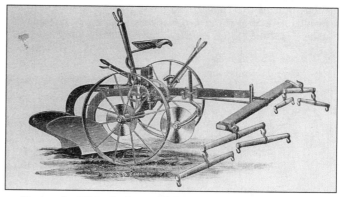

During the 1880s, the Imperial Gang Plow from Bucher & Gibbs took this form, using two wheels instead of the three-wheeled model made famous by Gilpin Moore. Note the four-horse evener on this plow. Every company had a different method of assuring that the plow moved forward in a straight line, crowding in neither direction. To achieve this desirable goal, many kinds of eveners and hitches were designed, some by companies specializing in this business.

Probably as comic humor, Bucher & Gibbs ran this 1900 advertisement of the Imperial Mobiliser, an auto-plow that existed only in the mind of the engraver. However, many readers took the ad seriously, deluging the factory with inquiries. Red-faced officials then had to reply that the whole thing was a joke. Ironically, the concept would become a reality in only a few more years.

At some point in its history, Bucher & Gibbs Plow Co. came under control of the Myer's interests at Ashland, Ohio. For some years, the company was actually owned by principals of F.E. Myers Co., the famous pump manufacturers. For 1903, Bucher & Gibbs offered this unusual Imperial Two Furrow Plow that would turn a furrow from 8 to 10 inches deep and 24 to 26 inches wide. Trade directories list the company into the late 1950s.

J.I. Case Co., Racine, Wisc.
(See Grand Detour Plow Co.)

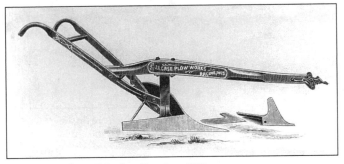

J.I. Case Plow Works, Racine, Wisc.
This company was formed by J.I. Case of threshing machine fame in 1878, when Case took over the firm of Case, Whiting & Co. This company was an entirely separate entity from J.I. Case

Threshing Machine Co. After Case's death in 1892, a bitter rivalry ensued between the two companies, finally ending when the Plow Works was sold to Massey-Harris in 1928. The latter then sold all rights to the "Case" name back to the Threshing Machine company. Shown here is the 1897 version of the Case Sod and Stubble Plow.

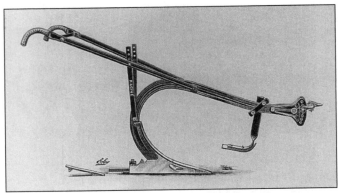

In 1890, Case introduced its Racine Sub-Soil Plow, a design not often seen in contemporary catalogs. It was built specifically to break up hardpan that occurs naturally in some soils. This provided a much better seed bed and crop growing conditions.

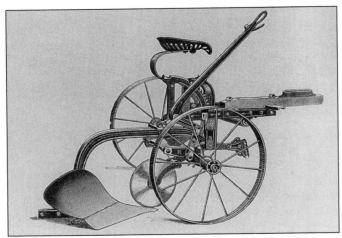

J.I. Case owned a famous race horse called Jay-Eye-See. His fame led to the introduction of numerous Jay-Eye-See implements, including the Jay-Eye-See Sulky Plow of the 1890s. This small two-wheeled design was quite popular.

Already in the 1890s, Case had introduced its Triumph line of plows, with its Triumph Gang Plow being illustrated here. This was a foot-lift plow that was easy to raise and lower by foot pedals.

An 1895 advertisement from J.I. Case Plow Works illustrates its Triumph Sulky Plow, noting that it "Triumphs over all hard ground." Since many plows would not penetrate hard ground, any company having such a plow would immediately gain the attention of interested farmers.

J.I. Case Plow Works often made claims for the lightness of draft in its plows. To prove the point they often conducted live demonstrations as shown here from April 1895. This test, done at Wyoming, Ill., shows one of the J.I. Case representatives "playing horse."

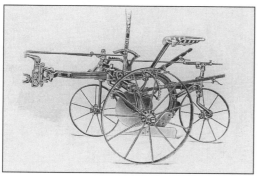

From 1906 comes this illustration of the J.I. Case Spinner Sulky Plow. The company built literally dozens of different plows dur-

ing its long career, ending in 1928. At that time, Massey-Harris Co. bought out J.I. Case Plow Works.

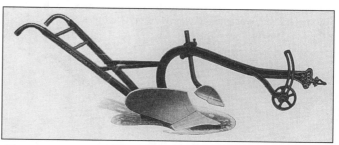

Chattanooga Plow Works, Chattanooga, Tenn.

International Harvester Co. bought out Chattanooga in 1919. The latter had developed a considerable business, particularly in the Southern states. Shown here is an example of its No. 95 chilled-iron walking plow, one of many different models from this company.

Cockshutt Farm Equipment Ltd., Brantford, Ontario

(See Frost & Wood)

Coffeyville Implement & Manufacturing Co., Coffeyville, Kan.

By the turn of the century, a few companies were building sulky attachments to convert the walking plow with a riding attachment. Shown here is a $15 set-up that consisted of axle and wheels, plus the suitable levers for leveling the plow and the raising device.

Reflecting the objection of some farmers to a riding plow, the Banner riding attachment was designed so that "it can be adjusted so there will be no more draft with the rider on the seat than there is to a walking plow." Since the Banner riding attachment was clamped to the plow beam, there was no need to drill any holes. All that was needed was a wrench that was supplied with the attachment kit.

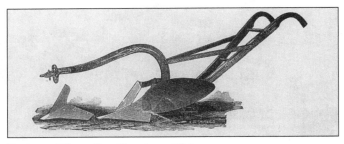

Dayton Plow Co., Dayton, Ohio

Numerous plow companies were in operation during the 1880s, including Dayton with its Perfected Perfection Plow of 1887. Like many plow companies, its products were not widely distributed, it did little advertising and was not in business for more than a few years. Thus for Dayton and many others, little information now exists.

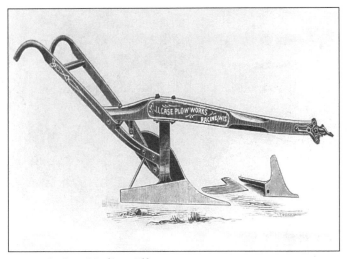

Deere & Co., Moline, Ill.

John Deere built his first plow in 1837, with many more in 1838. From then on, the story is well known of how John Deere built up a huge industry, beginning with a steel plow. A 1912 advertisement commemorates this achievement, illustrating an early example of the famous John Deere trademark.

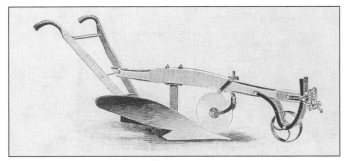

Deere perfected its breaking plow with the Prairie Queen model shown here; this one even included a rolling coulter, a definite improvement over the earlier knife coulter. Production of the Deere breaking plows continued at least into the 1920s; by then, most of the virgin prairie had come under the plow.

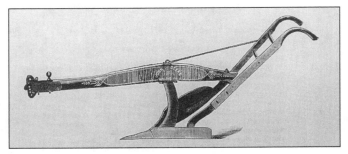

The John Deere Red Jacket Plow was a well-known walking plow built for decades. For reasons now unknown, some farmers referred to these plows as "stirring plows." Whatever they were called, plows were an essential part of frontier life. If tough conditions forced a wagon train to leave part of its load behind, seldom was the plow one of the victims. It was as necessary to the new life on the frontier as the ax and the hoe.

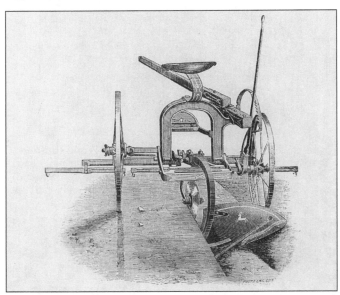

In 1875, Gilpin Moore patented a new sulky plow design, immediately put into production as the Gilpin Sulky Plow. This new design immediately launched Deere into a new era of the plow business, with the Gilpin and its successors continuing into the Deere line for decades to come.

For 1889, Deere illustrated its Gazelle Sulky Plow as part of the line. It was an improved style of the Gilpin sulky, pioneered several years earlier. New developments continued apace, with Deere & Co., remaining as a leader in the manufacture of steel plows.

A 1908 Deere catalog illustrates the company's Southern Sulky Middlebreaker. This style was developed especially for certain regions of the United States, particularly where semi-arid conditions were prevalent. Various kinds of Deere middlebreakers were offered in the following decades.

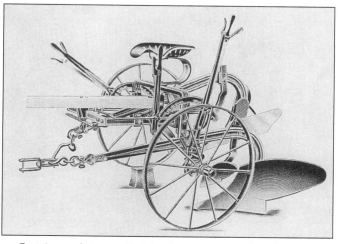

Certain conditions called for the two-way sulky plow. With this design, it was possible to start at one side of a field and plow to the other with no back furrows and no dead furrows. Two-way plows were particularly adapted to hilly ground and small, irregular-shaped fields.

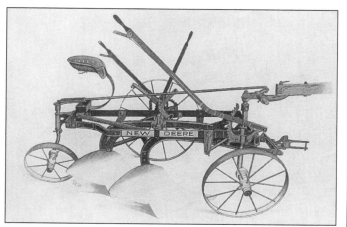

In the early 1900s, Deere & Co. came forth with its New Deere Gang Plow, an improved design that remained in the Deere catalogs for years to come. Immensely popular, the New Deere plows were marketed everywhere, including many foreign countries.

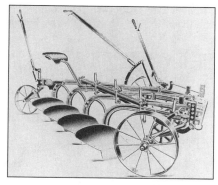

Recognizing the coming of motive power, whether from a steam traction engine or a tractor, Deere developed an engine gang plow in the early 1900s. This four-bottom engine gang of 1908 was but one of several early John Deere designs; the company built styles as large as a huge 14-bottom model designed for use with the largest steam-traction engines or tractors.

Deere & Co. pioneered the development of the tractor plow, beginning with its engine gangs in the early 1900s. By 1919, the small farm tractor had arrived. With its coming, Deere offered a series of tractor plows to meet the demand. The company continued to build plows until the changing tillage methods of recent years brought them to an end.

Economist Plow Co., South Bend, Ind.

In the 1880s, Economist Plow Co. offered its Solid Comfort Sulky Plow, a new design with a steel frame, but still using a wooden plow beam. Little is known of the company; by the early 1900s, the Solid Comfort was being built by Syracuse Chilled Plow Co., Syracuse, N.Y.

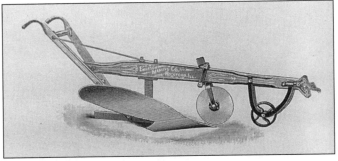

Emerson-Brantingham Co., Rockford, Ill.

Emerson Manufacturing Co. had a long career in the plow business, reaching back at least to the 1880s. One of its popular early designs was its Prairie Breaker, offered in 12-, 14- and 16-inch sizes. Made only in a wooden-beam design, this plow used the familiar prairie breaker moldboard designed to completely cover all the vegetation it turned over.

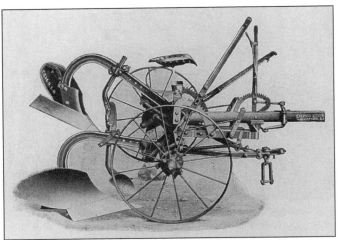

Like many other companies, Emerson-Brantingham offered a two-way plow, with this one having a built-in power-lift system. With this design it was only necessary to push a foot lever to raise the plow, with power from the wheel taking care of the mechanical duties.

Emerson-Brantingham was a pioneer in the farm tractor business and likewise was early to offer a tractor plow with a self-lift attachment. With this device, the operator pulled a rope to

engage the lifting mechanism. Pulling it again dropped the plow into the ground once more.

The E-B No. 90 Tractor Plow was one of many different designs offered over the years. This plow was of independent-beam design, meaning that each plow standard was on its own individual beam and the depth of each plow was controlled by a plowman on the large platform seen here. Individual gauge wheels controlled the depth of the plows.

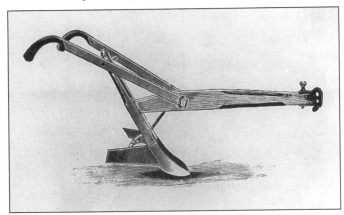

A.C. Evans Co., Springfield, Ohio

This company was one of the partners forming American Seeding Machine Co., in 1903. Prior to the merger, Evans built grain drills and numerous tillage implements. The wing shovel plow pictured here was for hilling potatoes and similar work. The steel wings were adjustable by means of spread rods.

A.B. Farquhar Co. Ltd., York, Pa.

By the 1870s, Farquhar was building the Reese Combination Plow, probably under license from its inventor. This tool is shown here with the beam alone, plus various kinds of plows to be attached to the plow stock.

Farquhar's Chilled Plow was offered in various styles and sizes into the early 1900s. Although the company remained in operation until the 1950s, there is no indication that it built sulky plows, gang plows or tractor plows.

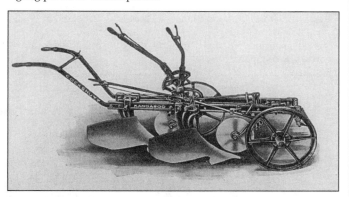

Frost & Wood Co. Ltd., Smiths Falls, Ontario

Little is known of Frost & Wood, but, from all appearances, much of its line was acquired from other companies. For instance, this 1910 illustration of the Kangaroo Gang Plow is actually one from Cockshutt Farm Equipment Ltd., of Brantford, Ontario, Canada. Cockshutt was a pioneer Canadian plow maker.

The 1910 Frost & Wood plow line was actually the Cockshutt plow line. The latter became widely known for its plows, particularly in Canada. Eventually, Cockshutt, Oliver and others were merged into White Farm Equipment Co.

Fuller & Johnson Manufacturing Co., Madison, Wisc.

Fuller & Johnson had its roots in the plow business, going back to the 1840s. During the 1880s and 1890s, the company was especially active, with its New Eclipse Riding Plow appearing about 1900. In 1911, the company sold out its entire implement business, opting to concentrate all its efforts on manufacturing gasoline engines.

Gale Manufacturing Co., Albion, Mich.

By the 1870s, Gale Manufacturing Co., was offering many kinds of plows, including the rod-beam plow shown here. This unusual design replaced the usual wooden beam for three heavy steel rods. Also of interest is the unusual knife coulter.

Being able to turn a square corner was always a desirable feature for plows and Gale Manufacturing Co. offered just such a plow in 1887. Known as the Big Injun, this plow had a rather unusual design, since the tongue or pole was mounted a couple of feet behind the evener, pivoting on the furrow wheel standard. Little is known of Gale Manufacturing Co., aside from a few illustrations.

Globe Plow Works, Davenport, Iowa

An 1888 advertisement illustrates the Hercules Tricycle Sulky Plow from Globe Plow Works. This unusual design lifted the moldboard vertically through a slide mounted to the rigid frame. Globe was a successor to Davenport Plow Co.; no information can be found on the latter entity.

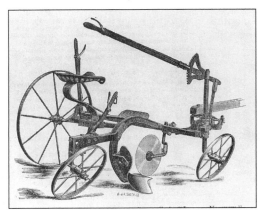

Grand Detour Plow Co., Dixon, Ill.

In 1837, this company was founded at nearby Grand Detour, Ill., but moved to Dixon in 1869. In 1879, the firm was incorporated as Grand Detour Plow Co.; by 1890, the company was building more than 100 styles and sizes of plows. Shown here is its Little Yankee sulky plow of 1887. The company was originally founded at Grand Detour by Major Andrus and John Deere. After a few years, however, the two parted company. J.I. Case Threshing Machine Co. bought Grand Detour in 1919.

Hackney Manufacturing Co., St. Paul, Minn.

By the early 1900s, a few farmers were looking for a plow that could be run with gasoline power rather than horse power. About 1910, Hackney came out with its Auto-Plow; a unique design that carried the plows beneath the tractor while the farmer sat in a seat with leather upholstery. Priced at $1,500 to $1,800, the Hackney was ahead of its time and soon left the scene.

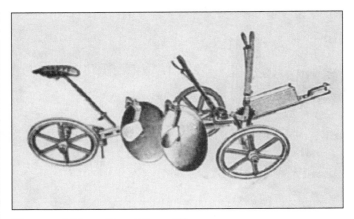

Hapgood Plow Co., Alton, Ill.

Hapgood was one of numerous small plow companies; small at least, when compared to Deere, P&O, Grand Detour and a few others. However, the company had developed an extensive line by the time this Hapgood-Hancock Disc Sulky appeared in 1902. Available in one-, two-, three- and four-gang models, it was designed especially for hard ground that the moldboard plow could scarcely penetrate.

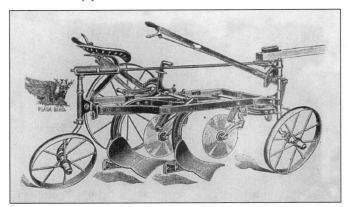

A 1906 offering was the Piasa Bird Double Lift Gang Plow from Hapgood Plow Co. Current research has not determined the origins of Hapgood Plow Co., but repairs for its plows were available into the late 1930s. However, during World War II, the company disappears from the trade directories.

Heilman Plow Company, Evansville, Ind.

Hundreds, perhaps thousands, of different makes and models of walking plows were made in the century following 1830. Included was the 1892 Vulcan Chilled Plow. As manufacturing and transportation both developed, most of the smaller companies ceased to exist. The development of wheeled plows in the 1870s left little need for the walking variety.

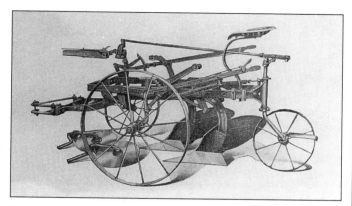

Independent Harvester Co., Milwaukee, Wisc.

Almost nothing is known of the plows built by Independent Harvester Co., or if they were built by Independent or bought under contract from another plow maker. However, parts were available from Independent as late as 1944, after which time the firm disappears from the implement trade directories.

International Harvester Co., Chicago, Ill.

In 1909, IHC contracted with P&O (Parlin & Orendorff) to sell its plows. This helped IHC broaden its product line and gave a great boost to the fortunes of P&O. Over the next 10 years, P&O made many developments, including its Little Chief sulky plow shown here. When IHC bought out P&O in 1919, the Little Chief remained in the IHC product line for several years to come.

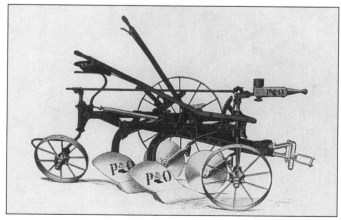

P&O plows included its No. 2 Diamond gang plow, developed in the early 1900s and remaining as part of the IHC plow line for several years after IHC bought out P&O in 1919. Despite the popularity of the recently designed tractor plows, horse-drawn plows remained with most manufacturers up to World War II.

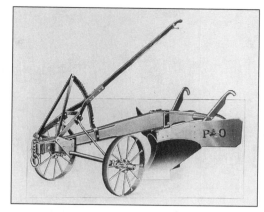

To drain low-lying areas, the farmer could sometimes achieve the goal with a ditching plow, such as this one developed by P&O. IHC sold this style for many years. Although it never sold in large numbers, this plow was an essential implement in some areas.

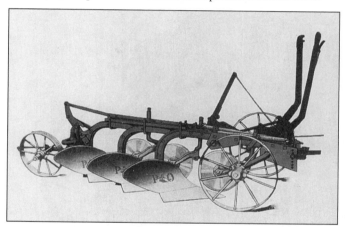

In the period around World War I, tractor plows gained new importance, especially since many of the nation's young men were off to war and every possible means had to be used for tilling the soil and planting the crop. This urgency greatly hastened the development of tractor plows, with the P&O Little Genius being one of the results. IHC continued to sell Little Genius plows in various models, but retained the Little Genius trade name into the 1950s.

Before 1920, IHC was offering the P&O power-lift tractor disk plow in various sizes, with this four-furrow model typifying the line. While Midwestern farmers had no need for the disk plow, it was essential in many crop-growing regions and remained an important part of the tillage arsenal until minimum tillage practices emerged.

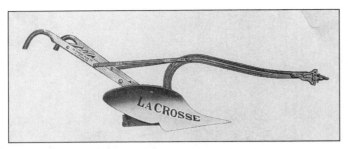

LaCrosse Plow Co., LaCrosse, Wisc.

When Allis-Chalmers bought out LaCrosse in 1929, A-C had its first line of tillage equipment. For a time after the purchase, the new line was advertised as Allis-Chalmers LaCrosse or A-C LaCrosse; it was simply a continuation of the old established LaCrosse line. One such item was the LaCrosse walking plow, offered in numerous styles and a design that the company had been marketing for years.

The origins of LaCrosse have not been made manifest during the present research; however, into the 1920s, the company was offering its LaCrosse Hustler Sulky Plow, advertised as an up-to-date and modern plow. As noted elsewhere in this section, tractor plows were becoming quite popular by the 1920s, but there were still many farms of this time using horse power almost exclusively for field work.

By 1915, LaCrosse was building this big tractor plow with a power-lift system. It could be operated entirely from the tractor, with no need for a plowman to raise and lower the independent beams. By the 1930s, this style was seldom sold. New designs were just as big and just as efficient, but with much less iron and much less weight than before.

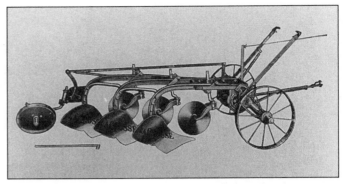

Tractor plows were developed by LaCrosse during World War I. At this point, there were many small tractors coming onto the market, with a consequent demand for tractor plows. One lever was used to control the plowing depth, another lever on the furrow wheel kept the plow level and a trip rope raised and lowered the plow at will. This plow was the foundation of the A-C line of plows manufactured after the 1929 buyout of LaCrosse.

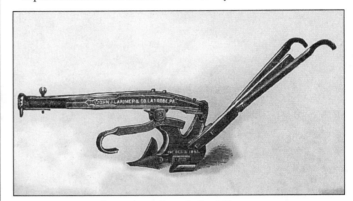

Larimer Manufacturing Co., Eola, Ill.

As noted elsewhere in this section, the ditching plow was an essential implement for farmers in many areas. Crops yielded poorly in wet ground and some system of drainage was essential. The Larimer Ditching Plow pictured here is equipped with a sub-soil attachment and tile-bed shovel so that underground drainage was possible, even though the operation had to be repeated occasionally. This design is from 1909.

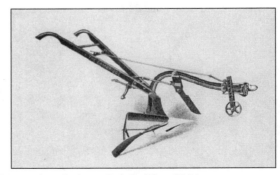

H.H. Lovejoy & Son, Cambridge, N.Y.

A small and indistinct illustration is the only clue found in the present research for this company. Shown here is its Cambridge Reversible Plow of 1906, one of more than 40 different styles available at the time. Reversible plows gained slight popularity in some areas, but the two-way sulky plows available by this time were probably better received by most farmers.

Lowell Steam Plow Co., Des Moines, Iowa

In 1905, the Lowell Steam Plow was announced. This huge plow was designed for use with steam-traction engines; the lift system used steam from the boiler for fully automatic operation. Little is known of the company or its plows; apparently the company didn't remain in business for more than a few years; it does however, appear until about 1910.

Madison Plow Co., Madison, Wisc.

Fuller & Johnson in Madison was in the plow business until 1911 when it sold out to private investors; the company then being known as Madison Plow Co. Shown here is its Madison New Eclipse Sulky Plow; this one is equipped with a breaker moldboard. Madison Plow Co. appears in the trade listings into the late 1940s.

Massey-Harris Co. Ltd., Toronto, Ontario

Although Massey-Harris was a well-known Canadian manufacturer, its career in the U.S. plow business was launched with the 1928 purchase of J.I. Case Plow Works at Racine, Wis. The latter was a well-known American manufacturer with many designs for almost every plowing application. By 1940, Massey-Harris had launched its new No. 28 tractor plow; it was built in two- and three-bottom sizes.

Mittendorf Manufacturing Co., Hermann, Mo.

An advertisement of about 1909 is the only evidence to surface thus far on the Mittendorf Plow Sulky. This device was attached to almost any walking plow, giving the farmer a continued use for the plow and providing a chance to ride instead of walk.

Moline Plow Co., Moline, Ill.

Established in 1865, Moline Plow Co. quickly grew into a major plow manufacturing enterprise. In 1906, the firm began expanding with acquisitions of other product lines. An engraving of the 1890s illustrates the plant facilities, dwarfed by the locomotive heading to the countryside with another load of Moline plows.

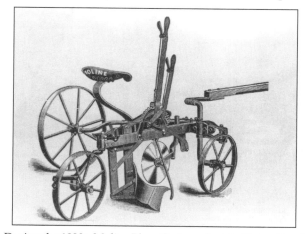

During the 1890s, Moline Plow Co. launched its Flying Dutchman sulky, a design that proved to be very popular. The Flying Dutchman trademark continued until the days of World War I when anti-German sentiment prompted the company to withdraw the slogan for fear of unsavory connotations. This design was marketed for almost 40 years.

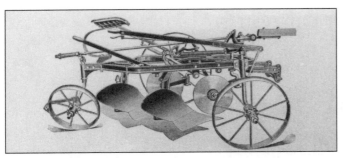

Moline Plow Co. offered its first foot-lift gang plow in 1897, as part of its Flying Dutchman line. Moline claimed to have revolutionized many aspects of plow manufacturing. Indeed, the company was among the most innovative of its time.

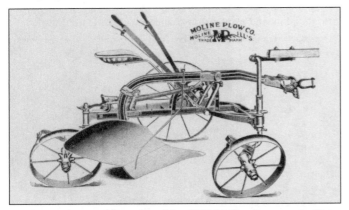

Yet another popular part of the 1900 Moline line was its Bismarck Sulky Plow. As part of the Flying Dutchman line, the Bismarck trade name had obvious German connotations and with many areas of the Midwestern states being dominated by farmers of German descent, the association was a beneficial one.

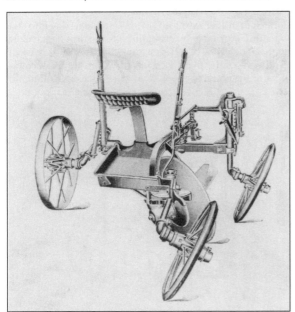

By the early 1900s, Moline Plow Co. had developed a disc plow for very hard ground and for use in certain areas where the moldboard plow was unsuccessful. Through the following years, Moline continued developing new designs, including a series of very successful tractor plows. Moline Plow Co. merged with others in 1929 to form Minneapolis-Moline Co.

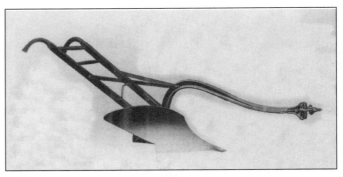

Monmouth Plow Co., Monmouth, Ill.

An advertisement of the early 1900s illustrates the Monmouth walking plows; at the time these sold from $8 to $10. By this time, most walking plows had taken the same general form, with the steel beam being the prevalent design. Few companies were now manufacturing plows with wooden beams.

The New I.D. plows of 1906 "are noted for their lightness of draft, simplicity of construction and satisfactory working qualities." By the mid-1940s, repairs for the Monmouth plows were available from Brown, Lynch, Scott Co., also of Monmouth. The latter firm fades from the trade directories by the late 1940s.

Morrison Manufacturing Co., Fort Madison, Iowa

Although the origins of Morrison Manufacturing Co. are unknown, the company was offering the Lenhart Sulky Plow as shown here in 1897. This interesting design used an exceptionally large tail wheel. The linkage between the furrow wheel and the tail wheel permitted square turns.

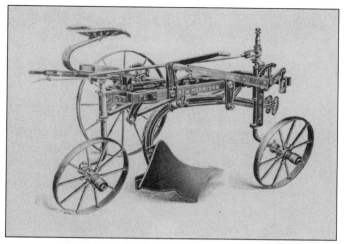

For 1903, Morrison offered a series of plows to its customers, including the New Morrison shown here. With great pride, the company pointed to the fact that when cutting 6 inches deep, a draft of only 338 pounds was required. By 1909, the company was known as Fort Madison Plow Co. The latter disappeared by 1918.

North River Agricultural Works, New York, N.Y.

In 1866, North River Agricultural Works offered several different plows, among them being this Mohawk Valley Clipper No. 1. It featured a steel moldboard and point; the latter being of an interesting design. The knife jointer is also of interest, but, at the time, rolling coulters were not yet a popular alternative.

Known as Fisher's Patent First Premium Lever Plow, this 1866 offering from North River Agricultural Works demonstrates one of the first sulky plows. It was invented by Samuel Fisher of West Windsor, N.J. He acquired Patent No. 30,727 on this design in 1860.

Norwegian Plow Co., Dubuque, Iowa

For 1887, Norwegian Plow Co. offered its Honest Abe Sulky Plow. This design has several interesting points, including the unusual design of the tail wheel. This was a foot-lift plow, operated by a lever attached to the rear of the plow beam. The Norwegian was built for only a few years before disappearing from the scene.

Oliver Chilled Plow Works, South Bend, Ind.

Through great adversity, James Oliver built a successful chilled plow. Instead of the soft-center plow steel used by many, the Oliver design was a special alloy of iron with an exceedingly hard surface that would scour and would last for years of work. Shown here is an early example of the Oliver Chilled Plow. James Oliver acquired a great many patents for plows during a long career in the business.

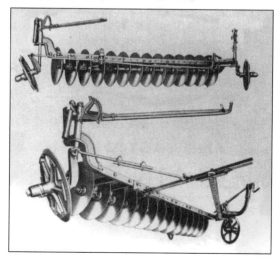

Through the years, the Oliver plows rose to the top of the market, being very popular in all parts of the United States and in many foreign countries. In 1929, Oliver was a partner in the formation of Oliver Farm Equipment Co. An extensive coverage of the Oliver plows can be found in the author's *Oliver Hart-Parr* (Motorbooks: 1993). Shown here is an Oliver one-way plow of 1929.

Parlin & Orendorff Co., Canton, Ill.

In 1842, William Parlin began building plows at Canton, Ill. The company operated under various titles until incorporating under the Parlin & Orendorff title in 1880. By this time, the Canton Clipper plows were well known; P&O was now known all over the United States and in many other parts of the world.

The P&O Clipper Tricycle Plow appeared in the 1880s; it is shown here being pulled by a team, although in heavy sod or certain other conditions, three horses were used. P&O built this style for a number of years, but followed it with many improved designs before the company was bought out by International Harvester in 1919.

An unusual style was this walking gang plow, offered by Parlin & Orendorff Co., in 1887. Sulky plows were then in vogue, so it

seems unusual that the company would offer a walking gang plow rather than one on which the farmer could ride. William Parlin remained active in the business until his death in 1891.

By 1898, the Canton Disc Plow was available from Parlin & Orendorff. This design was especially suited to hard ground and certain areas outside of the Midwestern prairies. P&O also built the first lister in the 1860s.

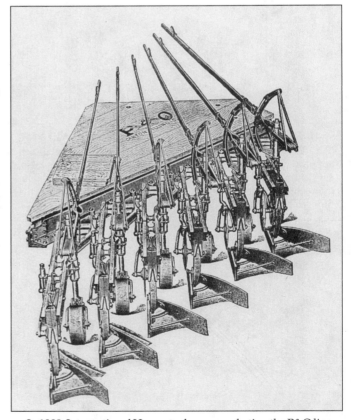

In 1909, International Harvester began marketing the P&O line, continuing in this manner until buying out the company in 1919. Already in 1910, P&O had developed its P&O Mogul Engine Gang Plow, a large and heavy design with individual beams. The plowman's platform was needed to raise and lower the individual plow beams.

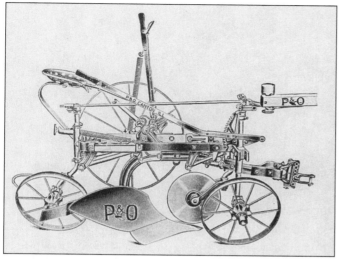

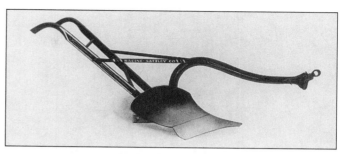

P&O was offering this modern sulky plow for the 1912 market. It featured its 3-in-1 X.X. adjustable moldboard. In fact, the latter design was furnished on all its Diamond and Success sulky and gang plows. When IHC bought out P&O in 1919, it purchased an established and respected member of the plow-making fraternity.

Racine-Sattley Co., Springfield, Ill.

Marshall Sattley began building plows in 1851. The success of the early plows caused him to locate at Taylorville, Ill., in 1858. Sattley was a self-made plow mechanic, having learned the trade from a local blacksmith who he later brought with him and continued in the plow business.

Plymouth Foundry & Machine Co., Plymouth, Wisc.

This company made feed cutters and other farm machines, but almost nothing can be found of its activities in the plow business except for this illustration. Pictured is Plymouth's Hero steel beam plow, available in a 12- or a 15-inch cut.

Sattley built his first successful gang plow already in 1863. From these beginnings, the Sattley line gained fame far and wide. Shown here is the company's 1899 Hummer plow, a sulky design which its makers said "will plow anything anywhere."

David Prouty & Co., Boston, Mass.

An 1861 issue of the *Boston Cultivator* illustrates the Michigan Double Plough, as built at the time by Prouty. Apparently, a few other companies had attempted building a "double plough" but none had been eminently successful. In demonstrations of the Prouty, it proved successful, even in the hands of a relatively inexperienced plowman.

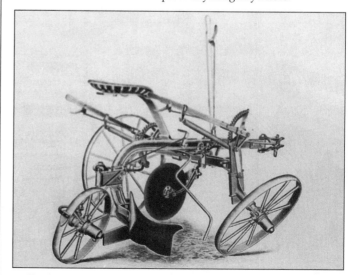

By the early 1900s, Sattley Manufacturing Co. reorganized as Racine-Sattley Co. One of its 1903 offerings was the Royal Blue Sulky shown here. This plow was arranged so that it could handle 12-, 14-, 16- or 18-inch bottoms simply by moving the beam to the appropriate position.

About 1915, Sattley was building the Wonder Gang Plow pictured here. It was a two-wheel walking plow, made especially for farmers who preferred this design to the three-wheeled sulky. Marshall Sattley died in 1907. Racine-Sattley continued into the 1920s. For some years after, the Sattley plows were built by Hummer Plow Works of Springfield, Ill.

Rock Island Plow Co., Rock Island, Ill.

With roots going back to the 1850s, Rock Island Plow Co. emerged as a major U.S. plow builder. When it is considered that the modern steel or chilled-iron plow did not appear until about 1840 and that there were thousands of farms needing a plow, it is a small miracle that American manufacturing capacity could fill the need. Most companies found their niche in the business and Rock Island found theirs with this New Model Walking Sulky of 1887.

Rock Island offered its New Rock Island Sulky to the market in 1903. Its "High-Low" design gained great popularity, along with the company's extensive line of farm tillage equipment. In addition, Rock Island built hay tools and many other items, even venturing into the tractor market.

An unusual offering was the Rock Island No. 10 Triple Gang Plow. This three-bottom plow was horse-drawn, probably requiring six or seven horses for easy operation. Very few companies built a three-bottom horse-drawn gang plow. Rock Island Plow Co., was purchased by J.I. Case Co. in 1937.

Ruggles, Nourse & Mason Co., Boston, Mass.

Famous by the 1860s, this company has now been almost forgotten. The company was an early manufacturer of the old cast-iron plows. After the introduction of the steel plow, it came out with its own design by the 1850s. Shown here is its plow of the early 1860s. In 1866, Ruggles, Nourse & Mason was bought out by Ames Plow Co., also of Boston.

M. Rumely Co., LaPorte, Ind.

From all appearances, Rumely built its own plows for a time in the early 1900s. While the specialty was in engine gang plows, the Rumely Hercules Brush Breaker shown here was a design intended for use with tractor power. The heavy design of this plow made it nearly indestructible. Aside from a brief entry into the plow business, Rumely laid claim to the famous OilPull tractors.

St. Paul Plow Works, St. Paul, Minn.

An 1897 illustration shows the newly designed St. Paul Sulky Plow. Among its other features, this plow claimed to be ideal for turning a square corner when plowing; this was achieved largely through the linkage from the furrow-wheel standard to the tail wheel. Little is known about this company or its duration in the plow business.

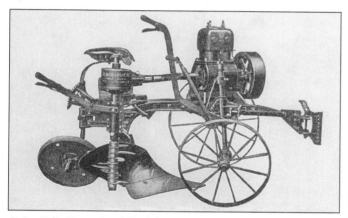

Scientific Farming Machinery Co., Minneapolis, Minn.

In 1917, Guy E. Lincoln designed the Once-Over Tiller as being the ideal approach to creating a seed bed. This design used a steel-tooth rotor powered by a gasoline engine; in this illustration, a Cushman 8-horsepower two-cylinder model is attached. The Once-Over Tiller could be attached to almost any sulky plow. The company disappears after 1924.

Skandia Plow Co., Rockford, Ill.

A unique feature of the Skandia plow was that it could easily be converted back and forth from a breaking plow to an ordinary

design with relative ease. For farmers having some of their land broken to the plow, with others remaining unbroken, this was cited as a distinct advantage. However, by the early 1900s, no further trace of the company has been found. The model shown here was illustrated in 1887.

South Bend Chilled Plow Co., South Bend, Ind.

This company goes back to the 1870s and the sulky plow designed by W.L. Casaday. Apparently, Casaday was associated with James Oliver for a time, but eventually formed his own company or at least associated himself with a company building his designs. Shown here is the Garland Riding Plow of 1890. Like many others of the time, it was designed to turn a square corner. As shown, the farmer is plowing from the center of the field outward, always turning the soil to the center. This left no dead furrows or back furrows.

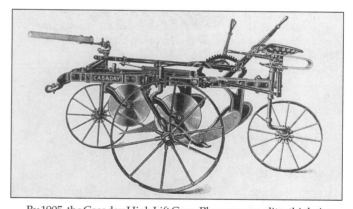

By 1905, the Casaday High Lift Gang Plow was a reality, this being another of the Casaday designs. The Casaday was one of the first to eliminate the landside, thus reducing the draft of the plow.

From 1910 comes this illustration of the Casaday Foot-Lift Sulky, a rather modern plow for its time. By this time, plow makers had approached most of the problems in design and this plow even included a special adjustment for the pole or tongue so that the center of draft was correct. Apparently, this firm came under control of Vulcan Plow Co. in the 1920s, with the latter joining in the 1930 merger that created Farm Tools, Inc.

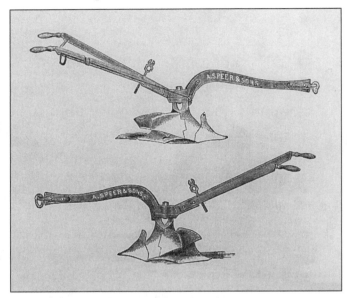

Alexander Speer & Sons, Pittsburgh, Penn.

For 1878, Speer offered this unique hillside plow that could be operated as either a right-hand plow or a left-hand plow. With this plow, a farmer could begin at one side of the field and plow to the other side, never having to make a back furrow or leave a dead furrow. Dozens of small companies like this one were in the plow business into the early 1900s.

Syracuse Chilled Plow Co., Syracuse, N.Y.

Shown here is the Syracuse Reversible Sulky Plow, also known as a two-way plow. With this design, it was possible to plow from one side of a field to the other without the need for back furrows or dead furrows. In 1912, this firm came under control of Deere & Co.

Did You Know?

In 1905, New Process offered its Long Knife Cultivator for $8.

J. Thompson & Sons, Beloit, Wisc.

In 1887, Thompson offered its Ole Olson Sulky Plow, the trade name being an obvious reference to immigrants of Scandinavian extraction. This plow remained on the market for some years, with parts being available from Thompson Plow & Engine Works at least into the late 1940s. After that time, the company slips into obscurity.

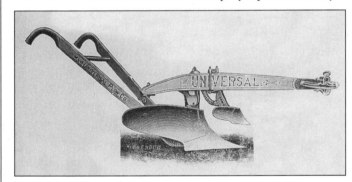

Universal Plow Co., Canton, Ohio

Advertised in the 1880s and 1890s, the Universal plow could be purchased with a steel moldboard or one of chilled iron. An 1887 advertisement lists the company at Canton, Ohio; by 1894, the firm is shown at Wooster, Ohio. After the 1890s, no further trace of Universal Plow Co. can be found.

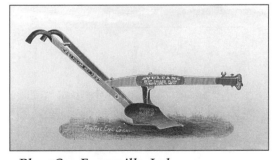

Vulcan Plow Co., Evansville, Ind.

Vulcan had a long history in the plow business, with much of its trade being in the Southern states. One of its late catalogs illustrates the Vulcan Chilled Plow with a wood beam, noting that many farmers still preferred this style to the steel beam design. At some point in the 1920s, it appears that Vulcan came into control of the South Bend Chilled Plow Works.

In 1930, Vulcan Plow Co., merged with Roderick Lean, Hayes Pump & Planter Co., and the Peoria Drill Co., to form Farm Tools, Inc. This bolstered the four companies by giving them better marketing power, as well as helping them weather the disastrous Great Depression. Shown here is the Vulcan Zephyr Tractor Plow of the 1930s. Vulcan had developed this plow prior to the merger and Farm Tools, Inc. continued to manufacture it for some years to come.

Weir Plow Co., Monmouth, Ill.

By 1887, Weir had come out with its "three-wheel plow," a new design with some unique features. Malleable iron chain transferred movement of the tongue to the furrow wheel, while the tail wheel was free to caster on its own. Weir continued in the plow business for some years; a well-known model was its Wild Irishman Sulky of the 1890s. By the 1920s, parts for Weir plows were available from Martin & Kennedy at Kansas City.

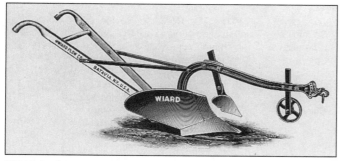

Wiard Plow Co., Batavia, N.Y.

George Wiard, who died in 1913, was the founder of Wiard Plow Co. His father before him was a plow maker. Shown here is a Wiard steel beam walking plow of the early 1900s. The company also built many different tillage implements and farm machines.

Parts for the Wiard plows were available at least into the late 1940s, after which time the company disappears from view. Shown here is the Wiard reversible sulky plow of the early 1900s. Curiously, George Wiard's nephew, Harry Wiard, was also in the plow business, being one of the organizers of the Syracuse Chilled Plow Co., noted previously in this section. In the 1870-1920 period, hundreds of plow makers built thousands of plow models; only a few are illustrated in this section.

Trade Names

Plows (Walking)

Name	Company	Location	Year
Aaron Varney	J. B. Varney Plow Co.	North Berwick, ME	1892
Acme	Hartig-Becker Plow Co.	Evansville, IN	1915
Acme	J. B. Varney Plow Co.	North Berwick, ME	1892
Acme	J. K. Wilder & Son	Monroe, MI	1892
Adamant	W. W. Packer & Son	Saddle River, NJ	1892
Adams	James A. Adams	Columbia, MO	1892
Adams	Sarah M. Adams	Galena, IL	1892
Advance	Ann Arbor Agricultural Co.	Ann Arbor, MI	1892
Ahnapee	A. Hamacek & Co.	Ahnapee, WI	1892
Akron	Akron Cultivator Co.	Akron, OH	1915
Albright	J. H. Albright & Sons	Mifflinburg, PA	1892
Alfalfa Clipper	Moline Plow Co.	Moline, IL	1915
American	American Plow Co.	Madison, WI	1905
American	B. F. Avery & Sons	Louisville, KY	1915
Ames Chilled	Ames Plow Co.	South Framingham, MA	1915
Amondson	L. O. Amondson	Gratiot, WI	1892
Appleton	J. E. Becker	Appleton, WI	1905
Armsby	Belcher & Taylor Agricultural Co.	Chicopee Falls, MA	1892
Armsby	Belcher & Taylor Agricultural Co.	Chicopee Falls, MA	1915
Arnold	G. W. Arnold's Son	Ionia, MI	1915
Atlanta	Atlanta Agricultural Works	Atlanta, GA	1905
Atlas	S. R. White & Bro.	Norfolk, VA	1892
Aughe	Aughe Plow Co.	Dayton, OH	1915
Aughe	Parrott Mfg. Co.	Dayton, OH	1892
Aurora	S. H. Peek	East Aurora, NY	1905
Aurora Clipper	Peek Bros.	East Aurora, NY	1892
Avery	B. F. Avery & Sons	Louisville, KY	1892
Banner	Ball, Mitchell & Co.	Maysville, KY	1892
Banner	Greenville Implement Co.	Greenville, MI	1905
Bantam	Deere & Co.	Moline, IL	1915

Trade Names (cont...)

Baxter	Evans Mfg. Co.	Hammond, NY	1905
Bay City	Bay City Plow Works	Bay City, MI	1905
Belcher & Taylor	Belcher & Taylor Agricultural Co.	Chicopee Falls, MA	1905
Bellevue	Ohio Cultivator Co.	Bellevue, OH	1915
Beloit	Gesley Mfg. Co.	Beloit, WI	1892
Bement	E. Bement & Sons	Lansing, MI	1892
Bement	E. Bement's Sons	Lansing, MI	1905
Bement Peerless	Parker Plow Co.	Richmond, MI	1915
Benicia	Benicia Agricultural Works	Benicia, CA	1892
Benson	H. J. Benson	Prairie du Chien, WI	1892
Bergstrom	Bergstrom Plow Works	Canton, SD	1905
Big Bolt	B. F. Avery & Sons	Louisville, KY	1915
Big Joe	Brillion Iron Works	Brillion, WI	1905
Bignell	F. B. Bignell	Smyrna, MI	1892
Billups Champion	C. Billups, Son & Co.	Norfolk, VA	1892
Bissel	Ohio Cultivator Co.	Bellevue, OH	1915
Bissell	T. M. Bissell Plow Co.	South Bend, IN	1892
Bissell's Improved	Bissell Chilled Plow Works	South Bend, IN	1892
Black Diamond	Parlin & Orendorff Co.	Canton, IL	1915
Black Prince	Thos. Meikle & Co.	Louisville, KY	1892
Blatchley	I. S. Matthews' Sons	Binghamton, NY	1892
Blount Daisy	Blount Plow Works	Evansville, IN	1915
Blount Darling	Blount Plow Works	Evansville, IN	1915
Blount Royal Beauty	Blount Plow Works	Evansville, IN	1915
Blount True Blue	Blount Plow Works	Evansville, IN	1915
Blount's	Henry F. Blount	Evansville, IN	1905
Blue Bird	Moline Plow Co.	Moline, IL	1915
Blue Jacket	J. Thompson & Sons Mfg. Co.	Beloit, WI	1892
Blue Jay	Parlin & Orendorff Co.	Canton, IL	1915
Blue Pony	E. Bement & Sons	Lansing, MI	1892
Blue Ribbon	Kingman Plow Co.	Peoria, IL	1915
Blue Ribbon	Weir Plow Co.	Monmouth, IL	1892
Bonanza	Madison Plow Co.	Madison, WI	1915
Boss	G. A. Kelly Plow Co.	Longview, TX	1915
Boss	R. W. Whitehurst Mfg. Corp.	Norfolk, VA	1915
Boss	Wrenn, Whitehurst & Co.	Norfolk, VA	1892
Boston Clipper	Ames Plow Co.	Boston, MA	1892
Boy Carbon	Harriman Mfg, Co.	Harriman, TN	1915
Boy Carbon	Southern Plow Co.	Columbus, GA	1915
Boy Dixie	Harriman Mfg, Co.	Harriman, TN	1915
Boy Dixie	Southern Plow Co.	Columbus, GA	1915
Boy Dixie	Starke's Dixie Plow Works	Richmond, VA	1915
Boy's Delight	St. John Plow Co.	Kalamazoo, MI	1892
Brinly	Brinly-Hardy Co.	Louisville, KY	1905
Brinly Blackland	Brinly-Hardy Co.	Louisville, KY	1915
Brinly Broncho	Brinly-Hardy Co.	Louisville, KY	1915
Brinly Combination	Brinly-Hardy Co.	Louisville, KY	1915
Brinly Duckbill	Brinly-Hardy Co.	Louisville, KY	1915
Brinly High Bed	Brinly-Hardy Co.	Louisville, KY	1915
Brinly Mixed Land	Brinly-Hardy Co.	Louisville, KY	1915
Brinly Mustang	Brinly-Hardy Co.	Louisville, KY	1915
Brinly Orange	Brinly-Hardy Co.	Louisville, KY	1915
Brinly's Universal	Brinly, Miles & Hardy Co.	Louisville, KY	1892

Trade Names (cont...)

Bristol	Sargent, Osgood & Roundy Co.	Randolph, VT	1915
Brookaw	Abram Brookaw	Bloomington, IL	1892
Bryan	Bryan Plow Co.	Bryan, OH	1892
Buckeye Clipper	Harriman Mfg, Co.	Harriman, TN	1915
Buckley	Charles E. Buckley	Amenia Union, NY	1892
Buckley Clipper	R. C. Buckley	Peoria, IL	1892
Buford	Rock Island Plow Co.	Rock Island, IL	1892
Bunker Hill	J. W. Murkland	Barton, VT	1915
Burch	Toledo Plow Co.	Toledo, OH	1892
Burch Chilled	J. W. Murkland	Barton, VT	1915
Burns	P. Burns & Co.	Hamilton, OH	1892
C. B. Ranger	South Bend Chilled Plow Works	South Bend, IN	1915
Cadet	B. F. Avery & Sons	Louisville, KY	1915
Calhoun	Wm. Clore's Sons	Rising Sun, IN	1892
Cambridge	Cambridge Steel Plow Co.	Cambridge, NY	1915
Cambridge	H. H. Lovejoy & Son	Cambridge, NY	1905
Canandaigua	Alexander Davidson	Canandaigua, NY	1905
Canton	Parlin & Orendorff Co.	Canton, IL	1905
Canton Clipper	Parlin & Orendorff Co.	Canton, IL	1892
Carolina	S. R. White & Bro.	Norfolk, VA	1892
Carolina	S. R. White's Sons	Norfolk, VA	1915
Carter	H. Carter & Sons	Canisteo, NY	1892
Carver	Carver Mfg. Co.	Carver, MN	1892
Case	J. I. Case Plow Works	Racine, WI	1892
Cass & McArthur	Cass & McArthur	Harlan, IA	1892
Cass City	Cass City Foundry & Machine Co.	Cass City, MI	1905
Castile	Castile Chilled Plow Co.	Castile, NY	1905
Castleton	S. R. Sargent & Son	Castleton, VT	1905
Castleton	Sargent, Osgood & Roundy Co.	Randolph, VT	1915
Centennial	Ames Plow Co.	South Framingham, MA	1915
Centennial	George Wagner	Effort, PA	1892
Challenge	Rock Island Plow Co.	Rock Island, IL	1915
Chamberlin	Bean-Chamberlin Mfg. Co.	Hudson, MI	1892
Champion	C. Billups, Son & Co.	Norfolk, VA	1915
Champion	A. H. Kirkland	Jackson, MS	1892
Champion	E. B. Marsh & Bro.	Snydersville, PA	1892
Champion	George Wagner	Effort, PA	1892
Champion	J. K. Wilder & Son	Monroe, MI	1892
Champion	Motherwell Iron & Steel Co.	Logan, OH	1892
Champion	Parrott Mfg. Co.	Dayton, OH	1892
Champion	Portland Foundry Co.	Portland, MI	1892
Champion	Richford Foundry Co.	Richford, VT	1905
Champion	William Ripson & Son	Youngstown, NY	1905
Champion	Smalley Mfg. Co.	Manitowoc, WI	1915
Champlain	W. G. Graves	Champlain, NY	1892
Chattanooga	Chattanooga Plow Co.	Chattanooga, TN	1892
Chicopee	Belcher & Taylor Agricultural Co.	Chicopee Falls, MA	1915
Childs	Chas. H. Childs & Co.	Utica, NY	1892
Clark	T. C. Clark	Russellville, KY	1892
Clayton	John Clayton Plow	Minneapolis, MN	1892
Climax	C. Billups, Son & Co.	Norfolk, VA	1915
Climax	J. H. Wagner & Co.	Vernon, IN	1892
Clipper	A. Bostick	Millington, MI	1892

Trade Names (cont...)

Clipper	A. Bostick & Son	Lapeer, MI	1905
Clipper	A. H. Kirkland	Jackson, MS	1892
Clipper	Brown-Manly Plow Co.	Malta, OH	1915
Clipper	Donaldson Bros.	Mt. Clemens, MI	1892
Clipper	Hartig-Becker Plow Co.	Evansville, IN	1915
Clipper	J. B. Varney Plow Co.	North Berwick, ME	1892
Clipper	Portland Foundry Co.	Portland, MI	1915
Clipper	Rock Island Plow Co.	Rock Island, IL	1915
Clipper	S. R. White's Sons	Norfolk, VA	1915
Collins	Collins Co.	Collinsville, CT	1892
Collins	Collins Plow Co.	Quincy, IL	1892
Columbia	Columbia Plow Works	Copake Iron Works, NY	1892
Columbus	Southern Plow Co.	Columbus, GA	1915
Conical	Belcher & Taylor Agricultural Co.	Chicopee Falls, MA	1892
Conquest	F. & J. H. Culver	West Oneonta, NY	1892
Cook's	H. O. Kerns	Sutherlin, VA	1892
Copenhagen	Alex R. Gebbie	Lowville, NY	1892
Cowley's	W. A. Cowley	Stamford, NY	1892
Creole	Deere & Co.	Moline, IL	1915
Crescent	Call-Watt Co.	Richmond, VA	1915
Crescent	Oliver Chilled Plow Works	South Bend, IN	1915
Crescent	Watt Plow Co.	Richmond, VA	1892
Cricket	B. F. Avery & Sons	Louisville, KY	1915
Crisler	Crisler Bros. & Co.	Lodi, WI	1892
Crothers	F. R. Crothers	Sparta, IL	1892
Crown	Call-Watt Co.	Richmond, VA	1915
Crown	Watt Plow Co.	Richmond, VA	1892
Cuban Sugarland	B. F. Avery & Sons	Louisville, KY	1915
Cummins	Wm. H. May & Son	Alexandria, VA	1892
Currier	Henry A. Currier	Almont, MI	1892
Curtis	Curtis Mfg. Co.	Albion, NY	1892
Curtis	Donaldson Bros.	Mt. Clemens, MI	1892
Curtis	G. W. Arnold & Son	Ionia, MI	1892
Curtis	J. K. Wilder & Son	Monroe, MI	1892
Curtis	Miller & Fernwood	Richmond, MI	1892
Curtis 22	Otter Lake Iron Works	Otter Lake, MI	1892
D Arrow	S. R. White's Sons	Norfolk, VA	1915
Daisy	Blount Plow Works	Evansville, IN	1915
Daisy	Charles City Mfg. Co.	Charles City, IA	1892
Daisy	S. R. White & Bro.	Norfolk, VA	1915
Daisy Clipper	Rock Island Plow Co.	Rock Island, IL	1915
Dandy	B. F. Avery & Sons	Louisville, KY	1915
David Bradley	David Bradley Mfg. Co.	Chicago, IL	1892
Davidson	Davidson-Dietrich Plow Co.	Evansville, IN	1905
Dayton	Parrott Mfg. Co.	Dayton, OH	1892
Deats	Hiram Deats Jr.	Pittstown, NJ	1892
Deer River	Alex R. Gebbie	Lowville, NY	1892
Deer River	Fulton Machine & Vise Co.	Lowville, NY	1915
Deer River	Wetmore Iron Works	Lowville, NY	1905
Defiance Clipper	Clipper Plow Co.	Defiance, OH	1905
Dew	Martin Dew	Cass City, MI	1892
Diamond	Lawrence & Chapin Co.	Kalamazoo, MI	1892
Diamond	Oliver Chilled Plow Works	South Bend, IN	1915
Diamond G.	George H. Snyder	Ghent, NY	1892

Dictator	Lehr Agricultural Co.	Fremont, OH	1892
Dirigo	J. B. Varney Plow Co.	North Berwick, ME	1892
Dixie	H. O. Kerns	Sutherlin, VA	1905
Dixie	Parlin & Orendorff Co.	Canton, IL	1915
Dixie	Starke's Dixie Plow Works	Richmond, VA	1915
Dixie Belle	Blount Plow Works	Evansville, IN	1915
Dixie Clipper	Rock Island Plow Co.	Rock Island, IL	1892
Dixie Pattern	S. R. White's Sons	Norfolk, VA	1915
Dodge	J. K. Wilder & Son	Monroe, MI	1892
Doe	Belcher & Taylor Agricultural Co.	Chicopee Falls, MA	1915
Doe's	Taylor & Gale	Chicopee Falls, MA	1892
Doe's Diamond	Wm. P. Ford & Co.	Concord, NH	1892
Dutton	E. Q. Dutton	Cato, NY	1892
Dutton	Eaton Plow Works	Pinckneyville, IL	1905
Eagle	A. B. Farquhar Co.	York, PA	1915
Eagle	Ames Plow Co.	Boston, MA	1892
Eagle	B. F. Avery & Sons	Louisville, KY	1915
Eagle	Eagle Mfg. Co.	Davenport, IA	1892
Eagle	Eagle Mfg. Co.	Kansas City, MO	1905
Eagle	Eagle Mfg. Co.	Muskogee, OK	1915
Eagle	Lehr Agricultural Co.	Fremont, OH	1892
Eagle	Wm. M. Johnson	Wilmot, OH	1892
Eagle Clipper	I. B. Rowell & Co.	Waukesha, WI	1915
Eagle Telegraph	Ames Plow Co.	Boston, MA	1892
Eaton's	E. C. Eaton	Pinckneyville, IL	1892
Eaton's	Eaton Plow Works	Pinckneyville, IL	1905
Eclipse	LaCrosse Plow Works	LaCrosse, WI	1915
Economist	Economist Plow Co.	South Bend, IN	1892
Eddy	W. Eddy Plow Co.	Greenwich, NY	1915
Edgecombe	Edgecombe Agricultural Works	Tarborough, NC	1892
Edinburgh	Edinburgh Agricultural Works	Edinburgh, VA	1892
Eggen	Eggen Bros.	Rushford, MN	1892
El Matador	B. F. Avery & Sons	Louisville, KY	1915
Emerson	Emerson Mfg. Co.	Rockford, IL	1905
Emperor	Plymouth Foundry & Machine Co.	Plymouth, WI	1915
Empire	Empire Plow Co.	Cleveland, OH	1892
Empire	Empire Plow Co.	Richmond, IN	1892
Empress	J. I. Case Plow Works	Racine, WI	1915
Empress	Moline Plow Co.	Moline, IL	1892
Empress	Texas Implement & Machine Co.	Dallas, TX	1915
Eureka	Benicia Agricultural Works	Benicia, CA	1892
Eureka	I. B. Rowell & Co.	Menomonee Falls, WI	1892
Eureka	J. I. Case Plow Works	Racine, WI	1915
Eureka	Painter & Frankland	Albion, IL	1892
Excelsior	Charles E. Buckley	Amenia Union, NY	1892
Excelsior	Cincinnati Plow & Bellows Works	Cincinnati, OH	1892
Excelsior	Geo. E. Bechtolt	Urbana, OH	1892
Excelsior	I. B. Rowell & Co.	Waukesha, WI	1915
Excelsior	R. I. Schlabach	Nazareth, PA	1892
Excelsior	Stringer, Dexter & Coe	Munnsville, NY	1892
Fair	G. Fair & Sons	Blaine, MI	1905
Fairfield Burch	Fairfield Plow Works	North Fairfield, OH	1905

Trade Names (cont...)

Famous	Hartig-Becker Plow Co.	Evansville, IN	1915
Famous	Moline Plow Co.	Moline, IL	1892
Famous	Roelker Plow Co.	Evansville, IN	1892
Farmer's Friend	Charles E. Hunter	Fredericksburg, VA	1892
Farmer's Friend	S. R. White & Bro.	Norfolk, VA	1892
Farquhar's	Pennsylvania Agricultural Works	York, PA	1892
Firefly Pony	Moline Plow Co.	Moline, IL	1915
Ford	Wm. P. Ford & Co.	Concord, NH	1892
Fort Madison	Fort Madison Plow Co.	Fort Madison, IA	1915
Frost	C. S. Frost	Watkins, NY	1892
Frye	Sargent, Osgood & Roundy Co.	Randolph, VT	1915
Frye's	John J. Frye	Portland, ME	1892
Fuller & Johnson	Fuller & Johnson Mfg. Co.	Madison, WI	1892
Furrow	Wm. P. Ford & Co.	Concord, NH	1892
Gale	Gale Mfg. Co.	Albion, MI	1892
Galena	Sarah M. Adams	Galena, IL	1892
Gammill	LaGrange Plow Works	LaGrange, GA	1892
Garden City Clipper	David Bradley Mfg. Co.	Bradley, IL	1905
Gardner	Gardner Foundry Co.	Lockport, NY	1892
Garnet	Oliver Chilled Plow Works	South Bend, IN	1915
Gate City Clipper	Southern Agricultural Works	Atlanta, GA	1892
Gem	Brinly-Hardy Co.	Louisville, KY	1915
Gem	Wrenn. Whitehurst & Co.	Norfolk, VA	1892
Gem City Clipper	Collins Plow Co.	Quincy, IL	1915
Genuine Bement	E. Bement & Sons	Lansing, MI	1892
Genuine Norwegian	J. Thompson & Sons Mfg. Co.	Beloit, WI	1892
George & Tweedale	George & Tweedale	Constantine, MI	1892
Gibson	Gibson Agricultural Works	Harriman, TN	1892
Goddard	Silas Goddard & Son	South Durham, ME	1892
Godfrey	H. M. Godfrey	Jonesburg, MO	1892
Gold Medal	Clipper Plow Co.	Defiance, OH	1905
Gopher	J. F. Lanfersieck Co.	New Bremen, OH	1892
Governor	Rock Island Plow Co.	Rock Island, IL	1892
Gowanda	Gowanda Agricultural Works	Gowanda, NY	1892
Grand Detour	Grand Detour Plow Co.	Dixon, IL	1892
Grand Rapids	Grand Rapids Mfg. & Implement Co.	Grand Rapids, MI	1892
Granger	C. Billups, Son & Co.	Norfolk, VA	1892
Green Mountain	Sargent, Osgood & Roundy Co.	Randolph, VT	1915
Gregg	Gregg & Co.	Trumansburg, NY	1892
Grier	Geo. S. Grier & Son	Milford, DE	1892
Ground Hog	Groundhog Plow & Foundry Co.	Clarksville, TN	1905
Hainline	V. C. Hainline	Levee, KY	1892
Hall	James H. Hall Plow Co.	Maysville, KY	1892
Hamburgh	Hamburgh Plow Works	Hamburgh, PA	1892
Hamilton	Millikin, Cisle & Co.	Peoria, IL	1892
Hapgood	Hapgood Plow Co.	Alton, IL	1892

Trade Names (cont...)

Harriman	Harriman Mfg. Co.	Harriman, TN	1915
Harrison	North Carolina Plow Co.	Cary, NC	1892
Hartford	Hartford Plow Works	Hartford, WI	1892
Hartig-Becker	Hartig-Becker Plow Co.	Evansville, IN	1905
Hartman	Hartman Mfg. Co.	Vincennes, IN	1905
Harvey	W. I. Harvey	Lock Haven, PA	1892
Hazel	Moline Plow Co.	Moline, IL	1915
Heckendorn	Sutton Bros. & Bell	Indiana, PA	1892
Hero	Harmon Machine Co.	Watertown, NY	1892
Hero	Plymouth Foundry & Machine Co.	Plymouth, WI	1915
Hersey	F. C. Merrill	South Paris, ME	1892
Highland	Evan Davis & Son	Butler, MD	1892
Hill Patent	George Fair	Blaine, MI	1892
Hillsdale	Hillsdale Plow Co.	Hillsdale, NY	1905
Hillsdale	Wm. A. Mallery	Hillsdale, NY	1892
Hilsinger	Cincinnati Plow & Bellows Works	Cincinnati, OH	1892
Hoffman	Wm. Clore's Sons	Rising Sun, IN	1892
Hoosier	Hartig-Becker Plow Co.	Evansville, IN	1915
Hoosier	Roelker Plow Co.	Evansville, IN	1892
Hoppes & Edwards	Hoppes & Edwards	Erin, TN	1892
Hubbell	J. W. Murkland	Barton, VT	1915
Hunter	Charles E. Hunter	Fredericksburg, VA	1892
Hunter Boy	Chas. E. Hunter's Plow Works	Fredericksburg, VA	1915
Huntington	Benj. E. Bond	Applegate, MI	1892
Huntington	E. Bement & Sons	Lansing, MI	1892
Huntington	Miller & Fernwood	Richmond, MI	1892
Hussey	Hussey Plow Co.	North Berwick, ME	1905
Hussey	Timothy B. Hussey	North Berwick, ME	1892
I. X. L.	W. G. Graves	Champlain, NY	1892
Ideal	Ames Plow Co.	South Framingham, MA	1915
Ideal	B. F. Avery & Sons	Louisville, KY	1915
Ideal	Sargent, Osgood & Roundy Co.	Randolph, VT	1915
Imperial	Bucher & Gibbs Plow Co.	Canton, OH	1892
Improved Lord	Kohler, Hayssen & Stehn Mfg. Co.	Sheboygan, WI	1892
Indian River Clipper	C. Wakefield & Son	Theresa, NY	1892
Ionia	G. W. Arnold & Son	Ionia, MI	1892
Iowa	Parlin & Orendorff Co.	Canton, IL	1915
Iowa Clipper	Kingman Plow Co.	Peoria, IL	1915
Ithaca	H. B. Wells & Co.	Ithaca, MI	1905
Janesville	Janesville Machine Co.	Janesville, WI	1905
Jarrell	J. I. Wells' Sons	Jackson, TN	1892
Jewel	Oliver Chilled Plow Works	South Bend, IN	1915
John Deere	Deere & Co.	Moline, IL	1892
Johnson	R. A. Johnson & Co.	Atlanta, GA	1892
Johnson & Smith	Johnson & Smith	Austin, MN	1892
Kelly	Daniel T. Kelly	Portland, ME	1892
Kelly	G. A. Kelly Plow Co.	Longview, TX	1905
Kelly Pony	E. Bement & Sons	Lansing, MI	1892
Kentucky	B. F. Avery & Sons	Louisville, KY	1915
Keystone	S. S. Messinger & Son	Tatamy, PA	1892
Keystone-Burch	Keystone Plow Co.	New Castle, PA	1892
Kingman	Kingman Plow Co.	Peoria, IL	1905

Trade Names (cont...)

Kirk	Weir Plow Co.	Monmouth, IL	1892
LaCrosse	LaCrosse Plow Works	LaCrosse, WI	1892
Lancaster	Frank Maute	Lancaster, NY	1892
Lanfersieck	J. F. Lanfersieck Co.	New Bremen, OH	1892
Lang	Lang & Bro.	Farmington, MO	1892
Le Roy	Le Roy Plow Co.	Le Roy, NY	1905
Lehr	Lehr Agricultural Co.	Fremont, OH	1905
Lewis	Henry Lewis	China, ME	1892
Lion	Belcher & Taylor Agricultural Co.	Chicopee Falls, MA	1892
Little Boy Blue	Gale Mfg. Co.	Albion, MI	1915
Little Captain	South Bend Chilled Plow Works	South Bend, IN	1915
Little Wonder	Fosmir Iron Works	Los Angeles, CA	1892
Livingston	Vesuvius Plow Works	Vesuvius, VA	1892
Lone Oak	Hartig-Becker Plow Co.	Evansville, IN	1915
Longview	Longview Kelly Co.	Longview, TX	1892
Look & Lincoln	Look & Lincoln	Marion, VA	1892
Lord Improved	I. B. Rowell & Co.	Waukesha, WI	1915
Louisiana	Moline Plow Co.	Moline, IL	1915
Louisville	E. Bement & Sons	Lansing, MI	1892
Lovejoy	Henry H. Lovejoy	Cambridge, NY	1892
Lynchburg	Lynchburg Foundry Co.	Lynchburg, VA	1905
Madison	Madison Plow Co.	Madison, WI	1915
Malta	Brown-Manly Plow Co.	Malta, OH	1915
Manny's	Thompson and Co.	Rockford, IL	1862
Marietta	Marietta Mfg. Co.	Marietta, PA	1892
Martin's Eagle	Ames Plow Co.	Boston, MA	1892
Martinsburg	Martinsburg Foundry Co.	Martinsburg, PA	1905
May's Crystal	Wm. H. May & Son	Alexandria, VA	1892
McWane	Graham Foundry & Machine Co.	Graham, VA	1892
McWane Boltless	Lynchburg Plow Works	Lynchburg, VA	1915
Mead's Conical	Belcher & Taylor Agricultural Co.	Chicopee Falls, MA	1915
Mellen	J. & D. Mellen	Alton, IL	1892
Meridian	Evarts & Co.	Meridian, NY	1905
Michigan	David Prouty and Co.	Boston, MA	1861
Miller	Miller & Fernwood	Richmond, MI	1892
Miller	Parker Plow Co.	Richmond, MI	1915
Mills	Marvin Mills	Memphis, MO	1892
Minor & Horton	Wm. H. May & Son	Alexandria, VA	1892
Mishawaka	Mishawaka Plow Co.	Mishawaka, IN	1905
Mishawaka Clipper	St. Joseph Mfg. Co.	Mishawaka, IN	1892
Mishawaka Scotchman	St. Joseph Mfg. Co.	Mishawaka, IN	1892
Mittendorf	Mittendorf Mfg. Co.	Hermann, MO	1909
Mitts	Mitts & Merrill	Saginaw, MI	1892
Modern Marvel	South Bend Chilled Plow Works	South Bend, IN	1892
Moffatt	Moffatt Mfg. Co.	Chester, SC	1892
Moline	Moline Plow Co.	Moline, IL	1905
Monitor	Harmon Machine Co.	Watertown, NY	1892
Monitor	Minneapolis Plow Works	Minneapolis, MN	1892
Monitor	Mt. Vernon Plow Works	Mt. Vernon, OH	1892
Monitor	R. I. Schlabach	Nazareth, PA	1892
Monroeton	Monroeton Mfg. Co.	Monroeton, PA	1892

Trade Names (cont...)

Moore	Moore Plow & Implement Co.	Greenville, MI	1905
Morrison	Fort Madison Plow Co.	Fort Madison, IA	1915
Morrison	Morrison Mfg. Co.	Fort Madison, IA	1892
Morse	Robt. E. Morse	Auburn, IL	1892
Munnsville	Munnsville Plow Co.	Munnsville, NY	1905
Murkland	J. W. Murkland	Barton, VT	1892
Murray Clipper	A. Strawn	Murray, IA	1892
Mustang	Brinly-Hardy Co.	Louisville, KY	1915
Nashua	Nashua Mfg. Co.	Nashua, IA	1892
National	Belcher & Taylor Agricultural Co.	Chicopee Falls, MA	1892
Nebraska City	Geo. F. Kregel	Nebraska City, NE	1892
Nebraska Clipper	Moline Plow Co.	Moline, IL	1915
Neufang	Boggs Mfg. Co.	Atlanta, NY	1928
New Bremen	J. F. Lanfersieck Co.	New Bremen, OH	1892
New Bremen	Laufersieck-Grothaus Co.	New Bremen, OH	1905
New Bremen	Shunk Plow Co.	Bucyrus, OH	1915
New Burch	Call-Watt Co.	Richmond, VA	1905
New England	Ames Plow Co.	Boston, MA	1892
New Era	C. Billups, Son & Co.	Norfolk, VA	1892
New Ground	E. Bement & Sons	Lansing, MI	1892
New Remington Clipper	A. M. Ross & Co.	Ilion, NY	1892
North Star	Thos. Meikle & Co.	Louisville, KY	1892
Norway Clipper	St. Paul Plow Works	St. Paul, MN	1892
Norwegian	Norwegian Plow Co.	Dubuque, IA	1892
Norwegian	Thompson Plow Works	Beloit, WI	1915
O. K.	F. C. Merrill	South Paris, ME	1892
O. K.	Heilman Plow Co.	Evansville, IN	1892
Old Style	Wrenn. Whitehurst & Co.	Norfolk, VA	1892
Oldendorph	Oldendorph Bros.	Waterloo, IL	1892
Oliver	Oliver Chilled Plow Works	South Bend, IN	1892
Oneida Valley Clipper	Munnsville Plow Co.	Munnsville, NY	1915
Oneida Valley Clipper	Stringer, Dexter & Coe	Munnsville, NY	1892
Oneonta Clipper	Belcher & Taylor Agricultural Co.	Chicopee Falls, MA	1892
Orange	B. F. Avery & Sons	Louisville, KY	1915
Orange	Brinly-Hardy Co.	Louisville, KY	1915
Oriole	B. F. Avery & Sons	Louisville, KY	1915
Oxford	Belcher & Taylor Agricultural Co.	Chicopee Falls, MA	1915
Pacific Coast Special	Moline Plow Co.	Moline, IL	1915
Painter & Frankland	Painter & Frankland	Albion, IL	1905
Paragon	B. F. Avery & Sons	Louisville, KY	1915
Paris	F. C. Merrill	South Paris, ME	1892
Parks	Parks Plow Co.	New Madrid, MO	1892
Peekskill	Stringer, Dexter & Coe	Munnsville, NY	1892
Peerless	Donaldson Bros.	Mt. Clemens, MI	1892
Peerless	George Fair	Blaine, MI	1892
Peerless	Peru Plow & Wheel Co.	Peru, IL	1915
Pekin	Pekin Plow Co.	Pekin, IL	1892
Penn Yan Improved	Reynolds & Lang	Ithaca, NY	1892
Peoria	Millikin, Cisle & Co.	Peoria, IL	1892
Peru	Peru Plow & Wheel Co.	Peru, IL	1892

Trade Names (cont...)

Phelps	Phelps Chilled Plow Works	Phelps, NY	1892
Pierce	Geo. M. Pierce	Brodhead, WI	1892
Pirate	Mast, Buford & Burwell Co.	St. Paul, MN	1892
Pony	E. Bement & Sons	Lansing, MI	1892
Pony	Moline Plow Co.	Moline, IL	1892
Pony Black Land	R. Ballauf & Co.	Jefferson , TX	1892
Portland Champion	Portland Foundry Co.	Portland, MI	1915
Prairie Clipper	Princess Plow Co.	Canton, OH	1892
Princess	Carnegie Plow & Mfg. Co.	Carnegie, PA	1905
Princess	Princess Plow Co.	Canton, OH	1892
Prouty & Mears	Ames Plow Co.	Boston, MA	1892
Queen	South Bend Chilled Plow Works	South Bend, IN	1915
Queen of the West	Benj. E. Bond	Applegate, MI	1892
Ranger	E. Bement & Sons	Lansing, MI	1892
Raymond	Cincinnati Plow & Bellows Works	Cincinnati, OH	1892
Red Bird	B. F. Avery & Sons	Louisville, KY	1915
Red Bird	Emerson-Brantingham Co.	Rockford, IL	1915
Red Bird	Kingman Plow Co.	Peoria, IL	1915
Red Jacket	Deere & Co.	Moline, IL	1915
Red Jacket	Princess Plow Co.	Canton, OH	1892
Remington	Donaldson Bros.	Mt. Clemens, MI	1892
Richards	A. H. Richards	Mendon, MI	1892
Richards'	Richards' Iron Works	Manitowoc, WI	1892
Risedorph	Risedorph Agricultural Works	Albany, NY	1892
Rival	Oliver Chilled Plow Works	South Bend, IN	1915
Robin Hood	Moline Plow Co.	Moline, IL	1915
Robinson	Robinson Chilled Plow Co.	Canandaigua, NY	1892
Robinson Chilled No. 22	E. R. Allen & Co.	Whitesville, NY	1892
Robison	J. Robison & Son	Curwensville, PA	1892
Rock Island	Rock Island Plow Co.	Rock Island, IL	1892
Rockford	Rockford Mfg. Co.	Rockford, IL	1892
Roland	Rawlings Implement Co.	Baltimore, MD	1905
Roland	Rawlings Implement Co.	Baltimore, MD	1915
Roland	Roland Plow Works	Baltimore, MD	1892
Root	Mountville Mfg. Co.	Mountville, PA	1905
Rose Clipper	Heilman Plow Co.	Evansville, IN	1892
Rose Clipper	Vulcan Plow Co.	Evansville, IN	1905
Rough & Ready	W. Eddy & Sons	Greenwich, NY	1892
Rowell	I. B. Rowell & Co.	Menomonee Falls, WI	1905
Royal Beauty	Blount Plow Works	Evansville, IN	1915
Rutherford	Z. P. Dederick	Sherman, TX	1892
Sandoval	Sandoval Mfg. Co.	Sandoval, IL	1892
Sanford	B. H. & J. Sanford	Sheboygan Falls, WI	1892
Sattley	Racine-Sattley Co.	Springfield, IL	1905
Sattley	Sattley Mfg. Co.	Springfield, IL	1892
Schroeder	E. Schroeder	Wellington, MO	1892
Schuerenberg	F. W. Schuerenberg	Brenham, TX	1892
Scotch	Donaldson Bros.	Mt. Clemens, MI	1892
Scotch Clipper	Kingman Plow Co.	Peoria, IL	1915
Scotch Clipper	Moline Plow Co.	Moline, IL	1892

Trade Names (cont...)

Scotch Clipper	Peru Plow & Wheel Co.	Peru, IL	1915
Scotch Clipper	Rock Island Plow Co.	Rock Island, IL	1915
Scotch Clipper	South Bend Chilled Plow Works	South Bend, IN	1915
Scotch Clipper	Vulcan Plow Co.	Evansville, IN	1915
Seward	Seward Co.	Bloomington, IN	1892
Seylar	G. W. Seylar	Hancock, MD	1892
Sheboygan Falls	Plymouth Foundry & Machine Co.	Plymouth, WI	1915
Shunk's New Model	Shunk Plow Co.	Bucyrus, OH	1892
Silver Steel	Brown-Manly Plow Co.	Malta, OH	1905
Simplex	Hamburgh Plow Works	Hamburgh, PA	1915
Sioux City Clipper	Bergstrom Plow Works	Canton, SD	1905
Sioux City Clipper	Sioux City Plow Co.	Sioux City, IA	1892
Skandia	Skandia Plow Co.	Rockford, IL	1892
Smalley	Smalley Mfg. Co.	Manitowoc, WI	1892
Smith & Amman	Smith & Amman	Columbus, OH	1892
Snoebergers & Bassler	Snoebergers & Bassler	Martinsburg, PA	1892
South Bend	South Bend Chilled Plow Works	South Bend, IN	1892
Southern Girl	Davidson-Dietrich Plow Co.	Evansville, IN	1915
Southern Queen	Davidson-Dietrich Plow Co.	Evansville, IN	1915
Sparta	Rock Island Plow Co.	Rock Island, IL	1892
Sparta	Sparta Plow Works	Sparta, IL	1905
Spaulding	Sutton Bros. & Bell	Indiana, PA	1892
Speer	Alexander Speer and Sons	Pittsburgh, PA	1878
Speer	Globe Plow Works	Pittsburgh, PA	1892
Spencer	T. J. Spencer	Hernando, MS	1892
St. Albans	St. Albans Foundry Co.	St. Albans, VT	1892
St. Joseph	St. Joseph Plow Co.	St. Joseph, MO	1892
St. Louis Clipper	J. I. Case Plow Works	Racine, WI	1915
St. Paul	St. Paul Plow Works	St. Paul, MN	1897
Standard	Charles City Mfg. Co.	Charles City, IA	1892
Stapler	W. T. Stapler	Harmony Grove, GA	1892
Star	Benicia Agricultural Works	Benicia, CA	1892
Star	Fairfield Plow Works	North Fairfield, OH	1892
Star	Star Mfg. Co.	Carpentersville, IL	1892
Starbuck	Donaldson Bros.	Mt. Clemens, MI	1915
Starke's Genuine Dixie	Starke's Dixie Plow Works	Richmond, VA	1905
Stevenson	Stevenson Bros. & Co.	St. Cloud, MN	1892
Stonewall	S. R. White & Bro.	Norfolk, VA	1892
Sturgis	W. B. Sturgis	Shelbyville, IL	1892
Success	H. O. Kerns	Sutherlin, VA	1892
Sunflower	Blount Plow Works	Evansville, IN	1915
Sunny South	W. A. Maloney	Telford, TN	1892
Sunset	Parlin & Orendorff Co.	Canton, IL	1915
Superior	D. P. Emrick & Co.	Germantown, OH	1892
Superior	D. P. Emrick & Co.	Germantown, OH	1905
Superior	Superior Drill Co.	Springfield, OH	1892
Sussex	O. J. Little	Deckertown, NJ	1892

Trade Names (cont...)

Syracuse	Syracuse Chilled Plow Co.	Syracuse, NY	1892
Tabor	Sargent, Osgood & Roundy Co.	Randolph, VT	1915
Tally Ho	Hartford Plow Works	Hartford, WI	1905
Texas	G. A. Kelly Plow Co.	Longview, TX	1915
Texas	Moline Plow Co.	Moline, IL	1892
Thompson	C. M. Thompson	Lexington, NC	1892
Thompson Norwegian	J. Thompson & Sons Mfg. Co.	Beloit, WI	1905
Throop & Huber	Novelty Iron Works	Priceburg, PA	1892
Tiger	Harmon Machine Co.	Watertown, NY	1892
Tiny Tim	B. F. Avery & Sons	Louisville, KY	1915
Toledo	Toledo Plow Co.	Toledo, OH	1892
Towers & Sullivan	Towers & Sullivan Mfg. Co.	Rome, GA	1892
Toy's	W. M. Toy	Sidney, OH	1892
Tripper	G. A. Kelly Plow Co.	Longview, TX	1915
True Blue	Henry F. Blount	Evansville, IN	1892
Universal	Universal Plow Co.	Canton, OH	1883
Universal	Universal Plow Co.	Wooster, OH	1892
Urie Clipper	Heilman Plow Co.	Evansville, IN	1892
Valley	Brown-Manly Plow Co.	Malta, OH	1915
Valley	Pearl River Foundry Works	Jackson, MS	1892
Varney	J. R. Varney Plow Co.	North Berwick, ME	1905
Vermonter	Sargent, Osgood & Roundy Co.	Randolph, VT	1915
Vernon	J. H. Wagner & Co.	Vernon, IN	1892
Veteran Cast	B. F. Avery & Sons	Louisville, KY	1915
Victor	McNaull Machine & Foundry Co.	Ronceverte, WV	1892
Victor	William Ripson & Son	Youngstown, NY	1892
Virginia	Vesuvius Plow Works	Vesuvius, VA	1892
Vulcan	Heilman Plow Co.	Evansville, IN	1892
Wachusett	J. W. Murkland	Barton, VT	1915
Wadley	A. K. Wadley	Arkabutla, MS	1892
Warsaw	Cress Bros. & Co.	Warsaw, IL	1892
Waterport	D. D. Bromley	Waterport, NY	1892
Watertown	Lee Bros.	Watertown, SD	1892
Watertown	Lee Bros.	Watertown , SD	1892
Watkins	Watkins Chilled Plow Co.	Watkins, NY	1892
Watt	Call-Watt Co.	Richmond, VA	1905
Waukon	Simonsen & Peterson	Waukon, IA	1905
Wayne	Wayne Agricultural Works	Goldsboro, NC	1905
Wedepohl	H. Wedepohl	Berger, MO	1892
Wells	H. B. Wells	Ithaca, MI	1892
Whiley	Evan Davis & Son	Butler, MD	1892
White's	S. R. White & Bro.	Norfolk, VA	1905
Wiard	Wiard Plow Co.	Batavia, NY	1892
Wild Irishman	Weir Plow Co.	Monmouth, IL	1887
Wilder	J. K. Wilder & Son	Monroe, MI	1892
Wilder	Wilder Mfg. Co.	Monroe, MI	1892
Wilder	Wilder-Strong Implement Co.	Monroe, MI	1905
Wilharm	Christoph Wilharm	Tripoli, IA	1892
Wilkinson	A. Bostick & Son	Lapeer, MI	1905
Wilkinson	Donaldson Bros.	Mt. Clemens, MI	1915
Wilkinson	Miller & Fernwood	Richmond, MI	1892
Wisconsin Clipper	Madison Plow Co.	Madison, WI	1915
Wm. J. Oliver	Wm. J. Oliver Mfg. Co.	Knoxville, TN	1915
Woodcock	Evan Davis & Son	Butler, MD	1892

Trade Names (cont...)

Woodward's	Frank L. Woodward	Clinton, MI	1892
Wooley	J. W. Murkland	Barton, VT	1905
Wright	F. N. Wright & co.	Greenville, MI	1892
Wright	Wright Bros. Mfg. Co.	Monroe, MI	1892
Wyman	W. F. Wyman	Oshkosh, WI	1892
Wytheville	Wytheville Foundry & Machine Co.	Wytheville, VA	1892
Yankee	Belcher & Taylor Agricultural Co.	Chicopee Falls, MA	1892
Zink	A. J. Zink & Son	Christiansburgh, VA	1892

Plows (Riding)

Admiral	Grand Detour Plow Co.	Dixon, IL	1905
Ajax	J. I. Case Plow Works	Racine, WI	1905
All-in-One	Gantt Mfg. Co.	Macon, GA	1913
American	American Plow Co.	Madison, WI	1905
American Chief	Matteson & Williamson Mfg. Co.	Stockton, CA	1892
Aunt Rhoda	Bergstrom Plow Works	Canton, SD	1905
Aunt Rhoda	Sioux Falls Plow Co.	Sioux Falls, SD	1913
Avery's Invincible	B. F. Avery & Sons	Louisville, KY	1905
Avery's Torpedo	B. F. Avery & Sons	Louisville, KY	1905
Avery's Uncle Sam	B. F. Avery & Sons	Louisville, KY	1905
Badger	Madison Plow Co.	Madison, WI	1913
Bement	E. Bement's Sons	Lansing, MI	1905
Best Ever	Moline Plow Co.	Moline, IL	1905
Best-of-All	Ohio Cultivator Co.	Bellevue, OH	1913
Big Injun	Gale Mfg. Co.	Albion, MI	1892
Bismarck	Moline Plow Co.	Moline, IL	1913
Bissell	Bissell Chilled Plow Works	South Bend, IN	1905
Blount	Henry F. Blount	Evansville, IN	1905
Blue Grass	B. F. Avery & Sons	Louisville, KY	1892
Blue Grass	Thos. Meikle & Co.	Louisville, KY	1892
Bonanza	Oliver Chilled Plow Works	South Bend, IN	1892
Boss of the U. S.	George Fair	Blaine, MI	1892
Bradley U. S. A.	David Bradley Mfg. Co.	Bradley, IL	1905
Brown	Galesburg Coulter-Disc Co.	Galesburg, IL	1905
Bryan	Bryan Plow Co.	Bryan, OH	1892
Buford	Rock Island Plow Co.	Rock Island, IL	1892
Buster Brown	Fort Madison Plow Co.	Fort Madison, IA	1913
Canton	Parlin & Orendorff Co.	Canton, IL	1913
Captain Bill	Kingman Plow Co.	Peoria, IL	1913
Casaday	Oliver Chilled Plow Works	South Bend, IN	1892
Case Foot Lift	J. I. Case Plow Works	Racine, WI	1913
Champion	David Bradley Mfg. Co.	Bradley, IL	1905
Clark	Mishawaka Plow Co.	Mishawaka, IN	1905
Clark Square Corner	St. Joseph Mfg. Co.	Mishawaka, IN	1892
Cock of the Walk	Peru Plow & Wheel Co.	Peru, IL	1892
Collins	Collins Plow Co.	Quincy, IL	1892
Columbia	Rock Island Plow Co.	Rock Island, IL	1905
Columbian	Oliver Chilled Plow Works	South Bend, IN	1905
Comet	B. F. Avery & Sons	Louisville, KY	1913
Commodore	Kingman Plow Co.	Peoria, IL	1905
Crothers	F. R. Crothers	Sparta, IL	1892
Curlew	Parlin & Orendorff Co.	Canton, IL	1905
Daisy	Gale Mfg. Co.	Albion, MI	1905

Trade Names (cont...)

Daniels	E. B. Daniels & Co.	Havana, NY	1892
Darling	Henry F. Blount	Evansville, IN	1892
Deere	Deere & Co.	Moline, IL	1892
Deere Ranger	Deere & Co.	Moline, IL	1905
Defiance	LaCrosse Plow Works	LaCrosse, WI	1905
Dew	Martin Dew	Cass City, MI	1892
Diamond	Parlin & Orendorff Co.	Canton, IL	1905
Duke	Peru Plow & Wheel Co.	Peru, IL	1905
Duke & Dewey	Peru Plow & Wheel Co.	Peru, IL	1913
Dutch Yankee	Pekin Plow co.	Pekin, IL	1892
Eagle	Eagle Mfg. Co.	Kansas City, MO	1905
Eagle	I. B. Rowell & Co.	Menomonee Falls, WI	1905
Eaton's	E. C. Eaton	Pinckneyville, IL	1892
Eclipse Jt.	Madison Plow Co.	Madison, WI	1913
Eddy	W. Eddy Plow Co.	Greenwich, NY	1913
Eli	Rock Island Plow Co.	Rock Island, IL	1892
Elk	Peru Plow & Wheel Co.	Peru, IL	1905
Elkhart	Elkhart Plow Sulky & Iron Co.	Elkhart, IN	1892
Emerson	Emerson Mfg. Co.	Rockford, IL	1905
Emerson	Emerson-Brantingham Co.	Rockford, IL	1913
Eureka	Benicia Agricultural Works	Benicia, CA	1892
Eureka	I. B. Rowell & Co.	Menomonee Falls, WI	1892
Eureka	Painter & Frankland	Albion, IL	1892
Eureka	Pekin Plow co.	Pekin, IL	1905
Farm King	Rockford Mfg. Co.	Rockford, IL	1892
Farm Queen	Rockford Mfg. Co.	Rockford, IL	1905
Farmer's Friend	H. B. Milmine & Co.	Toledo, OH	1892
Farquhar	Pennsylvania Agricultural Works	York, PA	1892
Flying Dutchman	Moline Plow Co.	Moline, IL	1892
Foot Lift	Gale Mfg. Co.	Albion, MI	1913
Fosmir	Fosmir Iron Works	Los Angeles, CA	1892
Fowler	Fowler & Farrington	Taughannock Falls, NY	1892
Fuller & Johnson	Fuller & Johnson Mfg. Co.	Madison, WI	1892
Gale	Gale Mfg. Co.	Albion, MI	1892
Garland	South Bend Chilled Plow Co.	South Bend, IN	1905
Gazelle	Deere & Co.	Moline, IL	1892
Gesley	Gesley Mfg. Co.	Beloit, WI	1892
Gilpin	Deere & Co.	Moline, IL	1892
Good Enough	Moline Plow Co.	Moline, IL	1905
Grand Detour	Grand Detour Plow Co.	Dixon, IL	1892
Granger	Houser & Haines Mfg. Co.	Stockton, CA	1913
Great West	Gale Mfg. Co.	Albion, MI	1905
Hamilton	Long & Alstatter Co.	Hamilton, OH	1913
Hancock	Hancock Disc Plow Co.	Alton, IL	1913
Hard Pan	J. Thompson & Sons Mfg. Co.	Beloit, WI	1913
Headlight	Pekin Plow Co.	Pekin, IL	1892
Hercules	J. I. Case Plow Works	Racine, WI	1913
High-Low	Rock Island Plow Co.	Rock Island, IL	1905
Hobson	Hobson & Co.	Tatamy, PA	1892

Trade Names (cont...)

Honest Abe	Norwegian Plow Co.	Dubuque, IA	1892
Hummer	Racine-Sattley Co.	Springfield, IL	1905
Hummer	Sattley Mfg. Co.	Springfield, IL	1892
Ideal	Madison Plow Co.	Madison, WI	1913
Imperial	Bucher & Gibbs Plow Co.	Canton, OH	1892
Improved Riggs	Thomas Peppler	Hightstown, NJ	1892
Invincible	B. F. Avery & Sons	Louisville, KY	1913
Iowa	Morrison Mfg. Co.	Fort Madison, IA	1905
Iron Age	Bateman Mfg. Co.	Grenloch, NJ	1913
Iron Negro	Sparta Plow Works	Sparta, IL	1905
James Oliver	Oliver Chilled Plow Works	South Bend, IN	1905
Janesville	Janesville Machine Co.	Janesville, WI	1905
Jaye Eye See	J. I. Case Plow Works	Racine, WI	1892
Jewel	Bucher & Gibbs Plow Co.	Canton, OH	1913
John Deere	Deere & Co.	Moline, IL	1913
K. O.	J. Thompson & Sons Mfg. Co.	Beloit, WI	1913
King	Hapgood Plow Co.	Alton, IL	1913
King Oscar	J. Thompson & Sons Mfg. Co.	Beloit, WI	1905
Kingman Klondike	Kingman Plow Co.	Peoria, IL	1905
Klondike	Kingman Plow Co.	Peoria, IL	1905
Kynett	H. P. Kynett	Lisbon, IA	1892
LaCrosse	LaCrosse Plow Works	LaCrosse, WI	1892
Leader	Norwegian Plow Co.	Dubuque, IA	1892
Little Giant	South Bend Chilled Plow Co.	South Bend, IN	1913
Little Injun	Gale Mfg. Co.	Albion, MI	1905
Little Jap	Pekin Plow Co.	Pekin, IL	1905
Little Yankee	Grand Detour Plow Co.	Dixon, IL	1892
Lone Star	Morrison Mfg. Co.	Fort Madison, IA	1905
Marsh	Oliver Chilled Plow Works	South Bend, IN	1905
Marsh Casaday	South Bend Chilled Plow Co.	South Bend, IN	1905
Miller's	F. W. Miller	Caledonia, NY	1892
Mishawaka	St. Joseph Mfg. Co.	Mishawaka, IN	1892
Model	Kingman Plow Co.	Peoria, IL	1913
Monarch	Skandia Plow Co.	Rockford, IL	1892
Monitor	Minneapolis Plow Works	Minneapolis, MN	1905
Monmouth	Monmouth Plow Co.	Monmouth, IL	1913
Montezuma	Benicia Agricultural Works	Benicia, CA	1892
Moore	Moore Plow & Implement Co.	Greenville, MI	1913
Morrison	Morrison Mfg. Co.	Fort Madison, IA	1892
Morrison Center Draft	Morrison Mfg. Co.	Fort Madison, IA	1905
National	Belcher & Taylor Agricultural Co.	Chicopee Falls, MA	1892
New American	Eagle Mfg. Co.	Davenport, IA	1892
New American	Eagle Mfg. Co.	Kansas City, MO	1905
New Casaday	South Bend Chilled Plow Co.	South Bend, IN	1905
New Casaday	South Bend Chilled Plow Co.	South Bend, IN	1905
New Deal	Deere & Co.	Moline, IL	1892
New Deere	Deere & Co.	Moline, IL	1905
New Departure	Oliver Chilled Plow Works	South Bend, IN	1905

Trade Names (cont...)

New Eclipse	Fuller & Johnson Mfg. Co.	Madison, WI	1905
New Eclipse	Madison Plow Co.	Madison, WI	1913
New I. D.	Monmouth Plow Co.	Monmouth, IL	1905
New Morrison	Fort Madison Plow Co.	Fort Madison, IA	1913
New Morrison	Morrison Mfg. Co.	Fort Madison, IA	1905
New Tornado	B. F. Avery & Sons	Louisville, KY	1913
New Triumph	Morrison Mfg. Co.	Fort Madison, IA	1905
New Yankee	Grand Detour Plow Co.	Dixon, IL	1905
None Such	David Bradley Mfg. Co.	Bradley, IL	1905
Northwestern	Janesville Machine Co.	Janesville, WI	1905
Nortwestern Clipper	Northwestern Steel & Iron Works	Eau Claire, WI	1913
Ohio	Bucher & Gibbs Plow Co.	Canton, OH	1913
Old Reliable	Hapgood Plow Co.	Alton, IL	1892
Old Reliable	Sparta Plow Works	Sparta, IL	1905
Ole Olson	J. Thompson & Sons Mfg. Co.	Beloit, WI	1892
Oliver	Oliver Chilled Plow Works	South Bend, IN	1892
P & O	Parlin & Orendorff Co.	Canton, IL	1913
Pacemaker	Peru Plow & Wheel Co.	Peru, IL	1913
Peerless	Benicia Agricultural Works	Benicia, CA	1892
Pekin Combined	Pekin Plow Co.	Pekin, IL	1905
Peru City	Peru Plow & Wheel Co.	Peru, IL	1892
Phelps	Phelps Chilled Plow Works	Phelps, NY	1892
Piasa Bird	Hapgood Plow Co.	Alton, IL	1892
Pirate	Mast, Buford & Burwell Co.	St. Paul, MN	1892
Pirate	Peru Plow & Wheel Co.	Peru, IL	1913
Pirate	St. Paul Plow Works	St. Paul, MN	1892
Poleza	David Bradley Mfg. Co.	Bradley, IL	1905
Prairie King	Sparta Plow Works	Sparta, IL	1905
Queen of the Prairie	Sparta Plow Works	Sparta, IL	1905
Quincy Beauty	Collins Plow Co.	Quincy, IL	1892
Quincy Queen	Collins Plow Co.	Quincy, IL	1905
Ranger	Deere & Co.	Moline, IL	1913
Red Bird	Parlin & Orendorff Co.	Canton, IL	1905
Reliance	Janesville Machine Co.	Janesville, WI	1905
Rex	Peru Plow & Wheel Co.	Peru, IL	1905
Riggs' Improved	Thomas Peppler	Hightstown, NJ	1913
Robin Hood	J. Thompson & Sons Mfg. Co.	Beloit, WI	1913
Robinson	Robinson Chilled Plow Co.	Canandaigua, NY	1892
Rock Island	Rock Island Plow Co.	Rock Island, IL	1892
Rockford	Rockford Mfg. Co.	Rockford, IL	1905
Rough & Ready	W. Eddy Plow Co.	Greenwich, NY	1913
Royal Beauty	Henry F. Blount	Evansville, IN	1892
Royal Blue	Racine-Sattley Co.	Springfield, IL	1913
Rue's	J. Chalmers Rue	Tennent, NJ	1892

Trade Names (cont...)

Sandow	Rock Island Plow Co.	Rock Island, IL	1913
Shaw	H. C. Shaw Plow Works	Stockton, CA	1892
Solid Comfort	Economist Plow Co.	South Bend, IN	1892
Solid Comfort	Syracuse Chilled Plow Works	Syracuse, NY	1905
Spinner	J. I. Case Plow Works	Racine, WI	1913
Square Corner	David Bradley Mfg. Co.	Chicago, IL	1892
Square Deal	Norwegian Plow Co.	Dubuque, IA	1892
St. Joseph	St. Joseph Plow Co.	St. Joseph, MO	1905
Stag	Deere & Co.	Moline, IL	1905
Star	John Clayton Plow Works	Minneapolis, MN	1892
Stark	Bucher & Gibbs Plow Co.	Canton, OH	1913
Stawana	Racine-Sattley Co.	Springfield, IL	1905
Stockton	Matteson & Williamson Mfg. Co.	Los Angeles, CA	1892
Success	Parlin & Orendorff Co.	Canton, IL	1905
Syracuse	Syracuse Chilled Plow Works	Syracuse, NY	1892
Texas Casaday	South Bend Chilled Plow Co.	South Bend, IN	1905
Texas Good Enough	Moline Plow Co.	Moline, IL	1913
Texas Ranger	Eagle Mfg. Co.	Davenport, IA	1892
Texas Special	Rock Island Plow Co.	Rock Island, IL	1905
Texas T. B. X.	Rock Island Plow Co.	Rock Island, IL	1913
Thompson XX Century	J. Thompson & Sons Mfg. Co.	Beloit, WI	1905
Townsend	Charles City Mfg. Co.	Charles City, IA	1892
Tricycle	Parlin & Orendorff Co.	Canton, IL	1892
Triumph	J. I. Case Plow Works	Racine, WI	1892
Twin Brother	Morrison Mfg. Co.	Fort Madison, IA	1905
Ugota	E. Bement's Sons	Lansing, MI	1905
Victor	Pekin Plow co.	Pekin, IL	1905
Victoria	Vulcan Plow Co.	Evansville, IN	1905
Wallaby	Parlin & Orendorff Co.	Canton, IL	1905
Weir	Weir Plow Co.	Monmouth, IL	1892
Western Star	Gale Mfg. Co.	Albion, MI	1905
Westervelt	South Bend Iron Works	South Bend, IN	1892
Wiard	Wiard Plow Co.	Batavia, NY	1892
Wild Irishman	Weir Plow Co.	Monmouth, IL	1892
Wilson	J. K. Wilder & Son	Monroe, MI	1892
Wright	Wright Bros. Mfg. Co.	Monroe, MI	1892
X X Rays	David Bradley Mfg. Co.	Bradley, IL	1905
York	Flinchbaugh Mfg. Co.	York, PA	1913

Plows (tractor)

Allis-Chalmers LaCrosse	Allis-Chalmers Mfg. Co.	Milwaukee, WI	1931
Athens Fordson	Athens Plow Co.	Athens, TN	1924
Automatic Self-Lift	Hart-Parr Co.	Charles City, IA	1915
Avery	B. F. Avery & Sons	Louisville, KY	1909
Avery SelfLift	Avery Co.	Peoria, IL	1913
Benicia	Benicia Iron Works	Benicia, CA	1913
Canton	Parlin & Orendorff Co.	Canton, IL	1909
Captor	South Bend Chilled Plow Co.	South Bend, IN	1924

Trade Names (cont...)

Casaday Power Lift	South Bend Chilled Plow Co.	South Bend, IN	1924
Case (E-B)	J. I. Case Co.	Racine, WI	1931
Case (Grand Detour)	J. I. Case Co.	Racine, WI	1931
Caterpillar	Holt Mfg. Co.	Peoria, IL	1924
Chattanooga	Chattanooga Plow Co.	Chattanooga, TN	1913
Deere	Deere & Co.	Moline, IL	1913
E-B	Emerson-Brantingham Co.	Rockford, IL	1924
Eddy	Eddy Plow Works	Greenwich, NY	1931
Emerson	Emerson-Brantingham Co.	Rockford, IL	1913
Enicar	J. I. Case Plow Works	Racine, WI	1924
Ferguson (Fordson)	Sherman Bros.	Evansville, IN	1931
Flying Dutchman	Moline Plow Co.	Moline, IL	1913
Hackney	Hackney Mfg. Co.	St. Paul, MN	1913
Haines Special	Holt Mfg. Co.	Stockton, CA	1915
Haines Special	Houser & Haines Mfg. Co.	Stockton, CA	1913
Hummer	Hummer Plow Works	Springfield, IL	1931
Imperial	Bucher & Gibbs Plow Co.	Canton, OH	1931
Independent	Independent Harvester Co.	Plano, IL	1931
J. I. Case	J. I. Case Plow Works	Racine, WI	1913
Janesville	Samson Tractor Co.	Janesville, WI	1931
John Deere	Deere & Co.	Moline, IL	1913
Jumbo	B. F. Avery & Sons	Louisville, KY	1913
LaCrosse	LaCrosse Plow Co.	LaCrosse, WI	1913
Little Genius	International Harvester Co.	Chicago, IL	1924
Little Wonder	International Harvester Co.	Chicago, IL	1924
Lowell Steam Lift	Lowell Steam Plow Co.	Des Moines, IA	1909
Maroa	Maroa Mfg. Co.	Maroa, IL	1913
Massey-Harris	Massey-Harris Co.	Racine, WI	1931
Minneapolis	Minneapolis Threshing Machine Co.	Hopkins, MN	1924
Mogul	Parlin & Orendorff Co.	Canton, IL	1913
Oliver	Oliver Chilled Plow Works	South Bend, IN	1913
P. & O.	Parlin & Orendorff Co.	Canton, IL	1913
Peerless	Geiser Mfg. Co.	Waynesboro, PA	1909
Pluto	B. F. Avery & Sons	Louisville, KY	1913
Reeves	Emerson-Brantingham Co.	Rockford, IL	1913
Rimple-Morgan	John Bean Mfg. Co.	San Jose, CA	1931
Rock Island	Rock Island Plow Co.	Rock Island, IL	1924
Rumely	M. Rumely Co.	LaPorte, IN	1913
Sanders	Newell Sanders Plow Co.	Chattanooga, TN	1913
Sattley	Racine-Sattley Co.	Springfield, IL	1909
Shaw	H. C. Shaw Co.	Stockton, CA	1913
Shaw	H. C. Shaw Mfg. Co.	Stockton, CA	1931
Syracuse	Syracuse Chilled Plow Co.	Syracuse, NY	1909
Thompson-Breese	Thompson-Breese Co.	Wapakoneta, OH	1913
Vulcan	Vulcan Plow Co.	Evansville, IN	1924
Vulcan-Fordson	Farm Tools Inc., Vulcan Division	Evansville, IN	1931

Trade Names (cont...)

Wonder	Racine-Sattley Co.	Springfield, IL	1913
Wray	Farm Tools Inc.	Evansville, IN	1931
Yuba	Yuba Mfg. Co.	San Francisco, CA	1931

Potato Machinery

Specialized equipment for planting and harvesting the potato crop came onto the market in the 1860s; by 1910, there were more than 50 different companies making various kinds of potato plows or potato digging machines. Unfortunately, many of these companies advertised only to a specialty market, so illustrations of their equipment are difficult to find. Even so, this heading offers a cross-section of the equipment used to plant and harvest potatoes.

Today, vintage potato harvesting equipment is still found in use quite often; sometimes a potato planter or potato digger has been within the same family or the same locality for 60, 70 or even 80 years. Thus this equipment often has a greater utilitarian value than an antique value. Under these circumstances, the $50-$100 a vintage machinery enthusiast might pay for a planter or digger will be exceeded several times by family or friends wishing to keep one of these machines within its locality where it can continue its annual task of planting or harvesting the crop.

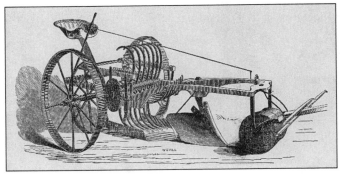

R.L. Allen & Co., New York, N.Y.
An 1869 issue of the *Boston Cultivator* illustrates the newly developed Empire Potato Harvester from R.L. Allen & Co., New York. The revolving tines separated the soil from the potatoes, leaving them on top of the row.

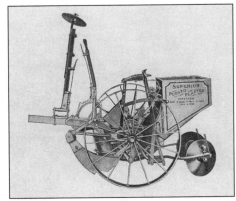

American Seeding Machine Co., Springfield, Ohio
For 1924, American offered this version of the Superior potato planter. By comparison, hand methods of planting were slow

and laborious. However, some farmers lessened the work by using a cultivator to make large furrows for planting the crop. It was then planted and covered by hand. In 1929, American merged with others to form Oliver Farm Equipment Co.; the latter then produced potato machinery for several years.

Aspinwall Manufacturing Co., Jackson, Mich.

L.A. Aspinwall began development of a potato planter in 1861. After 20 years of work, a few were sold. With this encouragement, Aspinwall opened a factory at Three Rivers, Mich., in 1884, selling 50 planters the first year. Business continued at Three Rivers until 1891 when the company moved to Jackson. Shown here is an Aspinwall model of 1889.

By the 1890s, the Aspinwall potato planter had gained a considerable reputation. This 1894 engraving illustrates the planter at work. The Aspinwall pioneered the concept of a machine that would furrow, plant and cover the seed potatoes in one operation.

By 1900, Aspinwall had the most complete line of potato machinery anywhere in the world. Other companies entered the business, but Aspinwall seemed to be the leader. The company augmented its line with other items from sprayers to barrel churns to lawn swings by 1900, but potato machinery was the specialty of the company.

In 1900, Aspinwall began marketing its potato sorter. This was intended primarily for the commercial grower who found it necessary to sort potatoes by size before marketing. The new machine also helped clean the potatoes of dirt; as they made their journey across the sorter, an attendant could spot any spoiled or inferior product.

Aspinwall introduced this engine-powered potato digging machine in 1919. It is powered by a New-Way engine. In the early 1920s, Aspinwall went out of business. For a few years after, parts were available from John A. Watson Co., Houlton, Maine. L.A. Aspinwall moved on to McKenzie Manufacturing Co., La-Crosse, Wis. In 1925, at the age of 83, Aspinwall was busy developing new potato machinery.

Associated Manufacturers, Waterloo, Iowa

For 1917, Associated offered its potato sorter, powered of course, by an Associated gasoline engine. Numerous companies built similar machines; their primary role was to sort out the small potatoes from the larger, more marketable sizes. This one was available in three different sizes, ranging in price from $98 to $150, complete with engine.

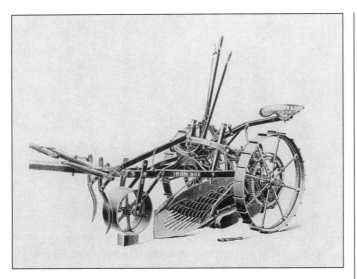

C.J. Cummings, Tully, N.Y.

An 1895 advertisement by Cummings notes that "over seventy-five different potato diggers have been built by me in the last twelve years." Little more is known of this venture; in the 1920s, the Cummings-Otsego potato diggers were being built by Babcock Manufacturing Co., Leonardsville, N.Y.

Bateman Manufacturing Co., Grenloch, N.J.

In 1906, Bateman announced its Iron Age potato diggers in two different styles. The company also built potato planters along with other farm equipment. Bateman continued in business until being bought out by A.B. Farquhar Co., York, Pa., in 1930.

Davenport & Prince, Downer's Grove, Ill.

Potato machinery development flourished in the 1890s, with Davenport's Automatic Potato Cutter and Planter appearing in 1895. This machine was designed to mark, furrow, cut, drop and cover the potatoes in one operation. Davenport planters remained on the market for some years, being offered by Davenport Planter Co., Wheaton, Ill., into the 1920s; parts for these planters were available at least into the late 1940s from this firm.

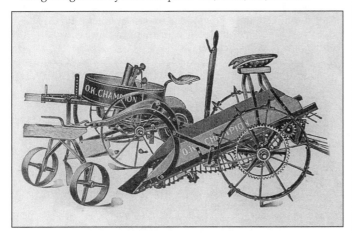

Champion Potato Machinery Co., Hammond, Ind.

For 1903, Champion offered a potato planter, as well as a two-horse digging machine. The potatoes and the soil were both carried up the open raddle chain, with the dirt falling through the chain and the potatoes landing on top of the ground to be picked up by hand. By the 1920s, Champion potato equipment was being offered from Messinger Manufacturing Co., Tatamy, Pa.

Deere & Co., Moline, Ill.

In 1896, Deere introduced the potato planter shown here, selling it through Deere & Mansur Co. Curiously, very little information can be found regarding this planter, aside from some announcements of 1896 for the new design, nor does it appear in the trade directories after 1907.

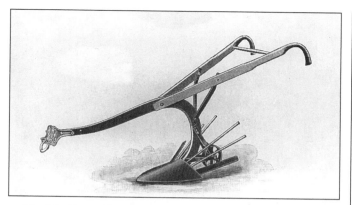

The John Deere Plow Co., catalog for 1908 illustrates the Deere potato digger. Potato plows like this one were common. These plows lifted the potatoes and, with the aid of a rake or a fork, the potatoes could be sacked for winter storage. Eventually, Deere got into the potato machinery business with its 1926 purchase of Hoover Manufacturing Co. Deere had sold the Hoover line for some years prior to the takeover.

Dowden Manufacturing Co., Prairie City, Iowa

In the 1890s, Dowden offered its potato cutter. It was designed to cut seed potatoes into a uniform size to work in any potato planter. The design of many planters was such that if the seed potatoes were too large, they lodged in the mechanism. A mechanical cutter was preferable to cutting by hand.

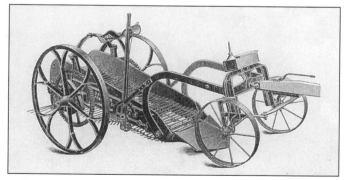

During the 1890s, Dowden began manufacturing its famous potato diggers. As shown, the machine straddled the row, actually taking dirt, potatoes and all and carrying everything over an open chain. The soil fell back through the chain, leaving the potatoes on top of the row. Dowden potato diggers remained on the market for decades; the company is listed in implement directories into the 1950s.

Emerson-Brantingham Co., Rockford, Ill.

Exactly when E-B entered the potato machinery business is unknown, but this attractive planter was available in its 1919 catalog. Among its many features, the E-B No. 1 planter also included an optional fertilizer attachment.

Emerson-Brantingham offered its E-B No. 2 potato digger in its 1919 catalog. As shown, it was furnished with the company's own Type N gas engine. The latter had been designed as a power for grain binders. Another feature was the use of steel over-tires, as portrayed in this illustration. For road transportation, the over-tires were easier to install than removing the lugs from the wheels.

A.B. Farquhar Co. Ltd., York, Pa.

Farquhar bought out the Iron Age line from Bateman Manufacturing Co., in 1930. Prior to that time, Farquhar had sold the Iron Age line for several years. Included was this No. 220 Iron

Age potato digger. Machines like this included a four-horse hitch, but engine-powered diggers required only two horses.

Hist Manufacturing Co., Barberton, Ohio

For 1907, Hist offered this potato digger, advertising it as "strictly a two-horse machine." At the time, many machines similar to the Hist required four horses for successful operation. By the 1920s, Hist potato diggers were being manufactured by Akron Cultivator & Manufacturing Co., Akron, Ohio.

Hoover Manufacturing Co., Avery, Ohio

In 1889, Hoover & Prout offered its potato sorter and sprouter. The revolving wooden reel permitted small potatoes to drop through, while the larger ones emerged from the end of the machine. In the process, any emerging sprouts were broken off so as to retard spoilage. Eventually, the company became known as Hoover Manufacturing Co.

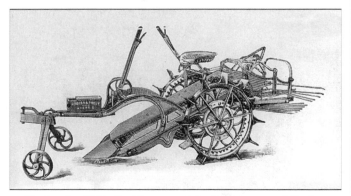

During the 1880s, the Hoover potato digger assumed the form shown here; it remained essentially in this form for many years. The Hoover became quite popular, especially because John Deere began selling the Hoover in the early 1900s. Deere bought out Hoover in 1926.

International Harvester Co., Chicago, Ill.

During the 1920s, IHC began developing various kinds of potato machinery. Included was this two-row potato digger of the 1920s. It was pulled by the company's new Farmall Row-Crop tractor, shown here in a large field with a large crop of potatoes coming off the chains.

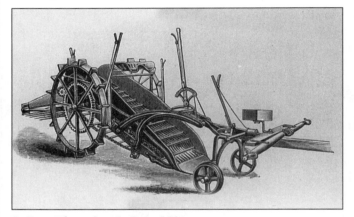

LeRoy Plow Co., LeRoy, N.Y.

Little is known of the Boss Potato Digger aside from this illustration of the early 1900s. The company was active into the late 1940s, but it appears that B.F. Avery Co. may have acquired the Boss potato digger at some point. In the late 1950s, parts for the Avery-LeRoy potato diggers were available from the Minneapolis-Moline Co.

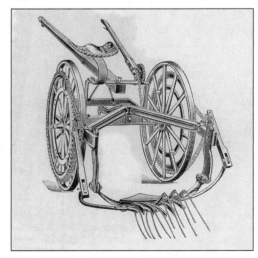

Oakfield Agricultural Works, Oakfield, N.Y.

An interesting design is shown with the Oakfield potato digger of 1895. This outfit lifted the potatoes after which they passed over a series of shaker bars to sift out the dirt, leaving the potatoes on top of the row. Aside from this illustration, no information has surfaced regarding the company.

Oliver Farm Equipment Co., Chicago, Ill.

From 1939 comes this photograph of an Oliver tractor hitched to an Oliver two-row potato digger. Not only was this a two-row machine, it was operated from the tractor PTO and rode on rubber tires. Eventually, the commercial potato harvest changed to include large self-contained units that would dig the potatoes, clean them and load them in a single operation.

S.H. Peek, East Aurora, N.Y.

For 1906, Peek offered the Reuther potato digger, a machine that became quite popular in many regions. By the 1920s, the Reuther digger was being built by U.S. Wind Engine & Pump Co., Batavia, Ill. Later, it was made by LeRoy Plow Co. noted above.

A.J. Platt, Sterling, Ill.

About 1910, the Keystone Hand-Drop Potato Planter appeared. This was a simple, but very popular design owned by many farmers for the household crop, as well as for commercial purposes. Seated above the press wheel, the farmer picked seed from the storage box, placing it in the chain slots shown beneath the hopper. The company remained active into the 1930s.

Alexander Speer & Sons, Pittsburgh, Pa.

By the 1870s, there were many plow makers offering some type of potato digger. One of these was the Speer & Sons digger exhibited at the Paris Exposition of 1878. This design typified the plow-type potato digger; thousands were built by many different companies in the following years.

Stearns Manufacturing & Foundry Co., Decatur, Ill.

In 1912, Stearns offered its Light-Draft Potato Digger. Instead of the usual open chain, this machine lifted the potatoes to the side of the row using revolving steel tines. Very little is known of this machine; the company disappears from the trade directories in the 1920s.

Trade Names

Acme	Traverse City Potato Planter Co.	Traverse City, MI	1892
American	Warner Implement Co.	Hammond, IN	1924
Ames	Ames Plow Co.	Boston, MA	1892
Ansley	A. Ansley	Geneva, NY	1892
Arnold	G. W. Arnold & Son	Ionia, MI	1892
Aspinwall	Aspinwall Mfg. Co.	Three Rivers, MI	1892
Avery	B. F. Avery & Sons	Louisville, KY	1892
Avery-LeRoy	B. F. Avery & Sons	Louisville, KY	1939
Babcock-Pugh	Babcock Mfg. Co.	Leonardsville, NY	1939
Banner	Greenville Implement Co.	Greenville, MI	1905
Bement	E. Bement & Sons	Lansing, MI	1892
Best	Wabers Mfg. Co.	Racine, WI	1924
Big Four	Pruyn Mfg. Co.	Hoosick Falls, NY	1892
Big Giant	Ohio Rake Co.	Dayton, OH	1924
Blount's	Henry F. Blount	Evansville, IN	1905
Blue Bell	Rock Island Plow Co.	Rock Island, IL	1905
Boss	LeRoy Plow Co.	LeRoy, NY	1924
Boss	Rawson & Thacher	Corning, NY	1892
Bradley	David Bradley Mfg. Co.	Bradley, IL	1905
Brown	Brown Mfg. Co.	Zanesville, OH	1913
Brown	Peter Brown & Son	Greeley, CO	1905
Canton	Parlin & Orendorff	Canton, IL	1905
Challenge	F. M. Thorn	Orchard Park, NY	1892
Champion	Messinger Mfg. Co.	Tatamy, PA	1905
Champion	Rock Island Plow Co.	Rock Island, IL	1892
Chattanooga	Chattanooga Plow Co.	Chattanooga, TN	1905
Clipper	Clipper Chilled Plow Co.	Elmira, NY	1905
Clipper	I. B. Rowell Co.	Menomonee Falls, WI	1905
Clipper	Northwestern Steel & Iron Works	Eau Claire, WI	1913
Clore's Improved	Wm. Clore's Sons	Rising Sun, IN	1892
Colgrove	Aetna Iron Works	St. Cloud, MN	1905
Colgrove	Granite City Iron Works	St. Cloud, MN	1939
Columbia	Wm. Fetzer Co.	Springfield, IL	1913
Common Sense	Star Mfg. Co.	Carpentersville, IL	1905
Daisy	Brown-Manly Plow Co.	Malta, OH	1905
David Bradley	David Bradley Mfg. Co.	Chicago, IL	1892
Davidson	Davidson-Dietrich Plow Co.	Evansville, IN	1913
Deere	Deere & Co.	Moline, IL	1892
Dorsch	John Dorsch & Sons	Milwaukee, WI	1905
Dowden	Dowden Mfg. Co.	Prairie City, IA	1905
Dunham	Dunham Co.	Berea, OH	1913
Eclipse	Deere & Co.	Moline, IL	1905
Egan	Egan Mfg. Co.	LaCrosse, WI	1913
Egan	Oliver Farm Equipment Co.	Chicago, IL	1939
Eureka	Eureka Mower Co.	Utica, NY	1905
Farquhar	A. B. Farquhar Co.	York, PA	1913
Fetzer	Wm. Fetzer Co.	Springfield, IL	1913
Giant King	Rice Mfg. Co.	Rochester, NY	1924
Gilt Edge	A. B. Farquhar Co.	York, PA	1913
Goodell	Lane Bros.	Holly, MI	1892
Gowanda	Gowanda Agricultural Works Co.	Gowanda, NY	1913
Great Northern	Eureka Mower Co.	Utica, NY	1924

Trade Names (cont...)

Greenberg	Edward Greenberg	Arlington Heights, IL	1905
H & D	Hench & Dromgold Co.	York, PA	1913
Hallock	A. B. Farquhar Co.	York, PA	1913
Hamburg	Hamburg Plow Works	Hamburg, PA	1905
Hamburg Improved	Hamburg Plow Works	Hamburg, PA	1892
Hench & Dromgold	Hench & Dromgold Co.	York, PA	1905
Hirsch	Hirsch Bros.	Milwaukee, WI	1905
Hist	Akron Cultivator Co.	Akron, OH	1913
Hitchcock's	Belcher & Taylor Agricultural Co.	Chicopee Falls, MA	1892
Hood	J. A. Hood	Philadelphia, PA	1892
Hoover	Hoover & Prout	Avery, OH	1905
Hoover	Hoover Mfg. Co.	Avery, OH	1913
Hudson	Riverhead Agricultural Works	Riverhead, NY	1892
Hustler	John Reuther	Marilla, NY	1892
Imperial	Bucher & Gibbs Plow Co.	Canton, OH	1905
Improved Boss	E. R. Allen	Corning, NY	1913
Improved Hallock	James Thornton	Philadelphia, PA	1892
Iron Age	Bateman Mfg. Co.	Grenloch, NJ	1913
John Deere-Hoover	Syracuse Chilled Plow Division	Syracuse, NY	1939
Junior	Schofield & Co.	Freeport, IL	1913
Keller	Keller Mfg. Co.	Minneapolis, MN	1924
Killarney King	Star Mfg. Co.	Carpentersville, IL	1905
King	Bernhardt Mfg. Co.	Edwardsville, IL	1913
King	Rice Mfg. Co.	Rochester, NY	1924
King of the Potato Field	H. W. Doughten	Moorestown, NJ	1905
Knocker	Moline Plow Co.	Moline, IL	1913
Knox	Gowanda Agricultural Works Co.	Gowanda, NY	1892
LaCrosse	LaCrosse Plow Co.	LaCrosse, WI	1913
Little Giant	Ohio Rake Co.	Dayton, OH	1924
Massey-Harris	Massey-Harris Co.	Racine, WI	1939
McCallum	J. McCallum Mfg. Co.	Elgin, IL	1892
McCormick-Deering	International Harvester Co.	Chicago, IL	1924
McKenzie Rotary	McKenzie Mfg. Co.	LaCrosse, WI	1924
McSherry	McSherry Mfg. Co.	Middletown, OH	1905
McSherry	Wm. Fetzer Co.	Springfield, IL	1913
Millikin	Millikin, Cisle & Co.	Peoria, IL	1892
Moline	Moline Plow Co.	Moline, IL	1892
Moore	Moore Plow & Implement Co.	Greenville, MI	1913
National	American Potato Machinery Co.	Hammond, IN	1913
National Junior	Warner Implement Co.	Hammond, IN	1924
New American	American Potato Machinery Co.	Hammond, IN	1913
New American Jr.	Warner Implement Co.	Hammond, IN	1924
New Burch	Burch Plow Works Co.	Crestline, OH	1905
New Hoover	Hoover & Prout	Avery, OH	1892
Northwestern	Northwestern Steel & Iron Works	Eau Claire, WI	1913
O. K. Champion	Champion Potato Machinery Co.	Hammond, IN	1905
Oldendorph	Oldendorph Bros.	Waterloo, IL	1892

Trade Names (cont...)

Otsego	Babcock Mfg. Co.	Leonardsville, NY	1913
Otsego-Pugh	Babcock Mfg. Co.	Leonardsville, NY	1924
P & O	Parlin & Orendorff	Canton, IL	1913
Peru	Peru Plow & Wheel Co.	Peru, IL	1905
Planet Jr.	S. L. Allen & Co.	Philadelphia, PA	1892
Pugh	B. H. Pugh Co.	Topeka, KS	1913
Rattler	Rock Island Plow Co.	Rock Island, IL	1905
Reuther	LeRoy Plow Co.	LeRoy, NY	1939
Reuther	S. H. Peek	East Aurora, NY	1905
Reuther	U. S. Wind Engine & Pump Co.	Batavia, IL	1924
Rice	Rice Mfg. Co.	Rochester, NY	1924
Rigby's Improved	Rigby & Burleigh	Houlton, ME	1892
Robbins	James Thornton	Philadelphia, PA	1892
Robinson	Robinson Chilled Plow Co.	Canandaigua, NY	1892
Root Hog or Die	Munnsville Plow Co.	Munnsville, NY	1913
Rowell	Hartford Plow Works	Hartford, WI	1905
Rue's	J. Chalmers Rue	Tennent, NJ	1892
Rustler	Racine-Sattley Co.	Springfield, IL	1913
Schofield	Schofield & Co.	Freeport, IL	1905
Shaker	B. F. Avery & Sons	Louisville, KY	1913
Shaker	Deere & Co.	Moline, IL	1905
Shangle	John R. Shangle	Hightstown, NJ	1905
Shunk	Shunk Plow Co.	Bucyrus, OH	1913
Smith	A. B. Smith	Fairfield, NE	1892
Smith	Thompson & Neill	Greeley, CO	1892
Splittsloser	Splittsloser Co.	North Branch, MN	1924
Spring	J. Spring & Son	York, PA	1892
Standard	Ohio Rake Co.	Dayton, OH	1924
Standard	Pruyn Mfg. Co.	Hoosick Falls, NY	1892
Standard	Standard Harrow Co.	Utica, NY	1905
Sterling	Sterling Mfg. Co.	Sterling, IL	1892
Stevens	Stevens Mfg. & Foundry Co.	Decatur, IL	1913
Success	A. B. Farquhar Co.	York, PA	1905
Success	D. Y. Hallock	York, PA	1892
The Best	Wabers Mfg. Co.	Racine, WI	1913
The Grange	Geo. W. Jessup	Moorestown, NJ	1913
The Wm. J. Oliver	Wm. J. Oliver Mfg. Co.	Knoxville, TN	1913
Throop & Huber	Novelty Iron Works	Priceburgh, PA	1892
Triumph	Frank M. Thorn	Orchard Park, NY	1892
True's	Belcher & Taylor Agricultural Co.	Chicopee Falls, MA	1892
U. S. Reuther	U. S. Wind Engine & Pump Co.	Batavia, IL	1924
Valley	Donaldson Bros.	Mt. Clemens, MI	1905
Vulcan	Vulcan Plow Co.	Evansville, IN	1913
Wabers	Wabers Mfg. Co.	Racine, WI	1913

Pumps

In 1924, there were more than 50 companies making wind mill pumps in more than 150 different models. In the previous 50 years, there were numerous companies that emerged and disappeared through merger or by simply going out of business. Considerable research would be required to determine even a rough estimate of the total numbers, but there is no doubt that it would be surprising. Many small firms sold their pumps locally, probably within a couple of counties in any direction. Most never made it as far as trade listings and probably had no great interest in a business which was already big enough to make a comfortable living. For this reason and due to the space constraints, the author has selected various kinds of pumps from many different manufacturers. This has been done to present a cross-section of pumps.

Today, an old pump standard will often sell from $60 to $100. Ornate or unusual designs will bring far more, but surprisingly few of the fancy and ornate pumps are seen today. After about 1900, the vast majority of pumps were rather simple in design; the extra costs involved in ornate iron castings gave way to maintaining a competitive edge in a very competitive business.

Aermotor Co., Chicago, Ill.

Aermotor Co. was the developer of the steel windmill, bringing it to the market in 1888. With it, the firm also built a variety of pump standards in various sizes and styles. A typical model is this one from the 1920s. As pictured here, it was priced at $10.

About 1909, Aermotor pioneered a small pumping engine, complete with pump jack. It was attached to the pump standard and took over when there wasn't enough wind for the windmill. Into the 1930s, Aermotor continued with various designs, including this

"Heavy Back-Geared Pumping Engine" of 1930. Equipped with a magneto, this one sold for $142.

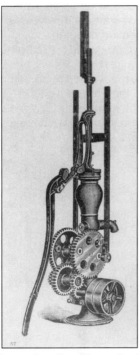

Appleton Manufacturing Co., Batavia, Ill.

Windmills were wonderful when there was a wind, but on those still summer days when not a leaf moved, the water supply disappeared. Virtually no one wanted to return to the days of pumping water by hand, so there was a great need for pump jacks to mechanize the process. They came in all sizes and styles imaginable, with this one from Appleton being pictured in its 1917 catalog. It was priced at $15.

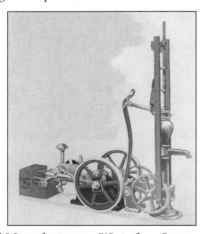

Associated Manufacturers, Waterloo, Iowa

Associated engines had become very popular by the time this 1917 combination appeared. It consisted of the company's Jack Boy engine to which was fitted its pumping attachment. The $52 list price did not include the pump standard.

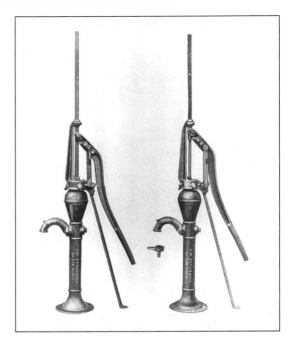

Baker Manufacturing Co., Evansville, Wisc.

Baker Manufacturing Co. began business in 1872, with windmills and pumps being the main product lines within a couple of years. By 1900, the Monitor line had grown to a huge industry, remaining so to the present time. Shown here are two examples of literally hundreds of different Monitor pump standards.

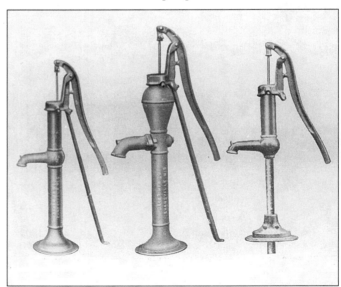

Monitor pumps were offered in almost every conceivable design to suit individual needs. Three styles of hand pumps are illustrated here; these were popular for pumping from cisterns or shallow wells.

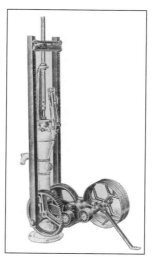

Pump jacks were another important part of the Monitor line. Over the years, the variety included this style from the 1920s. Since the pump jack clamped to the pump standard, the jack could be used on almost any windmill pump. Hand pumps were not fitted with the necessary guides for use with a pump jack.

By 1905, Baker had added gasoline engines to its thriving Monitor pump and windmill line. Eventually, the Little Monitor pumping engine appeared, becoming one of the most popular of all pumpers. Production of this style apparently ended in the 1930s.

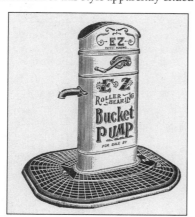

Butler Manufacturing Co., Kansas City, Kan.

A catalog of the 1920s illustrates the E-Z Roller Bearing Bucket Pump from Butler Manufacturing Co. As was sometimes the cus-

tom in those days, the pump came to the dealer with a place where the dealer's name could be stenciled on the unit for a constant reminder to anyone coming for a cool drink of water.

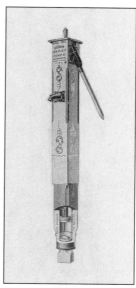

Cedar Rapids Pump Co., Cedar Rapids, Iowa

In the 1890s, this company was offering its new Cedar Rapids Pump, a wooden pump with a brass cylinder. At the time, there were many folks who preferred a wooden pump instead of cast iron, but the latter eventually won out. Cedar Rapids Pump Co. continued making these pumps into the 1940s or later.

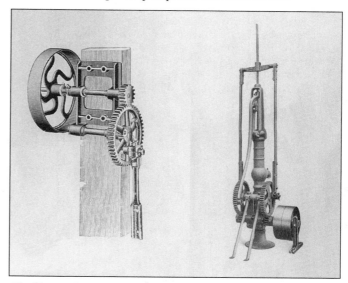

Challenge Co., Batavia, Ill.

This company went back to 1867 as Challenge Windmill & Feedmill Co. When these 1910 pump-jacks appeared, Challenge had been in business for more than 40 years. The coming of small gasoline engines by 1910 prompted the development of pump jacks so that farmers no longer had to pump water by hand when there wasn't enough wind for the windmill.

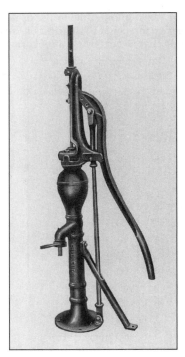

Challenge offered a variety of pump stands or pump standards, including this windmill standard of 1910. The handle was essential—when there wasn't enough wind for the windmill, the latter was disconnected and water had to be pumped by hand. This was no small task, even for a relatively shallow well.

By the 1920s, the Challenge line included this heavy-duty double-geared pump jack. Like most others, it clamped to the pump standard and was also bolted to the pump platform. By the late 1940s, the company had become U.S.-Challenge and subsequently disappears from the trade listings.

Chandler Pump Co., Cedar Rapids, Iowa

By the 1890s, Chandler was offering this wooden pump as part of its already extensive line. The company specialized in pumps for many years, broadening its product line to include various plumbing specialties. Production of wooden pumps slowed considerably after 1900, although this Chandler model was available at least into the 1920s.

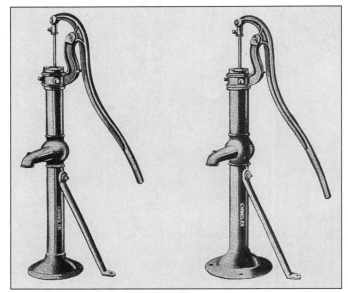

Typical of the time, these Chandler hand pumps were designed for shallow wells or cisterns. In many regions, a driven well was used; it consisted of a sand-point driven down to water. Sometimes, this was 10 feet or less.

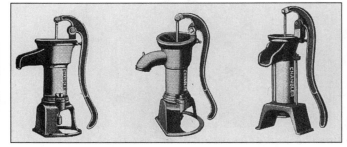

Pitcher pumps were an entirely separate category from the ordinary pump standard. These small pumps were used mainly for drawing water from cisterns or other applications with a small lift and were commonly seen at the kitchen sink or a laundry sink. Some were quite ornate.

About 1910, many farms were enjoying the benefits of running water piped to various places on the farm. Within the farm home, a pressurized water system was now a possibility. Chandler, among others, offered a geared pump, ostensibly powered by a gasoline engine through a small line-shaft hung on the basement ceiling. Thousands of these pumps were placed into service, many of them operating for 30 or 40 years with little attention.

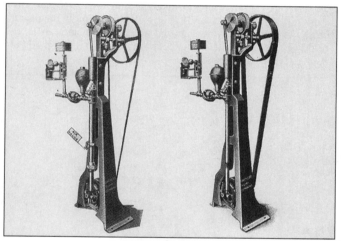

By the 1920s, electricity was available to many city dwellers and most farms could now have their own electric plant. One of the first electrified home water systems was the Hawkeye motor pump from Chandler Pump Co. First offered in the 1920s, these small pumps were installed by the thousands; some of them were in operation for 20 or 30 years before succumbing to newer designs.

Chase Pump Co., Canton, Ohio

Especially during the 1880s and 1890s, pump standards were often a very ornate affair. One of these was the Chase Pneumatic

Double-Acting Anti-Freezing Force Pump shown here. An important part of pump design was to prevent it from freezing in winter; this was usually accomplished by a device that permitted the stand-pipe to drain back to the well when the pump was not in use.

Cincinnati Pump Co., Cincinnati, Ohio

While the bucket pump or water elevator goes back to antiquity, it gained new status during the 1880s with numerous ornate designs coming to the market. For dug wells, this device was especially popular. The principles of operation are evident from the engravings.

Deming Co., Salem, Ohio

Deming became a well-known pump manufacturer by the early 1900s, with a unique product being its hydraulic ram pictured here. This simple device used low water pressure to force a smaller quantity of water to a greater height. While this device wasted water, it required no other form of energy, except for the head pressure of the supply. Hydraulic rams were very popular in some areas; many of them were also used in foreign countries.

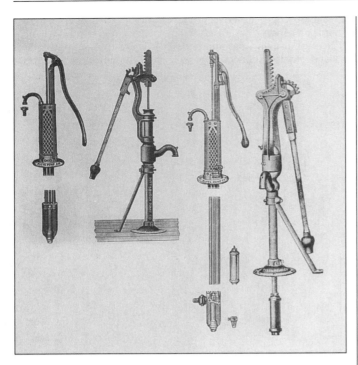

Duplex Manufacturing Co., Superior, Wisc.

Another of the well-known pump manufacturers was Duplex with its Superior hand and windmill pumps. A 1904 catalog lists dozens of different styles, with the four models shown here being especially interesting. Duplex remained active until the 1950s, but then the firm disappears from the trade directories.

Elgin Windmill Co., Elgin, Ill.

Elgin remained active until the 1940s; but, as with many of the firms in this book, its precise history is unknown. In 1930, the company offered this interesting motor-powered pump jack, reflecting the coming of electrical power to the farm. This eliminated the gas engine. Farm electrification spelled the end of the small gasoline engines for farm power purposes.

Fairbanks, Morse & Co., Chicago, Ill.

One of the earliest windmill manufacturers was Fairbanks-Morse. Its efforts were confined primarily to building windmills and pump jacks; well equipment and well pumps were not a major enterprise, at least for farm use. During the 1920s, the company offered its No. 3 Handy Pump Jack as a simple means of pumping water; this one clamped to the pump standard and could be operated with a small gasoline engine. It weighed 90 pounds and retailed at $6.20.

Goulds Manufacturing Co., Seneca Falls, N.Y.

This company was established in 1848. Its 1875 catalog illustrates this chain pump made of cast iron. Chain pumps or bucket pumps were a popular method of raising water from a dug well at the time and remained fairly popular into the 1920s. This one had an 1875 price of $9.

The 1875 Goulds pump line included a variety of pumps, including this small cistern pump. By the 1870s, the idea of building a cistern for storage of rain water was becoming quite popular. Underground cisterns and overhead water tanks were commonplace until the widespread use of pressurized water systems came along in the 1950s.

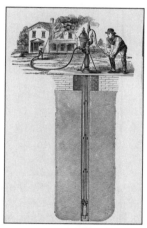

Drilled wells were becoming a reality by the 1870s. The 1875 Goulds catalog illustrates one in use as it attempts to save the house from fire. Graphic portrayals like this one were often used to make a point—in a time when fire protection was virtually non-existent, this represented

Hydraulic rams had come into use by the 1870s, with this 1875 engraving illustrating how the ram was set up and used. Usually the ram was set at least 25 to 50 feet from the water supply, giving

sufficient "drive pipe" for successful operation. A fall of 10 feet from the brook or spring was sufficient to raise water to a considerable height. To demonstrate the power of the ram, with a 10-foot fall, one gallon of every 14 could be raised to a height of 100 feet. These unique devices have become prized collector's items.

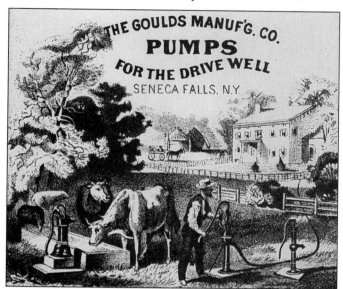

Driven wells were a reality by the 1870s and this engraving illustrates how they worked. The "point" seen at the bottom of the pipe was threaded to the pipe, a suitable cap was placed on top and the pipe was driven into the ground. Once it hit water, there was nothing left except to install the pump and secure water for the house and for the livestock.

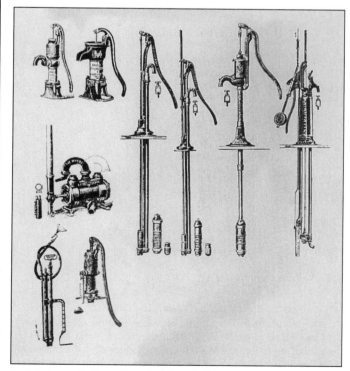

F.E. Myers & Bro. Co., Ashland, Ohio

Frank E. Myers began manufacturing pumps in 1875, along with his brother, Philip A. Myers. The latter was largely responsible for the design of the pumps, while F.E. Myers was a director of the Bucher & Gibbs Plow Co. at Canton, Ohio. Shown here is a sampling of the Myers pump line for 1903. Included are various pitcher pumps, hand pumps and well pumps. To the left of this illustration is a Myers thresher tank pump and at the bottom are two examples of Myers spray pumps.

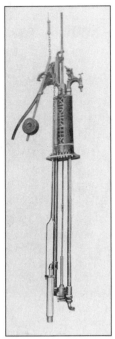

A 1910 style was the Myers Regulating Pump shown here. This pump used an ornate standard, along with a cog-tooth lifting device for the handle. Today, ornate pump standards are hard to find and command an excellent price as a collector's item.

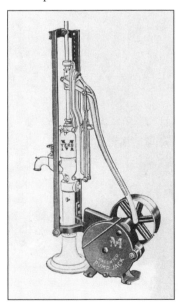

Along with its extensive line of pumps, Myers offered many styles of pump jacks, with this 1924 model being somewhat ahead of many competitors. This model operated in a completely enclosed gear case to keep out dust and moisture, all the while bathing the gears in oil. Also illustrated is a Myers windmill standard of the period.

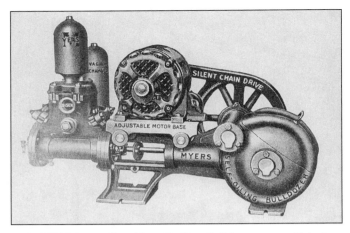

In 1927, Myers offered its self-oiling Bulldozer pump. This design could be furnished with an electric motor as shown and the latter could be controlled with a pressure switch for fully automatic operation. The company also made an early reputation for its haying equipment.

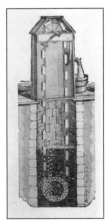

N.O. Nelson Manufacturing Co., St. Louis, Mo.

This illustration from 1884 demonstrates the operation of the bucket pump. One of the advantages claimed for these pumps was the constant aeration of the water. This was achieved by the entrapped air from each bucket as it descended into the well. These wells were dug out by hand, sometimes going down 20 feet or more.

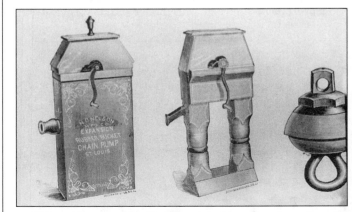

Nelson Manufacturing Co. offered a wide range of pumps and well supplies by 1884, with two of its pumps shown here. To the left is a bucket pump using small buckets to carry water to the spout. On the right is a curb pump or chain pump of wooden design. A lifting link of the chain pump is partially shown at the right.

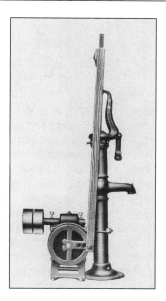

Stover Manufacturing & Engine Co., Freeport, Ill.

D.C. Stover was an early windmill designer; the Stover Ideal windmills were built until the company closed its doors in 1942. By the 1920s, Stover had developed a number of pump jacks, with the No. 18 and the No. 18-1/2 shown here. The No. 18 was for use with a gasoline engine, while the No. 18-1/2 was for use with an electric motor.

Red Jacket Manufacturing Co., Davenport, Iowa

Red Jacket emerged as a major pump manufacturer in the early 1900s. Shown above in this illustration is its hand-powered pump. This design was intended to pressurize a large tank, giving sufficient pressure for the house for a day or two. Then it was time to work the pump for 20 or 30 minutes again. Below is a Red Jacket pump jack designed for use with a gasoline engine. Thousands of these pumps were installed in farm basements and a surprising number still survive.

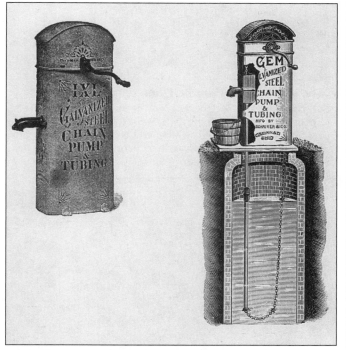

O.P. Schriver & Co., Cincinnati, Ohio

For decades, the IXL and GEM steel curb chain pumps were available from Schriver and later from Butler Manufacturing Co., Kansas City. While the bucket pump has been illustrated elsewhere in this section, the chain pump is shown with its rubber cups descending into the water, trapping it within the vertical tube and discharging it from the spout.

R

Reapers

The author's book *150 Years of International Harvester* (Crestline/Motorbooks: 1981) details much of the activity from 1830 onward, relative to the reaper. Briefly, Cyrus Hall McCormick invented his reaper in 1831, but delayed in getting a patent until 1834. Meanwhile, Obed Hussey in Baltimore patented his design. Therein came a battle that ran on for years, in the press and in the courts. The battle continued to rage into the 1890s. After McCormick's death, it was proposed that his portrait appear on a new banknote. An anonymous protest letter to the U.S. Treasury Department fueled the battle one again; this resulted in a small privately published book entitled *Who Invented the Reaper?* by Rodney B. Swift, privately published at Chicago in 1897. Various other titles appeared, some being favorable to McCormick's position, with others being quite antagonistic. Subsequent to 1845, many companies began building reapers with many of them being blatant copies of either the McCormick or the Hussey patents; the result being that the two inventors spent much of their time filing patent infringement suits.

Within this section are many reaper designs from various companies. Aside from the interesting reading provided by the untoward behavior of the parties involved, the fact is that the reaper made it possible to "mass-produce" wheat and small grains. John F. Steward's title, *The Reaper*, published in 1930, carried with it the subtitle: *A History of the Efforts of Those Who Justly May Be Said to Have Made Bread Cheap.* This was the bottom line: The reaper revolutionized the harvest, just as its descendant—the grain binder—would do once again in the 1870s. In another 50 years the combine would once again reshape the harvesting of grain. The reaper of the 1830s revolutionized the harvest, bringing to an end the methods going back for centuries. Yet, in less than 100 years, the reaper and the grain binder both came to an end; today, the harvest has been completely mechanized with the combine. Some of the early reapers were combination mowers and reapers, with references also occurring in the Mowers section of this book.

Old reapers are now quite a scarce item. Those in reasonably good condition usually sell for $300 and up. As with all vintage machinery, condition is the keyword and machines that are badly deteriorated often require more expense in their restoration than could ever be recouped when sold. Often, however, these old machines will be completely rebuilt as a labor of love.

Did You Know?

Today, old washing machines are often a valued collectors item. Popular ones—such as the early Maytag—often are valued at $300 or more.

Aetna Manufacturing Co., Salem, Ohio

Aetna was building this combination mower and reaper in the 1860s. Actually, this machine is a dropper. Cut grain accumulated on the wooden fingers behind the mower bar. At the appropriate time, a hand lever dropped the fingers, releasing a gavel of grain. However, this machine required a number of binders so that the cut grain was cleared before the dropper returned on the next round.

C. Aultman & Co., Canton, Ohio

During the 1860s, the Buckeye Mower and Dropper appeared, with this engraving showing the dropper folded away in its road position. A dropper could be adapted to either its Junior or the Senior mowers. Thus equipped, this Junior mower and dropper sold for $165, a substantial price for 1869.

Shown here from its 1869 catalog, the Buckeye dropper is at work. To the rear is seen a gavel of grain; in the distance are the binders, using wisps of straw to make the band for the sheave. By today's standards, this was very labor-intensive work. To the farmer of the 1860s, the dropper came as a godsend.

C. Aultman & Co., also produced a self-rake attachment for its Senior mowers during the 1860s, deeming the Junior mower too light and too small for this attachment. The self-raker had the advantage of sweeping the gavels of grain to the side, directly behind the machine. This permitted the farmer to continue cutting grain, even though the field workers had not caught up. For 1869, this outfit, complete with mower, sold for $200.

Cayuga Chief Manufacturing Co., Auburn, N.Y.

For the 1869 harvest, Cayuga Chief presented its No. 2 Combined Self-Raking Reaper & Mower, as shown here. However, the Cayuga Chief wasn't to remain on the market for very long; it was bought out by D.M. Osborne & Co., also of Auburn, in 1874.

Aultman, Miller & Co., Akron, Ohio

By the 1870s, Aultman, Miller & Co., was offering this style of the Buckeye Self-Rake Reaper. The revolving rakes swept grain from the table, then retreated quickly to a vertical position alongside the man at the helm. This was an ingenious device, quickly adopted in various forms by many different manufacturers.

Deering Harvester Co., Chicago, Ill.

By 1885, the Deering Ideal Reaper made its appearance. This machine was well proportioned and designed; after the 1902 IHC merger, the Deering reaper remained in the product line for decades. Despite the coming of the grain binder and even the combine, the reaper was still used in some areas of the United States, as well as in various parts of the world.

For 1901, the Buckeye self-rake reaper had assumed a much different form, with the farmer sitting well ahead of the rakes. An improved drive system was used, along with other features. This was purely a reaper; the days of the combination mower and reaper were gone. Aultman, Miller & Co. merged into International Harvester Co. in 1903.

Frost & Wood Manufacturing Co., Ltd., Smiths Falls, Ontario

For 1910, Frost & Wood continued to offer its Simplex reaper; it was built in two sizes; either a 4-foot cut or a 5-foot machine. The smaller one could be furnished as a one-horse reaper.

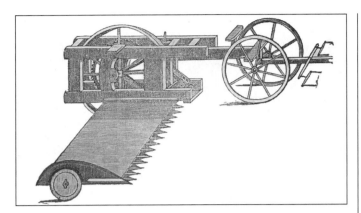

Obed Hussey, Wilmington, Del.

While it appears that Hussey began operations at Baltimore, this 1848 illustration from the pages of the *Boston Cultivator* show him at Wilmington, Del. This 1848 engraving is virtually the same machine illustrated elsewhere as the 1837 pattern.

Hussey's attempts to capture a portion of the reaper market met with disaster. The competing McCormick machine seemed to capture the market. By the 1850s, Hussey's machine took the form shown here. At this point, a seat was developed for the raker, besides having enough room for the driver.

International Harvester Co., Chicago, Ill.

A 1905 catalog illustrates the Champion reaper from International Harvester. It was essentially the same reaper as had been built at Springfield, Ohio, by Warder, Bushnell & Glessner Co. The Champion reapers remained in the IHC line for a number of years following the merger.

McCormick Daisy reapers came onto the market in the 1890s and remained in the IHC product line until 1934. Likewise, the Deering reaper of similar design was also carried by IHC into the 1930s. By this time, the company was well into the combine business, with the reaper remaining as a reminder of the past.

Johnston Harvester Co., Batavia, N.Y.

Johnston had its beginnings in the 1840s. Within 20 years, the company grew into a major manufacturer of mowers and reapers. Shown in this engraving is its 1878 version of the Johnston single-wheel sweep-rake reaper. It was a continuation of previous designs; the company went on to improved styles in later years. In 1910, the company came under stock control of Massey-Harris, with the latter buying out Johnston in 1917.

Long, Black & Alstatter Co., Hamilton, Ohio

Although the firm of Long & Alstatter survived in the cultivator business into the 1920s, very little information has surfaced regarding its activities. In the 1870s, the company was offering its Iron Harvester. It differed greatly from its contemporaries in its design and appearance, but aside from this engraving, no further information has emerged.

McCormick Harvesting Machine Co., Chicago, Ill.

McCormick's reaping machine of 1834 was crude, but it was the first reaper to employ all the necessities of design for a successful machine. This early design required a man to walk alongside the reaper with a special rake to pull the grain to the side as the reaper moved forward.

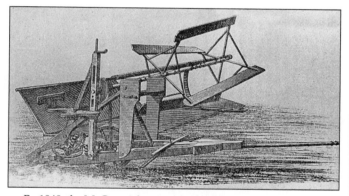

By 1848, the McCormick reaper had been improved with a raker's seat to ease the job of the person assigned to pull the grain from the table. With this design the McCormick reaper gained its first real commercial success; from 1855-59 the company sold some 15,000 machines.

Originally patented in 1858, the first McCormick self-rake design was sold in two main designs, the Advance and the Reliable. The Advance retailed for about $200 and the company sold thousands of these prior to 1875. Shown here is the 1871 version of the Advance Self-Rake Reaper.

In 1890, McCormick introduced its Folding Daisy reaper. Rather than being a combination mower and reaper, this dedicated design was strictly a reaper, leaving the mowing to machines designed specifically for the purpose. The Folding Daisy remained in production until about 1900.

About 1899, McCormick introduced a new model of its Folding Daisy reaper. This design remained in production while McCormick merged with others to form International Harvester Co. in 1902. Production of the Folding Daisy continued until 1934.

Miller & Moore, Louisville, Kty.

Little is known of the Kentucky Harvester, except that it was built under patents secured in 1856, 1857, and 1859. This was a combination machine, shown as a reaper and also as a mower. The company previously operated under the title of Miller, Wingate & Co.

Milwaukee Harvester Co., Milwaukee, Wisc.

Milwaukee Harvester had its beginnings in the 1850s with its production of the Fountain Harvester by Israel S. Love. After numerous changes, Milwaukee Harvester Co. was organized in 1884, becoming a part of International Harvester Co. in 1902. Shown here is a 1902 example of the Milwaukee Five-Rake Reaper.

D.M. Osborne & Co., Auburn, N.Y.

By 1866, Osborne was building Kirby's American Harvester, a hand-raker of substantial design. Osborne secured many sales points, including North River Agricultural Works in New York. This engraving is from its 1866 catalog.

By the 1870s, Osborne was building its No. 6 Combination Mower & Reaper, shown here as a reaping machine. It was a side-raker, meaning that the automatic sweep arms carried the gavels of grain to the side of the cut, leaving the stubble clear when the machine made its next pass along the grain.

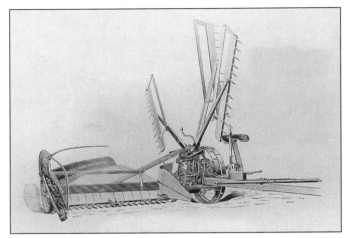

A 1900 catalog from Osborne displays its Osborne Columbia reaper, developed during the 1890s. This modernized version had a five-foot cut and was still part of the Osborne line when the latter was taken over by International Harvester Co. in 1905.

Plano Manufacturing Co., Plano, Ill.

The Plano line emerged subsequent to the formation of the company in 1881. By 1900, the firm had developed its Light Running Jones Reaper as shown here. This firm was part of the merger forming International Harvester Co. in 1902.

Seymour & Morgan, Brockport, N.Y.

This old firm had built some of McCormick's reapers at its factory in 1845, since McCormick had not yet removed to Chicago.

Subsequently, the company built other reapers, including the Improved Williams pictured here. This design was patented in 1851 by Aaron Palmer and S.G. Williams; it represented an important step in the development of the self-raker reapers.

Into the 1860s, Seymour & Morgan built the New Yorker reaper, a very popular design, particularly in the Eastern states. Eventually, the company withered into obscurity.

Thompson & Co., Rockford, Ill.

For 1862, this firm was offering John P. Manny's Combined Harvester & Mower; it is shown here as a reaper. John P. Manny was a significant figure in the development of mowers and reapers. After his death, in 1856, the partners of the company continued; eventually, the firm of Emerson-Brantingham emerged; the latter was acquired by J.I. Case Co. in 1928.

Warder, Bushnell & Glessner Co., Springfield, Ohio

In 1867, Warder, Mitchell & Co., began building the Marsh harvesters under license from the patentees. The company had also developed its Champion line of mowers and reapers; this illus-

tration of the 1860s shows the Champion No. 2 Mower with a hand-raking attachment. The raker stood against a substantial "leaning post" as he pulled the gavels of grain from the table.

An 1878 engraving shows Whiteley's Champion sweep-rake single-wheel reaper in the field. Much of the design for these machines came from William N. Whiteley. Eventually, the company took the title of Warder, Bushnell & Glessner Co., finally becoming a part of the International Harvester Co. merger of 1902.

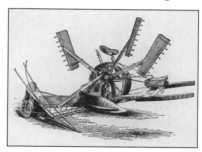

Walter A. Wood Mowing & Reaping Machine Co., Hoosick Falls, N.Y.

This company had its beginnings in the 1850s, with Walter A. Wood being its moving force. His inventive abilities added greatly to the design of mowers and reapers, with its 1878 design taking the form shown here.

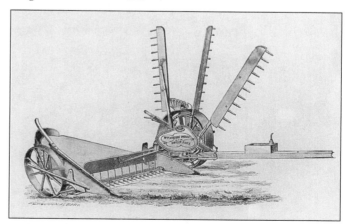

A significant improvement came with Wood's Chain-Rake Reaper, shown here from an 1887 catalog engraving. This design carried the cut grain to the side of the reaper by means of a chain-rake, eliminating the need for the sweep-rakes commonly used.

Wm. Anson Wood, Albany, N.Y.

Whether a connection existed between this firm and that of Walter A. Wood noted above, has not been determined. However, Wm. Anson Wood was offering this sweep-rake design in the 1880s.

Trade Names

Adriance	Adriance, Platt & Co.	Poughkeepsie, NY	1892
Aetna	Aetna Mfg. Co.	Salem, OH	1860
Bradley	Bradley & Co.	Syracuse, NY	1892
Buckeye	Aultman, Miller & Co.	Akron, OH	1870
Buckeye	C. Aultman & Co.	Canton, OH	1869
Cayuga Chief	Cayuga Chief Mfg. Co.	Auburn, NY	1869
Champion	B.F. Avery & Sons	Louisville, KY	1924
Champion	International Harvester Co.	Chicago, IL	1905
Champion	Warder, Bushnell & Glessner Co.	Soringfield, OH	1892
Continental	Johnston Harvester Co.	Batavia, NY	1892
Curtis	Curtis Mfg. Co.	Albion, NY	1892
Daisy	International Harvester Co.	Chicago, IL	1913
Deering	International Harvester Co.	Chicago, IL	1905
Deering	William Deering & Co.	Chicago, IL	1892
E-B	Emerson-Brantingham Co.	Rockford, IL	1924
Empire	J.F. Seiberling & Co.	Akron, OH	1892
Frost & Wood	Frost & Wood Mfg. Co. Ltd.	Smiths Falls, ON	1910
Gregg	Gregg & Co.	Trumansburgh, NY	1892
Hodges	Acme Harvester Co.	Peoria, IL	1905
Long & Alstatter	Long, Black & Alstatter	Hamilton, OH	1870
Manny's Combined	Thompson & Co.	Rockford, IL	1862
Massey-Harris	Massey-Harris Harvester Co.	Batavia, NY	1924
McCormick	International Harvester Co.	Chicago, IL	1905
McCormick	McCormick Harvesting Machine Co.	Chicago, IL	1892
Miller & Moore	Miller & Moore	Louisville, KY	1859
Milwaukee	International Harvester Co.	Chicago, IL	1905
Milwaukee	Milwaukee Harvester Co.	Milwaukee, WI	1860
Moline	Moline Plow Co.	Moline, IL	1924

Trade Names (cont...)

New Ideal	International Harvester Co.	Chicago, IL	1913
Osborne	D.M. Osborne & Co.	Auburn, NY	1892
Perry	Wyckoff & Co.	Perry, NY	1892
Plano	International Harvester Co.	Chicago, IL	1905
Royce	Geo. Sweet & Co.	Dansville, NY	1905
Royer Improved	Geo. Sweet & Co.	Dansville, NY	1892
Seymour & Morgan	Seymour & Morgan	Brockport, NY	1860
Standard	Emerson, Talcott & Co.	Rockford, IL	1892
Sweepstakes	Johnston Harvester Co.	Batavia, NY	1892
Triumph	D.S. Morgan & Co.	Brockport, NY	1892
Walter A. Wood	Walter A. Wood Mowing & Reaping Machine Co.	Hoosick Falls, NY	1892
Wood's	Wm. Anson Wood	Albany, NY	1880

Miscellany

Over the years the author has collected many different illustrations of reapers and, for a few of them, none of our research has attached company names to some rather interesting designs. Hopefully, some of our knowledgeable readers will be able to supply further information for subsequent editions of this book. If you have any information, contact the author in care of Krause Publications.

Dodge Self-Raker, a design of about 1870 from Dodge & Stevenson Co., but there is no address for this firm.

Excelsior Medium Reaper of about 1870; it is shown in its traveling position.

Improved Quaker Reaper at work.

A.R. Reese's Patent Self-Rake Reaper—this design is likely from the 1870s.

Another elusive firm is the builder of the Valley Chief Self-Rake Reaper from an engraving of the 1870s.

S

Sawmills

By the 1880s, the small sawmill had become a reality. Large sawmills were in place before this time, but most of them were commercial operations. With the coming of the steam-traction engine and even the large horse powers, a power source was finally available to those who didn't have water power.

During the 1880s, many companies appeared and their numbers swelled into the 1890s. Numerous engine and thresher manufacturers added sawmills to their line and, for years to come, sawmill companies flourished. Many sawmill advertisements encouraged threshermen to also become lumbermen, using their traction engine for more of the year than just the annual threshing run. By the early 1900s, many communities had at least one small sawmill in the neighborhood. Sometimes the mills were owned by a group of farmers so they could convert logs on their farm into lumber for farm buildings, fences or general repair work.

The mills illustrated in this section are a sidebar to the overall research for this book—in 1989, the author published a title, *The Circular Sawmill*, published at Lancaster, Pa., by Stemgas Publishing Co. This book details much of the development of the circular sawmill and it seemed redundant to reproduce all of that material here. Thus interested readers are invited to peruse the above title for additional information on circular sawmills.

While some items associated with sawmills have acquired collectible status, sawmills are so big and cumbersome that the average machinery collector shies away, leaving sawmills to those interested in same. However, an old mill can often bring several hundred dollars if in good condition. On the other hand, a mill with the wood all rotted away will seldom bring much more than scrap value.

Alexander, Bradley & Dunning, Syracuse, N.Y.

Aside from an 1889 advertisement, nothing is known of the Carley Saw Mill offered by this firm. This one is of the conventional circular sawmill design, but the husk, or frame, of the mill is of cast iron. By comparison, the majority of sawmill frames were of heavy wood construction, tied together with long threaded rods.

Did You Know?

Page & Clary's Patent Seed Drill was priced at $60 in 1869.

Aultman & Taylor Machinery Co., Mansfield, Ohio

In an 1890 catalog, Aultman Taylor remarked of its long experience in manufacturing and selling sawmills, noting that a good mill was a most profitable investment, but a poor mill was most vexatious. With plenty of lumber to cut, a new mill was capable of earning its purchase price within a couple of months. The Aultman Taylor Pony Mill, shown here, could cut lumber up to 34 feet in length.

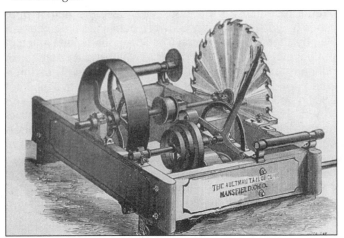

A 1915 catalog illustration shows the Aultman Taylor Standard Double Mill. This large mill carried a top blade to assist in making the cut through large logs. Over the years Aultman Taylor sold a great many mills, but this ended when the company was bought out in 1924 by Advance-Rumely Thresher Co., La Porte, Ind.

Crabb Gas Engine Co., Independence, Iowa

Organized at West Union, Iowa, about 1910, Isaiah Crabb began building gasoline engines and sawmills. In 1918, the company

moved to Independence to build sawmills exclusively, with this Crabb Model C Mill being of 1937 vintage. The company remained active into the 1950s when it removed to Vinton, Iowa, under the title of Schnoor Saw Co.

Curtis & Co. Manufacturing Co., St. Louis, Mo.

Curtis had plants in St. Louis and Chicago. By 1894, it was offering the design shown here, claiming its Dixie Mill to be the best mill for the price on the market. The feed system was always a point of interest—this one uses a single-lever belt feed.

DeLoach Mill Manufacturing Co., Atlanta, Ga.

In 1890, DeLoach advertised this mill, pointing to its "wonderful record" among sawyers. The DeLoach featured a friction-feed system that was infinitely variable. These popular mills were marketed for many years.

DeLoach advertised its mills in many farm magazines for years, with a special appeal to farmers. Advertising of 1910 noted that the company had more than 15,000 mills in use. By this time, the company had relocated to Bridgeport, Ala.

A.B. Farquhar Co., Ltd., York, Pa.

From the 1920s comes this illustration of the Farquhar No. 7 Tractor Sawmill. By the 1920s, the small farm tractor had come to stay and many sawmill manufacturers built small mills for light power. The truth was that even a small mill required considerable power, usually more than was available for fast sawing. It worked with a small tractor, but worked better with a big one. Farquhar continued building sawmills until selling out to Oliver in 1952.

Frick Co., Waynesboro, Pa.

By the early 1900s, Frick had become an established sawmill manufacturer, in addition to its thriving business in steam-traction engines and threshing machines. Shown here is its No. 0 or Pony Sawmill of 1920. By the late 1920s, Frick was opting out of the farm equipment business in favor of its thriving trade in building refrigerating machinery.

Hench & Dromgold, York, Pa.

Among its many products for 1902, Hench & Dromgold offered its sawmills. The mill shown here used a friction-feed system. While this advertisement also refers to engines, it is presently unknown if the company built its own engines or functioned as an agent for another manufacturer. This same advertisement appeared in farm magazines for many years.

Moses P. Johnson, St. Louis, Mo.

An 1890 illustration shows the Peerless No. 3 mill from Johnson. This big mill included a top saw attachment to handle large logs. Without it, sawyers were forced to "cut-and-turn" to reduce the log to lumber. Sometimes, a very large log could not be cut into lumber if it was too big for the local mills.

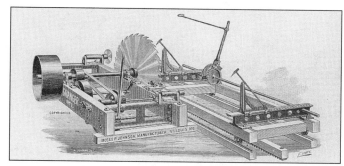

By 1894, Johnson was offering the Granger No. 1 mill, a small design with a belt-feed system. This mill was priced at $200, plus the cost of the blade. Also of note are the hammer dogs of this mill. They are shown on the headblocks and were set with a hammer each time the log was turned.

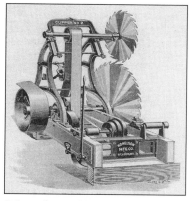

N.O. Nelson Manufacturing Co., St. Louis, Mo.

Already, in 1887, Nelson was offering this substantial sawmill that included a top-saw attachment. The belt-feed system for the carriage is obvious. The vast majority of the farm mills of this period were powered by a steam-traction engine. It took a bit of skill to fire the engine using green slabs from the mill.

Rockwood, Newcomb & Co., Indianapolis, Ind.

From 1887 comes this engraving of the Single "E" Mill from Rockwood, Newcomb & Co. The company does not appear in any other farm equipment category of the present research; presumably, the company was engaged solely in building sawmills.

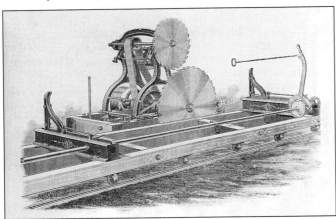

Rockwood, Newcomb & Co., appears in machinery listings until the 1890s, after which it either went onto other interests or sold out to another sawmill maker. This 1894 engraving shows its new Double E Mill, a large design with a top-saw rig. At the time, most farm mills had only two head blocks, as shown here. In later years, many mills were equipped with three headblocks to ease the job of setting the log.

L.M. Rumsey Manufacturing Co., St. Louis, Mo.

By the 1890s, Rumsey had become a prominent manufacturer and distributor of almost everything needed for the farm and factory. Its huge catalog included literally thousands of items.

From 1894 comes its Double Mill No. 1, a large and heavy design that included a top saw. Small sawmills converted thousands of trees into useable lumber on the farm.

Russell & Co., Massillon, Ohio

Of the steam engine and thresher manufacturers, Russell rose to prominence with its sawmills. A catalog of about 1900 illustrates its Massillon Medium Mill. This one was complete with a top rig. Successful sawmill operation required considerable experience, especially when problems arose.

Trade Names			
Advance	Advance Thresher Co.	Battle Creek, MI	1905
American	American Sawmill Machinery Co.	Hacketstown, NJ	1924
Aultman & Taylor	Aultman & Taylor Machinery Co.	Mansfield, OH	1890
Best	John Best Estate	Lancaster, PA	1905
Birdsall	Birdsall Co.	Auburn, NY	1892
Blandy	Blandy Machine Co.	Zanesville, OH	1892
Boss	Russell & Co.	Massillon, OH	1892
Cady	Geo. S. Cady & Co.	Moravia, NY	1905
Carley	A.C. Powell & Son	Syracuse, NY	1892
Carley	Alexander, Bradley & Dunning	Syracuse, NY	1889
Case	J.I. Case Threshing Machine Co.	Racine, WI	1892
Cole	R.D. Cole Mfg. Co.	Newnan, GA	1892
Comstock	Geo. S. Comstock	Mechanicsburg, PA	1892
Continental	Ritchie & Dyer Co.	Hamilton, OH	1892
Cooper	C. & G. Cooper Co.	Mt. Vernon, OH	1939
Crabb	Crabb Gas Engine Co.	Independence, IA	1935
Crowell	Crowell Mfg. Co.	Greencastle, PA	1892
Curtis	Curtis & Co.	St. Louis, MO	1895
DeLoach	DeLoach Mill Mfg. Co.	Atlanta, GA	1920
Eagle	Eagle Machine Works	Indianapolis, IN	1892
Eclipse	Fairbanks, Mporse & Co.	Chicago, IL	1913
Eclipse	Frick Co.	Waynesboro, PA	1892
Empire	Hagerstown Steam Engine & Mach.	Hagerstown, MD	1892
Farquhar	A.B. Farquhar Co.	York, PA	1920
Fay & Egan	J.A. Fay & Egan Co.	Cincinnati, OH	1905
Frick	Frick Co.	Waynesboro, PA	1920
Gaar-Scott	Gaar, Scott & Co.	Richmond, IN	1892
Gold Medal	Meadows Mill Co.	North Wilkesboro, NC	1939
Grier	Geo. S. Grier & Son	Milford, DE	1892
Griffith & Wedge	Griffith & Wedge Co.	Zanesville, OH	1892
Hamacek	A. Hamacek & Co.	Ahnapee, WI	1892
Hamburg	Hamburg Plow Works	Hamburg, PA	1892
Hege's Improved	Salem Iron Works	Salem, NC	1892

Trade Names (cont...)

Heilman	Heilman Machine Works	Evansville, IN	1892
Hench & Dromgold	Hench & Dromgold Co.	York, PA	1900
Hill-Curtis	Hill-Curtis Co.	Kalamazoo, MI	1924
Howell	R.R. Howell & Co.	Minneapolis, MN	1905
Industrial	Industrial Iron Works Co.	Clinton, MO	1913
Ireland	Bennett-Ireland Co.	Norwich, NY	1945
Ireland	Ireland Machine & Foundry Co.	Norwich, NY	1939
Johnson	J.S. Johnson	Waukon, IA	1892
June	D. June & Co.	Fremont, OH	1905
Keck-Gonnerman	Keck-Gonnerman Co.	Mt. Vernon, IN	1905
Kent	Kent Machinery Co.	Cuyahoga Falls, OH	1939
Kingsland-Douglas	Kingsland & Douglas Mfg. Co.	St. Louis, MO	1892
Kitten	F. Kitten	Ferdinand, IN	1892
Knight	Kent Machinery Co.	Cuyahoga Falls, OH	1939
Knight	Knight Mfg. Co.	Canton, OH	1913
Lansing	Lansing Iron & Engine Works	Lansing, MI	1892
Liddle	Liddell Co.	Charlotte, NC	1892
Lilliston	Lilliston Implement Co.	Albany, GA	1945
Lima	J.R. Ashton Machinery Co.	Lima, OH	1892
Lima	Lima Mfg. Co.	Lima, IN	1892
Lombard	Geo. R. Lombard & Co.	Augusta, GA	1892
Mansfield	Aultman & Taylor Machinery Co.	Mansfield, OH	1892
Marsh	E.B. Marsh & Bro.	Snydersville, PA	1892
Matchless	Aultman & Taylor Machinery Co.	Mansfield, OH	1892
Meadows	Meadows Mill Co.	North Wilkesboro, NC	1939
Monroeton	Monroeton Mfg. Co.	Monroeton, PA	1892
Mulay	Chandler & Taylor Co.	Indianapolis, IN	1892
Nelson	N.O. Nelson Mfg. Co.	St. Louis, MO	1885
New Buckeye	Enterprise Mfg. Co.	Columbiana, OH	1892
Novelty	Novelty Iron Works	Dubuque, IA	1892
Peerless	Moses P. Johnson	St. Louis, MO	1890
Plantation	Lane & Bodley Co.	Cincinnati, OH	1892
Pony E	Aultman & Taylor Machinery Co.	Mansfield, OH	1892
Port Huron	Port Huron Engine & Thresher Co.	Port Huron, MI	1905
Potts	C. & A. Potts & Co.	Indianapolis, IN	1892
Progress	Progress Engine & Machine Works	Fredericksburg, VA	1892
Reeves	Reeves & Co.	Columbus, IN	1905
Reynolds & Lang	Reynolds & Lang	Ithaca, NY	1892
Richmond	Richmond Machine Works	Richmond, IN	1892
Robinson	Robinson & Co.	Richmond, IN	1892
Rumsey	L.M. Rumsey Mfg. Co.	St. Louis, MO	1890
Russell	Russell & Co.	Massillon, OH	1900
Scheidler	Scheidler Machine Works	Newark, OH	1892
Single "E"	Rockwood, Newcomb & Co.	Indianapolis, IN	1887

Trade Names (cont...)

Southern	Southern Mfg. Co.	Eddyville, KY	1892
Southwestern	Brennan & Co.	Louisville, KY	1892
Spangler	Spangler Mfg. Co.	York, PA	1905
Standard	Hugh Wright & Sons	New Lisbon, OH	1892
Standard	Lyon Iron Works	Greene, NY	1892
Standard	Sergeant Mfg. Co.	Greensborough, NC	1892
Standard	T.M. Nagle	Erie, PA	1892
Star	C. Aultman & Co.	Canton, OH	1892
Thomas-Albright	Thomas-Albright Co.	Goshen, IN	1892
Turner	Turner Mfg. Co.	Statesville, NC	1945
U. S. Standard	Geo. S. Comstock	Mechanicsburg, PA	1913
Valley	Grand Rapids Mfg. & Implement Co.	Grand Rapids, MI	1892
Van Winkle	Van Winkle Gin & Machine Co.	Atlanta, GA	1892
Westinghouse	Westinghouse Co.	Schenectady, NY	1892
Wilson & Hendrie	Wilson & Hendrie	Montague, MI	1892
Winship	Winship Machine Co.	Atlanta, GA	1892
Woodruff	Woodruff Machinery Mfg. Co.	Winder, GA	1913
Zink's	A.J. Zink & Son	Christiansburg, VA	1892

Saws

With the first settlement of the American colonies, the saw and the ax came as necessary equipment. In the early days, saw steel hadn't yet been developed; into the late 1800s, sawing was done by hand; there were very few power saws of any kind except, of course, for sawmills. Chain saws were unheard of until the 1930s and never made real progress until after World War II.

This section deals primarily with power saws of various kinds, even including some of the engine-powered log saws that became popular in the 1920s. While a considerable number were sold, many farmers never used one—they continued to fell and buck trees as they had always done, first with a one- or two-man felling saw and then finishing the job with a buck saw or a circular saw.

Today, many of the old belt-powered saws have acquired collector status, although a plain saw mandrel still might be bought for only a few dollars. Engine-powered saws on the other hand, often bring $300 to $500 or more, depending on their condition.

Aermotor Co., Chicago, Ill.

By the 1930s, this famous windmill manufacturer had added saw frames to its product line. This all-steel saw weighed only

275 pounds, including a 100-pound flywheel. Usually, these saws were powered by a gasoline engine or a tractor. Occasionally, a farmer connected it to a horse power, using a speed jack to gain the desired saw speed.

Appleton Manufacturing Co., Batavia, Ill.

By 1917, Appleton offered several styles of saws, including this stationary drag saw. It was designed so that a log could be rolled onto the small carriage and moved forward for each cut. Since this was a stationary outfit, it was driven through a line shaft by the available power source.

As an alternative to the Hero drag saw, Appleton offered a circular saw design. Like the drag saw, this was a stationary unit, employing a small carriage to advance the log for each succeeding cut. The main shaft required a speed of 300 rpm and this was the usual speed for overhead line-shafting.

For farm use, Appleton offered its tilting table wood saws in various styles; the saw shown here is its No. 1 steel frame design. A flywheel was usually mounted on the saw mandrel to help it through large logs. Appleton also furnished saw frames using wood construction.

S.K. Campbell Co., Central Bridge, N.Y.

By the early 1900s, many companies were offering wood saws. One of these was the Campbell saw, shown here with a sliding-table design. Manufacturers and farmers alike had their preferences, whether it was for the sliding table shown here or the more commonly used tilting-table design.

A.B. Farquhar Co., Ltd., York, Pa.

By the 1890s, Farquhar was offering various kinds of sawing machines, including this drag saw, also known as a cross-cut sawing machine. These machines were designed for stationary installation rather than for portable use.

Circular sawing machines became popular in the 1890s, quickly relegating the time-honored buck saw to a hook in the tool shed. This one from Farquhar was of wooden design and employed the wooden slide table. Farquhar recommended this machine as being the best for overall farm use.

Folding Sawing Machine Co., Chicago, Ill.

An advertisement in an 1895 German edition of *American Agriculturist* illustrates the folding sawing machine. Loosely translated, the upper illustration shows the saw over the man's shoulder as he heads toward the woods. The center engraving shows the saw set up and felling a tree, while the lower engraving illustrates how the saw was then used to buck the log into firewood lengths.

R.R. Howell Co., Minneapolis, Minn.

A 1901 advertisement in the *American Thresherman* illustrates the Howell self-feed portable drag-saw machine. Like others of its time, this was a stationary unit, requiring considerable time to set up and align. Usually, the logs were brought to the machine where they were quickly dispatched into firewood.

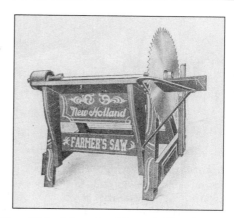

New Holland Machine Co., New Holland, Pa.

A catalog of the early 1900s illustrates the New Holland Farmer's Saw shown above with the swinging or tilting table. As noted in the lower figure, this saw could also be equipped with a special ripping attachment, making the saw useful for other duties.

Already in the 1930s, various companies built tractor-mounted saws that bolted onto the front of the tractor for complete portability. This New Holland tractor saw of the 1940s could also be converted to a stationary saw frame if so desired.

New Winona Manufacturing Co., Winona, Minn.

During the early 1900s, numerous companies organized to build saw frames. One of these was New Winona Manufacturing Co., a small company that also made feed grinders and other farm items. Shown here is its tilting table design of about 1910.

Ottawa Manufacturing Co., Ottawa, Kan.

In the 1920s, the engine-powered log saw became a reality. The Ottawa was one of the early designs; it remained on the market into the 1940s. This outfit also included an optional tree-felling attachment for complete mechanization of the job.

Port Huron Engine & Thresher Co., Port Huron, Mich.

In areas where coal was scarce, wood was often used to fuel a steam-traction engine. Port Huron offered this front-mounted wood saw in its 1899 catalog. It was the invention of Shore Bros., which owned a Port Huron engine. Several traction-engine builders made sawing attachments and many others were home-built by engine owners.

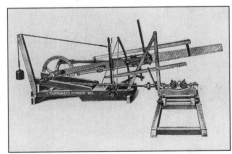

Plymouth Foundry & Machine Co., Plymouth, Wisc.

Originally built by F. Thurman & Co., Plymouth, Wis., the Plymouth Champion Drag Saw appeared in the Plymouth Foundry catalog of about 1910. This rather complicated design was stationary, with the log carriage having an automatic advance once a cut was completed.

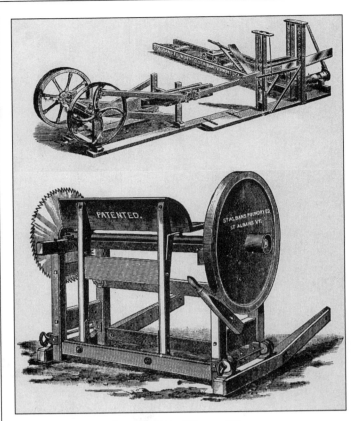

St. Albans Foundry Co., St. Albans, Vt.

St. Albans was one of the earliest manufacturers of saw frames. By 1881, its line included the combined saw frame shown above (top), plus the drag saw in the above (lower) illustration. At the time, the Combined Saw Frame sold for $50, with the Drag Saw Machine selling for $75.

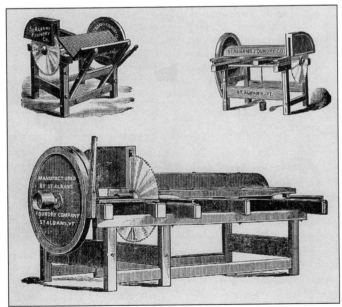

Many styles of saw frames were offered by St. Albans in its 1881 catalog, including three models illustrated here. All of these machines were dependent on having some form of motive power and that precluded most farmers from buying one at the time. By 1900, a few farmers would have a gasoline engine; within another decade, gasoline engines were on a great many farms.

For those with lots of wood to saw, St. Albans offered this outfit including a two-horse railway power and the St. Albans drag saw. Since this outfit was built more than a century ago, little information survives today. Chances are that sales of this unit came up to the company's hopes but, nevertheless, it represents a great move forward in mechanizing the work of cutting firewood.

Stover Manufacturing & Engine Co., Freeport, Ill.

Stover was a well-established manufacturer of gasoline engines, beginning in the early 1900s. About 1920, the firm came out with its Stover Drag Saw, an engine-powered saw that helped mechanize wood cutting. Shown here with the optional tree-felling attachment, the Stover was one of several such machines to appear in the 1920s.

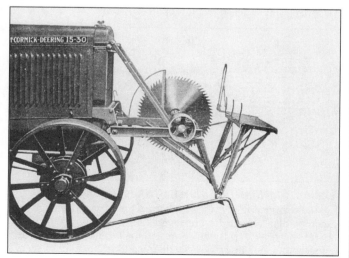

By 1930, Stover had come out with several styles of tractor-mounted saw frames, including this one mounted to the front of

a McCormick-Deering 10-20 tractor. These saws were fairly popular since they permitted taking the saw to the woods, rather than having to buck up much of the material by hand so that it could be loaded by hand for the trip to the saw. Stover solved the starting problem for the 10-20 by supplying a long crank that reached through the saw frame.

Witte Engine Works, Kansas City, Kan.

Witte had an aggressive marketing policy, selling many of its engines direct to the farmer or through local agents. In the 1920s, Witte developed its log and tree saws, selling them by the thousands in the following years. Shown here bucking a log, the saw could also be equipped with a special felling attachment. Witte log saws were built into the 1940s.

Scales

In 1830, E&T Fairbanks, St. Johnsbury, Vt., developed the Fairbanks Platform Scale. Its principles remain yet today, although diminished somewhat by the advent of electronic weighing methods. During the great period of farm mechanization, beginning about 1870, farm scales also came into widespread use. By the 1900s, many farms had their own scale for weighing livestock or grain. These larger wagon scales were simply a continuation of the development of scales, from small platform models to huge railroad scales.

Numerous companies were in the scale business and the great majority have long since gone from the scene. Today, small platform scales often sell for $100 or more, although wagon scales seem to have a limited market, possibly because there are so few left intact. This section includes a few representative examples, but many other companies were in the scale business, particularly in the 1900-1920 era.

American Scale Co., Kansas City, Kan.

In 1910, American offered its Pitless Scales. The company also made conventional pit scales, but this design was semi-portable and came as a complete unit, requiring little in the way of setup, except for leveling and adjusting.

Beckman Bros., Des Moines, Iowa

Little is known of Beckman Bros., aside from its scale advertisements of the early 1900s. Its American scale of 1909 was available in many sizes, from a small 400-pound platform scale to a huge 100-ton railroad track scale.

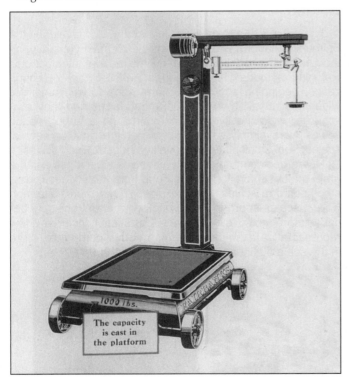

E&T Fairbanks Co., St. Johnsbury, Vt.

In the author's book *100 Years of Fairbanks-Morse: 1893-1993* (1993: Stemgas Publishing Co.), the history of the Fairbanks scale is well detailed. This 1,000 pound platform scale of 1916 sold for $14.85 and its smaller 500-pound brother was priced at only $12.50. Fairbanks scales were sold in the hundreds of thousands all over the world.

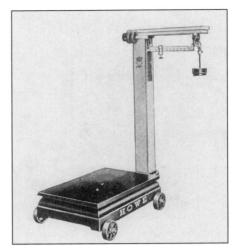

Along with numerous wagon scales and other styles, Howe built a wide variety of small portable platform scales with capacities of anywhere from 500 to 2,500 pounds. The Howe design was very popular. While there appears to have been nothing that exceeded the Fairbanks in popularity, the Howe was a close competitor.

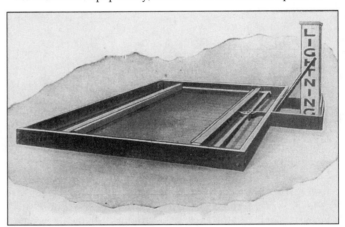

Kansas City Hay Press Co., Kansas City, Kan.

Kansas City Hay Press Co. began offering scales, at least by the early 1900s, with this one being its pitless scale design. The steel frame was only 7-inches high, making it a simple matter to build wooden ramps at each end for day-to-day use.

Lennox Machine Co., Marshalltown, Iowa

While this company was also known for its gasoline engines, Lennox also offered its Improved Pitless Scale by 1909. The gates shown with this one permitted the farmer to weigh livestock either for sale or to check their weight gain. Lennox went on to become a famous manufacturer of furnaces and air conditioning units.

McDonald Bros. Pitless Scale Co., Pleasant Hill, Mo.

A 1907 advertisement notes that the Economy Pitless Scale had already seen some "16 Years in Actual Use." Accordingly, the company was making pitless scales already in 1891. Pitless scales had the great advantage of being semi-portable and did not require the excavation of a pit to hold the weighing mechanism.

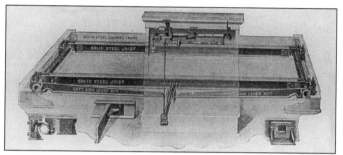

McDonald Bros. claimed it to be the original steel frame pitless wagon scale, illustrating it in a phantom view for 1910. Eventually, the company was bought out by Moline Plow Co., and the latter continued to sell McDonald scales for a number of years. However, about 1930, McDonald scales were available from American Scale Co., Kansas City.

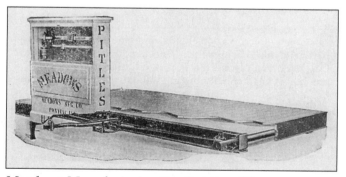

Meadows Manufacturing Co., Pontiac, Ill.

Meadows was a famous manufacturer of wagon dumps, elevators, washing machines and other farm equipment. About 1910, the company also began offering its Meadows Pitless Scale; like its contemporaries, this one was made of solid structural steel. Meadows continued building scales for a number of years. By 1930, it offered only repair parts.

Did You Know?

A farmer might sell an old abandoned hog oiler for $5 or $10, but a collector might give $100, or much more, for a particularly desirable style.

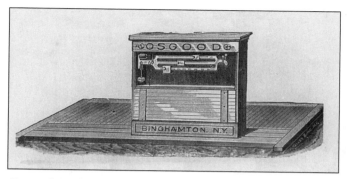

Osgood Scale Co., Binghamton, N.Y.

By 1889, Osgood & Thompson was offering wagon scales, with its 3-ton model priced at $35. A 1903 advertisement notes that the company had 30,000 in use, also noting the company's 40-year reputation in the scale business. The company remained under this title until about 1930 when Osgood scales were available from Binghamton Scale Co., also of Binghamton.

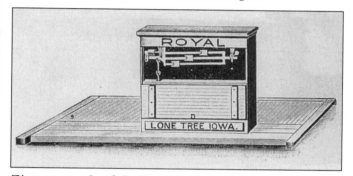

Zimmerman Steel Co., Lone Tree, Iowa

Stump pullers were the stock-in-trade for Zimmerman Steel Co. However, by 1909, the company was also offering its Royal Pitless Wagon Scale, along with the Zimmerman Pitless Wagon Scale. Little is known of its earlier history or its subsequent activities.

Sprayers

By the 1880s, many companies offered a variety of hand-operated sprayers. Usually, they were employed to protect growing fruit and vegetable crops from a variety of insects. At the time, arsenites such as Paris Green or London Purple were used; arsenate of lead was also popular, with thousands of gardens getting sprayed with this material every year. In addition, there was the horrible smelling mixture of lime-sulfur, made by mixing lime and sulfur together to rid livestock of insects or parasites.

In the early 1900s, power sprayers became a reality. Dozens of companies sprang into action for a time. After the usual shake-out period following a new development, the field narrowed, but a few companies emerged as leaders in the manufacture of spray equipment.

Old bucket sprayers were sometimes rather ornate and today are a conversation piece, although their collector value has not become more than $10 to $30, as a rule. Power sprayers are often desired more because of the vintage engine that powered the machine than for the pumping equipment. Thus, a power sprayer with the engine intact may often bring $300 to $500, this representing the value of the engine in most cases.

Aspinwall Manufacturing Co., Jackson, Mich.

In 1901, Aspinwall presented this cotton sprayer to the market. It was a powered sprayer, but power came from a chain drive from the wheels, rather than from an attached engine. Little is known of this machine aside from the initial announcement.

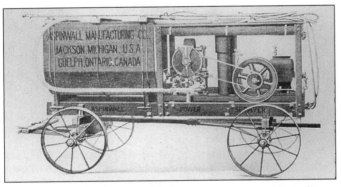

By 1912, Aspinwall had added two power sprayers to its line. As was usual at the time, the tank was made of wood and ordinarily carried anywhere from 50 to 200 gallons of spray mixture. This belt-driven model could also be supplied without the engine for those situations where the farmer preferred to install an engine of his own choosing.

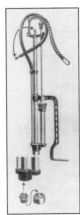

Bateman Manufacturing Co., Grenloch, N.J.

Bateman had a long history in the farm equipment business, offering various kinds of bucket sprayers already in the 1890s and perhaps even earlier. With this simple pump, all that was needed was a pail. The sprayer was simply set in the pail and held with the foot while spraying.

By the early 1900s, Bateman was offering various kinds of traction sprayers wherein the power to operate the spray pump came from the ground drive of the wheels. Of course, this sprayer was only useful for row crops, but it represented a forward step in the development of field sprayers.

Bateman offered various kinds of engine-power sprayers as part of its Iron Age implement line. In addition, A.B. Farquhar Co., York, Pa., carried the Iron Age line in its catalogs for a number of years, finally buying the Bateman Manufacturing Co. in 1930.

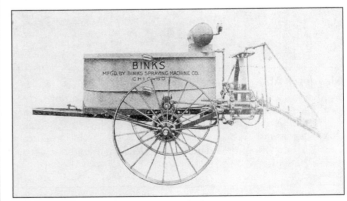

Binks Spraying Machine Co., Chicago, Ill.

Outside of this 1909 advertisement for the Binks Field Sprayer, nothing is known of this company's activities in the sprayer business. While the machine shown here was a traction-drive unit, Binks also offered a full line of power and hand sprayers for every purpose.

Crestline Manufacturing Co., Crestline, Ohio

The Crestline Whale Power Sprayer was unique for its time, since it could produce up to 150 pounds of pressure, using only a 2-horsepower gasoline engine. The extra pressure was important when spraying fruit trees and other applications requiring that the sprayer be able to reach a long distance. Aside from a 1912 advertisement, nothing more is known of this company.

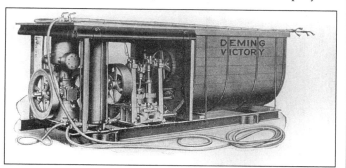

Deming Co., Salem, Ohio

In 1913, Deming announced its Victory sprayer, shown here on steel skids, but also available as a mounted unit. These sprayers used a Novo 3-horsepower engine to operate the pump and indeed, Novo shipped thousands of engines to Deming for this purpose. For reasons unknown, the Novo engine was very popular on sprayers, with many different companies using its 3-horsepower model for this purpose.

A.B. Farquhar Co., Ltd., York, Pa.

In 1930, Farquhar bought out Bateman Manufacturing Co., of Grenloch, N.J. Farquhar had been selling its Iron Age implement line for some years prior to the buy-out and continued with various Iron Age sprayers and other equipment. Shown here is the No. 512 Iron Age Traction Sprayer, a popular model that Farquhar continued to offer into the 1930s.

Even though dusters were not as popular as sprayers, a few companies offered them, including Farquhar. This one was a continuation of the Iron Age dusters formerly offered by Bateman Manufacturing Co. Farquhar sold out to Oliver Farm Equipment Co. in 1952.

Field Force Pump Co., Elmira, N.Y.

Field offered this Leader sprayer in 1910; it was furnished with a 3-1/2 horsepower gasoline engine; the pump was capable of delivering 200 PSI. The steel platform atop the sprayer was for the benefit of orchardists who now could ascend the tower and spray even the top-most parts of their fruit trees.

In the 1920s, Field had adopted its "Ospraymo" trademark and offered its Junior Leader Orchard Sprayer, among other items. The engine-powered pump used three cylinders set equally apart to stabilize the spray pressure. A convenient canvas side-curtain covered the engine and pump when not in use.

For 1925, Field offered its New Junior Outfit, a small unit for the average farm or orchard. It was operated by a Fairbanks-Morse engine through a chain-and-sprocket drive to the pump. This skidded design could be furnished truck-mounted or could be attached to a farm running gear.

Hardie Manufacturing Co., Hudson, Mich.

One of the important sprayer manufacturers was also one of the first to build a power sprayer. This 1902 model of the Hardie was an early attempt to mechanize the job; prior to this time, most orchard pumps were operated by hand.

By the 1930s, Hardie Manufacturing Co. was offering this Senior Duplex Cut-under Sprayer. The cut-under frame permitted short turns in orchards. This one is powered by a Stover engine. Like the Novo, the Stover was a popular power for spray pumps of various makes.

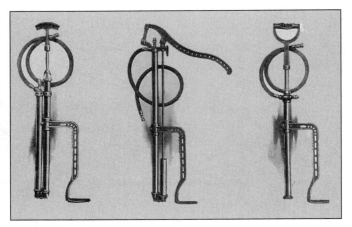

Hayes Pump & Planter Co., Galva, Ill.

Hayes had a history going back to the 1870s as a manufacturer of pumps, corn planters and other equipment. By the 1920s, the company had developed its "Fruit-Fog" sprayer line that included everything from the hand or bucket pumps shown here to large commercial orchard sprayers.

For small orchards, Hayes offered this wheelbarrow pump that enabled the gardener or farmer to load perhaps 15 gallons of spray and dispense it with a large hand pump. Wheelbarrow sprayers were very popular in some areas.

Equipped with a Fairbanks-Morse engine, this power sprayer was of the walking beam type. By comparison, many sprayers were gear driven styles. The protective canvas side-curtains are shown; when not in use, they could be rolled down to protect the engine and sprayer from the elements. Hayes also built its own engine for a time during the 1920s.

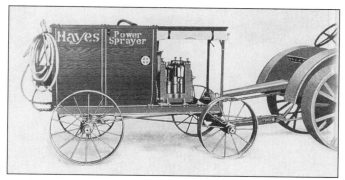

By the late 1920s, Hayes offered this tractor-driven sprayer. By utilizing the tractor's PTO shaft, the need for a separate engine was eliminated. In 1930, Hayes merged with others to form Farm Tools Inc.

International Harvester Co., Chicago, Ill.

About 1910, IHC began offering spray pump outfits complete with its own IHC engines. These outfits were built in many sizes and styles, with its 1-horsepower air-cooled engine (also known as the Tom Thumb engine) being the power source for this small portable outfit.

LeRoy Plow Co., LeRoy, N.Y.

In 1910, LeRoy Plow Co. announced its line of field sprayers; the model shown here was a traction sprayer deriving its power from the wheels through a series of chain drives. For a time, at least, LeRoy sprayers were sold by certain branches of John Deere Plow Co.

F.E. Myers & Bro., Ashland, Ohio

Already in 1887, Myers was offering its Knapsack Spray Pump. This outfit was loaded with solution, strapped onto the back and operated by pulling down on the weighted rope. From these beginnings, the Myers spray pump line expanded to include dozens of different models.

Myers sold thousands of its Duplex Spray Pumps over the years; this low-down design was a great advantage since filling the tank was much easier. The Duplex shown here is equipped with a Novo vertical engine, a very popular style for spray pumps of various makes.

In the 1920s, Myers offered this wheelbarrow pump that used an air chamber to provide even spraying despite the interval required for working the hand pump. At the time, Myers was offering dozens of different pumps with literally hundreds of available configurations.

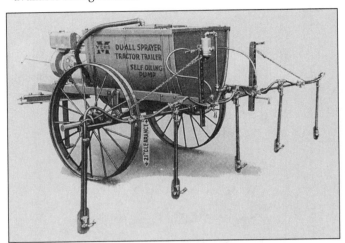

By 1940, the Myers spray-pump line had come to include its Du-All Junior Tractor Sprayer. Shown here with a mounted gasoline engine, the Du-All could also be furnished with a tractor PTO drive. For those having a tractor PTO, this eliminated the cost of the engine, diminishing the total price considerably.

Trade Names

Brunner	Brunner Foundry & Machy. Co.	Peru, IL	1915
Buckeye	Mast, Foos & Co.	Springfield, OH	1915
Bull Dog	Ward Pump Co.	Rockford, IL	1915
Bull Dog	Ward-Love Pump Co.	Rockford, IL	1924
Bulldozer	F. E. Myers & Bro.	Ashland, OH	1915
Charter Oak	W. & B. Douglas	Middletown, CT	1915
Climax	Thomas Peppler	Hightstown, NJ	1905
Climax Leader	Field Force Pump Co.	Elmira, NY	1931
Columbia	R. B. Collis Sprayer Co.	Benton Harbor, MI	1931
Crestline Hector	Crestline Mfg. Co.	Crestline, OH	1915
Cushman	Cushman Power Sprayer Co.	Lincoln, NE	1913
Daisy	Rippley Hardware Co.	Grafton, IL	1905
Deming	Deming Co.	Salem, OH	1905
Deyo	Deyo-Macey Engine Co.	Binghamton, NY	1915
Dobbins	Dobbins Mfg. Co.	Elkhart, IN	1945
Domestic	Domestic Engine & Pump Co.	Shippensburg, PA	1915
Dreadnaught	Goulds Mfg. Co.	Seneca Falls, NY	1924
Eastern Triplex	Hardie Mfg. Co.	Hudson, MI	1913
Eclipse	Morrill & Morley	Benton Harbor, MI	1905
Eclipse	Fairbanks, Morse & Co.	Chicago, IL	1913
Electric	Prairie Mfg. Co.	Indianapolis, IN	1913
Elmira King	Field Force Pump Co.	Elmira, NY	1915
Emperor	Goulds Mfg. Co.	Seneca Falls, NY	1915
Empire Duplex	Field Force Pump Co.	Elmira, NY	1915
Empire Leader	Field Force Pump Co.	Elmira, NY	1915
Eureka	Eureka Mower Co.	Utica, NY	1931
Excelsior	Field Force Pump Co.	Elmira, NY	1931
Excelsior	William Stahl	Quincy, IL	1905
Fairbanks-Morse	Fairbanks, Morse & Co.	Chicago, IL	1915
Flinchbaugh	Flinchbaugh Mfg. Co.	Greencastle, PA	1915
Friend	Friend Mfg. Co.	Gasport, NY	1905
Giant	Bean Spray Pump Co.	Lansing, MI	1915
Gile	Gile Boat & Engine Co.	Ludington, MI	1915
Goulds	Goulds Mfg. Co.	Seneca Falls, NY	1915
Granger	W. & B. Douglas	Middletown, CT	1924
Hardie Duplex	Hardie Mfg. Co.	Hudson, MI	1915
Hayes	Farm Tools Inc.	Galva, IL	1931
Hayes Duplex	Hayes Pump & Planter Co.	Galva, IL	1915
Hudson	H. D. Hudson Mfg. Co.	Chicago, IL	1931
Hurst	H. L. Hurst Mfg. Co.	Canton, OH	1905
I. X. L.	Wright Mfg. Co.	Pontiac, MI	1915
Ideal	Brandt Mfg. Co.	Minneapolis, MN	1913
Ideal	Terrill Mfg. Co.	Bridgman, MI	1924
IHC Famous	International Harvester Co.	Chicago, IL	1915
Imperial	Brandt Mfg. Co.	Minneapolis, MN	1913
Iron Age	A. B. Farquhar Co.	York, PA	1939
Iron Age	Bateman Mfg. Co.	Grenloch, NJ	1905
Junior Leader	Field Force Pump Co.	Elmira, NY	1924

Trade Names (cont...)

Kant-Klog	Rochester Spray Pump Co.	Rochester, NY	1913
King	Friend Mfg. Co.	Gasport, NY	1931
Leader	Field Force Pump Co.	Elmira, NY	1915
Little Giant	W. C. Akins Machine Co.	Rochester, NY	1915
Little Giant Duplex	John Bean Mfg. Co.	San Jose, CA	1939
Love	Love Tractor Inc.	Eau Claire, MI	1945
Medal Winner	Beck Sprayer Co.	Flushing, MI	1915
Mist	Fairbanks, Morse & Co.	Chicago, IL	1915
Myers Bulldozer	F. E. Myers & Bro.	Ashland, OH	1915
New Victor	Field Force Pump Co.	Elmira, NY	1905
New-Way	New-Way Motor Co.	Lansing, MI	1915
Niagara	Niagara Sprayer & Chemical Co.	Middleport, NY	1945
Nixon	Dayton Supply Co.	Dayton, OH	1905
Novo	Novo Engine Co.	Lansing, MI	1913
O. K. Champion	Champion Corp.	Hammond, IN	1924
Orchard Monarch	Field Force Pump Co.	Elmira, NY	1905
Ospraymo	Field Force Pump Co.	Elmira, NY	1931
Paragon	Campbell-Hausfeld Co.	Harrison, OH	1939
Park Leader	Field Force Pump Co.	Elmira, NY	1924
Peerless	Brandt Mfg. Co.	Minneapolis, MN	1915
Peerless	H. D. Hudson Mfg. Co.	Chicago, IL	1931
Peoria	Peoria Hydraulic Pump Co.	Peoria, IL	1924
Peppler	Thomas Peppler	Hightstown, NJ	1905
Perfection	Brandt Mfg. Co.	Minneapolis, MN	1913
Perfection	Thos. Peppler	Hightstown, NJ	1913
Pippin	Reierson Machinery Co.	Portland, OR	1915
Planet	Deming Co.	Salem, OH	1915
Pony Duplex	Bean Spray Pump Co.	Lansing, MI	1924
Prince	Friend Mfg. Co.	Gasport, NY	1931
Queen	Friend Mfg. Co.	Gasport, NY	1931
Quincy	Quincy Engine Co.	Quincy, PA	1915
R. E. A.	Rocklin Mfg. Co.	Sioux City, IA	1945
Reierson	Reierson Machinery Co.	Portland, OR	1915
Rippley	Rippley Hardware Co.	Grafton, IL	1913
Royal Leader	Field Force Pump Co.	Elmira, NY	1915
Schanck	John R. Shangle	Hightstown, NJ	1905
Silver Cloud	F. E. Myers & Bro.	Ashland, OH	1945
Simplex	Beck Sprayer Co.	Flushing, MI	1915
Simplicity	Turner Mfg. Co.	Port Washington, WI	1915
Simplicity Junior	Bean Spray Pump Co.	Lansing, MI	1924
Sturdy	Goulds Pumps Inc.	Seneca Falls, NY	1931
Suburban	W. & B. Douglas	Middletown, CT	1915
Tayoga	Field Force Pump Co.	Elmira, NY	1924
Union Leader	Field Force Pump Co.	Elmira, NY	1915
Utility	Terrill Mfg. Co.	Bridgman, MI	1924
Utility	Utility Sprayer Co.	Minneapolis, MN	1931

Trade Names (cont...)

Vice Admiral	Goulds Mfg. Co.	Seneca Falls, NY	1915
Victory	Deming Co.	Salem, OH	1915
Vulcan	Farm Tools Inc.	Evansville, IN	1931
Wallace	Wallace Machinery Co.	Champaign, IL	1905
Ward Jr.	Ward Pump Co.	Rockford, IL	1915
Ward Jr.	Ward-Love Pump Co.	Rockford, IL	1931
Ward Jr.	W. L. Davey Pump Corp.	Rockford, IL	1939
Warlo	Ward-Love Pump Co.	Rockford, IL	1931
Warlo	W. L. Davey Pump Corp.	Rockford, IL	1939
Watson	Field Force Pump Co.	Elmira, NY	1905
Western	Friend Mfg. Co.	Gasport, NY	1915
Whale	Crestline Mfg. Co.	Crestline, OH	1915
Wisconsin	Lauson-Lawton Co.	DePere, WI	1915
Wonder	Beck Sprayer Co.	Flushing, MI	1915
Woodland	W. & B. Douglas	Middletown, CT	1915
York	Flinchbaugh Mfg. Co.	York, PA	1913

Stalk Cutters

No significant stalk cutter patents were registered before 1860. During that decade, a few such machines appeared, but real progress wasn't made until the 1880s. Corn and cotton stalks both presented a unique problem. They were too long for the plow to cover successfully. Discing helped the problem slightly, but, given the disc harrows of the time, their assistance was not satisfactory. From this need, the stalk cutter arose. Virtually all the machines shown in this section depended on driving over the row and cutting the stalks into short pieces. Depending on various factors, this was more or less successful. Today, the vast majority of these machines have long since been relegated to scrap iron, so they are seldom seen; there seems to be no established collector value.

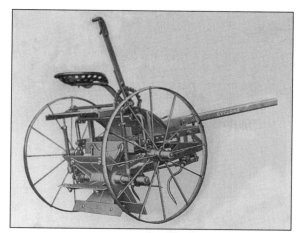

B.F. Avery & Sons, Louisville, Kty.

This long-time implement manufacturer had stalk cutters on the market at least by the early 1900s and perhaps much earlier. By 1915, the company was offering its Cyclone Cutter, a heavy machine with a series of hardened steel knives. Varying the cut length was achieved by varying the number of knives on the cylinder. The six-knife style shown here cut every 12-inches, but this machine could be purchased with seven-knife or 14-knife cylinders.

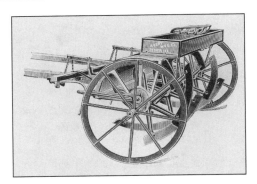

Avery Co., Peoria, Ill.

By the 1880s, the Avery Spiral Knife corn and cotton cutter was available. Built in one-row and two-row sizes, it used the spiral knives to minimize the jolting provided by straight knives. This machine was built until about 1910.

J.I. Case Plow Works, Racine, Wisc.

During the 1880s, Case Plow Works developed its Texan Stalk Cutter, designed especially to cut cotton stalks, but also useable for cutting corn stalks. The spiral knife was intended to minimize the constant jolting and jarring of straight-blade machines.

An 1897 Case Plow Works catalog illustrates its Steel Frame stalk cutter, noting that "probably no farming implement receives rougher usage than the stalk cutter." Although it was equipped with a seat, the ride was so rough that many farmers preferred to walk behind.

Deere & Co., Moline, Ill.

In addition to preparing the ground for plowing, farmers also recognized the value of cutting the stalks to help eradicate corn borers and other crop enemies. Deere & Co., offered this No. 12 steel frame stalk cutter in 1908, as part of its overall farm equipment line.

Emerson-Brantingham Co., Rockford, Ill.

By the early 1900s, Emerson added a stalk cutter to its farm implement line. Like its contemporaries, it featured a pair of fingers mounted ahead of the cutter blades. They were intended to align the stalks with the cutters; instead, they often became clogged with loose material and were then more of a detriment than a benefit.

Marseilles Manufacturing Co., Marseilles, Ill.

An 1898 illustration shows the Marseilles stalk cutter of the time, noting that it could be furnished with wood or steel wheels.

Also of note is the extensive Marseilles implement line at the time; everything from corn shellers to feed grinders to windmills.

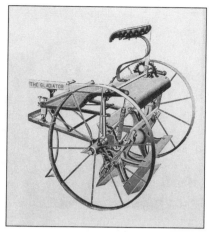

Moline Plow Co., Moline, Ill.

A 1906 catalog from Moline Plow Co. illustrates its Gladiator stalk cutter. It was part of its famous Flying Dutchman line; due to anti-German sentiment, Moline Plow Co. retired this famous trademark during World War I.

Stump Pullers

Whenever there was new ground to be cleared for farming, the age-old problem of removing the stumps reared its ugly head. In many cases, the larger ones were left to rot away, but this took many years. By the 1850s, a few manufacturers were devising stump pullers to achieve the task; by the end of the century, there were numerous firms offering machines to handle this work. Eventually, dynamite came along; for some, it was preferable, but it took experienced hands to set and fire the charge. Large bulldozers were unheard of, but the advent of the steam-traction engine was a major help because it was able to move many smaller stumps with relative ease. Eventually, the stump puller was no longer needed. Today, they are rarely found—most were converted to scrap iron many years ago.

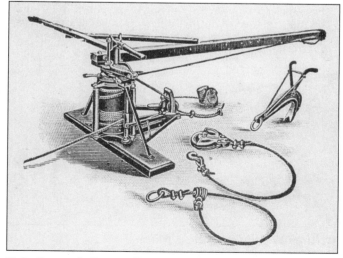

R.S. Caward, Cresco, Iowa

For reasons unknown, there were many stump-puller makers in Iowa. One of these was R.S. Caward, builder of the Faultless

puller; it had beginnings at least by 1900. Like most designs, the puller was suitably anchored; once set in place, it could clean all the stumps from a fairly large radius.

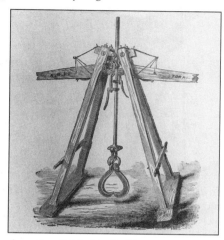

A.B. Farquhar Co., Ltd., York, Pa.

Unlike most stump pullers, Farquhar's Archimedean Stump Puller and Rock Lifter was available in three sizes; the No. 1, when worked by four hands, could lift 50,000 pounds, yet it weighed only 645 pounds. With this machine, Farquhar quoted the famous saying of Archimedes, "Give me a place for my fulcrum and I will move the World."

Milne Manufacturing Co., Monmouth, Ill.

By the early 1900s, Milne was established as a manufacturer of stump pullers, offering several different models. Shown here is its original design, the Hawkeye Grub & Stump Machine. Properly set, it could clear two acres of stumps with a single setting. Apparently, the company had already sold several thousand machines by the time this 1903 advertisement appeared.

Kansas City Hay Press Co., Kansas City, Kan.

Although this company is best known for its hay presses and other farm equipment, Kansas City Hay Press Co. also built its Lightning Stump Puller, as illustrated here from an 1895 advertisement. Suitably anchored, these machines could pull more than the cable of those days would bear.

Monarch Grubber Manufacturing Co., Lone Tree, Iowa

Little is known of Monarch Grubber Co., aside from this 1895 advertisement. A few years later, the Monarch machine was being built by Zimmerman Steel Co. in the same city. This one was guaranteed to stand a strain of 75 tons—150,000 pounds!

O.K. Grubber Co., Sigourney, Iowa

Many years ago, the author acquired an 1892 circular for this company, horribly printed on atrocious paper. Although this image is of poor quality, it is actually an improvement over the original. Nothing is known of this firm and this is equally true for many other companies encountered in our research for this book.

W. Smith Grubber Co., La Crescent, Minn.

About 1910, the Twentieth Century Stump Puller appeared from this firm. The puller shown here was capable of handling

32 tons; it remained on the market for a number of years and was sold by several leading machinery jobbers around the country.

Swenson Grubber Co., Cresco, Iowa

By the 1890s, the firm of Caward & Swenson Co. was building its Faultless Two-Horse Grubbing Machine, claiming it to be the best stump puller that man's knowledge and skill has ever been able to produce. Regardless of the claims, the Swenson remained on the market for decades to come.

Swenson apparently began building stump pullers in 1876; by 1909, the firm was offering five different sizes of machines. The company remained active into the 1920s. After 1930, it disappears from the trade directories.

William W. Willis, Orange, Mass.

The Boston Cultivator, in its July 26, 1851, issue illustrates Stewart's Patent Stump Puller. In an accompanying article, it offers pullers ranging in size up to 1,000 tons of capacity. The small machine shown here was priced at $50—a considerable sum of money in 1851. As might be expected, nothing more is known of this venture aside from the article cited.

Zimmerman Steel Co., Lone Tree, Iowa

In a 1914 advertisement, the Monarch Steel Stump Puller was guaranteed to pull stumps up to 7 feet in diameter and guaranteed for five years. This company was apparently a successor to the Monarch Grubber Manufacturing Co. of the same city. Zimmerman continued to offer this machine into the 1920s, but disappears from the trade directories by 1930.

Trade Names

Archimedean	A. B. Farquhar Co.	York, PA	1913
Armstrong	Armstrong Mfg. Co.	Waterloo, IA	1915
Bailey's	H. A. Currier	Almont, MI	1892
Bennett's Improved	H. L. Bennett & Co.	Westerville, OH	1892
Carter	H. Carter & Sons	Canisteo, NY	1892
Cast Iron Combination	Milne Mfg. Co.	Monmouth, IL	1913
Chamberlain Screw	Chamberlain Mfg. Co.	Olean, NY	1892
Chief	C. D. Edwards	Albert Lea, MN	1892
Climax	C. D. Edwards	Albert Lea, MN	1905
Corbett	Mohland & Co.	Burlington, IA	1909
Cyclone	Challenge Co.	Batavia, IL	1909
Cyclone	Snow Mfg. Co.	Batavia, IL	1905
Defiance	Smith Mfg. Co.	LaCrosse, WI	1905
Dorsey	Dorsey Bros.	Elba, AL	1939
Eclipse	Eclipse Hay Press Co.	Kansas City, MO	1909
Faultless	Faultless Stump Puller Co.	Cresco, IA	1924
Faultless	R. S. Caward	Cresco, IA	1905
Hawkeye	Milne Mfg. Co.	Monmouth, IL	1905
Hercules	Hercules Mfg. Co.	Centerville, IA	1905
Huston Fordson	Tom Huston Mfg. Co.	Columbus, GA	1924
I. X. L.	Milne Mfg. Co.	Monmouth, IL	1905
I. X. L. Grubber	James Milne & Son	Scotch Grove, IA	1892
Iron Giant	Milne Mfg. Co.	Monmouth, IL	1905
Iron Hawkeye	Mohland & Co.	Burlington, IA	1909
J. C. Sharp's	Duisdecker & Smith	Pekin, IL	1892
Jumbo	C. D. Edwards	Albert Lea, MN	1905
Kirstin	A. J. Kirstin Co.	Escanaba, MI	1945
Kring	Kring Bros.	Westerville, OH	1892
Leader	Waterloo Iron Works	Waterloo, IA	1905
Lightning	Kansas City Hay Press Co.	Kansas City, MO	1892
Little Giant	Mohland & Co.	Burlington, IA	1909
Little Giant	Smith Mfg. Co.	LaCrosse, WI	1892
Martin	Indiana Foundry Co.	Indiana, PA	1905
Martin	Sutton Bros. & Bell	Indiana, PA	1892
Milne's Combination	Milne Mfg. Co.	Monmouth, IL	1905
Mogul	Owatonna Fanning Mill Co.	Owatonna, MN	1915

Trade Names (cont...)

Monarch	Monarch Grubber Co.	Lone Tree, IA	1905
Monarch	Monarch Tractors Inc.	Watertown, WI	1924
Monarch	Zimmerman Steel Co.	Lone Tree, IA	1909
Novelty	Novelty Iron Works	Dubuque, IA	1892
Over	Ewald Over	Indianapolis, IN	1892
Pioneer	Mohland & Co.	Burlington, IA	1909
Sampson Screw	Dean Mfg. Co.	Seymour, WI	1905
Smith	Smith Grubber Mfg. Co.	LaCrosse, WI	1905
Smith	W. Smith Grubber Co.	LaCrescent, MN	1909
Sparta	Sparta Iron Works Co.	Sparta, WI	1905
St. Albans	St. Albans Foundry & Impl. Co.	St. Albans, VT	1905
Swenson's Malleable	Swenson Grubber Co.	Cresco, IA	1905
Waterloo	Waterloo Iron Works	Waterloo, IA	1905
Williams	Hazlehurst Mfg. Co.	Hazlehurst, GA	1905

T

Tank Heaters

The term "tank heaters" does not appear in the Subject Index of Patents, including all patents to 1873. Research during the course of this book does not find tank heaters prior to the 1890s. By that time, several companies were making tank heaters, with many more to follow. Additional examples will be found under the earlier heading of Farmstead Tools & Equipment.

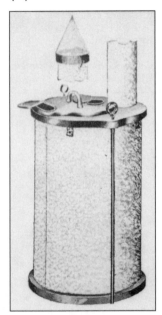

Brown Bros. Manufacturing Co., Nappanee, Ind.

A 1904 advertisement illustrates the Nappanee, which was adapted for either steel or wood tanks, said to be able to burn anything and included a cement bottom to sink it in the tank. Many such companies arose, but little information is now available.

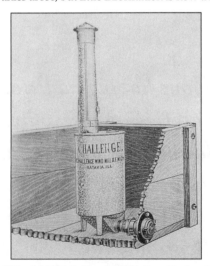

Challenge Wind Mill & Feed Mill Co., Batavia, Ill.

Challenge had become a major windmill and feed mill manufacturer by the time this 1895 advertisement appeared. The Chal-

lenge tank heater differed from most in its use of a side connection to provide draft and permit cleaning of ashes from the heater.

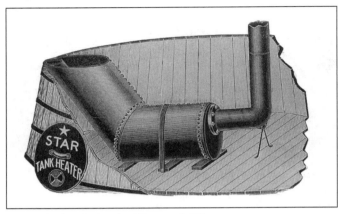

Hunt, Helm & Ferris, Harvard, Ill.

Its 1894 advertising read, "Hitch your wagon to a Star Tank Heater." This interesting design was one of many appearing in the 1890s. Farmers welcomed the coming of tank heaters instead of having to chop ice on almost a daily basis through the winter months.

U.S. Wind Engine & Pump Co., Batavia, Ill.

The 1890s spawned some interesting tank heater designs, including this IXL from U.S. Wind Engine & Pump Co. Although fed from the top, this one included a separate bottom draft and clean-out, bolted into the side of the tank. The entire unit was made of cast iron.

Threshing Machines

In the May 1887 issue of *Farm Machinery Magazine*, an editorial of old-time threshing methods states, "Agriculture is the acknowledged basis upon which all other works rest and upon its successful development depends all substantial progress. The rise in agriculture is readily traced in the improvement of agricultural implements and appliances, of which none present a more interesting study than the thrasher."

Of all aspects of farm life, one that was always held in high regard was threshing time. Few things inspired more enthusiasm than the sight of the steam threshing rig coming down the road or the plaintive whistle, sometimes heard for miles. The joy of the harvest also included farm wives who put together glorious feasts at threshing time. Even though the work was heavy, sweaty and dusty—not necessarily in that order—threshing time continues to inspire people to preserve a bit of our past. In the 1950s, "thresher reunions" began. These were mainly demonstrations of threshing as in days gone by. Eventually, the thresher reunions grew to the point that hundreds of these expositions are held every year.

The world's first successful threshing machine was built by Andrew Meikle in Scotland back in 1786. However, it simply threshed the grain; the thresher combined with a cleaner or separator did not come until much later. Hiram A. and John A. Pitts of Winthrop, Maine, are credited with building the first American threshing machine in 1830. (In the early days they were called "thrashing machines" as compared to the later term of "threshing machines.") As will be noted under the Buffalo-Pitts Co. heading below, the Pitts machines were indeed crude by later standards, but they marked the end of the flail and the beginning of a mechanical threshing machine.

About the same time as the Pitts Brothers were working out their design, Jacob A.V. Wemple in New York worked out a somewhat different design. In 1840, he went into partnership with George Westinghouse to build the machine and this was the beginning of the Westinghouse threshers. Wemple later went to Chicago, setting up a thresher factory there; it operated under the title of Wemple & Kline until 1857. Cyrus Roberts at Belleville, Ill., was the first to develop a vibrating separator about 1852. Subsequently, the Cox & Roberts machines were built; a manufacturing license was also issued to Kingsland & Ferguson at St. Louis for these machines. Cox eventually sold out his interests and Roberts moved to Three Rivers, Mich., where the Roberts, Throp Co. operated for some years.

Nichols & Shepard at Battle Creek, Mich., were the first to build threshers on the vibrating principle established in the Roberts patents. Its first Vibrator machines were built in 1858. Cornelius Aultman and H.H. Taylor organized the Aultman & Taylor Machinery Co., Mansfield, Ohio in 1867; this company manufactured machines under the Roberts patents.

Many other designs appeared, with some, like J.I. Case and Meinrad Rumely becoming quite famous. Unfortunately, the constraints of time and space do not permit a comprehensive review of the history associated with the thresher. To help this situation, many of the historic kernels are embedded within the captions that follow. Let it be noted, however, that the glory days of steam threshing only lasted about 40 years, beginning about 1890 and coming to a rapid close by 1930. Threshing remained on the scene for another 20 years. After 1930, the tractor replaced the steam engine; in the 1950s, the combine replaced the thresher.

Since so few threshing machines remain, especially the early wooden designs, they have now acquired collector status. Late model, all-steel machines of the 1920s and later, often bring $500 or more in good condition and some of the earliest wooden designs have acquired museum status. Hopefully, the remaining examples will survive for the enjoyment of future generations.

This section is presented in alphabetical order by manufacturers, rather than attempting to use a chronological sequence.

For centuries, the flail was used to beat the grain from the straw. In a day's time, the average worker could thresh from five to seven bushels of wheat using a flail. After this came the job of winnowing to separate the grain from the chaff. It is an interesting phenomenon that the flail continued to be used in certain areas of the country into the early 1900s.

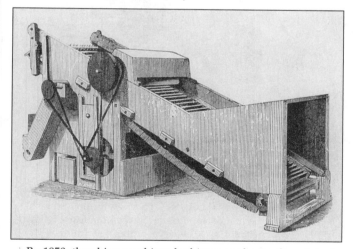

By 1850, threshing machines had improved over the original designs. Shown here is an unnamed design in which the cut grain was fed into the machine where the grain was threshed from the stems and cleaned after a fashion. Despite the crude appearance of these early machines, they represented a substantial improvement over the earlier methods.

Threshing machines of the 1840s were commonly known as "ground hog threshers" or "chaff pilers." These machines simply eliminated the flail, but did not winnow or clean the grain from the chaff. J.T. and E. Warren in New York received several patents for their "thrashing machine" in the 1830s and 1840s, an example of which is shown here. It could thresh as much as 120 bushels of wheat in a single day. One man with a flail would have been a month doing this much threshing.

Advance-Rumely Thresher Co., LaPorte, Ind.

An 1895 issue of *Farm Machinery Magazine* published an engraving of Meinrad Rumely, the founder of this company. He began building grain threshers at LaPorte in 1852, continuing in the business until his death in 1904. The company remained under the title of M. Rumely Co., until a reorganization of 1915, after which time the firm was known as Advance-Rumely Thresher Co. This firm remained in operation until selling out to Allis-Chalmers Manufacturing Co. in 1931.

An extensive history of M. Rumely Co. and Advance-Rumely Thresher Co. is contained in the author's *The Allis-Chalmers Story* (Crestline/Motorbooks: 1988). It details many of the early thresher designs by Rumely. However, the firm progressed until this basic design appeared about 1880. The New Rumely thresher continued on the market until replaced with the Rumely Ideal in 1904. Shown here is a 1903 version of the New Rumely.

Rumely's Ideal separator first appeared in 1904 and remained in production for 20 years. More than 20,000 Ideals of various sizes were built during that time. This one is equipped with a pneumatic stacker, also known as a wind stacker, but the slat stacker was also available.

Built in the 1909-1918 period, the Rumely Ideal Jr. was a small machine built in a 28 x 46 inch size. Thresher sizes refer first to the width of the cylinder, with the latter number referring to the width of the separator. This machine is illustrated with a slat stacker, a simple conveyor to carry the straw to the stack.

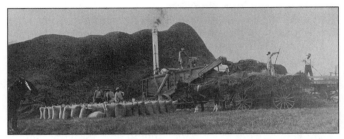

The discussion of threshing would be incomplete without showing what it was like in those days. In this photo, the grain is all being sacked, a common practice in some areas. Two men are pitching bundles into the machine, while the "separator tender" keeps an eye on things from a high vantage point.

In 1918, Advance-Rumely began building all-steel threshers, but also continued to offer the Rumely Ideal all-wood design. These machines were built in several sizes and remained in production until the Allis-Chalmers buy-out of 1931. The latter continued to offer Allis-Chalmers-Rumely threshers for a couple of years, mainly to use up the remaining parts inventory.

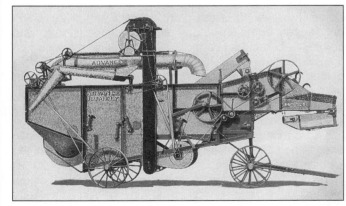

During the 1920s, Advance-Rumely introduced its small 22 x 36 inch All-Steel Thresher. This machine was intended for the farmer wishing to do his own threshing. With its easy running ball bearing design, it could even be pulled by the then-popular Fordson tractor. Small machines like this one were very popular in the 1920s and 1930s.

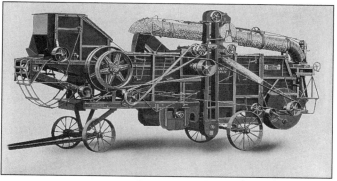

During the 1920s, Advance-Rumely offered a pea and bean thresher. Apparently, it was built for only a few years and probably in small numbers. A likely scenario is that this machine was a takeoff from the Aultman-Taylor pea and bean huller, since Rumely bought out Aultman & Taylor in 1924.

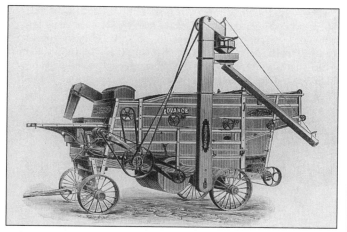

Advance Thresher Co., Battle Creek, Mich.

Advance opened its doors in 1881; 10 years later its thresher took this form. Known as the Advance No. 2 outfit, this separator was a hand-feed model but was equipped with a Washington grain weigher. Note the interesting construction of the weigher—even the delivery spout is made of wood.

Sattley stackers were widely known and used; this simple device was really no more than a conveyor to carry straw to the stack. Sattley was famous for its farm equipment line; among threshermen the Sattley stacker was equally famous. The Advance thresher shown here is of 1903; its machines stayed in essentially this same form until the company was bought out by M. Rumely Co. in 1911.

C. Aultman & Co., Canton, Ohio

Cornelius Aultman began building farm equipment in 1851. Subsequently, the firm began making threshing machines, with its Sweepstakes thresher gaining a great reputation. This was an early apron machine that antedated the vibrator threshers. The grain passed through the cylinder and over an endless open belt, permitting the grain to fall into the cleaning apparatus, then known as the "fan mill."

In the 1880s, the Aultman line included the New Model and Star separators. This one is equipped with a Perfection weigher made by Selby, Starr & Co., Peoria, Ill. The term "separator" became synonymous with the longer term, "threshing machine." Even the Aultman title calls this thresher a "separator."

By 1900, C. Aultman & Co. had developed its American thresher; this one is equipped with a Washington grain weigher made by Daniel Wilde & Son, Washington, Iowa. Numerous companies made grain weighers. Curiously, very few thresher manufacturers built their own feeders, stackers or weighers. In most instances, these items were extra-cost equipment supplied by specialty manufacturers.

Aultman & Taylor Machinery Co., Mansfield, Ohio

In 1866, Cornelius Aultman and H.H. Taylor formed a partnership to build threshers under the Cox & Roberts patents. Its new vibrator thresher evolved into the Globe thresher, shown here in its 1890 version. The smaller size was available in a geared model for use with a horse power, while the two largest sizes were only available as belted machines.

Reflecting the new advances in thresher design, the Aultman-Taylor took this form by 1893. After passing through the cylinder, the grain and straw traveled over vibrating straw racks with the grain falling to a grain pan beneath and the straw continuing to the back of the machine.

By 1915, the Aultman & Taylor New Century separator had already been on the market for about 15 years. Most separators used a feeder, stacker and weigher built by specialty houses; in this instance, a Ruth feeder, Peoria Double-Tube Weigher and a Farmer's Friend Wind Stacker were included.

During the early 1900s, Aultman & Taylor developed a bean and pea huller, continuing with these machines until being bought out by Advance-Rumely Thresher Co. in 1924. The latter then continued making these machines for a short time.

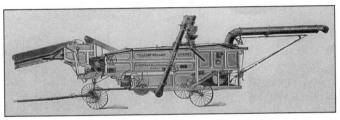

Avery Co., Peoria, Ill.

Avery had its beginnings in farm equipment at Galesburg, Ill., establishing a small factory there in 1877. Seven years later, the company moved to Peoria, Ill.; in 1891 it began building grain threshers, first under the title of Avery & Rouse Steam Thresher Co. Shown here is its 1898 model of the Yellow Fellow Thresher, distinctive because of its deep yellow color and fancy red decoration.

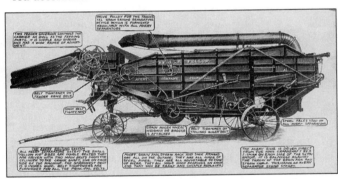

An early Avery catalog illustrates and describes many of the salient features of the Yellow Fellow separators. In those days the catalog was the main sales tool available to farm equipment dealers, aside from state and local fairs. The company's Yellow Fellow trademark was widely known, perhaps because it was so distinctive.

Avery Co. was incorporated in 1907. By that time, the Yellow Fellows were in use all over the United States, as well as in many foreign countries. The company also built steam-traction engines and other farm equipment, even including wagons. This catalog illustration typifies the usual cleanup at the end of the day or when finishing the job.

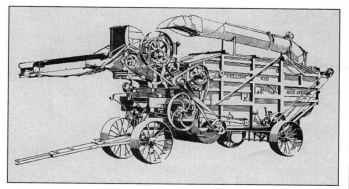

While the Avery Yellow Fellow was built in many sizes, even the smallest machine was too large for small farm tractors. Thus the company introduced its Yellow Kid machine about 1912; this one was specially set up for threshing rice.

By the early 1920s, Avery had come out with an all-steel thresher design; the smallest model was the Avery Yellow Baby. Unfortunately, the company went into bankruptcy, but recovered as Avery Farm Machinery Co. and continued to operate for a few more years.

Avery came out with a "Header-Thresher" in 1923. It was designed to be used in conjunction with a grain header for harvesting grain directly in the field. The thresher was powered by a mounted Avery engine. This unique alternative to the combine was only marketed for a short time.

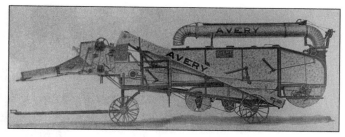

Avery Farm Machinery Co. continued building threshers into the 1930s but few, if any, were built after World War II. The company continued to supply repair parts for a time and eventually disappeared from the farm equipment business.

A.D. Baker & Co., Swanton, Ohio

A.D. Baker & Co. was organized to build steam-traction engines, with threshing machines also coming about the same time. By 1911, the company was building three different sizes of these machines. Advertising of the day notes that "our frame is made of carefully selected and thoroughly seasoned hard maple."

By the 1920s, Baker was offering an all-steel thresher in several sizes. This company was famous for its Baker Locomotive Valve Gear, used on steam locomotives all over the world. In later years, the company built some farm tractors, but production of threshers and tractors ended during World War II.

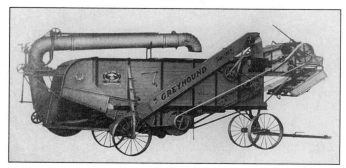

Banting Manufacturing Co., Toledo, Ohio

Research for this book details nothing concerning Banting Manufacturing Co. prior to 1919. At that time, its Greyhound Grain Thresher appears in five sizes, from a small 22 x 36 inch model up to a large 36 x 58 inch machine. By the 1930s, parts for the Greyhound threshers were available from A.D. Baker & Co.

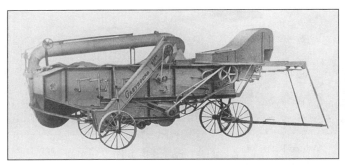

A 1919 Banting catalog illustrates the Greyhound Bean Thresher, a special design for hulling beans and peas. As with its grain threshers, little has been found in the present research concerning the history of the firm, although it entered the tractor business about this same time, and remained in this business for some years. However, its tractors appear to have been contracted from Allis-Chalmers. Curiously, the company remains in the trade directories into the late 1940s, offering repair parts for its steam-traction engines.

Belle City Manufacturing Co., Racine, Wisc.

Although our current research has not determined the origins of this company, an 1894 engraving shows its small Columbia thresher. The company specialized in small threshers and also built feed cutters and other farm equipment.

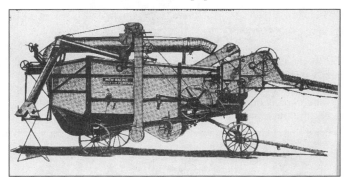

By the 1920s, Belle City had come out with a small all-steel separator; this 1925 style was hailed as "Fordson's Partner," an obvious suggestion to couple it to a Fordson tractor. Belle City continued to offer threshing machines at least until the late 1940s.

Did You Know?

Feed cutters, rare as they are today, have a limited value to vintage machinery collectors—often less than $50.

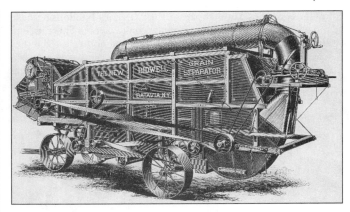

C.H. Bidwell Thresher Co., Batavia, N.Y.

The origins of Bidwell Thresher Co. are unknown; in 1908, the company announced its Bidwell Compound Grain Separator. This advertisement also notes that the company was offering traction engines, but no details are available. Apparently, this machine was built for only a short time.

The Bidwell trade name was well known in the specialty business of bean and pea threshers. By 1918, the Bidwell was being built by Batavia Machine Co., also of Batavia. By the 1930s, repair parts were available from Climax Corporation of the same city.

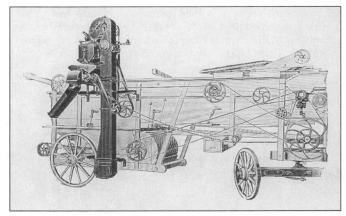

E.M. Birdsall Co., Auburn, N.Y.

This company had its beginnings with a small thresher factory at Penn Yan, N.Y., in 1860. By 1881, the firm was relocated to Auburn where it continued to build threshers and other machinery. Shown here is an 1893 example of its separator with a Perfection weigher. The company slips from view in the early 1900s.

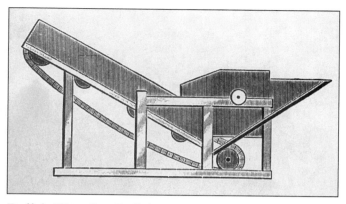

Buffalo Pitts Co., Buffalo, N.Y.

To Hiram and John Pitts go the credit for the beginning of the American threshing machine. In 1831, they built a "ground hog" thresher with their own improvement. This consisted of the open wood raddle chain which carried the threshed grain from the cylinder, permitting the grain and chaff to fall to the ground while elevating the straw to a pile.

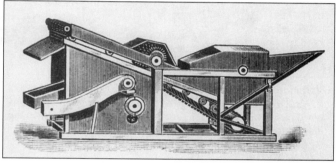

In the 1831-34 period the Pitts brothers experimented with various designs, eventually coming out with the first thresher having a built-in grain separator. This design was patented by the Pitts brothers in 1834. John A. Pitts eventually came to Buffalo, N.Y.; subsequently, his machines got the Buffalo Pitts name. Hiram A. Pitts went to Illinois in 1847 and built threshers in Chicago after 1851. His machines were known as the Chicago Pitts design.

By the 1850s, the Pitts mounted thresher appeared. This was a great forward step, since now the machine was portable and could be moved from farm to farm with relative ease. This was a so-called apron machine because the threshed grain was separated from the straw by traveling over an open wood apron. The straw went to the stack and the grain dropped below to the "fan mill" or separator. Eventually, threshers or threshing machines were simply referred to as separators.

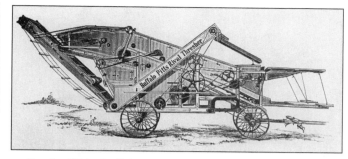

For the 1890s, Buffalo Pitts offered a variety of threshers, including its Rival design. This was an improved version of the early apron machine and was made in five different sizes.

An 1895 offering of Pitts Agricultural Works—as the company was then known—included its California Thresher, built in several sizes and designed specifically for the Western states. By this time, the California and other Pitts designs could be equipped with a self-feeder at extra cost.

Research has not determined when Pitts first built a vibrator thresher, that is, a thresher using shakers instead of the apron design. Its Niagara model of 1895 was a vibrator separator, shown here as a hand-fed machine with a slat stacker, also known to threshermen as a "common stacker."

By 1901, Buffalo Pitts had designed and built a special Bean, Pea and Cow Pea Thresher. Little is known of this design, aside from a few advertisements of the time. It would be an accurate assessment that few were built, even though they appear in Buffalo-Pitts catalogs as late as 1910.

The Buffalo Pitts catalog of 1910 illustrates the company's Rice Thresher. This crop had its own special requirements and most ordinary threshers could thresh and clean the crop only with difficulty. Thus some companies built special machines designed specifically for this crop.

By 1910, Buffalo Pitts had introduced its Niagara Second threshers. They were available in a steel-frame design, using wood to enclose the machine. For a time, these threshers were sold by International Harvester Co. to complement its vast implement line.

Buffalo Pitts Niagara Second threshers were available in steel-frame and wood-frame designs, with the latter being shown here. Although a few companies were building all-steel machines by 1910, the majority were still using wood construction, since this was preferred by many threshermen.

Buffalo Pitts went into receivership in 1914, but reorganized and continued for a few more years. However, by the early 1930s and perhaps sooner, repair parts only were available for these machines. Sometime during the 1930s, the repairs for the Buffalo Pitts separators could be secured from Wagner-Langemo Co., Minneapolis. The latter was then secured by Deere & Co., who began building threshing machines for several years.

Butterworth Universal Thresher Co., Trenton, N.J.

Aside from this 1905 advertisement, little is known of Butterworth. Its Patent Universal Thresher had apparently been on the market for a time, but subsequently was offered by New Jersey Agricultural Works, also in Trenton.

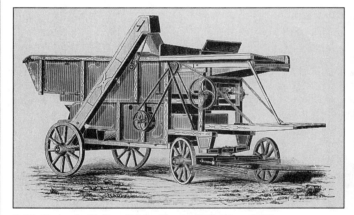

S.K. Campbell Co., Ltd., Central Bridge, N.Y.

Already in 1867, this company began building threshers. From the beginning, it built vibrator threshers. However, little information is now available beyond their descriptions from a 1920 catalog. Its small Thresher No. 2 shown here, had apparently been built in this form for many years.

Did You Know?

Old bucket sprayers were sometimes rather ornate and today are a conversation piece, although their collector value has generally not become more than $10 to $30.

The Campbell catalog of 1920 illustrates its Undershot Thresher No. 1-1/2, commenting that it was being offered in response to numerous demands. It was a small machine, having a cylinder width of 26 inches and a separating width of 36 inches.

The S.K.C. thresher line also included a straw-preserving rye thresher, designed for preserving the straw straight, as required for various industries. The company's 1920 catalog lists this special thresher—complete with the binding attachment—for $600.

Cape Manufacturing Co., Cape Girardeau, Mo.

In 1906, the first Cape separators appeared; this model was among the first to use a revolving rake instead of the time-honored vibrating straw racks. A 1920 catalog notes that the Cape design was made possible by "breaking away from the moss-grown principles" of the past.

Did You Know?

Today, hay knives might sell from $15 to $35.

For 1920, the Cape New Model Separators were built in six different sizes, ranging from a small 24 x 40 inch machine to a big 32 x 56 inch model. The rotary picker and raker system of the Cape New Model was unique; despite the advantages of this machine, it disappears from view by 1930.

J.I. Case Plow Works, Racine, Wisc.

In 1920, Case plow works announced its Wallis Thresher. This machine appears in an initial announcement, but subsequently disappears altogether. It is unknown if the Wallis was actually built at the Plow Works or contracted from another thresher manufacturer.

J.I. Case Threshing Machine Co., Racine, Wisc.

J.I. Case came to Wisconsin in 1842 and began building threshers. By the 1850s, the Case Sweepstakes threshers were on the market. Shown here is one of the earliest advertisements for the machine. At the time, Case built an apron machine like virtually everyone else; the agitator or vibrator design was not yet developed.

Case continued to promote its apron machines for some years after the vibrator designs had come to the market. Into the 1870s, Case built its Eclipse thresher, which was a continuing development over the earliest designs of the 1850s. The development of the Case threshers are detailed extensively in the author's *150 Years of J.I. Case* (Crestline/Motorbooks: 1991).

In 1880, J.I. Case introduced its famous Ironsides Agitator, an entirely new vibrator design. This machine was available with a belt pulley for steam power or it could be furnished as shown, with the necessary gearing to run the separator with a horse power.

Various improvements were introduced on the Case Agitator following its 1880 introduction. For instance, this 1898 model shows the unique tubular return elevator that Case had introduced 10 years earlier. Production of the Agitator continued into the earlier 1900s.

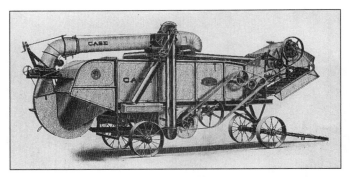

In 1904, J.I. Case Threshing Machine Co. was the first to come out with an all-steel thresher. Many improvements were made to these all-steel machines in subsequent years, but the same basic design remained intact until J.I. Case finally suspended production of threshing machines in 1953.

Caswell Bros., Cherokee, Iowa

In 1908, Caswell Bros. announced its new Gasoline Traction Thresher. This was a self-contained unit, complete with its own engine. When finished with one job, the traction gears could be engaged for moving to the next. Since nothing more is heard of this machine beyond its 1908 announcement, it is presumed that production ended almost before it began. Unfortunately, this very poor illustration is the only one that could be located; even this one is an improvement over the original.

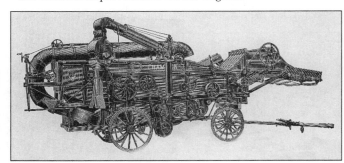

Champion Thresher Co., Orrville, Ohio

For 1903, Champion offered this machine in 24 x 40 and 33 x 52 inch sizes. This was a combined separator and clover huller, with the separate hulling cylinder noted behind the front wheels of the machine. Little is known of this firm aside from the advertisement shown here.

Did You Know?

B.F. Avery & Sons Co. was incorporated in 1877 for $1.5 million. Benjamin Franklin Avery founded the company in 1825 with $400 in capital.

Clark Machine Co., St. Johnsville, N.Y.

This company was building threshers in the early 1900s, but its origins are unknown. In the 1909-11 period, the company advertised its new line of gasoline engines extensively, but they disappear after that time. Shown here is the company's 1914 version of the Clark thresher.

Herman Cook, Sioux City, Iowa

From the May 1908 issue of *American Thresherman* comes an illustration of Cook's Auto-Thresher. It was intended to be a self-contained unit, complete with its own engine and traction wheels. Several different "auto-threshers" appeared about this time, but none of them achieved popularity.

Cripple's Revenge Thresher Co., LaCrosse, Wisc.

In a 1901 issue of *American Thresherman* is this drawing of Cripple's Revenge Thresher, but no other information has been located.

Deere & Co., Moline, Ill.

About 1930, Deere acquired Wagner-Langemo Co. of Minneapolis. From this purchase came the John Deere threshing ma-

chines, marketed for some years afterwards. This machine was built in 24 x 40 and 28 x 52 inch sizes, suitable for small- and medium-sized farms.

Dugan Manufacturing Co., Wichita, Kan.

The Dugan Rotary Separator first appeared in a number of 1909 advertisements, then quietly disappears from the various trade directories and product journals. This machine used a rotary separating system instead of the conventional straw racks, as shown in the sectional drawing.

Ellis Keystone Agricultural Works, Pottstown, Pa.

By the 1890s, Ellis Keystone was offering its Champion threshers in many styles, including this No. 3 Thresher and Cleaner, along with a two-horse railway or tread power. Probably responding to demand, this style remained available at least into the 1920s.

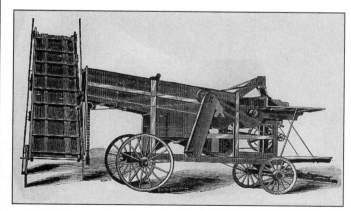

An 1898 engraving shows the No. 3 Ellis Keystone Champion thresher mounted on wheels and set up for operation by a steam-traction engine. This was a simple apron machine and the company continued to build it into the 1920s, long after most firms had opted for all-steel machines.

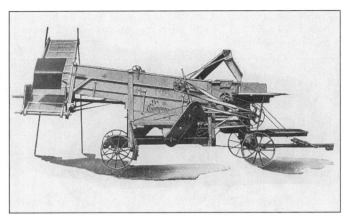

The Ellis Champion remained on the market at least into the 1940s. Trade directories of the late 1950s still show Ellis Keystone Co. as supplying parts for these machines. This small outfit had a 24-inch cylinder and was capable of threshing 35 to 60 bushels of wheat per hour.

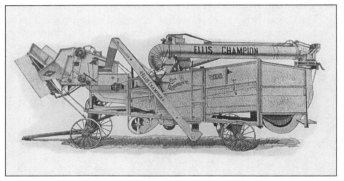

By the 1920s, the Ellis Champion Steel Thresher had arrived; it was a 28 x 46 inch machine capable of handling the work on small- to mid-sized farms. This machine weighed some 5,800 pounds (as shown). Very little is known of the company aside from various trade advertisements.

Emerson-Brantingham Co., Rockford, Ill.

Emerson-Brantingham Co. purchased Geiser Manufacturing Co. in 1912. For some years after, the company continued to build Geiser threshers, with this example coming from its 1919 catalog. E-B also marketed the Reeves threshers, having also bought this firm in 1912. In 1924, the company offered its remaining stock at bargain prices, as it phased out the sale of threshing machines.

Farmers' Independent Thresher Co., Springfield, Ill.

In 1917, this interesting machine appeared. It used two sets of corrugated rolls ahead of the cylinder to rub as much grain as possible from the heads prior to entering a conventional cylinder. The remainder of the machine was built along conventional lines. Aside from a 1917 catalog, little else is known of this firm.

A.B. Farquhar Co., Ltd., York, Pa.

An 1887 article in *Implement & Hardware Magazine* illustrated one of Farquhar's early threshers, called the Excelsior. Little is known of this model. Farquhar began a partnership with W.W. Dingee; after its factory burned in 1859, Dingee went to Racine and the J.I. Case Threshing Machine Co., while Farquhar remained to build his own fortune.

By the 1870s, Farquhar had developed his own apron thresher. Like other apron machines of the time, it carried the straw across an open wooden raddle chain to separate the grain. For many years, the cleaning mechanism was known as a separator or fan mill. The term "separator" eventually became synonymous with threshing machine or thresher, referring to the complete machine rather than one of its components.

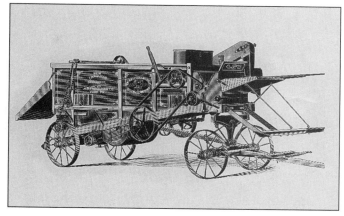

Plain threshers—consisting of a cylinder, feed table and open riddle—were probably among the first of the A.B. Farquhar's developments. This simple machine was fed by hand. The shaker table behind the cylinder served to separate grain and straw, leaving the grain on the floor to be winnowed and sacked as a separate operation. Farquhar continued to manufacture Plain Threshers well into the 1900s.

By 1900, Farquhar had introduced its New Farquhar Separator No. 26. It was an updated version of the earlier Vibrator Separator. Like others of its time, it used a massive wooden frame made of the best materials.

Farquhar's introduction of the Rake Separator is unknown, but presumably it was on the market by the 1880s, perhaps earlier. This machine was widely sold, primarily because of its simplicity and ease of operation. Farquhar continued to build these machines into the early 1900s; it appears that the company would continue to build them on order so long as the company remained in operation.

Recognizing the special needs of the rice crop, Farquhar introduced this special Rice Separator sometime prior to 1900. While it was similar to the standard machines in many respects, it was designed especially for the needs of this special crop. Originally Farquhar's firm was known as Pennsylvania Agricultural Works. In 1889, the official title was changed to A.B. Farquhar Co., Ltd., but the former title also remained in company advertising into the early 1900s.

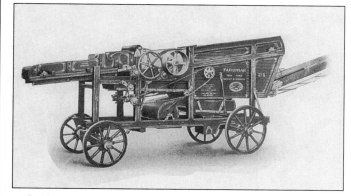

As with many other Farquhar machines, the year when this Vibrator Separator was introduced is now unknown, but probably by the 1880s. Although some farmers and threshermen were determined to hang onto their plain threshers or the simple rake separator, others were just as convinced that the vibrator design was faster and did a better job than the older designs.

In 1910, Farquhar offered this Pea Vine Thresher and Shredder, a machine designed to shed peas from their vines, then shred the vines for use as livestock feed. Presumably the production of this very specialized machine was rather low. Few details are available concerning the No. 1 Pea Huller.

Farquhar introduced its all-steel threshers by the 1920s; a decade later, it was still offering them in 22 x 36 and 28 x 48 inch sizes. The company continued in the business until being bought out by Oliver Corp. in 1952.

Frick Co., Waynesboro, Pa.

George Frick began building threshing machines in the 1840s, but virtually nothing is known of his early designs. By 1884, the company was offering the Vibrating Thresher shown here. It was of simple design and is shown with the common stacker folded over the machine, ready for the road.

By 1900, the company had launched its Landis Eclipse Thresher, an improved design with a distinctive appearance. This one is equipped with a sacking elevator, shown in the foreground. At the time, much of the grain was sacked for storage, rather than being stored in large open bins.

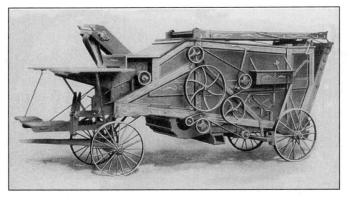

A smaller version of the Landis Eclipse was the Light Eclipse. This machine embodied all the design features of the larger machines but was smaller in size, making it ideal for the small farmer or the small "threshing ring." These groups were frequently formed to pool labor resources among farmers. Thus there was sufficient help to make quick work of the harvest as the separator moved from farm to farm.

About 1913, Frick introduced its Waynesboro Eclipse, a small thresher designed specifically for the farmer wanting to do his own threshing. This machine apparently was a successor to the Light Eclipse introduced some years earlier.

By 1913, Frick came out with its Improved Frick Thresher. This one is shown with a pneumatic stacker presumably, it could also be fitted with a self-feeder. Wind stackers, self-feeders and grain weighers were almost always supplied by specialty manufacturers. About 1930, the company moved toward its growing refrigerating machine business, eventually leaving the farm equipment trade entirely.

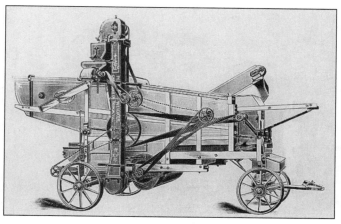

Gaar, Scott & Co., Richmond, Ind.

The firm of A. Gaar & Co. was organized in 1849 to build threshers and other items. After continuing success, the firm was incorporated as Gaar, Scott & Co. in 1870. By the 1890s, the firm was offering this attractive machine; it is fitted with a Perfection weigher from Selby, Starr & Co., Peoria, Ill.

By 1900, the company was offering a wide range of separators in the following sizes: 28 x 49, 31 x 52, 33 x 56, 36 x 60 and 40 x 64 inches. The company also built special Rice Separators. This model is equipped with a self-feeder, grain weigher and wind stacker.

M. Rumely Co., LaPorte, Ind., bought out the Gaar-Scott line in 1911. The latter continued to offer the Gaar-Scott line along with its own Rumely Ideal machines until about 1914. At that time, all thresher lines were combined under the Rumely title and Gaar-Scott disappeared from the scene. Shown here is a Gaar-Scott Junior Separator; this model was built in 20 x 40 and 24 x 44 inch sizes.

Garden City Feeder Co., Pella, Iowa

During the early 1900s, numerous companies specialized in making self-feeders for grain threshers. The Garden City is one such example. As the threshing machine industry developed, few thresher manufacturers developed their own feeder, for reasons now unknown. This firm was eventually bought out by Hart-Carter Co., Peoria, Ill.

Geiser Manufacturing Co., Waynesboro, Pa.

Peter Geiser began building threshing machines already in 1850, setting up a factory at Waynesboro 10 years later. Billed as "The Original Geiser" this machine appears in catalogs of the early 1900s, but no information has surfaced as to when the machine was first introduced. This small machine could be operated with a 6-horsepower steam engine.

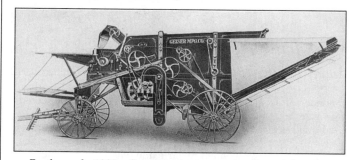

By the early 1900s, Geiser had an extensive line of threshers, including this small machine, designed especially for stack threshing or barn threshing. However, many barn threshers were furnished without wheels and were mounted within the barn. Unthreshed grain was stored in the barn and threshed in the winter months when other farm work was slack.

The No. 4 and No. 5 Geiser separators were built in 24 x 32 and 27 x 39 inch sizes. While this machine had a telescoping wind-stacker pipe, some of the smaller sizes would oscillate, but the blower pipe could not be extended beyond its fixed length. These small separators were very popular with the small farmer and with threshermen whose territory included many small farms.

While most Geiser separators were of the vibrator type, the company also built a raddle machine that dispensed with the shaking straw racks. Thus the company called this its New Peerless Sieveless Separator. A minority of threshermen preferred this style, objecting to the "shaking" of vibrator machines. In reality, well-designed vibrator threshers "shook" very little.

In the early 1900s, Geiser introduced its Peerless Rice Thresher, a machine especially designed for the peculiarities encountered in threshing and cleaning this crop. By this time, Geiser had adopted steel axles for its larger machines; they were less expensive and stronger than wood axles. However, many threshermen still insisted upon wooden construction wherever possible.

Geiser's time in the thresher business lasted until the 1912 buy-out by Emerson-Brantingham Co., Rockford, Ill. The latter continued building the Geiser separators into the 1920s, apparently ending production about 1924. Shown here is the Class A and AA New Peerless separator of 1912.

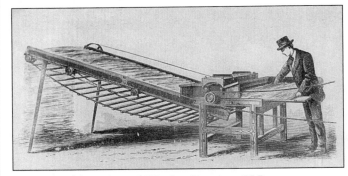

A.L. Gill Agricultural Works, Trenton, N.J.

Peerless Rye Threshers apparently had their beginnings in the 1860s, being built under patents of A.L. Gill. The machine shown here was for threshing rye without injuring the straw. The 66-inch cylinder was wide enough to accommodate the tallest rye. This engraving is from the 1880s.

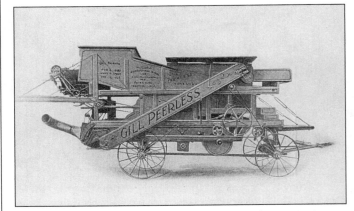

Gill Straight Straw Preserving Threshers included the large Peerless model shown here. To the left is shown the binding attachment; it was a conventional grain binder mechanism that put the straw in neat bundles after threshing. The latter was achieved with a tubular steel cylinder using wooden concaves covered with sheet steel. The straight straw was used for everything from thatched roofs to various industrial applications.

The Peerless grain thresher was a conventional separator, as compared to the company's straw-preserving models. This machine appears to have come onto the market at least by the 1890s, but no history of the firm—of its beginnings or its demise—have appeared.

John Goodison Thresher Co., Sarnia, Ontario, Canada

While the beginnings of this company are unknown, it appears that thresher production ended in the early 1920s. Perhaps as a testimony of its quality, a number of Goodison threshers were sold in the United States, despite the great number of American manufacturers. The machine illustrated here is of 1918 vintage.

Gopher Machine Co., New Prague, Minn.

In the 1920s, the Gopher thresher appeared for a few years—its designers, like many others, probably hoped for success in the very competitive business of building threshing machines. Since the company operated for only a few years, very little is known of its origins. By the late 1920s, the company was out of business and no repairs were available for these machines.

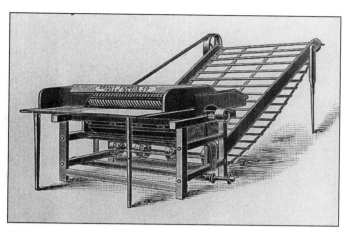

Grant-Ferris Co., Troy, N.Y.

This firm had its beginnings in 1822, it was incorporated under Grant-Ferris Co. in 1894. Virtually nothing is known of the company's history; in the 1890s, the company was still manufacturing this straw-preserving thresher, which it called its Plain Beater.

An 1897 issue of the Grant-Ferris catalog notes that its grain threshers were the inventive result of John G. Snyder of Rensselaer County, N.Y. One of the machines available at the time was this straw-preserving rye thresher, complete with cleaner and binder.

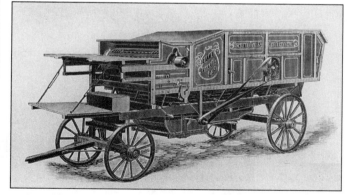

For 1897, Grant-Ferris offered this Combined Oat and Rye Thresher, claiming its Snyder design to be the only successful combination machine on the market. The company was also building grain drills and other farm equipment at the time. Apparently, the firm either sold out or ceased business in the early 1900s; a 1909 issue of the *Farm Implement News Buyer's Guide* lists no farm equipment manufacturers at Troy, N.Y.

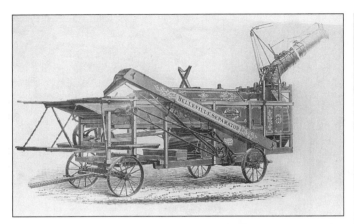

Harrison Machine Works, Belleville, Ill.

This company was originally founded in 1848. Although no direct evidence has been found, it appears that the firm was actually that of John Cox and Cyrus Roberts. The firm began building ground hog threshers at Belleville in 1848; the following year, it added a "vibrating pan" to separate grain from straw. These events are retold in an early Harrison catalog, although the Cox and Roberts names do not appear. The company continued building threshers, eventually organizing under the Harrison name in 1878. Shown here is its Belleville Separator of 1903.

The Belleville line of the early 1900s included many models, including this one with an attached grain weigher and wind stacker. A hand-feed table was furnished as standard equipment; by this time, however, the self-feeder was coming into use.

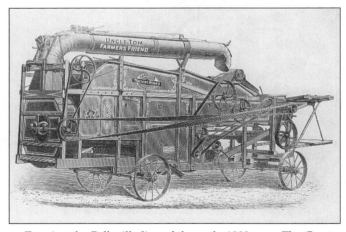

Topping the Belleville line of the early 1900s was The Great Western Separator, shown here with an attached Farmers' Friend Wind Stacker. Many of the early windstackers were mounted as shown, with the open bevel-gear drive being obvious. This machine was built in 32 x 53 and 36 x 57 inch sizes.

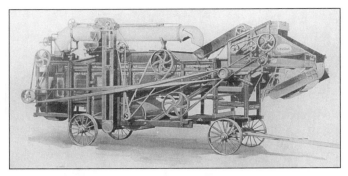

By the 1920s, Harrison Machine Works had redesigned the Great Western as the New Great Western. This machine was much the same as the original design, but embodied many improvements. A Langdon self-feeder is shown, but the plain feed table could still be furnished; instead of the wind stacker, this machine could be furnished with a common stacker if so desired.

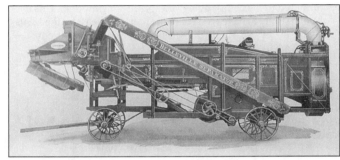

Harrison promoted its threshers into the 1940s and continued to offer repair parts at least into the late 1940s. Its designs changed but little over the years and this 1924 catalog illustration shows its Belleville separator of which it commented, "It has been built continuously by us since 1848."

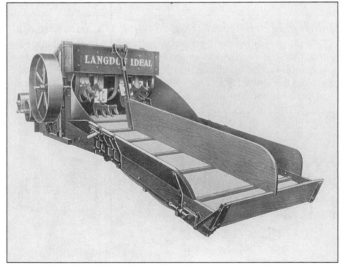

Hart Grain Weigher Co., Peoria, Ill.

In the early 1900s, Hart Grain Weigher rose to prominence as a leading manufacturer of self-feeders and grain weighers for threshing machines. Its equipment could be fitted to virtually any thresher. The company eventually came to a point of dominance, with numerous other product lines being absorbed into the Hart line. Shown here is its Langdon self-feeder of the 1920s.

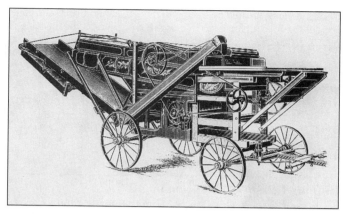

Heebner & Sons, Lansdale, Pa.

David S. Heebner began making various farm implements in 1840. Within a year or so, the company was also making threshers; by the 1890s, Heebner's Little Giant took the form shown here. These small machines were very popular in some regions; the company remained in business until 1926.

Heilman Machine Works, Evansville, Ind.

This company was in the thresher business in the early 1900s, but its origins are unknown. For 1905, the Heilman threshers took the form shown here, as extracted from an advertisement of the period. In the early 1920s, the firm apparently ceased making separators, although repair parts were available from the company into the late 1940s.

Heineke & Co., Springfield, Ill.

Many companies were manufacturing self-feeders for threshing machines in the ealry 1900s, including the Heineke designs. This firm also manufactured the Langdon self-feeder of the Langdon Feeder Co., Kansas City. Eventually, the Langdon came under control of Hart Grain Weigher Co., noted above. Heineke sold more than 3,500 self-feeders in 1919. The company continued in operation into the early 1940s.

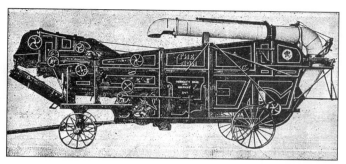

Herrgott Co., Mildmay, Ontario

The origins of the Lion thresher are now unknown, although it continued building threshers into the 1940s. Subsequently, the company was taken over by Lobsinger Bros., which continued to build separators at least into the 1950s.

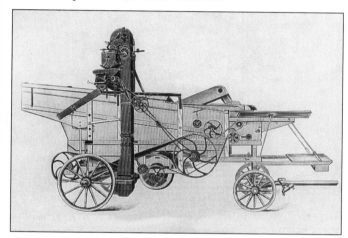

Huber Manufacturing Co., Marion, Ohio

Edward Huber began manufacturing hay rakes in 1865, followed by other machinery in the following years. Threshing machines came along in 1880, with the New Huber of the 1890s being illustrated here.

By 1900, the New Huber separator had been improved over earlier versions, with this model featuring the hand-feed table and a common stacker. This simple conveyor for the straw required little power but was unable to make the large stacks possible with the windstacker. Thus, it required resetting the machine once the straw stack had reached its maximum size.

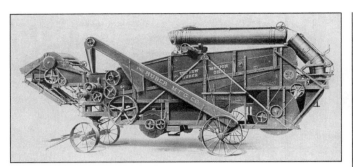

Into the 1900s, Huber came with its larger machines; this one being of about 1912 vintage. At some point, the design changed to the Huber Supreme and these machines were popular in many regions.

By the 1920s, Huber had developed a new all-steel thresher; this one had the new Huber Roto-Rack design. The company continued to build separators into the 1940s, but production was largely suspended because of World War II and never resumed afterward.

In the early 1900s, Huber designed a rice thresher, especially for this crop. A notable difference was that this was a combination machine that could also be converted back to a grain thresher. The backward conversion was relatively simple, but it was not nearly so easy to convert a grain thresher into one suitable for rice.

Built until about 1920, the Huber Bean and Pea Thresher was a special design intended only for this purpose; it was unsuitable for use as a grain thresher. This one is shown with a three-way stacker

for the vines; it could be swung to the left, straight back or to the right for three separate stacks before having to reset the machine.

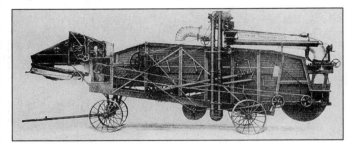

Illinois Thresher Co., Sycamore, Ill.

Wm. N. Rumely was a son of Meinrad Rumely, founder of M. Rumely Co. (see Advance-Rumely Thresher Co.). In 1911, he severed his interests in the company; by 1915, he formed the Illinois Thresher Co. The latter built threshers and traction engines for a number of years, but by the late 1920s, production had ended, although the firm continued to supply repair parts for a few more years.

Indiana Manufacturing Co., Indianapolis, Ind.

In 1891, Indiana Manufacturing Co., began selling windstackers and apparently built these, or contracted for them to be built, for direct sale to farmers. The company soon began buying up new windstacker patents and then sold manufacturing rights to various thresher manufacturers. Shown here is the Uncle Tom's Farmer's Friend stacker of 1895. Thousands of threshing machines were adorned with the famous Farmer's Friend trademark.

International Harvester Co., Chicago, Ill.

International Harvester began marketing threshing machines as early as 1909. These were not built by IHC, but by Belle City Manufacturing Co. About 1913, IHC contracted with Buffalo Pitts Co. for its Niagara Second threshers, selling these also for a time. Shown here is a New Racine thresher of 1911, made for IHC by Belle City.

In 1925, IHC began building its own all-steel threshing machines. These were available in 22 x 38 and 28 x 46 inch sizes. The latter size was large enough for medium sized farms and for small threshing rings. (A "threshing ring" was a group of farmers who banded together for the harvest, pooling their labor, bundle wagons and horses to bring the grain to the separator. They traveled from one farm to another until the harvest was completed). Production of this popular thresher ended in 1956.

Keck-Gonnerman Co., Mt. Vernon, Ind.

Established in 1873, Keck-Gonnerman built a variety of steam-traction engines, tractors, sawmills and threshing machines. Shown here is the K-G Steel Thresher of the late 1920s. This style remained in production into the late 1950s. It was one of the last companies to cease production of threshing machines.

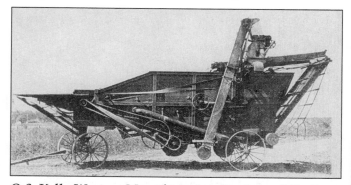

O.S. Kelly Western Manufacturing Co., Iowa City, Iowa

O.S. Kelly was a partner in the firm of Whiteley, Fassler & Kelly already in the late 1850s. This famous company developed the Champion line of harvesting machinery. Kelly got into the threshing machine business in 1882 with the Springfield Engine & Thresher Co.; the latter was eventually known as O.S. Kelly Co. In the late 1890s, Kelly established a factory at Iowa City, Iowa, building the Iowa Separator there for a few years.

Kingsland & Ferguson Manufacturing Co., St. Louis, Mo.

In the 1850s, Kingsland & Ferguson adopted the vibrator separator designs of Cox & Roberts (see Harrison Machine Works above) and commenced building separators in the following years. This 1884 example shows the state-of-the-art at that time, with this machine being set up for operation by steam power. Geared machines for use with a horse power were also available. By 1900, the company disappeared from the scene.

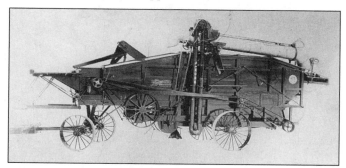

LaCrosse Threshing Machine Co., LaCrosse, Wisc.

Aside from a photograph found at a collector's fair, no information has been located concerning this company or the separator illustrated here. It appears to be a machine of the 1910-1920 period. The unique belting arrangement for driving the wind-stacker is evident, with two idler pulleys being used to keep the belt away from the left rear wheel of the machine.

McOsker Thresher Co., Turon, Kan.

In 1911, Frank McOsker determined to build a thresher suitable to his needs and one that would be the ultimate design. Accordingly, this machine was developed by 1912 in hopes of developing a company to manufacture it. Apparently, this did not materialize, since nothing else can be located in addition to this 1912 illustration from the *American Thresherman Magazine*.

Marion Manufacturing Co., Marion, Ohio

Marion Manufacturing Co. began building Leader engines and threshers in 1886. By 1900, its line included the Leader Northeastern Special shown here; it was equipped with the Leader self-feeder and a Farmer's Friend wind stacker. Like most threshers of its time, the Leader was of all-wood construction.

From all indications, Leader Manufacturing Co. left the thresher business about 1908 for reasons not shown in the present research. By this time, the threshing machine business was very competitive with many different companies trying for a portion of the market and the larger companies trampling the smaller ones with better prices and sometimes a better machine. For whatever reasons, the company does not appear in the trade directories after 1907.

Minneapolis Threshing Machine Co., Minneapolis, Minn.

This company was originally organized in 1874 at Fond du lac, Wis., as Fond du lac Threshing Machine Co. The firm failed. In 1887, it came back to life in Minneapolis under the heading shown here. By 1890, its Victory Separator was well on its way to fame, along with the company's newly designed steam-traction engines.

By the early 1900s, Minneapolis Threshing Machine Co. had become a major manufacturer of grain threshers, offering this model about 1913. Its design included large cylinder teeth—larger than those of any other manufacturer. The company continued in the grain thresher and tractor business until merging with others in 1929 to form Minneapolis-Moline Farm Machinery Co.

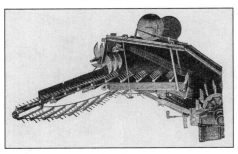

Morley Self Feeder Co., Sioux City, Iowa

In 1904, Morley announced its new self-feeder to the thresherman. At the time, this was the only self-feeder with a built-in automatic governor. Its purpose was to stop the feeder if the speed dropped below a certain level, to prevent slugging the separator. After a few 1904 advertisements, Morley Self Feeder Co. left the scene.

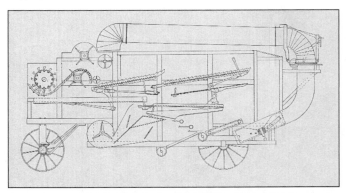

Morningstar Manufacturing Co., Napoleon, Ohio

For a short time, Morningstar advertised its new Napoleon separator, shown here in a cross-sectional view. Aside from a few advertisements, no information concerning this company has appeared. The illustration given here is from a 1903 issue of *American Thresherman Magazine*.

National Machine Co., Columbus, Ind.

A 1903 advertisement in *American Thresherman Magazine* provides an illustration of the National Self-Feeder. As shown, the bundles of grain were pitched into the side conveyors and carried sideways to the feeder for their journey to the threshing cylinder. Little is known of the company except for a few advertisements.

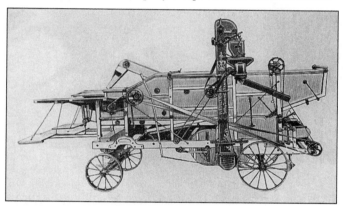

Nichols & Shepard Co., Battle Creek, Mich.

This company had its beginnings in 1848 building small threshers. In 1858, the company began building vibrator threshers, more or less following the earlier Cox & Roberts designs. Its Vibrator Separator was an immediate success and probably did more to revolutionize thresher design than any feature of its time. Shown here is the 1893 model of the Nichols & Shepard New Flag Separator.

About 1906, Nichols & Shepard introduced its entirely new threshing machine called the Red River Special. The name stuck and these machines became immensely popular. This was an all-wood machine and these remained in the line until about 1922, even though its all-steel machine had been introduced a few years earlier.

Responding to the coming of small tractors, Nichols & Shepard introduced its Junior Red River Special by 1914. It was built in 22 x 36 and 28 x 46 inch sizes. This one is equipped with self-feeder, wind stacker and grain weigher, but all of these accessories could be substituted for hand-feed parts and a common stacker.

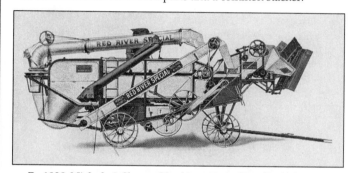

By 1920, Nichols & Shepard had introduced its all-steel version of the Red River Special. This machine was continued after the 1929 merger that formed Oliver Farm Equipment Co. A detailed history of the Nichols & Shepard line may be found in the Author's *Oliver Hart-Parr* (Motorbooks: 1993).

Northwest Thresher Co., Stillwater, Minn.

This company began building threshers in 1874; prior to that, it had functioned as Minnesota Thresher Manufacturing Co. Northwest threshers took the form shown here by 1903 when this engraving appeared in the pages of *American Thresherman Magazine*. In 1912, Northwest Thresher was taken over by M. Rumely Co., LaPorte, Ind.

J.L. Owens Co., Minneapolis, Minn.

While the origins of this company are presently unknown, a 1901 advertisement shows the Owens Bean Sheller, a hand-operated machine designed specifically for the purpose. Subsequently, the company specialized in this business, remaining active at least into the late 1940s.

In addition to its small hand-operated models, Owens also built various sizes and styles of belt-powered bean and pea threshers. Shown here is the 28 x 44 inch double-cylinder style with plain feed table and a common stacker.

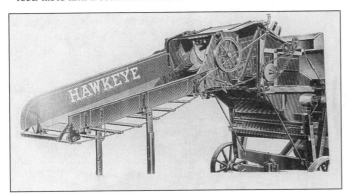

Parsons, Rich & Co., Newton, Iowa

One of the earliest self-feeder attachments was the Hawkeye, shown here in operating position. Subsequently, there were many models and company changes, including the famous Ruth feeders from Parsons Band Cutter & Self-Feeder Co., also at Newton. Few farmers and fewer threshermen were sorry to see the hand feeder become obsolete.

Pioneer Thresher Co., Shortsville, N.Y.

Pioneer Thresher Co. was a successor to the Westinghouse threshers of George Westinghouse. This company was still listed as a thresher manufacturer in the late 1950s. Pioneer threshers of the 1930s took the form shown here and were offered in various sizes and styles.

Port Huron Engine & Thresher Co., Port Huron, Mich.

An 1893 engraving of the Port Huron Rusher separator also illustrates one of the earliest examples of the Farmers' Friend Wind Stacker. Initially, it was a huge rectangular metal chute; in a short time, the latter was changed to the commonly known cylindrical design. Port Huron had its beginnings in 1851, taking its final name in 1890.

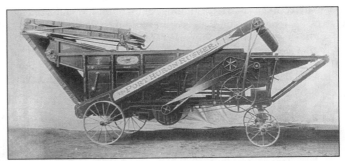

By 1900, the Port Huron Rusher had been upgraded from earlier years, but still retained the same essential design. This machine of that period is equipped with a web stacker, also known as a slat stacker or a common stacker; all three names mean the same thing.

In the early 1900s, Port Huron built a new machine. Although it was of all-wood design, this model of 1910 was offered in several sizes and featured the Port Huron Razor-Back cylinder teeth, guaranteed by the company to save up to $200 a season in grain that would otherwise be lost in the straw pile.

The Port Huron line included a small 20 x 34 inch "Tractor Special" thresher by the 1920s. This small machine was designed to thresh all kinds of grain in addition to its normal fare of wheat and oats. The company continued to build threshers into the 1940s.

Quick & Thomas Co., Auburn, N.Y.

The origins of Quick & Thomas are unknown, but the firm continued building Wide Awake threshers into the 1920s and had parts available for its machines for some years after. Numerous firms built small threshers for those regions in which small farms predominated. Few were sold in the large grain-growing regions.

Randolph Manufacturing Co., Newton, Iowa

In 1904, Randolph announced its new windstacker for grain separators. This unique design used the Randolph "Twin-Fan" system, actually employing two separate fans and discharge spouts as shown. Little else is known of the company aside from the 1904 illustration from *American Thresherman Magazine*.

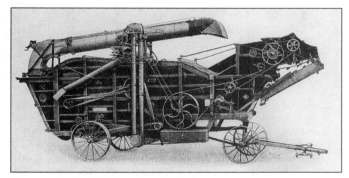

Reeves & Co., Columbus, Ind.

Reeves began building threshers in 1874, coming up through the ranks to a dominant position by 1900. Its 1905 Reeves Compound Thresher took the form shown here, complete with wind stacker, self-feeder and weigher (it was also available without these accessories). The company functioned until 1912 when taken over by Emerson-Brantingham Co., Rockford, Ill. The latter continued building Reeves separators until 1924.

Roberts & Cox, Belleville, Ill.

Cyrus Robert and John Cox began building plain threshers at Belleville in 1848. The following year they adapted a vibrating pan behind the cylinder to separate grain from straw. This was the beginning of the vibrator thresher. About 1856, Cox sold his interest in the company; a year or so later, Roberts also sold out and moved to Three Rivers, Mich. At this location, he became involved again in the thresher business under the title of Roberts, Throp & Co.

Roberts, Throp & Co., Three Rivers, Mich.

As noted under Roberts & Cox above, Cyrus Roberts moved to Three Rivers about 1857. Subsequently, he became involved in the thresher business. Roberts was the originator of the vibrator system of grain separation and this cross-sectional view of the Three Rivers Invincible Thresher of 1884 illustrates how the straw and grain were separated.

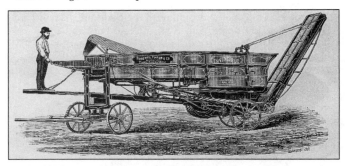

An 1884 engraving shows the Three Rivers Invincible Separator in operating position. The feeder, usually also the owner and the thresherman, is shown standing on the feeder's platform. In the early days of grain binders (when wire was used to tie the band), bits of wire often went through the machine, to the later detriment of livestock. After twine came into use, thresherman held a sharp cutter in one hand; sometimes these were attached with small leather straps to the hand. The bundle was then spread out and fed evenly into the cylinder.

Robinson & Co., Richmond, Ind.

This company had its beginnings in 1842 as a machine shop and later as a farm equipment manufacturer. The company began building threshers in its early days and by 1893 the Bonanza

Separator took the form shown here. This one is equipped with a Perfection weigher from Selby, Starr & Co., Peoria, Ill.

For many years, the company operated under the title of Swayne, Robinson & Co. This illustration of about 1915 shows its Money Maker Separator. Hart-Parr Co., Charles City, Iowa, sold the same machine for a time as the Hart-Parr Money Maker. The company continued building threshers into the 1920s and supplying repair parts into the 1940s.

Russell & Co., Massillon, Ohio

In the 1840s, this company began making simple threshers and building on its early success, the company remained in this business until being sold at auction in March 1927. By 1883, the company was offering the New Massillon shown here with its Patent Lateral Moving Stacker. Russell & Co. had introduced this machine already in 1863 and sold 150 separators the first year.

An 1887 article in *Farm Machinery Magazine* regarding "Modern Threshing Machinery" illustrates the New Massillon thresher of that time. It was a simple and sturdy machine. Eventually, the company would refer to itself as building "the old reliable Russell line."

By 1900, Russell had come out with several new thresher designs, including the Massillon Cyclone shown here. It was built in various sizes and was available with the usual attachments, although this one is shown with a hand-feed table and a common stacker.

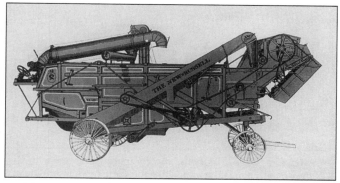

Toward the end of its career in the separator business, the company came out with its New Russell, equipped here with the Massillon Farmers' Friend Stacker, Boss Feeder and Peoria Grain Weigher. When this 1921 model came out, the company was not much longer in business, being sold at auction in 1927. However, parts were available until 1942.

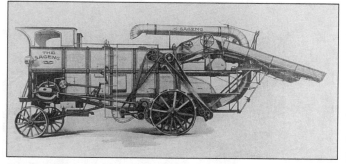

Sageng Threshing Machine Co., St. Paul, Minn.

In 1908, the Sageng Combination Gasoline Thresher appeared. A company was organized to raise $1 million in capital to build the new machine, but the entire plan failed. Sageng had been a missionary in Madagascar for about six years and had developed his ideas for the machine during that time. The Sageng machine was equipped with a 40-horsepower engine.

Did You Know?

Challenge's Daisy Hog Waterers had a 1910 price of $3.

St. Albans Foundry Co., St. Albans, Vt.

This interesting company was building an extensive line of farm equipment by 1880. An engraving of the time shows its "One Horse Power and Thresher." This small outfit with the drive belt sold for $232 a handsome price for the early 1880s. The one-horsepower was also known as a railway power.

Snyder Combined Thresher Co., Troy, N.Y.

Calling it "the two best threshing machines produced," the Snyder Combined was an oat and rye thresher, as well as being a straight straw rye thresher. A small folder in the Author's files gives no indication as to whether this company preceded Grant-Ferris Co. with the Snyder design or whether the firm appeared after Grant-Ferris went out of business. Regardless, John G. Snyder was involved with both companies.

Springfield Engine & Thresher Co., Springfield, Ohio

Organized in 1882, this firm was offering its Improved Springfield Pitts Over-Blast Separator in 1885. This was one of the company's first designs and reflects the use of the Pitts design. The overblast or overshot cleaning fan was designed to direct its blast beneath the riddle, blowing through the grain without blowing it over into the stacker.

One of the finest engravings found in our research for this entire book is represented with this rendering of the New Springfield Vibrating Separator of 1885. This machine was quite modern for its time and brought immediate success for its makers.

To build a large straw stack, the swinging stacker was a necessity. It attached to the back of the separator and received its power from a small belt. After leaving the common stacker, straw was carried to the stack for leveling by men with pitchforks. Eventually, the name of the company was changed to O.S. Kelly Co., reflecting the name of its principal owner.

A.W. Stevens Co., Marinette, Wisc.

This firm began building threshers at Genoa, N.Y., in 1842, moving to Auburn, N.Y., in 1878. For 1893, the company offered the Stevens Apron Thresher shown here. It was built to the preferences of some threshermen who disliked the vibrator machines, although the latter had become the dominant form by this time.

The Stevens New Vibrating Separator of 1893 was essentially the same as the firm had been building for several years. The design was attractive, especially when embellished with extensive decoration. The company moved to Marinette in 1898.

After moving to Marinette, the company emerged with the New Stevens, a machine much like the same model built in Auburn. However, the company designated it thus so as to set it apart from the Stevens Apron Thresher, an older design that still remained with the company in 1903. The firm continued for a few years, but disappears from the farm equipment directories after 1909.

Twin City Co., Minneapolis, Minn.

The Twin City Jr. wood frame thresher was announced in 1922. This design was made in 22 x 36, 24 x 42 and 28 x 46 inch sizes. The Twin City Co. was actually a division of Minneapolis Steel & Machinery Co., builders of the Twin City tractors. Current research has not determined its activity in the threshing machine business prior to this 1922 announcement. In 1929, the firm joined with others to form Minneapolis-Moline.

Waterloo Threshing Machine Co., Waterloo, Iowa

In 1905, Waterloo Threshing Machine Co. advertised its Winnishiek separator, an impressive design shown here with self-feeder, wind stacker and grain weigher. Virtually nothing is known of the firm except that by about 1909, the same machine was being offered by Cascaden Manufacturing Co., also of Waterloo. After that, the Winnishiek disappears from the scene.

Weber Implement Co., St. Louis, Mo.

A few advertisements about 1905 illustrate the Illinois Special Separator, noting that Weber Implement had exclusive sales for this machine. Nothing has surfaced in the present research to indicate the manufacturer of the machine; obviously it was not Weber. After a short time, the Illinois Special disappeared and various trade directories make no mention of it in subsequent years.

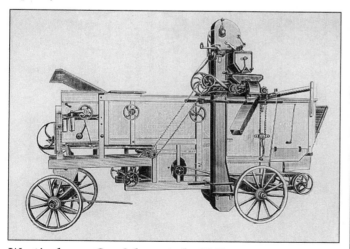

Westinghouse Co., Schenectady, N.Y.

About 1835, George Westinghouse began building threshing machines at Central Bridge, N.Y., moving to Schenectady in 1856. By 1893, the firm had a machine with the appearance shown here from a catalog of Selby, Starr & Co., Peoria, Ill. The latter was illustrating how its Perfection grain weigher could be attached to the Westinghouse machines.

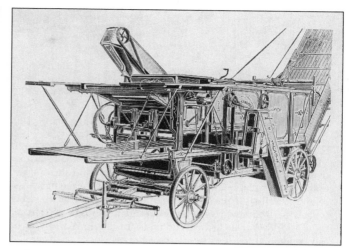

By 1912, the Westinghouse Improved Grain Thresher had already made its name in the marketplace. This 1912 catalog illustration comments that its threshers at the time had steel wheels instead of the wooden ones shown. The company continued into the 1920s, with Pioneer Thresher Co. continuing to supply parts for the Westinghouse machines, as well as building its own designs.

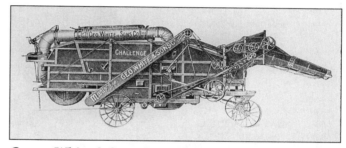

George White & Sons Co., Ltd., London, Ontario

Although this company began building steam-traction engines in the 1870s, the firm did not enter the threshing machine business until 1898. Subsequently, the George White separators became very popular, particularly in the Canadian provinces. The company ended production of traction engines in 1924, but it is unknown when separator production came to a close.

Wood Bros. Thresher Co., Des Moines, Iowa

In the 1890s, F.J. and R.L. Wood began building harvesting machinery, moving their plant to Des Moines in 1899. At this time, the company was incorporated as Wood Bros. Steel Self Feeder Co., reflecting its invention of a self-feeder for separators. Shortly after, the firm began building the Humming Bird separators in various sizes. This one is of 1905 vintage.

In 1911, Wood Bros. Thresher Co. was incorporated as a successor to the Self-Feeder Co. Its line of threshers and steam-traction engines remained very popular. By the 1930s, the firm was offering an all-steel machine; it continued on the market for some time, with production apparently coming to a close with the onset of World War II. As often noted in this book, World War II can be likened to a great curtain in the history of farm implements. After its end, many of the time-honored farming methods ended, to be replaced with new and innovative ideas.

Trade Names

Advance	M. Rumely Co.	LaPorte, IN	1913
Advance	Advance Thresher Co.	Battle Creek, MI	1892
Advance Jr.	M. Rumely Co.	LaPorte, IN	1913
Advance-Rumely	Advance-Rumely Thresher Co.	LaPorte, IN	1915
Agitator	J. I. Case Threshing Machine Co.	Racine, WI	1892
America	Doylestown Agricultural Co.	Doylestown, PA	1909
Andes	W. D. Andes & Son	Leacock, PA	1905
Avery Individual	Avery Co.	Peoria, IL	1924
Avery Yellow Baby	Avery Co.	Peoria, IL	1924
Avery Yellow Kid	Avery Co.	Peoria, IL	1909
Baby Belleville	Harrison Machine Works	Belleville, IL	1924
Baby Huber	Huber Mfg. Co.	Marion, OH	1905
Baker	A. D. Baker Co.	Swanton, OH	1909
Batavia	Batavia Machine Co.	Batavia, NY	1915
Batavia	Climax Corp.	Batavia, NY	1939
Belle City	Belle City Mfg. Co.	Racine Junction, WI	1905
Belleville	Harrison Machine Works	Belleville, IL	1892
Bidwell	C. H. Bidwell Thresher Co.	Batavia, NY	1905
Bonanza	Robinson & Co.	Richmond, IN	1892
Boss	Russell & Co.	Massillon, OH	1913
Bowers	E. Q. Bowers & Son	Hackettstown, NJ	1905
Brasher	P. E. Kennehan's Son & Co.	Brasher Falls, NY	1931
Buch	A. Buch & Sons	Wlizabethtown, PA	1892
Buffalo Pitts	Pitts Agricultural Works	Buffalo, NY	1892
Butterworth	New Jersey Agricultural Works	Trenton, NJ	1892
Campbell	S. K. Campbell Co.	Central Bridge, NY	1905
Campbell	Schoharie Agricultural Works	Central Bridge, NY	1892
Cardwell's	Cardwell Machine Co.	Richmond, VA	1892
Carter Disc	Carter-Mayhew Co.	Minneapolis, MN	1924
Case	J. I. Case Threshing Machine Co.	Racine, WI	1909
Caswell	Caswell Mfg. Co.	Cherokee, IA	1913

Trade Names (cont...)

Cayuga Chief	Birdsall Co.	Auburn, NY	1892
Champion	Champion Thresher Co.	Orrville, OH	1905
Climax	Scheidler Machine Works	Newark, OH	1892
Colean	Colean Mfg. Co.	Peoria, IL	1905
Colorado Special	Harrison Machine Works	Belleville, IL	1915
Columbia	Belle City Mfg. Co.	Racine, WI	1892
Columbia	Blake & Elliott	Racine, WI	1892
Crowell	Crowell Mfg. Co.	Greencastle, PA	1892
Cyclone	Russell & Co.	Massillon, OH	1892
Dakota	Geiser Mfg. Co.	Waynesboro, PA	1892
Daniel Best	Daniel Best Agricultural Works	San Leandro, CA	1892
Davies	Davies Threshing Machine Co.	Oshkosh, WI	1913
Deere	Deere & Co.	Moline, IL	1931
Dixie	Aultman & Taylor Machinery Co.	Mansfield, OH	1892
Doylestown Jr.	Daniel Hulshizer	Doylestown, PA	1892
Dugan Rotary	Dugan Mfg. Co.	Wichita, KS	1909
Dwarf	Roberts Machine Co.	Collegeville, PA	1892
E-B Geiser	Emerson-Brantingham Co.	Rockford, IL	1924
E-B Peerless	Emerson-Brantingham Co.	Rockford, IL	1924
E-B Reeves	Emerson-Brantingham Co.	Rockford, IL	1924
Eddy	W. Eddy & Sons	Greenwich, NY	1892
Ellis Champion	Ellis Keystone Agricultural Works	Pottstown, PA	1892
Empire	Hagerstown Steam Engine & Mach.	Hagerstown, MD	1892
Empire	S. S. Messinger & Son	Tatamy, PA	1892
Farquhar	A. B. Farquhar	York, PA	1892
Fearless	Minard Harder	Cobleskill, NY	1892
Fleetwood	Fleetwood Foundry & Mach. Works	Fleetwood, PA	1905
Freed	Y. C. Freed & Co.	Royersford, PA	1892
Gaar-Scott	Gaar, Scott & Co.	Richmond, IN	1892
Gaar-Scott	M. Rumely Co.	LaPorte, IN	1913
Geiser Peerless	Emerson-Brantingham Co.	Rockford, IL	1913
Globe	Aultman & Taylor Machinery Co.	Mansfield, OH	1892
Gopher	Gopher Machine Mfg. Co.	New Prague, MN	1924
Gray Line	A. W. Gray's Sons	Poultney, VT	1924
Gray's	A. W. Gray's Sons	Middletown Spgs., VT	1892
Great Western	Harrison Machine Works	Belleville, IL	1905
Greyhound	Banting Mfg. Co.	Toledo, OH	1924
Harrisburg	Harrisburg Car Mfg. Co.	Harrisburg, PA	1892
Hart-Parr Money Maker	Hart-Parr Co.	Charles City, IA	1915
Harvey	W. I. Harvey	Lock Haven, PA	1892
Heebner	Heebner & Sons	Lansdale, PA	1892
Heilman	Heilman Machine Works	Evansville, IN	1905
Hirsch	C. V. Hirsch Threshing Machine Co.	Kansas City, MO	1931
Hobson	Hobson & Co.	Tatamy, PA	1892

Trade Names (cont...)

Hooverizer	Wagner-Langemo Co.	Minneapolis, MN	1924
Humming Bird	Wood Bros.	Des Moines, IA	1909
Ideal	Messinger Mfg. Co.	Tatamy, PA	1905
Illinois	Illinois Thresher Co.	Sycamore, IL	1916
Independent	Farmer's Independent Thresher Co.	Springfield, IL	1924
Indiana	Keck-Gonnerman Co.	Mt. Vernon, IN	1924
Invincible	A. D. Baker Co.	Swanton, OH	1905
Invincible	Roberts, Throp & Co.	Three Rivers, MI	1892
Jumbo	John Wolff	Albany, NY	1892
Junior America	Doylestown Agricultural Co.	Doylestown, PA	1924
K. G.	Keck-Gonnerman Co.	Mt. Vernon, IN	1913
Keck-Gonnerman	Keck-Gonnerman Co.	Mt. Vernon, IN	1905
Kingsland	Kingsland Mfg. Co.	St. Louis, MO	1905
Kingsland-Douglas	Kingsland & Douglas Mfg. Co.	St. Louis, MO	1892
Kitten	F. Kitten	Ferdinand, IN	1905
Koger	Koger Pea & Bean Thresher Co.	Morristown, TN	1915
Landis Eclipse	Frick Co.	Waynesboro, PA	1905
Leader	Marion Mfg. Co.	Marion, OH	1905
Leader	Ohio Tractor Mfg. Co.	Marion, OH	1913
Lessig	Lessig & Bro. Agricultural Works	Reading, PA	1892
Lewis	Keystone Farm Machine Co.	York, PA	1913
Little Giant	Heebner & Sons	Lansdale, PA	1892
Little Wonder	Hiram Deats Jr.	Pittstown, NJ	1892
Lucas	John Lucas Co.	Hastings, MN	1892
Marsh	E. B. Marsh & Bro.	Snydersville, PA	1892
Massillon Cyclone	Russell & Co.	Massillon, OH	1905
Massillon Low-Down	Russell & Co.	Massillon, OH	1905
McCormick-Deering	International Harvester Co.	Chicago, IL	1924
McOsker	McOsker Thresher Co.	Turon, KS	1911
Minneapolis	Minneapolis Threshing Machine Co.	Hopkins, MN	1905
Minnesota Chief	Minnesota Thresher Mfg. Co.	Stillwater, MN	1892
Money Maker	Robinson & Co.	Richmond, IN	1905
Monitor	Aaron Wissler	Brunnerville, PA	1892
Morningstar	Morningstar Mfg. Co.	Napoleon, OH	1905
Napoleon	Napoleon Mfg. Co.	Napoleon, OH	1905
New Century	Aultman & Taylor Machinery Co.	Mansfield, OH	1905
New Chalfant	John N. Chalfant & Sons	Lenover, PA	1892
New Champion	Krauss Bros.	Geryville, PA	1892
New Champion	Orrville Machine Co.	Orrville, OH	1892
New Champion	R. I. Schlabach	Nazareth, PA	1892
New Elward	Avery & Rouse Steam Thresher Co.	Peoria, IL	1892
New Era	Heilman Machine Works	Evansville, IN	1892
New Farquhar	A. B. Farquhar	York, PA	1905
New Huber	Huber Mfg. Co.	Marion, OH	1892
New King	Fleetwood Foundry & Mach. Works	Fleetwood, OH	1905
New Model	Cape Mfg. Co.	Cape Girardeau, MO	1924
New Model	Groton Bridge & Mfg. Co.	Groton, NY	1892

Trade Names (cont...)

New Peerless	Geiser Mfg. Co.	Waynesboro, PA	1892
New Process	LaCrosse Threshing Mach. Mfg. Co.	LaCrosse, WI	1905
New Racine	Belle City Mfg. Co.	Racine, WI	1915
New Racine	International Harvester Co.	Chicago, IL	1913
New Rumely	M. Rumely Co.	LaPorte, IN	1892
New Stevens	A. W. Stevens Co.	Marinette, WI	1905
New Vibrator	Nichols & Shepard Co.	Battle Creek, MI	1892
Newtown	A. Blaker & Co.	Newtown, PA	1892
Niagara	Buffalo Pitts Co.	Buffalo, NY	1905
Niagara Junior	Buffalo Pitts Co.	Buffalo, NY	1905
Niagara Second	Buffalo Pitts Co.	Buffalo, NY	1905
Nichols & Shepard	Oliver Farm Equipment Co.	Chicago, IL	1931
Northwest	Northwest Thresher Co.	Stillwater, MN	1905
Ohio Favorite	Ohio Thresher & Engine Co.	Upper Sandusky, OH	1892
Oscillator	John S. Davis' Sons	Davenport, IA	1892
Owens	J. L. Owens & Co.	Minneapolis, MN	1892
Paris Broomcorn	Paris Foundry & Mach. Works	Paris, IL	1913
Peerless	A. L. Gill Agricultural Works	Trenton, NJ	1870
Peerless	Ezra F. Landis	Lancaster, PA	1892
Peerless	Trenton Agricultural Works	Trenton, NJ	1892
Pennsylvania	Heebner & Sons	Lansdale, PA	1892
Pioneer-Westinghouse	Pioneer Thresher Co.	Shortsville, NY	1931
Port Huron Rusher	Port Huron Engine & Thresher Co.	Port Huron, MI	1892
Prairie Queen	Prairie Queen Mfg. Co.	Newton, KS	1909
Pride of Shenendoah	Edinburgh Agricultural Works	Edinbirgh, VA	1892
Pride of Washington	Gilbert Hunt & Co.	Walla Walla, WA	1892
Racine	Johnson & Field Co.	Racine, WI	1892
Red River Special	Nichols & Shepard Co.	Battle Creek, MI	1905
Red River Special	Oliver Farm Equipment Co.	Chicago, IL	1931
Reeves	Reeves & Co.	Columbus, IN	1905
Richardson	E. D. Tichardson Mfg. Co.	Cawker City, KS	1929
Richmond	H. M. Smith & Co.	Richmond, VA	1892
Roberts & Cox	Roberts & Cox	Belleville, IL	1848
Robison	J. Robison & Son	Curwensville, PA	1892
Rumely	M. Rumely Co.	LaPorte, IN	1905
Rumely Ideal	M. Rumely Co.	LaPorte, IN	1909
Rusher	Port Huron Engine & Thresher Co.	Port Huron, MI	1905
S. K. C.	S. K. Campbell Co.	Central Bridge, NY	1913
Sageng	Sageng Threshing Machine Co.	St. Paul, MN	1908
Samson	Samson Tractor Co.	Janesville, WI	1929
Seneca	New Birdsall Co.	Auburn, NY	1905
Spence	L. Spence & Son	Martin's Ferry, OH	1892
Springfield	O. S. Kelly Co.	Springfield, OH	1892
St. Albans	St. Albans Foundry Co.	St. Albans, VT	1892
St. Johnsville	St. Johnsville Agricultural Works	St. Johnsville, NY	1892
Star	C. Aultman & Co.	Canton, OH	1892

Trade Names (cont...)

Sterling	International Harvester Co.	Chicago, IL	1913
Stevens	A. W. Stevens & Son	Auburn, NY	1892
Tiger	Gaar, Scott & Co.	Richmond, IN	1909
Tiger	J. S. Rowell Mfg. Co.	Beaver Dam, WI	1892
Turner	Turner Mfg. Co.	Statesville, NC	1931
Twin City	Minneapolis Steel & Machy. Co.	Minneapolis, MN	1924
Union	J. E. Armour	Philadelphia, PA	1892
Victory	Minneapolis Threshing Machine Co.	Minneapolis, MN	1892
Wagner-Langemo	Deere & Co.	Moline, IL	193
Wallis	Massey-Harris Co.	Racine, WI	1927
Westinghouse	Westinghouse Co.	Schenectady, NY	1892
Wheelock	Stephen G. Cree	Wheelock, VT	1892
White's 20th Century	Orangeville Agricultural Works	Orangeville, PA	1905
Whitman's	Whitman Agricultural Works	Auburn, ME	1892
Wide Awake	Bowen & Quick	Auburn, NY	1905
Williams	Clark Machine Co.	St. Johnsville, NY	1913
Winnishiek	Waterloo Threshing Machine Co.	Waterloo, IA	1905
Yellow Fellow	Avery Co.	Peoria, IL	1905
Young Chief	Aaron Wissler	Brunnerville, PA	1892

Transplanters

By the early 1900s, various companies approached the mechanization of planting small seedlings. Until that time, small plants such as tobacco, cabbage, tomatoes and similar truck crops were planted by hand. Transplanters saved many hours of hard work compared to hand methods. They became fairly popular with large growers. During the research for this book, we came across several different makes, although there surely are more that we were unable to access.

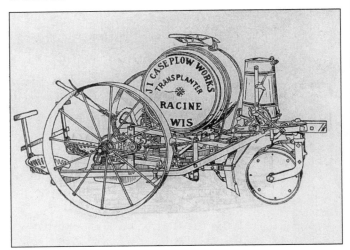

J.I. Case Plow Works, Racine, Wis.

In the 1920s, the J.I. Case Transplanter appeared; it has a great similarity to the Bemis transplanter from Madison Plow Co. The water tank was provided to give the seedlings an extra drink of water upon landing in their new home.

A.B. Farquhar Co., Ltd., York, Pa.

Farquhar bought out Bateman Manufacturing Co., of Grenloch, N.J., in 1930. The latter had developed a transplanter some years earlier. Farquhar sold them for at least a decade prior to buying the company.

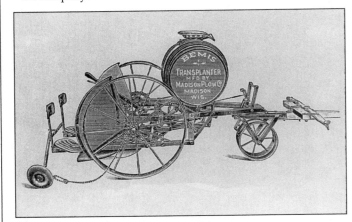

Madison Plow Co., Madison, Wisc.

A 1912 catalog of Madison Plow Co., illustrates its Bemis Transplanter. The Bemis had previously been built by Fuller & Johnson Manufacturing Co., but when it opted out of the farm machinery business, Madison took over the line, including the Bemis Transplanter.

New Idea Inc., Coldwater, Ohio

By 1940, perhaps earlier, New Idea was offering a transplanter for truck gardeners of the style shown here. It differed from most others because the laborers were seated forward instead of at the back of the machine. The transplanter became especially valuable when labor was scarce during World War II.

J.L. Owens Co., Minneapolis, Minn.

By the 1920s, this firm was offering the Owens Transplanter as an automatic and self-setting machine, somewhat more advanced than some of its competitors. The company continued to make these machines for a few years; by the late 1930s, it was out of production, although the company continued to supply repair parts.

Tread Powers

Under the heading of Horse Powers will be found a number of tread powers, also called tread mills or railway powers. The latter name is a reference to the wheel and track arrangement similar to a train. The tread power was fairly well developed by the 1830s and was one of the first means of rotary power available to the average farmer. A fortunate few were near a stream where water power could be secured and wind power was entirely dependent on windy days to accomplish any work.

J.S. Brubaker, Freeport, Ill.

From about 1885, comes this engraving of a small dog power, suitable for turning a sausage grinder or other light duties. At the time, the centrifugal cream separator was not a reality, nor were there any power washing machines, so the applications for a small power were quite limited.

S.S. Messinger & Son, Tatamy, Pa.

From the 1880s comes this illustration of Messinger's railway power, complete with a separator. The advertisement notes that the power could be furnished for one, two or three horses. This early manufacturer was offering an extensive line of farm equipment by 1885.

Search Manufacturing Co., Sheboygan Falls, Wisc.

Most railway powers were inclined, although some were built in a horizontal pattern as shown. Search Manufacturing Co. also built threshers and other farm machines, but current research has not found any illustrations aside from this Horizontal Tread Power.

Whitman Agricultural Co., St. Louis, Mo.

By the 1880s, Whitman was manufacturing a large number of farm machines, including the Whitman Tread Power. This one was of the usual inclined design. As is obvious in this engraving, the movement of the tread turned a pair of large gears meshing with pinions on the pulley shaft. This greatly increased the belt speed and it was further enhanced by the use of a large band wheel.

Trade Names

All-Right	Sperry Mfg. Co.	Owatonna, MN	1905
Baby	Messinger Mfg. Co.	Tatamy, PA	1905
Bay State	B. F. Rollins & Co.	St. Johnsbury, VT	1892
Belle City	Belle City Mfg. Co.	Racine, WI	1892
Bowers	R. Q. Bowers & Son	Hackettstown, NJ	1905
Buch	A. Buch & Son	Elizabethtown, PA	1892
Butterworth	New Jersey Agricultural Works	Trenton, NJ	1892
Campbell	Schoharie Agricultural Works	Central Bridge, NY	1892
Carpenter's	Carpenter & Genung	Independence, IA	1892
Case	J. I. Case Threshing Machine Co.	Racine, WI	1892
Chalfant	John N. Chalfant & Sons	Lenover, PA	1892
Champion	Fleetwood Foundry & Machine Co.	Fleetwood, PA	1905
Champion	Krauss Bros.	Geryville, PA	1892
Chief	Appleton Mfg. Co.	Appleton, WI	1892
Comstock	Geo. S. Comstock	Mechanicsburg, PA	1892
Doylestown	Daniel Hulshizer	Doylestown, PA	1892
Emery's	Ann Arbor Agricultural Co.	Ann Arbor, MI	1892
Emery's	D. O. Everest Co.	Pine Grove Mills, MI	1892
Empire	S. S. Messinger & Son	Tatamy, PA	1892
Enterprise	Harder Mfg. Co.	Cobleskill, NY	1905
Enterprise	J. McDermaid	Rockford, IL	1905
Excelsior	Daniel Hulshizer	Doylestown, PA	1892
Excelsior	Doylestown Agricultural Works	Doylestown, PA	1905
Farmer's Friend	Morton Mfg. Co.	Romeo, MI	1892
Farquhar's	A. B. Farquhar Co.	York, PA	1892
Fearless	Minard Harder	Cobleskill, NY	1892
Gowanda	Gowanda Agricultural Works	Gowanda, NY	1905
Gray's	A. W. Gray's Sons	Middletown Spgs, VT	1905
Heebner's	Heebner & Sons	Lansdale, PA	1892
Hildreth	Hildreth Bros.	Harvard, MA	1892
Ideal	Stoddard Mfg. Co.	Rutland, VT	1905
Keystone	Ellis Keystone Agricultural Works	Pottstown, PA	1892
Lamb's	Lamb & Co.	Freeport, IL	1905
Lessig's	Lessig & Bro. Agricultural Works	Reading, PA	1892
Little Giant	E. W. Ross Co.	Springfield, OH	1892
Lyon	Lyon Iron Works	Greene, NY	1905
Marsh	E. B. Marsh & Bro.	Snydersville, PA	1892
McDermaid's	J. McDermaid	Rockford, IL	1905
Monarch	Smalley Mfg. Co.	Manitowoc, WI	1905
Morton's	Morton Mfg. Co.	Romeo, MI	1892
New Champion	R. I. Schlabach	Nazareth, PA	1892
New Model	Roberts Machine Co.	Collegeville, PA	1892
Newtown	A. Blaker & Co.	Newtown, PA	1892
Novelty	Novelty Iron Works	Dubuque, IA	1892
Owatonna	Owatonna Fanning Mill Co.	Owatonna, MN	1905
Peerless	Trenton Agricultural Works	Trenton, NJ	1892
Pittstown	Hiram Deats Jr.	Pittstown, NJ	1892
Robison	J. Robison & Son	Curwensville, PA	1892
Ross	E. W. Ross Co.	Springfield, OH	1892
Royal	Appleton Mfg. Co.	Appleton, WI	1892

Trade Names (cont...)

Search	Search Mfg. Co.	Oshkosh, WI	1905
Smalley	Smalley Mfg. Co.	Manitowoc, WI	1892
St. Albans	St. Albans Foundry Co.	St. Albans, VT	1892
St. Johnsville	St. Johnsville Agricultural Works	St. Johnsville, NY	1892
Star	Star Mfg. Co.	Carpentersville, IL	1905
Star	Wilder-Strong Implement Co.	Monroe, MI	1905
Success	Appleton Mfg. Co.	Batavia, IL	1905
Tally Ho	Hartford Plow Works	Hartford, WI	1905
Triumph	Daniel Hulshizer	Doylestown, PA	1892
Union	Ames Plow Co.	Boston, MA	1892
Union	B. F. Rollins & Co.	St. Johnsbury, VT	1892
Union	J. E. Armour	Philadelphia, PA	1892
V. F. M.	Vermont Farm Machine Co.	Bellows Falls, VT	1905
Westinghouse	Westinghouse Co.	Schenectady, NY	1892
White	Orangeville Agricultural Works	Orangeville, PA	1905
Whitman's	Whitman Agricultural Works	Auburn, ME	1892
Whitman's	Whitman Agricultural Co.	St. Louis, MO	1892
Wolff	John Wolff	Albany, NY	1892

W

Wagons & Carriages

Research for this book discovered literally hundreds of carriage and wagon manufacturers. In addition to those we found, there were hundreds more for which we had no access and legions beyond that which were small companies that sold all of their product within a 50-mile radius. In fact, complete books have been written about wagons and other vehicles, so this volume makes no pretense of being in any way complete.

In reality, wagons and carriages were two separate industries. Some manufacturers produced both kinds of vehicles, but many of them specialized in one or the other. Many frontier farmers considered themselves lucky to have a wagon; a carriage was only something to be admired and wished for. In addition, wagons were usually pulled with draft horses; pulling a carriage with draft horses would have been as silly as hauling a load of hogs to town with a pair of fancy driving horses. Eventually, most farmers were able to afford both, a wagon for daily work and a carriage for attending church or going for an occasional visit. Today, most farm wagons in reasonably good condition will bring $500 or more, while a good carriage will be much more expensive. Nicely restored carriages—especially one that is quite fancy and equipped with brass driving lights and other paraphernalia—can often bring $2,000 or more.

Ordinarily, the farm wagon was supplied as a double box—that is, the main box, plus one set of sideboards and endgates. A triple-box wagon usually had the second set of sideboards furnished at extra cost. Wagons used in hilly country were usually fitted with brakes. In the level country of the plains, brakes were seldom used. If the farmer wanted to sit down while driving, a board placed across the box was sufficient; for an extra cost, a spring seat could be purchased.

For reasons unknown, wagons were almost always painted green. Seldom did wagon makers use any other color. Likewise, the wheels were almost always painted red. Many wagons were adorned with ornate striping and lettering and this could be almost any color. Carriages were almost always painted a very dark green or simple black. The dark green may be likened to Brewster Green or Quaker Green. Ironically, the fancy coachwork of the 1890s helped bring the carriage to an end. Those experimenting with horseless carriages aptly named them at the time, for many of them were little more than a carriage powered by a gasoline engine. Most wagon and carriage makers continued business as usual for as long as they could. A few used their talents in the emerging automobile business, but most of them slowly vanished in the 1920s. Of those still holding on, most were then vanquished by the Great Depression.

F.A. Ames & Co., Owensboro, Kty.

In 1895, Ames offered this fine carriage—No. 65 Mascot—complete with driving lights and a fringed top.

Ames-Dean Carriage Co., Jackson, Mich.

For 1898, Ames-Dean offered its No. 46 End Spring Surrey, a two-seater with upholstered seats and likely a leather dashboard. The company also built Banner wagons and other vehicles.

Appleton Manufacturing Co., Batavia, Ill.

For 1917, Appleton offered this steel-wheeled running gear, suitable for any standard 10-foot wagon box. It was made in four sizes, ranging from a capacity of about 500 pounds up to a heavy gear capable of two tons. Steel wheels on wagons first appeared in the 1890s.

The Aultman Co., Canton, Ohio

With the coming of the steam-traction engine came the need for a water wagon. Many engine builders supplied water wagons, including the 1902 Star wagon, shown here from Aultman.

Bain Wagon Co., Kenosha, Wisc.

Bain Wagon Co. had its beginnings in the 1860s. By the time this 1906 model appeared, the company had more than 40 years of experience in the wagon business.

J. G. Baumann, Clarence, Cedar County, Iowa

An 1875 Iowa Atlas illustrates the Baumann Carriage & Wagon Shop. Building even the simplest wagons required extraordinary skill, usually acquired through a long apprenticeship. Prior to the days of power woodworking machinery, this occupation also required above average physical skill.

Beggs Bros., Carrollton, Mo.

Beggs Bros. began building wagons about 1880. By 1895, it offered this attractive design; the tailgate shown in the engraving was highly decorated, as was the remainder of the wagon.

Given some of the design similarities, Beggs-Goodson Wagon Co., Hannibal, Mo., was likely connected with the Beggs Bros. firm. A 1903 advertisement shows the Beggs-Goodson of the time; Beggs-Goodson billed itself as "wholesale wagon manufacturers."

Birdsell Manufacturing Co., South Bend, Ind.

Aside from being manufacturers of the renowned Birdsell clover hullers, this firm also built wagons for many years; like the hullers, Birdsell wagons were of the finest quality. A spring seat was often sold with a wagon, but usually as an extra-cost item.

Wm. W. Boob, Coburn, Pa.

A few companies specialized in building road carts, while others included them as part of an overall line of vehicles. Shown here is the Champion Phaeton road cart.

Brown Manufacturing Co., Zanesville, Ohio

As with many wagon manufacturers, little is known of Browns' early history. The company remained in business for some years, with this being a 1924 example of the Brown wagon.

Buerkens Manufacturing Co., Pella, Iowa

In the early 1900s, Buerkens built a series of wagons, pointing to its use of hickory axles and white oak wheel hubs. Wagons were sometimes subjected to horrendous strains, especially when roads turned to a sea of mud.

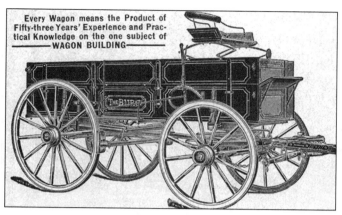

Burg Wagon Company, Burlington, Iowa

Going back to 1851, Burg had been established for over half a century when this 1905 advertisement appeared. The company reached a considerable market in the midwestern states, as well as distribution points on the Pacific coast.

Burnham Mfg. Company, Charles City, Iowa

An early 1900s advertising folder illustrates the Gem City Wood Wheel Truck. It noted: "Each [wagon] is the result of 25 years of successful experience." In many instances a small wagon maker might have several employees and a thriving business. When the owner, (likely the resident expert), retired or died, no one with the money or expertise, was left to carry on. A large number of these companies operated for only 30 to 40 years.

For the 1910 market, Burnham offered their steel Improved Bryson Truck. In many instances, certain parts, such as the bolsters, were built of wood. Burnham noted all running gear parts were hand painted, using the "best quality of red lead paint, ground in oil." Almost all running gears were adorned with attractive pinstripes, then given two or three coats of varnish.

Capital City Carriage Co., Des Moines, Iowa

For 1906, this firm built a wide range of carriages, buggies, surreys and other vehicles. Nothing is known of the company history; it presumably ended with the coming of the automobile.

Columbia Carriage Company, Hamilton, Ohio

An endless variety of carriages and vehicles emerged from hundreds of manufacturers, especially in the 1890-1920 period. Included was this elegant 1905 design from Columbia Carriage Company.

Columbian Wagon & Body Company, Columbia, Pa.

Farm wagons were built in various patterns, depending on the region. This Columbian style was made expressly for "Maryland, Delaware, and Southern States. "

An early 1900s Columbian catalog notes: "These wagons are built after the pattern of one-horse wagons built in local shops of that territory." Columbian called the style shown here "Our New England One-Horse Wagon."

Shown here is the Columbian Pennsylvania or Eastern Style Wagon. It was built after the pattern dictated by local custom in the region.

Ordinarily, this Maryland, Delaware, and Southern Wagon was built with plain-banded wheels. It could also be furnished with Sarven wheels. Depending on local custom, it could be equipped with slip, drop, or half stiff tongues.

The South New Jersey wagon pattern was built in keeping with the customary design used in South New Jersey. Of particular note are the unique Jersey standards mounted to the front and rear bolsters.

The New York Columbian Wagon was a style developed in much of the state in observance of local custom and to meet customer needs. Sarven or Warner wheels were commonly used on this style.

Sarven Patent wheels were standard equipment for this wagon of the early 1900s. Columbian billed it as their "New England Two-Horse Wagon."

In the early 1900s, Columbian offered this Special Pennsylvania Style Hay Wagon, apparently based on a pattern developed in Lancaster and Lebanon Counties. The body could be 16- or 18-feet long.

In addition to an extensive line of farm wagons, Columbian also offered numerous municipal styles. Included was the Dumping Wagon shown here. Its capacity was 1 ½ or 2 cubic yards, as desired. Columbian sold this style as The Susquehanna.

An unusual design was the Columbia Wet Garbage Wagon, offered in three different sizes. The body was built of boiler plate and included a center-hinged lid.

J. M. Childs & Company, Utica, N.Y.

From an 1878 catalog comes an engraving of the Childs Farm and Freight Wagon. This firm operated as a farm machinery manufacturer and wholesaler. It began business in the 1850s.

For 1898, Columbus offered this No. 118 Extension Top Carriage. The majority of carriage makers offered their vehicles to dealers. A minority sold them direct to the consumer. Silverplated hub bands could be furnished at no additional cost.

Instead of an extension top carriage like the No. 118, this style could also be furnished as a canopy top carriage, complete with side curtains for those rainy days.

The 1898 Columbus No. 114 Surrey was regularly furnished with fenders and driving lamps. A black body was standard, but running gear and wheels could be finished in black, Brewster Green, or carmine.

Quite often, a phaeton like this No. 250 from Columbus was hung on two springs. For those who desired, it could be furnished with a three-spring mounting. Storm curtains often were stored under the seat.

Although using conventional elliptic end springs, the No. 49 Columbus also featured longitudinal side springs. While this gave greater support and stability, it also provided a stiffer ride.

The Columbus No. 46 buggy was identical to the No. 40, except for spring suspension. The No. 46 Brewster used the patented Thomas coil springs on each corner. This design only was used on the Brewster. No other buggy styles were equipped with Thomas coils.

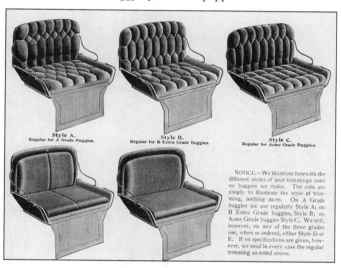

NOTICE.—We illustrate herewith the different styles of seat trimmings used on buggies we make. The cuts are simply to illustrate the style of trimming, nothing more. On A Grade buggies we use regularly Style A; on B Extra Grade buggies, Style B; on Acme Grade buggies Style C. We will, however, on any of the three grades use, when so ordered, either Style D or E. If no specifications are given, however, we send in every case the regular trimming as noted above.

These illustrations represent the style trimmings which we use in Carriages, Surreys, Phaetons and Park Wagons. Style F is the regular trimming for all these vehicles, and when no specifications are given they will always be trimmed in this way. We will, however, on any of the vehicles trim either in Style G or H when so ordered.

On page 45 we show a buggy seat ironed. This cut is submitted to show our customers the manner in which we iron our buggy seats. The seat of every buggy which leaves our factory is ironed in this manner.

It will be apparent, we think, to the casual observer that the work is done in a very substantial way. With any reasonable care the seat should stay intact for years.

Carriage, Surrey, Phaeton and Park Wagon seats are also ironed in equally as substantial way.

All carriage makers offered various kinds of seats for use with their vehicles. The plain ones were less expensive, and the detailed styles embodied far more material and work. Fabric choices included various grades of wool, or even leather.

Compressed Band Hub.   Sarven Hub.

Two distinct wheel styles were used from 1890 onward. On the left is the compressed band hub. Steel bands either were shrunk over the hub, or pressed in place hydraulically. This style was used almost exclusively on farm wagons and heavier running gears. On the right, is the Sarven Patented Hub. It used solid iron flanges, pressed onto the hub hydraulically and secured with rivets through both halves. This style was popular on light wagons and most kinds of vehicles.

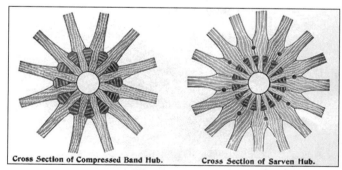

The Thomas coil spring suspension system was an early production venture for a torsion spring suspension system. Although it probably functioned satisfactorily, elliptic springs would be the most popular choice for decades to come.

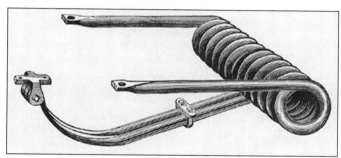

Cross Section of Compressed Band Hub.   Cross Section of Sarven Hub.

Shown here are cross-sectional views of the compressed band hub and the Sarven hub. Regardless of the hub used, it was imperative to keep the iron tire tight. It was the only wearing surface and kept all the part: hubs, spokes, and felloes in tension at all times. No wheel would stand up for any time with a loose tire.

Did You Know?

Today, old incubators are hard to find. When they appear, those still complete can often bring $100 or more.

There were numerous kinds of vehicles. In addition to buggies and surreys there were driving wagons, phaetons, and run-abouts. The Stanhope was essentially a topless phaeton and was priced at $55.

Priced at $200, the Columbus Station Wagon was designed to convey people and their luggage from the train station to their hotel or other destinations. The driver sat in the front seat and passengers occupied the rear compartment. Wherever glass was used, as in the doors and front panels, it was beveled plate glass.

This Physician's Closed Stop Stanhope was designed with storage beneath the seat for medicines or surgical cases, an ideal design for summer. It provided an open-air atmosphere with protection from the burning sun.

New Conklin Wagon Co., Olean, N.Y.

With a career in the wagon business back to the 1860s, the Conklin wagons were unusual in that they used two extra spokes in the wheels. Ordinarily, wagons were made with 12 spokes in the front and 14 spokes in the rear wheels. The New Conklin used 14 spokes in the front and 16 spokes in the rear.

Conner Brothers, Ada, Ohio

An 1890 advertisement for "The Famous Ada Road Cart" claimed it to be the "most beautiful, practical and easiest riding two-wheel vehicle ever invented." It is unknown if this firm specialized in carts, or if its line included other vehicles.

No. 50 BIKE WAGON

Connersville Buggy Company, Connersville, Indiana

Along with the conventional designs came the unusual. One such example is the No. 50 Bike Wagon for 1905 from Connersville Buggy Company. It was an ultra-lightweight design as evidenced by the wheels.

Consumers Carriage & Manufacturing Co., Chicago, Ill.

An 1895 advertisement in the *American Agriculturist* offers this $28.50 buggy to farmers on a 30-day free trial. From this ad, it is determined that the company began building carriages in 1874.

A.A. Cooper Wagon & Buggy Co., Dubuque, Iowa

Cooper wagons were sold by many dealers, as well as being handled through the warehouses of Parlin & Orendorff Plow Co. In areas where flax was grown, the adage was that a wagon box had to be water-tight to haul this seed; Cooper advertised having a Flax-Tight wagon.

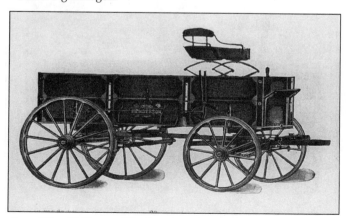

Coquillard Wagon Works, Henderson, Kty.

Established in 1865, this company functioned well into the early 1900s. It built Henderson and Coquillard farm and log wagons, carts and drays.

Deere & Co., Moline, Ill.

John Deere Plow Co., and its branch warehouses were heavily into the wagon and carriage business by 1900. Shown here is a light vehicle of 1905, advertised by Deere as "the best in the world."

A John Deere Vehicle Catalog of 1909 illustrates its Quick-Shift Auto-Seat Buggy of the time, being built at the John Deere Buggy Factory in St. Louis. In 1909, Deere made a very short excursion into the automobile business and then withdrew.

By the early 1900s, Deere was selling most or all the production from Davenport Wagon Co., Davenport, Iowa. The latter pioneered the steel-wagon gear, having it for sale already in the 1890s. Deere bought out the firm in 1912.

In 1910, Deere bought out Moline Wagon Co. The following year, the company bought Fort Smith Wagon Co., Fort Smith, Ark. The latter built its wagons from southern hardwoods, primarily hickory and white oak.

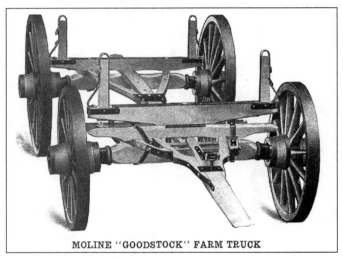

MOLINE "GOODSTOCK" FARM TRUCK

Deere & Company, Moline, Illinois

From about 1910, comes this illustrated Moline "Goodstock" wagon, then sold by Deere. Prior to about 1910, Deere often contracted with other companies, such as Moline Wagon Company, for at least a part of their production. In many instances, Deere would eventually buy out suppliers.

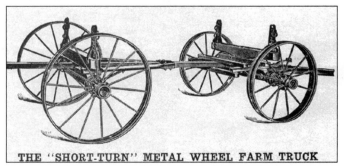

THE "SHORT-TURN" METAL WHEEL FARM TRUCK

By 1910 or earlier, Deere offered an all-steel farm truck such as the "Short Turn" shown here. Farmers gradually saw the usefulness of this design. One example was using this style of farm truck to load hay. "Wagon" usually referred to a conventional wooden wheel design. The "farm truck" was generally of the low-profile all-steel design shown here.

A 1927 advertisement illustrates the John Deere wagons on the road. By this time, many of the smaller wagon companies had vanished and those who still survived were battered even worse in the 1930s, due to the changing agricultural scene and the Great Depression. Few wagon companies remained in business by the beginning of World War II.

DeKalb Wagon Company, DeKalb, Ill.

In the early 1900s, DeKalb produced an elaborate catalog of their carriages and specialized vehicles. Formerly known as the Sycamore Wagon Works, Sycamore, Illinois, the firm transplanted to DeKalb. One of their offerings was this attractive milk or bakery wagon with panel sides.

Bevel-edged plate glass was featured in the DeKalb Casket Wagon. Ordinarily, this vehicle was furnished in a high-grade black finish with no striping. It also could be finished in white or gray, at extra cost.

For retail stores, DeKalb offered this attractive panel-side Furniture Wagon with running gear in red or yellow. The body could be finished in Brewster Green, Black, Yellow, Red, or Coach Painter's Green.

This unusual vehicle was not likely found in small towns. It was the DeKalb Piano and Organ Wagon. The bed was designed with anchor points, and at extra cost it could be furnished with the necessary tie downs, blankets, and other required equipment.

The American Livestock Wagon was an interesting DeKalb design. Instead of driving livestock over the roads, they could be loaded onto this wagon and transported to their destination.

The Eagle Carriage Co., Cincinnati, Ohio

Presumably, this firm built a full line of carriages, but also made the small pony vehicle shown here. Fortunate indeed was the youngster having a pony, plus a carriage to match.

Electric Wheel Company, Quincy, Ill.

Walton Farm Wagons were a part of the Electric Wheel Company line. This high-quality wagon had a capacity of 4,500 pounds.

COOK HOUSE TRUCK

The huge EWC line included specialties like the Cook House Truck. It was available in track widths of 6'-8" and 8-foot. Everything from cattle drives to threshing crews needed plenty of grub while on the move.

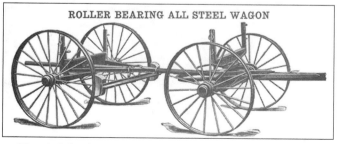

ROLLER BEARING ALL STEEL WAGON

Electric Wheel All-Steel Wagons were first built in the 1890s. Early on they attracted a small market. Meanwhile, the company continued building the Calkins and other conventional wood wagons. By the 1930s, the all-steel design achieved a dominant position in the industry.

Emerson-Brantingham Co., Rockford, Ill.

About 1911, Emerson-Brantingham acquired the Newton Wagon Co., Batavia, Ill. Subsequently, E-B produced Newton wagons until the company was bought out by J.I. Case Co. in 1928.

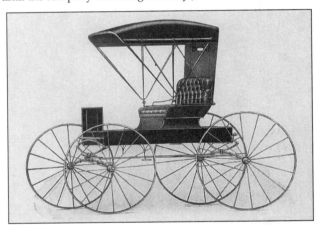

Presumably with the purchase of Newton Wagon Co. in 1911, the company also offered a line of buggies and other vehicles. This one is from the 1919 E-B catalog; by this time, demand for buggies and carriages was waning.

E.D. Etnyre & Co., Oregon, Ill.

While most wagon companies specialized in farm wagons, logging wagons and similar designs, a few firms offered other specialties. One of these was the Etnyre Patent Sprinkler Wagon; this offering is from 1907.

Eureka Carriage Company, Rock Falls, Ill.

Aside from this 1892 advertisement, little is known of the Eureka line. They specialized in spring wagons, road wagons, and road carts.

Farmers Handy Wagon Co., Saginaw, Mich.

From 1906 comes this illustration of the Farmers No. 4 Log Truck, a huge and heavy running gear with a capacity of 7-1/2 tons. This one is built with solid wooden wheels; the firm also made steel wheels.

Florence Wagon Works, Florence, Ala.

Wagon companies abounded in the early 1900s; after all, wagons and railroads were the only means of transporting goods from one point to another. The Florence wagons were made of select white oak, a favorite wood among wagon makers.

James Goold & Co., Albany, N.Y.

This firm had beginnings in the early 1800s; by 1877, it had an extensive line of carriages and sleighs. Shown here is its Chester Wagon of the time.

Harrison Wagon Co., Grand Rapids, Mich.

Harrison and New Harrison wagons were widely sold by the time this 1906 advertisement appeared. Selected white oak was used for the wheels and running gear, with the box having poplar sides and a floor made of Norway pine.

Havana Metal Wheel Co., Havana, Ill.

In the late 1890s, wagons with steel wheels began to appear; often, these were called "farm trucks" (as compared to "farm wagons") when furnished with wooden wheels. Eventually, the steel wheels would predominate; by the 1930s, wooden wheels were rapidly leaving the scene.

Hickman-Ebbert Co., Owensboro, Kty.

For 1907, the Ebbert Farm Wagon took the form shown here. The Ebbert was very popular in many regions. Most wagons of the time were highly ornamented with striping and decorations.

Hoffman & Co., Albion, Ind.

This firm was a wholesale manufacturer, meaning that another company could secure its vehicles and sell them under its own name, even though the buyer had no facilities for building wagons. Many of these vehicles were sold through mail-order catalogs.

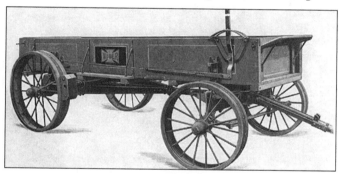

International Harvester Company, Chicago, Ill.

All-steel farm wagons were marketed already in the 1890s, but never gained great popularity until the 1930s. This IHC All-Purpose Farm Truck of 1939 had a relatively short market life. Pneumatic tires would soon become universal, to the point of completely excluding wood and steel wheels.

James & Graham Wagon Company, Memphis, Tenn.

For 1905, James & Graham offered an extensive line of high quality farm wagons. A specialty was their Model Log Wagon in various styles. As with many other wagon builders, few specific details can be found.

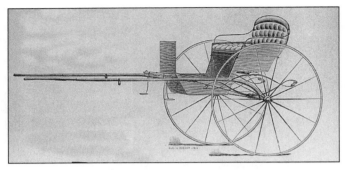

James & Mayer Buggy Co., Cincinnati, Ohio.

An 1890 advertisement reveals that this large manufacturer had a plant at Lawrenceburg, Ind., in addition to its operation at Cincinnati. Shown here is its Dream Cart, with the body finished in a choice of black, wine or green.

Kalamazoo Cart Co., Kalamazoo, Mich.

An engraving of the 1880s illustrates the company's Excelsior Drop-Bar Cart, also noting that the firm was the second oldest cart manufacturer in Michigan. In 1887, the company sold more than 7,000 of the carts shown here.

Karges Wagon Company, Evansville, Ind.

These well-known wagons were marketed in the thousands, especially in southern Indiana and surrounding environs. However, wagon patterns varied from one region to another, so an Indiana Pattern would not likely be found in Pennsylvania.

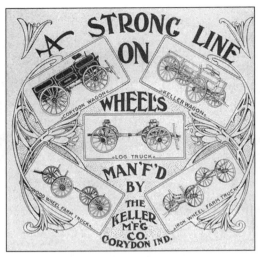

Keller Mfg. Company, Corydon, Ind.

For 1905, Keller offered an extensive line of farm trucks and wagons. Included were the Keller wagons, as well as the Corydon Series. A great many of the thousands of wagon models offered by hundreds of manufacturers have been lost to time. Finding any one of the wagons in this section still in their original, unspoiled condition, has become increasingly difficult.

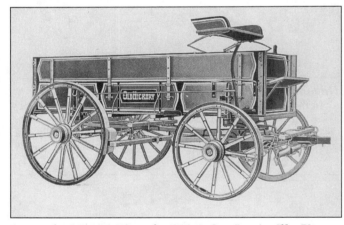

Kentucky Wagon Manufacturing Co., Louisville, Kty.

The origins of this firm are unknown, but Kentucky Wagon Co. endured at least into the late 1950s. Shown here is its Old Hickory farm wagon of the 1920s.

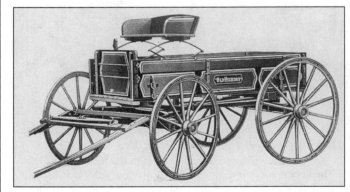

Old Hickory wagons were made in many different styles and sizes, with this illustration of the 1920s showing its one-horse wagon, complete with a spring seat. Kentucky Wagon Co. offered its miniature wagons for some years, with this one being built in the 1920s. It was available with a hand tongue or could be furnished with shafts (as shown), with a goat doing the work.

"Old Hickory" Solid Steel Axle Miniature Wagons.

Kentucky Wagon Mfg. Company, Louisville, Ky.

In addition to their line of farm wagons, a few companies offered a small miniature wagon that could be pulled with a small horse, or perhaps even another farm animal, as shown here. This classy little wagon sold for about $10 in the early 1900s.

Linstroth Wagon Co., St. Louis, Mo.

Linstroth remained in the wagon business until the 1940s. By then, demand for wagons like the one shown had disappeared. The wagon business kept many blacksmiths busy making repairs and resetting the iron tires. Many shops were equipped with a large cast-iron trough that held hot linseed oil. The wheels were periodically soaked with hot oil to preserve the wood and prevented it from shrinking.

Luedinghaus-Espenschied Wagon Co., St. Louis, Mo.

For most farmers, it was a point of pride to drive into town with an attractive team and wagon. However, when it came to

buying a wagon, strength and durability were paramount. Most manufacturers recognized this need and described their wagons in exhaustive detail.

Litchfield Mfg. Company, Waterloo, Iowa

Litchfield was a well-known manufacturer of manure spreaders by the early 1900s. The company was quite successful in this endeavor. The Litchfield Farm Truck appeared early in the 1920s. Little is known of this venture, although it had an attractive and durable design.

A. McAvoy & Son, Racine, Wisc.

By 1890, this company was offering a dozen different kinds of road carts, plus two different styles of road wagons. Aside from this 1890 engraving, nothing is known of McAvoy's Triumph or other company products.

McCallum Steel Wheel Wagon Co., Aurora, Ill.

In 1895, this company was promoting its steel-wheel wagons, noting that it had taken "Highest Award at the World's Fair," referring to the Chicago World's Fair of 1893. The built-up design of these wheels is of particular interest.

McCallum Steel Wagon Company, Elgin, Ill.

An 1890 advertisement noted the "McCallum Steel Wheel Wagon is Climate Proof." This carried an element of truth, since rain, mud, and snow all deteriorated wooden wheels. Steel wheels had no such problems. It would be a couple of decades before steel wheels gained wide acceptance.

McFarlan Carriage Co., Kansas City, Kan.

Shown here in its 1905 version, this McFarlan carriage typifies the state-of-the-art in carriage building. While there were extra-fancy carriages on the market, the average buyer was overjoyed to have a classy vehicle of this kind. By 1915, the demand for carriages was fast diminishing. The 1931 issue of *Farm Implement News Buyer's Guide* lists only three companies still in the carriage and buggy business.

T.G. Mandt, Stoughton, Wisc.

Mandt wagons acquired a sterling reputation from its beginnings. As a result, the company became very prominent. Moline Plow Co. bought out Mandt in 1906, continuing to build "The Genuine T.G. Mandt Wagon" for decades to come.

Milburn Wagon Co., Toledo, Ohio

Grocery wagons were a familiar sight by the early 1900s. Some farms were not near anything more than a small village, so the itinerant grocer appeared occasionally. Milburn Wagon Co. offered this specially designed Grocer's Wagon in 1895.

The Milburn line included its Milburn Hollow-Axle Wagon made of steel (instead of the commonly used oak or hickory) axles. The company remained active into the 1920s, but disappeared from the trade directories by 1930.

Miller Wagon Company, Edina, Mo.

From the early 1900s, comes this Miller wagon illustration. First built in 1867, the company noted that all wagons were made of "bone dry stock, handsomely finished." All wood parts were soaked in boiling linseed oil prior to assembly. Iron parts were usually finished in black, and most wagons had a red running gear with black striping. Almost all farm wagons built in the United had a green box.

Mitchell & Lewis Co., Racine, Wisc.

A part of the 1882 Mitchell & Lewis line was this open-spring buggy, a small outfit for one or two people and storage of rain coats or a picnic basket behind the seat.

The Mitchell, Lewis & Co. Annual Catalog for 1882 illustrates various Mitchell wagons, including this farm wagon. Most wagons were furnished as shown here, with a double box. For picking corn and various other duties, a triple box was needed. Often, the latter was built to fit by a local blacksmith, but the additional sideboards could also be secured from the manufacturer.

Mitchell & Lewis wagons took the form shown here for 1903. By 1915, the company is listed as Mitchell Wagon Co.; by 1918, the Mitchell wagons were being built by John Deere Wagon Co., Moline, Ill.

Moline Plow Co., Moline, Ill.

Moline Plow Co. had apparently been selling wagons prior to its 1906 buy-out of T.G. Mandt, Stoughton, Wis. Subsequently, the firm operated this facility as its Mandt Wagon Branch. Shown here is a Mandt triple box wagon of the 1920s.

During 1906, Moline Plow Co. bought Henney Buggy Co., Freeport, Ill., as well as buying the Freeport Carriage Co. of the same city. Some years earlier, Moline began marketing the Crescent wagons, noting its long experience in the business since 1861.

The Crescent line of wagons was apparently a competitively priced series, with its Mandt wagons being at the top of the line.

A 1920 illustration shows the Crescent running gear, together with a Wisconsin box, as offered by Moline Plow Co.

Wisconsin steel-wheel farm trucks were a part of the Moline Plow Co. line by 1920. Many farmers preferred the low profile of the farm truck for loading hay or loading bundles for their trip to the threshing machine.

Moline Wagon Co., Moline, Ill.

This company had its beginnings in the 1850s; 30 years later, it was offering the Moline Road Cart shown in this engraving. Road carts were very popular in some regions, particularly for pleasure driving.

Moline Wagon Co. sold many of its wagons through the John Deere Plow Co. warehouses by the early 1900s. Shown here is a Moline wagon of 1906. Deere & Co. bought out Moline Wagon Co. in 1910.

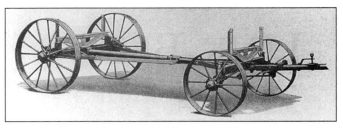

New Idea Spreader Co., Coldwater, Ohio

This company became famous in the early 1900s with its line of manure spreaders. Shown here is its 1930 edition of the New

Idea Harvest Wagon, a new design. The stakes were adjustable to 38 or 42 inches. The standard wagon box was 3-by-10 feet inside measurements, thus the stake width of 38 inches.

Newton Carriage Co., Kalamazoo, Mich.

As evidenced by this 1888 engraving, Newton was a wholesale manufacturer, building and selling large quantities of its vehicles for other jobbers and distributors. Shown here is its Newton 2-Seat Farmer's Wagon No. 3.

Northwestern Manufacturing Co., Fort Atkinson, Wisc.

About 1900, Northwestern was offering this attractive spring wagon, a small, light-weight design with slight hauling capacity in the rear. This style was often used for hauling milk or cream to the local creamery or the eggs to market.

The origins of this company are unknown, but Northwestern appears in the trade directories until about 1920. After that, it disappears. Shown here is an attractive Northwestern wagon of 1905.

Northwestern Mfg. Company, Fort Atkinson, Wis.

The Northwestern No. 80 was also billed as the Northwestern Milk Wagon. This model used steel axles, with hickory rims and spokes for the wheels. The frame also was made of hickory.

Shown here is the Northwestern No. 33 Spring Wagon. This one was the three-spring design, and included two seats. The body was furnished in black, the gear could be black or wine and the wheels were red.

The Northwestern No. 48 was a half-platform spring wagon. It used an elliptic spring on the front axle, and platform springs in the rear. It was furnished with leather-cushioned seats with high backs. The spring wagon also had an oil carpet on the floor and used a leather dashboard.

The 1900 No. 52 Northwestern Buggy was equipped with Sarven wheels, elliptic springs, and leather seat cushions. Although not shown here, it could be outfitted with an extension top, if desired.

Ohio Carriage Mfg. Company, Columbus, Ohio

Ohio's Split Hickory Runabout shown here was of the short-turn or cut-under design. This one had a black body and a handsome red gear. It sold for $57 plus freight to your depot.

Priced at $66.75, this Concord Spring Buggy could be furnished with a set of Goodyear solid rubber tires for another $15. Sometimes these were called a Drummer's Buggy. The nickname for traveling salesmen of those times was "drummers."

Did You Know?

Old reapers are now quite a scarce item. Those in reasonably good condition usually sell from $300 and up.

This attractive Split Hickory Phaeton was priced at $71. The upholstery and top were dark green wool fabric. The body was finished in black with Brewster Green accents, and the gear was painted Brewster Green. The entire vehicle was enhanced with gold pinstripes.

Ohio Steel Wagon Co., Wapakoneta, Ohio

In 1910, Ohio Steel Wagon Co., announced that it experienced a change in management and was "cleaning house," with the remaining stock of the wagons shown here being sold at "prices below the actual cost of manufacture." Nothing more is known of the company except for this advertisement.

Olds Wagon Works, Fort Wayne, Ind.

Except for this 1895 illustration of the "Old Reliable Olds" wagon, nothing is known of this venture, nor is it known if this company was connected with P.F. Olds & Son, which eventually built the famous Oldsmobile automobiles.

Pekin Wagon Co., Pekin, Ill.

Pekin wagons were first built in 1849, with a 1910 version illustrated here. The company continued into the 1930s; by the end of the decade, repair parts were available only from Springfield Wagon & Trailer Co., Springfield, Mo.

Peru Plow & Implement Co., Peru, Ill.

By the 1890s, Peru had built up a considerable trade in farm implements, as well as developing a large trade in buggies and other vehicles. Shown here is the No. 201 Standard Grade Buggy. It was available in two widths, the narrow track of 56 inches and the wide track of 60 inches. The track was always measured from outside to outside, at the bottom of the wheels.

The Peru line included various models of surreys. This one with driving lanterns was a cut above the ordinary, since most "farmer surreys" did not include lanterns or other extra features. By definition, a buggy was a four-wheeled vehicle with one seat; a surrey had two seats.

Pioneer Implement Company, Council Bluffs, Iowa

Little is known of Pioneer, but their 1896 catalog illustrated numerous vehicles. Included was their Racine-Jackson Spring Buggy. It was equipped with long double side springs, rather than the front- and rear-mounted elliptical springs.

Phaetons were a single seat style with an extension top. Rear fenders were usually standard equipment, as were kerosene driving lamps.

A surrey was a two-seated vehicle. It could be furnished with an extension top, or the shorter straight top. Most were of the straight-

sill type, but many styles could be ordered in a cut-under design for an additional cost. The cut-under design permitted shorter turns.

Shown here is the Bennett & Frantz buggy offered by Pioneer in 1898. Many of Pioneer vehicles were trimmed in hand-buffed leather, finished with Sherwin & Williams paints, then varnished.

Those desiring a substantial, well-furnished surrey could choose a Pioneer No. 38, shown here. It was equipped with double fenders, kerosene driving lights, and a fancy patent leather dash. The whipcord trimming on the top was a rather common surrey accessory.

Piqua Wagon Co., Piqua, Ohio

For 1895, Piqua offered this attractive one-horse wagon, noting that it was available in two different sizes. The previous year, the company built more than 2,000 wagons. For reasons now unknown, the company disappeared in the early 1900s.

Pitts Agricultural Works, Buffalo, N.Y.

Many of the steam-traction engine builders offered water wagons as a necessary accessory for its engines. Some built a combined coal and water wagon to ease the life of the engineer. Shown here is an 1895 version from Buffalo Pitts.

A.L. Pratt & Co., Kalamazoo, Mich.

Road carts had become very popular by the 1880s, providing an easy way to travel without riding horseback. Shown here is Pratt's Perfection Cart of 1888.

Racine-Sattley Co., Springfield, Ill.

About 1905, Sattley Manufacturing Co. of Springfield, Ill., joined forces with Racine Wagon Co. of Racine, Wis., to form Racine-Sattley Co. Shown here is a 1905 Racine farm wagon. This firm eventually left the business, but, into the 1930s, repairs for the Racine wagons were available from Hummer Plow Works at Springfield, Ill.

Randolph Wagon Works, Randolph, Wis.

Mandt Farm Wagons were built by Randolph, although the connection with T. G. Mandt is presently unknown. Perhaps Randolph built the Mandt wagons under a licensing or royalty arrangement.

The Mandt wagon line from Randolph Wagon Works was extensive. In addition to many styles of farm wagons, the company also built mountain wagons and other specialties.

Randolph Wagon Works, Randolph, Wis.

Farm wagon designs varied from one region to another. The Mandt Sunny South wagon was built especially for the southern trade. A Randolph catalog notes that all lumber was air dried, rather than being kiln dried. All painting was done with a brush, instead of parts being dipped in mass production operations.

D.F. Sargeant & Sons, Geneseo, Ill.

For 1888, this firm offered a small two-wheeled buggy, built over the Geneseo Road Cart. Aside from this engraving, nothing is known of the company, its beginnings or its subsequent destiny.

Peter Schuttler Co., Chicago, Ill.

One of the earliest midwestern wagon makers was Peter Schuttler. His wagons gained a wide reputation for their quality and remained on the market into the 1920s. By the early 1930s, repair parts for Schuttler wagons could be secured from Springfield Wagon & Trailer Co., Springfield, Mo.

D.M. Sechler Carriage Co., Moline, Ill.

For 1910, this company offered numerous kinds of buggies and other vehicles, including this No. 08. By this time, Sechler was also building the Black Hawk corn planter, the Black Hawk manure spreader and other farm equipment.

Seidel Buggy Co., Richmond, Ind.

In a catalog of the early 1900s, this firm billed themselves as "Vehicle Builders." Obviously, the company had specialized in this business, offering an extensive line, including this straight-sill surrey with phaeton seats.

J.T. Sharkey, Taunton, Mass.

From its 80-page catalog of the 1890s, comes this engraving of the company's No. 150 St. Louis Storm Wagon. Its simple design included convenient side curtains that could be rolled down in case of inclement weather.

Sprague & French, Norwalk, Ohio

Instead of buying a top buggy, those so inclined could buy a buggy canopy as shown for protection from rain or sun. A few companies specialized in building canopies in an 1895 setting.

Standard Wagon Company, Cincinnati, Ohio

For 1888, Standard offered a large number of buggies, road wagons, cabriolets, surreys, and spring wagons. Like many other manufacturers, their Annual Catalog took the form of an almanac. One example is their Stratton Improved Jump Seat Buggy.

Star Tank Co., Goshen, Ind.

Every thresherman needed a water tank for his steam-traction engine; the Stutz Steel Thresher Tank was built especially for this. It is shown mounted on a heavy steel farm truck, although the tank could be purchased separately.

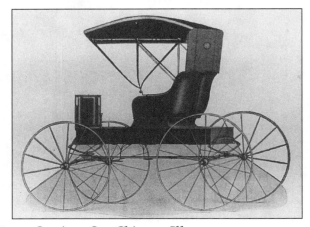

Staver Carriage Co., Chicago, Ill.

In 1910, Staver offered its No. 224 buggy with a leather quarter top and a twin auto seat. By this time, the carriage industry was

badly hurt by the emerging automobile. One of the farm equipment directories for 1906 listed some 150 different manufacturers of buggies and surreys. The numbers began to dwindle by 1910; by 1917, the same directory listed but 30 manufacturers.

Stoughton Wagon Co., Stoughton, Wisc.

This company began building wagons in 1866. By the early 1900s, the Moline Plow Co. was acting as General Agents for the Stoughton wagons and eventually came into control of the company.

Studebaker Bros. Manufacturing Co., South Bend, Ind.

By 1872, the Studebaker billed itself as "The Largest Vehicle Builders in the World." This 1903 example of a Studebaker wagon typifies the line at that time. Studebaker went on to become a major manufacturer of motor cars.

This attractive one-horse business wagon was built by Studebaker for many years. Frequent applications of black axle grease to the wheels and the king pin helped to keep a wagon or vehicle in service for years.

Studebaker farm wagons came by the thousands from the South Bend factory. Farm wagons were offered in numerous sizes and styles. Wagon hubs were made of New England Black Birch, and reinforced with steel bands.

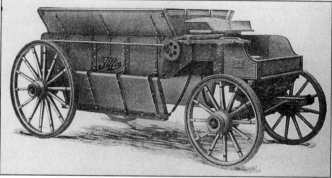

Tiffin Wagon Co., Tiffin, Ohio

By the early 1900s, Tiffin had established a reputation for its farm wagons, as well as the heavy self-dumping wagons shown here. The firm also built garbage, stone and asphalt wagons.

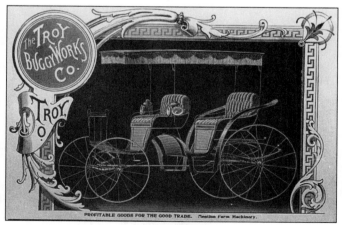

Troy Buggy Works Co., Troy, Ohio

In the 1890s, Troy offered this elaborate surrey, complete with a fringe-top canopy. The average farmer couldn't or wouldn't afford a fancy vehicle like this—their surrey might have a fringe top, but few other frills.

Troy Wagon Works Co., Troy, Ohio

For 1895, Troy offered this attractive farm wagon, continuing with virtually the same design for some years to come. By the 1930s, the firm had become Troy Trailer & Wagon Co.

J. Turney & Company, Fairfield, Iowa

Established in 1856, the Turney Company had already experienced a half-century in the wagon business when this 1905 Charter Oak wagon appeared. Chances are that the design varied but little from the original.

Velie Carriage Co., Moline, Ill.

W.H. Velie was a grandson of John Deere. In 1902, Velie organized Velie Carriage Co., hoping to build horseless carriages, eventually bringing out the Velie automobile. Meanwhile, the firm also built many carriages and light wagons, with this No. 920 Delivery Wagon appearing in the company's 1916 catalog.

No. 32 Driving Wagon

Velie Carriage Company, Moline, Ill.

Driving wagons were a popular part of any carriage line, with Velie offering numerous styles. Included was this extremely high quality No. 32 model.

Velie driving wagons were made in numerous styles, such as their popular No. 622. Like much of the Velie line, the body could be finished in black, red, maroon, or green. This model is from 1915.

The Velie Open Riser Concord was similar to a driving wagon. A major difference was the use of side springs, as shown on the No. 626 illustrated here.

The Corning Buggy was but one of several styles offered by Velie. This one could be trimmed in cloth or leather. Standard features were a padded dash and nickel-plated trimmings.

Toward the top of the 1915 Velie carriage line was their Auto Seat Top Buggy. This model was furnished with a luxurious seat, nickel-plated trim, and a padded wing dash.

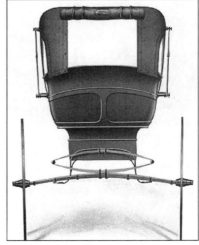

A rear view of the Velie No. 368 Top Buggy illustrates the handsomely carved rear panel. The entire Velie line epitomized quality, yet often featured prices that were not for the fainthearted.

The Velie DeLuxe was an unusual design having a one-piece steel body and seat. Imported fabric was used for the top. Battery-operated lights were standard, along with a 36-hour, dash-mounted clock.

The cut-under body design of the Velie No. 482 surrey permitted short turns and added an extra touch of class. Although not shown here, a canopy top and double fenders came as an extra-cost option.

This attractive surrey with a fringe top came with double fenders and a pair of kerosene driving lamps as standard equipment. Usually, these were furnished with red jewels that served as tail lights.

Vorwick Road Cart Co., Monmouth, Ill.

For 1890, Vorwick offered this small road cart, noting that it used raw linseed oil on the shafts, while the wheels were painted a wine color or bright red.

Weber Wagon Co., Chicago, Ill.

This firm was organized in 1845; when it sold out to International Harvester in 1904, it had 59 years of wagon building experience to its credit. IHC continued to market Weber wagons for many years.

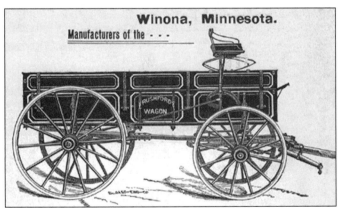

Winona Wagon Company, Winona, Minn.

Farm wagons were almost always painted attractively, and usually were finished with elaborate striping. In addition, the overall design was very important, including the highest quality lumber. By 1870, mass-produced wagons entered the market and many small wagon shops and wheelwrights drifted into other endeavors.

Winkler Bros., South Bend, Ind.

An 1899 engraving illustrates the Winkler Milk Wagon, a familiar sight at the time, especially in larger cities. Occasionally, a farmer would build up a local trade in milk, making deliveries every day or two.

Trade Names

Abingdon	Abingdon Wagon Co.	Abingdon, IL	1905
Acme	Acme Wagon Co.	Emigsville, PA	1892
Albion	Painter & Frankland	Albion, IL	1892
Ames	F. A. Ames & Co.	Owensboro, KY	1892
Amondson	L. O. Amondson	Gratiot, WI	1892
Anderson	Anderson Bros.	Moorhead, MN	1892
Anderson	Anderson Co.	St. Paul, MN	1915
Appleton	Appleton Mfg. Co.	Batavia, IL	1915
Atlas	B. F. Avery & Sons	Louisville, KY	1915
Auburn	Auburn Wagon Co.	Martinsburg, WV	1905
Avery	Avery Mfg. Co.	Peoria, IL	1905
B & G	Bristol & Gale Co.	Chicago, IL	1915
Badger	Fuller & Johnson Mfg. Co.	Madison, WI	1905
Badger	Moline Plow Co.	Moline, IL	1915
Bailey	Alpheus Bailey	Sand Lake, NY	1892
Bain	Bain Wagon Co.	Kenosha, WI	1892
Baldrick	J. J. Baldrick	Lakeland, FL	1892
Beggs	Beggs Wagon Co.	Kansas City, MO	1905
Beggs-Goodson	Beggs-Goodson Wagon Co.	Hannibal, MO	1905
Belknap	Belknap Wagon Co.	Grand Rapids, MI	1905
Benson	H. J. Benson	Prairie du Chien, WI	1892
Best Yet	Turnbull Wagon Co.	Defiance, OH	1915
Bettendorf	Bettendorf Axle Co.	Bettendorf, IA	1905
Bettendorf	International Harvester Co.	Chicago, IL	1909
Bible	Ionia Wagon Co.	Ionia, MI	1905
Birdsell	Birdsell Mfg. Co.	South Bend, IN	1892
Blount	Davidson, Blount & Co.	Evansville, IN	1892
Bode	Bode Wagon Co.	Cincinnati, OH	1905
Border Alliance	North Carolina Plow Co.	Cary, NC	1892
Boscobel	Ruka Bros. Mfg. Co.	Boscobel, WI	1892
Boso	B. F. Avery & Sons	Louisville, KY	1915
Brown	Brown Buggy Co.	Waterloo, IA	1905
Brown	Brown Mfg. Co.	Zanesville, OH	1892
Brown	Brown Wagon Co.	Macon, GA	1913
Buchanan	Rough Bros. Wagon Works	Buchanan, MI	1892
Buckeye	International Harvester Co.	Chicago, IL	1913
Buckeye	Turnbull Wagon Co.	Defiance, OH	1915

Trade Names (cont...)

Buerkens	Buerkens Mfg. Co.	Pella, IA	1909
Bugbee	Jonathan Bugbee	Hartford, VT	1892
Burch	L. M. Burch	Baylis, IL	1892
Burg	Burg Wagon Co.	Burlington, IA	1892
Burnham	Burnham Mfg. Co.	Charles City, IA	1924
Buster	Pekin Wagon Co.	Pekin, IL	1915
Calkins & Walton	Electric Wheel Co.	Quincy, IL	1924
Calmar	Miller Wagon Co.	Calmar, IA	1924
Cambridge	D. W. Scobie	Cambridge, WI	1892
Campbell	W. J. Campbell	Port Austin, MI	1892
Capital	Capital Wagon Works	Ionia, MI	1892
Capital	Ionia Wagon Co.	Ionia, MI	1905
Champion	Champion Wagon Co.	Owego, NY	1892
Champion	H. J. Buhr & Co.	Washington, MO	1905
Champion	Joliet Strowbridge Co.	Joliet, IL	1892
Charter Oak	Joel Turney & Co.	Fairfield, IA	1892
Chase City	Chase City Mfg. Co.	Chase City, VA	1905
Chattanooga	Chattanooga Wagon Co.	Chattanooga, TN	1909
Chockelt	John A. Chockelt	South Bend, IN	1892
Clinton	Abingdon Wagon Co.	Abingdon, IL	1905
Clipper	Avery Mfg. Co.	Peoria, IL	1913
Columbia	James A. Adams	Columbia, MO	1892
Columbian	Columbia Wagon Co.	Columbia, PA	1905
Columbus	Columbus Wagon Co.	Chicago, IL	1905
Columbus	International Harvester Co.	Chicago, IL	1913
Commonwealth	Abingdon Wagon Co.	Abingdon, IL	1915
Conklin	W. H. & D. C. Conklin	Olean, NY	1892
Conqueror	Kentucky Wagon Mfg. Co.	Louisville, KY	1915
Cook	Cook Carriage Co.	Cincinnati, OH	1892
Cooper	A. A. Cooper Wagon & Buggy Co.	Dubuque, IA	1892
Coquillard	Coquillard Wagon Works	South Bend, IN	1892
Coquillard	Coquillard Wagon Works	Henderson, KY	1909
Corydon	Keller Mfg. Co.	Corydon, IN	1905
Coweta	Coweta Wagon Co.	Newnan, GA	1892
Crescent	Mandt Div., Moline Plow Co.	Moline, IL	1913
Cruzan	N. A. Cruzan	Astoria, IL	1892
Daisy	Lansing Wagon Works	Lansing, MI	1915
Dakin	J. H. Dakin	Schenectady, NY	1892
Dandy	Turnbull Wagon Co.	Defiance, OH	1915
Davenport	Davenport Wagon Co.	Davenport, IA	1905
Davis	Davis Wagon Co.	Columbus, GA	1905
Diamond	Kentucky Wagon Mfg. Co.	Louisville, KY	1915
Dixie	Mandt Wagon Co.	Stoughton, WI	1909
Donaldson	Donaldson Bros.	Mt. Clemens, MI	1905
Dunnavant	J. H. Dunnavant	Birmingham, AL	1892
Dutch	Buerkens Mfg. Co.	Pella, IA	1915
Ebbert	Hickman-Ebbert Co.	Owensboro, KY	1909
Eclipse	Columbia Wagon Co.	Columbia, PA	1892
Edgecombe	Edgecombe Agricultural Works	Tarborough, NC	1892
Edgerton	Edgerton Wagon Co.	Edgerton, WI	1915
Electric	Electric Wheel Co.	Quincy, IL	1905
Eli	Columbia Wagon Co.	Columbia, PA	1913
Empire	A. W. Hawks	Phoenix, NY	1892

Trade Names (cont...)

Empire	Empire Mfg. Co.	Quincy, IL	1915
Erin	Hoppes & Edwards	Erin, TN	1892
Evans	B. A. Evans	Hammond, NY	1915
Excelsior	Geo. E. Bechtolt	Urbana, OH	1892
Fairfield	Joel Turney & Co.	Fairfield, IA	1915
Fish Bros.	Fish Bros. Mfg. Co.	Clinton, IA	1905
Fish Bros.	Fish Bros. Wagon Co.	Racine, WI	1905
Fitzhugh	J. R. Fitzhugh	Centreton, NJ	1892
Flint	Flint Wagon Works	Flint, MI	1892
Florence	Florence Wagon Works	Florence, AL	1905
Fort Smith	Fort Smith Wagon Co.	Fort Smith, AR	1905
Fosston	Fosston Mfg. Co.	St. Paul, MN	1924
Fresno	Fresno Implement Co.	Fresno, CA	1913
Fuller & Johnson	Fuller & Johnson Mfg. Co.	Madison, WI	1905
Garth	Geo. S. Garth & Sons	Mill Hall, PA	1892
Gate City	Winona Wagon Co.	Winona, MN	1915
Geneva	Geneva Metal Wheel Co.	Geneva, OH	1915
Georgia	O. H. Miller	Fort Valley, GA	1892
Goetzinger	Nic. Goetzinger Sons Co.	Dyersville, IA	1924
Grain King	Anderson Co.	St. Paul, MN	1924
Grand Detour	Grand Detour Wagon Co.	Dixon, IL	1905
Grand Rapids	Harrison Wagon Works	Grand Rapids, MI	1905
Green	Samuel Green	Florida, NY	1892
Gregory	Chase City Mfg. Co.	Chase City, VA	1913
Hackney	Hackney Wagon Co.	Wilson, NC	1924
Hanna	Hanna Wagon Co.	Peoria, IL	1892
Hannibal	Hannibal Wagon Co.	Hannibal, MO	1915
Harrison	Harrison Wagon Works	Grand Rapids, MI	1892
Harvard	Turnbull Wagon Co.	Defiance, OH	1915
Harvest Queen	B. F. Avery & Sons	Louisville, KY	1915
Hatcher	Hatcher Iron Wagon Co.	Columbus, GA	1892
Hauge & Christopherson	Hauge & Christopherson	Albert Lea, MN	1892
Havana	Havana Metal Wheel Co.	Havana, IL	1915
Henderson	Coquillard Wagon Works	Henderson, KY	1909
Henderson	M. P. Henderson & Son	Stockton, CA	1892
Hercules	Abingdon Wagon Co.	Abingdon, IL	1915
Hickman	Hertwick, Baltzer & Co.	Hickman, KY	1892
Hickman	Hickman Wagon Co.	Hickman, KY	1909
Hickory	Piedmont Wagon Co.	Hickory, NC	1909
Holly	Patterson & Brown Bros. Mfg. Co.	Holly, MI	1905
Hoosier	Birdsell Mfg. Co.	South Bend, IN	1915
Huggins & Griffith	Huggins & Griffith	Anamosa, IA	1892
Huntingburg	Huntingburg Wagon Works	Huntingburg, IN	1905
I. X. L.	F. MacKinnon Mfg. Co.	Wisconsin Rapids, WI	1924
Ideal	Owensboro Wagon Co.	Owensboro, KY	1915
Indiana	Indiana Wagon Co.	Lafayette, IN	1905
Iowa	Iowa Wagon Co.	Shenendoah, IA	1913
Ironclad	Moline Wagon Co.	Moline, IL	1913

Trade Names (cont...)

Ithaca	Williams Bros.	Ithaca, NY	1905
J. I. Nissen	C. F. Nissen	Winston-Salem, NC	1905
Jack Rabbit	Springfield Wagon Co.	Fayetteville, AR	1945
Jackson	Austin, Tomlinson & Webster	Jackson, MI	1892
James & Graham	James & Graham Wagon Co.	Memphis, TN	1905
Jefferson	O. C. Vaughn	Jefferson, WI	1892
Jefferson	Vaughn Mfg. Co.	Jefferson, WI	1909
Jewel	Kentucky Wagon Mfg. Co.	Louisville, KY	1915
John Deere	John Deere Wagon Co.	Moline, IL	1915
Karges	Karges Wagon Co.	Evansville, IN	1905
Keller	Keller Mfg. Co.	Sauk Center, MN	1905
Kemp & Burpee	Kemp & Burpee Mfg. Co.	Syracuse, NY	1892
Kentucky	Kentucky Wagon Mfg. Co.	Louisville, KY	1905
Kerns	H. O. Kerns	Sutherlin, VA	1892
Ketchum	Ketchum Wagon Co.	Marshalltown, IA	1892
Keystone	International Harvester Co.	Chicago, IL	1915
Kiel Anti-Tip	Kiel Machine Co.	Kiel, WI	1924
King & Hamilton	King & Hamilton Co.	Ottawa, IL	1892
Knapheide	Henry Knapheide Wagon Co.	Quincy, IL	1909
Kramer	Kramer Wagon Co.	Oil City, PA	1905
Kustum Bilt	Corl & Fleming	Fillmore, CA	1945
L. R. V.	Auburn Wagon Co.	Martinsburg, WV	1924
La Fayette	Indiana Wagon Co.	Lafayette, IN	1913
LaBelle	LaBelle Wagon Works	South Superior, WI	1892
LaBelle	Fish Bros. Wagon Co.	Racine, WI	1905
LaCrosse	Smith Mfg. Co.	LaCrosse, WI	1892
Lake City	Neal, Johns & Co.	Lake City, MN	1892
Lang	Lang & Bro.	Farmington, MO	1892
Lansing	Lansing Wagon Works	Lansing, MI	1905
Lenhart	Lenhart Wagon Co.	Minneapolis, MN	1905
Lindsey	Lindsey Wagon Co.	Laurel, MS	1905
Linstroth	Linstroth Wagon Co.	St. Louis, MO	1905
Litchfield Little Giant	Litchfield Mfg. Co.	Waterloo, IA	1915
Little	Owen J. Little	Deckerton, NJ	1892
Little Gem	Acme Wagon Co.	Emigsville, PA	1892
Look & Lincoln	Look & Lincoln	Marion, VA	1892
Love	Love Wagon Co.	Durant, MS	1892
Lucas	Thomas T. Lucas	Pattonville, MO	1892
Luedinghaus	Luedinghaus-Espenschied Co.	St. Louis, MO	1905
MacKinnon	E. MacKinnon Mfg. Co.	Grand Rapids, WI	1905
Macomb	Macomb Wagon Co.	Macomb, IL	1892
Macomber	S. M. Macomber	Adams, VT	1892
Madison	Fuller & Johnson Mfg. Co.	Madison, WI	1905
Madisonville	Madisonville Wagon Co.	Madisonville, KY	1905
Majestic	Kentucky Wagon Mfg. Co.	Louisville, KY	1915
Mandt	Mandt Wagon Co.	Stoughton, WI	1909
Mandt	Moline Plow Co.	Moline, IL	1909
Marietta	Ohio Valley Wagon Co.	Marietta, OH	1905

Trade Names (cont...)

McCallum	J. McCallum Mfg. Co.	Elgin, IL	1892
McCallum	McCallum Steel Wheel Wagon Co.	Elgin, IL	1892
McCormick-Deering	International Harvester Co.	Chicago, IL	1924
Michigan	Lansing Wagon Works	Lansing, MI	1915
Michigan	Patterson Mfg. Co.	Holly, MI	1915
Michigan	Pekin Wagon Co.	Pekin, IL	1915
Milburn	Milburn Wagon Co.	Toledo, OH	1892
Miller	Miller Wagon Co.	Edina, MO	1905
Mills	Marvin Mills	Memphis, MO	1892
Minnesota	Winona Wagon Co.	Winona, MN	1913
Missouri Mule	Springfield Wagon Co.	Fayetteville, AR	1945
Mitchell	Fort Smith Wagon Co.	Fort Smith, AR	1924
Mitchell	John Deere Wagon Works	Moline, IL	1924
Mitchell	Mitchell & Lewis Co.	Racine, WI	1892
Mitchell	Mitchell-Lewis Motor Co.	Racine, WI	1913
Model	Abingdon Wagon Co.	Abingdon, IL	1915
Mogul	Forbes Mfg. Co.	Hopkinsville, KY	1905
Moline	Moline Buggy Co.	Moline, IL	1892
Moline	Moline Wagon Co.	Moline, IL	1892
Moline	Moline Wagon Co.	Moline, IL	1909
Morse	Robt. E. Morse	Auburn, IL	1892
Nashua	Nashua Mfg. Co.	Nashua, IA	1892
National	National Carriage Works	Vineland, NJ	1892
National	Turnbull Wagon Co.	Defiance, OH	1915
New Bettendorf	International Harvester Co.	Chicago, IL	1909
New Conklin	New Conklin Wagon Co.	Olean, NY	1905
New Ebbert	Pekin Wagon Co.	Pekin, IL	1913
New Idea	New Idea Spreader Co.	Coldwater, OH	1931
New Jefferson	Vaughn Mfg. Co.	Jefferson, WI	1915
New Lenhart	Lenhart Wagon Co.	Minneapolis, MN	1915
New Moline	Moline Wagon Co.	Moline, IL	1905
New Randolph	Randolph Wagon Works	Randolph, WI	1915
New Sattley	Racine-Sattley Co.	Racine, WI	1909
New Smith	Pekin Wagon Co.	Pekin, IL	1909
New South	Auburn Wagon Co.	Martinsburg, WV	1913
New Stoughton	Stoughton Wagon Works	Stoughton, WI	1915
New Western	Miller Wagon Co.	Calmar, IA	1924
Newton	Emerson-Brantingham Co.	Rockford, IL	1913
Newton	Newton Wagon Co.	Batavia, IL	1892
Nissen	Geo. E. Nissen & Co.	Winston-Salem, NC	1905
Northwestern	Northwestern Mfg. Co.	Fort Atkinson, WI	1892
O. K.	Columbia Wagon Co.	Columbia, PA	1913
Oakland	Patterson Mfg. Co.	Holly, MI	1915
O'Brien	Indiana Wagon Co.	Lafayette, IN	1905
O'Brien	O'Brien Wagon Co.	Lafayette, IN	1892
Old Hickory	Kentucky Wagon Mfg. Co.	Louisville, KY	1892
Oldendorph	Oldendorph Bros.	Waterloo, IL	1892
Olds	Olds Wagon Works	Fort Wayne, IN	1892

Trade Names (cont...)

Orchard City	Orchard City Wagon Co.	Burlington, IA	1905
Original Moline	Moline Wagon Co.	Moline, IL	1913
Ottawa	King & Hamilton Co.	Ottawa, IL	1905
Overland	Emerson-Brantingham Co.	Rockford, IL	1924
Owego	Champion Wagon Co.	Owego, NY	1909
Owego	Joliet Strowbridge Co.	Joliet, IL	1892
Owensboro	Owensboro Wagon Co.	Owensboro, KY	1892
P. B.	Patterson Mfg. Co.	Holly, MI	1913
Pacific Special	Hannibal Wagon Co.	Hannibal, MO	1915
Painter & Frankland	Painter & Frankland	Albion, IL	1905
Pekin	Pekin Wagon Co.	Pekin, IL	1909
Peoria	Avery Mfg. Co.	Peoria, IL	1909
Peoria	Peoria Wagon Co.	Peoria, IL	1905
Peru	Peru Plow & Wheel Co.	Peru, IL	1915
Peter Schuttler	Peter Schuttler Co.	Chicago, IL	1915
Piedmont	Piedmont Wagon Co.	Hickory, NC	1892
Pioneer	Smith Mfg. Co.	LaCrosse, WI	1909
Planter	W. P. Horner Wagon Mfg. Co.	Danville, VA	1913
Platform Democrats	B. W. Bramer	Fabius, NY	1892
Popular	Kentucky Wagon Mfg. Co.	Louisville, KY	1915
Pride of St. Louis	Linstroth Wagon Co.	St. Louis, MO	1909
Quincy	Knapheide Wagon Co.	Quincy, IL	1915
Racine	Racine-Sattley Co.	Racine, WI	1909
Randolph	Randolph Wagon Works	Randolph, WI	1905
Rasmussen	R. N. Rasmussen	Randolph, WI	1892
Red Hickory	Florence Wagon Works	Florence, AL	1924
Rhoads	Samuel Rhoades	Anderson, IN	1892
Rock City	Emerson-Brantingham Co.	Rockford, IL	1915
Rock Island	Rock Island Plow Co.	Rock Island, IL	1913
Rossow	Rossow Bros.	Chicago, IL	1892
Rud	L. O. Rud & Co.	Lansing, IA	1905
Ruka	Ruka Bros. Mfg. Co.	Boscobel, WI	1892
Rushford	Winona Wagon Co.	Winona, MN	1892
Sames	Peter Sames	Rockford, IL	1892
Samson	B. F. Avery & Sons	Louisville, KY	1915
Sandow	Emerson-Brantingham Co.	Rockford, IL	1915
Scheer & Schweikert	Scheer & Schweikert	Lincoln, IL	1892
Schmitt	W. F. Schmitt	Wright City, MO	1913
Schreiber	Schreber Carriage Mfg. Co.	Chariton, IA	1905
Schroeder	E. Schroeder	Wellington, MO	1892
Schuerenberg	F. W. Schuerenberg	Brenham, TX	1892
Schuttler	Schuttler & Hotz	Chicago, IL	1892
Schuttler	Peter Schuttler Co.	Chicago, IL	1909
Schuttler	Springfield Wagon Co.	Fayetteville, AR	1945
Smith	Henry M. Smith	Frankfort, MI	1892
Smith	T. & H. Smith Co.	Pekin, IL	1892
Snyder	Snyder Wagon Works	Danville, IL	1892
Soilfitter	General Implement Co.	Cleveland, OH	1945

Trade Names (cont...)

South Bend	South Bend Wagon Co.	South Bend, IN	1892
Southwest	Fort Smith Wagon Co.	Fort Smith, AR	1924
Springfield	Springfield Wagon Co.	Springfield, MO	1905
Square Deal	Kentucky Wagon Mfg. Co.	Louisville, KY	1915
Standard	Standard Wagon Co.	Cincinnati, OH	1892
Stapler	W. T. Stapler	Harmony Grove, GA	1892
Steel King	International Harvester Co.	Chicago, IL	1913
Sterling	A. B. Spies	Clinton, IA	1892
Sterling	Abingdon Wagon Co.	Abingdon, IL	1905
Sterling	International Harvester Co.	Chicago, IL	1913
Stoughton	Stoughton Wagon Works	Stoughton, WI	1892
Streich	A. Streich & Bro. Co.	Oshkosh, WI	1909
Studebaker	Studebaker Bros. Mfg. Co.	South Bend, IN	1892
Sturdy	Abingdon Wagon Co.	Abingdon, IL	1915
Success	Kentucky Wagon Mfg. Co.	Louisville, KY	1915
Sunny South	Mandt Div., Moline Plow Co.	Moline, IL	1913
Superior	Abingdon Wagon Co.	Abingdon, IL	1915
Swab	Swab Wagon Co.	Elizabethville, PA	1905
Sweet's	B. F. & H. L. Sweet	Fond du Lac, WI	1892
Tanner	D. F. Tanner	Holland, NY	1909
Teddie	Turnbull Wagon Co.	Defiance, OH	1915
Tennessee	Kentucky Wagon Mfg. Co.	Louisville, KY	1892
Thomas	Thomas Wagon Co.	Vernon, NY	1905
Thornhill	Thornhill Wagon Co.	Lynchburg, VA	1905
Tiffin	Tiffin Agricultural Works	Tiffin, OH	1892
Tiffin	Tiffin Wagon Co.	Tiffin, OH	1905
Triumph	Fort Smith Wagon Co.	Fort Smith, AR	1924
Triumph	John Deere Wagon Works	Moline, IL	1924
Troy	Troy Wagon Works	Troy, OH	1892
Turnbull	Turnbull Wagon Co.	Defiance, OH	1892
Vanderburgh	H. S. Vanderburgh	Lithgow, NY	1892
Virginian	Auburn Wagon Co.	Martinsburg, WV	1924
Wadley	A. K. Wadley	Arkabutla, MS	1892
Wagner	J. H. Wagner & Co.	Vernon, IN	1892
Walker	Geo. S. Cady & Co.	Moravia, NY	1905
Warsaw	Cress Bros. & Co.	Warsaw, IL	1892
Weber	International Harvester Co.	Chicago, IL	1909
Weber	Weber Wagon Co.	Chicago, IL	1892
Wedepohl	H. Wedepohl	Berger, MO	1892
West Bend	Schmidt & Stork	West Bend, WI	1905
Western	Western Wheeled Scraper Co.	Aurora, IL	1892
White Hickory	Blount & Bell	East Point, GA	1892
White Hickory	White Hickory Wagon Co.	Atlanta, GA	1905
Wilharm	Christoph Wilharm	Tripoli, IA	1892
Williams	Williams Bros.	Ithaca, NY	1892
Winner	Kentucky Wagon Mfg. Co.	Louisville, KY	1915
Winona	Winona Wagon Co.	Winona, MN	1905

Trade Names (cont...)

Wisconsin	Moline Plow Co.	Moline, IL	1915
Wisconsin	Vaughn Mfg. Co.	Jefferson, WI	1915
Wise	Wise Wagon Works	Buena Vista, VA	1892
Woodchuck	Moline Plow Co.	Moline, IL	1915
Yale	Turnbull Wagon Co.	Defiance, OH	1915

Washing Machines

Knight's American Mechanical Dictionary of 1876 includes descriptions of many washing machines, even classifying them in their various methods of operation. The washing machine had come of age, but it would take until the early 1900s before washing machines appeared in most American farm homes. Numerous styles certainly were sold in the 1880-1900 period, but many of them were a picture of mediocrity, at best—a virtual waste of time, at worst. However, in defense of these early designs, let it be said that the washing machine was one of the greatest labor-saving devices to appear in the farm home. The hand-powered ones could often be operated by the youngsters in the household, as part of their daily or weekly chores. By 1910, the coming of small gasoline engines mechanized the process, making washday easier than it had ever been in history.

Although this section covers many different makes of washers, it certainly does not include all that were built from the 1870s onward. By 1890, it appears that there were literally hundreds of companies making washing machines. Many of these were small factories or even a one-room shop, with their sales area rarely extending into the adjacent counties.

Today, old washing machines are often a valued collectors item. Popular ones—such as the early Maytag—often are valued at $300 or more, depending on their condition. Sometimes, a power washer with a mounted engine will be valued much more, because of the value of the engine, in addition to the value of the washer itself. As with many of the implements and machines included in this book, there is no established market value as might be the case with antique coins or other antiques. The prices realized often reflect local demand and personal preferences. As with most antique items, the best bargains are often secured through private treaty.

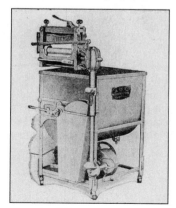

Altorfer Bros., Peoria, Ill.

This company was among the first to offer an electric washer, doing so in 1918. At the time, many washers were still hand-operated, with many others being operated by a gasoline engine. Altorfer Bros., called this its A.B.C. Super-Electric machine.

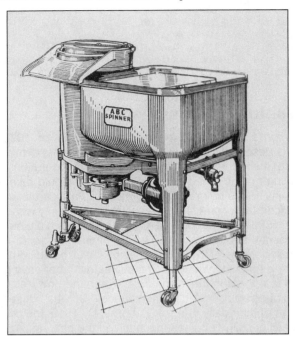

By the 1930s, Altorfer Bros. had refined its line of washing machines to include the ABC Spinner shown here. The company highly recommended the electric motor to power its washers. As an alternative, they could also be fitted for use with a gasoline engine.

American Washer Co., St. Louis, Mo.

The O-Joy washing machine of 1907, was unique in that it was powered by a self-propelling water motor. Pressurized water was used to operate the agitator; while wasteful of water, the design was simple and efficient.

Associated Manufacturers, Waterloo, Iowa

For 1917, Associated offered its Amanco Hand and Power Washer, a machine that could be operated through a belt pulley as shown; or lacking that, could be worked by hand. This machine included a power wringer, a feature welcomed on washday.

At Last Washing Machine Co., Perry, Iowa

This belt-powered washer was advertised in 1912 for $18. The company continued to supply repair parts for its machines at least into the late 1940s, although it appears that production ended by the late 1920s.

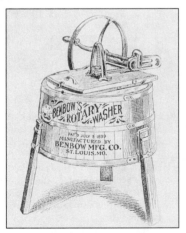

Benbow Manufacturing Co., St. Louis, Mo.

An advertisement of 1900 illustrates Benbow's Rotary Washer. A feature was the use of cedar for the tank. This machine could be cranked by hand or driven from a line-shaft or gasoline engine, if available. By 1905, the company was known as Benbow-Brammer Manufacturing Co.; shortly after, it disappears from the trade directories.

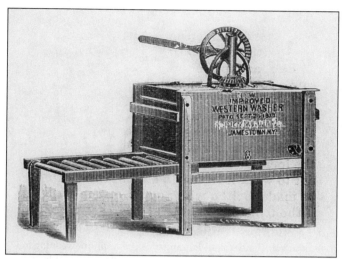

Blackstone Manufacturing Co., Jamestown, N.Y.

When this 1888 advertisement appeared for the New Improved Western Washer, the company had already been in business for some time, since it had already secured a sales agent at St. Louis. The Western remained on the market at least until 1910.

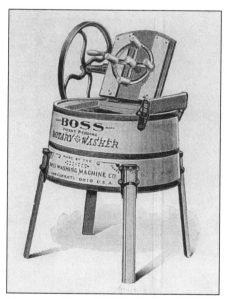

Boss Washing Machine Co., Cincinnati, Ohio

Advertising for the Boss washing machine first appears in 1901, although the rocker machine shown at the bottom of this illustration likely came onto the market sometime earlier. The company remained active in the business into the 1940s and continued to offer repair parts into the latter part of the 1940s, perhaps later.

H.F. Brammer Manufacturing Co., Davenport, Iowa

By 1899, Brammer was offering the B.B. Rotary Washer from his factory at Davenport, Iowa, and continued building washing machines at least into the 1930s, with parts still being available into the late 1940s. It is unknown if this company was connected with Benbow Manufacturing Co., noted previously in this section.

Buckeye Churn Co., Sidney, Ohio

The Queen Washer took the form shown here for 1892. This was strictly a hand washer, with no provision to be converted to a power machine. However, compared to the time-honored scrub board, this machine was a tremendous improvement.

The Dexter Co., Fairfield, Iowa

In 1917, Dexter announced its Dexter Power Washer, with its Model 3P Duchess Style being shown here. Like many others of its time, the external belt pulley permitted operation from an overhead line-shaft or directly from a gasoline engine; a lucky few were able to use an electric motor.

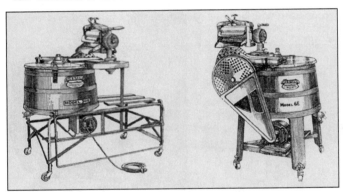

By 1930, the Dexter line included many models and styles. Its Long Bench Electric, Model 30-E was priced at $107, complete with a Westinghouse motor and insulated cord. The Dexter Special Electric, Model 6-E was priced at only $85. These machines could also be equipped with a small gasoline engine.

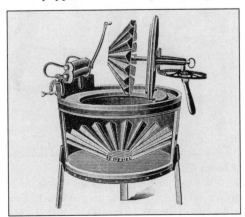

Diether & Barrows, Fort Wayne, Ind.

From 1892 comes this engraving of the Weisell Washer, probably in reference to its inventor. The bottom of the tub was equipped with raised wooden ribs and the revolving element was of heavy rubber. This machine was designed to rub and squeeze the clothes during the washing cycle.

Fairbanks, Morse & Co., Chicago, Ill.

About 1913, Fairbanks-Morse introduced its line of washing machines, all of them being power washers. They were built under Eclipse trademark of Fairbanks-Morse and ostensibly were to be used with the company's small Eclipse gasoline engines.

Globe Manufacturing Co., Perry, Iowa

This company offered the Quicker Yet washing machine shown here in 1917. At the time, the firm was building various washers and remained active into the 1920s. However, the 1931 trade listings indicate that parts were available from Barker Produce Equipment Co., Ottumwa, Iowa. By the late 1940s, parts could be secured from Dilenbeck Investment Co., Perry, Iowa.

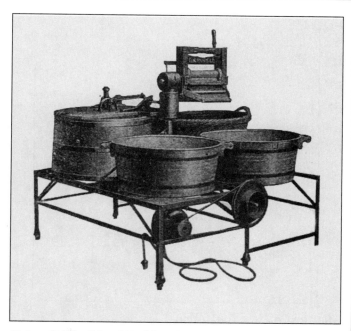

Grinnell Washing Machine Co., Grinnell, Iowa

This company began building an electric washer in 1912, known as the Big 4, continuing for some years. Little is known of this firm except that it continued under this name, offering repair parts as late as 1948.

Haag Bros. Co., Peoria, Ill.

This company apparently began building washing machines about 1912, with its 1914 model illustrated here. Bench machines like this one could hold various wash tubs and rinse tubs, with the wringer being workable on any of up to four tubs.

A 1927 advertisement shows the Haag washing machine equipped with a small gasoline engine, although it was also available with an electric motor. Subsequent activities of the firm have not been determined, although it supplied repair parts into the late 1940s.

Horton Manufacturing Co., Fort Wayne, Ind.

An 1894 advertisement illustrates the Western Combination Washer of the time, a rocker washer, complete with a wringer. This simple washer had no gears or other mechanism to get out of order; at the time, this was a great advantage.

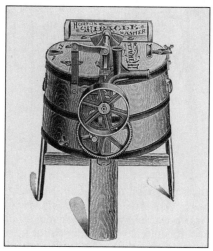

In 1911, Horton announced its No. 22 Horton Miracle Washer. It was a combination machine that could be operated by hand, but could easily be changed over for gasoline engine operation. The company noted in its advertising that many farmers already had an engine on the farm and it could easily be belted to this machine.

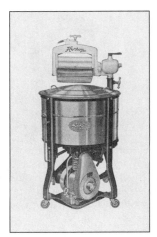

Horton announced its No. 34 Power washer in 1927; this machine could be powered by a gasoline engine as shown or could be operated with an electric motor. The company remained in the washer business at least into the late 1940s, but subsequent activities are unknown.

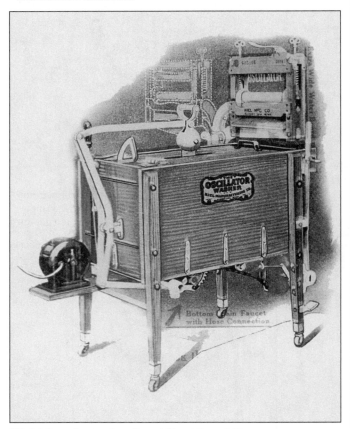

Kiel Manufacturing Co., Albert Lea, Minn.

As described in 1915, the Kiel was sold as "the washer without a fault." It was powered by an electric motor, although it is presumed that it could also be equipped for gasoline engine power. Little is known of the company; subsequently, parts were furnished from American Gas Machine Co., also at Albert Lea, Minn.

Maytag Co., Newton, Iowa

This firm began building washing machines in 1909 and continues under the same name today. Its early Maytag Power Washer shown here became an immediate success, with thousands being sold.

A 1910 offering from Maytag was its small Pastime Washer, with sales promotions noting that "A Pastime Washer with a five-year old kid attached will do your washing in twenty minutes with no more wear on the kid than would result in twenty minutes playing marbles."

Meadows Manufacturing Co., Pontiac, Ill.

By 1910, Meadows was offering this interesting power-washer design. By the 1920s, the company was offering new designs such as the Meadomotor; the company had also moved to Bloomington, Ill. Meadows was supplying repair parts into the late 1940s.

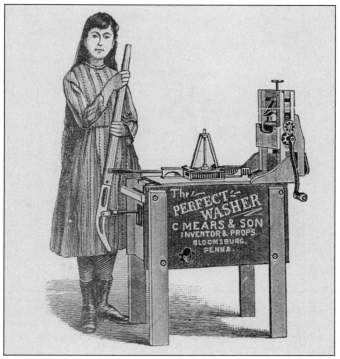

C. Mears & Son, Bloomsburg, Pa.

An 1892 advertisement shows a young woman at work on the Perfect Washer, invented and built by this company and also offered for sale by Rector & Wilhemy Co., Omaha, Neb. It was built in three sizes, the No. 2 for the common family, the No. 3 for a large family and the No. 4 for hotels or laundries.

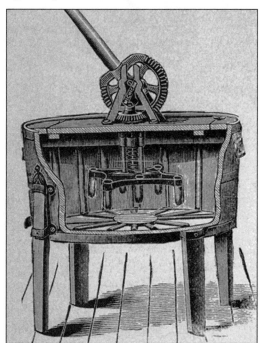

Michigan Washing Machine Company, Muskegon, Mich.

By the 1890s, hand-operated washing machines were gaining in popularity. By 1900, the majority of American households had some type of washing machine. By 1920, the majority of these

were powered by a small engine or an electric motor. Much of the housewife's drudgery was mitigated.

Muir Washing Machine Co., Muir, Mich.

Dilley's Laundry King was the title given to Muir's newest model, apparently just coming to the market in 1893. Subsequent activities of this company are unknown.

Willis R. Munger, St. Joseph, Mo.

Apparently, Munger had recently developed this machine when this 1905 advertisement appeared. Aside from this advertisement, nothing is known of the company, but it does not appear in 1909 trade directories.

One Minute Manufacturing Co., Newton, Iowa

This company emerged with a power washer in 1909; it was similar in design to the Maytag washer noted above. The company also manufactured butter churns and other items, including a small gasoline engine to power the washer.

In addition to its 1909 power washer, One Minute Manufacturing Co. also offered a hand-powered machine, calling this one its No. 5. A few years later, the company noted that thousands of its dealers were very satisfied with the machine. One Minute Manufacturing Co. remained active at least into the late 1940s, but its eventual disposition is unknown.

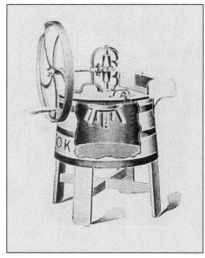

Perfection Manufacturing Co., Cowan, Ind.

Its 1905 advertising noted that "The Neff Perfection washes everything but the dishes, and the baby, and does it well." Despite these qualities, the company appears to have lasted for only a short time and does not appear in subsequent listings of the trade directories.

Rawleigh Manufacturing Co., Freeport, Ill.

About 1912, W.T. Rawleigh expanded his established home remedy business to include gasoline engines, washing machines and other items. All went well until a fire in 1916 wiped out the manufacturing enterprises. Subsequently, Rawleigh withdrew from these activities; the company remains active with Rawleigh home products.

Red Jacket Manufacturing Co., Davenport, Iowa

This famous company is listed under Pumps in a previous section of this book; in 1905, it took a short diversion by adding the Simplex washing machine to its product line. The venture apparently lasted for only a short time, since the Simplex later appears under the auspices of Superior Machine Co., Sterling, Ill.

Did You Know?

Very early wooden forks might bring $100 or more, while common metal forks usually sell from $10 and upwards.

Victor Manufacturing Co., Leavenworth, Kan.

A 1914 announcement illustrated the Wonder Washer from Victor Manufacturing Co. This power washer could be operated from any gasoline engine or electric motor. Subsequent activities of the firm are unknown, but it does not appear in subsequent farm implement trade directories.

Voss Bros. Manufacturing Co., Davenport, Iowa

Ocean Wave washing machines appeared from Voss Bros., in 1905, perhaps earlier. This one could be hand-operated or power-driven. Voss continued in the washing machine business at least into the late 1940s, but its eventual destiny is unknown.

Waverly Woodenware Works, St. Joseph, Mo.

For a short time around 1906, the Waverly power washer was available, but no details of the firm have come to the present research, aside from this single advertisement.

Anthony Wayne Manufacturing Co., Fort Wayne, Ind.

In 1893, the Wayne Combination Washer took the identity shown here; this was a rocker machine, worked by rocking the tub back and forth.

White Lily Washer Co., Davenport, Iowa

A 1905 advertisement from this firm noted that they already had 6,000 dealers for the White Lily washer. In 1906, this advertisement appeared, showing the While Lily, the White Rose and the White Daisy, each being distinctly different models. Also illustrated was its White Lily gasoline engine. White Lily was one of the first companies to offer a successful power washer. The White Lily line continued into the 1920s; by 1931, parts for these machines could be secured from Brammer Manufacturing Co., also located at Davenport.

Trade Names

1900 Cataract	1900 Washer Co.	Binghampton, NY	1924
20th Century	Twentieth Century Mfg. Co.	Mansfield, OH	1909
2-in-1	S. E. Schroeder Mfg. Co.	Minier, IL	1915
A.B.C.	Altorfer Bros.	Peoria, IL	1915
Acme	H. H. Palmer Co.	Rockford, IL	1892
Aerowing	Boss Washing Machine Co.	Cincinnati, OH	1931
Alco	Altorfer Bros.	Peoria, IL	1915
Amanco	Associated Manufacturers Co.	Waterloo, IA	1915
Am-Co	American Woodenware Mfg. Co.	Toledo, OH	1915
American	American Woodenware Mfg. Co.	Toledo, OH	1905
American	Bluffton Mfg. Co.	Bluffton, IN	1892
American	Horton Mfg. Co.	Fort Wayne, IN	1905
American Beauty	Getz Power Washer Co.	Cedar Falls, IA	1924
American Union	Blackstone Mfg. Co.	Jamestown, NY	1905
Anthony Wayne	Anthony Wayne Mfg. Co.	Fort Wayne, IN	1905
Anthony Wayne	Wayne Mfg. Co.	St. Louis, MO	1909
Apex	Apex Appliance Co.	Chicago, IL	1924
At Last	At Last Washer Co.	Perry, IA	1915
Atlantic	Spicer Mfg. Co.	New Philadelphia, OH	1892
Automatic	Automatic Electric Washer Co.	Newton, IA	1913
Automatic	Boss Washing Machine Co.	Cincinnati, OH	1913
Automatic	Voss Bros. Mfg. Co.	Davenport, IA	1909
Awco	American Washer Co.	St. Louis, MO	1915
B & G	One Minute Mfg. Co.	Newton, IA	1915
B.B.	Benbow-Brammer Mfg. Co.	St. Louis, MO	1905
B.B. Rotary	H. F. Brammer Mfg. Co.	Davenport, IA	1909
Baby Grand	Maytag Co.	Newton, IA	1924
Baldwin	Baldwin Woodenware Co.	Lafayette, IN	1892
Banner	Boss Washing Machine Co.	Cincinnati, OH	1905
Becker	N. C. Baughman	York, PA	1909
Big 3	Barlow & Seelig Mfg. Co.	Ripon, WI	1915
Big 4	Grinnell Washing Machine Co.	Grinnell, IA	1915
Billy Twister	Dexter Co.	Fairfield, IA	1913
Blackstone	Blackstone Mfg. Co.	Jamestown, NY	1905
Blue Ribbon Rotary	H. F. Brammer Mfg. Co.	Davenport, IA	1909
Boss	Boss Washing Machine Co.	Cincinnati, OH	1905
Brammer	H. F. Brammer Mfg. Co.	Davenport, IA	1892
Brammer	H. F. Brammer Mfg. Co.	Davenport, IA	1905
Buckeye	M. Brown & Co.	Wapakoneta, OH	1905
Busy Girl	Associated Manufacturers Co.	Waterloo, IA	1915
Camp	Camp Mfg. Co.	Washington, IL	1924
Cascade	Wahle Foundry & Machine Works	Davenport, IA	1909

Trade Names (cont...)

Challenge	Blackstone Mfg. Co.	Jamestown, NY	1905
Champion	Boss Washing Machine Co.	Cincinnati, OH	1924
Champion	Glascock Bros. Mfg. Co.	Muncie, IN	1905
Champion	Manuel Drumm	Tipton, MO	1905
Champion Rotary	Boss Washing Machine Co.	Cincinnati, OH	1909
Chautauqua	Blackstone Mfg. Co.	Jamestown, NY	1905
Chicago	Chicago Dryer Co.	Chicago, IL	1924
Chief	Wayne Mfg. Co.	St. Louis, MO	1909
Cincinnati Square	Boss Washing Machine Co.	Cincinnati, OH	1909
Cincinnati Western	Boss Washing Machine Co.	Cincinnati, OH	1905
Clarinda	Clarinda Mfg. Co.	Clarinda, IA	1924
Clarinda	Lisle Corp.	Clarinda, IA	1939
Climax	Climax Washer Co.	Oakville, IN	1905
Climax	Dexter Co.	Fairfield, IA	1915
Clinton	Kelly-Sorenson Furniture Co.	Clinton, IA	1915
Clover Leaf	United Engine Co.	Lansing, MI	1931
Coffield	Coffield Motor Washer Co.	Dayton, OH	1924
Coffield	P. T. Coffield & Son	Dayton, OH	1909
Columbia	Benbow-Brammer Mfg. Co.	St. Louis, MO	1905
Columbia	H. F. Brammer Mfg. Co.	Davenport, IA	1909
Columbia Standard	Wayne Mfg. Co.	St. Louis, MO	1909
Companion	Altorfer Bros.	Peoria, IL	1931
Conlon	Graybar Electric Co.	Chicago, IL	1931
Conlon	Western Electric Co.	New York, NY	1924
Crown Princess	Princess Mfg. Co.	Cincinnati, OH	1913
Cruiser	Dexter Co.	Fairfield, IA	1924
Cyclone	Kirksville Mfg. Co.	Kirksville, MO	1905
Daley	M. H. Daley	Charles City, IA	1913
Dandy	Union Foundry & Machine Co.	Ottawa, KS	1915
Daylight	Puffer-Hubbard Co.	Minneapolis, MN	1924
Decker	L. M. Decker Co.	Omaha, NE	1931
DeForest	Miller Products Co.	Waterloo, IA	1931
DeLuxe	White Lily Washer Co.	Davenport, IA	1924
Dexter	Dexter Co.	Fairfield, IA	1915
Dietz	Boss Washing Machine Co.	Cincinnati, OH	1905
Drumm's Best	Manuel Drumm	Tipton, MO	1905
Duchess	Dexter Co.	Fairfield, IA	1924
Duplex	Dexter Co.	Fairfield, IA	1924
Duplex	Voss Bros. Mfg. Co.	Davenport, IA	1913
Duro	Rotary Washing Machine Co.	St. Louis, MO	1913
Eagle	Wayne Mfg. Co.	St. Louis, MO	1909
Eagle High Speed	Voss Bros. Mfg. Co.	Davenport, IA	1905
Easiest Way	Easiest Way Mfg. Co.	Sandusky, OH	1915
Easy	Syracuse Washing Machine Corp.	Syracuse, NY	1931
Easy Clean	Hiawatha Mfg. Co.	Hiawatha, KS	1909
Eclipse	Fairbanks, Morse & Co.	Chicago, IL	1915
Eclipse	Voss Bros. Mfg. Co.	Davenport, IA	1913
Eden	Brokaw-Eden Mfg. Co.	Chicago, IL	1915

Trade Names (cont...)

Eden	Eden Washer Corp.	Chicago, IL	1931
Electric Lady	Michigan Washing Machine Co.	Muskegon, MI	1915
Electric Maid	Grinnell Washing Machine Co.	Grinnell, IA	1915
Electric Star	Wayne Mfg. Co.	St. Louis, MO	1915
Elite	Minier Mfg. Co.	Minier, IL	1924
Elmo	Grinnell Washing Machine Co.	Grinnell, IA	1915
Emerald	Horton Mfg. Co.	Fort Wayne, IN	1931
Empire	Empire Washer Co.	Jamestown, NY	1892
Everede	Brokaw-Eden Mfg. Co.	Alton, IL	1924
Ever-Ready	Brokaw-Eden Mfg. Co.	Chicago, IL	1915
F.K.	Kostlan Mfg. Co.	Traer, IA	1913
Fairday	Fairbanks, Morse & Co.	Chicago, IL	1924
Fairfield	Dexter Co.	Fairfield, IA	1924
Farmer's Friend	G. & D. Mfg. Co.	Streator, IL	1924
Fastwin	Dexter Co.	Fairfield, IA	1939
Faultless	Wenzelman Mfg. Co.	Galesburg, IL	1931
Favorite	James Groenendyke	Middletown, IN	1892
Federal	Federal Electric Co.	Chicago, IL	1924
Five Minutes	Walker Mfg. Co.	Council Bluffs, IA	1905
Flanders	Moses P. Flanders	Sharon, VT	1892
Gainaday	Gainaday Electric Co.	Pittsburgh, PA	1931
Gainaday	Pittsburgh Gauge & Supply Co.	Pittsburgh, PA	1924
Gearless	Walker Mfg. Co.	Council Bluffs, IA	1913
Gee Whiz	Gee Whiz Mfg. Co.	Des Moines, IA	1905
G-E-M	Grinnell Washing Machine Co.	Grinnell, IA	1915
Genesee	Genesee Valley Mfg. Co.	Mt. Morris, NY	1924
Getz	Getz Power Washer Co.	Cedar Falls, IA	1924
Getz	Getz Power Washer Co.	Morton, IL	1915
Geyser	Geyser Electric Co.	Chicago, IL	1924
Geyser	Geyser Electric Co.	Chicago, IL	1931
Gibson Jr.	H. F. Brammer Mfg. Co.	Davenport, IA	1939
Globe	Boss Washing Machine Co.	Cincinnati, OH	1913
Globe	Horton Mfg. Co.	Fort Wayne, IN	1905
Golden West	Grinnell Washing Machine Co.	Grinnell, IA	1915
Grand	Davenport Washing Machine Co.	Davenport, IA	1915
Great Western	Benbow-Brammer Mfg. Co.	St. Louis, MO	1905
Grinnell	Grinnell Washing Machine Co.	Grinnell, IA	1924
Guarantee	Michigan Washing Machine Co.	Muskegon, MI	1905
Haag	Haag Bros.	Peoria, IA	1924
Handy	Glascock Bros. Mfg. Co.	Muncie, IN	1905
Hero	Buckeye Churn Co.	Sidney, OH	1905
Herschel	R. Herschel Mfg. Co.	Peoria, IL	1931
High Speed Rotary	Voss Bros. Mfg. Co.	Davenport, IA	1905
Home Gem	Wm. S. Miller	Meyersdale, PA	1905
Home Model	Miller Mfg. Co.	Meyersdale, PA	1913
Horton	Horton Mfg. Co.	Fort Wayne, IN	1905

Trade Names (cont...)

Huenefeld	E. H. Huenefeld	Cincinnati, OH	1905
Huffer	J. M. Flook & Bro.	Myersville, MD	1892
Hummer	White Lily Washer Co.	Davenport, IA	1913
Ideal	Bluffton Mfg. Co.	Bluffton, IN	1915
Ideal	Haag Bros.	Peoria, IL	1915
Ideal	Ideal Gas Engine Co.	Independence, IA	1915
Illinois	C. E. Ross	Lincoln, IL	1913
Improved Doty	J. G. Henderson & Co.	Keokuk, IA	1892"
Improved Globe	Boss Washing Machine Co.	Cincinnati, OH	1905
Improved Globe	Boss Washing Machine Co.	Cincinnati, OH	1909
Improved Thor	Hurley Machine Co.	Chicago, IL	1924
Improved Western	B. Wright & Son	Hudson, MI	1892
Improved Western	Vandergrift Mfg. Co.	Jamestown, NY	1892
Iowa King	Kostlan Mfg. Co.	Traer, IA	1913
Jensen	Jensen Mfg. Co.	Palmyra, NY	1913
Jewel	American Washer Co.	St. Louis, MO	1915
Jewel	Wayne Mfg. Co.	St. Louis, MO	1909
Judd	Judd Laundry Machine Co.	Chicago, IL	1924
Kibby's	At Last Washer Co.	Perry, IA	1931
Kill Kare	Michigan Washing Machine Co.	Muskegon, MI	1924
Kill-Kare	S. E. Schroeder Mfg. Co.	Minier, IL	1915
King	Winger-Blume Mfg. Co.	Wolcott, IN	1915
Klean Kwick	Acme Mfg. Co.	Cedar Falls, IA	1931
Klean Kwick	Klean Kwick Washer Co.	Cedar Falls, IA	1924
Klean-Kwick	DuMond Mfg. Co.	Cedar Falls, IA	1915
Kleenette	Horton Mfg. Co.	Fort Wayne, IN	1939
Klotz	Klotz & Kromer Machine Co.	Sandusky, OH	1892
Klymax	Home Utilities Co.	Chicago, IL	1924
Knoxall	H. F. Brammer Mfg. Co.	Davenport, IA	1945
Lachance	Keller Mfg. Co.	Sauk Center, MN	1892
Ladies' Friend	D. L. Bates & Co.	Dayton, OH	1913
Laundry Maid	One Minute Mfg. Co.	Newton, IA	1924
Laundry Queen	Grinnell Washing Machine Co.	Grinnell, IA	1915
Leader	Elgin Combination Wagon Box Co.	Elgin, IL	1905
Leader	Leader Iron Works	Decatur, IL	1915
Lennox	Lennox Machine Co.	Newton, IA	1915
Lewis	Grinnell Washing Machine Co.	Grinnell, IA	1915
Liberty Bell	Altorfer Bros.	Peoria, IL	1915
Litchfield	Litchfield Mfg. Co.	Waterloo, IA	1915
Little Princess	Princess Mfg. Co.	Cincinnati, OH	1913
Lockhart	Gilbert Lockhart	Bryan, OH	1892
Magic Disc	H. F. Brammer Mfg. Co.	Davenport, IA	1945
Magic Wash	Holland-Rieger Corp.	Sandusky, OH	1945
Marvel	Eagle Mfg. Co.	Cincinnati, OH	1915
Maumee	American Woodenware Mfg. Co.	Toledo, OH	1915
Maytag	Maytag Co.	Newton, IA	1915
Meadows	Meadows Mfg. Co.	Pontiac, IL	1915
Merry Widow	Bluffton Mfg. Co.	Bluffton, IN	1909
Messinger	Messinger Mfg. Co.	Tatamy, PA	1924

Trade Names (cont...)

Michigan	Michigan Washing Machine Co.	Muskegon, MI	1892
Miracle	Horton Mfg. Co.	Fort Wayne, IN	1915
Mitchell	Wiard & Eggleston	East Avon, NY	1892
Modern Maid	Holland-Rieger Corp.	Sandusky, OH	1945
Monarch	American Woodenware Mfg. Co.	Toledo, OH	1905
Monarch	Dexter Co.	Fairfield, IA	1913
Moore	Given Moore Co.	Spring Valley, IL	1915
Mount Gilead	Hydraulic Press Mfg. Co.	Mt. Gilead, OH	1924
Muskegon	Michigan Washing Machine Co.	Muskegon, MI	1915
Myers Perfect	J. W. Myers Co.	Ashland, OH	1905
National	National Motor Co.	Springfield, OH	1915
New Awco	American Washer Co.	St. Louis, MO	1915
New Century	Climax Washer Co.	Oakville, IN	1905
New Era	Glascock Bros. Mfg. Co.	Muncie, IN	1905
New Home	Wells Hay Press Co.	Streator, IL	1913
New Liberty	Fosston Mfg. Co.	St. Paul, MN	1924
New Miller	N. C. Baughman	York, PA	1905
New Process	Meadows Sheet Metal Works	Meadows, IL	1915
New Standard	Boss Washing Machine Co.	Cincinnati, OH	1905
New Standard	G. Lockhart	Bryan, OH	1905
New Wayne	Wayne Mfg. Co.	St. Louis, MO	1909
New Western	Wayne Mfg. Co.	St. Louis, MO	1909
Newdisco	Newton Disc Plow Co.	Newton, IA	1913
Nineteen Hundred	Nineteen Hundred Washer Co.	Binghamton, NY	1905
Nuway	Haag Bros.	Peoria, IL	1924
O.I.C.	H. F. Brammer Mfg. Co.	Davenport, IA	1905
O.K.	H. F. Brammer Mfg. Co.	Davenport, IA	1905
Ocean Wave	Voss Bros. Mfg. Co.	Davenport, IA	1905
Ocean Wave	Voss Bros. Mfg. Co.	Davenport, IA	1924
O-Joy	American Washer Co.	St. Louis, MO	1913
One Minute	One Minute Mfg. Co.	Newton, IA	1909
Original Brammer	H. F. Brammer Mfg. Co.	Davenport, IA	1909
Oscillator	California Garden Tool Co.	Ferndale, CA	1892
Over	Ewald Over	Indianapolis, IN	1892
Packard	Dexter Co.	Fairfield, IA	1924
Pan American	Blackstone Mfg. Co.	Jamestown, NY	1905
Paragon	Chas. G. Allen & Co.	Barre, MA	1892
Paragon	Paragon Mfg. Co.	Chicago, IL	1915
Pastime	Parsons Hawkeye Mfg. Co.	Newton, IA	1909
Peacemaker Rotary	H. F. Brammer Mfg. Co.	Davenport, IA	1909
Pedigo Perfection	Oakes Mfg. Co.	Bloomington, IN	1905
Peerless	Michigan Washing Machine Co.	Muskegon, MI	1905
Peerless	Oakes Mfg. Co.	Bloomington, IN	1905
Pendulum	Voss Bros. Mfg. Co.	Davenport, IA	1913
Peoria	Clark, Quien & Morse	Peoria, IL	1905
Peoria	Haag Bros.	Peoria, IL	1915

Trade Names (cont...)

Perfect	C. Mears	Brooklyn, NY	1905
Perfect	Horton Mfg. Co.	Fort Wayne, IN	1931
Perfection	Perfection Mfg. Co.	Cowan, IN	1905
Perfection	W. H. Neff	Cowan, IN	1892
Perry Pride	At Last Washer Co.	Perry, IA	1924
Perry Pride	Perry Washer Co.	Perry, IA	1915
Prima	Prima Mfg. Co.	Sidney, OH	1931
Princess Automatic	Princess Mfg. Co.	Cincinnati, OH	1913
Progress	Altorfer Bros.	Peoria, IL	1924
Queen	Buckeye Churn Co.	Sidney, OH	1892
Queen	Jas. H. Knoll	Reading, PA	1915
Quick Action	Wahle Foundry & Machine Works	Davenport, IA	1909
Quick Time	Blackstone Mfg. Co.	Jamestown, NY	1909
Quick Time	Blackstone Mfg. Co.	Jamestown, NY	1913
Quicker Yet	Globe Mfg. Co.	Perry, IA	1915
Quickest Ever	Blackstone Mfg. Co.	Jamestown, NY	1913
Quite-An-Easy	Gee Whiz Mfg. Co.	Des Moines, IA	1909
Rainbow	Bluffton Mfg. Co.	Bluffton, IN	1905
Red Electric	Hurley Machine Co.	Chicago, IL	1924
Regal	Blackstone Mfg. Co.	Jamestown, NY	1913
Rex	Blackstone Mfg. Co.	Jamestown, NY	1913
Richmond	Richmond Cedar Works	Richmond, VA	1915
Roanoke	Altorfer Bros.	Peoria, IL	1915
Rocker	Peerless Mfg. Co.	Fort Wayne, IN	1913
Rocker	Rocker Washer Co.	Fort Wayne, IN	1892
Ross	C. E. Ross	Lincoln, IL	1892
Rotary	Rotary Washing Machine Co.	St. Louis, MO	1913
Royal	Haag Bros.	Peoria, IL	1915
Royal	Wayne Mfg. Co.	St. Louis, MO	1909
Royal Blue	H. F. Brammer Mfg. Co.	Davenport, IA	1909
Royale	Dexter Co.	Fairfield, IA	1939
Rural	Davenport Washing Machine Co.	Davenport, IA	1915
Rustler	Newton Disc Plow Co.	Newton, IA	1913
Sandow	Sandy McManus Inc.	Waterloo, IA	1915
Sandusky	One Minute Washer Co.	Sandusky, OH	1915
Sani	Wenzelman Mfg. Co.	Galesburg, IL	1915
Schroeder	Benbow-Brammer Mfg. Co.	St. Louis, MO	1905
Schroeder Rotary	H. F. Brammer Mfg. Co.	Davenport, IA	1909
Sea Wave	Voss Bros. Mfg. Co.	Davenport, IA	1931
Sheldon	Sheldon Engine & Sales Co.	Waterloo, IA	1924
Sieverkropp	Sieverkropp Engine Co.	Racine, WI	1924
Silent	Silent Washer Co.	Appleton, WI	1915
Simplex	Simplex Washer Co.	Davenport, IA	1905
Simplex	Superior Machine Co.	Sterling, IL	1915
Snow Ball	Wahle Foundry & Machine Works	Davenport, IA	1909
Snow Flake Rotary	H. F. Brammer Mfg. Co.	Davenport, IA	1909
Snowhite	Globe Mfg. Co.	Perry, IA	1905
Snowhite Rotary	H. F. Brammer Mfg. Co.	Davenport, IA	1909
Solo	Dexter Co.	Fairfield, IA	1924
Speedex	Dexter Co.	Fairfield, IA	1939

Trade Names (cont...)

Speedy High Speed	H. F. Brammer Mfg. Co.	Davenport, IA	1909
Spinner	Altorfer Bros.	Peoria, IL	1931
Square Deal Rotary	H. F. Brammer Mfg. Co.	Davenport, IA	1909
St. Louis	Wayne Mfg. Co.	St. Louis, MO	1909
Standard	G. Lockhart	Bryan, OH	1905
Standard Champion	Boss Washing Machine Co.	Cincinnati, OH	1909
Standard Perfection	Boss Washing Machine Co.	Cincinnati, OH	1909
Star	C. E. Ross	Lincoln, IL	1905
Steel King	Hiawatha Mfg. Co.	Hiawatha, KS	1909
Sterling	American Woodenware Mfg. Co.	Toledo, OH	1915
Sterling	Superior Machine Co.	Sterling, IL	1915
Streator	Wells Hay Press Co.	Streator, IL	1915
Success	Superior Machine Co.	Sterling, IL	1915
Sucker State	Chas. H. Trappe	Mascoutah, IL	1905
Sucker State	Trappe Bros.	Mascoutah, IL	1892
Sun	Blackstone Mfg. Co.	Jamestown, NY	1905
Sunbeam Surf	Sunbeam Electric Co.	Evansville, IN	1924
Sunny Monday	Dexter Co.	Fairfield, IA	1915
Sunshine	Voss Bros. Mfg. Co.	Davenport, IA	1913
Superior	Horton Mfg. Co.	Fort Wayne, IN	1909
Superior	Superior Machine Co.	Sterling, IL	1915
Superior	Wayne Mfg. Co.	St. Louis, MO	1909
Thermo	Boss Washing Machine Co.	Cincinnati, OH	1931
Thrift	H. F. Brammer Mfg. Co.	Davenport, IA	1931
Toledo	American Woodenware Mfg. Co.	Toledo, OH	1915
Twin	DuMond Mfg. Co.	Cedar Falls, IA	1915
Twin-Tex	Haag Bros.	Peoria, IL	1931
Two-in-One	Minier Mfg. Co.	Minier, IL	1924
Uncle Sam	Uncle Sam Washer Co.	Des Moines, IA	1909
Uneeda American	Boss Washing Machine Co.	Cincinnati, OH	1905
Union	Union Foundry & Machine Co.	Ottawa, KS	1915
United	United Engine Co.	Lansing, MI	1915
United States	M. Brown & Co.	Wapakoneta, OH	1892
United States	M. Brown & Co.	Wapakoneta, OH	1905
United States	United States Washing Machine Co.	Racine, WI	1905
Universal	Voss Bros. Mfg. Co.	Davenport, IA	1915
Upton	Upton Machine Co.	St. Joseph, MI	1931
USA	Fosston Mfg. Co.	St. Paul, MN	1909
Utility	G. & D. Mfg. Co.	Streator, IL	1924
Van Buren	Van Buren & Bitler	Carey, OH	1892
Veribest	Boss Washing Machine Co.	Cincinnati, OH	1909
Vortex	Haag Bros.	Peoria, IL	1931
Voss	Voss Bros. Mfg. Co.	Davenport, IA	1915
Wamanco	Wayne Mfg. Co.	St. Louis, MO	1915
Washmaster	Holland-Rieger Corp.	Sandusky, OH	1945
Water Witch	H. F. Brammer Mfg. Co.	Davenport, IA	1909
Waverly	Waverly Woodenware Works	St. Joseph, MO	1905
Wayne	Horton Mfg. Co.	Fort Wayne, IN	1905
Wayne	Wayne Mfg. Co.	St. Louis, MO	1909
Weisell Fair	Diether & Barrows	Fort Wayne, IN	1892

Trade Names (cont...)

Western	American Woodenware Mfg. Co.	Toledo, OH	1905
Western	Blackstone Mfg. Co.	Jamestown, NY	1905
Western	Bluffton Mfg. Co.	Bluffton, IN	1905
Western	Horton Mfg. Co.	Fort Wayne, IN	1892
Western	Horton Mfg. Co.	Fort Wayne, IN	1905
Western American	Bluffton Mfg. Co.	Bluffton, IN	1905
Western American	Bluffton Mfg. Co.	Bluffton, IN	1909
Western Defender	Boss Washing Machine Co.	Cincinnati, OH	1905
Western Star	Wayne Mfg. Co.	St. Louis, MO	1909
Whirlpool	Horton Mfg. Co.	Fort Wayne, IN	1913
White Daisy	White Lily Washer Co.	Davenport, IA	1909
White Lily	White Lily Washer Co.	Davenport, IA	1905
White Rose	White Lily Washer Co.	Davenport, IA	1909
White Swan	Davenport Washing Machine Co.	Davenport, IA	1905
White Washer	White Lily Washer Co.	Davenport, IA	1909
White's DeLuxe	H. F. Brammer Mfg. Co.	Davenport, IA	1931
Wiard's Standard	Wiard Mfg. Co.	East Avon, NY	1905
Winner	Wayne Mfg. Co.	St. Louis, MO	1909
Wizard	International Mfg. Co.	Omaha, NE	1905
Wolverine	Michigan Washing Machine Co.	Muskegon, MI	1924
Woman's Friend	Fosston Mfg. Co.	St. Paul, MN	1909
Wonder	Victor Mfg. Co.	Leavenworth, KS	1915
Woodrow	Woodrow Mfg. Co.	Newton, IA	1924
World	C. E. Ross	Lincoln, IL	1905
Worldbeater	M. H. Daley	Charles City, IA	1913
X.L.	Boss Washing Machine Co.	Cincinnati, OH	1905
Yost	Yost Gearless Motor Co.	Springfield, OH	1913

Well Drilling Machinery

The dug well goes back to the beginning of time, the simplest form being a hole dug in the ground and the water then being dipped out with a jar or bucket. The dug well was an important part of early farm life, since it was about the only means available to secure water, aside from living near a stream, pond or lake. In areas where the soil was unstable, a curb was set as the digging progressed. This kept the well from caving in and sometimes the curb remained. In other instances, brick was used to line the outside of the well.

A driven well was a shallow well whereby water was secured by driving a sand point down to water. The point was attached to a piece of pipe and driven downward, with sections being added as the job progressed. The drilled well was well established for various purposes by the 1870s, with the portable well drilling rigs shown in this section appearing in the following years. Various drills appeared, eventually being mounted on a motor truck for easy portability. In recent years, the well drill has all but left the scene, with the new rotary drills taking their place.

A bored well is a shallow well that is dug by means of an auger, instead of being dug by hand. Bored wells can be much deeper than would be feasible to dig by hand. Artesian wells are not so common. These are natural wells in which water flows to the surface from subterranean supplies and needs nothing except a means of securing the well head and controlling the flow. Likewise, springs are still common. Water rises to the top of the ground or nearly so, giving plenty of water in normal seasons, but often drying up in dry weather. Today, the ancient well machinery shown here is almost impossible to find, having long ago made its trip to the scrap yard.

American Well Works, Aurora, Ill.

An 1885 catalog of American Well Works displays its Challenge Well Boring Rig. The was essentially a well auger, operated by hand or horse power. When the auger filled it was hoisted to the top, emptied and returned for another lift. It could be fitted with augers anywhere from 6 to 20 inches in diameter.

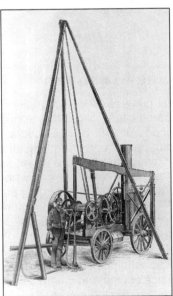

By 1885, American Well Works was providing the Keystone Portable Steam Drill, a large outfit designed to drive deep wells. The company held nearly 70 patents covering various kinds of

well drilling machinery, including those of M.C. and M.T. Chapman, specifically covering the machinery for drilled wells.

F.C. Austin Manufacturing Co., Harvey, Ill.

By the 1890s, Austin emerged as a major manufacturer of well-drilling equipment. One of its larger outfits was this big drill with a self-contained engine and boiler. With thousands of farms being settled and most of them having a less than desirable water supply, well drillers found ample work for many years.

By 1910, Austin refined and improved its line to include everything from a small one-man drilling rig, to a huge engine-powered, self-propelled well drill. Many of the small outfits were owned by threshermen who drilled wells for their neighbors.

Canton Well Drilling Machine Co., Canton, Ohio

For 1888, this firm offered the Poor Man's Well Drilling Machine. At the time, most well drilling outfits were expensive;

this was obviously an attempt to convince prospective buyers that the machine shown here was built to fit their pocketbook. Aside from this illustration, nothing is known of the company or its activities.

Chicago Tubular Well Works, Chicago, Ill.

In 1888, this firm offered the Goulds & Austin Acme Rock-Drilling Machine. Despite the long title, it was essentially a well drill. This one is folded up and moving to the next job. The majority of these machines were used to drill for water, but occasionally found their way to jobs requiring test bore holes, prospecting for mineral deposits and the like.

Edward Christman, Massillon, Ohio

A 1908 advertisement illustrates the Christman machine, typical of the small well drills usually found in rural areas at the time. This one had its own engine and boiler, with traction wheels added for portability.

Did You Know?

Among collectors of vintage farm equipment, old mowing machines have acquired a market value that is quite variable. Very old machines often bring $250 or more, even in poor condition. Later machines, usually after 1920, can sometimes sell for $100 or more, but many can be bought for much less.

Dempster Mill Manufacturing Co., Beatrice, Neb.

For 1900, Dempster offered this well drill as one of eight different styles available at the time. It is shown in the operating position. While a steam engine is visible in the engraving, no boiler is seen; presumably, steam could be secured from a steam-traction engine in the locality. This company also made windmills, gasoline engines and many other items.

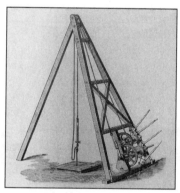

Fort Scott Foundry & Machine Works, Fort Scott, Kan.

An 1888 engraving illustrates the Williams & Kanning No. 1 drilling machine, a small outfit with a folding tripod. This small machine was operated entirely by hand, so there is no doubt that plenty of work was involved in operating this machine. Despite this, it was probably a welcome sight in a time when there was little else other than hand power or horse power.

Ft. Scott offered this huge semi-portable well drill in 1888. It was operated by a steam engine through a belt. Given the size, weight and bulk of the engine, setting up to drill a well would indeed have been a long and heavy process.

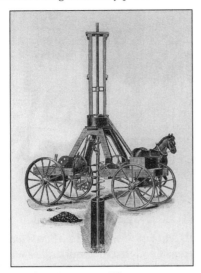

Globe Well Works, Ottawa, Ill.

Well augers were very popular in some areas where water was relatively close to the surface. The engraving shows how the machine was worked, with a horse walking around the drill, feeding it into the earth. A suitable lifting mechanism is also visible.

Kalamazoo Tubular Well Co., Kalamazoo, Mich.

An 1889 advertisement is one of the few remaining items found in regards to this firm, but a study indicates that the company had already been selling these outfits for eight years, putting its origins back to at least 1881.

Kelley & Taneyhill, Waterloo, Iowa

This 1895 engraving shows the Osage Well Drill, complete with the company's own gasoline engine, probably one of the first

such combination machines to be built. Although the origins of the firm are unknown, it is presumed that the company had been building this equipment for a number of years prior to 1895.

An 1896 illustration shows a new well drilling design from Kelly & Taneyhill. This one had heavier proportions than the 1895 model and was powered from an outside source, likely to be a nearby steam-traction engine. Oftentimes, threshermen bought a well drill so as to have more work for their traction engine outside of the annual threshing run.

Although Kelly & Taneyhill was very active in the well drilling business for several years, the company disappears from the scene prior to 1910. Shown here is its 1902 model, a complete portable rig with its own self-contained engine and boiler.

Lisle Manufacturing Co., Clarinda, Iowa

A 1910 illustration shows The Improved Powers Boring Machine in operation. Well augers like this one were powered by the horse walking around the machine behind a sweep. When the auger filled, it was raised and emptied. By using additional sections of drill rod, the well could be bored to a considerable depth.

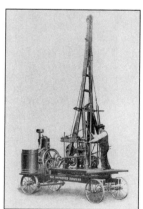

Lisle Manufacturing Co. offered a complete gasoline-powered boring machine by 1910, perhaps earlier. This one was similar in design to the horse-powered machine, but was probably faster, even though it had a higher first cost.

Loomis & Nyman, Tiffin, Ohio

This firm offered the Advance Deep Well Machine shown here in 1895. It was capable of drilling wells up to 12 inches in diameter and anywhere from 50 to 2,500 feet in depth. Nothing is known of the company except for this 1895 illustration.

Gus Pech Foundry & Manufacturing Co., Le Mars, Iowa

By 1900, Pech was offering a complete line of well drilling and well boring machinery. This illustration from a 1902 issue of *American Thresherman Magazine* was one of many different advertisements of well drilling machinery to appear in this and similar journals. Thus many threshermen also became well drillers.

Sioux City Engine & Iron Works, Sioux City, Iowa

Twenty different styles of well drills were available from this firm in 1895. The machine shown here has a small steam engine mounted beneath the frame, with power likely coming from a traction-engine boiler. Rumors persist that the company built gasoline engines for a time, but none have ever been located.

Sparta Iron Works Co., Sparta, Wisc.

This illustration of about 1915 shows the Sparta Portable Drill No. 10 in its working position. By this time, most well drills were equipped with their own engine, usually a gasoline engine, since the latter required little attention during the day. This 5,500 pound machine had a drilling capacity of 300 feet.

Western Forge & Tool Works, St. Louis, Mo.

Shown here is the Victor Well Auger at work. While visitors observe, the horse walks the circle, filling the auger. To the right

is a horse-operated capstan which lifts the filled auger so that it can be discharged for another load.

Trade Names

Advance	Loomis Machine Co.	Tiffin, OH	1905
Advance	Sparta Iron Works	Sparta, WI	1905
Alamo	Alamo Iron Works	San Antonio, TX	1914
American	American Well Works	Aurora, IL	1892
Artesian	Pech Mfg. Co.	Sioux City, IA	1892
Austin	F. C. Austin Mfg. Co.	Chicago, IL	1892
Banner	Loomis Machine Co.	Tiffin, OH	1905
Challenge	St. Louis Well Machine & Tool Co.	St. Louis, MO	1909
Champion	Loomis Machine Co.	Tiffin, OH	1905
Chapman	American Well Works	Aurora, IL	1909
Christman	Christman Co.	Massillon, OH	1909
Climax	Armstrong-Quam Mfg. Co.	Waterloo, IA	1909
Climax	Kelly & Taneyhill	Waterloo, IA	1905
Clipper	Loomis Machine Co.	Tiffin, OH	1905
Crookston	Crookston Mfg. Co.	Crookston, MN	1909
Cyclone	Cyclone Drilling Machine Co.	Orrville, OH	1905
Dakota	Pech Mfg. Co.	Sioux City, IA	1892
Dakota Special	Kelly & Taneyhill	Waterloo, IA	1905
Dederick	Z. P. Dederick	Sherman, TX	1892
Dempster	Dempster Mill Mfg. Co.	Beatrice, NE	1905
Dimock	Dimock Mfg. Co.	Newman Grove, NE	1905
Double Walking Beam	Reierson Machinery Co.	Portland, OR	1914
Eagle	Williams Bros.	Ithaca, NY	1905
Economy	Cherokee Mfg. Co.	Cherokee, IA	1905
Elliptic	Kelly & Taneyhill	Waterloo, IA	1905
Ferguson	Ferguson Mfg. Co.	Waterloo, IA	1909
Fort Scott	Fort Scott Foundry & Mach. Works	Fort Scott, KS	1892
Fort Worth	Fort Worth Iron Works	Fort Worth, TX	1892
Goulds	Goulds Mfg. Co.	Seneca Falls, NY	1892
Gray	Gray Bros.	Milwaukee, WI	1892
Great Western	R. R. Howell & Co.	Minneapolis, MN	1924
Haight's	W. E. Haight	Winnebago City, MN	1892
Hawkeye	Pech Mfg. Co.	Sioux City, IA	1892
Hoosier	Flint & Walling Mfg. Co.	Kendallville, IN	1892
Howell	R. R. Howell & Co.	Minneapolis, MN	1905
Hydraulic	Armstrong Mfg. Co.	Waterloo, IA	1922
Ideal	Brass Iron Works Co.	Fostoria, OH	1892
Ithaca	Treman, Waterman & Co.	Ithaca, NY	1892
K. & T.	Kelly & Taneyhill	Waterloo, IA	1905
Kalamazoo	Kalamazoo Tubular Well Co.	Kalamazoo, MI	1892
Kelly-Taneyhill	Armstrong-Quam Mfg. Co.	Waterloo, IA	1909
Keystone	Keystone Driller Co.	Beaver Falls, PA	1924
Knox & McLynn	Knox & McLynn	Baker City, OR	1892
Leader	Sparta Iron Works	Sparta, WI	1905
Lewis	Wm. Moritz	Hastings, NE	1892
Lockwood	Dempster Mill Mfg. Co.	Beatrice, NE	1892
Loomis & Nyman	Loomis & Nyman	Tiffin, OH	1892
Monarch	Armstrong-Quam Mfg. Co.	Waterloo, IA	1909

Trade Names (cont...)			
Monarch	Morgan, Kelly & Taneyhill	Waterloo, IA	1892
Monitor	Gus Pech Foundry & Mfg. Co.	Lemars, IA	1905
Morris	Morris Drive Well Point Co.	Chicago, IL	1892
National	National Drill & Mfg. Co.	Chicago, IL	1905
Newman	American Well Works	Aurora, IL	1931
North Star	R. R. Howell & Co.	Minneapolis, MN	1924
Novelty	Novelty Iron Works	Dubuque, IA	1892
Ohio	Loomis Machine Co.	Tiffin, OH	1905
Pech	Pech Mfg. Co.	Sioux City, IA	1892
Peck	A. D. Peck	Jordan, NY	1892
Pierce	Pierce Artesian & Oil Well Supply	New York, NY	1892
Plattner Yale	Yale & Hopewell Co.	Lincoln, NE	1922
Powers	Lisle Mfg. Co.	Clarinda, IA	1909
Powers	Powers Mfg. Co.	Clarinda, IA	1905
Reliable	Wm. Moritz	Hastings, NE	1892
Reliance	Cherokee Mfg. Co.	Cherokee, IA	1905
Reliance	Pech Mfg. Co.	Sioux City, IA	1892
Rockford	Rockford Well Drill Co.	Rockford, IL	1905
Seneca Chief	Loomis Machine Co.	Tiffin, OH	1909
St. Louis	St. Louis Well Machine & Tool Co.	St. Louis, MO	1892
Standard	Brass Iron Works Co.	Fostoria, NY	1892
Standard	Morgan, Kelly & Taneyhill	Waterloo, IA	1892
Standard	Reierson Machinery Co.	Portland, OR	1914
Standard	St. Louis Well Machine & Tool Co.	St. Louis, MO	1909
Standard Gearless	Reierson Machinery Co.	Portland, OR	1924
Star	Star Drilling Machine Co.	Akron, OH	1892
Strang	Strang Engine Co.	Harvey, IL	1922
Sumner	Sumner Mfg. Co.	Hutchinson, MN	1892
Teetzel	Globe Well Works	Ottawa, IL	1892
Tiffin	Loomis Machine Co.	Tiffin, OH	1909
Walburn-Swenson	Walburn-Swenson Mfg. Co.	Fort Scott, KS	1892
Walker	E. W. Walker & Co.	Goshen, IN	1892
Waterloo	Armstrong-Quam Mfg. Co.	Waterloo, IA	1909
Waterloo	Kelly & Taneyhill	Waterloo, IA	1905
Williams	Williams Bros.	Ithaca, NY	1892

Windmills

In 1900, a book appeared under the title of *The Windmill as a Prime Mover* by Alfred R. Wolff. Originally written in 1885, it details much of the early history of the windmill, noting that they were probably first used in Germany about a thousand years ago. This book then goes on to discuss and illustrate the American windmill in detail. Several illustrations in this heading are extracted from the above title.

It is not the purpose of this section to detail the history of the windmill, except as it applies to individual inventors and companies. Our goal has been to illustrate as many different windmills as possible. Even so, we have likely missed a great many during our research. Hopefully, the blank spaces will be filled in for future editions of this book. Windmills have gained considerable status as collector items. In Midwestern states, it is not uncommon to see a nicely restored windmill as a bit of landscape architecture. Even though there are no longer any American windmill manufacturers, considerable numbers are still in daily use in some regions.

An engraving of the 1880s illustrates a portable windmill built by Friedrich Filler at Einsbüttel-Hamburg, Germany. Although our research has never found anything like this in American windmill design, it stands as a very clever idea.

Aermotor Co., Chicago, Ill.

Aermotor began building all-steel windmills in 1888, being the first company to adopt this design. By 1890, the firm had developed the tilting tower design for easy servicing of the windmill head as necessary.

About 1916, Aermotor announced its "Auto-oiled" windmill design, with every moving part running in a bath of oil and only requiring an oil change once a year. The Aermotor rose to a point of dominance in the industry, being one of the most widely sold of all makes.

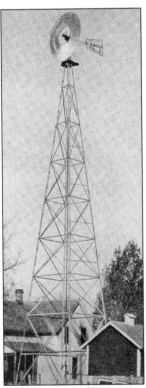

This scene from the 1920s is a typical windmill setting. Aermotor could furnish towers from stock as high as 80 feet. Depending on trees, groves and surrounding buildings, it was often necessary to have a tower high enough to provide the wheel with an undiminished breeze.

Althouse-Wheeler Co., Waupun, Wisc.

This company was active in the windmill business into the 1920s, with its 1885 Waupun mill being shown here. This is a geared power mill, intended for operating small grinders and other equipment.

American Well Works, Aurora, Ill.

During the 1880s, American Well Works was actively promoting everything from windmills to well drills. Its American Advance shown here was available in many different sizes, with the average farm using one having a diameter of 8 to 12 feet.

An 1885 American Well Works catalog notes that the Turbine Challenge shown here was "for farm, ornamental and general domestic use." The 8-foot mill was capable of about 3/4 horsepower; it sold for $108. The largest model had a 12-foot wheel, was capable of 1-1/2 horsepower and was priced at $136.

American Well Works offered a range of power or pumping mills, with this one being a large railway pumping combination. The largest size carried a 30-foot wheel capable of about 9 horsepower; this huge mill was priced at $960.

Appleton Manufacturing Co., Batavia, Ill.

In the early 1900s, Appleton had its Goodhue windmills on the market and continued making them at least into the 1930s; parts were available from Appleton into the late 1940s and perhaps later. Shown here is a 1917 model of the Goodhue mill.

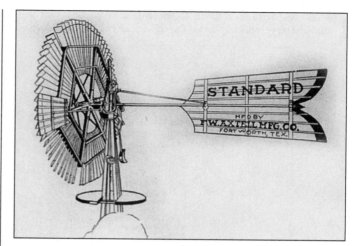

F.W. Axtell Manufacturing Co., Fort Worth, Tex.

Standard windmills from Axtell appeared in the early 1920s, but seem to have remained on the market for only a short time. Aside from this 1923 illustration, nothing more has been found regarding the company.

Baker Manufacturing Co., Evansville, Wisc.

Baker began building windmills in the 1870s, eventually under its "Monitor" trademark. The company built numerous sizes and styles, including this vaneless wooden mill.

Monitor steel windmills were made in 8-, 10- and 12-foot sizes. The windmill required little attention, had a low first cost, long life and cost virtually nothing to operate. The company also developed a large trade in pumps and other waterworks equipment.

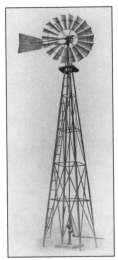

Windmill towers were the subject of considerable design; it took a substantial tower to remain unscathed when heavy storms came through. Shown here is a typical Monitor mill with its heavily braced steel tower. Despite heavy winds and storms, relatively few towers ever collapsed as a result.

Bean-Chamberlin Manufacturing Co., Hudson, Mich.

This company was established in 1869; 30 years later, it announced the Wolverine windmill shown here. For reasons unknown, the company disappeared from the trade directories before 1910.

Buchanan Wind Mill Co., Buchanan, Mich.

In the 1880s, Buchanan was building the mill shown here. It was an all-wood design with ornate fretwork on the sail. In windmill

parlance, the tail was often referred to as a "fan" or "vane." While the wheel looked like a fan, it was usually called the "wheel" or "sail." No information can be found on this company by 1900.

Butler Co., Butler, Ind.

Butler was making windmills by the early 1900s, apparently continuing at least into the 1930s and continuing to offer repair parts for some years after. Little other history has been found regarding this firm.

Perry S. Carter, Des Moines, Iowa

The Carter Bros. mill was an early design, with this engraving coming from a 1904 issue of *American Thresherman Magazine*. The advertisement implies that the company had been in business for a time prior to 1904, but trade directories of a few years later reveal no trace of the firm.

Challenge Co., Batavia, Ill.

Organized in 1867, Challenge Wind Mill & Feed Mill Co. offered this huge power mill in 1887. At the time, wind power seemed a logical choice as a source of cheap power. It was all the more attractive in an age when many looked to the windmill as being the major prime mover on the farm.

At the Chicago World's Fair of 1893, Challenge had this large display, having the highest steel tower, among other things. The company even mounted one mill on the platform of the large power mill to the right, so that it swung in the breeze as the large mill responded in changes of wind direction.

During the 1890s, the Dandy steel windmills became very popular, remaining in production for years to come. Shown here is a 1910 version of the Dandy mill.

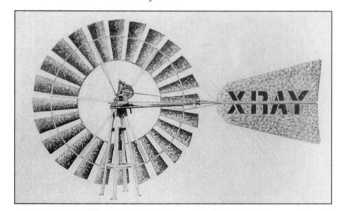

By 1910, Challenge had introduced its XRAY mill, a small mill that was more competitive in price than the Challenge design, but still using the same basic design as other Challenge mills of the time.

Some farmers preferred the vaneless mill shown here. Challenge continued to build these mills for many years, although by

1910 the majority of windmills were using the vane design. With this design, the speed was governed by centrifugal force. Once this speed was reached, the mill would go no faster, no matter how hard the wind might blow.

Challenge Daisy mills were of the solid-wheel design in which the wheel was bolted rigidly together and depended on turning the face of the wheel away from the wind once the maximum speed had been reached. This mill is a 1910 design.

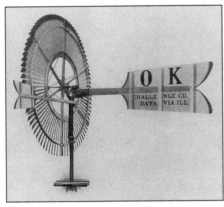

Yet another design from Challenge was the O.K. mill of 1910. It was similar in design to the Daisy mill, having a solid wheel and a large wooden vane.

By the 1920s, the Challenge line included a series of all-steel mills with Timken roller bearings to reduce friction. These mills

were offered in sizes from 6 to 18 feet. Challenge continued building windmills into the 1940s. Originally known as Challenge Wind Mill & Feed Mill Co., the company changed the name to Challenge Co., in 1905.

Chicago Tubular Well Works, Chicago, Ill.

This company was building various kinds of well drilling equipment in 1888, the year that this engraving appeared for its Acme windmill. It was available in wheel diameters from 8 to 30 feet.

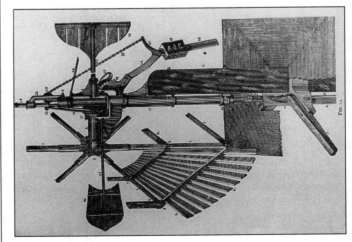

A.J. Corcoran, New York, N.Y.

By the 1880s, the Corcoran mill was well developed and was available either as a pumping mill or as a power mill. Subsequently, the Corcoran mill disappeared; our research has found no subsequent references to this design.

Cornell Wind Engine & Pump Co., Big Rapids, Mich.

The Cornell was on the market in the 1880s, but our research has shown no traces of it after that time. Likewise, the company's activity in pumps, tanks and similar items is unknown.

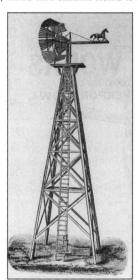

Benjamin Danforth, Batavia, Ill.

Danforth's Improved Wind Mill appeared in the 1880s, being of the vaneless design, but including a handsome ornament at the tail. This mill was of all-wood construction, the general practice at the time.

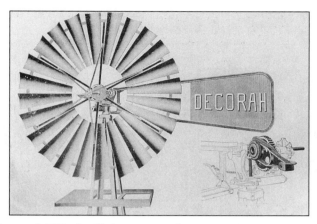

Decorah Windmill Co., Decorah, Iowa

The Decorah mill was on the market by 1890, remaining in the windmill business into the early 1900s. The firm was apparently bought out by Challenge Co., Batavia, Ill., since the latter continued supplying repair parts for the Decorah mills into the late 1940s.

Dempster Mill Manufacturing Co., Beatrice, Neb.

Established in 1878, this firm had a long career in the windmill business, continuing to manufacture windmills at least into the late 1940s, perhaps later. Shown here is a 1927 example of the Dempster mill; this one was equipped with Timken tapered roller bearings.

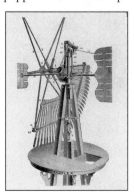

Duplex Manufacturing Co., Superior, Wisc.

When this 1889 example of the Duplex mill appeared, the company was known as Duplex Wind Mill Co., Brooklyn, Wis. This firm remained in the windmill business into the 1930s and continued to offer repair parts for some years after.

Elgin Windmill Co., Elgin, Ill.

For 1899, the Lady Elgin mill appeared as part of the Elgin line; at this time, the company was selling pumping mills or power mills. The latter were often used for grinding grain; a small grinder was connected to the power shaft, the hopper filled with grain and left to do its work, largely unattended.

By the 1920s, Elgin was offering its Model L Hummer mill, a vaneless design that used a steel wheel instead of the usual all-wood design. This was a direct-stroke mill with no intermediate gearing.

The New Improved Elgin Wonder mills appeared in the 1920s and remained on the market at least into the 1940s. This mill was entirely enclosed with all the gears running in oil. Given minimal attention, these mills would run for years, with some of them operating for 40 and 50 years.

Enterprise Windmill Co., Sandwich, Ill.

An 1889 advertisement lists this firm as Enterprise Co., with the change in name coming between that time and 1907, when this advertisement appeared. At the time, Enterprise was building the Enterprise, Sandwich, Perkins and Carter designs, but trade directories of 1910 do not list Enterprise as a mill builder. By the 1920s, parts for Enterprise mills were available from D.A. Hinman & Co., Sandwich, Ill., while parts for the Carter mills were available from Wistrand Manufacturing Co., Galva, Ill. Sandwich-Enterprise and Sandwich-Perkins parts were also available from Hinman.

Fairbanks, Morse & Co., Chicago, Ill.

L.H. Wheeler & Son was organized at Beloit, Wis., in 1867. The firm was reorganized as Eclipse Wind Engine Co., in 1880, with Fairbanks-Morse eventually coming into control of the firm. The Eclipse wood mill was built until 1925.

Two illustrations from a 1913 Fairbanks-Morse catalog illustrate the position of the vaneless mills in and out of the wind. Being "open" was to be in the wind so it could work; being "furled" it was out of the wind and at rest. Fairbanks-Morse windmills are covered extensively in the author's *Fairbanks-Morse: 1893-1993* (1993: Stemgas Publishing Co.).

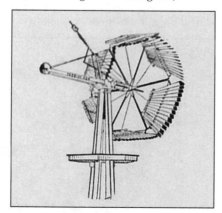

Fairbury Iron Works & Windmill Co., Fairbury, Neb.

The Fairbury as shown was illustrated in 1905, but subsequent years remain barren and no later references can be found. This was a vaneless mill; the company built cultivators along with making all sorts of brass and iron castings.

Flint & Walling Manufacturing Co., Kendallville, Ind.

David C. Walling and Simeon Flint organized this firm in 1866; in 1872, they organized as Flint, Walling & Co. The name was changed as shown above in 1886. Windmills were added to the line in 1872; in 1878, Walling invented the Star windmill which the company built for decades. Shown here is one of the earliest examples, this being an 1890 model.

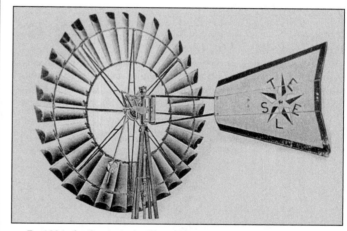

By 1894, the Star windmill was an improved all-steel design as shown. In addition, the company built a wide variety of plumbing and water supply goods.

By the 1920s, the Star mill was redesigned with all gears running in oil for trouble-free operation and a long operating life. The company continued building Star windmills at least into the late 1940s and perhaps longer, but current research has not determined precisely when production ended.

Fort Wayne Wind Mill Co., Fort Wayne, Ind.

This all-steel mill appears in the early 1900s and apparently remained active until about 1915. Subsequently, repair parts were available from Ragan-Brown-Lange Co., Napoleon, Ohio. The auther has found no information at all on the latter company.

S. Freeman & Sons Manufacturing Co., Racine, Wisc.

This company was among the early windmill manufacturers, having this all-steel Freeman mill on the market before 1895. The company continued in the mill business into the 1930s; subsequently, parts were available from Harvey Manufacturing Co., also of Racine.

Did You Know?

Singletrees today sell for anywhere from $5 to $20.

Goold & Austin Manufacturing Co., Chicago, Ill.

From 1887 comes this view of the Acme Wind Mill from Goold & Austin. The company pioneered in windmills and well equipment, but subsequently disappeared, either through a reorganization, a name change or simply going out of business.

Heller-Aller Co., Napoleon, Ohio

This company first appears in the trade directories about 1910, with the company remaining in the windmill business into the late 1940s, perhaps longer. An illustration of the 1920s shows the Baker self-oiling design; it was made in 8- and 10-foot sizes.

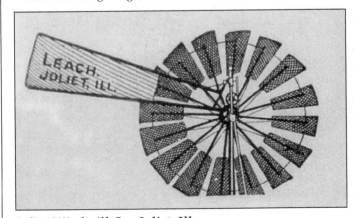

Joliet Windmill Co., Joliet, Ill.

A single small advertisement is the only information uncovered thus far for the Leach windmill from this firm. The firm was building mills with steel or wood towers; the extent of its windmill line is unknown.

R. G. Marcy Manufacturing Co., Bluffton, Ind.

A 1901 illustration shows the Red Cross mill with a tank mounted half way up the tower. This scheme for a gravity-water system had its faults, since it was almost impossible to keep the center opening (for the pump rod) from leaking sooner or later. Subsequently, the firm was known as Red Cross Manufacturing Co.; it continued to supply repair parts into the late 1940s.

Marseilles Manufacturing Co., Marseilles, Ill.

This company was building windmills in the 1880s or sooner. By 1900, its line was extensive, including the Steel Queen, Princess, Splendid and Adams mills. The company left the windmill business in the early 1900s. Subsequently, John Deere Plow Co. supplied repair parts for the Steel Queen for some years; the latter bought out Marseilles in 1911.

Did You Know?

An ordinary hay carrier might now bring $40.

Mast, Foos & Co., Springfield, Ohio

An 1887 advertisement notes that there were "thousands of [Iron Turbine] mills in use." Thus it would seem logical that this design had already been on the market for several years.

From all appearances, Mast, Foos & Co. continued building Imperial windmills into the 1920s; by the early 1930s, the company is listed only as having repair parts and continued to be listed in this manner until at least the late 1940s. Shown here is an Imperial mill of 1906.

Monitor Manufacturing Co., Auburn Junction, Ind.

An 1890 advertisement illustrates the Monitor Wind Mill, complete with automatic regulator. The company was offering pumping and power mills, along with other necessities. Except for this lone advertisement, nothing more is known of the firm.

Perkins Wind Mill Co., Mishawaka, Ind.

In the late 1880s, this company was known as Perkins Windmill & Ax Co., changing to Perkins Wind Mill Co., prior to this 1895 advertisement. At the time, the company was making mills up to 20-feet in diameter. The company continued building mills into the 1920s, then disappeared from the scene. In later years, the firm was known as Perkins Corp.

Phelps & Bigelow Wind Mill Co., Kalamazoo, Mich.

During the 1880s, Phelps & Bigelow offered the IXL windmill shown here, along with pumps, tanks and related supplies. About 1920, the firm took the name of I.X.L. Windmill Co., remaining in business into the 1940s.

Did You Know?

Hartman offered its Majestic Saw Frame in the 1920s for $31.10, including a 60-pound flywheel, plus the cost of the blade. Moving upward to a 100-pound flywheel raised the price another $2.20.

Powell & Douglas, Waukegan, Ill.

An illustration from 1885 shows the Powell & Douglas Geared Mill. Bevel gears at the top joined the wheel to a vertical shaft extending down to ground level. Suitable gearing and belt pulleys then permitted the mill to operate small grinders and other equipment.

Engine & Machine Works, Summerfield, Md.

Kirkwood's Iron Wind Engine was depicted in this 1890 engraving. Aside from this illustration, nothing is known of the company. Like other firms, it may have merged into another or simply gone out of business.

Sandwich Manufacturing Co., Sandwich, Ill.

This company is best known for its feed grinders, elevators and corn shellers. However, by the 1880s, Sandwich had developed the Regulator Windmill shown here. Subsequently, though, Sandwich opted out of the windmill market, selling its interest to Enterprise Manufacturing Co., also of Sandwich.

Smith & Pomeroy Wind Mill Co., Kalamazoo, Mich.

An advertisement in an 1895 issue of *American Agriculturist* illustrates its Eureka windmill of the time, posing the question, "Which mill shall I buy?" By the 1920s, parts for the Eureka were available from IXL Windmill Co., also of Kalamazoo.

Springfield Machine Co., Springfield, Ohio

Leffel's Improved Iron windmill took the form shown here in an 1889 engraving. At the time, the company was also making pumps and hay tools, but none of the subsequent activities have appeared during the research of this book.

Geo. L. Squier Manufacturing Co., Buffalo, N.Y.

For 1887, Squier offered the Hercules Wind Engine, shown here on an elaborate tower. Since no subsequent information had been located regarding the novel design of the Hercules, it is presumed that it remained in production for a short time.

Star Manufacturing Co., Carpentersville, Ill.

An 1890 advertisement illustrates the Butler Wind Mill from Star Manufacturing Co. Subsequently, a Butler mill was made by the Butler Co., but we have made no connection between the two, if one existed. Like the early Aermotor, this mill used a tilting-tower design, as shown in the engraving.

Stover Manufacturing Co., Freeport, Ill.

An 1889 advertisement shows the Stover Ideal mill. D.C. Stover's experience in windmills went back to the early 1870s; by the time this advertisement appeared, the company was well into the windmill business.

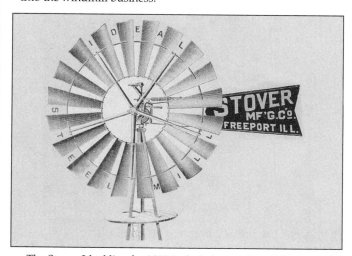

The Stover Ideal line for 1893 included several models of wood and steel windmills, along with the choice of wood or steel towers. Ideal mills had an excellent reputation, with thousands being sold.

Freeport mills were built for only a few years, but the Samson, introduced about 1900, was the backbone of the Stover windmill line until the company closed its doors in 1942. Shown here is the 1900 model; in the 1920s, Stover revamped the Samson with roller bearings and a complete oiling system.

Two-Wheel Windmill Manufacturing Co., Hutchinson, Kan.

In the early 1920s, the Twin Wheel mills appeared, remaining for only a few years. By the 1930s, repairs only were available. Little else is known of this venture.

U.S. Wind Engine & Pump Co., Batavia, Ill.

By the 1880s, U.S. Wind Engine Co., had adopted the Halladay designs, with its Standard Wind Mill No. 2 being illustrated in this 1888 engraving. It is shown here "out of gear" or as the company termed it, "out of sail."

During the 1880s, the company promoted its Halladay power mills, illustrating a typical setup in this 1888 engraving. However, using the wind as a prime mover had one basic drawback; there had to be a wind!

By the 1890s, the Gem windmill had been developed and shown here in an all-steel design. To the right of this engraving is shown the company's vaneless model. This illustration is from an 1895 issue of *American Agriculturist*.

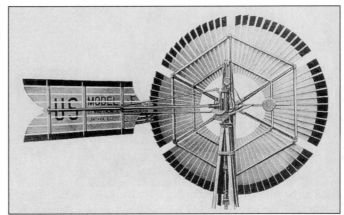

By the early 1900s, U.S. was offering its Model E mill, shown here "out of sail." A mechanism worked from ground level permitted the farmer to put the mill into or out of gear; in the latter position, the vane was pulled to a right angle with the wheel, thus keeping it out of sail. The speed governor mechanism worked on the arm carrying the vane so that in strong winds the mill worked more or less out of sail to maintain the maximum speed at a safe level.

Into the 1920s, U.S. came with its Model B, all-steel mill. Even though this mill had become very popular, a few buyers still preferred the wooden wheel, despite its obvious disadvantages.

Winger, The Windmill Man, Freeport, Ill.

Winger's Royal Wind Mill is pictured in an 1889 advertisement; the company also made a feed grinder, tank heaters, tanks and other items. Further information on this operation is unknown.

Winchester & Partridge Manufacturing Co., Whitewater, Wisc.

On Sept. 11, 1888, Wm. and Charles H. Tuckwood of Janesville, Wis., received Patent No. 389,342 for "Balanced Gearing for Windmills." By the following year, the Tuckwood mill was being offered from Winchester & Partridge.

Trade Names

1900	D. H. Bausman	Bausman, PA	1892
Abbott	A. M. Abbott	Stockton, CA	1892
Acme	Goold & Austin Mfg. Co.	Chicago, IL	1887
Adams	Marseilles Mfg. Co.	Marseilles, IL	1892
Advance	American Well Works	Aurora, IL	1892
Aera	Aera Mfg. Co.	Henry, IL	1892
Aerial	Enterprise Wind Mill Co.	Sandwich, IL	1913
Aermotor	Aermotor Co.	Chicago, IL	1892
Air King	Sandwich Enterprise Co.	Sandwich, IL	1892
Airmaster	Woodmanse Mfg. Co.	Freeport, IL	1939
Albion	Cook Mfg. Co.	Albion, MI	1905
Albion	Union Steel Screen Co.	Albion, MI	1915
Aldrich	Lourie Implement Co.	Keokuk, IA	1892
Alta	Walterscheid Bros.	Wichita, KS	1905
Althouse-Raymond	Althouse-Wheeler Co.	Waupun, WI	1905
American Multiple Wheel	Kansas City Hay Press Co.	Kansas City, MO	1922
Andrew	Duplex Mfg. Co.	Superior, WI	1931
Appleton-Goodhue	Appleton Mfg. Co.	Batavia, IL	1905
Aquarius	W. Wetherbee	Barre Center, NY	1892
Arrow	Dempster Mill Mfg. Co.	Beatrice, NE	1913
Automatic	Automatic Mower & Mfg. Co.	Harvey, IL	1892
B & Y	Barlow & Youmans	Galesburg, MI	1892
B.B.	Beckman Bros.	Des Moines, IA	1909
Badger	Winchester & Partridge Mfg. Co.	Whitewater, WI	1892
Baker	Heller-Aller Co.	Napoleon, OH	1905
Banner	Banner Mfg. Co.	La Otto, IN	1892
Banner Vaneless	Challenge Wind Mill & Feed Mill Co.	Batavia, IL	1905
Batavia	Batavia Windmill Co.	Batavia, IL	1892
Bausman	D. H. Bausman	Bausman, PA	1892
Beatrice	Dempster Mill Mfg. Co.	Beatrice, NE	1892
Beckman	Beckman Bros.	Des Moines, IA	1905
Bell	Breyer Bros., Whiting & Co.	Waupun, WI	1909
Beloit	Eclipse Wind Engine Co.	Beloit, WI	1892
Beloit	Fairbanks, Morse & Co.	Chicago, IL	1892
Ben Franklin	James Mossman	Westerville, OH	1892
Bird	St. John Plow Co.	Kalamazoo, MI	1892
Blue Star	Blue Star Mfg. Co.	Galva, IL	1939
Boss	H. F. Batcheller & Son	Rock Falls, IL	1892
Boss Vaneless	Dempster Mfg. Co.	Des Moines, IA	1915'
Buchanan	Buchanan Wind Mill Co.	Buchanan, MI	1880
Buckeye	Mast, Foos & Co.	Springfield, OH	1913
Bushnell	Bushnell Pump Co.	Bushnell, IL	1909
Butler	Butler Co.	Butler, IN	1909
Butler	Butler Mfg. Co.	Butler, IN	1892
Butler	Star Mfg. Co.	Carpentersville, IL	1892
California	Byron Jackson	San Francisco, CA	1892
California	California Wind Mill Co.	Somonauk, IL	1922

Trade Names (cont...)

Capital	Dempster Mfg. Co.	Des Moines, IA	1905
Carroll	Carroll Iron Works	Chicago, IL	1905
Carter	Carter Bros. Co.	Des Moines, IA	1892
Carter	Perry S. Carter Co.	Des Moines, IA	1905
Carter	Wistrand Mfg. Co.	Galva, IL	1915
Centennial	Elgin Wind Power & Pump Co.	Elgin, IL	1892
Centennial	Pech Mfg. Co.	Sioux City, IA	1892
Challenge	Challenge Wind Mill & Feed Mill Co.	Batavia, IL	1892
Champion	R. J. Douglas & Co.	Waukegan, IL	1892
Chief	Althouse-Wheeler Co.	Waupun, WI	1909
Climax	Sandwich Enterprise Co.	Sandwich, IL	1892
Columbia	Mast, Foos & Co.	Springfield, OH	1892
Columbia	W. H. Aldrich	Logansport, IN	1892
Comet	U. S. Wind Engine & Pump Co.	Batavia, IL	1905
Cook	Union Steel Screen Co.	Albion, MI	1915
Corcoran	Andrew J. Corcoran	New York, NY	1892
Corn Belt	Freeman Mfg. Co.	Racine, WI	1931
Cornell	Cornell Mfg. Co.	Louisville, KY	1892
Cornell	Cornell Wind Engine & Pump Co.	Big Rapids, MI	1880
Crown	Duplex Mfg. Co.	Superior, WI	1913
C-S	Cornell-Searl Co.	Lincoln, NE	1922
Currie	C. W. Turner	Mason City, IL	1892
Currie	Currie Wind Mill Co.	Topeka, KS	1905
Cyclone	Pacific Mfg. Co.	San Francisco, CA	1892
Cyclone Proof	Althouse-Wheeler Co.	Waupun, WI	1915
Daisy	Challenge Wind Mill & Feed Mill Co.	Batavia, IL	1892
Daisy	Empire Mfg. Co.	Keokuk, IA	1892
Daisy	Monitor Mfg. Co.	Auburn Junction, IN	1892
Dana	Dana Wind Engine Co.	Fairhaven, MS	1892
Dandy	Challenge Wind Mill & Feed Mill Co.	Batavia, IL	1892
Dandy	Challenge Wind Mill & Feed Mill Co.	Batavia, IL	1905
Dandy	D. U. Brown & Co.	Sac City, IA	1892
Danforth's Improved	Benjamin Danforth	Batavia, IL	1880
Decorah	Decorah Wind Mill Co.	Decorah, IA	1892
Decorah	Snow Mfg. Co.	Batavia, IL	1905
Defender	Mast, Foos & Co.	Springfield, OH	1913
De-mand-a	Chas. H. Myers & Co.	LeRoy, IL	1905
Dempster	Dempster Mill Mfg. Co.	Beatrice, NE	1892
Diamond	Monitor Mfg. Co.	Auburn Junction, IN	1892
Diamond	Temple Pump Co.	Chicago, IL	1905
Double Power	Double Power Mill Co	Appleton, WI	1909
Double Power	Killen-Strait Mfg. Co.	Appleton, WI	1922
Duplex	Duplex Mfg. Co.	Superior, WI	1905
Duplex	Duplex Wind Mill Co.	Brooklyn, WI	1892
Eagle	Eagle Mfg. Co.	Decatur, IN	1892
Eagle	F. W. Krogh & Co.	San Francisco, CA	1892
Eagle	I. E. Phelps	Wahoo, NE	1892
Eagle	U. S. Wind Engine & Pump Co.	Batavia, IL	1905

Trade Names (cont...)

Eclipse	Eclipse Wind Engine Co.	Beloit, WI	1892
Eclipse	Fairbanks, Morse & Co.	Chicago, IL	1892
Economy	F. W. Krogh & Co.	San Francisco, CA	1892
Elgin	Elgin Wind Power & Pump Co.	Elgin, IL	1905
Eli	Geo. F. Kregel	Nebraska City, NE	1892
Eli	Kregel Wind Mill Co.	Nebraska City, NE	1922
Emperor	Perkins Wind Mill Co.	Mishawaka, IN	1905
Enterprise	Sandwich Enterprise Co.	Sandwich, IL	1892
Ess-Tee	Smith-Talbott Co.	Cedar Rapids, IA	1905
Eureka	F. W. Krogh & Co.	San Francisco, CA	1892
Eureka	Smith & Pomeroy	Kalamazoo, MI	1892
Everlasting	D. U. Brown & Co.	Sac City, IA	1892
Fairbanks	Fairbanks, Morse & Co.	Chicago, IL	1905
Fairbury	Fairbury Wind Mill Co.	Fairbury, NE	1905
Falcon	Dempster Mfg. Co.	Des Moines, IA	1905
Famous	Thos. Cascaden Jr.	Waterloo, IA	1892
Favorite	Cornish, Curtis & Greene	Fort Atkinson, WI	1892
Favorite	D. U. Brown & Co.	Sac City, IA	1892
Favorite	Zimmerman Mfg. Co.	Auburn, IN	1892
Fleming & Creager	Fleming & Creager	Portland, IN	1892
Flying Dutchman	Elgin Wind Power & Pump Co.	Elgin, IL	1909
Fort Wayne	Fort Wayne Wind Mill Co.	Fort Wayne, IN	1905
Fort Wayne	Fort Wayne Wind Mill Co.	Fort Wayne, IN	1909
Fountain	H. L. Bennett & Co.	Westerville, OH	1892
Freeman	Freeman Mfg. Co.	Racine, WI	1922
Freeman	S. Freeman & Sons Mfg. Co.	Racine, WI	1905
Freeport	Stover Mfg. Co.	Freeport, IL	1909
Garland	Valley Wind Engine & Iron Co.	Bay City, MI	1905
Gem	Panhandle Machy. & Improvement	Fort Worth, TX	1892
Gem	U. S. Wind Engine & Pump Co.	Batavia, IL	1892
Geneva	Geneva Iron & Wind Mill Co.	Geneva, NE	1892
Geneva	Snow Mfg. Co.	Batavia, IL	1905
Giant	Althouse-Wheeler Co.	Waupun, WI	1909
Giant	Charles Kaestner & Co.	Chicago, IL	1892
Gibraltar	Elgin Wind Power & Pump Co.	Elgin, IL	1922
Globe	Globe Implement Co.	Goshen, IN	1892
Goodhue	Goodhue Wind Engine Co.	St. Charles, IL	1892
Goodhue Special	Appleton Mfg. Co.	Batavia, IL	1909
Gudnuf	Clay City Wind Mill & Foundry Co.	Clay Center, KS	1909
Gudnuf	Okmulgee Implement & Mfg. Co.	Okmulgee, OK	1922
Gusher	Dempster Mfg. Co.	Des Moines, IA	1905
Halladay	U. S. Wind Engine & Pump Co.	Batavia, IL	1892
Hazen	F. W. Winter & Co.	Faribault, MN	1892

Trade Names (cont...)

Trade Name	Maker	Location	Year
Hazen	S. Hazen & Son	Ripon, WI	1892
Hazen	W. S. Hazen	Ripon, WI	1905
Hill	H. N. Hill	Pontiac, MI	1892
Holdredge	Hultquist Bros.	Holdredge, MI	1905
Hoosier	Fort Wayne Wind Mill Co.	Fort Wayne, IN	1909
Horicon	Breyer Bros., Whiting & Co.	Waupun, WI	1915
Horicon	Horicon Windmill Co.	Horicon, WI	1892
Hudson	Hudson Mfg. Co.	Minneapolis, MN	1924
Hummer	Elgin Wind Power & Pump Co.	Elgin, IL	1915
I.X.L.	Jones, Woodruff & Co.	Rockford, IL	1892
I.X.L.	Phelps & Bigelow Wind Mill Co.	Kalamazoo, MI	1892
Ideal	Stover Mfg. Co.	Freeport, IL	1892
Imperial	Mast, Foos & Co.	Springfield, OH	1905
Improved California	Clark & Co.	Somonauk, IL	1892
Improved Climax	C. A. Miller	Urbana, OH	1892
Improved Monitor	Monitor Mfg. Co.	Auburn Junction, IN	1892
Industrious	Avery Planter Co.	Peoria, IL	1892
Iron Turbine	Mast, Foos & Co.	Springfield, OH	1892
Irrigator	Dempster Mfg. Co.	Des Moines, IA	1905
IXL	IXL Wind Mill Co.	Kalamazoo, MI	1922
Jackson's California	Byron Jackson Machine Works	San Francisco, CA	1905
Joker	R. S. Scott	Peabody, KS	1892
Joliet Star	Leach Wind Mill Co.	Joliet, IL	1892
Junior	Phelps & Bigelow Wind Mill Co.	Kalamazoo, MI	1913
Kalamazoo	Kalamazoo Tank & Silo Co.	Kalamazoo, MI	1905
Kalamazoo	Kalamazoo Wind Mill Co.	Kalamazoo, MI	1892
Keith	James C. Keith	Battle Creek, MI	1892
Kenwood	Sears, Roebuck & Co.	Chicago, IL	1931
Keokuk	Lourie Implement Co.	Keokuk, IA	1892
King	Gustav Wenzelmann	Missal, IL	1892
Kirkwood	Kirkwood Mfg. Co.	Arkansas City, KS	1892
Kirkwood's	Engine & Machine Works	Summerfield, MD	1890
Knox & McLynn	Knox & McLynn	Baker City, OR	1892
Kregel	Kregel Wind Mill Co.	Nebraska City, NE	1922
Kring	Kring Bros.	Westerville, OH	1892
Lamb	Lamb & Co.	Freeport, IL	1892
Leach	Leach Wind Mill Co.	Joliet, IL	1892
Leader	Flint & Walling Mfg. Co.	Kendallville, IN	1913
Leffel's	Springfield Machine Co.	Springfield, OH	1892
Little Giant	Elgin Wind Power & Pump Co.	Elgin, IL	1909
Mammoth	Eclipse Mfg. Co.	Middlebury, IN	1892
Manvel	Gilbert Hunt & Co.	Walla Walla, WA	1892
Manvel	Kalamazoo Tank & Silo Co.	Kalamazoo, MI	1905
Manvel	Williams Mfg. Co.	Kalamazoo, MI	1892
Maud S.	Ideal Motor Co.	Lansing, MI	1909
Maud S.	Lansing Iron & Engine Works	Lansing, MI	1892
Maud S.	Lansing Motor & Pump Co.	Lansing, MI	1915
Maud S.	Maud S. Wind Mill & Pump Co.	Lansing, MI	1905
May	May Bros.	Galesburg, IL	1892
McDonald	A. Y. McDonald Co.	Dubuque, IA	1939
Meyer Improved	Jacob S. Meyer	Bloomville, OH	1892
Michigan	Smith & Pomeroy	Kalamazoo, MI	1892
Midland	Midland Mfg. Co.	Tarkio, MO	1905
Miller	C. H. Miller	Millington, IL	1892
Milo	Althouse-Wheeler Co.	Waupun, WI	1892
Model A	Stover Mfg. Co.	Freeport, IL	1909
Mogul	Woodmanse Mfg. Co.	Freeport, IL	1909
Monarch	Celina Mfg. Co.	Celina, OH	1913
Monarch	Zimmerman Mfg. Co.	Auburn, IN	1892
Monitor	Baker Mfg. Co.	Evansville, WI	1892
New Era	McDaniel & Son	Litchfield, IL	1905
New Royal	E. B. Winger	Chicago, IL	1892
New Wolcott	National Engineering Co.	Saginaw, MI	1905
Niagara	Novelty Iron Works	Dubuque, IA	1892
O.K.	Challenge Wind Mill & Feed Mill Co.	Batavia, IL	1905
Ohio	Genoa Mfg. Co.	Genoa, OH	1905
Okmulgee	Okmulgee Implement & Mfg. Co.	Okmulgee, OK	1909
Opfer	Genoa Mfg. Co.	Genoa, OH	1905
Ottawa	Ottawa Mfg. Co.	Ottawa, KS	1909
Over	Ewal Over	Indianapolis, IN	1892
Pattengill	Red Cross Mfg. Co.	Bluffton, IN	1931
Paxton	Samuel Paxton	Boone, IA	1892
Perkins	Perkins Wind Mill & Ax Co.	Mishawaka, IN	1892
Perkins	Perkins Windmill Co.	Mishawaka, IN	1905
Pfouts	J. H. McClain Machine Co.	Canton, OH	1892
Pilot	Flint & Walling Mfg. Co.	Kendallville, IN	1892
Pirate	Heller-Aller Co.	Napoleon, OH	1905
Plattner	Plattner Implement Co.	Denver, CO	1915
Plattner-Yale	Yale & Hopewell Co.	Lincoln, NE	1922
Powell & Douglas	Powell & Douglas	Waukegan, IL	1885
Queen	Lima Mfg. Co.	Lima, IN	1892
Queen City	Dempster Mill Mfg. Co.	Beatrice, NE	1931
Racine	Winship Mfg. Co.	Racine, WI	1892
Red Cross	Red Cross Mfg. Co.	Bluffton, IN	1905
Red King	Burke-Bollmeyer Mfg. Co.	Wauseon, OH	1905
Red King	Red King Co.	Wauseon, OH	1915
Reese	John Reese	Florin, CA	1892
Regulator	Stearns Mfg. Co.	Los Angeles, CA	1892
Reliance	Cornish, Curtis & Greene	Fort Atkinson, WI	1892
Relief	John Stowell	Stockton, CA	1892
Rex	Rex Mfg. Co.	Manchester, IN	1892
Rex	Ross Supply Co.	Anderson, IN	1905
Rork	James Rork & Bro.	Lansing, MI	1905
Royal	Winger, the Windmill Man	Freeport, IL	1889
Sailor	Heller-Aller Co.	Napoleon, OH	1905
Samson	Stover Mfg. Co.	Freeport, IL	1905
Sandwich-Perkins	Enterprise Wind Mill Co.	Sandwich, IL	1913
Sandwich-Perkins	Sandwich Enterprise Co.	Sandwich, IL	1892

Trade Names (cont...)

Simpson	Nebraska Foundry & Mfg. Co.	Omaha, NE	1922
Smith & Pomeroy	IXL Wind Mill Co.	Kalamazoo, MI	1931
South Bend	Koontz Mfg. Co.	South Bend, IN	1892
Spencer	Spencer Mfg. Co.	Blue Springs, NE	1892
Splendid	Marseilles Mfg. Co.	Marseilles, IL	1892
Standard	D. J. Howenstine	Mansfield, OH	1892
Standard	F. W. Axtell Mfg. Co.	Fort Worth, TX	1920
Standard	Standard Scale & Mfg. Co.	Des Moines, IA	1909
Star	Flint & Walling Mfg. Co.	Kendallville, IN	1892
Star	O. P. Benjamin Mfg. Co.	Lafayette, IN	1892
Stearns	Stearns Mfg. Co.	Connersville, IN	1892
Steel Chief	Althouse-Wheeler Co.	Waupun, WI	1909
Steel Giant	Althouse-Wheeler Co.	Waupun, WI	1909
Stover	Lamb & Co.	Freeport, IL	1892
Stover	Stover Mfg. Co.	Freeport, IL	1922
Strait	A. D. Peck	Jordan, NY	1892
Strait	Strait Wind Mill Co.	Galesburg, MI, NE	1892
Success	Hastings Foundry & Iron Works	Hastings, NE	1915
Sun	Sunderland Machy. & Supply Co.	Omaha, NE	1922
Superior	American Well Works	Aurora, IL	1892
Superior	Duplex Mfg. Co.	Superior, WI	1905
Superior	Superior Co.	Streator, IL	1905
Terrible Swede	Elgin Wind Power & Pump Co.	Elgin, IL	1909
Texas	Butler Co.	Butler, IN	1913
Times	D. H. Bausman	Bausman, PA	1892
Tip Top	Elgin Wind Power & Pump Co.	Elgin, IL	1924
Toledo	Merrell Mfg. Co.	Toledo, OH	1892
Tom Thumb	Tom Thumb Machine Co.	Dublin, IN	1892
Tucker Automatic	Temple Pump Co.	Chicago, IL	1909
Tuckwood	Winchester & Partridge Mfg. Co.	Whitewater, WI	1892
Two-Wheel	Two-Wheel Wind Mill Co.	Hutchinson, KS	1939
U.S.	U. S. Wind Engine & Pump Co.	Batavia, IL	1892
U.S. Star	O. G. Stowell	Delavan, WI	1892
Union	Union Steel Screen Co.	Albion, MI	1915
Van Buren & Bitler	Van Buren & Bitler	Carey, OH	1892
Wallenbeck	Geo. Wallenbeck	Ithaca, NY	1892
Ward	Ward Pump Co.	Rockford, IL	1892
Waupun	Althouse-Wheeler Co.	Waupun, WI	1892
Waupun Bell	Breyer Bros., Whiting & Co.	Waupun, WI	1913
Waupun Raymond	Breyer Bros., Whiting & Co.	Waupun, WI	1913
Western	Geise Mfg. Co.	Grand Island, NE	1909
Western	Western Land Roller Co.	Hastings, NE	1945
Weston	Vail & Smith Co.	Weston, MI	1909
Wetherbee	W. Wetherbee	Barre Center, NY	1892
Whizz	Elgin Wind Power & Pump Co.	Elgin, IL	1905

Trade Names (cont...)

Wichita	Waterscheid Machinery Co.	Wichita, KS	1913
Windmotor	Duplex Mfg. Co.	Superior, WI	1922
Winner	Sandwich Enterprise Co.	Sandwich, IL	1892
Wolcott's	Union Wind Mill & Mfg. Co.	Albion, MI	1892
Wolverine	Bean-Chamberlin Mfg. Co.	Hudson, MI	1869
Wonder	Elgin Wind Power & Pump Co.	Elgin, IL	1913
Woodmanse	Woodmanse & Hewitt Mfg. Co.	Freeport, IL	1892
Woodmanse	Woodmanse Mfg. Co.	Freeport, IL	1905
Wyatt	Wyatt Mfg. Co.	Salina, KS	1945
X Ray	Challenge Wind Mill & Feed Mill Co.	Batavia, IL	1905
Yankee	Mt. Pulaski Wind Mill Co.	Mt. Pulaski, IL	1892
Yellow Star	May Wind Mill Co.	Galesburg, IL	1924
Zenith	Lamb & Co.	Freeport, IL	1892
Zenith	Lamb & Co.	Freeport, IL	1905
Zephyr	Deacon Hdwe. & Mercantile Co.	Harrisonville, MO	1905

Anyone having additional materials and resources relating to American farm implements is invited to contact C.H. Wendel, in care of Krause Publications, 700 E. State St., Iola, WI 54990-0001.